Great Lives from History

Asian and Pacific Islander Americans

Great Lives from History

Asian and Pacific Islander Americans

Volume 3
Gabby Pahinui – Caroline Zhang

Editor
Gary Y. Okihiro
Columbia University

SALEM PRESS
A Division of EBSCO Publishing
Ipswich, Massachusetts   Hackensack, New Jersey

Cover Photos (pictured left to right, from top left): Troy Polamalu (© Gene J. Puskar/AP/Corbis); Kristi Yamaguchi (© Neal Preston/Corbis); Jim Yong Kim (Dartmouth College/Joseph Mehling '69); Amy Tan (© Reuters/Corbis); Martin Yan (© Craig Lee/San Francisco Chronicle/Corbis).

The paper used in these volumes conforms to the American National Standard for Permanence of Paper for Printed Library Materials, X39.48-1992 (R1997).

Library of Congress Cataloging-in-Publication Data

Asian and Pacific Islander Americans / editor, Gary Okihiro.
      p. cm. — (Great lives from history)
   Includes bibliographical references and index.
   ISBN 978-1-58765-860-0 (set) — ISBN 978-1-58765-861-7 (volume 1) — ISBN 978-1-58765-862-4 (volume 2) — ISBN 978-1-58765-863-1 (volume 3) — ISBN 978-1-58765-864-8 (ebook set) 1. Asian Americans—Biography. 2. Pacific Islander Americans—Biography. I. Okihiro, Gary Y., 1945–
   E184.A75A85 2013
   973'.0495—dc23

                                                                            2012019469

PRINTED IN THE UNITED STATES OF AMERICA

CONTENTS

VOLUME 3

KEY TO PRONUNCIATION

Many of the names of personages covered in *Great Lives from History: Asian and Pacific Islander Americans* may be unfamiliar to students and general readers. For difficult-to-pronounce names, guidelines to pronunciation have been provided upon first mention of the name in each essay. These guidelines do not purport to achieve the subtleties of all languages but will offer readers a rough equivalent of how English speakers may approximate the proper pronunciation.

Vowel Sounds

Symbol	Spelled (Pronounced)
a	answer (AN-suhr), laugh (laf), sample (SAM-puhl), that (that)
ah	father (FAH-thur), hospital (HAHS-pih-tuhl)
aw	awful (AW-fuhl), caught (kawt)
ay	blaze (blayz), fade (fayd), waiter (WAYT-ur), weigh (way)
eh	bed (behd), head (hehd), said (sehd)
ee	believe (bee-LEEV), cedar (SEE-dur), leader (LEED-ur), liter (LEE-tur)
ew	boot (bewt), lose (lewz)
i	buy (bi), height (hit), lie (li), surprise (sur-PRIZ)
ih	bitter (BIH-tur), pill (pihl)
o	cotton (KO-tuhn), hot (hot)
oh	below (bee-LOH), coat (koht), note (noht), wholesome (HOHL-suhm)
oo	good (good), look (look)
ow	couch (kowch), how (how)
oy	boy (boy), coin (koyn)
uh	about (uh-BOWT), butter (BUH-tuhr), enough (ee-NUHF), other (UH-thur).

Consonant Sounds

Symbol	Spelled (Pronounced)
ch	beach (beech), chimp (chihmp)
g	beg (behg), disguise (dihs-GIZ), get (geht)
j	digit (DIH-juht), edge (ehj), jet (jeht)
k	cat (kat), kitten (KIH-tuhn), hex (hehks)
s	cellar (SEHL-ur), save (sayv), scent (sehnt)
sh	champagne (sham-PAYN), issue (IH-shew), shop (shop)
ur	birth (burth), disturb (dihs-TURB), earth (urth), letter (LEH-tur)
y	useful (YEWS-fuhl), young (yuhng)
z	business (BIHZ-nehs), zest (zehst)
zh	vision (VIH-zhuhn)

COMPLETE LIST OF CONTENTS

VOLUME 1

VOLUME 2

Volume 3

Appendixes

Indexes

GABBY PAHINUI

Musician

An iconic Hawaiian guitarist and singer, Pahinui was best known for his use of the slack-key guitar style, which lent a unique sound to recordings such as "Hi'ilawe." He played a significant role in the development of Hawaiian music and was a major figure in the Hawaiian Renaissance of the 1960s and 1970s.

Born: April 22, 1921; Honolulu, Hawaii
Died: October 13, 1980; Waimanalo, Hawaii
Full name: Charles Philip Pahinui (pah-hee-NEW-ee)
Birth name: Charles Kapono Kahahawai
Also known as: Gabby Pahinui; Pops
Area of achievement: Music

EARLY LIFE

Charles Philip Pahinui was born Charles Kapono Kahahawai in Honolulu, Hawaii. He acquired the last name Pahinui from his adoptive parents, while Gabby became his nickname. As a child, Pahinui learned to play the upright bass and guitar by ear, without any formal musical training. He was drawn to hula and other traditional Hawaiian music styles as well as jazz and swing. Pahinui began playing the popular slide guitar with local singers and bands while also mastering the open tunings of *kī hōalu*, or slack-key guitar, and honing his falsetto singing voice.

LIFE'S WORK

Pahinui played popular music in bars and clubs throughout his career, accompanying bands such as Andy Cummings and His Hawaiian Serenaders and the Eddie Spencer Band. To support his wife and ten children,

he worked on a road-maintenance crew as well. Despite his frequent live performances, his early recordings featuring slack-key guitar, including the classic "Hi'ilawe" (1946), went largely unnoticed, though Pahinui developed a dedicated following among local musicians.

Gabby Pahinui. (Michael Ochs Archives/Getty Images)

In 1960, Pahinui cofounded the music group Sons of Hawaii with fellow musicians Eddie Kamae, Joe Marshall, and David Rogers. Pahinui's fame increased as he played with the Sons of Hawaii, releasing several albums with the group. By the mid-1970s, Pahinui was at the forefront of the Hawaiian cultural movement, or Hawaiian Renaissance, of the period and was recognized for his mastery of the slack-key guitar throughout Hawaii and the mainland United States. He released several solo records and recorded with guitarist Ry Cooder and other mainstream musicians.

SIGNIFICANCE

An innovative master of the slack-key guitar, Pahinui continued to inspire later generations of guitarists long after his death in 1980. His recordings have been re-released multiple times, and he is remembered annually with the Gabby Pahinui Waimanalo Kanikapila Festival, which supports Hawaiian cultural projects. In

2002, he was inducted into the Hawaiian Music Hall of Fame.

Sally Driscoll

FURTHER READING

Berger, John. "This One's for Gabby." *Honolulu Star Advertiser*. Honolulu Star Advertiser, 6 Aug. 2010. Web. 1 Mar. 2012. Explores Pahinui's enduring legacy in Hawaii and discusses the annual Gabby Pahinui Waimanalo Kanikapila Festival.

Houston, James D. "When Eddie Met Gabby." *Honolulu.* Aio, Nov. 2004. Web. 1 Mar. 2012. Discusses Pahinui's meeting with musician Eddie Kamae in 1959, the development of the Sons of Hawaii, and the beginnings of the Hawaiian traditional music revival.

Lewis, George H. "Storm Blowing from Paradise: Social Protest and Oppositional Ideology in Popular Hawaiian Music." *Popular Music* 10.1 (1991): 53–67. Print. Places Pahinui within the context of the much larger cultural and political Hawaiian Renaissance.

NAM JUNE PAIK

Korean-born artist

A musical composer who blended technology with numerous art forms, Paik is widely considered to be the first video artist. His work, reflecting his role as a major member of the Fluxus movement, challenged the seriousness traditionally associated with art.

Born: July 20, 1932; Seoul, Korea (now South Korea)
Died: January 29, 2006; Miami, Florida
Full name: Nam June Paik (NAHM joon PAYK)
Areas of achievement: Art, music

EARLY LIFE

Born in Korea to a prosperous family, Nam June Paik took piano and composition lessons as a child. The Korean War forced his family to flee the country in 1950; they lived briefly in Hong Kong and then settled in Japan. At the University of Tokyo, Paik studied music and art history before earning a degree in aesthetics in 1956. He wrote his thesis on twentieth-century composer Arnold Schoenberg. Paik then moved to Germany to study music at the University of Munich and the Conservatory of Music in Freiburg. In Germany, he began experimenting with technology in his compositions, including using tape recorders as instruments. While in Darmstadt

in the late 1950s, Paik met American composer John Cage, who became one of his biggest musical influences. Paik was inspired by Cage's use of "found sounds" and silence in musical compositions.

Paik built on Cage's ideas by creating musical sculptures that added the sounds of everyday objects, such as telephones and radios, to the sound of a piano. Paik presented his "Action Music" performances and musical sculptures at the WDR Studio für Elektronische Musik in Cologne, Germany, from 1958 to 1963. Paik did not set out with any concrete artistic objectives but instead worked from a few given conditions. Essentially, he made do with what he could obtain and present.

In the 1960s, Paik became closely associated with the Fluxus movement, an anarchic global coalition of artists founded by George Maciunas in 1961. The group aimed to challenge the seriousness and formal conventions of high art through performances, publications, manifestos, and music. Paik met Maciunas in 1961 and began to participate in Fluxus events throughout Europe. Reflecting Fluxus thought, Paik favored collages and found objects while deriding the view of artists as elite creators existing apart from the common folk.

Nam June Paik. (AP Photo)

LIFE'S WORK

Although he was renowned among his peers in the art world, Paik struggled throughout his career to attain commercial success. He never developed a particular artistic style, in part because he had no financial imperative to remain stylistically consistent. Paik's first solo exhibition in 1963, *Exposition of Music–Electronic Television* at the Galerie Parnass in Wuppertal, Germany, featured a video sculpture displaying a continuous image of abstract forms on a television set. The installation included pianos, noise machines, and other televisions transformed by altered electronics. Following the exhibition, Paik traveled to Japan to collaborate with electronics engineer Shuya Abe in the construction of *Robot K-456*, a remote-controlled robot made out of found parts that walked, talked, and defecated beans.

Paik moved to New York City in 1964 to work with other Fluxus artists. He collaborated with cellist Charlotte Moorman in a performance of John Cage's *26'1.1499" for a String Player*. During the performance, which took place at the Café a Go-Go in New York City in 1965, Moorman played a "cello" that was actually a half-dressed Paik. The piece questioned why serious music always had to be played by serious-looking people dressed in black.

Increasingly focused on television, Paik wanted to exploit the medium as though it were a musical instrument by retuning, altering circuits, and distorting the image with magnets, as in his 1965 piece *Magnet TV*. Paik, who is credited with coining the term *superhighway* as it relates to telecommunication, sought to overturn the passive, one-way flow of data typical of the electronic media in the 1970s and 1980s. He described his work as "time art" rather than sculpture.

Paik often laboriously transformed technological objects by hand to alter their appearance and purpose. He created the template for the video artists who followed him by abandoning narrative structure as well as video editing in such works as *Video Fish* (1975) and *TV Garden* (1982). For *Time Is Triangular* (1993), he created a blizzard of pulsating, morphing images shown on an array of monitors.

In 1996, Paik suffered a stroke that paralyzed the left side of his body and required him to use a wheelchair. He died on January 29, 2006, at the age of seventy-four. His work remains a part of public art collections all over the world, including the collections of the National Museum of Contemporary Art in Seoul, the Smithsonian American Art Museum in Washington, DC, and the Walker Art Center in Minneapolis, Minnesota.

SIGNIFICANCE

Never bound by convention, Paik explored the impact of technology on human existence through his art. His optimistic vision asserted the ascendancy of the human spirit over the machine. By creating new realms of experience and new forms of sound, he celebrated new opportunities for creative play and adventure. His artworks reflect a faith in the benign power of technology to enhance understanding and communication between cultures.

Caryn E. Neumann

FURTHER READING

Decker-Phillips, Edith. *Paik Video*. Barrytown, NY: Station Hill, 1998. Print. An illustrated biography of Paik's work until 1984, originally published in German in 1988.

Hanhardt, John G. *The Worlds of Nam June Paik*. New York: Guggenheim, 2003. Print. Includes a summary of Paik's life, written to accompany one of his exhibitions.

Herzogenrath, Wulf, and Andreas Kreul, eds. *Nam June Paik: There Is No Rewind Button for Life*. Bremen, Germany: Kunsthalle Bremen, 2006. Print. A collection of tributes to Paik that were given at his memorial service.

Kellein, Thomas, ed. *Nam June Paik: Video Time, Video Space*. New York: Abrams, 1993. Print. Offers a number of essays on Paik's work as well as several interviews with the artist.

Zurbrugg, Nicholas, ed. "Nam June Paik." *Art, Performance, Media.* Minneapolis: U of Minnesota P, 2004. Print. Contains an interview with Paik in the twilight of his life.

ORHAN PAMUK

Turkish-born novelist

Orhan Pamuk has been referred to as the most acclaimed Turkish novelist of his generation, embracing universal themes and winning the Nobel Prize for Literature.

Born: June 7, 1952; Istanbul, Turkey
Full name: Ferit Orhan Pamuk (fay-DEET or-HAHN pah-MOOK)
Areas of achievement: Literature

EARLY LIFE

Orhan Pamuk was born in Istanbul, Turkey, and grew up in the middle-class Nişantaşi district, the setting for many of his novels. Pamuk, his parents, his older brother, his grandmother, and several aunts and uncles lived on different floors of an apartment building, and Pamuk would continue living there as an adult. The family was well-to-do through a fortune amassed in the 1930s by Pamuk's grandfather, a civil engineer and industrialist. Upon the grandfather's death, Pamuk's father and paternal uncle, both engineers, took over the estate and lost much of the family fortune. His father often disappeared to Paris, and his parents eventually divorced.

Pamuk attended Robert College, an elite, Americanized high school in Istanbul. Young Pamuk wanted to become a painter, but his family expected him to become an engineer. He studied architecture at Istanbul Technical University, his grandfather's alma mater, and took part unenthusiastically in the school's left-wing culture, preferring William Faulkner, Thomas Mann, Marcel Proust, and Virginia Woolf to Marxist tracts. Pamuk was pleased that both his grandfather and Faulkner's built railroads.

Never taking architecture too seriously, Pamuk dropped out before completing his degree. Determined to become a writer, he completed his undergraduate education by obtaining a degree in journalism from the University of Istanbul in 1976. When he was twenty-two, he locked himself in his bedroom to write but seemed to be unproductive for eight years, while his mother begged him to apply to medical school. In 1980, he discarded a novel about student revolutionaries, inspired by Joseph Conrad, and began a new work.

LIFE'S WORK

In 1982, Pamuk married Aylin Tofajjal Türegün, a historian, and published his first novel, *Cevdet Bey ve oğullari* (1982; *Cevdet Bey and His Sons*). The novel

Orhan Pamuk. (Getty Images)

looks at the influence of Western capitalism on Turkish society as represented by Cevdet Bey, a Muslim businessman, and his descendents. While Bey considers himself responsible for his family and indebted to his nation, his sons prefer to define themselves as individuals.

If Pamuk's first novel was said to resemble the fiction of Thomas Mann, his second reminded critics of the modernism of Faulkner and Woolf. *Sessiz ev* (1983; *Silent House*) tells its story from five points of view and presents a week in the life of three upper-class siblings amid the political chaos of Turkey in the early 1980s.

Pamuk began breaking away from his modernist models with *Beyaz kale* (1985; *The White Castle*). Its protagonists seem to be mirror images—one Turkish, the other Venetian—and one among many examples of doubles appearing in Pamuk's fiction. A fantasy set in the 1690s, the novel has been described as having an intellectual playfulness that helped establish Pamuk's reputation as a cerebral writer and won him his first international acclaim.

Pamuk was in New York from 1985 to 1988 as a visiting scholar at Columbia University while his wife attended graduate school. He wrote *Kara kitap* (1990; *The Black Book*) in the university's main library. In this novel, Pamuk tells the story of a lawyer who roams Istanbul's streets looking for his missing wife. The lawyer assumes the identity of his wife's half-brother, who has also disappeared. *Yeni hayat* (1994; *The New Life*) also presents a man searching for a lost woman, as well as a group of people devoted to a mysterious book offering the hope of a new life.

Set in the sixteenth century, *Benim adim Kirmizi* (1998; *My Name Is Red*) is a postmodern mystery about the murder of an artist. Its narrators include a corpse, a horse, a tree, a coin, and the color red. *Kar* (2002; *Snow*), his first novel translated by Maureen Freely, with whom Pamuk attended high school, looks at the clash between Islamic fundamentalism and the ideals of the secular West as a writer returns to Turkey from exile in Germany. *Masumiyet müzesi* (2008; *The Museum of Innocence*) is another treatment of lost love. The novel, encompassing the changes in Turkish society over the final quarter of the twentieth century, features characters from earlier novels and a cameo by Pamuk himself. Pamuk also published several nonfiction works, including the memoir *İstanbul: Hatiralar ve şehir* (2003; *Istanbul: Memories and the City*).

Pamuk was the subject of considerable controversy in Turkey through his campaigns for Kurdish rights and

---

Orhan Pamuk's *My Name Is Red*

Pamuk's novel *My Name Is Red* (1998) is a historical murder mystery set in the sixteenth century. Much of the plot is focused on figuring out why court miniaturist Elegant Effendi was murdered, and by whom. The novel comprises fifty-nine short chapters, each narrated by a different character, including the murder victim, the murderer, a dog, and even a gold coin. Each character conveys information about the murdered Elegant Effendi as well as opinions about art, love, and daily life on the fringes of the sultan's court. Framed as a mystery, Pamuk's novel weaves together multiple plot lines. Against the backdrop of the murder investigation, the reader follows the clandestine but increasingly dangerous romance between the characters Black and Shekure, the growing power of religious fundamentalism and its threat of physical violence against opponents, and rising tensions from an increase of foreign influences in Ottoman society.

Many reviewers note that Pamuk plays with literary conventions in *My Name Is Red*. The story is told from multiple first-person points of view and even incorporates nonhuman narrators. Readers with knowledge of medieval Islamic art and philosophy texts, which form the substrate of the novel, will interpret the narrative on a deeper level. Unacquainted readers will learn much about Ottoman society. Pamuk's use of clashing symbols for East-West relations surfaces in this novel and was one of the reasons Pamuk was awarded the Nobel Prize in Literature in 2006.

---

against police brutality and other authoritarian practices. In 2005, after Pamuk told a Swiss journalist that Turkey was ignoring its history of killing thirty thousand Kurds and a million Armenians, he was charged with "insulting Turkish identity" and faced three years in prison. Following an international uproar, the threat of prosecution was dropped. During this turmoil Pamuk, divorced since 2001, lived for a time in New York, and Columbia University hired him to teach one semester a year.

SIGNIFICANCE

Pamuk has won international acclaim unprecedented for a Turkish novelist. Only Yaşar Kemal came close to finding as many readers outside Turkey. Pamuk was also popular in his native country, with many of his novels reaching the top of the Turkish best-seller list. The consistent quality and scope of his fiction and the universality of his themes helped Pamuk become the first Turk to earn the Nobel Prize in Literature in 2006, an honor dismissed as politically motivated by some Turks but acclaimed by the international literary community.

Michael Adams

FURTHER READING

Eberstadt, Fernanda. "The Best Seller of Byzantium." *New York Times Magazine* 4 May 1997: 33–37.

Print. Biographical profile of Pamuk emphasizing Turkish politics.

McGaha, Michael D. *Autobiographies of Orhan Pamuk: The Writer in His Novels*. Salt Lake City: U of Utah P, 2008. Print. Places Pamuk's work within the context of Turkish history and literature. Includes a brief biography.

Mirze, Z. Esra. "Implementing Disform: An Interview with Orhan Pamuk." *PMLA* 123.1 (Jan. 2008): 176–80. Print. Pamuk discusses his fiction, Turkish politics, and artistic freedom.

SAKHARAM GANESH PANDIT

Lawyer, philosopher, teacher

Sakharam Ganesh Pandit, a lecturer and practicing California attorney, fought to retain his US citizenship when the government moved against naturalized South Asian Americans in the mid-1920s. In 1927, he won a final decision in his favor before the US Supreme Court in United States v. Pandit.

Born: November 1, 1875; Gujarat, British India
Died: August 7, 1959; Los Angeles, California
Full name: Sakharam Ganesh Pandit
Also known as: S. G. Pandit
Areas of achievement: Law, philosophy

EARLY LIFE

Little is known of Sakharam Ganesh Pandit's early life, other than that he was the eldest son in a wealthy Brahman family in the state of Gujarat in western India. After university studies in India (then a British colony), he left to lecture in Paris and London in 1906, and settled in the United States, becoming a citizen in 1914. As the eldest son, he would have inherited his ancestral property in India, which consisted of about four hundred acres of agricultural land, a house, and personal property, but he gave all this up for a life in the United States. By 1910, he was living in Chicago as a boarder, in the home of Thomas and Lillian Stringer. He continued to live for a number of years with the Stringers, and developed a relationship with Lillian.

LIFE'S WORK

Pandit spent time as a traveling lecturer in the United States, and promotional material published in 1910 described him as a high-caste (Brahman) teacher from India. He traveled throughout the country, giving lectures on Hindu philosophy, yoga, evolution, religion, and Sanskrit, among other topics. Pandit's speaking engagements were handled by the Redpath Lyceum Bureau, the largest booking agency for the Circuit Chautauqua, an enterprise in the early twentieth century that brought thousands of performers and lecturers together under large tents before millions of small-town residents across the country. The Circuit Chautauqua introduced new ideas to rural America and helped to provoke discussion about important political, social, philosophical, and cultural issues of the time. Religion, temperance, and politics thrived as the most popular subjects, and Pandit took full advantage of the venue, bringing new ideas to grassroots America.

In 1914, Pandit applied for and was granted US citizenship, based on his education and employment background. At this time, most Asians were barred from becoming US citizens, but a certain number of Indians got around this by arguing that South Asians were in fact Caucasian. By the time World War I began, Pandit and Lillian Stringer had moved to California, where they eventually married. Pandit finished law school and became an attorney in Los Angeles, where he was also active in the Indian nationalist movement against British rule.

In 1923, the Supreme Court ruled definitively in *United States v. Bhagat Singh Thind* that South Asians were not eligible for US citizenship, and the government began the process of revoking the citizenship of naturalized Americans from the Indian subcontinent. As an attorney, Pandit represented a number of his fellow South Asian Americans in their denaturalization

Sakaram Pandit's Fight for US Citizenship

In 1923, the US Supreme Court ruled that natives of India could not become naturalized US citizens. Between 1923 and 1926, the Department of Justice revoked about fifty naturalization certificates previously issued to Asian Indians. Pandit represented spiritual teacher A. K. Mozumdar in a hearing held on November 30, 1923, where he presented a strong case but failed to save Mozumdar's citizenship. The practice served him well, however, when the United States government sought to cancel his own naturalization certificate in 1926; he represented himself in the subsequent lawsuit. Rather than focusing on proof that he was "white" within the meaning of the naturalization law, Pandit instead appealed to principles of equity. It was a less confrontational strategy. Pandit successfully argued that the United States could not cancel the certificate of naturalization because, having granted it in 1914, they waited nine years too long before instituting an action to cancel it. In addition, Pandit had spent those nine years exercising the rights and privileges of an American citizen: he married a white American woman and completely changed his life. At this point in his life, he argued, it would be impossible to reestablish the original advantageous position that he had occupied prior to his naturalization, and the losses he would suffer as a result would be irreparable. The government allowed Pandit to keep his citizenship and ceased its revocation campaign.

citizenship and therefore their property rights, and their marriages to American citizens became void—Pandit successfully challenged his own denaturalization before the Supreme Court in 1927. In *United States v. Pandit*, Pandit cited his personal history as an upstanding citizen and also invoked a rule that a decision (such as his naturalization) could not be appealed after three years.

SIGNIFICANCE

United States v. Pandit provided precedent for alternative interpretations of the immigration legislation in the late 1920s. Pandit's victory in the Supreme Court resulted in the government ending its denaturalization proceedings against Indian Americans. In addition, his success as a lawyer and lecturer carved a South Asian foothold in American law and popular culture during a time of great nationalistic fervor and active discrimination against Asian Americans.

Jan Voogd

FURTHER READING

Daniels, Roger. "Aspects of the Asian American Experience: Rights Denied and Attained." *American Studies Journal* 51 (2008). Web. 15 Mar. 2012. Describes the various legislative and constitutional statutes that denied specific rights to Asian immigrants and their descendants, with reference to Pandit's case.

Lal, Vinay. *The Other Indians: A Political and Cultural History of South Asians in America*. Los Angeles: UCLA Asian American Studies Center, 2008. Print. An illustrated, pocket-sized political and cultural history of South Asians in America.

Shah, Nayan. *Stranger Intimacy: Contesting Race, Sexuality and the Law in the North American West*. Berkeley: U of California P, 2011. Contains a section on the denaturalization campaign against South Asian Americans and Pandit's experience.

proceedings, including the spiritual teacher A. K. Mozumdar, with whose New Thought movement Pandit had been associated as a Chautauqua lecturer. Although Mozumdar and many other South Asian Americans lost their cases and were denaturalized—meaning they lost their

VIKRAM PANDIT

Business executive, investor, philanthropist

Vikram Pandit, one of the founders of the hedge fund and private equity firm Old Lane Partners, sold his business to Citigroup, the world's largest bank, for $800 million. Within nine months, Pandit had risen up the ranks in Citigroup to become the chief executive officer in a company facing a dire financial crisis.

Born: January 14, 1957; Nagpur, Maharashtra, India
Full name: Vikram Shankar Pandit
Areas of achievement: Business, philanthropy

EARLY LIFE

Vikram Pandit was born on January 14, 1957, in Nagpur, in the state of Maharashtra, India. He was the

Vikram Pandit. (Getty Images)

second child born to Shankar B. Pandit, a pharmaceutical representative, and his wife, Shailaja. Pandit was raised in the Hindu faith in an affluent family. Since his father's job required frequent relocation, Pandit attended several schools in India, as well as schools in Mombasa, Kenya, and in Flushing, New York. In each of these schools, Pandit excelled as a student. He graduated from Dadar Parsee Youth Assembly High School in Mumbai. When he was sixteen, he moved to the United States with his parents and his sister, Alka. Pandit enrolled at Gannon University in Pennsylvania and later attended Columbia University, where he earned a bachelor of science in electrical engineering in 1976 and a master's in electrical engineering in 1977. Pandit earned a master's in business administration from Columbia Business School in 1980.

From 1980 until 1983, Pandit taught economics at Columbia University and at Indiana State University in Bloomington. He became president and chief operating officer of the Institutional Securities and Investment Banking Group at Morgan Stanley in 1983. Three years later, he earned his PhD in finance at Columbia. On August 2, 1986, Pandit married Swathi

Sathaye. The couple has a son, Rahul, and a daughter, Maya.

LIFE'S WORK

In 2005, Pandit and two of his colleagues, John Haven and Guru Ramakrishnan, left Morgan Stanley and joined forces to form the hedge fund Old Lane Partners. The hedge fund generated high returns on investment almost immediately. In 2007, Citigroup acquired Old Lane, and Pandit became the leader of Citi Alternative Investments. On December 11, 2007, he was named the new chief executive officer (CEO) of Citigroup.

The global financial crisis of 2008 posed numerous challenges to Pandit in his new role as CEO. At a time of drastically falling shares and mayhem in the mortgage market, Pandit worked to revitalize Citigroup by closing down risky hedge funds, including the one he had founded. He also moved to reduce executive salaries and attract outside investors. In the short term, Pandit's efforts were not enough: Citigroup required two financial bailouts from the US government totaling $45 million. Many critics blasted Pandit for requiring taxpayer dollars to save his company and questioned his ability to maintain his role as CEO. After Citibank incurred billions of dollars in net losses in 2008 and 2009, Pandit testified before a congressional committee, stating that he would receive a one-dollar annual salary until Citigroup made a profit.

In December 2009, the company repaid the US Treasury $20 billion. A year later, Citigroup reported a net income of $10.6 billion, and the Treasury sold its shares in the company to private investors at a net profit of $12 billion. In early 2011, Citigroup officials praised Pandit for his outstanding performance, and rewarded him with a multimillion-dollar, multiyear retention package. In 2009, Pandit announced that Citigroup had been looking toward developing countries for its growth. The company's investments in Latin America and Asia, particularly in India, Brazil, and Mexico, increased. By 2010, less than one-third of Citigroup employees were employed in the United States.

In January 2011, Pandit and other high-ranking Citi officials were named in a fraud complaint filed in India in connection with an investment scam. However, investigators cleared Pandit of wrongdoing, and the investigation centered on local Citi officials.

SIGNIFICANCE

During the market turmoil of the 2008 financial crisis, amid much controversy and criticism, Pandit successfully led Citigroup from despair to profitability. Throughout his career, he has remained an active supporter of philanthropic efforts and nonprofit organizations. Citigroup sponsors the group Junior Achievement of Southern California, a financial education program for youth leaders. In memory of his mother, Pandit founded the Maina Foundation for Raising Breast Cancer Awareness. Pandit has served as a trustee of Columbia University and on the Board of Overseers for the Columbia Business School, as well as for the Indian School of Business and the Trinity School of New York City. Pandit has also served as an executive director of the American India Foundation, a director of the Institute of International Finance, and a board member of the NASDAQ.

Cynthia J. W. Svoboda

FURTHER READING

Dash, Eric. "Citigroup's Chief Shrinks Company, Eyeing Growth." *New York Times*. New York Times, 5 Apr. 2010. Web. 16 Mar. 2012. Discusses Pandit's moves to steer Citigroup through the financial crisis and its government bailout.

Davidson, Andrew, and Marshall Goldsmith. *1000 CEOs*. New York: Dorling Kindersley, 2009. Print. Provides an overview of Pandit's life and reviews his best business decisions.

Smith, Randall. "Citi CEO Gets a Big Retention Deal: Package Aims to Keep Pandit at the Helm Through 2015; His Pay Draws Fire from Critics." *Wall Street Journal* (Eastern Edition) 18 May 2011: C1. Print. Discusses Citigroup's deal to retain Pandit and reviews his compensation since 2007.

THAKOON PANICHGUL

Fashion designer

Best known for his work as a fashion designer, Thakoon Panichgul was an established writer for a major fashion publication before moving into design.

Born: September 25, 1974; Chiang Rai, Thailand
Full name: Thakoon Panichgul (TAH-kewn PAH-nihch-guhl)
Area of achievement: Fashion

EARLY LIFE

Thakoon Panichgul was born on September 25, 1974, in Chiang Rai province, Thailand. Throughout his childhood, he was surrounded by clothing production and fashion design, as both his mother and grandmother worked as tailors. Panichgul was taught how to sew at an early age. Panichgul's family relocated to the United States when he was still a young boy, settling in Omaha, Nebraska. Panichgul attended Bellevue West High School, where he excelled as a student, earning a scholarship to Boston University. Although Panichgul was interested in fashion design, he studied business in college, graduating in 1997. After completing his degree, Panichgul decided to pursue a career in the fashion industry. He moved to New York and took a position as a merchandiser for J. Crew. Three years later, he accepted a job as a fashion writer for *Harper's Bazaar*. During

Thakoon Panichgul. (Getty Images)

his time at the magazine, Panichgul enrolled in night courses at Parsons School of Design.

LIFE'S WORK

In 2004, after three years of working with *Harper's Bazaar* and taking courses at Parsons, Panichgul started his own fashion label, called Thakoon. The first Thakoon collection, which Panichgul financed using money he saved as a down payment for an apartment, was presented in September 2004. The collection consisted of ten pieces and was well received by editors, buyers, and others in the fashion industry. Following his successful debut, Panichgul received the Ecco Domani Fashion Foundation Award, which recognizes emerging talent in the fashion design industry. Because of the award, Panichgul and his Thakoon brand received increasing attention and interest. In 2006, he was nominated by the Council of Fashion Designers of America (CFDA) for the CFDA/Vogue Fashion Fund, from which Panichgul won fifty thousand dollars and a mentorship with Mark Lee, CEO of Gucci. Panichgul debuted his first collaboration, a shoe and accessory partnership with the retail chain Nine West, in September of 2006.

With a new mentorship and growing brand, Panichgul experienced a wealth of opportunities in 2007, with major collaborations that furthered the recognition of his brand and design aesthetic. Panichgul launched his first eyewear collaboration with Cult eyewear, as well as a collaboration with the clothing retailer Gap. The Gap Design Editions white t-shirt collaboration was a nationwide launch, and was featured on the cover of *Vogue*. Thakoon became a lead womenswear designer for the Hogan label, and designed their first ready-to-wear collection.

Michelle Obama, the wife of then-Senator Barack Obama, wore a dress from Thakoon's 2008 fall collection at that year's Democratic National Convention. The dress was seen by all in attendance and watching on television as Senator Obama accepted the Democratic Party presidential nomination. The event helped Thakoon to become a household name, and led to a successful 2009 capsule collection for the retailer Target.

After Obama was elected president, the Thakoon label became a favorite of the First Lady. She wore a Thakoon tweed coat on her first European visit as First Lady in 2009. Adding to his list of collaborations, Thakoon debuted his footwear collaboration with Guiseppe Zanotti, which was featured during Mercedes Benz Fashion Week in New York.

Panichgul was nominated for the 2009 CFDA Swarovski's Perry Ellis Award for Womenswear, as well as the Swiss Textile Foundation's Stella Contemporary Fashion Award. Panichgul also launched a new clothing line, Thakoon Addition, which is sold at retail for a lower price point than his Thakoon label. Panichgul was appointed creative director for the Japanese jeweler Tasaki in 2009.

SIGNIFICANCE

Panichgul has become one of the best-known and best-selling designers of the early twenty-first century. Critics have commended his work as being appreciative of past styles while remaining forward-looking. Designs by Thakoon are available worldwide, and sold by exclusive retailers such as Saks and Barney's.

Quentin D. Washington

FURTHER READING

Calloway, Libby. "Thakoon Panichgul's Omaha" *Travel and Leisure*. American Express, November 2010. Web. 19 Mar. 2012. Panichgul discusses the inspiration he draws from his United States hometown of Omaha, Nebraska.

"Thakoon Fashion Shows: Designer Directory on Style.com." *Style.com*. Condé Nast Digital, 2012. Web. 23 April 2011. Visual reference to the collections Thakoon Panichgul has presented since his debut in 2004.

Norwood, Mandi. *Michelle Style: Celebrating the First Lady of Fashion*. William Morrow, May 2009. Print. Detailed look at the fashion of First Lady Michelle Obama; the iconic reverse kimono dress designed by Thakoon Panichgul is featured.

GRACE PARK

Actor

Grace Park's role as Sharon "Boomer" Valerii in the reimagined television series Battlestar Galactica *has made her an icon of the science-fiction world. Her work as an actor on television, on the stage, and in films and video games has earned her critical acclaim.*

Born: March 14, 1974; Los Angeles, California

Full name: Grace Park
Birth name: Jee Un Park
Areas of achievement: Acting, television

EARLY LIFE

Grace Park was born Jee Un Park in Los Angeles, California, on March 14, 1974, to Korean American parents. Her family relocated to Canada shortly before her second birthday. Raised in Vancouver, Canada, Park attended the University of British Columbia, where she earned a degree in psychology. She holds both American and Canadian citizenship and is fluent in Korean. Park identifies herself as Canadian, although she was born in the United States, and she is proud of her Korean heritage.

Park worked for a time as a model before trying her hand as an actor. Her conservative parents assumed her interest in acting would just be a phase; Park herself had never considered acting as a career choice, having never regarded herself as a performer. After her father asked her when she was going to give it up, she made up her mind to do the best that she could as an actor.

Park began her career with small roles in the television series *The Outer Limits* and *Beyond Belief: Fact or Fiction*. She then moved on to a recurring role in the series *The Immortal*. Her first film role was a small part in the Jet Li action movie *Romeo Must Die* (2000). She also appeared in the television movie *LA Law: The Movie* (2002).

LIFE'S WORK

Park's big break came when she was offered a recurring role in the Canadian daytime drama *Edgemont*. Her performance in the series was praised by critics. Park also made appearances in episodes of *Stargate SG-1* and *Dark Angel*, which, along with some of her previous work, brought her some notice among the science-fiction community.

In 2003, Park capitalized on her previous work in the science-fiction genre by accepting a role in the miniseries of the reimagined *Battlestar Galactica* as Lt. Sharon "Boomer" Valerii. Before *Battlestar Galactica*, Park had had roles on the science-fiction television shows *Andromeda* and *The Dead Zone*. She played multiple characters in the ensuing *Battlestar Galactica* series and had some creative control over her character development. Her performance in the first season earned her a spot in *TV Guide*'s list of the "100 Most

Grace Park. (Getty Images)

Memorable TV Moments." *Battlestar Galactica* was critically acclaimed and earned multiple awards. Meanwhile, Park continued in her role as Shannon Ng on *Edgemont* until the show ended in 2005.

In 2007, Park appeared in the video game *Command & Conquer 3: Tiberium Wars*. She was also in the stage production of *The Boys Next Door* in Vancouver. Also in 2007, Park costarred in the crime drama film *West 32nd*. She then worked with actor Benjamin Bratt on the series *The Cleaner* and had a starring role in the Canadian series *The Border*, both in 2008. *Battlestar Galactica* concluded production in 2009, but Park continued her career in television, appearing on the popular series *CSI: Crime Scene Investigation* and reprising the role of Lt. Valerii in the television movie *Battlestar Galactica: The Plan* in 2009.

In 2010, Park made a guest appearance in the television series *Human Target*. That same year, she took a role in the CBS remake *Hawaii Five-0* as Kono Kalakaua, a character who had been cast as male in the original television series. The show has been generally well received by viewers and critics.

SIGNIFICANCE

Park has become one of the most successful Asian American television actors in the entertainment industry. Her role on *Battlestar Galactica* earned her a large fan base and helped make the show a cult classic. Over the course of her career, Park has worked in film, television, stage, and video games. She was nominated for an AZN Asian Excellence Award for Best Newcomer in 2006.

James J. Heiney

FURTHER READING

Park, Grace. "Boom Town." Interview by Steven Eramo. *Starburst Special* 77 (2006): 26–30. Print. An exclusive on-set interview in an issue celebrating *Battlestar Galactica*'s third season.

---. "IGN Interviews Grace Park." By Eric Goldman. *IGN*. IGN Entertainment, 10 Mar. 2006. Web. 15 Mar. 2012. Park discusses her experiences auditioning for and filming *Battlestar Galactica*.

LINDA SUE PARK

Writer, poet

Linda Sue Park is a Korean American writer of children's literature who won the Newbery Medal in 2002 for her work A Single Shard*, a historical novel set in Korea.*

Born: March 25, 1960; Urbana, Illinois
Full name: Linda Sue Park
Area of achievement: Literature

EARLY LIFE

Linda Sue Park was born in Urbana, Illinois, to Korean immigrants Eung Won Ed and Susie Kim. She was raised in Park Forest, a suburb of Chicago. When Park was a child, her mother cut the alphabet out of the newspaper and pasted the characters onto a college textbook for her to use as a reading primer. Her father took her to the public library regularly; Park later learned that he had referenced lists of recommended children's books to help him select books for her to read. As a child, Park was such a voracious reader that her parents had to force her to try other activities.

After earning a bachelor of arts degree in English from Stanford University, Park attended graduate school at Trinity College Dublin and Birkbeck, University of London, known at the time as Birkbeck College. She married Irish journalist Ben Dobbin in 1984. The couple have two children, Sean and Anna. Before becoming a writer, Park worked in a number of other jobs, including public relations, food journalism, education, and teaching English as a second language.

Park's parents did not speak Korean at home, seeking to Americanize their children as much as possible. When Park had her own children, she realized that they were learning a lot about the Irish side of their heritage but little about their Korean heritage. This prompted her to begin studying Korean history and culture, which has informed her work as a writer.

LIFE'S WORK

Park is best known for winning the prestigious Newbery Award for *A Single Shard* (2001), her third novel. By the time *A Single Shard* was published, she had already established a reputation as a writer for children; in 1997, Dinah Stevenson, her editor at Clarion, had discovered

Linda Sue Park. (Sonya Sones)

Park's manuscript for *Seesaw Girl* (1999) in the submissions pile and immediately offered her a contract. *Seesaw Girl* was inspired by something Park discovered when reading Frances Carpenter's *Tales of a Korean Grandmother* (1947): during the Joseon dynasty (1400–1900), tradition held that Korean girls did not leave their homes until marriage. Park wanted to explore how it might have felt to be a young girl during that time in Korean history.

Park's father inspired her to write her second novel, *The Kite Fighters* (2000). Her third, *A Single Shard*, came about because Park wanted to create a story that explored Korea's art history, particularly its tradition of pottery making; she envisioned that the orphan character, Tree Ear, would grow up to produce examples of Korean pottery that would become the envy of the East. In 2005, playwright Katie Leo adapted *A Single Shard* for the stage in Hopkins, Minnesota.

Family stories serve as a basis for Park's fourth novel, *When My Name Was Keoko* (2002), in which Park attempts to make young readers aware of Korea's struggles and triumphs before and during World War II. Similarly, *Keeping Score* (2008), also set in the mid-twentieth century, tells the story of a young girl in New York named Maggie who learns about the Korean War through her friend Jim.

Park has also written novels set in present day. In *Project Mulberry* (2005), a Korean American girl named Julia Song undertakes a silkworm science project, through which she learns about both the biology of silkworms and the complications of race relations and prejudices harbored by her mother. Similarly, *Archer's Quest* (2006) takes place in the present day, although history makes a magical appearance when a Korean leader from the past appears in the protagonist's bedroom. By bringing the past into the present, Park links elements of Korean history with the American experience.

Other works by Park include *The Firekeeper's Son* (2003), *Mung-mung* (2004), and *Bee-bim Bop* (2005). *Mung-mung* is a concept book filled with onomatopoeias of the sounds that animals make; "mung-mung" is the sound a dog makes in Korea. *Bee-bim Bop* is a picture book depicting a young Korean girl and her mother preparing a popular Korean dish, bee-bim bop, a mixed casserole of meat and vegetables. In 2010, Park published *Storm Warning* and *A Long Walk to Water*.

SIGNIFICANCE

Park's work represents significant and important contributions to the growing body of Asian American children's literature. Over the course of her career, Park has explored underrepresented histories with nuance and precision and has been praised for creating compelling characters and meticulously researched temporal and geographic settings. Park has received numerous accolades and awards, including the Chicago Tribune Young Adult Fiction Award and the Asian/Pacific American Award for Literature. In addition to being an author of children's fiction, Park is also a poet.

Sarah Park

FURTHER READING

Park, Linda Sue. "Interview with the 2002 Newbery Medal Winner, Linda Sue Park." By Nancy J. Johnson and Cyndi Giorgis. *Reading Teacher* 55.6 (2002): 394–98. Print. Discusses Park's personal history and her work as a writer.

---. "Newbery Medal Acceptance Speech." *Horn Book Magazine* 78.4 (2002): 377–84. Print. Park's Newbery acceptance speech, in which she discusses her impetus for writing *A Single Shard* and what the award means to her.

---. "Staying on Past Canal Street: Reflections on Asian Identity." *Booklist* 98.9 (2002): 832. Print. Park addresses the ways that race and culture affect her work as a writer.

Stevenson, Dinah. "Linda Sue Park." *Horn Book Magazine* 78.4 (2002): 387–91. Print. Park's literary agent discusses her development as a writer.

RACHEL PAULOSE

Indian-born lawyer

Soon after Rachel Paulose was named US Attorney for the District of Minnesota at an unusually young age, she was forced to resign because of criticisms of her management style and accusations of political bias. She nevertheless continued to be employed as a lawyer *for the federal government, taking a position with the Securities and Exchange Commission in 2011.*

Born: March 12, 1973; Kerala, India
Full name: Rachel Kunjummen Paulose

Area of achievement: Law

EARLY LIFE

Born in India in 1973, Rachel Paulose is the daughter of Joseph Paulose, a school administrator, and Lucy Paulose, the CEO of an electronics company. Paulose's maternal grandparents, Daniel and Sara Kunjummen, had immigrated to the United States in the 1960s, and her parents moved to the United States soon after her birth. Although raised primarily in Ohio, Paulose moved with her family to Minnesota when she was seventeen.

Paulose attended the University of Minnesota, graduating summa cum laude. Afterward she enrolled at Yale Law School. In addition to serving as editor of the *Yale Journal of Law and Feminism*, she was a board member of both the Asian American Students' Association and, as a devout and conservative Protestant, the Yale Law Christian Fellowship.

LIFE'S WORK

Paulose began her legal career in 1997 as a law clerk for the US Court of Appeals for the Eighth Circuit. From 1998 to 1999, she served as a trial lawyer in the US Attorney General's Honors Program, the Justice Department's recruiting program for entry-level attorneys. After working as an assistant US attorney from 1999 to 2002, she spent the next two years in private law firms, first in Washington, DC, and then in Minneapolis, Minnesota. After she successfully represented the Republican Party in an election lawsuit, Paulose's communication skills and charismatic personality attracted the attention of influential leaders of the party.

In January 2006, Paulose left the private sector and returned to the Justice Department. After briefly serving as senior counsel to Acting Deputy Attorney General Paul McNulty, she was promoted to special assistant to Attorney General Alberto Gonzales, in the administration of President George W. Bush. On February 17, 2006, Gonzales appointed Paulose to serve as the US Attorney, or federal prosecutor, for the District of Minnesota. Her nomination was confirmed by the US Senate in August 2006. Paulose became the first woman, and at thirty-three the youngest person, to hold this position. She pledged to enforce the law vigorously, emphasizing the need for robust prosecution of illegal pornography and corruption among elected public officials.

Shortly after Paulose's confirmation, Democratic legislators accused the Attorney General's office of firing eight federal prosecutors for partisan and ideological reasons. Some Democrats were hostile toward Paulose, claiming her more liberal predecessor had been pressured to resign. These critics also objected to the fact that her nomination occurred "out of committee," meaning without a hearing or committee vote, as part of a rarely utilized "discharge resolution." In addition, there were criticisms regarding her swearing-in ceremony, which took place before three hundred people at the St. Thomas School of Law in Minneapolis. After a local television station criticized the event as too extravagant, resembling "a coronation," a spokesperson for Paulose replied that the event only cost taxpayers approximately two hundred dollars.

Soon after Paulose took over management of the Minnesota US District Attorney's office, several employees complained that her management style was authoritarian, and objected to her frequent use of biblical quotations on the job. On April 5, 2007, three of the office's top lawyers voluntarily reverted to lower positions to avoid working under Paulose's supervision. Paulose's defenders argued that the three attorneys were partisan liberals who were either unable or unwilling to cooperate with an aggressive supervisor determined to bring the office more in line with the policies of the Bush administration.

Criticisms of Paulose's actions continued to grow. The *Los Angeles Times* reported allegations that she had removed an assistant US attorney because he was a strong supporter of the voting rights of Native Americans. On September 24, 2007 the *Washington Post* reported that Paulose was under investigation for allegedly making racist remarks and mishandling classified information. On November 19, 2007, Paulose resigned her position and returned to Washington, DC, to work as an official for the Department of Justice.

The following year, she accepted a position as senior trial counsel for the US Securities and Exchange Commission in Miami, Florida. Paulose's resignation did not end the controversy over her work as a federal prosecutor. The US Office of Special Counsel (OSC) investigated the circumstances for her earlier dismissal of a lawyer, and on December 3, 2008, it released a report stating that there "were reasonable grounds to believe that a prohibited personnel practice had occurred that warranted corrective action." Although the dismissed lawyer was given compensation for lost wages, Paulose was never personally accused of any wrongdoing. The *New York Times*, moreover, reported that the OSC official responsible for the report was investigated for having possibly "mixed politics with official business."

Significance

Paulose has always been recognized as an outstanding lawyer. Following her appointment as US attorney, she became caught up in the polarized political climate of the late 2000s. It has been speculated that she was promoted too quickly, without the administrative experience necessary to manage a US attorney's office successfully. Nonetheless, her appointment as a federal prosecutor in Minnesota represented a landmark for women in the history of the state's judicial system.

Thomas Tandy Lewis

Further Reading

Iglesias, David, and Davin Seay. *In Justice: Inside the Scandal That Rocked the Bush Administration.* Hoboken: Wiley, 2008. Discusses the partisan rancor within the US judicial system during the second term of US President George W. Bush.

Minutaglio, Bill. *The President's Counselor: The Rise to Power of Albert Gonzales.* New York: Rayo, 2006. Print. Provides information on Paulose's tenure as US attorney for Minnesota.

Shenon, Philip. "Amid Turmoil, US Attorney Will Shift to Headquarters." *New York Times.* New York Times, 20 Nov. 2007. Web. 27 Mar. 2012. Summarizes the controversy concerning Paulose's work in Minnesota.

I. M. Pei

Architect

Blending Asian influences with modern design elements, architect I. M. Pei has designed buildings all over the world. Paying close attention to the buildings' surroundings and purpose, he creates urban spaces that are inviting and useful. Although his buildings are very geometric, they are a part of the landscape in which they exist. Pei is one of the most prominent figures in twentieth-century architecture and has maintained his stature in the early twenty-first century.

Born: April 26, 1917; Canton, China
Full name: I. M. Pei
Birth name: Ieoh Ming Pei
Areas of achievement: Architecture and design

Early Life

I. M. Pei was born on April 26, 1917, to a wealthy and prestigious family in Canton, China. His father, a banker, moved the family to Hong Kong in 1918 and then to Shanghai in 1927. Shanghai, known as the Paris of the East, was more cosmopolitan than anything Pei had ever known. Architecturally, the city was a blend of the old and the new. Pei spent time visiting the Suzhou and Shizilin Gardens, where manmade and natural artifacts coexisted in a single landscape.

As a high school student, Pei developed a love of American cinema, especially musicals, and when offered the opportunity to study abroad he chose America over England, where his father wanted him to go. He enrolled at the University of Pennsylvania, where he planned to study architecture. However, Pei found himself disappointed by their old-fashioned course listings,

I. M. Pei. (FilmMagic)

which focused on classical architecture. He transferred to the Massachusetts Institute of Technology (MIT) to study architectural engineering. Pei developed a love of modernism after studying the work of Le Corbusier and Frank Lloyd Wright. While Pei was a freshman at MIT, Le Corbusier visited the school and Pei had the opportunity to meet him. This proved to be very important to Pei. He decided to study modern design. Pei was encouraged by the dean of the architecture school, who noticed his gifts in the field of architecture, to switch out of engineering and into architecture. Pei graduated at the top of his class at MIT, earning the American Institute of Architects' Gold Medal award upon graduating in 1940.

LIFE'S WORK

After graduation, Pei took a position at Bemis Corp. He married Eileen Loo in 1942. Loo was a student at the Harvard School of Landscape Architecture, and introduced Pei to the Harvard School of Design. Pei enrolled there in 1942, studying under the renowned modernist designers Walter Gropius and Marcel Breuer. Pei learned from Gropius and Breuer how to design structures without showing visible support elements such as columns. Beginning in 1943, he was under contract for two years to the National Defense Research Committee in Princeton, New Jersey. What Pei did there remains secret. During these years away from Harvard, he formed a company with some other students and began designing low-cost housing using prefabricated parts. Pei returned to Harvard in 1945, and after graduating, became an assistant professor of design. He also worked with architect Hugh Stubbins. In 1948, Pei joined the New York architectural firm Webb and Knapp, owned by real estate developer William Zeckendorf. For Zeckendorf, Pei designed large-scale urban developments, and gained experience overseeing big projects. Most of these projects involved demolishing run-down areas and rebuilding entire neighborhoods. Pei's work included urban renewal projects in Chicago and Denver.

Pei split from Webb and Knapp in 1955, with Zeckendorf's blessing, and founded I. M. Pei and Associates, which later became I. M. Pei and Partners. Pei's firm began working on urban renewal projects in New York City, designing the Kips Bay Towers, and in Philadelphia, building the Society Hill project. He also designed Montreal's Place Ville Marie, a commercial center, and, in England, the University of Cambridge's Green Building, using the grid pattern he employed in the Kips Bay project. Although these projects helped to make Pei famous in

---

The Louvre Pyramid

In 1981, French president François Mitterand assigned Émile Biasini to find an architect to design an entrance for the Louvre museum in Paris. After visiting the National Gallery's East Wing, Biasini decided on I. M. Pei and brought him to Paris. Pei made multiple secret visits to view the site before accepting the commission in 1983. Pei needed to visualize a way to organically incorporate his modernist style in the middle of the traditional French buildings. The original Louvre, begun in the thirteenth century, had been rebuilt and added onto throughout France's history. The existing building was a massive, sprawling, three-sided structure. Pei decided to fill the large courtyard with a giant pyramid, thereby opening up the underground entranceway and filling it with light. The glass and metal structure, in the center of the open space in front of the Louvre, allows passersby to see through the modern addition to the ancient buildings on all sides. Inside the structure there is an inverted pyramid, suspended from the base of the exterior, which draws the eye from the ceiling to the floor of the entrance. Despite its clear and delicate appearance, the pyramid is a strong, stable structure. Many people opposed Pei's design, including the Louvre's chief architect, who resigned in protest. When the pyramid was unveiled in 1989, only about half of the people who responded liked it. Through the years, however, it has become a beloved addition to the Parisian landscape and Pei's most famous piece.

---

the architectural world, many criticized them for destroying historic buildings and changing the look and feel of long-established neighborhoods. These early projects utilized what became significant elements of Pei's signature style, concrete structures with large expanses of glass.

In 1962, Pei accepted a commission to design the National Center for Atmospheric Research in Boulder, Colorado. It was the first time he was asked to design a nonurban structure. The buildings were to be built in front of a massive mesa, with no other manmade structures nearby. Pei envisioned a building that seemed a part of its natural surroundings. He researched the region's indigenous population, and incorporated the shapes and structures prevalent in their architecture into his design. This philosophy of building in harmony with nature became a central principle of Pei's work.

Pei's first highly public commission came in 1964 when Jacqueline Kennedy chose him to design the Kennedy Library in Cambridge, Massachusetts. Pei felt honored to be selected; however, the project became fraught with problems, including numerous site changes, which caused a twelve-year delay in its completion. For Pei, the experience was frustrating and unsatisfactory. He has never been satisfied with the building, believing it should have been more extraordinary in order to better honor its subject, President John F. Kennedy.

However, the fame he attained from the Kennedy Library commission made Pei's firm more visible. In 1966, he helped to revamp downtown Oklahoma City, and in 1968, he was commissioned to build an addition to Washington DC's National Gallery of Art. Pei and Partners were responsible for building Boston's John Hancock Building in 1976, another important commission. A soaring skyscraper, it was made almost entirely of glass. Learning from the mistakes of the early urban buildings, Pei's design allows the building to blend in with the more intimate neighborhood in which it stands. Its reflective surface serves as a mirror, highlighting the historical buildings at its base and making it seem to disappear into the sky as it moves upwards.

Pei's firm designed the Dallas City Hall in 1978, which became a popular and critical success. Built like a tree, with a wider top and narrower base, it has a large overhang that provides shade over the entrance plaza. In subsequent years, Pei and his firm earned more commissions from the city of Dallas.

Over the course of his career, Pei has designed and constructed many internationally acclaimed buildings, including the Louvre Pyramid in Paris, the Museum of Islamic Art in Qatar, the Luce Memorial Chapel in Taiwan, the Suzhou Museum in China, the Miho Museum in Japan, the Macao Science Center in Macao, Raffles City in Singapore, and the Bank of China in Hong Kong. His other works in the United States include Dallas's Morton H. Myerson Symphony Center, New York's Jacob Javitz Center, and Cleveland's Rock and Roll Hall of Fame.

Pei has received dozens of architecture honors and received recognition for his achievements in the field by design and construction bodies in France, Japan, China, Israel, Great Britain, and the United States.

SIGNIFICANCE

Pei is one of the best-known architects of the late twentieth and early twenty-first centuries. Drawing on both Western and Asian influences, his building have been acclaimed for their design aesthetics and functionality. Pei believes that his buildings should serve the people who use them, and not exist as mere artistic statements that are detached from their surrounding environment. He has received praise for his use of glass and geometry to create open, light-filled buildings that invite users in and connect them with their community. He is a champion of modernism, using clean sight lines and eschewing ornamentation. Some have criticized Pei for his use of concrete in design, claiming it imparts an industrial heaviness to structures. Nonetheless, many of Pei's buildings have become icons of modernism, such as the Louvre pyramid and the East Wing of the National Gallery.

Leslie Neilan

FURTHER READING

Cannell, Michael. *I. M. Pei: Mandarin of Modernism.* New York: Clarkson Potter, 1995. Print. Analyzes Pei's work and his place in the history of architecture. Discusses his successes and failures and the process behind the building of Pei's architectural designs.

Jodido, Phillip, and Janet Adams Strong. *I. M. Pei: Complete Works.* New York: Rizzoli, 2008. Print. Large-format book of photographs and commentary on Pei's work and that of his partners.

Von Boehm, Gero, and I. M. Pei. *Conversations with I. M. Pei: Light Is the Key.* New York: Prestel, 2000. Print. Features interviews with Pei about his early influences and his style of design. Includes discussions on how he designed various buildings and why.

KAL PENN

Actor

An actor who has appeared in numerous roles in film and television, Penn is best known for playing Kumar Patel in the 2004 comedy Harold & Kumar Go to White Castle *and its sequels. Penn has also worked for the United States government, serving as an associate director of public engagement for the Obama administration.*

Born: April 23, 1977; Montclair, New Jersey
Full name: Kalpen Suresh Modi (KAL-pehn soo-
REHSH MOH-dee)
Areas of achievement: Film, television

Early Life

The son of immigrants from the Indian state of Gujarat, the actor known as Kal Penn was born Kalpen Suresh Modi in Montclair, New Jersey. His mother worked for a perfume company and his father was an engineer. As a child, Penn lived in the town of Wayne, New Jersey, and attended Marlboro Middle School, where he became involved with the school's drama club. In eighth grade, Penn played the Tin Man in a school production of *The Wiz*. He received a standing ovation from the audience for his performance, an experience that led him to consider a future career as an actor. Penn attended the Fine and Performing Arts Academy at Howell High School in Farmingdale and later transferred to Freehold Township High School for his senior year, graduating in 1995. He then enrolled in the sociology and acting programs at the University of California, Los Angeles (UCLA), where he earned his bachelor's degree.

Kal Penn. (FilmMagic)

Life's Work

While attending UCLA, Penn auditioned for various film and television roles but soon discovered that opportunities for minority actors, especially those of Indian descent, were limited. Around this time, friends and industry professionals suggested that he assume an anglicized stage name in order to better his chances. Penn sought to test this theory and began to audition for roles under the name Kal Penn, a modified version of his birth name, Kalpen. He experienced an immediate increase in auditions and callbacks, and he decided to use the name Kal Penn while acting but retain Kalpen Modi as his legal name.

Penn began his film career with roles in *Express: Aisle to Glory* (1998) and *Freshmen* (1999), but television was his primary source of work during his early years as an actor. He appeared in guest roles on shows such as *Buffy the Vampire Slayer*, *Spin City*, *ER*, *NYPD Blue*, and *Sabrina, the Teenage Witch*, then returned to film projects with *American Desi* (2001). After working primarily in television and on low-budget films for several years, Penn obtained the role of Indian foreign-exchange student Taj Mahal Badalandabad in the comedy *Van Wilder* (2002), his most major role to that date. Penn would later state in interviews that while he very much disagreed with the racial stereotypes associated with the part, he took the role as an opportunity to transform a stereotypical representation into a more well-rounded character. He reprised the role in *Van Wilder 2: The Rise of Taj* (2006), for which he also served as executive producer.

After appearing in *Love Don't Cost a Thing*, *Malibu's Most Wanted*, and *Where's the Party Yaar?*, all of which were released in 2003, Penn starred as Kumar Patel in the comedy *Harold & Kumar Go to White Castle* (2004) alongside John Cho. In the film, Kumar and roommate Harold Lee (Cho) embark on an outlandish journey to the fast-food restaurant White Castle, encountering bizarre characters along the way. Though the stoner comedy was not particularly successful at the box office, it increased in popularity after its DVD release and was praised by many critics for featuring Asian American actors in the lead roles and depicting multifaceted Asian American characters. Penn went on to costar in *Harold & Kumar Escape from Guantanamo Bay* (2008) and *A Very Harold & Kumar 3D Christmas* (2011).

Penn was named one of the fifty most eligible bachelors by *People* magazine in 2004. The following year, he appeared in small roles in various films,

Kal Penn and the Impact of *Harold & Kumar*

While *Harold & Kumar Go to White Castle* (2004), *Harold & Kumar Escape from Guantanamo Bay* (2008), and *A Very Harold & Kumar 3D Christmas* (2011) are somewhat reminiscent of earlier cult stoner comedies such as those starring Cheech Marin and Tommy Chong, the film franchise has broken new ground in its depiction of Asian American characters. Penn's Kumar Patel and John Cho's Harold Lee struggle to overcome the biased perceptions of Asian Americans prevalent in American media and society, as well as the expectations of their first-generation immigrant parents. In *Harold & Kumar Go to White Castle*, Kumar rejects his family's expectation that he become a doctor, while Harold confronts coworkers who perceive him as a stereotypically hardworking Asian who should do their work for them. The two continue to encounter racism both subtle and blatant in the sequels, particularly in *Harold & Kumar Escape from Guantanamo Bay*, in which they are labeled as terrorists by a xenophobic Homeland Security official. Although the franchise's comedic style and pervasive vulgarity have not appealed to all critics, many have praised the films for their multi-faceted depictions of Asian American characters. Penn's appearance in the Harold & Kumar franchise has garnered him significant attention, making him one of the most recognizable Indian American actors in the United States and leading him to appear in major roles in a number of films and television series.

including *Dancing in Twilight*, *Son of the Mask*, and *A Lot Like Love*. In 2006, he played an assistant to the villainous Lex Luthor in *Superman Returns*. Taking on his first major dramatic role, Penn appeared as Gogol, a young man struggling with his Indian identity and unusual name, in the critically acclaimed film *The Namesake*, which played at various film festivals in 2006 and opened in the United States in 2007. The film, based on a 2003 novel by Jhumpa Lahiri, was nominated for several awards. Penn went on to appear as a terrorist in several episodes of the television show *24*. In 2007, he became a regular on the series *House M.D.*, playing Dr. Lawrence Kutner; he remained in the role until 2009.

In 2008, Penn was hired as a guest instructor at the University of Pennsylvania to teach two courses, Images of Asian Americans in the Media and Contemporary American Teen Films. The same year, he campaigned in support of then–presidential candidate Barack Obama. Penn remained politically active after Obama's successful election to the presidency, leaving *House* to accept the position of associate director of the Office of Public Engagement in 2009. In this role, Penn focused on public outreach related to youth demographics, the arts, and Asian Americans. In 2010, he temporarily resigned his White House post to film *A Very Harold & Kumar 3D Christmas*, returning to Washington, DC, several months later. He resigned again in 2011 to resume acting, taking on a significant guest role in the television comedy *How I Met Your Mother*.

SIGNIFICANCE

As one of the relatively few well-known actors of Indian descent in the United States, Penn has increased the visibility of Indian Americans in entertainment and confronted pervasive stereotypes through a number of his film and television roles. Throughout his tenure with the Office of Public Engagement, he worked to call attention to the concerns and needs of the Asian American community and promote dialogue between the community and the federal government.

Kyle Bluth

FURTHER READING

Amdur, Neil. "Still in Touch with His Jersey Roots, an Actor Mines His Talent." *New York Times* 18 Mar. 2007: L6. Print. Describes Penn's early life and career and his role in *The Namesake*.

Penn, Kal. "The GQ&A: Kal Penn." Interview by Mickey Rapkin. *GQ*. Condé Nast, Nov. 2011. Web. 23 Feb. 2012. Discusses Penn's work at the White House, his return to acting, and his experiences with racial profiling.

---. "*How I Met Your Mother*: Kal Penn on Getting Back into Acting, Dating Robin, and More." Interview by Rick Porter. *Zap2it*. Tribune Media Services, 3 Oct. 2011. Web. 23 Feb. 2012. Features discussion about Penn's return to acting and his role in *How I Met Your Mother*.

---. "Kal Penn." Interview by Brandon Routh. *Interview* Apr. 2007: 154–57. Print. Explores Penn's shift from comedy to drama with his role in *The Namesake* and discusses his childhood in New Jersey.

DAT PHAN

Vietnamese-born entertainer

Stand-up comic Dat Phan is best known as the winner of the first season of NBC's stand-up comedy competition Last Comic Standing, *which aired in 2003. He has also appeared in small roles in a variety of television shows and films and has released recordings of his comedy acts.*

Born: January 25, 1975; Saigon, South Vietnam (now Ho Chi Minh City, Vietnam)
Full name: Dat Tien Phan (DAT tee-EHN FAN)
Area of achievement: Entertainment

EARLY LIFE

Dat Tien Phan was born in Saigon, South Vietnam, the youngest of ten children. As a young child, Phan immigrated to the United States with his family and settled in San Diego, California. The family lived in poverty, but Phan has stated in interviews that he had a good childhood and credited his mother with preventing him from joining any San Diego gangs. The family later moved to suburban Santee, California. Phan graduated from West Hills High School and enrolled in Grossmont College in El Cajon, California. He changed his major four times before dropping out to pursue a career in stand-up comedy.

During his early years as a stand-up comic, Phan experienced financial difficulties and was homeless for a time. He worked to hone his craft by breaking down and analyzing each performance, and he has noted that while he realized at an early age that he had a talent for telling stories and anecdotes, he found it difficult to adjust to the structure of stand-up joke telling, which typically features setup and a distinct punch line.

LIFE'S WORK

Phan's stand-up comedy career took off when he auditioned for the first season of NBC's stand-up comedy competition *Last Comic Standing*, which aired in the summer of 2003. He successfully proceeded through the qualifying rounds and earned a spot as a finalist. Phan competed against nine other comics and performed a variety of challenges, eventually proceeding to the final rounds, in which audience votes determined which comics would be eliminated. Phan ultimately defeated nearly two thousand comics, including more established entertainers such as Ralphie May and Rich Vos, to win the competition. His success was unusual, as he

was young and relatively new to the stand-up scene. He returned to *Last Comic Standing* in 2004 for its third season, which featured the final ten comics from each of the two previous seasons. He was eliminated in the sixth episode along with three other comics. Nevertheless, his appearance on the show garnered him additional attention and further opportunities as a comic.

After appearing on *Last Comic Standing*, Phan served as a guest on numerous talk shows, including *The Tonight Show with Jay Leno* and *The Late Late Show with Craig Kilborn*. His 2009 guest appearance on *The Tyra Banks Show* was not particularly comedic in nature; rather, Phan and the other guests discussed and answered audience questions about racial stereotypes. He also played various small roles in films and television shows, appearing in the television drama *The West Wing* and the thriller *Cellular* (2004). He also found work as a voice actor, performing voice work for the animated series *Family Guy* and *Danny Phantom*. Phan has also appeared as himself in several comedy specials, including an episode of *Comedy Central Presents*, a

Dat Phan. (Getty Images)

series that features a different stand-up comic in each episode. He produced his own stand-up comedy DVD, *Dat Phan Live* (2010), as well as the comedy CD release *You Touch, You Buy* (2009).

Since *Last Comic Standing*, Phan has regularly toured the United States as a headlining comedian, appearing in venues in major cities as well as at universities and casinos. His stand-up routines frequently feature observations about race, Asian American stereotypes, and prejudice he has encountered due to his Vietnamese heritage. Phan has also worked to support the Jade Ribbon Campaign, an educational program operated by the Asian Liver Center at the Stanford University School of Medicine that raises awareness of liver cancer and hepatitis B in the Asian American community.

SIGNIFICANCE

One of the relatively few well-known American comics of Asian descent, Phan has increased the visibility of Asian Americans in comedy through his appearances on *Last Comic Standing* and nationwide tours. In recognition of his accomplishments, Grossmont College honored Phan as an outstanding alumnus with a place on the college's walk of fame. Beginning in 2007, the Smithsonian Institution included information about Phan in its traveling exhibition *Exit Saigon, Enter Little*

Saigon, which recognizes the culture and achievements of Vietnamese Americans.

Joseph F. Sanders

FURTHER READING

Bloom, Stephen. "Dat Phan: From Homeless to Headliner." *Sacramento Press*. Macer Media, 10 Mar. 2010. Web. 23 Feb. 2012. An article focusing on Phan's childhood and his early attempts to begin his career in stand-up comedy.

Curran, James. "Locally Raised Comedian Phan Grateful to Be Working." *North County Times*. North County Times, 2 Jan. 2008. Web. 23 Feb. 2012. A profile of Phan focusing on his humble beginnings, including his experiences with homelessness and his early career.

Duck, Allison. "Dinner at the Peppermill with Dat Phan." *Las Vegas Weekly*. Greenspun Media, 30 Sept. 2009. Web. 23 Feb. 2012. An article providing some insight into Phan's mindset during a performance as well as what happens after the show is complete.

Phan, Dat. "Dat Phan: Homeless to Hilarious." Interview with Allison Duck. *Las Vegas Weekly*. Greenspun Media, 21 Sept. 2009. Web. 23 Feb. 2012. An interview with Phan offering information about his experiences on *Last Comic Standing* and his thoughts on being recognized as an influential Vietnamese American by the Smithsonian Institution.

LOU DIAMOND PHILLIPS

Philippine-born actor

During a successful career as an actor that has lasted over three decades, Lou Diamond Phillips has appeared in a wide range of roles on film, television, and the Broadway stage.

Born: February 17, 1962; Subic Bay United States Naval Station, Zambales, Philippines
Full name: Lou Diamond Phillips
Birth name: Lou Diamond Upchurch
Areas of achievement: Acting, film, television

EARLY LIFE

Lou Diamond Phillips was born on February 17, 1962, on the Subic Bay United States Naval Base in Zambales, Philippines. His father, Gerald Upchurch, was a naval aircraft mechanic of Scottish, Irish, and Cherokee descent; his mother, Lucita Aranas, was born in

Candeleria, Zambales, and was of Spanish, Chinese, Hawaiian, and Japanese descent. Lou was the couple's only child. His father died when he was two years old. Years later, his mother married US naval officer George Phillips, who adopted Lou and gave him the surname Phillips.

Due to his stepfather's military career, Phillips's family relocated throughout the United States several times during his childhood. When he was a teenager, the family made Texas their permanent home. Phillips graduated from Flour Bluff High School in Corpus Christi, Texas, in 1980. He then enrolled at the University of Texas at Arlington, where he earned an undergraduate degree in drama. Between 1983 and 1986, Phillips studied acting at the Adam Roarke Film Actors Laboratory in Dallas, Texas, during which time he began performing with the Fort Worth Stage West Theater Company.

Lou Diamond Phillips. (FilmMagic)

In 1984, he made his acting debut in the horror movie *Interface*. Then, in 1987, he starred in the low-budget movie *Trespasses*.

LIFE'S WORK

In 1987, Phillips starred in the blockbuster film *La Bamba*. His role as rock-and-roll musician Richie Valens, who died tragically in a plane crash in 1959, earned him widespread fame and popularity as an actor. For the role, Phillips had to gain weight and learn to play the guitar. The movie was a commercial success and was nominated for a Golden Globe Award for Best Picture.

In March 1987, Phillips made a guest appearance on the NBC television series *Miami Vice*. He married girlfriend Julie Cypher in September of that year. In 1988, he appeared alongside Edward James Olmos in the drama *Stand and Deliver*, which won him a Golden Globe nomination for Best Performance by an Actor in a Supporting Role. Later in 1988, Phillips costarred alongside Emilio Estevez, Keifer Sutherland, and Charlie Sheen in the Western movie *Young Guns*. The movie was a box-office hit, and the sequel, *Young Guns II*, was released in 1990.

In August 1990, Phillips and his wife divorced. Throughout the early 1990s, he continued to earn roles in numerous movies, although none matched the success of his previous films. These films included *The Dark Wind* (1991), *Extreme Justice* (1993), *Wind in the Wire* (1993), *Dangerous Touch* (1994), and *Boulevard* (1994). In 1994, Phillips married Kelly Preston Phillips. The couple had twin daughters on October 5, 1997.

In April 1996, Phillips made his stage debut as the king of Siam in the Broadway production of Richard Rodgers and Oscar Hammerstein's *The King and I*. His performance as the king earned him a Tony Award nomination in 1996. He also starred alongside Denzel Washington and Meg Ryan in the action movie *Courage under Fire*, released in that same year. In 1998, he starred alongside Mark Wahlberg in the action-comedy movie *The Big Hit*.

Phillips divorced his second wife in July 2007 and married Yvonne Boismier the following month. The couple had a daughter in October 2007. In September 2007, Phillips joined a touring production of *Camelot* in the role of King Arthur. He also continued to obtain roles in numerous feature films and television shows, including the recurring role of Agent Ian Edgerton on the CBS hit television show *Numb3rs* (2005–10) and that of Colonel David Telford on the Syfy series *Stargate Universe* (2009–11). In 2009, he won the second season of the NBC reality series *I'm a Celebrity . . . Get Me Out of Here!* The following year, Phillips appeared in a supporting role in the horror movie *The Invited* (2010).

SIGNIFICANCE

Phillips has proven himself to be a talented and versatile actor. Over the course of his career, he has found success in film, in television, and on stage. While he remains best known for his portrayal of Richie Valens in *La Bamba*, Phillips continues to entertain audiences worldwide with his quality performances.

Bernadette Zbicki Heiney

FURTHER READING

Hollandsworth, Skip. "Lou Diamond Phillips." *Texas Monthly*. Emmis, Sept. 1996. Web. 27 Feb. 2012. Includes a short biography of Phillips and discusses his role in the Broadway revival of *The King and I*.

Phillips, Lou Diamond. "An Interview with Lou Diamond Phillips." By Ken P. *IGN*. IGN Entertainment, 12 June 2003. Web. 15 Mar. 2012. A discussion of Phillips's lengthy career, following the release of three of his films in a boxed set.

TROY POLAMALU

Athlete

Professional football player Troy Polamalu is a member of the National Football League's (NFL) Pittsburgh Steelers. Drafted by the Steelers in the spring of 2003, he made his NFL debut that fall. In his first eight seasons with the Steelers, he has been selected for numerous awards and honors, including six Pro Bowl selections and the NFL's Defensive Player of the Year Award.

Born: April 19, 1981; Garden Grove, California
Full name: Troy Aumua Polamalu
Birth name: Troy Aumua
Also known as: The Samoan Headhunter
Area of achievement: Sports

EARLY LIFE

The youngest of five children, Troy Polamalu was born in Garden Grove, California, on April 19, 1981. He is of Samoan descent. Polamalu's parents divorced when he was young, leaving his mother to raise her children on her own. She was unable to keep Polamalu under control,

Troy Polamalu. (Getty Images)

and by the age of eight, surrounded by crime, he was already on the streets and breaking into homes. Polamalu's mother sent him to live in Oregon with his uncle and cousins, whereupon his fortunes changed; surrounded by a strong community of family and friends, he began to behave better.

Polamalu's first experience with football was at Douglas High School in Winston, Oregon, where he excelled as both a running back and a defensive back. He also showed talent in baseball and basketball, but while he received accolades for his abilities in all sports, it was his success on the football field that would guide his future.

Throughout his high school career, Polamalu averaged six touchdowns a year, and he was chosen for the 1998 Super Prep All-Northwest team. He was named one of the top one hundred high-school football players in the western United States by the *Tacoma News* and was selected to the second team of the All–Far West League. After graduating from high school, Polamalu was offered a full scholarship to play football at the University of Southern California (USC).

LIFE'S WORK

Polamalu began his career at USC in 1999. He spent his freshman year as a backup player, appearing in eight games. Polamalu made the most of his time on the field, recording two sacks, forcing two fumbles, and blocking a punt. The following season, he began appearing as a starter at the strong-safety position, where he improved on his statistics from the previous season. By the time he concluded his playing career at USC, Polamalu was a three-year starter. He collected 278 tackles and six interceptions and was twice named to the college football All-American team.

Although an injury during his senior year forced him to miss the Orange Bowl, the Senior Bowl, and the NFL Scouting Combine, Polamalu was still able to impress Pittsburgh Steelers scouts during workouts at the USC-hosted Pro Day. The Steelers selected Polamalu as the sixteenth overall pick in the 2003 NFL draft, making him the only safety ever selected by the organization in the first round. Amid high expectations, he signed a five-year contract with the Steelers that was worth over $8 million. Polamalu quickly developed into the centerpiece of the Pittsburgh defense, his incredible speed and ability to anticipate, read, and react to an opposing offense making him the perfect candidate to lead an NFL-caliber defense. His hard work during his first season was acknowledged by the Steelers organization when they presented him with the Joe Greene Great Performance Award, which is presented annually to an outstanding Steelers rookie.

In 2003, Polamalu made three sacks in a single game, tying the NFL record. He was selected for the 2004, 2005, and 2006 Pro Bowls and won a Super Bowl championship with the Steelers in February 2006. Prior to the 2007 season, the Steelers awarded Polamalu the largest contract in team history: a four-year contract extension worth over $30 million, making him the highest-paid safety in the league.

On and off the field, one of Polamalu's most identifiable characteristics is his long, black, fluffy hair. In 2010, he insisted that it had been at least eight or nine years since he had cut his hair. Polamalu's hair has become his trademark, leading Procter & Gamble to contract with him to endorse their Head & Shoulders shampoo. Polamalu won his second career Super Bowl championship with the Steelers in February 2009.

SIGNIFICANCE

In addition to winning two championship rings, Polamalu has become one of the most decorated defensive players in the NFL and has been selected for seven Pro Bowls. At the conclusion of the 2010 season, he received the Steelers' Most Valuable Player award and was named NFL Defensive Player of the Year. Off the field, Polamalu and his wife, Theodora, have founded the Harry Panos Fund in support of wounded soldiers. The fund is named for Theodora's grandfather, a World War II veteran.

Michael D. Cummings Jr.

FURTHER READING

Breer, Albert, and Bob Bratkowski. "You Can't Stop: 'Once-in-a-Decade Talent.'" *Sporting News* 5 Jan. 2009: 24–25. Print. Discusses what opposing teams need to prepare for when facing Polamalu.

Demasio, Nunyo. "The Mane Man." *Sports Illustrated* 28 Nov. 2005: 44–45. Print. Examines the contrast between Polamalu's quiet off-field demeanor and his hard-hitting style on the field.

Layden, Tim. "Like a Bolt of Pure Energy." *Sports Illustrated* 24 Jan. 2011: 114. Print. Appearing during the 2011 playoffs, provides insight into how Polamalu impacts the game.

WHILCE PORTACIO

Artist

Often described as an artistic legend, Whilce Portacio came to prominence in the 1990s as a penciller and inker for Marvel Comics. He later cofounded Image Comics and advocated for greater intellectual property rights for comic book artists and writers.

Born: July 8, 1963; Cavite City, Philippines
Full name: William Portacio (por-TAH-see-oh)
Areas of achievement: Animation, art

EARLY LIFE

Whilce (pronounced "Wills") Portacio was born at the US Naval Station Sangley Point, a major US naval supply and repair facility on Manila Bay in the Philippines. Because his father was in the military, Portacio and his family moved frequently during Whilce's childhood, living briefly on Midway Island near Hawaii and in New Mexico before finally settling in San Diego, California.

As a young child, Portacio dreamed of becoming an astronaut, but when he was ten years old, he discovered his love for comic books after a neighbor threw out her husband's collection. He was inspired by the art of Neal Adams and Jack Kirby, the two most significant influences on Portacio, and as a teenager he began to create comic books with his friend Scott Williams. Williams would later achieve success as an inker of *Batman, Superman, The Uncanny X-Men,* and *Iron Man.* Portacio and Williams forged a working relationship that continued throughout their professional careers.

LIFE'S WORK

Portacio's first visit to a comic book convention was in San Diego in 1985. It was there that he showed his portfolio to Carl Potts, a Marvel Comics editor, who then hired Portacio to work as an inker on *Alien Legion,* interpreting, enhancing, and finishing the art of more

Whilce Portacio. (Getty Images)

established pencillers Chris Warner and Frank Cirocco. Later that year, Portacio inked the well-received *Longshot* miniseries. Eventually, he was promoted to penciller and assigned to create the visuals for the Count Nefaria character profile in *The Official Handbook of the Marvel Universe* in February 1987. He then contributed artwork for *Strikeforce: Morituri* in 1987 and *Strange Tales* in 1988. A noteworthy twelve-issue run on *The Punisher* between May 1988 and June 1989 helped to cement Portacio's popularity. Other early career assignments included *Daredevil* and *Power Pack* in 1989; *The Punisher Magazine* in 1990; and *Conan the Barbarian*, *Dreadstar*, *The Legion of Night*, *Meta-4*, and *X-Factor* in 1991. Among his best-known work is his eleven-issue stint as a penciller on the prominent series *The Uncanny X-Men* between September 1990 and July 1992; in November 1991, Portacio, along with John Byrne and Jim Lee, created the popular *X-Men* character Bishop.

In December 1991, Portacio made one of his most significant contributions to the comic book industry. He and a group of seven other prominent illustrators and writers, disenchanted by the barely adequate rates and royalties they received, asked Terry Stewart, president of Marvel Comics, for greater creative control and

ownership of their work. When the publishing giant balked at their request, the group, which included Jim Lee, Rob Liefeld, Chris Claremont, Marc Silvestri, Jim Valentino, Todd McFarlane, and Erik Larsen, founded Image Comics. Unlike the preeminent publishers at the time, Marvel Comics and DC Comics, Image Comics retained possession of only the company name and logo; ownership and editorial control of the artists' and writers' work remained in the hands of the creators. News of Image Comics' innovations caused Marvel's stock to drop by $3.25 per share. By the mid-1990s, Image Comics was the third-most-successful comics publisher in the country.

Nevertheless, family matters forced Portacio to withdraw from the partnership. As his sister struggled with systemic lupus erythematosus, a chronic autoimmune disorder, Portacio reduced his workload. After her death, he put his career on hold to grieve. Despite numerous delays, his own title, *Wetworks*, cowritten by Korean American writer Brandon Choi, debuted under Image Comics' Wildstorm Studio in June 1994. It ran for forty-three issues until August 1998. A second *Wetworks* series ran for fifteen issues, from November 2006 to January 2008.

In 1998, Portacio started his own studio at Image Comics, and later formed Avalon Studios with artist Brian Haberlin. Their first title, *Stone*, featured many elements of Filipino culture and characters from the country's folklore. Later that year, Sony Music Philippines released a soundtrack to accompany the comic and featured the music of Razorback, a Filipino heavy metal band.

Portacio's career suffered another setback in August 2000 when he fell into a diabetic coma. He came out of the coma after seven days, but he found he could not stand or draw. After months of physical therapy, Portacio was able to return to drawing and has since worked on the *Heroes Reborn*, *Batman*, *The Incredible Hulk*, and *Strikeforce* series. Whilce has also continued drawing for *The Uncanny X-Men* and *Punisher* comics.

SIGNIFICANCE

Whilce Portacio's drawings have contributed to the diversity of the comic book industry. With South Korean–born artist Jim Lee, Portacio cofounded Image Comics, which allowed artists to retain creative control of their work. Portacio has developed some of the most popular comic book characters, including the African American X-Man, Bishop, as well as a host of Filipino folklore-inspired characters in *Stone*. He also cocreated

Wetworks, which blended genres, stylistic elements, and cultural influences from around the world.

Leon James Bynum

FURTHER READING

Blosser, Betsy J. "Ethnic Differences in Children's Media Use." *Journal of Broadcasting and Electronic Media* 32.4 (1988): 453–70. Print. Explores the impact of ethnic diversity in children's media, including comic books.

Singer, Marc. "'Black Skins' and White Masks: Comic Books and the Secret of Race." *African American Review* 36.1 (Spring 2002): 107–19. Print. Considers racial stereotypes in superhero comics.

Sulat, Bert B. "Whilce Myth." *Gerry Alanguilan Interview Page*. Komikero Dot Com, 20 Sept. 1998. Web. 21 Feb. 2012. Discusses Filipino influences in *Stone* and provides background information on Portacio's life and insights into his career.

Wright, Bradford W. *Comic Book Nation: The Transformation of Youth Culture in America*. Baltimore: Johns Hopkins UP, 2003. Print. Provides historical and cultural contexts for popular comics from the 1930s through present day.

VIJAY PRASHAD

Indian-born scholar, educator, and activist

A scholar, professor, and left-wing activist, Vijay Prashad is best known for his award-winning books The Darker Nations: A People's History of the Third World *and* The Karma of Brown Folk. *His scholarly interests include South Asian history and politics, imperialism, and issues of race and class in the United States and elsewhere.*

Born: 1967; Calcutta (now Kolkata), India
Full name: Vijay Prashad
Areas of achievement: Scholarship, education, activism

EARLY LIFE

Vijay Prashad was born in 1967 in Calcutta, the capital of the Indian state of West Bengal. He attended the Doon Public School in New Delhi before immigrating to the United States, where he earned a bachelor's degree in history from Pomona College in 1989. He pursued graduate studies at the University of Chicago, earning a master's degree in 1990 and a PhD in 1994 with a thesis titled "Revolting Labor: The Making of the Balmiki Community." While at the University of Chicago, Prashad received fellowships from such institutions as the John D. and Catherine T. MacArthur Foundation.

LIFE'S WORK

Prashad completed visiting professorships at Syracuse University and Cornell University in 1995 and 1996 and then accepted the position of assistant professor of international studies at Trinity College in Hartford, Connecticut. He became an associate professor and director of the Department of International Studies in 2000 and was named the George and Martha Kellner Chair of South Asian History in 2006, becoming a full professor the same year. In 2010, Prashad became codirector of the Trinity Institute for Interdisciplinary Studies. He has taught classes on such topics as nonviolent protest, imperialism, and the South Asian diaspora.

A prolific writer, Prashad has published scholarly papers in a variety of journals and anthologies, including *Critical Asian Studies* and *Total Chaos: The Art and Aesthetics of Hip-Hop* (2008), and his articles have appeared in magazines such as *Counterpunch*. He has written more than a dozen books, including *The Karma of Brown Folk*, which the *Village Voice* included in its list of the best books of 2000. His work *The Darker Nations: A People's History of the Third World* (2007) received the Muzaffar Ahmad Award for 2009. In addition to writing, Prashad has edited several books, including *Dispatches from Latin America: Experiments against Neo-Liberalism* (2006).

Prashad has also been involved in a number of community and activist organizations, having served on the executive board of the Center for Third World Organizing and as a member of the advisory board for the Connecticut Union Community Fund. In 1996, he helped found Youth Solidarity Summer, a summer program for young South Asian activists.

SIGNIFICANCE

Through his work as an educator and numerous publications, Prashad has made significant contributions to the field of South Asian history as well as twenty-first-century leftist thought. In recognition of his work, he was awarded an Indian American Achievement Award in Arts and Letters by the Global Organization of People of Indian Origin in 2011.

Narayanan Komerath

Further Reading

Prashad, Vijay. "Community Scholarship." *Radical History Review* 79 (2001): 116–19. Print. An article in which Prashad explains how his leftist political and economic beliefs developed during his early life in India.

---."'If Power Is Not Seized, Counter-Revolution Will Rise': Vijay Prashad on the Arab Revolt." Interview with Pothik Ghosh. *Radical Notes*. Radical Notes, 31 Jan. 2011. Web. 23 Feb. 2012. An interview in which Prashad discusses his thoughts on the Arab Spring uprisings of 2011 and their significance.

---. "Smashing the Myth of the Model Minority." Interview by Michelle Caswell. *Asia Society*. Asia Society, n.d. Web. 23 Feb. 2012. An interview in which Prashad explains the goals of Youth Solidarity Summer and discusses his beliefs regarding the perception of Indian Americans as a model minority.

Mary Abigail Kawena Pukui

Scholar

A notable Hawaiian scholar and translator, Pukui worked with the Bishop Museum in Honolulu, Hawaii, from the 1930s through the 1980s. She is best known for publishing more than fifty books on Hawaiian language and culture, including Hawaiian Folk Tales, Hawaiian-English Dictionary, *and* Echo of Our Song: Chants and Poems of the Hawaiians.

Born: April 20, 1895; Kau, Hawaii
Died: May 21, 1986; Honolulu, Hawaii
Full name: Mary Abigail Kawena Pukui (kah-VEH-nah POO-kew-ee)
Birth name: Mary Abigail Kawena Wiggin
Also known as: Kawena
Area of achievement: Scholarship

Early Life

Mary Abigail Kawena Pukui was born to Henry Nathaniel Wiggin and Mary Paahana Kanakaole Wiggin in 1895. Her father was from Massachusetts and worked as an overseer at a Hutchinson Sugar plantation in Naalehu, Hawaii, while her mother came from a family of Hawaiian priestesses. In accordance with Hawaiian tradition, Pukui lived with her maternal grandmother for much of her early childhood. From her grandmother, Pukui learned about Hawaiian language and culture, including traditional medicine, music and dance, and genealogy and history.

Fluent in both Hawaiian and English, Pukui attended public schools in several towns on the island of Hawaii. Following the family's move to Honolulu, on the island of Oahu, she enrolled in Central Grammar School and later in Kawaiahao Seminary. She eventually graduated from Hawaiian Mission Academy. Her education, bilingual fluency, and firsthand knowledge of Hawaiian culture directed her toward a career as a scholar devoted to recording and translating stories and oral history and promoting the study of the Hawaiian language. In 1913, she married Kalolii Pukui. The couple later adopted two daughters, Patience and Faith, and in 1931 had a biological daughter, Asenath.

Life's Work

Pukui began to work for the Bishop Museum in Honolulu in the 1920s, taking an official position with the institution in 1937. She worked as a researcher, translator, and ethnographer and began to contribute to scholarly publications in 1923, when Vassar College anthropologist Martha Beckwith and Bishop Museum anthropologist Laura Green published *Hawaiian Stories and Wise Sayings* with Pukui's assistance. Pukui visited older members of the Hawaiian community and recorded stories about customs and lore, building a collection of notes and audio recordings housed at Bishop Museum. Beckwith encouraged Vassar's publication of Pukui's *Hawaiian Folk Tales* (1933), and together they translated the works of Hawaiian scholars such as John Papa Īī as well as newspapers and other documents written in Hawaiian.

Pukui's research often paralleled her personal life, and her growing children may have inspired the writing of *Hawaiian Beliefs and Customs during Birth, Infancy, and Childhood* (1942). Scholarly and government interest in Hawaii and the Pacific increased during World

War II, and Pukui worked with researchers such as Kenneth P. Emory, the first archaeologist to use carbon-14 to date Pacific archaeological sites, and linguist Samuel Elbert, who worked as an intelligence officer and created dictionaries of various Pacific languages. Pukui and her husband, who died in 1943, also worked briefly with the US Army Corps of Engineers to camouflage Hawaii's military installations during the war. After the war, Pukui continued her Hawaiian language work with Elbert. Their scholarly collaboration produced books such as the *Hawaiian-English Dictionary* (1957), *Place Names of Hawaii* (1974), and *Hawaiian Grammar* (1979).

Over the course of her career, Pukui published more than fifty books, many of which were collaborations with scholars from a variety of fields. With anthropologist Green, Pukui published *The Legend of Kawelo and Other Hawaiian Folktales* (1936), and she coauthored *Outline of Hawaiian Physical Therapeutics* (1934) with anthropologists Edward Smith Craighill Handy and Katherine Livermore. For the latter work, Pukui drew heavily on her knowledge of traditional medicine gained during her childhood studies with her grandmother. Pukui collaborated with Handy again on *The Polynesian Family System in Kau, Hawaii* (1972), and she worked with Bishop Museum librarian Margaret Titcomb on the volume *Dog and Man in the Ancient Pacific, with Special Attention to Hawaii* (1969).

While many of Pukui's individual and collaborative publications focused on topics such as Hawaiian language and medicine, Pukui was also known for her expertise in Hawaiian music and dance. She composed more than one hundred songs and chants during her lifetime, many of which were later recorded, and cowrote the volumes *The Echo of Our Song: Chants and Poems of the Hawaiians* (1973) and *Hula: Historical Perspective* (1980). In recognition of her commitment to these aspects of Hawaiian culture, Bishop Museum held the first annual Mary Kawena Pukui Arts Festival in 2001, celebrating Hawaiian music, dance, and storytelling traditions.

SIGNIFICANCE

A widely respected scholar of Hawaiian language and culture, Pukui received honorary doctorates from the University of Hawaii in 1960 and from Brigham Young University–Hawaii in 1974. She was awarded the State of Hawaii Order of Distinction for Cultural Leadership in 1974 and named to the Hawaiian Music Hall of Fame in 1995.

Barbara Bennett Peterson

FURTHER READING

Blair, Chad. "Kawena's Legacy." *Hana Hou!* Hawaiian Airlines, Aug.-Sept. 2007. Web. 27 Feb. 2012. Discusses Pukui's early life, work as a scholar, and legacy in Hawaii.

Pukui, Mary. "Sharing from the Source." Interview with Pat Pitzer. *Honolulu* 18.5 (1983): 109+. Print. Explains Pukui's scholarly objectives in a lengthy interview.

Williamson, Eleanor. "Introduction." *Olelo Noeau*, by Mary Pukui. Honolulu: Bishop Museum, 1983. Print. Discusses Pukui's scholarly work in an introduction to one of her volumes of proverbs.

MILTON QUON

Artist and animator

A pioneer in animation and commercial art, Quon was one of the first Chinese Americans to work for Walt Disney Studios and to hold the position of art director at a major advertising agency. He is best known for his work on such films as Fantasia *and* Dumbo.

Born: August 22, 1913; Los Angeles, California
Full name: Milton Quon
Also known as: Milt Quon
Areas of achievement: Art, animation

EARLY LIFE

Milton Quon was born on August 22, 1913, in Los Angeles, California. He was the eldest of eight children and the only boy. His parents were from Guangzhou, China, and had settled in Los Angeles, where his father operated a produce shop. Quon attended Polytechnic High School, graduating in 1932. He went on to attend Frank Wiggins Trade School and also studied art and engineering at Los Angeles Junior College. His mother wanted him to become an architect or engineer, but his uncle convinced her to allow Quon to pursue a career in art. Quon won a scholarship to Chouinard Art Institute in 1936 and graduated in 1939.

LIFE'S WORK

Quon's art began to gain public recognition in 1939, during which year he won the Latham Foundation International Poster Contest and designed the lettering for the cover of an issue of *California Arts and Architecture*. Also in 1939, Quon took a position as an animator for Walt Disney Studios, remaining in the role until 1942.

His first feature film was *Fantasia* (1940). For the film, Quon helped complete animated sequences set to portions of Ludwig van Beethoven's *Pastoral Symphony* and Pyotr Tchaikovsky's *Nutcracker Suite*. He served as first assistant animator for *Dumbo* (1941) and was also an animator for various short films.

Quon left Disney during World War II and became an illustrator for Douglas Aircraft, leading a team of artists who contributed to the war effort by illustrating repair handbooks and catalogs of airplane parts. In 1946, Quon returned to Disney, joining the publicity and promotions department as a designer and artist. He was responsible for the marketing campaigns for *Song of the South* (1946) and *Make Mine Music* (1946), among other projects.

After leaving Disney again in 1949, Quon became an art director at the advertising agency Batten, Barton, Durstine, and Osborn (BBDO) in 1951. He was one of the first Chinese Americans to obtain a senior position at an advertising agency. As art director at BBDO, Quon spearheaded the design of advertisements that appeared in a variety of print publications. In 1964, Quon took the position of senior design artist at Sealright, a packaging company. Beginning in 1974, he also taught art courses at Los Angeles Trade-Technical College. Quon retired from corporate work in 1980.

In the years following his retirement, Quon began to work as a film and television extra, appearing in small roles in such television shows as *NYPD Blue* and *Mighty Morphin' Power Rangers*. He appeared in the films *Sweet Jane* (1998) and *The Cat Killers* (2000) and is best known for playing one of the passengers on the out-of-control bus in *Speed* (1994). Quon also continued to create artwork, particularly watercolor paintings inspired by his travels in Los Angeles and throughout the world. His art was the subject of the retrospective exhibition *Impressions: Milton Quon's Los Angeles* at the Los Angeles Chinese American Museum in 2005 and 2006. His work has also been featured in the group exhibitions *Inspiring Lines: Chinese American Pioneers in the Commercial Arts*, held at LMAN Studio and the El Pueblo Gallery in 2001 and 2002, and *'Round the Clock: Chinese American Artists Working in Los Angeles*, held at the Vincent Price Art Museum in 2012, among others.

SIGNIFICANCE

One of the first Chinese Americans to work in animation and the commercial arts, Quon has contributed greatly to the visibility of Asian Americans in art through the many public exhibitions of his artwork. His work on films such as *Fantasia* helped to establish Disney as one of the world's most successful media companies.

Jenny Cho

FURTHER READING

Friedrich, Kristin. "Bridging the Generation Gap: Chinese American Museum Displays the Young at Heart, and a Youthful Old Soul." *Los Angeles Downtown News* 6 May 2005: n. pag. Print. An article about two exhibitions at the Chinese American Museum, *Milton Quon's Los Angeles* and Sam Boi Lee's *A Portrait of My Mother*.

Poundstone, William. "'Round the Clock: Chinese American Artists." *Los Angeles County Museum on Fire*. Blouin Artinfo, 16 Feb. 2012. Web. 27 Feb. 2012. An article discussing the *'Round the Clock* exhibition, which featured Quon and four other Chinese American artists.

Sandell, Scott. "Through a Native Son's Eyes: In Watercolors and More, Milton Quon Chronicles Decades of Life in Los Angeles." *Los Angeles Times*. Los Angeles Times, 1 Sept. 2005. Web. 27 Feb. 2012. An article discussing Quon's exhibition at the Chinese American Museum as well as his early life and career.

A. K. Ramanujan

Indian-born poet and scholar

As a poet and scholar, Ramanujan made numerous cross-disciplinary contributions to the fields of linguistics, anthropology, history, and literature. His scholarship has contributed greatly to academic study of the languages and literatures of Tamil and Kannada, and he is particularly remembered for his translations of classic Indian literature.

Born: March 16, 1929; Mysore, British India (now India)
Died: July 13, 1993; Chicago, Illinois
Full name: Attipat Krishnaswami Ramanujan (AH-tee-paht KRIHSH-nuh-SWAH-mee rah-MAH-new-jahn)
Areas of achievement: Poetry, literature, scholarship

Early Life

Attipat Krishnaswami Ramanujan was born in Mysore, British India, in 1929. His family spoke Tamil, Sanskrit, and English, and Ramanujan also learned Kannada, a language spoken mainly in the southwest Indian state of Karnataka, where Mysore is located. Ramanujan attended D. Bhanumaiah's High School and later Maharaja College of Mysore. He continued his studies at Deccan College in Pune, earning a graduate degree in theoretical linguistics, then traveled to the United States in 1959 to attend Indiana University, where he earned his PhD in linguistics in 1963. Ramanujan married Molly Daniels, with whom he later had two children.

While completing his doctorate, Ramanujan began to work at the University of Chicago in 1961, specializing in South Asian languages, and was appointed assistant professor a year later. At the University of Chicago,

he served in the Department of Linguistics and notably helped to develop the Department of South Asian Languages and Civilizations, which he chaired from 1980 to 1985.

Life's Work

Ramanujan received significant attention and praise from fellow scholars for his English translations of classic literature from the Indian subcontinent. *The Interior Landscape: Love Poems from a Classic Tamil Anthology* (1967), his first published translation, made the classical Tamil poetry anthology *Kuruntokai* (ca. 100–300 CE) accessible to an English-reading audience. Acknowledging the limits of translation, Ramanujan strove to render the poetic elements of the Tamil text in modern English while retaining the imagery and effect of the poems.

As he was fluent in several Indian languages and familiar with many more, Ramanujan translated works from a variety of regions and cultures, expanding the breadth of Indian literature available for study in English. *Speaking of Siva*, first published in 1973, contains translations of free-verse poems originally written in Kannada between 900 and 1100 CE. Ramanujan's *Folktales from India: A Selection of Oral Tales from Twenty-Two Languages* (1991) collects folklore originally written or told in a variety of languages and includes translations of written stories, adaptations of oral tales, and rewritten versions of stories from earlier English-language texts. Languages represented within the collection include Punjabi, Urdu, and Rajasthani.

In addition to publishing numerous English translations of Indian literature, Ramanujan became known for

A. K. Ramanujan's Scholarship on the Folktales of India

A. K. Ramanujan compiled more than one hundred Indian folktales from across the subcontinent in his collection *Folktales from India: A Selection of Oral Tales from Twenty-two Languages* (1991). As the title indicates, the folktales have been translated from twenty-two different languages into English and represent a broad spectrum of Indian culture. In his scholarly introduction to the collection, Ramanujan points out that the people of India speak one hundred different languages and sixteen hundred distinct dialects. In addition to Sanskrit, the language of ancient written texts, and English, which is read and spoken throughout the entire subcontinent, India has fifteen "major" vernacular languages.

Ramanujan organizes the collection by major themes in Indian folklore and classifies the folktales that pervade South Asian society by subject matter. He provides explanatory notes throughout the volume. Some tales feature strong men; others feature strong women. Many deal with family relationships. There are stories of the supernatural and stories about animals, grim stories and humorous stories, and even stories about storytelling. As Ramanujan observes, folktales still permeate South Asian culture. They are familiar in cities and in villages, among those of every faith and every caste, or class. India's celebrated short fiction owes much to this ancient tradition, which Ramanujan's collection has helped bring to a wider readership.

fusing Indian and American styles in his own poetry. *The Striders* (1966), his first collection of original poetry, displays traces of Tamil in its tone and conventional Indian metaphors. He went on to publish several more volumes of poetry, including *Relations* (1971), *Selected Poems* (1976), and *Second Sight* (1986). *The Collected Poems of A. K. Ramanujan* was published posthumously in 1995. Ramanujan's poems, which typically concern themes of mortality and impermanence, the cyclic forces of nature, and the tension between institutional time and personal time, have inspired numerous critical studies by scholars of Indian, postcolonial, and Asian American literature.

Ramanujan published widely in a variety of anthologies and journals and is known particularly for

such scholarly papers as "Is There an Indian Way of Thinking?" (1990) and the controversial "Three Hundred Ramayanas: Five Examples and Three Thoughts on Translation" (1987), the latter of which was removed from the Delhi University curriculum in 2011 following protests from conservative Hindu groups. He served as a visiting lecturer at institutions in the United States and throughout the world, speaking about subjects related to Indian language and literature as well as his own poetry. In 1983, he was honored with a fellowship from the John D. and Catherine T. MacArthur Foundation.

SIGNIFICANCE

Ramanujan reinvigorated South Asian studies in India and the United States by reintroducing the literatures and languages of Tamil and Kannada to a discipline that was largely focused on Sanskrit texts. Through his translations, poems, and essays, he promoted the study of these languages and made significant contributions to international scholarship. In 1976, the government of India awarded Ramanujan the title of Padma Shri, a civilian award recognizing his scholarly contributions. The A. K. Ramanujan Book Prize for Translation, first awarded by the Association for Asian Studies in 1996, was named in his honor.

Trevor Lee

FURTHER READING

Bhatnagar, Manmohan Krishna, ed. *The Poetry of A. K. Ramanujan.* New Delhi: Atlantic, 2002. Print. Provides diverse perspectives on Ramanujan's poetry with a series of scholarly essays on his biography, his search for identity, and his Buddhist beliefs.

Biswas, Soutik. "Ramayana: An 'Epic' Controversy." *BBC News South Asia.* BBC, 19 Oct. 2011. Web. 2 Mar. 2012. Explores the controversy caused by Delhi University's decision to remove Ramanujan's essay "Three Hundred Ramayanas" from the curriculum following religious protests.

King, Bruce. *Three Indian Poets.* Oxford: Oxford UP, 1991. Print. Includes chapters that track Ramanujan's evolving poetic style, providing both in-depth close readings and broad overviews of his poetic collections.

Ramanujan, A. K. *Uncollected Poems and Prose.* Ed. Molly Daniels-Ramanujan and Keith Harrison. Delhi: Oxford UP, 2001. Print. Reveals Ramanujan's creative process through a collection of previously unpublished manuscripts.

KEANU REEVES

Lebanese-born actor and musician

Keanu Reeves is one of the more successful and better known actors in the entertainment industry. Although he has had many popular roles, Reeves is perhaps most famous for his role as Neo in the science-fiction blockbuster The Matrix *(1999) and its sequels.*

Born: September 2, 1964; Beirut, Lebanon
Full name: Keanu Charles Reeves
Area of achievement: Film

EARLY LIFE

Keanu Reeves is the son of Samuel Nowlin Reeves, a geologist, and Patricia Taylor, a showgirl and costume designer. His father is of Hawaiian and Chinese descent, and his mother is English. Reeves's first name means "cool breeze over the mountain" in Hawaiian. He has a younger sister, Kim. When Reeves was a child, his father was arrested for drug possession and sentenced to prison. He and his sister spent a year in Australia with their mother before settling in New York City. In 1970, Patricia, who had divorced Reeves's father, married Paul Aaron, a Broadway and Hollywood director, and the family moved to Toronto. During the six-month marriage, Aaron sparked Reeves's interest in acting.

Growing up, Reeves played ice hockey and considered becoming a professional hockey player. However, visits to Aaron in Hollywood inspired his interest in acting. Reeves enrolled in drama classes and tried out for television shows and films that were shooting in Canada. His first acting role was at De La Salle College (a high school) in a production of Arthur Miller's *The Crucible*. Reeves was accepted at the Toronto High School for the Performing Arts, but was expelled following a disagreement with a teacher, and he never finished high school. He started taking acting classes at Lea Poshuns, a community theater school, and began to get some acting jobs. Interested in Shakespeare, he auditioned for Canada's Stratford Shakespeare Festival, but was not accepted. Instead, he spent a summer at the Hedgerow Theatre in Pennsylvania, studying under actor-director Jasper Deeter. In 1984, Reeves won his first legitimate theater role in Brad Fraser's *Wolfboy* (1981). He portrayed a boy in a psychiatric hospital victimized by another boy who believes he is a werewolf. Although the play was a hit in Toronto's gay community, it was not well received by critics. Reeves next earned a role on the Canadian television show *Hangin' In*. This led to other work on television shows and commercials. Reeves moved to Los Angeles in 1984.

Reeves's feature film debut came as a result of his skill at hockey as well as his acting experience. He played the role of a hockey goalie in *Youngblood* (1986), starring Patrick Swayze and Rob Lowe. In 1986, he appeared in another sports-themed movie, *Flying*. His role as Matt, a troubled teen in the true-crime drama *River's Edge* (1986), won favorable reviews from Vincent Canby of the *New York Times* and Richard Schickel, film critic for *Time*. In 1988, Reeves appeared in two comedies: He was a rebellious teen motorcycle rider in *The Prince of Pennsylvania* and a teen racecar driver in the film *Parenthood*.

LIFE'S WORK

After a number of auditions, Reeves earned the role of Ted in the teen comedy *Bill and Ted's Excellent Adventure* (1989). The film was a box office success, but Reeves's performance as a teenage airhead led many

Keanu Reeves. (Getty Images)

Keanu Reeves as Neo in *The Matrix* Series

In many ways, Reeves's previous roles led to his success in *The Matrix*. In 1997, Andy and Lana Wachowski, the film's directors, were looking for someone who could play both an adventure and romantic lead role in their science fiction film. Reeves's quiet introspection, often displayed in previous films, was appropriate for the role of Thomas A. Anderson, alias Neo, a computer programmer by day and hacker by night whose questioning of "the matrix" leads him into an alternative world. A bonus was the fact that Reeves could and did do most of his own stunts. The first film shows the birth of a hero who has to fight for humankind in a world run by machines. In an interview for *Newsweek* magazine (4 May 2003), Reeves stated that playing Neo is "like playing the best part of us." Neo is a man who has superhuman abilities; he is also a man who can love. The combination of science fiction and action made the film one of the top hits of 1999. It earned $460 million worldwide and created a cult of followers intrigued by the allusions the Wachowski siblings packed into the film. The film's success led to two other films that focused on Neo, *The Matrix Reloaded* and *The Matrix Revolutions*, both released at different times in 2003. Reeves did not hesitate in signing on for the sequels.

fans of the movie to believe that this was his true personality. Nonetheless, the film was a surprise hit, and a sequel, *Bill and Ted's Bogus Journey*, was released in 1991. In an attempt to alter his teenaged image, Reeves tried other roles. He appeared alongside Patrick Swayze as an undercover FBI agent in the 1991 action film *Point Break*. Reeves learned to surf for his role in the film, which became a box office hit. The success of *Point Break* led to many other roles for Reeves. He portrayed a gay male hustler in *My Own Private Idaho* (1991). In 1992, he played a young English lawyer in *Bram Stoker's Dracula*. Reeves also appeared in Kenneth Branagh's 1993 film version of Shakespeare's *Much Ado About Nothing*. Reeves played the young Buddha in *Little Buddha* (1994). Reviews were mixed. Some critics still spoke of seeing hints of "Ted" in Reeves's performance. Reeves's performance as Jack Traven, a bomb squad police officer in the film *Speed* (1994), helped establish him as a credible action hero. Critics were impressed by Reeves's work in the film, which included a variety of stunts. The film helped earn Reeves a new audience of appreciative fans.

Reeves appeared in several other films throughout the 1990s, including *A Walk in the Clouds* (1995), *Feeling Minnesota* (1995), and *Chain Reaction* (1996). He also appeared as Hamlet in Shakespeare's play on stage in Winnipeg, Manitoba, to positive reviews. During the late 1990s, Reeves started touring as a bass player with his band, Dogstar. The band began opening for major musical acts and touring in Japan and New Zealand. Reeves declined to appear in *Speed 2* in 1997, opting instead for a role opposite Al Pacino in *The Devil's Advocate* (1997).

Although he had established himself as a well-known Hollywood actor, Reeves's role as Neo in the 1999 science-fiction film *The Matrix* (1999) made him a superstar. The film was a critical success and earned tens of millions of dollars worldwide. Reeves also appeared as Neo in the sequels *The Matrix Reloaded* and *The Matrix Revolutions*, both released in 2003.

Reeves has never married. His longtime girlfriend, actor Jennifer Syme, was killed in an automobile accident in 2001. In 2010, Reeves announced that he will reprise his role as Ted in the film *Bill and Ted 3*, planned for release in 2013.

SIGNIFICANCE

Reeves has become one of the most successful Hollywood actors of his generation. His character Neo in *The Matrix* film series has become an icon of the science-fiction genre. In addition to his success as an action film star, Reeves is also known for his comedic roles. He continues to work as a musician as well.

Marcia B. Dinneen

FURTHER READING

Corliss, Richard. "Unlocking *The Matrix*." *Time* 12 May 2003: 64–74. Print. Includes many details on each of the *Matrix* films.

Grossman, Lev. "The Man Who Isn't There." *Time* 21 Feb. 2005: 54–56. Print. Profiles Reeves's personal life and selected film roles.

Robb, Brian J. *Keanu Reeves: An Excellent Adventure*. Rev. ed. London: Plexus, 2003. Print. Includes biographical information, as well as a behind-the-scenes look at many of Reeves's films.

Dave Roberts

Athlete

A left-handed outfielder, Roberts played professional baseball for such teams as the Cleveland Indians, the Boston Red Sox, and the San Francisco Giants prior to retiring to become a coach. He was a member of the 2004 Red Sox and assisted the team in winning its first World Series in more than eighty years.

Born: May 31, 1972; Naha, Okinawa, Japan
Full name: David Ray Roberts
Area of achievement: Sports

Early Life

David Ray Roberts was born in Naha, Japan, on May 31, 1972, to American marine Waymon Roberts and Okinawan Eiko Roberts. When Roberts was young, his family moved to California following his father's reassignment to a military base there. Roberts attended Rancho Buena Vista High School in Vista, where he excelled at sports, especially baseball and football. His athletic abilities earned him a scholarship to the University of California, Los Angeles (UCLA). Roberts played for the UCLA Bruins baseball team while earning his bachelor's degree in history.

Life's Work

Roberts was originally drafted by the Cleveland Indians in the forty-seventh round of the 1993 amateur draft but did not sign. In the 1994 draft, he was selected by the Detroit Tigers in the twenty-eighth round and signed on June 9. Roberts married his wife, Tricia, in 1997; the couple later had two children. After playing for minor-league teams associated with the Tigers for several years, Roberts was traded from Detroit to Cleveland on June 24, 1998. He made his major-league debut with the Cleveland Indians on August 7, 1999, stealing eleven bases in his first season. In July and August of 1999, he also competed as a member of the US baseball team at the Pan American Games in Winnipeg, Canada; the team won a silver medal.

The Indians traded Roberts to the Los Angeles Dodgers after the 2001 season. While with the Dodgers, Roberts continued to establish himself as a strong player, stealing 118 bases during his tenure and placing third in the National League for stolen bases in 2002 and 2003. On July 31, 2004, the trade deadline for the 2004 season, the Boston Red Sox acquired Roberts. While he had been a major contributor to the Dodgers,

he was largely a bench player for the Red Sox, appearing in only forty-five games.

During the 2004 postseason, the Red Sox entered the American League Division Series as a wild-card team and eventually defeated the Los Angeles Angels of Anaheim. The team went on to compete in the American League Championship Series (ALCS), facing its historical rival, the New York Yankees. After the Yankees won the first three games in the series, winning a fourth would have ended the ALCS and sent them to the World Series, and in the ninth inning of the fourth game, the score was 4–3 in the Yankees' favor. However, after Red Sox batter Kevin Millar was walked to first base, Roberts entered the game as a pinch runner, taking Millar's place. He quickly stole second base, and when the next batter hit a single, Roberts scored. His run tied the score, allowing the game to continue into extra innings. The Red Sox won the game 6–4 in twelve innings and went on to win the next three games, then swept the St. Louis Cardinals for the team's first World Series win since 1918. Although Roberts did not play with the Red Sox in the World Series, his steal was one of the plays credited with making his team's victory possible.

Dave Roberts. (MLB Photos via Getty Images)

Roberts was traded to his hometown team, the San Diego Padres, on December 20, 2004. He played two seasons for the Padres as a major contributor and then signed as a free agent with the San Francisco Giants following the 2006 season. He retired in early 2009 after two seasons with the Giants. Over the course of his career in major-league baseball, Roberts stole 243 bases, appeared in a total of 832 games, and achieved a batting average of .266.

Following his retirement, Roberts worked as a part-time Red Sox analyst for the sports television station NESN in 2009, then took a job as an assistant to baseball operations with the Padres for the 2010 season. Early in 2010, Roberts was diagnosed with Hodgkin's lymphoma, a cancer of the lymphatic system. After undergoing chemotherapy, he was declared cancer-free in late 2010 and was promoted to first-base coach for the Padres for the 2011 season. He returned to the position in 2012, accompanying the team to spring training in Peoria, Arizona.

SIGNIFICANCE

Playing for five teams over the course of his major-league career, Roberts established himself as a successful hitter and outfielder with a skill for stealing bases. His stolen base in the 2004 ALCS helped the Red Sox achieve the team's first World Series victory in eighty-six years, beginning a new era for the team. Along with the other members of the Red Sox, Roberts was named Sports Illustrated Sportsman of the Year for 2004.

Jonathan E. Dinneen

FURTHER READING

McCauley, Janie. "Healthy Once Again, Dave Roberts Ready to Coach." *NBCSports*. NBC Universal, 2 Feb. 2011. Web. 23 Mar. 2012. Discusses Roberts's bout with cancer and his career as a coach.

Shaughnessy, Dan. *Reversing the Curse: Inside the 2004 Boston Red Sox*. New York: Houghton, 2005. Print. Chronicles the Boston Red Sox's 2004 season, including Roberts's contributions, and culminates with the team's first World Series win in eighty-six years.

Verducci, Tom. "Take That, New York!" *Sports Illustrated* 10 Nov. 2004: 44. Print. Details Roberts's career-defining moment at the ALCS.

NINOTCHKA ROSCA

Philippine-born activist, feminist, and writer

A leftist activist forced into political exile during the reign of Philippine president Ferdinand Marcos, Rosca is the author of numerous works that critique US imperialism, satirize Philippine dictatorship, and advocate for social reform. Working with women's solidarity organizations such as GABRIELA, she has sought to end human-rights violations in the Philippines and elsewhere.

Born: 1946; Philippines
Full name: Ninotchka Rosca (nih-NOCH-kuh ROS-kuh)
Areas of achievement: Literature, activism, women's rights

EARLY LIFE

Ninotchka Rosca was born in the Philippines in 1946, the year the United States granted the nation independence after forty-eight years of rule. A bright student and outspoken activist, she attended the University of the Philippines during the 1960s, where she studied comparative literature. After earning her degree, Rosca began to work as a freelance journalist, publishing articles critical of the regime of Philippine president Ferdinand Marcos, an ardent opponent of communism whose rule was supported by the US government as part of its efforts to prevent the spread of communist influence in Asia.

In September of 1972, Marcos declared martial law, taking control of the media, curtailing civil liberties, and cracking down on political opponents such as the Communist Party of the Philippines (CPP). Rosca was arrested in 1973 and sent to the Camp Crame Detention Center for six months. In 1977, threatened with a second arrest for her continued activism, Rosca fled the Philippines for the United States, where she obtained a position at the University of Hawaii at Manoa. She later moved to New York to write and organize for social justice.

LIFE'S WORK

A poetic writer and ardent activist, Rosca interweaves personal experience and Philippine history in her fiction. Her first book, the short-fiction collection *Bitter Country and Other Stories* (1970), was published while she was still living in the Philippines. Rosca went on to publish *The Monsoon Collection* (1983) and the novels *State of War* (1988), which chronicles the lives of ordinary Filipinos under dictatorial rule, and *Twice Blessed* (1992), which recasts and satirizes Marcos's rise to power. *Twice Blessed* won the American Book Award in 1993. In 2006, Rosca published *Sugar and Salt*, which originally appeared as a short story in *Ms.* magazine.

Rosca has also gained recognition for her nonfiction works, which include *Endgame: The Fall of Marcos* (1987) and *Jose Maria Sison: At Home in the World; Portrait of a Revolutionary* (2004). The latter work includes a profile of and extensive interview with Jose Maria Sison, the controversial founder of the CPP and a professor whom Rosca met while attending the University of the Philippines. Rosca writes frequently for such periodicals as *Ms.*, *Village Voice*, the *Nation*, *Filipinas*, and *Q*. In 2006, she began to publish essays and informal writings on her blog, *Lily Pad*.

As a feminist activist, Rosca focuses particularly on issues related to women's rights and human trafficking. In the 1990s, she cofounded the US branch of the General Assembly Binding Women for Reforms, Integrity, Education, Leadership, and Action (GABRIELA), a women's solidarity organization founded in the Philippines in the previous decade. This organization later evolved into the Association of Filipinas, Feminists Fighting Imperialism, Re-feudalization, and Marginalization (AF3IRM). Rosca has also worked with Amnesty International and the PEN American Center.

In 1993, in a cowritten statement distributed at the United Nations' World Conference on Human Rights in Vienna, Austria, Rosca introduced the phrase "modern-day slavery" in reference to human trafficking. She later helped plan the fourth United Nations World Conference on Women, held in Beijing, China, in 1995, which highlighted such issues as sex tourism, violence against women, and the mail-order bride industry. Rosca worked as a media liaison for the Women's International War Crimes Tribunal on Japan's Military Sexual Slavery in 2000, which convicted Japan's wartime government for its role in the "comfort women" system during World War II. Influenced by her own experiences under Philippine martial law, Rosca has also served as a member of the Survivors Committee, a group of activists and former political prisoners.

SIGNIFICANCE

Rosca blends poetry with activism, nationalism with transnationalism, and women's rights with human rights, highlighting the intersections of race, class, and gender in order to build connections and alliances. Although deeply rooted in her own experience as a political exile living in the United States, Rosca connects her struggle with that of women fighting for an end to imperialism, oppression, and injustice around the world. In 1998, Rosca was recognized by the Bread and Roses Cultural Project as one of twelve Asian American Women of Hope for her outstanding dedication to human rights.

Evyn Lê Espiritu

FURTHER READING

Davis, Rocio G. "Postcolonial Visions and Immigrant Longings: Ninotchka Rosca's Versions of the Philippines." *World Literature Today* 73.1 (1999): 62–70. Print. Analyzes Rosca's novels *Twice Blessed* and *State of War* within the context of the Philippines' historical and contemporary politics.

Rosca, Ninotchka. "Interview with Ninotchka Rosca." By Braden Goyete. *Maisonneuve.* Maisonneuve, 16 May 2010. Web. 29 Feb. 2012. Discusses Rosca's views on immigration and her work as a writer and activist.

---. "Rosca Discusses Women's Rights and American Public's 'Willful Ignorance' of US Presence in Philippines." *Open Hand.* Open Hand, n.d. Web. 29 Feb. 2012. Explores Rosca's connections to Filipino activist Jose Maria Sison, with whom she wrote *Jose Maria Sison: At Home in the World.*

S

Seito Saibara

Japanese-born agriculturist

One of the first Japanese citizens to settle permanently in Texas, Saibara was instrumental in establishing rice farming as a major industry along the Gulf Coast. His introduction of Japanese varieties of rice to the area dramatically increased harvests and contributed to the development of a Japanese settlement in Webster, Texas.

Born: 1861; Kochi, Japan
Died: April 11, 1939; Webster, Texas
Full name: Seito Saibara (SAY-toh si-BAH-rah)
Areas of achievement: Agriculture, business, pioneering

Early Life

Seito Saibara was born in Kochi, Japan, on October 11, 1861. Trained as a lawyer, he initially pursued a career in politics and became the first Christian member of the Japanese Diet, or parliament. In 1899, he became president of Doshisha University in Kyoto, Japan, an institution founded by American Congregationalists. Saibara traveled to Hartford, Connecticut, in 1901 to study theology at the Hartford Theological Seminary. His wife, Taiko, and their children remained in Japan.

Life's Work

After studying in the United States for a time, Saibara wished to remain in the country, and he was soon presented with an opportunity that would allow him to do so. Rice as a crop had been introduced into Texas in the nineteenth century, but it had never been a high-yield crop. However, farmers and commercial interests in Texas, especially the Southern Pacific Railroad, hoped to make rice a major cash crop in the state. On behalf of the Houston Chamber of Commerce and the Southern Pacific Railroad, Japanese consul general Sadatsuchi Uchida asked Saibara if he would be interested in establishing a rice plantation in Texas. Saibara gladly accepted and traveled to Texas in August of 1903. Not long after, his family and thirty other Japanese immigrants settled in Webster, a small town in Harris County, Texas.

Saibara leased a tract of land near Webster and began growing Shinriki rice, a Japanese variety of the plant, the original seed having been provided by the emperor of Japan and brought to Texas by Saibara's son Kiyoaki. The success of the rice plantation allowed Saibara to purchase the land he had leased and build a house, further establishing his family's presence in Webster. The Texas Historical Commission would later place a marker detailing Saibara's contributions to the rice industry at the former site of his home. The Saibaras were reasonably well accepted in town; they were active members of the local Presbyterian church, and Saibara received permission from the Galveston Board of Trustees for his son to enroll in Ball High School.

While a number of Japanese citizens had settled in Texas, Saibara hoped to develop an even larger Japanese rice-farming community. Several more families did immigrate to Webster, but the homesickness experienced by some immigrants and the increasing anti-Japanese sentiment in the United States prevented Saibara from creating the extensive community he had envisioned. The Naturalization Act of 1790 had denied

Seito Saibara as a Texan Rice Farmer

Saibara is credited with establishing rice as a successful cash crop in Texas. Although he had no previous experience as a rice farmer, he wished to stay in the United States and bring his family over. He also wanted to establish a Japanese community in Texas. Creating rice plantations gave him the opportunity to carry out this project. Saibara became an active rice farmer as well as an advisor and consultant to other Texan farmers cultivating the crop.

When Saibara's son Kiyoaki arrived in Webster, Texas, he brought with him three hundred pounds of Shinriki rice seed. Previously, all rice seed had come from Honduras or the Carolinas. Saibara leased one thousand acres of land and planted the Japanese rice, which proved far superior to the previously used varieties. The Shinriki rice seed produced an average of thirty-four barrels of rice per acre, almost twice the production of the American seed. The first three crops produced were primarily intended as seed crops and were dispensed to rice farmers in Texas and Louisiana. The improved strains of rice and new farming techniques that Saibara and his family developed played a key role in establishing the rice industry in Texas.

naturalization to immigrants from Asia, so while the Japanese colonists were welcomed by the rice industry for their abilities to improve the quality and production of rice, they remained aliens, unable to participate in the American political process. In addition, the Immigration Act of 1924, also known as the Johnson-Reed Act, prohibited Japanese immigration to the United States entirely, as it excluded all potential immigrants ineligible for naturalization. Saibara was thus unable to expand his rice-farming community, but he nevertheless declined an invitation to return to Japan and serve as minister of education. The Naturalization Act would remain in place throughout Saibara's life, preventing him from attaining US citizenship; Kiyoaki, his oldest son, would later be one of the first Japanese Texans to become a naturalized citizen.

Eventually, Saibara and his wife left Texas for South America, establishing settlements along the Amazon River. He ultimately spent eight years in Brazil, where a major Japanese immigrant community was forming. During this time, he continued to influence the Texas rice industry through the work of Kiyoaki, who managed the rice plantation in Texas. Saibara returned to Japan for a time and then, due to ill health, rejoined his children in Texas in 1937, remaining there until his death.

SIGNIFICANCE

Through his work as a grower, experimenter, and consultant, Saibara established the rice industry in Texas and the Gulf Coast as a major commercial business.

He was also instrumental in encouraging Japanese immigration to the United States and in fostering positive relations between the United States and Japan. Saibara has been recognized by a number of organizations for his contributions to Texas agriculture. In 2000, the *Houston Chronicle* included him in a list of one hundred "tall Texans," individuals who played an important role both in Texas and elsewhere. On March 28, 2004, a memorial service for the pioneer families of Webster was held to honor the Saibaras and other Japanese families who immigrated to Texas early in the twentieth century.

Shawncey J. Webb

FURTHER READING

Brady, Marilyn Dell. *The Asian Texans*. College Station: Texas A&M UP, 2004. Print. Provides information on the religion, customs, and culture of Saibara and his family and fellow colonists.

"The Saibara Family of Webster, Texas." *Japanese American Citizens League, Houston Chapter*. Japanese American Citizens League, Houston Chapter, n.d. Web. 15 Mar. 2012. Explores the history of the US branch of the Saibara family, beginning with Seito Saibara.

Tang, Irwin A, ed. *Asian Texans: Our Histories and Our Lives*. Austin: it Works, 2008. Print. Discusses problems encountered in establishing rice plantations in Texas, including those related to anti-Asian prejudices, and places Saibara within a social and cultural context.

Edward W. Said

Palestinian-born scholar, activist, and educator

A scholar and educator, Said made significant contributions to the fields of literary and cultural criticism through his writings and is best known for his book Orientalism, *an early work in the field of postcolonial studies. As a political activist, he was particularly interested in the issue of Palestinian nationhood.*

Born: November 1, 1935; Jerusalem, Palestine (now Israel)
Died: September 25, 2003; New York, New York
Full name: Edward Wadie Said (WA-dee sah-EED)
Areas of achievement: Scholarship, activism, education

Early Life

Edward Wadie Said was born in Jerusalem, Palestine, on November 1, 1935, the son of William and Hilda Said. His father was an American citizen and had changed his name from Wadie to William while living the United States. Said's affluent family spoke English and French and discouraged the speaking of Arabic. The family split its time between Palestine, Egypt, and Lebanon and in 1947 left Palestine permanently. Said received his early education at the British preparatory school Victoria College. Upon his expulsion, his parents sent him to the United States to attend Mount Hermon School, a boarding school (now called Northfield Mount Hermon School).

Said enrolled in Princeton University after graduation, earning a bachelor's degree in 1957. He went on to attend graduate school at Harvard University and received a master's degree in English literature in 1960. In 1962, he married Maire Jaanus. The following year, he accepted a position as an instructor in the English Department at Columbia University. He completed his PhD, also in English literature, at Harvard in 1964. During his years at school, Said acquired native fluency in English, French, and Arabic and a reading knowledge of Latin, Spanish, Italian, and German.

Life's Work

Said remained at Columbia for his entire teaching career. Becoming an assistant professor in 1965, he was later promoted to associate professor and in 1970 was appointed a full professor of English and comparative literature. He married Mariam Cortas that year, his first marriage having ended in divorce in 1967; the couple had a son and a daughter. During his career at Columbia, Said served as Parr Professor of English and Comparative Literature, Old Dominion Foundation Professor in the Humanities, and University Professor of English and Comparative Literature.

As well as being a respected educator, Said was a prolific writer. A specialist in English and comparative literature, he wrote books dealing with English and anglophone authors and the craft of writing. He published his first scholarly book, *Joseph Conrad and the Fiction of Autobiography*, in 1966. This text was followed in 1975 by a book addressing literary creativity, *Beginnings: Intention and Method.*

Throughout his life, Said felt a close tie to Palestine and his Palestinian heritage. He also had a strong sense of being out of place in the Western culture of the United States and the British-run schools of his youth. The Six-Day War in 1967 between Israel and several of the Arab nations was particularly distressing to Said, as it dispossessed a large number of Palestinians and placed many more under Israeli rule. As a result, Said began to question the West's representation of the Orient, or East, in literature and art and in cultural attitudes. In 1978, Said published *Orientalism*, a book that would shape

Edward W. Said. (Getty Images)

Edward Said on Orientalism and Postcolonialism

In his book *Orientalism*, Said questions the representation of Asian cultures in Western thought and culture. He proposes that this representation is inaccurate and based on a colonizing sense of superiority, a desire to exploit the East economically, and a thirst for colonial power and domination. The inaccurate representation of the East relies on stereotypes that portray Eastern culture as based on irrationality, degeneracy, and violence. Said illustrates the existence of these stereotypical representations in the journalistic and scholarly writing of the West, as well as in its literary and popular fiction and art. Said's theory laid the foundation for the development of the field of postcolonialism, broadly defined as discourse concerning the interaction between colonizing nations (primarily European) and colonized nations (primarily non-European) and the legacy of that interaction. Postcolonial studies represent a significant area of cultural and literary studies in which writers and critics examine the problems of identity faced by individuals who lived or grew up under colonial dominance.

the field of postcolonial studies and influence numerous later scholars and authors.

Beginning in 1977, Said was actively involved in the Palestinian pursuit of nationhood. That year, he became a member of the Palestinian National Council; he served on the council until 1991, when he resigned due to his belief that it was making too many concessions. In 1979, he published his first book directly addressing the situation in the Middle East, *The Question of Palestine*. Through the 1980s, he became a visible advocate for the rights of Palestinians, writing articles and making public and televised appearances. At the time, he supported the establishment of two independent political entities, Palestine and Israel; by the 1990s, he would come to advocate the creation of one democratic country comprising both states.

Although deeply involved in the politics of the Middle East, Said continued to address the issue of East versus West in theoretical terms through literary and cultural criticism. In 1983, he published *The World, the Text, and the Critic*, proposing ways in which critics could confront their own cultural preconceptions and biases. Early in the 1990s, Said was diagnosed with leukemia; however, treatment for the illness allowed him to continue his work. In 1994, he published another book on the Palestinian situation, *The Politics of Dispossession: The Struggle for Palestinian Self-Determination, 1969–1994*. He published a memoir chronicling his childhood and education, *Out of Place*, in 1999.

In 2000, disillusioned with the peace negotiations between Palestine and Israel, Said published *End of the Peace Process: Oslo and After*. A lover of music and accomplished pianist, he coauthored the book *Parallels and Paradoxes: Explorations in Music and Society* (2002) with conductor Daniel Barenboim, with whom he also organized an Arab and Israeli youth orchestra. Several of Said's books were published following his death in 2003, including *Humanism and Democratic Criticism* (2004), *From Oslo to Iraq and the Road Map* (2004), and *On Late Style: Music and Literature against the Grain* (2006).

SIGNIFICANCE

One of the most influential literary and cultural critics of the twentieth century, Said challenged the West's concept of Eastern culture and provided the base for the development of the field of postcolonial studies. Throughout his academic career, Said urged scholars to address their own preconceptions and prejudices and move beyond them. His work concerning Palestinian nationhood called attention to the issue and presented the Palestinian perspective to a wide academic and general audience. In 2001, the Lannan Foundation awarded Said a lifetime achievement award for his work in literature.

Shawncey J. Webb

FURTHER READING

Iskandar, Adel, and Hakem Rustom, eds. *Edward Said: A Legacy of Emancipation and Representation*. Berkeley: U of California P, 2010. Print. Discusses Said's influence in the development of criticism in a broad range of fields and his involvement in politics.

Said, Edward. *Out of Place: A Memoir*. New York: Vintage, 2000. Print. Explores Said's early life and education, focusing particularly on his relationship with his parents and his sense of not belonging.

Varisco, Daniel Martin. *Reading* Orientalism: *Said and the Unsaid*. Reprint. Seattle: U of Washington P, 2007. Print. Provides a comprehensive survey of Said's writing and thinking as well as a history of the debate caused by *Orientalism* in several fields of scholarship.

Veeser, H. Aram. *Edward Said: The Charisma of Criticism*. New York: Routledge, 2010. Print. Presents an intimate portrait of Said as an intellectual and critic written by a former student and featuring interviews, transcripts, and other primary sources.

JAMES Y. SAKAMOTO

Activist and journalist

A journalist and proponent of cooperation between Japanese and non-Japanese Americans, Sakamoto edited the first English-language newspaper for the Japanese community in the United States, the Japanese American Courier. *He also helped found the Japanese American Citizens League and served as president of the organization from 1936 to 1938.*

Born: 1903; Seattle, Washington
Died: December 3, 1955; Seattle, Washington
Full name: James Yoshinori Sakamoto (yoh-shee-NOH-ree sah-kah-MOH-toh)
Also known as: Yoshinori Sakamoto; Jimmie Sakamoto; Jay Esse
Areas of achievement: Activism, journalism

EARLY LIFE

James Yoshinori Sakamoto was born in Seattle, Washington, to Osamu and Tsuchi Sakamoto, Japanese immigrants who had settled in Washington late in the nineteenth century. Sakamoto attended Franklin High School, where he excelled at sports, particularly football, baseball, and boxing. In 1921, he cofounded the Seattle Progressive Citizens League, a forerunner of the Japanese American Citizens League (JACL), which he helped to found in 1929. During the 1920s, Sakamoto took college courses, worked as an English editor for a Japanese newspaper, and also began a career in professional boxing. Injuries sustained while boxing left him nearly blind, and he returned to Seattle in 1927. In 1928, he married Misao Nishitani.

LIFE'S WORK

Sakamoto began publishing the *Japanese American Courier* in Seattle in 1928, at times writing editorials for the paper under the pen name Jay Esse. The newspaper, the first in the United States to be written entirely in English for a Japanese audience, encouraged *nisei*, or second-generation Japanese Americans, to become fully Americanized. In addition to disseminating news and other information, the *Courier* sponsored sports teams as a form of community outreach. Though the newspaper was never a profitable venture, particularly during the Great Depression, it continued to be published until 1942. In 1936, Sakamoto also became the second president of the JACL, a position he held until 1938.

Following the Japanese attack on Pearl Harbor in 1941, Japanese Americans living on the West Coast of the United States, Sakamoto among them, were relocated to internment camps. In February of 1942, Sakamoto appeared before the Tolan Commission to protest this relocation; however, he agreed to cooperate with the government, and the JACL worked to ease the transition for the Japanese American community. While at an assembly center in Puyallup, Washington, Sakamoto was appointed chief supervisor of the internees there. Sakamoto and his family were later sent to the Minidoka

---

The Japanese American Citizens League

Japanese immigration to the United States began in the late nineteenth century. While more than seventy thousand Japanese settled on the mainland of the United States, by 1910 they faced racial discriminatory practices in education, housing, and landownership. *Nisei* (second-generation Japanese Americans) began to form many small political groups to cope with the anti-Japanese movement. The American Loyalty League of Fresno, California, founded in 1923, was among them. Similar nisei leagues were organized in Washington and Oregon during the 1920s. These regional groups in the Pacific Northwest and in California united in 1929 to become a national nisei organization called the Japanese American Citizens League (JACL). The first JACL national convention took place on August 29, 1930, in Seattle, Washington.

In early 1931, JACL successfully petitioned Congress to amend the Cable Act of 1922, which stated that any female citizen who married an alien ineligible for citizenship would cease to be a citizen of the United States. In 1935, JACL helped the passage of the Nye-Lea bill, granting citizenship to *issei* (first-generation Japanese American) World War I veterans. Thanks to the long-term efforts of JACL to help with the recovery of property losses caused by the relocation of Japanese Americans during World War II, Congress passed the Civil Liberties Act of 1988, which granted each surviving internee about twenty thousand dollars in compensation. Still active in the twenty-first century, JACL is the largest Asian American civil rights advocacy organization in the United States.

camp in Idaho and remained there until 1945. After the end of World War II, Sakamoto returned to Seattle, where he lived and worked until his death.

SIGNIFICANCE

Through his efforts as a journalist and activist, Sakamoto worked to break down racial barriers and build connections between Japanese Americans and other groups. Due in part to the continued efforts of the JACL, in 1988, President Ronald Regan authorized the payment of financial compensation to Japanese Americans interned during World War II and issued a formal apology for the event.

Judy A. Johnson

FURTHER READING

Hosokawa, Bill. *JACL in Quest of Justice: The History of the Japanese American Citizens League*. New York: Morrow, 1982. Print. Chronicles the history of the JACL, paying special attention to its attempts at obtaining redress for those interned during World War II.

---. *Nisei: The Quiet Americans*. Rev. ed. Niwot: UP of Colorado, 2002. Print. Highlights contributions of second-generation Japanese Americans such as Sakamoto to the development of the Western United States and details their experiences in the internment camps.

Ichioka, Yuji. "A Study in Dualism: James Yoshinori Sakamoto and the *Japanese American Courier, 1928–1942*." *Before Internment: Essays in Prewar Japanese American History*. Ed. Gordon H. Chang and Eiichiro Azuma. Stanford: Stanford UP, 2006. Print. Includes a brief biography of Sakamoto, along with a discussion of the dual emphasis of the *Japanese American Courier* on both Americanism and cooperation between cultures.

HAROLD SAKATA

Actor and athlete

An athlete and actor, Sakata won a silver medal in weight lifting at the 1948 Olympic Games in London, England, and gained notoriety as the professional wrestling villain Tosh Togo. He is best known for his performance as Oddjob, the silent, intimidating, bowler-hat-throwing henchman in the 1964 James Bond film Goldfinger.

Born: July 1, 1920; Holualoa, Hawaii
Died: July 29, 1982; Honolulu, Hawaii
Full name: Harold Toshiyuki Sakata (TOH-shee-YEW-kee SAH-kah-tah)
Also known as: Toshiyuki Sakata; Tosh Togo
Areas of achievement: Film, sports

EARLY LIFE

Harold Toshiyuki Sakata was born in Holualoa, Hawaii, to Risaburo and Matsue Sakata. At age sixteen, he left school to work as a laborer on his parents' coffee farm and, later, on pineapple and sugar plantations throughout the Hawaiian islands. Sakata eventually settled in Honolulu, where he would spend the majority of his life.

As a young man, Sakata had a very small frame; he stood five feet eight and weighed around 113 pounds. While in Honolulu, he began working out at the local

Harold Sakata. (Getty Images)

Asian-only YMCA and developed an interest in competitive weight lifting. He competed frequently, placing high in numerous weight-lifting events in Hawaii and on the mainland. In 1944, Sakata joined the US Army, serving in an engineering unit in Hawaii that worked to build roads, runways, and other structures. Because he was stationed close to home, he was able to continue lifting weights during his military service.

After the war, Sakata continued to compete in weight-lifting competitions, setting several Hawaiian records in the process and winning the title of Mr. Hawaii in 1947. He then set his sights on earning a place on the US weight-lifting team for the 1948 Olympic Games in London, England. Sakata placed second at the US Nationals in May 1948 and at the Olympic tryouts two months later, earning a spot on the Olympic team. Sakata went on to win a silver medal in the light-heavyweight division at the London Games.

LIFE'S WORK

Despite his success as a weight lifter, Sakata struggled financially after the Olympics, and his search for a more lucrative profession led him to explore a career in professional wrestling. He began wrestling in 1950 as Mr. Sakata, the Human Tank, a "face" (hero). It was unusual for foreigners and especially Asian Americans to portray heroes in the ring, as promoters frequently played upon lingering racial prejudices and stereotypes to draw crowds. Sakata kept a busy schedule, wrestling in both the United States and Japan. In 1953, Sakata began wrestling as Tosh Togo, a "heel" (villain), at times portrayed as a stereotypical Japanese villain. During his wrestling career, Sakata divided his time between Japan and Hawaii, enjoying a great deal of success in both places.

While wrestling in a televised match in London, Sakata drew the attention of James Bond film producers Harry Saltzman and Albert Broccoli, who were impressed by the wrestler's imposing build and apparent suitability for the role of Oddjob, the mute Korean bodyguard of villain Auric Goldfinger (Gert Fröbe) and enemy of Bond (Sean Connery) in the film *Goldfinger*. Sakata had no acting experience, but his impressive physical presence secured him the part of the menacing henchman, whose deadly, razor-lined bowler hat

became an iconic symbol in popular culture. *Goldfinger* was released in 1964 and became a critical and financial success. The widespread popularity of the film made Oddjob a household name, and Sakata's performance came to define his acting career.

Sakata continued to pursue acting after *Goldfinger*, appearing in a variety of films and television programs. Because of his close association with the character of Oddjob, Sakata was often typecast as a menacing henchman in subsequent roles, including a guest appearance on *Gilligan's Island*, and was at times credited as Harold "Odd Job" Sakata. In the 1970s, Sakata appeared as Oddjob in a commercial for Vicks Cough Syrup; he later parodied the commercial on the *Tonight Show*.

SIGNIFICANCE

As an early Asian American professional wrestler and one of the first athletes of Asian descent to win an Olympic medal for the United States, Sakata made a significant contribution to the visibility of Asian Americans in sports. The character of Oddjob remained a recognizable and iconic figure long after Sakata's death; in 1998, the bowler hat worn and thrown by Sakata in *Goldfinger* was sold for more than ninety thousand dollars at auction.

Aaron D. Horton

FURTHER READING

Niiya, Brian, ed. *More Than a Game: Sport in the Japanese American Community*. Los Angeles: Japanese Amer. Natl. Museum, 2000. Print. Discusses the role of sports in the Japanese American community, placing Sakata within a greater cultural and social context.

"Sakata, Harold T." *Newsweek* 9 Aug. 1982: 68. Print. Memorializes Sakata and discusses his life and career.

Svinth, Joseph R. "Harold Sakata: Olympic Weightlifter and Professional Wrestler." *InYo: The Journal of Alternative Perspectives on the Martial Arts and Sciences*. Electronic Journals of Martial Arts and Sciences, Apr. 2001. Web. 1 Mar. 2012. Chronicles Sakata's career as a weight lifter and wrestler and discusses his experience portraying Oddjob.

LEA SALONGA

Philippine-born actor and singer

Filipina child star Salonga became internationally famous as an adult for her work as a singer and actor. Best known for originating the role of Kim in the award-winning musical Miss Saigon, *she has also received critical and popular recognition for her vocal performances in the Disney films* Aladdin *(1992) and* Mulan *(1998).*

Born: February 22, 1971; Manila, Philippines
Full name: Maria Ligaya Carmen Imutan Salonga (sah-LON-guh)
Also known as: Lea Salonga-Chien
Areas of achievement: Theater, music

EARLY LIFE

Maria Ligaya Carmen Imutan Salonga, known as Lea Salonga, was born in 1971 to Feliciano Genuino Salonga, the owner of a shipping company, and Ligaya Alcantara Imutan, who later became Salonga's manager. She grew up in Angeles City, in the Philippine province of Pampanga, and moved to Manila at the age

Lea Salonga. (Getty Images)

of six. Salonga has a younger brother, Gerard, and an adopted sister, Sheila.

Salonga enjoyed performing even as a child, and in 1978 she became active in Repertory Philippines, securing a role in the company's production of the musical *The King and I.* She appeared in various productions and eventually auditioned for and won the lead in *Annie.* In 1981, she recorded her first album, *Small Voice,* which became a hit in the Philippines. The same year, she appeared in her first film, *Tropany Bulilit,* and was nominated for the Filipino Academy of Movie Arts and Sciences Award for Best Child Actress.

Salonga continued to perform in plays and musicals, appearing in such shows as *Fiddler on the Roof,* *The Goodbye Girl,* and *Paper Moon,* and won several Aliw Awards for Best Child Performer. In addition, she hosted the television show *Love, Lea* with her brother. In 1985, she appeared in her second film, *Like Father, Like Son,* and opened for the Puerto Rican pop group Menudo during their tour of the Philippines. Salonga went on to appear in more films and musicals and in 1988 released a second album, *Lea.*

Despite her many commitments, Salonga graduated from high school as valedictorian and enrolled in Ateneo de Manila University as a premedical student. However, during her first year of college, seventeen-year-old Salonga auditioned for the female lead in the new musical *Miss Saigon.* Asked to sing "On My Own" from *Les Misérables* and then "Sun and Moon" from the new musical, she bested the competition and was selected to play Kim, a Vietnamese woman who falls in love with an American soldier.

LIFE'S WORK

Salonga debuted as Kim on September 20, 1989, at London's Theatre Royal. Her acting and clear, lyric soprano voice thrilled audiences, and she was awarded the Laurence Olivier Award for Best Performance by an Actress in a Musical. The show opened on Broadway two years later, with Salonga again playing the part of Kim. American audiences were no less enthusiastic, and her performance earned her a Tony Award for Best Actress in a Musical in 1991.

After leaving *Miss Saigon,* Salonga took on the role of Éponine in the Broadway production of *Les Misérables* in 1992. That year, she was featured as the singing voice of Princess Jasmine in the Disney film

Lea Salonga as Kim in *Miss Saigon*

Based on Giacomo Puccini's opera *Madame Butterfly* (1904), the musical *Miss Saigon* (1989) was written by Claude-Michel Schönberg and Alain Boublil, with lyrics by Boublil and Richard Maltby Jr. Schönberg and Boublil had previously collaborated on the successful musical *Les Misérables* (1985). Seeking a young, innocent-looking singer to play the lead role of Kim, producer Cameron Mackintosh auditioned more than one thousand young women. He cast Salonga in the role after hearing her sing in Manila, Philippines.

Salonga was a critical and popular success in the London production of *Miss Saigon*. The producers planned for her to reprise her role in the United States, but the Actors' Equity Association, an American labor union, wanted the lead roles to be sung by American actors of Asian descent. After Mackintosh threatened to cancel the US production, which at that point had sold a significant number of advance tickets, the matter was brought to arbitration. Mackintosh prevailed, and Salonga played Kim on Broadway when the show opened in April of 1991. She won numerous awards for her performance, including a Tony. Salonga remained in the role until 1992 and later returned to the show twice, eventually playing Kim in the show's final Broadway performance on January 28, 2001.

Aladdin; the song "A Whole New World," performed by Salonga at the Academy Awards in 1993, won the Academy Award for Best Original Song. Salonga released the album *Lea Salonga* in 1993 and the following year appeared in *My Fair Lady* in Manila as well as in a Singapore production of *Into the Woods*. In 1995, she joined an all-star cast for the tenth-anniversary production of *Les Misérables* at the Royal Albert Hall, again in the role of Éponine. Salonga was featured in another animated Disney film in 1998, providing the singing voice for the eponymous protagonist of *Mulan*. She would later reprise the role in the sequel, *Mulan II* (2004).

In 2000, Salonga joined the first Asian tour of *Miss Saigon*, which opened in the Philippines in October. After returning to the United States, she appeared on television in a 2001 episode of the hospital drama series *ER* and took on the recurring role of Lien Hughes in the daytime soap opera *As the World Turns*—a role originally played by Ming-Na Wen, who had provided the speaking voice for Mulan. Also in 2001, Salonga took on the role of Mei-Li in the revival of the 1958 musical *Flower Drum Song* in Los Angeles. The show was successful in California, and Salonga continued to perform in the musical when it opened on Broadway in 2002. In January of 2004, Salonga married businessman Robert Charles Chien, whom she had met while performing in *Flower Drum Song* in Los Angeles. Their daughter, Nicole, was born in May of 2006.

During her 2005 concert tour of the United States, Salonga became one of the first solo artists from the Philippines to perform at New York's Carnegie Hall. She went on to appear as Fantine in the Broadway revival of *Les Misérables* in 2007, Cinderella in the international tour of Richard Rodgers and Oscar Hammerstein's *Cinderella* in 2008, and Grizabella in the Asian tour of *Cats* in 2010. Salonga was named a goodwill ambassador for the Food and Agriculture Organization of the United Nations in October of 2010.

SIGNIFICANCE

Widely recognized as a talented singer and actor, Salonga has received numerous awards for her performances in musical theater and film. In recognition of her contributions to the international visibility of Filipino performers and culture, the government of the Philippines awarded her a Presidential Award of Merit in 1990 and the Order of Lakandula in 2008.

Marcia B. Dinneen

FURTHER READING

Behr, Edward, and Mark Steyn. *The Story of Miss Saigon*. New York: Arcade, 1991. Print. Includes information about the making of *Miss Saigon*, focusing on the casting process, rehearsals, and the Broadway opening.

Defensor, Teresa. "A Busy Woman." *BusinessWorld* 17 June 2002: 23. Print. Focuses on Salonga's performance in *Flower Drum Song* and her career as a recording artist.

Roura, Phil. "Diva on the Boardwalk." *Daily News* [New York] 13 Feb. 2005, Sunday Now sec: 40. Print. Discusses the beginning of Salonga's first US tour and touches on her early career in the Philippines.

Witchel, Alex. "The Iron Butterfly within Miss Saigon." *New York Times* 17 March 1991, sec. 2: 5. Print. Presents a detailed portrait of Salonga early in her career.

E. SAN JUAN JR.

Philippine-born poet, literary critic, and scholar, and writer

E. San Juan is best known for theoretical interventions in the areas of cultural and ethnic studies, literary theory, and postcolonial studies. San Juan is credited for his pioneering rediscovery of Carlos Bulosan as well as his utilization of dialectical thinking to confront the causes and consequences of the Philippine diaspora. A prolific writer and astute social theorist, San Juan has made indelible contributions to the landscape of critical theory and cultural critique.

Born: December 29, 1938; Manila, Philippines
Full name: Epifanio San Juan Jr. (EP-ee-FAHN-yoh)
Also known as: Sonny San Juan
Areas of achievement: Poetry, literary criticism, scholarship

EARLY LIFE

Epifanio San Juan Jr. was born in the Santa Cruz district of Manila, the Philippines, on December 29, 1938, to Epifanio San Juan and Loreto Samia San Juan. Entering into adulthood in the Philippines during the 1950s, San Juan was influenced by the asymmetrical relationship between the United States and his homeland, evident in the US cultural and military influence in the country after World War II as well as the emergent responses of popular democracy. In 1958, San Juan graduated magna cum laude from the University of the Philippines Diliman. In 1959, while completing his master's degree at the same university, San Juan met his future wife, Delia D. Aguilar, in a graduate course on literary criticism. The two married and had their first child, Karin Aguilar-San Juan, in 1962. Their second child, Eric San Juan, was born in 1966.

LIFE'S WORK

In 1960, San Juan received a Rockefeller Fellowship to complete his doctorate at Harvard University in Cambridge, Massachusetts. In 1964, San Juan won the Siglo de Oro award from Spain for his critique of the poems of Spanish Baroque poet Luis de Góngora. He also published his own poetry in collections such as *Godkissing Carion/Selected Poems: 1954–1964* (1964) and *The Exorcism and Other Poems* (1967). Upon completing his PhD in 1965, San Juan taught at the University of California, Davis, for a year before returning to the Philippines to teach English and comparative literature at his alma mater (1966–67). In 1966 he translated the

poetry of the renowned Filipino labor leader Amado V. Hernandez and published the collection as *Rice Grains: Selected Poems of Amado V. Hernandez* (1966). San Juan returned to the United States in 1967 as an associate professor of English at the University of Connecticut (1967–79).

In 1972, martial law was declared in the Philippines by the US-supported president, Ferdinand Marcos, and San Juan was no longer allowed back in his homeland. The same year, San Juan published *Carlos Bulosan and the Imagination of Class Struggle*, about the early-twentieth-century Filipino American novelist. This book, along with earlier published essays, revived interest in Bulosan's literature and politics concerning racism and Filipino immigrants to the United States during the first half of the twentieth century. His works on Bulosan as well as his edition of Georg Lukacs's essays in *Marxism and Human Liberation* (1972) situated E. San Juan as a prominent Marxist scholar as he began to utilize historical materialism as the central lens through which to explore the historical constraints and emancipatory possibilities of a Philippine political organization.

San Juan also analyzed the unique qualities of the Philippine diaspora as a committed intellectual in the United States. He held various professorships at Brooklyn College, City University of New York (1977–79), the University of Connecticut (1979–94), and Bowling Green State University (1994–98). San Juan also served as professor and chair of the Department of Comparative American Cultures at Washington State University, Pullman (1998–2001).

The 1990s were a prolific period in San Juan's scholarship. In 1992 he published *Racial Formation/Critical Transformations* (1992), which received numerous awards for its incisive critique of multiculturalism and the dominant theoretical modes of analyzing race and difference. For his groundbreaking work on this text, San Juan received numerous accolades and human rights awards. In 1995, E. San Juan returned to the works of Carlos Bulosan, publishing posthumous selections of his poetry, short stories, and letters in the volume *On Becoming Filipino* (1995). The same year, he facilitated the publication of Bulosan's unfinished novel, *The Cry and the Dedication* (1995), which depicted the struggle of Philippine peasants against colonial governments. Other important publications where San Juan confronts class exploitation and the global mechanisms of patriarchy and racialization include *From Exile to Diaspora* (1998), *After Postcolonialism* (2000), *Racism and Cultural Studies* (2002), *Working through the Contradictions* (2004), and *In the Wake of Terror* (2007). All of these texts solidify his place in the canon of cultural, ethnic, and Asian American studies.

With the escalation of human rights abuses in the Philippines in 2001, San Juan founded and has since directed the Philippine Cultural Studies Center in Storrs, Connecticut. With analysis focused upon the American empire in the Philippines, San Juan's growing catalog also includes: *US Imperialism and Revolution in the Philippines* (2008), *Balikbayang Sinta: An E. San Juan Reader* (2008), and *Toward Filipino Self-Determination* (2010). In 2009, he was a fellow at the W.E.B. Du Bois Institute for African and African American Research at Harvard University.

SIGNIFICANCE

For more than five decades, E. San Juan's poetry, literary criticism, and scholarly works have addressed and explained the totalizing contours of global capitalist development, enabling committed activists and scholars in the United States to situate their aspirations for social transformation within the human struggles taking place in the Philippines and throughout the developing world. His writing continually reminds his readers that the earth does not have to be so wretched.

Michael Joseph Viola

FURTHER READING

San Juan, Epifanio, Jr. *In the Wake of Terror: Class, Race, Nation, Ethnicity in the Postmodern World*. Maryland: Lexington, 2007. Print. Presents San Juan's positions in a multitude of scholarly debates pertaining to race, class, culture, and nationalism.

---, ed. *On Becoming Filipino: Selected Writings of Carlos Bulosan*, Philadelphia: Temple UP, 1995. Print. Includes an important introduction to Bulosan's work by San Juan and selected short stories, poetry, and letters written by Bulosan.

---. *Toward Filipino Self-Determination: Beyond Transnational Globalization*. Albany: State U of New York P, 2009. Print. A collection of essays chronicling the contradictions in the Filipino American experience and throughout the Philippine diaspora.

BIENVENIDO N. SANTOS

Philippine-born novelist, poet, and writer

The author of several novels and numerous short stories and poems, Santos is best known for works such as the American Book Award–winning collection Scent of Apples. *His writings chronicle the development of Filipino American identity amid the political upheaval of the twentieth century.*

Born: March 22, 1911; Manila, Philippines
Died: January 7, 1996; Legazpi, Philippines
Full name: Bienvenido Nuqui Santos (BEE-ehn-veh-NEE-doh NEW-kee SAN-tohs)
Also known as: Mang Ben; Ben Santos
Area of achievement: Literature

EARLY LIFE

Bienvenido Nuqui Santos was born and raised in Tondo, a low-income district in Manila, Philippines, then a US territory. He received a bachelor's degree in education from the University of the Philippines in 1932 and taught school while also writing short stories. Santos traveled to the United States on a student scholarship in 1941 and earned a master's degree in English from the University of Illinois, also studying at Columbia University.

LIFE'S WORK

Santos's plans to return to the Philippines after completing his studies were thwarted by World War II, and he instead took a position in the Washington, DC, office of the Philippine government. His first collection of short stories, *You Lovely People* (1955), draws heavily on this period of exile and alienation. After the war, Santos attended Harvard University and then returned to the Philippines, becoming a professor at Legazpi College and later its president (1957–58). He became a fellow of the University of Iowa Writers' Workshop in 1958. In the 1960s, Santos was awarded a Guggenheim Fellowship and completed the novel *Villa Magdalena* (1965) and the collections *Brother, My Brother* (1960) and *The Day the Dancers Came* (1967).

Filipino American Long Fiction

Filipino Americans occupy a unique place in US history. From the end of the Spanish-American War in 1898 to the independence of the Philippines in 1946, Filipinos were considered subjects of the United States. This unique historical phenomenon created ambivalent feelings among Filipino Americans toward the United States. While many appreciated its economic opportunities, Filipino American writers such as Joaquin Legaspi, José Garcia Villa, Alfred A. Robles, Bayani L. Mariano, N. V. M. Gonzalez, Samuel Tagatac, J. C. Dionisio, and Bienvenido N. Santos also aspired to reconnect with native Filipino culture, literature, and art. Filipino American long fiction is largely built on this aspiration; it grows out of the fear of losing what Mariano, in his poem "What We Know," calls the "best of ourselves."

Cecilia Manguerra Brainard and Jessica Hagedorn are two leading Filipino American novelists who have represented Filipino Americans' efforts to reclaim their history and identity. The main event of Brainard's *When the Rainbow Goddess Wept* (1994) occurs during World War II. With her family, nine-year-old Yvonne Macaraig flees the Japanese invasion of the Philippines to join the resistance effort. In the jungle, she is nourished by the legends of Bongkatolan, the Woman Warrior, and the merciful rainbow goddess. In Jessica Hagedorn's 1996 novel *The Gangster of Love*, the protagonist is a new immigrant from the Philippines who, while excited about his new life in the United States, is haunted by the memory of the homeland he left behind.

During the regime of Philippine dictator Ferdinand Marcos, Santos went into exile in the United States, where he became a citizen and served as distinguished writer in residence at Wichita State University for nearly a decade. He began to split his time between the United States and the Philippines in the 1980s. In 1981, his short fiction collection *Scent of Apples* (1979) won the American Book Award. He went on to publish the novels *The Man Who (Thought He) Looked Like Robert Taylor* (1983) and *What the Hell for You Left Your Heart in San Francisco* (1987), among other works.

SIGNIFICANCE
Santos's work spans the postcolonial decades of the twentieth century, from Philippine independence through the dictatorship of Ferdinand Marcos, and gives voice to the emerging Filipino American community. In recognition of his accomplishments in the field of literature, Santos was awarded several honorary doctorates and received numerous awards, including four Carlos Palanca Memorial Awards for Literature and the Philippine Republic Cultural Heritage Award.

Sally Driscoll

FURTHER READING
Cruz, Isagani R. *The Lovely Bienvenido N. Santos*. Quezon: U of the Philippines P, 2005. Print. Includes two biographical plays that feature quotes from Santos's works as well as from his unpublished manuscripts, letters, and other primary sources.
Espiritu, Augusto Fauni. "Fidelity and Shame: Bienvenido Santos." *Five Faces of Exile: The Nation and Filipino American Intellectuals*. Stanford: Stanford UP, 2005. Print. Discusses Santos's relationship with the United States and the Philippines, his experiences with colonialism, and his identity as an expatriate.
Palomar, Al Camus. "World Literature in Review: Philippines." *World Literature Today* 67.2 (1993): 455. Print. Provides a portrait of Santos based on the autobiographical component of his poetry collection *The Wounded Stag* (1956).

DALIP SINGH SAUND
Indian-born politician and judge

Best remembered as the first Asian American Congressman, Saund also played an important role in the campaign to secure US citizenship rights for immigrants of Asian origin in the 1940s. A talented mathematician and successful farmer and businessman, Saund also served as a judge in California.

Born: September 20, 1899; Chhajulwadi, Punjab, India
Died: April 22, 1973; Hollywood, California
Full name: Dalip Singh Saund (THLEEP SIN-gah sah-OOND)
Areas of achievement: Government and politics, activism

Early Life

Dalip Singh Saund was born in Chhajulwadi, a small village in British India. His Sikh parents, Natha Singh and Jeoni Kaur, were uneducated, but his father became quite wealthy as a government contractor, and Saund's mother taught him to value his Indian cultural heritage. His parents were determined that their seven children should have the best possible education, and when he was eight years old, Saund was sent to boarding school in the town of Amritsar. Saund's father died when he was ten years old, leaving his mother to raise the family on her own.

Saund was interested in the United States from an early age and was inspired by the ideals of self-government expressed in the Gettysburg Address. Following his 1919 graduation from the University of Punjab with a degree in mathematics, Saund decided to go to the United States to study food preservation. His family was not supportive of this decision, but he assured them that he would return to India afterward to set up a mango canning plant.

Saund sailed from Bombay (now known as Mumbai) to the United States via England. After arriving at Ellis Island in New York, he traveled by train to San Francisco, California, to enroll at the University of California, Berkeley, and he lived in the clubhouse of the Sikh Temple in Stockton, California, where Indian students were able to live rent-free.

Saund enrolled in the Department of Agriculture at Berkeley but continued taking courses in mathematics. He decided to change programs, and he obtained a master's degree in mathematics in 1922. Politically active, Saund joined the Hindustan Association of America, whose members supported Indian independence from Great Britain. He was later elected its national president.

Life's Work

After receiving his PhD in 1924 from Berkeley, Saund decided against returning to India, despite receiving job offers from several universities there. There were few opportunities for an educated Indian in California, however, and the Alien Land Act of 1913 prevented noncitizens from owning or leasing farm land. After meeting other Indians who were farming in the Imperial Valley in Southern California, Saund decided to go there in the summer of 1925.

His first job was as foreman of a cotton-picking crew. Working hard, he managed to save enough money to begin farming his own crops. Saund was also active in the local community, joining the Lions Club, becoming a toastmaster, and speaking to civic organizations and church groups on topics such as Mahatma Gandhi and the fight for Indian independence.

In the summers when it was too hot to work the land, Saund spent time in libraries in Los Angeles. He was commissioned by a Sikh organization to write a book, *My Mother India* (1930), a response to the book *Mother India* (1927) by the American writer Katherine Mayo, which presented negative and stereotyped views of his homeland.

In the mid-1920s, Saund was invited to speak at the Unitarian Church in Hollywood, where he met a Czech American, Emil Kosa, who later invited Saund home to meet his parents. Realizing that he had already met Emil's mother and sister on board the ship bound for the United States in 1920, Saund soon became close friends with the family. In 1928, he married Emil's sister, Marian, and the couple moved to Westmorland, California, in 1930. They had three children.

Dalip Saund's Election as California Congressman

Saund was supported in his candidature for Congress by leaders of the Democratic Party in California. He stood against a formidable Republican opponent, Jacqueline Cochran, a famous aviator and the wife of Floyd Bostwick Odlum, one of the wealthiest men in the country. Cochran was also a personal friend of the extremely popular president, Dwight D. Eisenhower. Despite attempts by Saund's opponents and even some members of his own party to present him as Indian rather than American, Saund won the election.

As a congressman, Saund favored policies that benefited his largely agricultural constituency, supporting farm subsidies and immigration, which was important for farmers who depended on Mexican workers during the harvest. His knowledge of foreign affairs led him to be appointed to the House Foreign Affairs Committee, which was unusual for a new congressman. In 1957, he returned to his home country for the first time in over three decades when he visited on behalf of the House of Representatives. Saund was reelected twice: in 1958 and 1960, each time with a majority of over 60 percent. During his second term in office, Saund wrote an account of his career entitled *Congressman from India* (1960). Although he won the Democratic Party nomination for a fourth term, a stroke ended his congressional career.

Saund admired the United States and its democratic system, but he deplored the discrimination against the Asian population, especially as evidenced in state and national legislation. He was also frustrated to be denied US citizenship.

Saund registered as a Democrat and attended local party meetings despite being unable to vote. He then initiated a campaign to lift the restrictions preventing Asians from becoming naturalized citizens. His organization, the India Association of America, and several other Indian welfare group, lobbied Congress for change. In 1946, the Luce-Cellar Act was passed, which granted naturalization rights to Indians and Filipinos.

Saund became an American citizen in December 1949. The next year he ran for and won the position of justice of the peace of Westmorland, but the result was reversed after it was determined that he had been a citizen for less than the required year. Undeterred, Saund ran again and took office in January 1953. Saund was then elected unopposed to the Imperial County Democratic Central Committee, and in 1954 he was elected its chairman. In November 1955, he was nominated to run for Congress, winning the seat against a strong Republican candidate and becoming the first Asian American and first Sikh to serve in Congress.

Singh served three terms but suffered a severe stroke in 1962 during his campaign for a fourth term. Saund was partially paralyzed and never regained his speech. He died on April 22, 1973 and was buried in Forest Lawn Cemetery in Glendale, California.

SIGNIFICANCE

Saund successfully overcame the discrimination and anti-immigrant legislation of his time to pursue an outstanding political career. He opened the way for later generations of Asian American politicians and fought for the rights of all Asian Americans. As a congressman, he used his political influence to promote the interests of immigrants. In 2005, a US Post Office building in Temecula (Imperial County), California was named after him. In 2006, Saund was ranked among the most prominent foreign-born Americans in *The Citizen's Almanac*, published for new citizens by the US government.

Christine Ayorinde

FURTHER READING

Roots in the Sand. Dir. Jayasri Majumdar Hart. PBS, 2000. Film. Documentary consisting of archival information, interviews, and a 1937 amateur documentary on Sikh, Muslim, and Hindu immigrants to the United States, including a segment on Dalip Singh Saund.

Saund, Dalip Singh. *Congressman from India.* New York: Dutton, 1960. Autobiography recounting Saund's early life in India and his struggle to gain acceptance in his adopted country.

Tajitsu, Nash. "Centennial of Asian American Pioneer Dalip Singh Saund." *IMDiversity.com.* IMDiversity, 2011. Web. 12 Mar. 2012. Reports on the life and accomplishments of Saund and his contributions to the Asian American community.

ALLEN SAY

Japanese-born writer and artist

A 1994 Caldecott Medal winner and 1988 Caldecott Honor Book award winner, Allen Say is renowned for his watercolor illustrations of multicultural stories that often focus on social outsiders who are searching for their place in the world.

Born: August 28, 1937; Yokohama, Japan
Full name: Allen Say
Areas of achievement: Art, literature

EARLY LIFE

Allen Say, son of a Korean father and Japanese American mother, grew up in circumstances that often made him feel ostracized. Born in Japan, Say grew up during the tumultuous period of World War II as the son of a discriminated-against Korean father. He, and all Japanese citizens, experienced the difficulties of wartime, the US bombing of Japanese cities, and the subsequent American occupation of the country. His parents divorced when he was nine, and he was sent to live with his maternal grandmother.

His passion for art began early, but his parents were not supportive and instead urged him to become a businessman. His second-grade teacher, though, recognized his talent, encouraged him, and sent one of his pictures to a competition, which he won.

At the age of twelve, Say began living on his own and in his own apartment, and he soon apprenticed himself to famed cartoonist Noro Shinpei, a man who became his spiritual mentor and father figure. Say remained with his teacher for four years and then moved to San Francisco with his father and his father's new family. Though he knew no English, he was enrolled in a military academy; he was expelled after a year for smoking cigarettes. Say then enrolled himself in a public high school in Azusa, California. The principal, who had fought in Japan during World War II, befriended Say and helped him finish high school and find a job. Say then attended art school.

LIFE'S WORK

Say enrolled in architecture school at the University of California, Berkeley, in 1960. Two years later his student deferment was revoked due to a technicality, and he was drafted into the military and stationed in Germany for two years. As a distraction from his work, Say began taking photographs, which were published regularly in the Army newspaper *Stars and Stripes*.

When Say returned to California after his military service, he began attending the San Francisco Art

Allen Say. (Time & Life Pictures/Getty Images)

Institute to study photography and to pursue commercial photography as a career. For the next twenty years, Say worked as a photographer and freelance illustrator. His first children's book was *Dr. Smith's Safari* (1972).

Say published a novel, *The Ink-Keeper's Apprentice* (1979), an autobiography of his time with Noro Shinpei, and in 1984, Say illustrated *How My Parents Learned to Eat.* He was so discouraged by the production and printed quality of his drawings in this book that he decided to never again illustrate a children's book. Three years later, however, Houghton Mifflin editor Walter Lorraine persuaded him to illustrate Dianne Snyder's book *The Boy of the Three-Year Nap* (1988), which was awarded the Boston Globe–Horn Book Award. His success with this book, which was also selected as a Caldecott Honor Book in 1988, convinced him to devote all of his energy to children's books, and in 1994, Say won the Caldecott Medal for *Grandfather's Journey* (1993). Since then, he has won numerous awards and recognitions for his work writing and illustrating children's books.

Say explains that as a photographer he learned the importance of light and of capturing a significant action, important skills for illustrating his stories. In 2000, his illustrations were featured in the exhibit *Allen Say's Journey: The Art and Words of a Children's Book Author* at the Japanese American National Museum in Los Angeles.

Say's books explore in word and picture a variety of both first- and second-hand experiences. *Grandfather's Journey* reflects on his maternal grandfather's travels to and from Japan and explores his own feelings as an immigrant and the conflicting feelings grandfather and grandson undoubtedly shared being caught between two different cultures and two distant places. Say's work also draws on stories and fairy tales he heard as a child, and they often blend dream with reality and demonstrate that at times dreams are as vivid and compelling as reality. Say's stories often focus on individuals who are trying to find their place in a world that treats them as outsiders. For instance, *El Chino* (1990), a story he heard from a friend, is a biography of a Chinese American boy who longed to be an athlete and fulfilled his dream by becoming a famous matador in Spain.

SIGNIFICANCE

Allen Say's books have become touchstones of multicultural literature for children. They often present the struggle of individuals longing to express their uniqueness in environments where they are culturally stereotyped. Some of his protagonists find they can best express their longing for self-expression in another culture. His illustrations successfully depict the struggle, the conflict, and the emotion felt by his protagonists as they celebrate an accomplishment or a goal or simply gain insight into the human condition.

Bernadette Flynn Low

FURTHER READING

"The Gentle Art of Allen Say." *USA Today Magazine* Nov. 2000: 44–49. Print. Recounts Say's artistic training and career experiences, with information on his 2000 exhibit.

Rodia, Becky. "The Strange Journey of Allen Say." *Teaching Pre K–8* Jan. 2003: 43–44. Print. Highlights Allen Say's important career and personal milestones.

Say, Allen. "Caldecott Medal Acceptance." *Horn Book Magazine* July/Aug. 1994: 427–31. Print. Discusses Say's "lucky" opportunities throughout his life, the importance of his dreams, and what he tries to capture in his work.

---. "Musings of a Walking Stereotype." *School Library Journal* Dec. 1991: 45–46. Print. Say reflects on his work and his inspirations, noting the recurring theme of trying to overcome stereotypes.

NICOLE SCHERZINGER

Musician and singer

Pop singer, songwriter, and dancer Nicole Scherzinger first came to fame as the lead singer of the all-female group the Pussycat Dolls. She also has a solo recording career, and in 2010, she was the winner of the ABC television series Dancing with the Stars.

Born: June 29, 1978; Honolulu, Hawaii
Full name: Nicole Prescovia Elikolani Valiente Scherzinger (prehs-KOH-vee-uh eh-lee-KOH-lah-nee va-lee-EHN-teh SHUR-zihng-ur)
Birth name: Nicole Prescovia Elikolani Valiente
Also known as: Nicole Kea
Areas of achievement: Music, entertainment, dance

EARLY LIFE

Nicole Scherzinger was born Nicole Prescovia Elikolani Valiente on June 29, 1978, in Honolulu, Hawaii, to a Filipino father and a mother of Hawaiian and Russian descent. Her parents separated when she was a baby, and her mother, Rosemary, later married Gary Scherzinger, who officially adopted Nicole and gave her his last name. When Scherzinger was six years old, she and her sister, Keala, moved with their mother and stepfather to Louisville, Kentucky.

In Kentucky, Scherzinger attended the Youth Performing Arts School at duPont Manual High School and began performing with the Actors Theatre of Louisville. In 1996, she was first runner-up in the Kentucky State Fair talent contest. After graduating from high school, Scherzinger attended Wright State University in Dayton, Ohio, as a drama and musical theater major. She left school in 1999 to pursue a music career after being hired as a backup singer for the experimental rock band Days of the New.

Nicole Scherzinger. (FilmMagic)

675

LIFE'S WORK

In 2001, Scherzinger appeared on the WB television network show *Popstars* and won a spot in the all-female pop group Eden's Crush. The group signed with Warner Bros. affiliate London-Sire Records and recorded one album. Their first single, "Get over Yourself," reached the top ten on the *Billboard* Hot 100 chart and was at the top of the Canadian Singles Chart. In 2001, Eden's Crush was the opening act for both Jessica Simpson's DreamChaser Tour and *NSYNC's PopOdyssey Tour. The group disbanded in December 2001.

After Eden's Crush, Scherzinger began singing under the name Nicole Kea, contributing songs to the soundtrack for the film *50 First Dates* (2004) and the compilation album *Exposition of Global Harmony* (2003). She also appeared in several television shows, including *My Wife and Kids* and *Sabrina the Teenage Witch*, and had a role in the 2003 film *Love Don't Cost a Thing*. In addition, Scherzinger appeared in several commercials in Southeast Asia, particularly the Philippines.

In 2003, Scherzinger joined the all-female dance and performance group the Pussycat Dolls and soon became their lead singer. The group's music debuted on the soundtracks for the 2004 films *Shark Tale* and *Shall We Dance?* Their first album, *PCD*, was released in 2005, debuting at number five on the *Billboard* Hot 200 album chart. The first single from the album, "Don't Cha," peaked at number two on the Hot 100. The second single from the album, "Stickwitu," was nominated for a Grammy for Best Pop Performance by a Duo or Group in 2005.

Scherzinger's success with the Pussycat Dolls led to opportunities with other performers, such as Shaggy, Vittorio Grigolo, Diddy, Enrique Iglesias, and 50 Cent. She also began working on her first solo album, *Her Name Is Nicole*, in 2006. The project was intended to showcase a softer, more vulnerable side of the singer than was seen with the Pussycat Dolls. She worked with several well-known producers and performers on the album, including T.I. and will.i.am from the Black Eyed Peas. Ultimately, four singles were released, but the album never was.

In 2007, the Pussycat Dolls began working on their second album, which featured some of the songs originally recorded by Scherzinger for her solo album. The album, *Doll Domination*, was released in 2008, and although it debuted higher on the Hot 200 chart than their first album, it did not sell nearly as well overall. In January 2009, the group began their Doll Domination Tour in Europe with Lady Gaga and Ne-Yo. They were then the opening act for Britney Spears's The Circus Starring Britney Spears tour in North America later that year.

Following the tour, the Pussycat Dolls went on hiatus, and rumors began to circulate that internal tensions between members were surfacing over what was seen as preferential treatment for Scherzinger. The group's manager denied the rumors and claimed preparations were under way for a third album. In the meantime, Scherzinger recorded a song with rock icons Slash and Alice Cooper for Slash's solo album and performed on the Artists for Haiti recording of "We Are the World." She also began working on a new solo album.

Scherzinger appeared as a guest judge on Simon Cowell's reality series *The X Factor* and competed in ABC's 2010 season of *Dancing with the Stars*, which she won. In August 2010, Scherzinger played the role of Maureen in the musical *Rent* under the direction of Neil Patrick Harris. There were also reports that she was working with Andrew Lloyd Webber on a sequel to his blockbuster musical *The Phantom of the Opera* entitled *Love Never Dies*.

SIGNIFICANCE

Coming from a poor family, Nicole Scherzinger used her talent to become a successful singer and performer. She has been a part of six *Billboard* top-ten songs, ten international top-ten songs, and two top-five albums, and she has been invited to perform with such top rap performers as Diddy and 50 Cent, as well as mainstream artists such as Enrique Iglesias and Celine Dion. In addition, Scherzinger has become a national celebrity in her father's native Philippines.

Eric S. Strother

FURTHER READING

Henderson, Jessica. "Reality Queen: Nicole Scherzinger." *Marie Claire*. Hearst, 9 Aug. 2011. Web. 12 Mar. 2012. Reports on Scherzinger's solo album, *Killer Love*, and her experience as a judge on television's *The X Factor*.

Scherzinger, Nicole. "Cat Power." Interview by Laura Checkoway. *Vibe* May 2007: 36. Print. A brief interview that focuses mainly on Scherzinger's perception of herself.

---. Interview by Nick Levine. *Digital Spy*. Hearst, 2 Nov. 2007. Web. 27 Mar. 2012. Discusses the making of Scherzinger's first solo record.

ROB SCHNEIDER

Actor, comedian, writer

Rob Schneider is an internationally known comedian who has expanded his career into film and television as an actor, director, producer, and screenwriter. First becoming well known as a Saturday Night Live *cast member in the early 1990s, Schneider has gone on to star in numerous comedy films, often in collaboration with fellow SNL alumnus Adam Sandler.*

Birth: October 31, 1963: San Francisco, California
Full name: Robert Michael Schneider
Areas of achievement: Comedy, film, television

EARLY LIFE

Rob Schneider was born on October 31, 1963, in San Francisco, California. His father, Marvin Schneider, worked as a real estate broker, while his mother, Pilar, taught kindergarten. Schneider's father is Jewish and his mother is half Filipino; he is the youngest of five children. His early days were spent in Pacifica, a suburb south of San Francisco, in a section known as Pedro Point. He graduated from Terra Nova High School in Pacifica.

Rob Schneider. (FilmMagic)

During high school Schneider followed the careers of comedians and entertainers such as Richard Pryor, Gene Wilder, and Peter Sellers. At age fifteen he started writing and performing his own comedy routines locally. After graduating from high school, he decided to pursue his career in comedy clubs. Gaining rave reviews for his comedy, he worked as the opening act for well-known comedians such as Jerry Seinfield, Jay Leno, and Dana Carvey. In 1987 Schneider was invited to perform on the David Letterman show, making his debut on a major television network.

LIFE'S WORK

Schneider's career moved forward when he opened for comedian Dennis Miller and was then invited to perform on HBO's *Thirteenth Annual Young Comedians Special*, which Miller hosted in 1989. Lorne Michaels, creator and producer of the sketch comedy show *Saturday Night Live* (*SNL*), saw Schneider on the show and offered him work as a writer for *SNL*. Before long Schneider was performing as a regular *SNL* cast member. Fellow comedian Adam Sandler was hired as a writer about the same time, and the two forged a friendship that outlasted Schneider's tenure at *SNL* and would lead to partnerships in several later film ventures. Schneider left *SNL* in 1994 to pursue an acting career.

As early as 1991, Schneider was working in film. The movie *Necessary Roughness,* a football saga about the Texas State University team, cast Schneider as sportscaster and announcer Chuck Neiderman. In 1992 he played Cedric, the hotel bellman, in the popular *Home Alone 2: Lost in New York.* In 1993 Schneider appeared in the films *Surf Ninjas* and *The Beverly Hillbillies.* By 1995 he had a chance to play a supporting role as Herman "Fergee" Ferguson alongside well-known actor Sylvester Stallone in *Judge Dredd.* Though Schneider continued in films, his next few years proved unremarkable. However, in 1998 he appeared alongside his friend and *SNL* costar Adam Sandler in *The Waterboy.* A year later, in 1999, he again teamed up with Sandler, as the delivery guy in *Big Daddy.* That year, Schneider also landed his first starring role, as Deuce Bigalow, the house-sitting fish tank cleaner who is mistaken for a gigolo, in *Deuce Bigalo: Male Gigolo,* the script for which he wrote with screenwriter Harris Goldberg. The success of this film with audiences led to his next big role, as Marvin in the comedy *The Animal* in 2001.

In 2002, Schneider played the Chinese waiter and voice-over narrator in Adam Sandler's *Eight Crazy Nights*. That year he also produced and starred in *The Hot Chick*, a script he wrote with director Tom Brady. In 2005 Schneider appeared as Punky in *The Longest Yard*, again with lead actor and executive producer Adam Sandler. His next lead role was Gus in the 2006 film *The Benchwarmers*.

Over time Schneider expanded his career beyond acting to include directing, screenwriting, and producing. His brother, John Schneider, has managed and coproduced many of Schneider's films through their company From Out of Nowhere Productions. Schneider's mother often appears in cameo roles in his films. In 2007 Schneider directed and starred in *Big Stan* with David Carradine. In 2010 he cowrote, directed, and acted in *The Chosen One* and played in *Grown Ups* with Sandler. He continues to work as director, producer, and actor in various film endeavors and perform stand-up comedy. In 2012, Schneider tried his hand at television, creating and starring in his own sitcom, *Rob*.

SIGNIFICANCE

Rob Schneider has found success through his various talents: comedian, actor, director, screenwriter, and producer. Schneider was nominated for three Emmy Awards and a Peabody Award during his tenure as writer and actor at *SNL*. He established the Rob Schneider Music Foundation to provide financial support for music education at Pacifica schools, paying for teacher salaries and musical instruments. In the summer of 2010 Schneider performed at a benefit in Rochester, New York, for the Renee Julian Cattron Memorial Foundation, established in memory of a family friend who died of lung cancer. An environmentalist, Schneider served as host of the 2004 Environmental Media Awards.

Marylane Wade Koch

FURTHER READING

Marin, Rick. "Rob Schneider; Call Him Busy. He's the Smarminator." *New York Times*. New York Times, 21 Nov. 1993. Web. 29 Mar. 2012. Positive review of Rob Schneider as a successful cast member of *SNL*.

"Rob Schneider" *New York Times*. 2010. Web. 29 Mar. 2012. Provides a succinct biography of Schneider from his family roots through his film and professional accomplishments.

Vizcarra, Gian Carlo. "The Pinoy Side of Rob Schneider." *Philippine Star*. Philstar, 9 Sep. 2006. Web. 29 Mar. 2012. Article on a Philippine website, based on an interview with Schneider's mother, about his status as part Filipino.

JUNIOR SEAU

Athlete

Junior Seau lived the American dream, growing up in near squalor and earning immense amounts of money and respect as an adult. He was one of the most decorated linebackers in the history of the National Football League (NFL). Seau was a smart, instinctive player whose natural athleticism and energy made him a well-respected competitor.

Born: January 19, 1969; San Diego, California
Died: May 2, 2012; Oceanside, California
Full name: Tiaina Baul Seau Jr. (tee-i-EE-nuh SAY-ow)
Area of achievement: Sports

EARLY LIFE

Tiaina Seau Jr. was born in San Diego, California, on January 19, 1969, to Tiaina Sr. and Luisa Seau, who had moved to San Diego from the island of Aunuu in American Samoa in 1964, seeking lung surgery for their son David. They took their paternal grandmother's name, Seau, as a gesture of love for the family. Tiaina Sr. worked on an assembly line and Luisa took a laundry job to support their growing family and pay for David's surgery. Tiaina Jr. was born in 1969 and grew up in a very poor section of San Diego. The family was close knit and strictly adhered to their Samoan culture; Seau didn't learn English until age seven. He slept with his three brothers on the concrete floor of the family's garage in deplorable conditions while his two sisters slept in the house.

At an early age, Junior started lifting dumbbells and working out intensely, a practice he would continue for decades. All the Seau children worked and played sports after school, but Junior stood out as a good student and a talented athlete, starring on the basketball and track teams. But Junior truly excelled at football, playing linebacker and tight end at Oceanside High School. As a senior, he led the team to the city championship, earning most valuable player (MVP) honors.

LIFE'S WORK

Junior was aggressively recruited out of high school by many colleges and universities and chose a football scholarship offer from the University of Southern California (USC). He was unable to play his freshman year after scoring a 690 on his Scholastic Aptitude Test (SAT), ten points below the required minimum score. Junior was dealt another setback just before his sophomore season, injuring his ankle, and he missed another year of football.

At the beginning of his junior season, two starting linebackers were injured, making room for Seau on the field. He had a tremendous season, earning All-American honors and the conference Defensive Player of the Year award. Rather than risk another year playing college football, where he could be injured again, Seau declared himself eligible for the 1990 NFL draft. He was selected as the fifth overall pick by the San Diego Chargers.

Seau had an instant impact on his hometown Chargers and was selected to go to the Pro Bowl, the NFL all-star game, by the end of his second season. Junior's family and friends attended all of his home games wearing their traditional Samoan clothing covered by a Seau jersey.

Seau played twelve seasons in San Diego, becoming arguably the best and most decorated linebacker of the decade, and was a perennial all-pro player. He took the Chargers to the 1995 Super Bowl only to lose to the San Francisco 49ers. Seau was the face of the San Diego franchise, and he always gave his time and money back to the community.

In April 2003, the Miami Dolphins traded a draft pick to acquire Seau. He had a great season, earning his twelfth straight Pro Bowl selection, but lost most of the next two seasons to injury. He was released on March 6, 2006, later signing a one-day contract with the Chargers on August 14, 2006, and retiring. Four days later, Seau was offered a spot with the New England Patriots. He came out of his four-day retirement to sign with the Patriots, wanting another chance at a championship. He played the first ten games before he broke his arm and was sidelined for the rest of the season. Seau played three more seasons with the Patriots, including the undefeated regular season of 2007, in which the Patriots fell to the New York Giants in the Super Bowl. Seau announced his second retirement on January 13, 2010.

Junior Seau. (Forza LLC via Getty Images)

After his first year in the NFL, Junior established the Junior Seau Foundation, which funds programs for child abuse prevention, educational opportunities, and other services for children and young adults. He used his money and celebrity to build the foundation, which had distributed $4 million by 2010. He also owned a successful restaurant in San Diego called Seau's and a clothing line called Say-Ow.

He married Gina Deboer in 1991, and they had three children. They divorced after twelve years. Seau died on May 2, 2012, of a self-inflicted gunshot wound to the chest. He was forty-three.

SIGNIFICANCE

For many, Junior Seau represents the American rags-to-riches story. He came from meager surroundings and made himself into one of the greatest linebackers in the NFL. He played in two Super Bowls, was selected for twelve straight Pro Bowls, and won numerous other football and humanitarian honors. He has been a model to other American Samoans, inspiring a number of other Samoan football players, many of whom share his strong moral base and work ethic.

Jonathan E. Dinneen

FURTHER READING

"Junior Seau to Enter Chargers' HOF." *ESPN.com.* ESPN, 23 Aug. 2011. Web. 27 Mar. 2012. Description of Seau's retirement and induction into the Chargers' Hall of Fame.

Layden, Tim. "Welcome to the 'Backerhood." *Sports Illustrated* 12 Nov. 2007: 42–48. Print. Detailed article about Seau, the veteran, coming out or retirement to be the glue holding the Patriots linebacking corps and defense together.

Lieber, Jill. "Hard Charger." *Sports Illustrated* 6 Sep. 1993: 64–66; 71–73. Print. Feature article about Seau as a youth, through school, college, and his rise to NFL stardom.

LISA SEE

Novelist and writer

Lisa See, a Chinese American writer, is best known for portraying the lives and thoughts of Chinese women in Snow Flower and the Secret Fan, Peony in Love*, and* Shanghai Girls. *Her other critically acclaimed book is* On Gold Mountain.

Born: February 18, 1955; Paris, France
Full name: Lisa See
Also known as: Lisa See Kendall
Area of achievement: Literature

EARLY LIFE

Lisa See was born in Paris, France, to Richard Edward See, an anthropologist, and Carolyn Laws See, a novelist and writer. She grew up in Los Angeles, living with her mother after her parents divorced in 1959, but remaining close with her father's family. During her childhood, she spent weekends and summer vacations in Los Angeles's Chinatown with her paternal grandparents, great uncles, and great aunts, listening to their family stories.

See's great-great-grandfather emigrated from China to the United States in 1867 to work on the transcontinental railroad. Fong See, his fourth son, left China to join him at age sixteen. He eventually opened a successful importing business, which would grow into an empire. He helped build Chinatown in Los Angeles and is considered one of its founding fathers. See has been influenced by the Chinese side of her family immensely and is deeply interested in Chinese customs, traditions, and culture.

See graduated from Loyola Marymount University with a BA in 1979. Before graduation, she worked in sales and public relations for Triad Graphic Workshop in Los Angeles for two years. She was also an event coordinator for the Sun Institute in Los Angeles. She married Richard Becker Kendall, an attorney, in 1981, and they have two sons.

LIFE'S WORK

After completing her college education, See worked as a freelance writer and published articles in several magazines. In her early writing career, See wrote novels with her mother, Carolyn, and her friend John Espey under the joint pseudonym Monica Highland.

Encouraged by her great aunt, See penned her first book, *On Gold Mountain: The One-Hundred-Year Odyssey of My Chinese-American Family* (1995), a memoir of her family history from 1866 to 1991. The book begins with her great-great-grandfather's journey to

Lisa See. (FilmMagic)

Gold Mountain in California and ends with her visit to his village in China. To write the book, See interviewed more than one hundred family members in the United States and China, visited her ancestors' village, and spent endless hours in the National Archives and the Immigration Office. The book became a national bestseller and a *New York Times* Notable Book of 1995. While doing research for *On Gold Mountain*, See was inspired to write a mystery, *Flower Net* (1997), which was followed by *The Interior* (1999) and *Dragon Bones* (2003). *Flower Net* also became a national best-seller, a *New York Times* Notable Book, and an Edgar Award nominee.

Snow Flower and the Secret Fan (2005), a highly acclaimed book domestically and internationally, tells the story of the friendship of two women living in small villages in China in the nineteenth century. They communicate using *nu shu*, a secret script used by women for written communication in a remote county in Hunan Province, China, for hundreds of years. They share their private lives by writing messages in *nu shu* on a fan and passing it back and forth. To research *nu shu*, See traveled to Hunan Province. The book became a *New York Times* best-seller and was published in thirty-nine languages. A film based on the novel was released by Fox Searchlight in 2011.

The two books that followed also made the *New York Times* best-seller list. Based on an ancient text about three lovesick maidens*, Peony in Love* (2007) portrays the sixteen-year-old Peony yearning for true love in seventeenth-century China. *Shanghai Girls* (2009) is the story of two sisters who live a glamorous life in 1937 Shanghai as models for artists. By a twist of fate, they go to America, where they face discrimination and hardship.

In addition to realizing these literary accomplishments, See was a guest curator for an exhibition on the Chinese American experience for the Autry Museum of Western Heritage and the Smithsonian Institution. She also developed the Family Gallery for the Autry Museum, which portrays Los Angeles in the 1930s from her father's perspective as a young boy. She designed a walking tour and guidebook for Los Angeles's Chinatown. She serves as a Los Angeles City Commissioner on the El Pueblo de Los Angeles Historical Monument Authority. For her contributions to many cultural events in Los Angeles and Chinatown, See was named the National Woman of the Year in 2001 by the Organization of Chinese American Women.

SIGNIFICANCE

See's *On Gold Mountain* is not just her family history but also a history of Chinese immigrants to California struggling to make a life for themselves during the nineteenth and twentieth centuries. It is also a history of Los Angeles's Chinatown, which See's great-grandfather played an important part in building. See claims her favorite part of writing a book is doing the research for it. Through her painstaking research, she has shed light on Chinese and Chinese American history and culture for her readers.

Shu-Hsien L. Chen

FURTHER READING

Kinsella, Bridget. "Seeing China." *Publishers Weekly* 11 July 2005: 28–29. Print. Provides background on See's parents and great-grandparents.

See, Lisa. "Have Roots, Will Travel." *Smithsonian* 38.7 (October 2007): 27–30. Print. See talks about her childhood in Los Angeles's Chinatown with her grandparents, and emphasizes the characteristics of cultural and racial diversity of the city.

---. *On Gold Mountain*. New York: St. Martin's, 1995. Print. An account of See's family history spanning one hundred years, from her great-great-grandfather's journey to America to her visit to his small village in China.

Teisch, Jessica. "Lisa See." *Bookmarks* (September-October 2009): 18–23. Print. Discusses See's background and presents a few reviews of her books.

JAMES SHIGETA

Actor and singer

A Hawaiian-born actor, singer, and nightclub performer, Shigeta was one of the first Asian actors to play leading roles in Hollywood films and to portray interracial romances on-screen.

Born: June 17, 1933; Honolulu, Hawaii
Full name: James Shigeta (shee-GEH-tuh)
Also known as: Jimmy Shigeta
Areas of achievement: Film, television, theater

EARLY LIFE

James Shigeta is the *nisei* (second-generation Japanese) son of a building contractor, one of six children. Shigeta attended New York University, originally as a creative-writing major, but he switched to music after his first year. A talented singer, he competed on and won the Ted Mack–hosted *Original Amateur Hour*, a televised talent show that launched the careers of such stars as Frank Sinatra and Ann-Margret. Shigeta went on to perform in Las Vegas, but the Korean War put his developing career on hold; he was drafted and served two and a half years as a marine, achieving the rank of staff sergeant.

After being discharged, Shigeta sang for a time at the Los Angeles Players' Club, then moved to Japan when he was offered a lead role in a musical revue. Although of Japanese descent, Shigeta had to hire a tutor to learn the language. In Japan, he became a popular singer, starred in stage productions, and played the lead in four movie musicals, coming to be known as the "Frank Sinatra of Japan." In 1958, he traveled to Australia as the male lead in *Cherry Blossom Show*, produced by the Nichigeki Theatre of Tokyo.

James Shigeta. (Getty Images)

Later, Shigeta was recruited by producer Steve Parker and his wife, actor Shirley MacLaine, to star in their revue production *Holiday in Japan*, slated for the New Frontier Hotel and Casino in Las Vegas. In 1959, Shigeta returned to the United States to perform in the show and also appeared on the *Dinah Shore Show*. As he resumed his career as a singer and dancer in America, his good looks caught the attention of Hollywood film producers.

LIFE'S WORK

Shigeta's first film role was in 1959 as Detective Joe Kojaku in *The Crimson Kimono*, produced and directed by Sam Fuller. The film follows the story of two detectives, one white and one of Japanese descent, who investigate a murder in Chinatown. Both fall in love with their key witness, a white woman named Christine. Ultimately, Christine chooses Detective Kojaku over his white counterpart—a first in American cinema. It was also unusual at that time to have an actual Asian playing an Asian character and for that character to speak in non-pidgin English. In addition, the film was one of the first to address racial tension within the Japanese American community.

In his next role, Shigeta played Chinese immigrant Cheng Lu in *Walk like a Dragon* (1960), costarring with actor Jack Lord. Other important roles followed. In *Flower Drum Song* (1961), he played the romantic lead, Wang Ta, showcasing his singing and dancing abilities. He went on to play Hidenari Terasaki, a World War II Japanese diplomat, in the drama *Bridge to the Sun* (1961). Based on a true story, the film was about a racially mixed marriage set during the war between the United States and Japan. Critics view it as Shigeta's best screen performance.

Shigeta costarred with Elvis Presley in *Paradise Hawaiian Style* (1966), his last starring role. He went on to play Brother To-Lenn in the musical *Lost Horizon* (1973), Vice Admiral Chuichi Naguma in *Midway* (1976), Joseph Takagi in *Die Hard* (1988), and Sugimoto in *Brother* (2001). He was also the voice of General Li in Disney's *Mulan* (1998).

Shigeta worked extensively in television as well. In 1961, he played a Chinese communist who tortured the hero in an episode of the television series *Alcoa Premiere*. He was cast as a lawyer in the 1965 *Perry Mason* episode "The Case of the Wrongful Writ," and he appeared with *Perry Mason* lead Raymond Burr again in two episodes of *Ironside*, in 1969 and 1971. In *Medical Center*, he played two different recurring roles between

1969 and 1972. Shigeta also had parts in a number of other series, including *The Outer Limits*, *The Streets of San Francisco*, *Little House on the Prairie*, and *The Love Boat*. He appeared on *Magnum, P.I.* in 1983 and 1986, as two different characters, and had three separate parts in *Simon & Simon* in 1984, 1987, and 1988. Shigeta appeared in *Murder, She Wrote* in 1987 and 1992 and played the part of Ben Sosna in three episodes of *Beverly Hills, 90210* in 1999.

Shigeta continued his film and television career into the twenty-first century. In 2004, he and Nancy Kwan, his costar from *Flower Drum Song*, reunited in playwright A. R. Gurney's *Love Letters*. Their performance was well received, and they have reprised it in various venues. Shigeta is interviewed in the 2006 documentary *The Slanted Screen*, which depicts the discrimination against Asian actors in Hollywood and includes clips of his films. He is also featured in Arthur Dong's documentary *Hollywood Chinese* (2007).

SIGNIFICANCE

Shigeta is one of very few Asian Americans who have played romantic leads in Hollywood films. He shared the Golden Globe Award for Most Promising Male Newcomer with three other actors. He starred in five important films between 1959 and 1961, and it appeared that Hollywood was promoting him as a leading man, although that promise was ultimately not fulfilled. In 2005, he received a Visionary Award from the East West Players, an Asian American theater organization.

Marcia B. Dinneen

FURTHER READING

Niiya, Brian, ed. *Japanese American History: An A-to-Z Reference from 1868 to the Present*. New York: FOF, 1993. Print. Includes a biographical entry on Shigeta.

Prasso, Sheridan. *The Asian Mystique*. New York: Public Affairs, 2005. Print. The chapter entitled "Matters of Men and Country" particularly relates to Shigeta and his experiences in finding positive masculine roles in film and television.

Shigeta, James. "James Shigeta: The Leading Man." Interview by Roger Garcia. *Out of the Shadows: Asians in American Cinema*. Ed. Garcia. Milan: Olivares, 2001. 116–19. Print. An interview discussing Shigeta's background and career.

GEORGE SHIMA

Farmer, entrepreneur, business executive

An industrious, enterprising farmer, George Shima reclaimed and rehabilitated thousands of acres of unwanted swampland near rivers in San Joaquin County, California. He grew wealthy while cornering the market on tubers, and became known as the "Potato King" during the early twentieth century.

Born: ca. 1864; Kurume, Fukuoka, Japan
Died: March 27, 1926; Los Angeles, California
Full name: George Shima (SHEE-mah)
Birth name: Seikichi Ushijima
Also known as: Kinji Ushijima
Areas of achievement: Agriculture, business

EARLY LIFE

George Shima was born as Seikichi Ushijima near the port of Fukuoka on Kyushu, Japan's southernmost island. He descended from a long line of prosperous, landowning farmers. Shima was privately tutored during his early years and developed a lifelong love of Chinese classical poetry. He entered private middle school as a teenager, where he was called Kinji to avoid confusion with a similarly named student. In 1885, Shima moved to Tokyo to continue studying Chinese classics at Hitotsubashi University. However, he flunked the entrance examinations because he could not read or write English. After taking private lessons for a time, he booked passage to the United States to immerse himself in English.

Shima arrived in San Francisco, California, in 1889. Unlike many Japanese immigrants, he did not come penniless to America, but sought work nonetheless in order to save money and improve his prospects. He landed a position as a "schoolboy"—a derogatory term for someone working as a servant while attending classes—and became fluent in English. Shima soon traded domestic servitude for farm work, moving from San Francisco to Stockton to become a field laborer. A fast, efficient worker, he won numerous friendly potato-picking contests with American farmhands. Eventually,

George Shima's Career as California's "Potato King"

Shima helped bring efficient, high-yield farming techniques to the United States. He bought land that was thought worthless, including swampy parcels and seasonally submerged islands along rivers, for $3 to $5 per acre—at a time when farmland typically cost $150 and up per acre. Shima and co-investors dug ditches and installed pumps to drain the land, used dredges to deepen natural river channels, built levees to control flooding, and built dikes to provide irrigation. Weeds and brush were plowed under as fertilizer to enrich the soil. Shima's farming project, which eventually salvaged nearly 29,000 acres and employed more than five hundred workers, was one of the West Coast's largest reclamation efforts.

To help determine what would best grow on the refurbished land, Shima consulted with agriculturalists at Stanford University and the University of California–Berkeley. He settled on the versatile potato as his primary crop. Spuds were more resistant to damp and cold than grains, and potatoes were a staple that could be shipped to distant markets. Shima's six-thousand-acre Empire Delta Farms formed the core of his agricultural holdings. His packing facility loaded red bags of what became famously trademarked as "Shima Fancy" potatoes. The US government was one of Shima's first major customers, buying tons of potatoes for soldiers fighting in the Spanish-American War. Until the local market began to slump around the time of his death, Shima supplied markets with more than 85 percent of all California-grown potatoes.

Shima became a labor contractor, supplying for a fee other Japanese migrant workers to area farms in the fertile San Joaquin Valley.

LIFE'S WORK

As he provided workers to California farmlands, Shima noticed that certain low-lying areas east of San Francisco along the Sacramento and San Joaquin rivers were not being used because of regular flooding. He thought that he could make use of the land. Shima and a group of Japanese friends began buying up cheap property near the rivers and for a decade worked to improve the land. At first, Shima grew beans while he experimented with other crops. Rice proved to be a disaster; mites, mildew, improper insecticides, and other factors made it impractical to undertake the crossbreeding necessary to create specimens appropriate for local conditions. Finally, he settled on potatoes.

Shima returned to Japan in 1900 and married Shimeko Shimomura, converting to Christianity at her request. They began a family after returning together to the United States: daughter Taye was born in 1902, son Togo in 1904, son Takuji in 1906, and final son Rindge in 1908.

With the assistance of both Japanese and non-Japanese financial backers, Shima continued buying and reclaiming land. By the first decade of the twentieth century, he had transformed thousands of acres into productive farmland. Though he grew such cash crops as fruits, berries, and onions, most of the land was planted with potatoes. Within twenty years of starting his American farming enterprise, Shima grew the great majority of potatoes produced in California.

By 1909, Shima was a wealthy man. He bought a large home in one of Berkeley's most exclusive neighborhoods and an adjacent empty lot that he landscaped with rare, imported shrubs and plants. The purchase, coming in the midst of a rising tide of anti-Asian sentiment, spawned racist headlines in local newspapers. To counter the prejudice, Shima and other successful businesses formed the Japanese Association of America to promote a positive image and defend the rights of the *issei* (first-generation Japanese Americans) and *nisei* (second-generation Japanese Americans). Shima was elected the first president of the association, remaining in office from 1909 to 1926. His position made him a prime target for those opposed to the Japanese.

Despite the association's efforts, California's xenophobia continued and grew. In 1911, twenty-seven new anti-Japanese bills were introduced into the state legislature. In 1913, the Alien Land Law was passed. This affected Shima and other farmers by placing a three-year limit on agricultural land leases to issei. Like other issei, Shima made leases and purchases in the names of his children, Americans by birth. This loophole was closed in 1920 through a new law instigated by the Native Sons, American Legion, labor unions, competing farmers, and others. That new law prohibited issei from buying or leasing land through any means. In 1922 a US Supreme Court ruling prohibited Japanese from becoming naturalized citizens. The 1924 National Origins Act halted Japanese immigration for almost thirty years.

By the mid-1920s, the "Potato King" had been dethroned by increased competition from other potato-growing regions, notably southern California, Idaho, and Oregon. George Shima died of a stroke in 1926 while on a business trip to Los Angeles, leaving an estate valued at more than $15 million. By the mid-1930s, Shima's widow had moved the family to New York, thus avoiding the ignominy of internment that West Coast Japanese were subjected to during World War II.

SIGNIFICANCE

The first issei to become a millionaire in California, George Shima prospered through hard work and determination despite an atmosphere of hatred, suspicion, and jealousy toward successful Asians that dominated in the state. Shima carved a thriving farm out of wilderness and created a profitable market for potatoes that he sustained for twenty-five years. As longtime president of the Japanese Association of America, he advocated eloquently—though fruitlessly—for the assimilation of issei and nisei into American society. Shima shrugged off insults while quietly performing charitable acts; he donated fresh produce to victims of the 1906 San Francisco earthquake, supported the YMCA, and beautified the neighborhood where he lived. It is a measure of the esteem in which he was held in the non-Asian community that pallbearers at his funeral included Stanford University President David Starr Jordan and San Francisco Mayor James Rolph. On the day of his death, Japanese Emperor Hirohito bestowed on Shima the Order of the Rising Sun, an award given for outstanding civil or military merit. Posthumous honors include the naming of a center at San Joaquin Delta College after Shima and a monument to his memory in his hometown in Japan.

Jack Ewing

FURTHER READING

Daniels, Roger. *Coming to America: A History of Immigration and Ethnicity in American Life*. New York: HarperCollins, 2002. Print. Encompasses more than two hundred years of United States history, emphasizing the reactions of established Americans to successive waves of newcomers from Europe, China, Japan, and elsewhere.

---. *The Politics of Prejudice: The Anti-Japanese Movement in California and the Struggle for Japanese Exclusion*. Berkeley: U of California P, 1999. Print. A new edition of a well-researched 1960s examination of the racist attitudes and xenophobic political climate that prevailed in California during Shima's heyday between the late nineteenth and early twentieth centuries.

Street, Richard Steven. *Beasts of the Field: A Narrative History of California Farmworkers, 1769–1913*. Palo Alto: Stanford UP, 2004. Print. An overview using manuscripts, letters, and other documents to detail nearly 150 years of California's agricultural industry through the eyes of the people who worked the land.

Yoshimura, Toshio. *George Shima, Potato King and Lover of Chinese Classics*. Fukushima, Japan: Taiseido Insatsu Shuppanbu, 1981. Print. A brief biography of Shima in English, incorporating his years in both Japan and the United States.

MIKE SHINODA
Musician, visual artist

With his bandmates in Linkin Park, Mike Shinoda has sold over fifty million albums and won two Grammy Awards. A skilled guitarist, percussionist, keyboardist, and rapper, Shinoda has helped to create the group's award-winning, genre-blending sound. Shinoda has been recognized by a number of organizations for his work as a musician, visual artist, and humanitarian. His Japanese American identity has been a recurrent theme in his music.

Born: February 11, 1977; Agoura Hills, California
Birth name: Michael Kenji Shinoda

Areas of achievement: Music, visual arts

EARLY LIFE

Michael Kenji Shinoda was born on February 11, 1977 in Agoura Hills, California, a suburb of Los Angeles. His mother, Donna, is an American of European descent. His father, Muto, is a second-generation Japanese American who was interned during World War II. Shinoda has a brother, Jason, who is two years his junior. When he was six years old, Shinoda's mother enrolled him in piano lessons. This early musical training inspired his interest in jazz, hip-hop, and guitar. Shinoda has cited Public Enemy, Dr. Dre, Nine Inch Nails, and The Police among his major musical influences. In addition, the work of contemporary visual artists Corey Sandelius, Mark Ryden, and Banksy has also influenced Shinoda's artistic development.

Shinoda attended Agoura Hills High School, where he met one of his future bandmates, guitarist Brad Delson. The two began writing and recording songs in a makeshift studio in Delson's bedroom. They soon recruited drummer Rob Bourdon to join them.

Shinoda attended the Art Center College of Design in Pasadena. He graduated one year early with a bachelor's degree in illustration in 1998. While in college, he met Joseph Hahn, a DJ, and Dave "Phoenix" Farrell, a bass guitarist. It was at this time that Shinoda began to understand the gradations of difference between identifying as Japanese American and Japanese.

LIFE'S WORK

Shinoda, Hahn, Farrell, and singer Mark Wakefield formed the band Xero in 1996. With record executives encouraging them to alter their image and music, Wakefield was replaced by Chester Bennington in 1998. The band changed its name briefly to Hybrid Theory, before settling on Linkin Park, named in honor of an area in Santa Monica. The band was signed by Warner Bros. Records in 1999 and released its debut album, *Hybrid Theory*, on October 24, 2000. The album sold nearly five million units within a year, and was the best-selling album of 2001.

Linkin Park's second album, *Meteora*, was released on March 25, 2003, and was also a huge success, the third-best-selling album of that year. The follow-up, *Minutes to Midnight*, was released in May 2007. The band released its fourth studio album, *A Thousand Suns*, in September 2010.

As a trained illustrator, Shinoda played a major role in designing and developing Linkin Park's merchandise, website, and album and production artwork.

Looking for an outlet to express his interest in hip-hop music, Shinoda formed the group Fort Minor, with Ryan "Ryu" Maginn and Rakbir "Tak" Bashir, in 2004. They released the album *The Rising Tied* in November 2005, executive produced by hip-hop superstar Jay-Z. The critically and commercially successful album produced two *Billboard* Top 100 singles and included the song "Kenji," discussing the Japanese internment camps during World War II.

On November 19, 2006, Shinoda's first art show, entitled *Diamonds, Spades, Hearts & Clubs*, premiered

Mike Shinoda. (WireImage)

at Los Angeles's Gallery 1988. Between July and October 2009, Shinoda's paintings were exhibited in *Glorious Excess (BORN)* and *Glorious Excess (DIES)*, two installations on consumerism and celebrity culture at the Japanese American National Museum in Los Angeles. The Art Center College of Design in Pasadena, Shinoda's alma mater, awarded him an honorary doctorate of humane letters in 2009.

Shinoda has worked with numerous charitable organizations, including groups assisting the victims of Hurricane Charley and Hurricane Katrina, the 2004 Indian Ocean tsunami, and the 2010 Haitian earthquake. He has also worked with the Special Operations Warrior Foundation, Live 8, and Music for Relief. He established the Michael K. Shinoda Endowed Scholarship at the Art Center College of Design in 2004, to assist graphic design and illustration students with financial need.

Shinoda married Anna Hillenger on May 10, 2003. Their son, Otio Akio Shinoda, was born in 2009.

SIGNIFICANCE

The sound that Shinoda engineered with Linkin Park helped make the rap-rock and nu-metal genres accessible to a wider audience. In December 2006, the music magazine *Hit Parader* named Shinoda number seventy-two on its list of the Top 100 Metal Vocalists of All Time. MTV2 ranked Linkin Park the third-greatest band of the millennium in 2003. Linkin Park won the Grammy Award for Best Hard Rock Performance for "Crawling" in 2002 and Best Rap/Sung Collaboration in 2006 for *Collision Course*, an album the band made in collaboration with Jay-Z.

Leon James Bynum

FURTHER READING

Naison, Mark. "Hip Hop and Oral History: Turning Students into 'Griots for a New Age.'" *Organization of American Historians Magazine of History* 22.3 (2008): 46–48. Print. Discusses the manner in which Shinoda uses hip-hop to address challenges faced by immigrant groups in America.

Schlund-Vials, Cathy. "Asian American Family, Memory, and Folklore." *Encyclopedia of Asian American Folklore and Folklife*. Ed. Kathleen Nadeau and Jonathan H. X. Lee. Santa Barbara: ABC-CLIO, 2010. Print. Analyzes the expression of Japanese American identity within the context of Shinoda's music.

Wang, Oliver. "Rapping and Repping Asian: Race, Authenticity, and the Asian American MC." *Alien Encounters: Popular Culture in Asian America*. Ed. Mimi Thi Nguyen. Durham: Duke UP, 2007. Print. Discusses the role ethnicity plays in the music of Asian American rappers.

ERIC SHINSEKI

US secretary of veterans affairs (2009–present), military leader, and business executive

Eric Shinseki was the first Japanese American to be appointed chief of staff of the United States Army. When he left this position, he became the first Japanese American head of the Veterans Administration. A wounded combat veteran, Shinseki has also established himself as a renowned business leader.

Born: November 28, 1942; Lihue, Hawaii
Full name: Eric Ken Shinseki
Areas of achievement: Military, government, business

EARLY LIFE

On November 28, 1942, as the attack on Pearl Harbor was nearing its first anniversary, Eric Ken Shinseki was born in the small Hawaiian town of Lihue, on the island of Kauai. His grandparents had emigrated from Hiroshima, Japan, to Hawaii in 1901. His parents were native-born Americans, but like other Americans of Japanese ancestry, they were subject to relocation and internment by the US government during World War II. However, since nearly one-third of the population of Hawaii was Japanese American, few were sent to relocation camps. In fact, three of Shinseki's uncles fought in the European theater of World War II, as part of the famed 442nd Regiment Combat Team, made up predominantly of Japanese American soldiers. He and his older brother, Paul, therefore grew up with tales of combat etched in their minds. A model student both academically and socially, Shinseki was elected student body president at Kauai High School. After graduating from West Point in 1965, he married his high school sweetheart, Patricia Yoshinobu, and they have two children.

Eric Shinseki. (Getty Images)

In June 1965, Second Lieutenant Eric Shinseki entered combat in Vietnam, assigned to the 9th Infantry Division. Three months later, on a dangerous reconnaissance mission he was badly wounded by mortar fire, and was near death from additional head and chest trauma after his medevac helicopter crashed. After a seven-month recuperation, Shinseki attended advanced armor school. He returned to Vietnam in 1970 to command an armored cavalry unit attached to the 5th Cavalry Regiment. After two months and two missions, he stepped on a land mine and blew off part of one foot. He returned to Hawaii for a year to recover and to adjust to life with an artificial right foot.

Between 1971 and 1974, Shinseki served as a personnel staff officer at Fort Shafter in Hawaii. He then took a two-year leave to obtain a master's degree from Duke University. After teaching English at West Point from 1976 to 1978, he began studying at the Army Command and Staff College at Fort Leavenworth, Kansas.

Life's Work

From 1980 to 1981, Shinseki served as a regimental adjutant and then as executive officer of an armored cavalry regiment at Fort Bliss, Texas. Promoted to colonel, he was sent to West Germany, where he served as deputy chief of staff for operations and planning from 1982 to 1984. After graduating from the National War College in 1986, he was sent back to Europe, where he commanded the 2d Brigade, 3d Infantry Division (1987–89) and served as assistant chief of staff with the VII Corps (1989–90). In 1990, Shinseki was promoted to deputy chief of staff of Allied Land Forces in Southern Europe. He was promoted to assistant division commander, 3d Infantry Division, in 1992. By 1996, Shinseki was serving simultaneously as commanding general of the United States Army in Europe, commanding general of NATO Land Forces in Central Europe, and commander of the NATO-led Stabilization Force in Bosnia-Herzegovina. At the conclusion of the Balkans conflict, Shinseki commanded the NATO peacekeeping force in Bosnia-Herzegovina from 1997 to 1998. In June 1999, US President Bill Clinton named Shinseki chief of staff of the United States Army, making him the highest-ranking officer in the Army.

During his four years as Army chief of staff, Shinseki was a proponent of transforming the American military, particularly in light of the dissolution of the Soviet Union, the terrorist attacks of September 11, 2001, and the global war on terrorism. He wanted to make the Army lighter, more modular, and more deployable. To make the army more mobile in urban warfare, peacekeeping missions, and emergency actions, he created the Stryker Interim-Force Brigade Combat Teams. In addition, Shinseki was the main architect of the Future Combat Systems program, a long-term strategic plan to transform the Army to meet the defense needs of the twenty-first century.

As chief of staff, Shinseki sought to make heavy forces more mobile and lighter forces more lethal. His strategy was often at odds with that of Defense Secretary Donald Rumsfeld, who envisioned future wars being fought from the air with precision weapons. Shinseki and Rumsfeld also disagreed about the strategy for the American-led invasion of Iraq, which sought to remove Iraqi dictator Saddam Hussein from power. Shinseki stated before the Senate Armed Services Committee that several hundred thousand soldiers would be needed to stabilize postwar Iraq, a significantly higher number than that advocated by Rumsfeld and other officials in the administration of President George W. Bush. In the wake of this public disagreement, Shinseki opted in June 2003 to end his thirty-eight-year career in the Army and enter private industry.

Business Leader

Shinseki's political connections, military know-how, and leadership experience made him highly valuable to the business community. He was appointed a director for a number of corporations, including the aerospace technology developer Honeywell International and the defense contractor Ducommun. Shinseki also served on the boards of Grove Farm Corporation, First Hawaiian Bank, DC Capital Partners, Banc West Corporation, and the Guardian Life Insurance Company of America. In addition, Shinseki was recruited to become a member of the advisory board at the Center for Public Leadership of the John F. Kennedy School of Government at Harvard University and advisor to the US Comptroller General.

In January 2009, President Barack Obama nominated Shinseki to join his cabinet as secretary of the Department of Veteran Affairs. As leader of the department, Shinseki has worked to improve medical care for veterans of the Iraq and Afghan wars. In addition, he has worked to make more employment opportunities available to US service members. Among the challenges Shinseki has faced as veterans affairs secretary has been how to cope with the increase among veterans in the rates of post-traumatic stress disorder (PTSD), homelessness, and suicide.

Eric Shinseki's Stance on the Iraq War

As planning for the US invasion of Iraq took place several weeks before the operation, a clash of views occurred between Army Chief of Staff General Shinseki and Defense Secretary Donald Rumsfeld. Concerned that the most difficult part of the invasion was not in toppling Saddam Hussein but in stabilizing an ethnically divided Iraq in the aftermath, Shinseki argued before the Senate Armed Services Committee on February 25, 2003, that several thousand troops were needed. Drawing upon his leadership in the war against Serbia and NATO's occupation of Kosovo, he argued that showing a preponderance of power during the first few days of occupation was critically important in preventing opposition.

Infuriated, Rumsfeld accused Shinseki of being "wildly off the mark" and said that it was impossible to imagine that occupying Iraq would be more difficult than conquering it. Ultimately, an unhappy Rumsfeld was pressured into increasing the number of troops from seventy-five thousand to two hundred thousand. The inability of US forces to prevent looting and maintain any semblance of order after the fall of Hussein indicated that this was still far too few. Three months after their clash of views, Shinseki, whose influence over the Joint Chiefs of Staff was waning, retired from the military. Neither President Bush nor Rumsfeld attended his retirement ceremonies.

SIGNIFICANCE

During a military career that has lasted most of his life, Shinseki has become one of the most decorated officers in the US military. As a soldier, Shinseki earned two Purple Hearts, a Bronze Star, and a Distinguished Service Medal. He is the first Asian American to become a four-star general and US Army chief of staff, and the first to serve as secretary of veterans affairs. In addition to helping to modernize the American military, he has worked to move the Veterans Administration into a more active role in taking responsibility for the needs of US veterans.

Irwin Halfond

FURTHER READING

Boyer, Peter. "A Different War." *New Yorker*. Condé Nast Digital, 1 July 2002. Web. 9 Mar. 2012. Lengthy, in-depth article on Chief of Staff Shinseki's ambitious plans to modernize the Army, and the obstacles to his success.

Dao, James, and Thom Shanker. "No Longer a Soldier, Shinseki Has a New Mission." *New York Times*. New York Times, 10 Nov. 2009. Web. 9 Mar. 2012. Discusses Shinseki's work as secretary of veterans affairs.

Shanker, Thom. "New Strategy Vindicates Ex-Army Chief Shinseki." *New York Times*. New York Times, 12 Jan. 2007. Web. 9 Mar. 2012. Discusses Bush administration moves to increase troop strength in Iraq, as Shinseki had recommended before being forced out as Army chief of staff.

M. NIGHT SHYAMALAN

Indian-born film director, producer, and screenwriter

Of the accomplishments of his nearly two-decade career, Indian American writer and director M. Night Shyamalan is perhaps best known for the acclaimed 1999 film The Sixth Sense. *With nine feature films grossing nearly $2 billion combined, Shyamalan has been placed in a very select category of filmmakers who consistently deliver works that combine critical and commercial appeal.*

Born: August 6, 1970; Pondicherry, India
Full name: M. Night Shyamalan (SHAH-muh-LAHN)
Birth name: Manoj Nelliyattu Shyamalan
Area of achievement: Film

EARLY LIFE

Manoj Nelliyattu Shyamalan, the younger of two siblings, was born in Pondicherry, India. His mother, Jayalakshmi, and father, Nelliate, were both doctors. When he was eight months old, his family moved to the United States and settled in the wealthy Philadelphia suburb of Penn Valley. He was raised in the Hindu religion, but, to instill values of discipline, his parents enrolled him at Waldron Mercy Academy, a Catholic grammar school.

As early as age seven, Shyamalan was captivated by the cinematic adventures of one of his biggest influences, Steven Spielberg. When he first watched *Star*

Wars (1977) and later *Raiders of the Lost Ark* (1981), he realized his calling. At the age of ten, he received a Super 8 film camera, with which he started making his own action and horror movies. By twelve, Shyamalan was watching and making movies at fast as he could. Friends, cousins, and even the family dog were cast in his productions. By the time he graduated from high school, Shyamalan had already completed forty-five short films.

As his high school graduation approached, Shyamalan's parents assumed that he would follow in their footsteps and attend medical school. Instead, he announced his dream of a career in the movie industry and his plans to attend school in New York. His parents were concerned with his choice of profession, but the ever-confident teenager went on to make an audacious prediction during his senior year at Episcopal Academy, outside Philadelphia. He created a full-page mock-up of a *Time* magazine cover for the yearbook with his photo and a caption that read, "Best Director: NYU Grad Takes Hollywood by Storm." Shyamalan graduated from high school in 1988 and headed for New York City.

During the summer before Shyamalan left for college, he decided to change his name. The inspiration for his new name came from an affinity for Native American culture. By adopting a new middle name, *Night*, and shortening his first name to just one initial, M. Night Shyamalan was born. With his new name, he set off for New York City to attend New York University's Tisch School of the Arts.

Life's Work

Shyamalan was a prolific writer in college, completing numerous screenplays before he graduated. One of his screenplays was made into his first feature film, *Praying with Anger* (1992). Thanks to his generous family, who supplied the $750,000 needed to make the film, Shyamalan shot his semi-autobiographical pilgrimage story entirely in India. Initially, the investment seemed to be a mistake, earning only $7,000, but the real rate of return came when Shyamalan mailed a copy of the film to the 1992 Toronto Film Festival. Many people noticed the promise represented by the film, and it went on to win the American Film Institute's award for best feature debut. This was all before Shyamalan graduated from NYU in 1993.

The exposure sparked a studio deal with Miramax for his second picture, *Wide Awake* (1998). Unfortunately, the project was riddled with problems, cursed from the start due to a strained relationship between

M. Night Shyamalan. (Getty Images)

the director and studio executives. Shyamalan felt he lacked creative freedom during the making of the film as well as final say on the finished product. The movie was finally made in 1995, with portions shot in one of Shyamalan's boyhood schools. After completion, *Wide Awake* drifted along, finally releasing in 1998. Lacking any sense of fluidity or redeeming qualities, the film was a box office failure, earning a mere $300,000. The experience left the young director wondering if his parents were right about medical school.

After this setback, Shyamalan bounced back quickly when he earned $600,000 to cowrite the screenplay for the family film *Stuart Little* (1999). This credit was to become little more than a footnote to Shyamalan's career, however, as he became a marquee director overnight with the release of the psychological thriller *The Sixth Sense* (1999), which he wrote and directed, about a boy who can communicate with the dead. The movie was wildly popular, earning six Academy Award nominations, including Best Picture and Best Director.

For his next project, Shyamalan again teamed up with Bruce Willis, who had starred in *The Sixth Sense*, on the comic-book-influenced thriller *Unbreakable* (2000). Though it had good earnings, some critics who

---

The Sixth Sense

The Sixth Sense (1999), M. Night Shyamalan's third film, flashed through theaters and captivated the imaginations of audiences, grossing nearly $700 million in worldwide box-office sales. The film earned six Academy Award nominations, including Best Director and Best Picture. A tour de force, *The Sixth Sense* offered a befuddling plot twist which shook the entertainment world. It launched Shyamalan's career and landed him on the cover of a 2002 issue of *Newsweek*, crowned as "The New Spielberg."

Set in Philadelphia, the film follows the story of child psychologist Dr. Malcolm Crowe, played by actor Bruce Willis. Crowe acquires a new patient, a boy named Cole Sear. Cole, played by Haley Joel Osment, claims that he can see ghosts and that these ghosts haunt him until he helps them settle unfinished business on earth. Crowe follows the boy through a terrifying world where the living and the dead collide. It is only at the very end of the film that Crowe discovers his true purpose in counseling Cole.

---

had held high expectations felt it paled in comparison to Shyamalan's previous work.

Shyamalan was then approached by Steven Spielberg, who offered him an opportunity to write the screenplay for a fourth *Indiana Jones* film. Tempting as the proposition was, Shyamalan turned it down and instead wrote and directed *Signs* (2002), which spun the tale of a preacher who had lost his faith in God, only to regain it during an alien invasion. This film was also extremely successful; a year later, Shyamalan donated $1.5 million toward the refurbishment of a South Philadelphia neighborhood where he had shot many scenes for *The Sixth Sense*.

His next thriller, set in the late nineteenth century, was *The Village* (2004). Despite the string of blockbusters that

Shyamalan had churned out, his partnership with Disney dissolved after creative differences got in the way of his next script, *Lady in the Water* (2006). Warner Brothers embraced the project, but it proved to be a disappointment, earning a subpar $42 million and a cornucopia of scornful reviews from critics, many of whom suggested that Shyamalan's best days were behind him. He did bounce back to cash in with his first-ever R-rated movie, *The Happening* (2008), and most recently, the live-action screen adaptation of the popular Nickelodeon cartoon *Avatar: The Last Airbender* (2010).

Shyamalan lives in Wayne, Pennsylvania, with his wife, Bhavna, whom he met during college, and their two daughters.

SIGNIFICANCE

The themes that carry Shyamalan's films are deeply rooted in myth, the unknown, the mystical, and people's search for meaning in their lives. He has been compared with Steven Spielberg and Alfred Hitchcock for his highly imaginative screenplays and signature plot twists. He continues to create suspenseful, popular, and thought-provoking movies that not only entertain, but comment on societal norms and theological questions.

Kyle Bluth

FURTHER READING

Bamberger, Michael. *The Man Who Heard Voices: Or, How M. Night Shyamalan Risked His Career on a Fairy Tale*. New York: Gotham, 2006. Print. Follows Shyamalan throughout the process of producing and directing *Lady in the Water*.

Buschel, Bruce. "The Super Natural." *Rolling Stone* 7 Dec. 2000: 46. Print. An overview of the director and his movies, including a discussion of his spiritual journey.

Humphries, Stephen. "A Different Take." *Christian Science Monitor*, 28 July 2004. Print. An inside look at Shyamalan's departure from Disney.

MUZAMMIL H. SIDDIQI

Indian-born religious scholar and theologian

A renowned scholar of Islamic law, Siddiqi promotes a positive image of Islam and encourages American Muslims to reject the violence advocated by extremist jihadists.

Born: 1943; British India (now India)
Birth name: Muzammil Husain Siddiqi (mew-ZUHM-mil hoo-SAYN sid-DEE-kee)
Areas of achievement: Religion and theology

EARLY LIFE

Born in India in 1943 and raised in a middle-class family, Muzammil Siddiqi pursued his undergraduate studies at the Aligarh Muslim University and the Darul Uloom Nadwatul Ulama in Lucknow, India. In 1965, he earned graduate degrees in Arabic and Islamic studies from the Islamic University of Medina in Saudi Arabia. He then earned a master's degree in theology from Birmingham University in England. After completing his thesis, which addressed Muslim views of Christianity in the Middle Ages, Siddiqi earned a PhD in comparative religion from Harvard University in 1978. As a PhD candidate, he worked with several Islamic organizations in England, Switzerland, and the United States. Siddiqi served as chair of the Religious Affairs Committee of the Muslim Association in the United States and Canada.

LIFE'S WORK

After earning his doctorate, Siddiqi moved to southern California. In 1981, he was named president of the Islamic Society of Orange County (ISOC), located in the city of Garden Grove. He held the presidency of the ISOC for the next thirty years, and thereafter he continued to be one of the society's major leaders and regularly delivered its Friday sermon. By 2000, the ISOC had grown to become one of the largest Muslim centers in the Americas, occupying over five acres and serving some seven thousand worshippers.

From 1997 to 2001, Siddiqi served two terms as president of the Islamic Society of North America, based in Indiana. He remained a member of the society's board of trustees for the next ten years. Among his other leadership roles, Siddiqi has served as chair of the eighteen-member Fiqh Council of North America, which makes legal rulings about Islamic jurisprudence. He has also served as a member of the Supreme Council of Mosques in Mecca, Saudi Arabia, and the Supreme Islamic Council of Egypt.

Siddiqi has been an active participant in many interreligious dialogues. In 1983, he spoke at the sixth assembly of the World Council of Churches in Vancouver, Canada. In 1999, Siddiqi was named Humanitarian of the Year by the National Council of Christians and Jews. Following the terrorist attacks of September 11, 2001, Siddiqi received an invitation from US President George W. Bush to lead a Muslim prayer at an interfaith prayer service at the Washington National Cathedral. He is also a founding member of the World Economic Forum's Council of 100 Leaders, which works to increase tolerance and understanding between the Islamic world and the West.

Between 1982 and 2004, Siddiqi conducted a weekly radio broadcast from Pasadena. A committed teacher, he has worked for many years as an adjunct professor of Islamic studies and comparative religion at Chapman University in Orange, California. In 2011, Siddiqi visited Islamic studies programs at several foreign universities, including programs in South Africa, Pakistan, and India. Siddiqi has contributed many articles to academic and Islamic journals, and he has written numerous articles for mainstream newspapers. Several of his conversations, essays, and fatwas (religious findings or declarations) are available on the Internet.

In his articles and sermons, Siddiqi has consistently called for religious tolerance and has criticized Muslims who oppose religious freedom for Christians. However, Siddiqi has at times been controversial in his opinions. In 1989, for instance, when a journalist from the *Los Angeles Times* asked him if he agreed with an Iranian fatwa calling for the death of author Salman Rushdie, whose work is considered blasphemous by some Muslims, Siddiqi replied that the issue would have to be determined according to Islamic law. In addition, Siddiqi is not tolerant of compromises with homosexuality and other practices condemned in the Koran. He has endorsed the death penalty for homosexuality in countries where Muslims constitute a majority.

Siddiqi teaches that sharia (Islamic law) is the only infallible path to "truth and justice." In applying sharia, which is taken from the Koran and the Hadith (deeds and statements of Muhammad), he insists on the need for careful scholarly interpretations based on critical analysis of the views of differing Islamic scholars. In 2000, Siddiqi advocated that Muslims participate in the American legal system in order to protect Muslims' interests and promote justice. Yet he made it clear that his ultimate goal was to bring about the establishment of sharia in all countries, including the United States. Siddiqi shared his belief that the city of Jerusalem belongs to Islam and cannot be turned over to Israel as part of negotiations aimed at settling the Israeli-Palestinian conflict.

In 2002, federal authorities raided the headquarters of the Fiqh Council in search of suspected terrorists, but the raid resulted in no arrests. In 2005, Siddiqi attached his name to the Fiqh Council's fatwa that strongly condemned terrorism and religious extremism as contrary to Islamic principles. The council has also issued declarations arguing that the death penalty for *murtad* (apostasy) violates the teachings of the prophets, despite the fact that other Islamic leaders have justified the practice.

SIGNIFICANCE

During the first decade of the twenty-first century, Siddiqi's mosque became one of the largest in North America. Serving as a leader in many of the nation's most important Islamic institutions, he has remained calm and knowledgeable in an age of religious turbulence. At a time when proponents of extremist jihadism fueled xenophobia, he provided a voice in favor of moderation, nonviolence, and tolerance. In 2006, the *Los Angeles Times* recognized Siddiqi as one of the hundred most influential persons in Southern California.

Thomas Tandy Lewis

FURTHER READING

Ali, M. M. "Islamic Society of North America: President Dr. Muzammil Siddiqi." *Washington Report on Middle East Affairs* 19.7 (2000): 47–48. Print. Discusses Siddiqi's personality and summarizes his ideas, emphasizing his opposition to extremism.

Gordis, David M., George B. Grose, and Muzammil H. Siddiqi. *The Abraham Connection: A Jew, Christian, and Muslim in Dialogue*. Notre Dame, IN: Cross Cultural, 1994. Print. A dialogue about mutual tolerance and respect, while recognizing the major differences among the three religions.

Hallaq, Wael. *History of Islamic Legal Theories: An Introduction to Sunni Usul Al-Fiqh*. New York: Cambridge UP, 1997. Print. Introduction to the history of Islamic jurisprudence.

Kone, Kassim. *Muslims in the United States*. Westport, CT: Greenwood, 2006. Print. Discusses the ways of life and challenges faced by Muslims in a country dominated by Christian and secular values.

BAPSI SIDHWA

Indian-born feminist and writer

Writer Bapsi Sidhwa is a renowned spokesperson for women's rights, both in her native Pakistan and throughout the world.

Born: August 11, 1938; Karachi, British India (now Pakistan)
Full name: Bapsi Sidhwa (BAP-see SIHD-wah)
Birth name: Bapsy Bhandara
Also known as: Bapsy Kermani; Bapsy Sidhwa
Areas of achievement: Literature, film, women's rights

EARLY LIFE

Bapsi Sidhwa was born Bapsy Bhandara on August 11, 1938, in Karachi, British India. Her father, Peshotan Bhandara, was a businessman. Though her maternal grandmother named her Bapsy, when Sidhwa became an adult, she decided to change the *y* in her first name to *i*. Sidhwa grew up in Lahore, India, which became part of Pakistan following the British partition of India. As Parsis, or Zoroastrians, the Sidhwa family was part of a small, close-knit community that remained neutral during the conflicts between Hindus, Sikhs, and Muslims before and after the 1947 partition. Although her own family remained safe, the bloody conflict all around her made an indelible impression on Sidhwa.

Bapsi Sidhwa. (India Today Group/Getty Images)

Sidhwa contracted polio as a young girl, which forced her to spend most of her childhood at home. After one of her tutors gave her a copy of *Little Women* (1869) by Louisa May Alcott, Sidhwa became a voracious reader. At fifteen, she entered the Kinnaird College for Women in Lahore, where she majored in psychology and ethics, earning her degree in 1957.

After finishing college, Sidhwa married Gustad Kermani and moved to Bombay (now Mumbai), India, where she joined a large, cosmopolitan Parsi community. She and her husband had two children, a son and a daughter, but divorced after five years of marriage. Sidhwa moved back to Lahore, taking her daughter with her; her son remained with his father until Kermani's death in 1975, at which point he returned to Sidhwa. In 1963, she married Noshir Sidhwa. The couple had one child, a daughter.

Sidhwa led a busy life, tending to her children, supervising a household full of servants, and performing her many social obligations. However, during a trip with her second husband to northern Pakistan, she heard the story of a young Punjabi girl who was sold into marriage. When the girl ran away from her husband, the men of his tribe hunted her down, killed her, and threw her decapitated body into a river. For some years, Sidhwa had been a vocal supporter of women's rights, but although she had written about the issue, she had never submitted any of her writing for publication; in fact, only her husband knew that she was a writer. However, Sidhwa felt compelled to tell the world the story of the Punjabi girl from the north.

LIFE'S WORK

After returning to Lahore, Sidhwa began work on what she thought would be a short story, but the narrative gradually evolved into a novel. Sidhwa's story is told from the viewpoint of three characters: Qasim, a tribesman; Zaitoon, his adopted daughter; and Carol, an American woman married to a Pakistani. Sidhwa treats the tribesmen sympathetically, depicting them as trapped by a society with an inflexible definition of honor. In contrast to them, the character Carol represents Western social values, and her presence makes it possible for Zaitoon to be smuggled out of the hill country and thus to survive. Unlike the incident that inspired it, Sidhwa's story has a happy conclusion.

Since English-language novels were not being published in Pakistan at the time Sidhwa completed her novel, she submitted her work to publishers outside the country. They all rejected it. In fact, *The Bride* was not accepted for publication until 1983, after the success of

---

Bapsi Sidhwa and Deepa Mehta as Collaborators

In the 1990s, Indian Canadian filmmaker Deepa Mehta planned a trilogy about life on the Indian subcontinent. All of the films would point out how social and religious attitudes resulted in oppression, especially in the repression of women. In the first film, *Fire* (1996), two wives find deliverance from their boredom by venturing into a lesbian relationship. The second film, *Earth*, which was shot in 1998, is based on Bapsi Sidhwa's novel *Cracking India* (1991). Its focus is on how racism, religious intolerance, and violence destroy relationships and ruin lives. The final film in Mehta's trilogy, *Water* (2005), is set in India in the 1930s and deals with the systematic expulsion of widows from society. Due to demonstrations and protests, the filming had to be moved from Varanasi to West Bengal. Nevertheless, *Water* set audience records in Canada and in the United States. After she saw the film, Sidhwa was inspired to write a novel fleshing out Mehta's characters. Four months later, *Water* (2006) appeared in bookstores.

Sidhwa's second novel. In 1990, *The Bride* was republished as *The Pakistani Bride*.

Sidhwa's second novel, *The Crow Eaters* (1978), is very different from her first. It is a comic novel, set in Lahore's Parsi community and told from a male point of view. Though he is a successful businessman, the character Faredoon Junglewalla is regularly defeated at home by his tyrannical mother-in-law. Sidhwa originally self-published *The Crow Eaters*. In 1980 and 1981, it was republished in London and New York.

Sidhwa relocated to Houston, Texas, in 1983. She made the city her permanent home, becoming a naturalized American citizen in 1992. Over the course of her career, she taught at a number of universities, including the University of Houston, Rice University, Columbia University, and Brandeis University.

Sidhwa's third novel, *Ice-Candy-Man* (1988), published in the United States under the title *Cracking India* (1991), is the story of a young Parsi girl who sees her community torn apart by the 1947 partition. Even though the Parsis are largely unaffected by the violence, the main character bears witness to neighbor turning against neighbor, friend against friend, and men against defenseless women. Women's issues also play a prominent role in Sidhwa's novel *An American Brat* (1993). The central characters in the novel are a young Parsi woman, who has come to the United States to complete her education, and her mother, who travels to the United States from Pakistan because she fears her daughter is learning too much. A stage adaptation of *An American Brat* was performed in England in 2003 under the title *Sock 'Em with Honey*. In 2007, a revised production debuted in Houston, Texas, under the original title.

In 2005, Sidhwa edited the anthology *City of Sin and Splendour: Writings on Lahore*. Her fifth novel, *Water*, appeared in 2006. Sidhwa's work as a writer has earned her many honors, including a New York Times Notable Book of the Year Award in 1991 for *Cracking India* and a Lila Wallace–Reader's Digest Award in 1993. Also in 1991, Sidhwa was awarded the Sitara-i-Imtiaz, Pakistan's highest honor in the arts.

SIGNIFICANCE

Sidhwa consistently focuses on the unjust and inhumane treatment of women in Pakistan and India, societies where social and religious systems are profoundly patriarchal. Her work describes the purchase of wives, the abuse of widows, violence against women in the aftermath of colonialism, and the difficulties faced by a South Asian woman living in the Western world. Her compelling characters and vivid storytelling have led many critics to describe her as Pakistan's greatest novelist.

Rosemary M. Canfield Reisman

FURTHER READING

Jussawalla, Feroza, and Reed Way Dasenbrock. *Interviews with Writers of the Post-Colonial World*. Jackson: UP of Mississippi, 1992. Print. Compares the influence of the colonial past on Mexican American authors and on those from the Commonwealth.

Rushdie, Salman, and Elizabeth West. *Mirrorwork: 50 Years of Indian Writing, 1947–1997*. New York: Holt, 1997. Print. Discusses such issues as language, style, and dominant themes. Includes "Ranna's Story," an excerpt from Sidhwa's *Ice-Candy-Man* (*Cracking India*).

Zaman, Niaz. *A Divided Legacy: The Partition in Selected Novels of India, Pakistan, and Bangladesh*. New York: Oxford UP, 2001. Print. Analysis of novels written in Bengali and Urdu, as well as in English, with many references to Sidhwa.

MONICA SONE

Writer

In her memoir Nisei Daughter, *Japanese American author Monica Sone chronicled her upbringing in Seattle, Washington, and her family's internment during World War II. The book is an important account of Japanese American lives in the United States during years of strong anti-Asian prejudice and discrimination.*

Born: September 1, 1919; Seattle, Washington
Died: September 5, 2011; Canton, Ohio
Full name: Monica Sone (SOH-nay)
Birth name: Kazuko Monica Itoi
Area of achievement: Literature

EARLY LIFE

Monica Sone was born in 1919 in Seattle, Washington. Her father, Seizo Itoi, ran the Carrollton Hotel in the Skid Row area of Seattle, known for its rough and impoverished population. The Carrollton was also home to the Itoi family, which included Monica's mother, Benko, her brothers Henry and Ken, and her sister Sumiko.

Sone's father had studied and practiced law in Tokyo before immigrating to the United States in 1904 with the hope of entering law school at the University of Michigan. However, despite years of hard work in Washington state and Alaska, he was unable to pursue his dream. Instead, while working in Seattle, he met and married Benko Nagashima, whose father, a Congregational minister from Japan, had brought his family there in the 1910s.

Monica and her siblings grew up considering themselves to be thoroughly American until, when she was six, the Itois decided to enroll their children in a Japanese after-school program to learn the Japanese language and Japanese cultural practices. Throughout her childhood, Sone pursued her American identity while facing pressure from her parents to embrace her Japanese ancestry and encountering anti-Japanese sentiments in the wider society.

LIFE'S WORK

Bowing to her father's demand that she pursue practical training instead of a college education, Sone learned secretarial skills at the Edison Vocational School. While attending the school she contracted tuberculosis, and spent nine months recuperating at Seattle's Firland Sanatorium, in company with another future writer, Betty MacDonald. Sone had just regained her health when Japan attacked the US naval base at Pearl Harbor on December 7, 1941. Following the attack, she and her family were forced into an assembly center in Puyallup, Washington, then moved to Camp Minidoka, an Idaho internment center for Japanese Americans. Throughout her internment, she wrote many letters to MacDonald, describing her family's efforts to adapt to and survive their incarceration.

Following her release in 1943, Sone moved to Indiana. After earning a bachelor's degree at Hanover College in Indiana, she earned a master's in clinical psychology from Case Western Reserve University in 1949. By the time she married Geary Sone, a Japanese American war veteran from California pursuing a career as a microbiologist, her friend MacDonald had become a prominent author. Having shared Sone's letters with a literary agent who praised her writing, MacDonald urged Sone to write a book about her life as a *nisei*, or American citizen born to Japanese immigrant parents. Sone published *Nisei Daughter* in 1953, and it received favorable reviews.

Nisei Daughter outlines Sone's evolution from a child uncertain as to whether she was Japanese or American, to a confident adult who viewed herself as both, and happily so. Sone's mild-mannered treatment of the racism and incarceration she experienced in her life made the book more palatable to white readers. However, Sone did not ignore the existence of anti-Asian discrimination and used wit and sarcasm to criticize the injustices she had experienced.

Following the book's publication, Sone and her husband had four children and settled in Canton, Ohio, where she worked as an adoption counselor. In 1979, as Japanese Americans began to pursue legal redress for the wrongs done to them during World War II, *Nisei Daughter* was reissued. The republished book drew widespread critical acclaim. A strong supporter of the redress movement, Sone provided a foreward to the 1979 edition that identified her book as an early testimony about the injustices inflicted upon Japanese Americans by the United States government. Monica Sone died in 2011.

Significance

Nisei Daughter represents one of the earliest memoirs by an Asian American who experienced internment under the auspices of the US government during World War II. For this reason, the work maintains a prominent position in the canon of twentieth-century Asian American literature. Although *Nisei Daughter* is Sone's only book, its widespread use in schools since 1979 has made Sone an important author. While her apparent willingness to downplay anti-Asian prejudices in the book drew some criticism in the 1980s and 1990s, others argued that her work must be understood in its historical context and was actually bold for its time. Throughout her life, Sone shunned the spotlight and preferred to view herself as a spouse, parent, and counselor. Yet, to the multiple generations of readers moved by *Nisei Daughter*, she stands out as a storyteller of great power.

Further Reading

Hoffman, Warren D. "Home, Memory, and Narrative in Monica Sone's *Nisei Daughter*." *Recovered Legacies: Authority and Identity in Early Asian American Literature*. Ed. Keith Lawrence and Floyd Cheung. Philadelphia: Temple UP, 2005. Print. Analyzes *Nisei Daughter* as a chronicle of Sone's ongoing development of her Japanese American identity from 1919 to 1979.

Lim, Shirley Geok-lin. "Japanese American Women's Life Stories: Maternality in Monica Sone's *Nisei Daughter* and Joy Kogawa's *Obasan*." *Asian-American Writers*. Ed. Harold Bloom. Philadelphia: Chelsea House, 1999. Print. Discusses the treatment of ethnic assimilation and gender as subjects in *Nisei Daughter*.

Sumida, Stephen H. "Protest and Accommodation, Self-Satire and Self-Effacement, and Monica Sone's *Nisei Daughter*." *Multicultural Autobiography: American Lives*. Ed. James Robert Payne. Knoxville: U of Tennessee P, 1992. Print. Sumida discusses Sone's use of humor in response to the racism and injustice faced by Japanese Americans.

Yamamoto, Traise. "*Nisei Daughter*." *A Resource Guide to Asian American Literature*. Ed. Sau-ling Cynthia Wong and Stephen H. Sumida. New York: Modern Language Association, 2001. Print. Discusses *Nisei Daughter*'s historical context and its use in classroom settings.

BRENDA SONG

Actor and singer

Best known for her many accomplishments in film and television, Song became a model at age three and a professional actress at the age of six. Since 2000, she has appeared in numerous Disney Channel productions.

Born: March 27, 1988; Carmichael, California
Full name: Brenda Julietta Song
Areas of achievement: Film, television

EARLY LIFE

Brenda Song was born on March 27, 1988, in Carmichael, California, to a Hmong Chinese father and a Thai American mother—a second-grade schoolteacher and a homemaker, respectively. She is the oldest of three children, with two younger brothers. Her father's family emigrated from Laos to America in 1976. Song was homeschooled starting in fourth grade; in ninth grade, she was named an All-American Scholar, a recognition given for outstanding scholastic achievement by the United States Achievement Academy. Song graduated from high school at age sixteen and then took courses in business at a community college.

Early in her life, Song received attention for her exceptional looks and poise, becoming a model when she was just three years old. At age six, she appeared on television in a commercial for Little Caesars Pizza. Her family moved from Sacramento to Los Angeles to support Song's budding career, and she landed roles in other commercials, such as Mattel's Barbie advertisements.

Although Song wanted to take ballet, her brother wanted to learn tae kwon do, and their mother decided they would both study martial arts. Song earned her black belt in 2004 at age fourteen, providing additional skills that would bolster her acting opportunities later on in her career.

LIFE'S WORK

Though young, Brenda Song has had a busy and successful professional life, having experienced fame as a fashion model and actor in television and film. Between 1994 and 2003, she made various guest appearances in programs such as *Thunder Alley*, *MADtv*, *Bette*, *Judging Amy*, *ER*, *7th Heaven*, *The Bernie Mac Show*, and *That's So Raven*. In 1996, Song made her movie debut with professional wrestler Hulk Hogan in the independent film *Santa with Muscles*; the following year, she appeared as Susan Acustis in the film *Leave It to Beaver* (1997). She also played Sariffa Chung in thirteen episodes of the Nickelodeon family television series *100 Deeds for Eddie McDowd*, from 2000 to 2002.

Song's role as Samantha Elizabeth Kwan in *The Ultimate Christmas Present* (2000), a Disney Channel movie, resulted in her receiving a Young Hollywood Award in 2001. Her career continued to escalate when she landed a role in *Get a Clue* (2002), a Disney Channel original movie starring Lindsay Lohan. She then played Reg Stevens, best friend to main character Calvin, in *Like Mike* (2002), a film about a teenage orphan who becomes an NBA star after finding a pair of magic sneakers. In 2004, she was back at Disney in another TV movie, *Stuck in the Suburbs*.

From then on, Song worked almost exclusively for Disney. In 2005, she was cast in Disney's television series *The Suite Life of Zack and Cody*, in which she played London Tipton, a role she reprised in the many

Brenda Song. (FilmMagic)

spinoffs of the show. In 2006, Song put her tae kwon do training to good use as the title character in *Wendy Wu: Homecoming Warrior*, an Asian female warrior who has been reincarnated as an American teen with a mission to save the world from destruction.

Song continues to expand her talents and accrue acting credits. In 2008, she played Nancy in the Disney production *College Road Trip*, and she was cast as Christy Lee in the successful film *The Social Network* in 2010. The following year, she reprised the role of London Tipton in *The Suite Life Movie* (2011), a Disney Channel original movie based on the television series.

SIGNIFICANCE

Brenda Song has had many outstanding accomplishments in her young life. In 2001, while still in her early teens, Song won the Young Artist Award for Best Performance in a TV Movie (Comedy), Supporting Young Actress for her role in *The Ultimate Christmas Present*. Two years later, she was nominated for the same award for her performance in *The Bernie Mac Show*. In 2006, Song was nominated for the Asian Excellence Newcomer Award for *The Suite Life of Zack and Cody*, and in 2011, she was nominated for a Nickelodeon Kids' Choice Award for Favorite TV Sidekick in the sequel series *The Suite Life on Deck*.

Song is also active in philanthropy, working for select causes. She participated in the thirteenth annual Susan G. Komen Los Angeles County Race for the Cure in support of breast-cancer awareness, and she walked the red carpet in 2011 at the Cancer Research Foundation's Hot Pink Party. Other philanthropic groups she supports are the Lakers' Youth Foundation and the Make-a-Wish Foundation.

Marylane Wade Koch

FURTHER READING

Orr, Tamra. *Brenda Song.* Hockessin, DE: Mitchell Lane, 2010. Print. Robbie Readers. Provides an overview of Song's major accomplishments as a positive role model for youth.

Rawson, Katherine. *Brenda Song.* New York: Rosen, 2010. Print. Kid Stars. Part of a series written at the elementary level, providing basic biographical information and pictures.

Song, Brenda. "Brenda Song—The New Interview." By Audrey Fine. *Seventeen.* Hearst, n.d. Web. 29 Mar. 2012. Addresses Song's role in *Pass the Plate*, Disney's effort to encourage young people to eat and exercise for better health, as well as her love of cooking and her personal eating habits.

Steinberg, Jacques. "Brenda Song Turns Warrior in Disney's *Wendy Wu*." *New York Times*. New York Times, 15 June 2006. Web. 29 Mar. 2012. Discusses the shift from Song's role in *The Suite Life of Zack and Cody* to her character in *Wendy Wu*.

CATHY SONG

Poet and educator

Hawaiian native Song has won considerable acclaim and a number of awards for her poetry, which focuses on her Asian heritage and her experiences with her family.

Born: August 20, 1955; Honolulu, Hawaii
Full name: Cathy-Lynn Song
Area of achievement: Literature

EARLY LIFE

Cathy Song is the daughter of Andrew Song, a Korean American airline pilot, and Ella Song, a Chinese American seamstress. Song, her older sister Andrea, and her younger brother Alan lived with their parents in Wahiawa, a small plantation town in central Oahu devoted to the cultivation of pineapple and sugar, until Song was seven. They then moved to Honolulu. The family traveled a lot, and at age nine, Song decided to chronicle their stories and travels. Her stories about her family filled so much paper that her father bought surplus Army target paper to accommodate her writing. This early work and her family's travels would later become the nucleus of her poetry.

Song attended Kalani High School, where her writing was encouraged, and went on to work with poet and biographer John Unterecker at the University of Hawaii at Manoa, who encouraged her to develop her talent. After two years at the University of Hawaii, Song transferred to Wellesley College in Massachusetts, where she earned a BA in English in 1977. Although she published a short story, "Beginnings (For Bok Pil)," in 1976, Song otherwise focused on writing poetry. Some of the poems

Cathy Song's *Picture Bride*

Cathy Song's first collection of poetry, *Picture Bride* (1983), was originally titled *From the White Place*, after the title of the poem she dedicated to Georgia O'Keeffe, her favorite painter. The publisher suggested that Song change the book's title to *Picture Bride*, which seemed more ethnically appealing. Song's mentor, Kathleen Spivak, proposed the thirty-one poems be divided into five sections, each named for a flower painting by Georgia O'Keeffe.

In his introduction to the book, poet Richard Hugo refers to Song's poems as "bouquets" containing "moments in life" that initially seem unimportant but in "retrospect count the most." The book focuses on Song's world in Hawaii. It begins with the title poem "Picture Bride," which is based on her Korean grandmother's experience coming to Hawaii in 1921 to meet a man she had "married" in a ceremony in Korea but had never met, except through his picture. Such arranged marriages were not uncommon among Japanese and Korean immigrants before World War II.

Picture Bride provides insights into Song's life through its descriptions of her family and past events. For example, "Easter, Wahiawa: 1959" describes a family Easter celebration, and "Hotel Genève" remembers a family trip to Mexico City. The final poem, "The Seamstress," shows how her mother's world of sewing and Song's world of crafting poems are not all that different. *Picture Bride* also celebrates the work of two visual artists: Georgia O'Keeffe and the nineteenth-century Japanese printmaker Kitagawa Utamaro.

advanced poetry workshop. It was Spivak who suggested that Song seek publication from mainstream presses, not just those that focused on ethnic authors.

LIFE'S WORK

In 1982, Song submitted her first book of poetry, *Picture Bride*, to the Yale Series of Younger Poets, one of the most prestigious literary competitions in the nation. The book, which centers on Song's Asian American heritage and reflects her experiences as a child and young woman in Hawaii, was selected from a field of 625 entries. *Picture Bride* was nominated for the National Book Critics Circle Award and brought Song to national attention.

While living in Boston, Song met Douglas McHarg Davenport, a medical student at Tufts University. They married in 1979 and relocated to Denver, Colorado, where Davenport completed his residency and the couple had two children. While in Denver, Song worked on her second book of poetry, *Frameless Windows, Squares of Life* (1988). The title alludes to moments of the present that stimulate memories of the past and other experiences. Song's experiences with her brother in the past recur in the present, with some differences, as her own son grows up and interacts with his sister. The book continues to explore the ties that bind women to parents and children, as well as to their community and traditions. The poem "Humble Jar" attracted considerable critical acclaim. It describes the mayonnaise jar filled with buttons kept by Song's mother, a seamstress; some of the buttons are for practical use, while others are kept as memories of other times and places.

In the summer of 1987, Song, her husband, and their two children moved to Honolulu, where their third child was born. Back in Hawaii, Song continued to write, and she also began teaching poetry workshops at several universities. She became involved in Poets in the Schools, a program that gives public school children, from kindergarten through high school, the opportunity to work with and learn from published poets. Song also joined the Bamboo Ridge study group of Hawaiian poets and fiction writers and worked for the Bamboo Ridge Press. However, her principal activity remained the writing of poetry.

School Figures (1994), Song's third book of poetry, again uses family stories as subjects. It explores many aspects of family life, including the joyous and the devastating. The book's title refers to the figures that ice skaters practice repeatedly; the poems examine Song's world and the experiences of her family to recreate the images. In the poem "The Grammar of Silk," Song revisits the

she wrote while a student at Wellesley were later published in *Picture Bride* (1983), her first book of poetry. Song later remarked that her feelings of being homesick and far from her family were reflected in the title poem about her paternal grandmother, a picture bride sent to Hawaii to marry a man she had never met.

When she was a student at Wellesley, Song discovered American artist Georgia O'Keeffe's book *Georgia O'Keeffe* (1976). O'Keeffe's work and life impacted Song's writing, both providing her with subject material and influencing her artistic use of images in her poetry. In 1981, Song completed an MFA in creative writing at Boston University; while there, she encountered a second mentor, writer Kathleen Spivak, who taught an

concept of sewing as a typically creative act for women and recalls learning to sew as a child.

Song's collection *The Land of Bliss* (2001) also focuses specifically on her own family. She writes about the reality of aging parents, mixed with the memories of her grandparents. The poem "Ghost" reflects on racial differences in a multiethnic society; historically, the term *ghost* was often used by Chinese and Chinese American people to refer to people of other races, usually Caucasians. Her fifth book, *Cloud Moving Hands* (2007), is named for a movement in tai chi. The book is infused with Buddhist teachings and reiterates the importance of suffering as an opportunity for change, such as in the poem "The Man Moves Earth." In addition to writing poetry, Song also coedited the anthology *Sister Stew: Fiction and Poetry by Women* (1991) with Juliet S. Kono.

SIGNIFICANCE

Song is the first Native Hawaiian writer to be nationally recognized for her work. She earned her reputation as a poet by writing about her family as well as her Korean and Chinese heritage. Her poetry has been heavily anthologized, and her books of poetry have received several awards. In 1993, she became the youngest person to have won the Hawaii Award for Literature and was also awarded the Shelley Memorial Award from the Poetry Society of America. Other awards Song has received include *Poetry* magazine's Frederick Bock Prize, the Elliot Cades Award for Literature, and the Pushcart Prize.

Marcia B. Dinneen

FURTHER READING

Chen, Fu-Jen. "Body and Female Subjectivity in Cathy Song's *Picture Bride*." *Women's Studies* 33.5 (2004): 577–612. Print. Includes biographical material and a detailed analysis of the visual nature of Song's poetry.

Fujita-Sato, Gayle K. "'Third World' as Place and Paradigm in Cathy Song's *Picture Bride*." *MELUS* 15.1 (1988): 49–72. Print. Focuses on Song's interpretation of the role of women in both Asian and American societies.

Hugo, Richard. Foreword. *Picture Bride*. By Cathy Song. New Haven, CT: Yale UP, 1983. Print. Discusses the visual nature of Song's poetry and her sense of "quietude" in the precision and control in her poems.

Song, Cathy. "Cathy Song." Interview by David Choo. *Honolulu Weekly* 15 June 1994: 6–8. Print. Discusses how Song became a poet.

JACK SOO

Actor, entertainer, and singer

One of the first Asian Americans to star on Broadway and in television, Jack Soo became known for his wisecracking and wry performances. He helped to open the door for future Asian American actors and entertainers by refusing to portray Asian stereotypes.

Born: October 28, 1917; Oakland, California
Died: January 11, 1979; Los Angeles, California
Full name: Jack Soo
Birth name: Goro Suzuki
Also known as: Jack Suzuki
Areas of achievement: Acting, television, entertainment

EARLY LIFE

Jack Soo was born Goro Suzuki to Japanese American parents on October 28, 1917. Wanting their child to be born in Japan, the Suzukis sailed from California, hoping to arrive in time for the birth; however, Soo was born on the boat before they could reach Japan, and his birthplace is listed as Oakland, California, the Suzukis' home. After high school, Soo worked for a time as a farm laborer and melon buyer before enrolling at the University of California, Berkeley, where he majored in English. While in college, he began appearing in San Francisco nightclubs as a comedian, singer, and emcee.

Soo's career was put on hold by the bombing of Pearl Harbor and the subsequent relocation of Japanese Americans into internment camps. In 1941, he and his family were moved into Tanforan Assembly Center in San Francisco, then sent to Utah's Topaz Relocation Center. While interned at the camp, Soo entertained the residents by performing stand-up comedy and singing. He became very well known and was eventually released by the US government to work in military intelligence in Cleveland, Ohio.

After the war, Soo was determined to break into show business. He worked as a butcher to pay the bills, but continued to perform stand-up throughout the Midwest and the East Coast. During this time, he befriended another struggling comic, Danny Arnold, who was hoping to break into television production; Arnold promised Soo that one day he would hire him. In the meantime, Soo's comedy career got a big boost when he was paired with Joey Bishop in 1949. He played straight man to Bishop, perfecting his sarcastic and droll delivery. The partnership lasted only a year and a half, however, as Bishop's agents were worried that being linked to an Asian would hurt his career and thus fired Soo.

In the late 1950s, Soo began working regularly at two Asian American nightclubs in San Francisco, Andy Wong's Sky Room and Charlie Low's Forbidden City. His big break came when Gene Kelly enjoyed Soo so much as the club's announcer that he offered him the role of the nightclub emcee in the upcoming Broadway musical *Flower Drum Song.*

LIFE'S WORK

By the time Soo was hired to play Frankie Wing in *Flower Drum Song*, he wanted to change his stage name back to Suzuki. However, the producers convinced him that it was not a good idea due to lingering anti-Japanese sentiment and that his current name would seem more authentic for the Chinese character he was about to portray. Soo kept his name, took the part, and moved to New York City in 1958. His portrayal of Wing received positive reviews, and he was promoted to the role of Sammy Fong, a romantic lead. The show was a great success, and Soo became a star. He was again cast as Fong in the 1961 film version, for which he sang his own songs. This performance helped to launch his singing career; in 1965, he was one of the first non–African American performers signed to Motown Records, for which he recorded "For Once in My Life," a song that singer Stevie Wonder would cover in 1968.

After *Flower Drum Song*, Soo found it difficult to get work. Despite his popularity, roles for Asian actors were sparse and were generally limited to gardeners, houseboys, and other service-related parts, and Soo refused to take any role that reinforced Asian stereotypes. Although proud of the early Asian actors who had to take these roles, he felt that the time for stereotyping was over. Then, in 1964, he was offered a leading role on *Valentine's Day*, a TV sitcom, alongside actor Tony Franciosa. The show only lasted for one season, and Soo spent the next eleven years guest starring in many television shows and movies.

Soo's biggest success came in 1975, when his old friend Danny Arnold's new show *Barney Miller* was picked up by the networks. Making good on the promise he had made to Soo twenty years earlier, Arnold cast him as one of a group of diverse New York City policemen. For the next four years, Soo played Detective Nick Yemana, once again using the sarcastic and caustic persona developed in his early stand-up career. Many Asian jokes were written into the show, mostly revolving around people's inability to tell his ethnicity and mistaking him for Chinese or Korean.

At the height of his popularity, Soo was diagnosed with esophageal cancer. He died while filming the fifth season of *Barney Miller* and was buried in Los Angeles, California.

SIGNIFICANCE

Jack Soo's role in the 1964 series *Valentine's Day* made him the first Asian actor to play a lead in a television show. He promoted the idea that Asian American actors could play any parts, not just domestics or gardeners, and should not be limited to portraying exaggerated stereotypes for comic effect.

Leslie Neilan

FURTHER READING

Hamamoto, Darrell Y. *Monitored Peril: Asian Americans and the Politics of TV Representation.* Minneapolis: U of Minnesota P, 1994. Print. A description of the struggles of Asian American actors on television. Mentions Soo and his various television roles.

Lewis, David H. *Flower Drum Songs: The Story of Two Musicals.* Jefferson, NC: McFarland, 2006. Print. Compares the histories of the original 1958 Broadway version of *Flower Drum Song* and the rewritten revival of 2002.

Niiya, Brian, ed. *Japanese American History: An A-to-Z Reference from 1868 to the Present.* New York: FOF, 1993. Print. Includes a brief synopsis of Soo's life and career.

PATRICK SOON-SHIONG

South African-born physician, entrepreneur, philanthropist

A self-made billionaire, Patrick Soon-Shiong created his fortune by founding pharmaceutical and health product companies that focus on using new technology to cure diseases. He is best known for creating the chemotherapeutic drug Abraxane to treat metastatic breast cancer.

Born: 1952; Port Elizabeth, South Africa
Full name: Patrick Soon-Shiong (SOON-shong)
Areas of achievement: Medicine, technology

EARLY LIFE

Patrick Soon-Shiong was born to Chinese parents living under apartheid (racial segregation) in South Africa. His parents left China during World War II. When Soon-Shiong's father lived in China, he was the village physician and herbalist. Soon-Shiong excelled in school, graduating from high school early, at age sixteen. He was motivated to become a physician by the work his father did as an herbalist. Soon-Shiong attended college at the University of the Witwatersrand in Johannesburg,

Patrick Soon-Shiong. (AP Photo)

South Africa, where he earned a bachelor of arts and bachelor of science as well as a degree in medicine. He graduated when he was twenty-three years old, finishing fourth in his class. He remained in Johannesburg for his internship at Johannesburg General Hospital (now the Charlotte Maxeke Johannesburg Academic Hospital) where he became the first Chinese student to intern in the all-white hospital. He had to get special permission from the South African government to do so.

In 1977, Soon-Shiong finished his internship and relocated to Vancouver, Canada, for residency at the University of British Columbia because of South Africa's racially discriminatory system, which would only pay him half of the salary of a white physician. In addition to receiving multiple honors throughout his residency, including the American College of Surgeons Schering Scholar, Association for Academic Surgery Award for Research, and the Royal College of Physicians and Surgeons of Canada Research Award, Soon-Shiong also earned a master of science degree in 1978. In 1980 he moved to the United States for surgical training at the University of California, Los Angeles (UCLA). Soon-Shiong subsequently became board certified in surgery.

LIFE'S WORK

Soon-Shiong remained at UCLA after completing his medical training and became a faculty member of the School of Medicine at the age of thirty-one, in 1983. He began a new organ transplant program, and in 1987 Soon-Shiong performed the first whole pancreas transplant. He left UCLA in 1991 in frustration over the lag in time between when medical discoveries were made and when they actually became available to patients. Thus, the remainder of his career has been devoted to forming companies that deliver quality and innovative medications and health care products to the public at a faster pace.

Soon-Shiong first formed the company VivoRx, and later VivoRx Diabetes, both of which were devoted to diabetes research. Soon-Shiong recognized that the whole-pancreas transplant was difficult. He modified the procedure and performed the first encapsulated islet transplant in a patient with diabetes in 1993. This procedure transplanted just the insulin-producing portion of the organ. Soon-Shiong pioneered using seaweed to surround the islets to avoid transplant rejection and the need for immunosuppressive medication. He also was the first surgeon to transplant an islet from a pig to a human.

In 1998 Soon-Shiong bought his first company, American Pharmaceutical Partners (APP). He was chairman of the board of directors and chief executive officer (CEO) and was named president of the company in 2001. Through APP, Soon-Shiong and his team created Abraxane, a chemotherapy drug that works on the nanoparticle level. It was the first one of its kind to win Federal Drug Administration (FDA) approval. In addition, APP was the only company to supply untainted heparin, a blood thinner that was responsible for more than sixty deaths in 2008 due to tainted doses. Soon-Shiong sold his share of the company in 2008.

Soon-Shiong went on to cofound the biotechnology company Abraxis BioScience, which focused on cancer drug development. Starting in 2007 he served as the executive chairman and CEO. He continued the refinement and marketing of Abraxane, a now-famous treatment for breast cancer, at Abraxis BioScience. Soon-Shiong sold the company in 2010.

In 2006 Soon-Shiong began to focus on the American health care system. He founded the National Coalition for Health Integration, whose goal is to create computer networks for the sharing of secure patient medical information throughout the country. In February 2011 he acquired the company Vitality, Inc. as part of his crusade to increase medical care effectiveness through technological advancements. Vitality, Inc. recently developed the GlowCap, a pill bottle cover that lights up or plays music to remind a patient to take his or her medication. The technology has been shown to increase adherence to taking medication and overall health. Since 2009, Soon-Shiong has been the executive director for the UCLA Wireless Health Institute and recently collaborated with Toumaz Limited, a company focused on creating new wireless health care technology especially for athletes.

Awards and honors for Soon-Shiong include the Humanitarian of Vision Award (2010), Pancreatic Cancer Action Network's Medical Visionary Award (2008), St. Mary's Medical Center Lifetime Achievement Award (2007), Ellis Island Medal of Honor (2007), Gilda Club Award (2006), Peter Kiewit Distinguished Membership in Medicine Award, and the International J. W. Hyatt Award for Service to Mankind. He is a member of the advisory board for the RAND Corporation and the Institute of Technology Advancement (ITA) at the UCLA School of Engineering and Applied Science. Soon-Shiong sits on the board of directors for the Mendez National Institute of Transplantation, Northwestern University's Technology Council for the Center for Cancer Nanotechnology Excellence, and Fresenius Kabi Pharmaceuticals Holding, Inc. He also sits on the board of two nonprofit organizations, the Dossia Foundation and FAIR Health. Soon-Shiong additionally is the chairman of the Steering Committee of Life Sciences for the X Prize Foundation.

Soon-Shiong currently resides in Los Angeles, California, where he enjoys playing basketball and surfing. He is married to former actress Michele Chan, and has two children. He is a fellow of the American College of Surgeons and of Canada's Royal College of Surgeons. To date he has authored over one hundred scientific publications and holds fifty patents. He was recently ranked by Forbes magazine as the 196th wealthiest person in the world, with a net worth of approximately seven billion dollars in 2011.

Soon-Shiong donates much of his earnings to health care and the community through the Chan Soon-Shiong Family Foundation. He has publicly

Patrick Soon-Shiong's Nanotechnology Cancer Research

While Patrick Soon-Shiong was conducting diabetes research, he found that albumin—the most common blood protein, responsible for transporting nutrients in the body—was attracted to cancer cells. Soon-Shiong hypothesized that using the albumin nanoparticle to encase a chemotherapeutic drug would allow the medication to target cancer cells. Previously, paclitaxel (Taxol) was the most effective chemotherapy for treating breast cancer, but it used a toxic solvent to deliver the medication, causing negative side effects. Abraxane was a repackaging of paclitaxel with the albumin wrapped around the medication. This decreased the side effects dramatically. Abraxane was released to the pharmaceutical market in 2005 with initial studies demonstrating thirty percent better efficacy than with paclitaxel. The drug was the first protein nanoparticle delivery technology approved by the Federal Drug Administration (FDA) to treat metastatic breast cancer. It has since been approved for this use in thirty-eight countries. The drug is being studied for the treatment of other cancers, including lung, pancreatic, stomach, and melanoma. Clinical trials for additional nanoparticle albumin-bound drugs are also under way.

vowed to donate 50 percent of his money to charity through the Giving Pledge. In 2007 he donated $35 million to create a research facility at St. John's Health Center in Santa Monica, California. In 2009 his philanthropic efforts allowed the reopening of Martin Luther King Jr. Hospital in Los Angeles. The foundation also promotes educating students on newer technology; in 2009 it donated the largest gift ever to Marymount High School for Girls in Los Angeles. In addition to philanthropic efforts, Soon-Shiong became known for purchasing basketball legend Earvin "Magic" Johnson's shares of the Los Angeles Lakers in 2010.

Significance

Soon-Shiong is a visionary who seeks to use new-generation technology to revolutionize the medical field. He has, for example, proposed that cell phones should carry patient medical information and data, so that any treating physician can have access to a patient's most up-to-date and accurate records. These forms of "telemedicine" are already emerging as a means to better care for patients. Thus, Soon-Shiong's vision of having a system that focuses on promoting overall wellness and prevention, rather than on treating medical problems, is becoming a reality.

Janet Ober Berman

Further Reading

Armstrong, David. "Vindication." *Forbes.com.* Forbes, 6 Oct. 2003. Web. 30 Mar. 2012. Outlines Soon-Shiong's triumphs and controversies as a scientist and pharmaceutical executive, focusing on his work with Abraxane.

Hawkins M. J., Patrick Soon-Shiong, and Neal Desai. "Protein nanoparticles as drug carriers in clinical medicine." *Advanced Drug Delivery Reviews* 60, 8 (May, 2008): 876–85. Describes new technology employed by Soon-Shiong and colleagues in order to develop Abraxane.

Soon-Shiong, Patrick. "Treatment of type I diabetes using encapsulated islets." *Advanced Drug Delivery Reviews* 35.2–3 (February 1999): 259–70. Soon-Shiong details his theory behind the encapsulated islet transplantation and the success and challenges of the procedure.

Shannyn Sossamon

Actor

A dancer turned actress, Sossamon won a Young Hollywood Award for Breakthrough Female Performance for her role in A Knight's Tale. *Many of her films have been very successful at the box office and she has branched successfully into television roles.*

Born: October 3, 1978; Honolulu, Hawaii
Full name: Shannyn Sossamon
Birth name: Shannon Marie Kahololani Sossamon
Areas of achievement: Film, music

Early Life

Shannyn Sossamon was born in Honolulu, Hawaii, to Sherry Sossamon and Todd Lindberg. She is of Hawaiian and Filipino heritage and also has Dutch, French, Irish, and English roots. She and her parents moved to Reno, Nevada, when she was a year old. At the age of seven, Sossamon began dance lessons. She continued to dance throughout high school, training in various styles and competing for a number of years.

During high school, Sossamon changed the spelling of her name from *Shannon* to *Shannyn.* The day after she graduated from high school, she moved to Los Angeles to try to become a professional dancer. Sossamon supported herself by modeling for fashion magazine *Sassy,* various major clothing catalogs, and Planned Parenthood. She also appeared in television commercials and in music videos for multiple artists. In the meantime, Sossamon also began a career as a DJ and appeared at several clubs around town. She was helping a friend DJ at a birthday party for actress Gwyneth Paltrow when she was discovered by noted casting director Francine Maisler. The support of Maisler eventually led her to audition for the lead female role in the movie *A Knight's Tale* (2001). She worked her way through six casting calls before she finally landed the role of Lady Jocelyn, beating out Kate Hudson and numerous other actors.

Life's Work

A Knight's Tale was Sossamon's breakout role. She starred opposite the rising actor Heath Ledger and was nominated for various MTV movie awards as well as the Fox Channel's Teen Choice awards. Her portrayal

Shannyn Sossamon. (Getty Images)

of Lady Jocelyn did earn her the Young Hollywood Award for Breakthrough Female Performance in 2002. In 2002 she appeared in the movie *40 Days and 40 Nights* with Josh Hartnett, which garnered another Teen Choice Award nomination for her. Both of her initial movies performed well at the box office. They launched her acting career and she took a variety of movie and television projects. However, her next film, *The Rules of Attraction* (2002), received mixed reviews from critics. Despite its shaky start, it has achieved cult classic status.

As her career progressed, Sossamon earned a reputation for being spontaneous on the set and in her scenes, making her stand out among other up-and-coming actors.

In 2003, Sossamon had a son with her then-boyfriend, children's author and illustrator Dallas Clayton. Audio Science Clayton was born that May, after which Sossamon returned to work. She reunited with Heath Ledger and Brian Helgland, director of *A Knight's Tale*, to make *The Order*. She also appeared on the popular

television drama *Law & Order: Special Victims Unit* in 2004, marking her first notable television role and her only performance of the year. She appeared in a few low-grossing films in 2005.

In 2006, Sossamon landed a supporting role in the film *The Holiday*, where she appeared next to Hollywood stars Kate Winslet and Cameron Diaz. She also starred in *Wristcutters: A Love Story*, which received multiple award nominations and was cited as her best performance to date. Sossamon appeared as Kira Klay on the series *Dirt* with Courteney Cox in 2007. That year also saw her in the horror movie *Catacombs* as the female lead. Sossamon had a major role in the short-lived CBS vampire series *Moonlight*, in which she played Coraline Duvall. She starred in the box office hit *One Missed Call*, which earned her a Teen Choice Award nomination in the Choice Film Actress: Horror category. She appeared in the movie *Life Is Hot in Cracktown* to mixed reviews in 2009. In 2010, she was cast in the recurring role of Gingy Wu in the HBO series *How to Make It in America*. Critics praised her performance in the film *Road to Nowhere* (2010), which was nominated for a Golden Lion award at the Venice Film Festival.

Aside from her acting, Sossamon was also in the band Warpaint, along with her sister, Jenny Lindberg. She played drums and recorded with the band on their 2009 EP, *Exquisite Corpse*.

SIGNIFICANCE

A dancer turned actress by chance, Shannyn Sossamon has made a name for herself in the entertainment industry. She is a sought-after actress and has appeared in over twenty movies in a short period of time. She is known for her ability to enhance a scene with her spontaneity. Sossamon has appeared in multiple television series in recurring roles. She has acted alongside big Hollywood names and done admirably well, gathering critical notice.

James J. Heiney

FURTHER READING

"Come as You Are." *Teen People* Oct. 2002: 152. Print. A review of Sossamon's personal style.

E. H. "Shannyn Sossamon." *Rolling Stone* 11 Apr. 2002: 83. Print. Brief profile on Shannyn Sossamon.

Smith, Krista. "Shannyn Sossamon." *Vanity Fair* Feb. 2001: 99. Print. A profile of Sossamon's work as a DJ and actress.

GAYATRI CHAKRAVORTY SPIVAK

Indian-born feminist, scholar, and translator

A frequently cited authority in subaltern studies, Gayatri Chakravorty Spivak has increased awareness of oppressed minorities who have no voice within dominant social power structures. She argues not that those in power should speak for the subaltern, but for the construction of a space in which the subaltern is able to speak for him- or herself, thereby losing the subaltern identity.

Born: February 24, 1942; Calcutta, British India (now Kolkata, India)

Full name: Gayatri Chakravorty Spivak (GI-uh-tree CHAK-ruh-VOR-tee SPEE-vak)

Birth name: Gayatri Chakravorty

Areas of achievement: Education, literature, scholarship

EARLY LIFE

Gayatri Chakravorty Spivak was born Gayatri Chakravorty in Calcutta (now Kolkata), India, to middle-class parents. When Spivak was five, India won independence from British rule. Her father died when she was thirteen. In 1959, she graduated from the University of Calcutta with a degree in English. Following graduation, she worked as a tutor for two years in order to earn money to attend graduate school in the United States. She enrolled at Cornell University and studied comparative literature, earning her master's degree in 1961. Spivak taught at the University of Iowa while working on her doctoral dissertation, on poet William Butler Yeats, under the direction of Cornell literary critic Paul de Man; she finished her doctorate in 1967. She was briefly married to American Talbot Spivak. Her dissertation, *Myself Must I Remake: The Life and Poetry of W. B. Yeats,* was published in 1974. She taught at the University of Texas, Emory University, and the University of Pittsburgh before her tenure at Columbia University, which began in 1991. She was appointed University Professor at Columbia University, the highest academic rank at the school, in 2007.

LIFE'S WORK

Spivak earned recognition early in her career when she introduced English speakers to the work of the French philosopher Jacques Derrida, who developed the influential postmodern literary theory known as deconstruction. Specifically, she translated Derrida's *De la grammatologie* (1967), published in 1976 as *Of Grammatology*. Most notable about Spivak's translation was her lengthy preface, in which she not only introduced Derrida but applied his theory of deconstruction to the preface itself as a genre of writing.

Perhaps Spivak's most influential original work is her 1988 essay, "Can the Subaltern Speak?" published in *Marxism and the Interpretation of Culture*, edited by Cary Nelson and Larry Grossberg. In this essay, Spivak introduces the concept of the subaltern, or cultural subordinate, with a description of a Hindu widow performing the traditional rite of *sati,* in which, upon the death of her husband, she is burned alive on his funeral pyre. The widow is represented by the cultural elite (Western white males) and, therefore, cannot speak, as she is only an object in this representation and not a subject; hence, she may only be spoken for or about. Significantly, Spivak's political program calls for a space in which the subaltern can speak for him- or herself, and thus will no longer be identified as a subaltern.

Spivak's work on subaltern identity, among other topics, is associated more broadly with postcolonial theory, a critical scholarly approach to the intellectual and cultural legacy of imperialism in former European colonies around the world. After publication of her dissertation on Yeats, Spivak turned to cultural studies and literature by authors from the developing world. Her second published volume, *In Other Worlds: Essays on Cultural Politics* (1987), moves from studies of British literature to political and feminist studies, to studies on the Bengali fiction of Mahasweta Devi. (In addition to translating Derrida, Spivak has translated numerous works by Devi.) *The Post-Colonial Critic: Interviews, Strategies, Dialogues,* published in 1990, contains a dozen interviews with Spivak. The dialogic nature of the interview and its clear location in space, time, and occasion serve to complement the more static nature of Spivak's traditional prose in the form of argument. In addition, the published interviews with Spivak are often more accessible than her academic prose, which many readers find difficult.

Outside in the Teaching Machine (1993) continues Spivak's exploration of Derrida, Karl Marx, feminism, cultural studies, and her position on the margins of American academia. *The Spivak Reader*, edited by Donna Landry and Gerald Maclean, appeared in 1995 and serves to introduce Spivak to novice readers. *A Critique of Postcolonial Reason: Toward a History of the*

Vanishing Present (1999) was faulted by critic Terry Eagleton for the inaccessible nature of its prose, but admired for its range of scholarly influences. *Death of a Discipline* (2003) presents Spivak's vision of a new and improved discipline of comparative literature.

SIGNIFICANCE

Although she received wide recognition early in her career for *Of Grammatology*, her English translation of Derrida's famous work, Spivak is best known as a postcolonial critic. Her writing is often described as inaccessible, but she is one of the most cited authorities in subaltern studies and is sometimes referred to as a founding member of the discipline. However, her most influential work, "Can the Subaltern Speak?," remains uncollected in her own published collections. Spivak did not grant permission for the essay to be republished in *The Spivak Reader*, as she was in the process of revising it and considered the original version outdated.

Nettie Farris

FURTHER READING

Chakraborty, Mridula Nath. "Everybody's Afraid of Gayatri Chakravorty Spivak: Reading Interviews with the Public Intellectual and Postcolonial Critic." *Signs* 35.3 (Spring 2010): 621–45. Focuses on the interview as a prevalent genre in the published discourse of Spivak and argues that this genre is a site of transformation for her thought and work.

Kapoor, Ilan. "Hyper-Self-Reflexive Development? Spivak on Representing the Third World 'Other.'" *Third World Quarterly* 25.4 (2004): 627–47. Highlights the relevance of Spivak's work for developmental specialists in relation to representing third-world marginal groups.

Landry, Donna, and Gerald Maclean, eds. *The Spivak Reader*. New York: Routledge, 1996. This volume provides texts specifically for readers not familiar with the works of Spivak. Also includes a short introduction by the editors, which briefly addresses biographical information on Spivak, her work, and her audience.

McMillen, Liz. "The Education of Gayatri Spivak." *Chronicle of Higher Education* 54.3 (2007): B16–19. Provides background on Spivak's activism, specifically her literacy project that aims to educate tribal students in West Bengal, India. Spivak's interaction with these students serves to educate her as well.

Spivak, Gayatri. "Can the Subaltern Speak?" *Marxism and the Interpretation of Culture*. Ed. Cary Nelson and Larry Grossberg. Urbana: U of Illinois P, 1988. 271–313. Spivak's most influential essay, illustrating the concept of the subaltern.

ERIK SPOELSTRA

Athlete

Erik Spoelstra, who was named the head coach of the National Basketball Association's Miami Heat in 2008, is the first Filipino American head coach of any professional sports team, and one of the few current Asian American head coaches. In 2008, he was also the youngest coach in the NBA.

Born: November 1, 1970; Evanston, Illinois
Full name: Erik Spoelstra (SPOHL-struh)
Area of achievement: Sports

EARLY LIFE

Erik Spoelstra grew up in Portland, Oregon, and was the son of Jon Spoelstra, who worked with several different NBA franchises, including the Portland Trail Blazers. His father's profession, in part, led young Spoelstra to try basketball, and he was quite successful. During his playing days, Spoelstra was a practice fanatic, and he credits this with some of his success. He graduated from Jesuit High School in Portland and then attended the University of Portland, staying close to home. Spoelstra was very successful there; he was a four-year starter and was named the West Coast Conference Freshman of the Year. He ranked among Portland's historic leaders in three-pointers, free throws, and assists, among other categories. He scored over one thousand points in his career. (As a team, Portland had limited success during his time there, enduring four losing seasons.) After graduating from college, Spoelstra joined a professional team in Germany for two years as a player and coach.

LIFE'S WORK

Spoelstra joined the Miami Heat in 1995 as a video coordinator. He had demonstrated his desire to be a coach previously as a player and coach in Germany. After serving as video coordinator, Spoelstra was promoted to the role of both assistant coach and video coordinator. His job transitioned after another few years, as he was put in charge of scouting opponents for the team, at which time he was both a scout and an assistant coach. In 2001, Spoelstra was promoted again, becoming the director of scouting in addition to being an assistant coach. He continued in this role, working directly with the Miami Heat's main star, Dwayne Wade. Spoelstra's success in navigating the politics of basketball was shown in Miami's going through four different head coaches (Pat Riley, with two terms as head coach, counts twice) and Spoelstra's managing to keep his job throughout the transitions. He worked as an assistant coach under Stan Van Gundy, who resigned in December 2005 and was replaced by Pat Riley—also the general manager. Riley kept Spoelstra on, and in 2008 Riley returned to being solely general manager, appointing Spoelstra as coach and arguing publicly that the players would work harder with Spoelstra as coach.

At this time, Spoelstra was presented as the future of coaching, as he was familiar with video work, scouting, and coaching. The team had finished poorly in 2007–08, winning only fifteen games and trading away

Erik Spoelstra. (Getty Images)

Shaquille O'Neal. In 2008–09, the team improved by twenty-eight games, finishing 43 and 39. This record qualified them for the playoffs, where they lost in seven games to the Atlanta Hawks. In 2009–10, the team improved its record by four wins, notching forty-seven wins versus thirty-five losses. The results did not improve in the division, however, as the Heat were still third. They exited the playoffs in the first round, losing to the Boston Celtics in five games. The real news for the Heat came in July 2010, after the end of the playoffs, when LeBron James, a free agent and the two-time most valuable player, decided to join the Heat rather than stay with his hometown team, the Cleveland Cavaliers. The team also added power forward Chris Bosh, who had been an all-star and a leading scorer for his previous team, the Toronto Raptors. The roster was expected to do well, and some (players with the Miami Heat among them) predicted that the team would challenge the historic winning record of seventy-two games set by the Chicago Bulls, led by Michael Jordan, in 1995–96. The team did not fare as well as these rosy forecasts predicted; the Heat did, however, improve significantly. It did not help, of course, that Spoelstra and the team were in the midst of a media feeding frenzy during the entire year. The Heat were in third place in the conference for most of the 2010–11 season, winning the Southeast Division and finishing in first, much better than in previous years. Spoelstra also had the difficult job of managing all of the egos on the team, which he managed somewhat successfully.

Spoelstra began his fourth season with the Miami Heat in December 2011.

Significance

Erik Spoelstra was the first Filipino American head coach of a major professional sport. He was also, at the time of the 2008–09 season, the youngest coach in the NBA. He assembled a superstar roster in the 2010–11 season, with Chris Bosh, LeBron James, and Dwayne Wade. Spoelstra's appeal as a head coach likely played a significant role in the decision of both Bosh and James to pick the Miami Heat over the other teams campaigning to acquire them.

Scott A. Merriman

Further Reading

"Erik Spoelstra." *NBA.com.* NBA Media Ventures, n.d. Web. 29 Feb. 2012. A comprehensive profile of Spoelstra's professional career, including season records and a brief biography.

Kelley, K. C. *Miami Heat*. New York: Children's World, 2009. Print. Profiles the Miami Heat and includes information on past stars of the team, features on the Heat's history and past coaches, and a discussion of current players.

Osier, Dan. *LeBron James*. New York: Rosen, 2011. Print. Discusses the top star of the Heat's 2011 season, including material on James's relationship with Spoelstra.

YELLAPRAGADA SUBBAROW

Indian-born physician and scientist

Yellapragada SubbaRow was a biochemist regarded as an eminent leader in the field because of his numerous laboratory discoveries. He is best known for describing the function of adenosine triphosphate in muscle contractions, as well as synthesizing numerous novel chemotherapeutic agents, vitamins, and antibiotics.

Born: January 12, 1895; Bhimavaram, British India
Died: August 9, 1948; Pearl River, New York
Full name: Yellapragada SubbaRow (YEL-ah-prah-GAH-dah SOO-bah-ROW)
Also known as: Yellapragada Subbarow; Yellapragada Subbarao; Yellapragada Subba Rao
Areas of achievement: Medicine, science and technology

EARLY LIFE

Yellapragada SubbaRow was born the fourth of seven children to father Jagganadham, a revenue inspector, and mother Venkamma. His father and two siblings died at an early age from tropical sprue, a chronic intestinal disease, leaving the family in poverty. The loss of his family members would later motivate SubbaRow to pursue a medical career. SubbaRow's mother sold her possessions in order to send her son to school. However, SubbaRow initially lacked an interest in schooling and even ran away to avoid it, but he credits his mother with instilling in him an understanding of the value of an education and a career.

After switching secondary schools several times, SubbaRow enrolled at Hindu High School in Triplicane, Madras (now Chennai). He graduated after taking the final examination three times. SubbaRow subsequently attended the Madras Presidency College, where he originally pursued a major in religion, with the intention of entering a Hindu monastic order. His mother and his spiritual teachers eventually convinced him to concentrate on mathematics, physics, and chemistry in order

to study medicine. At college, SubbaRow supported the movement for Indian independence from the British Empire. As his professors were British, they denied SubbaRow a full medical degree, awarding him a certificate instead.

It was SubbaRow's hope to immigrate to the United States for further studies in tropical medicine at Harvard University. He was denied admission on his first attempt, and became an anatomy and physiology lecturer at Madras Ayurvedic College. Here he hoped to perform scientific research that would standardize the practice of using Indian herbs in medical care. However, the college environment did not permit such research. SubbaRow then applied to join the Madras Medical Service, but was also rejected.

On his second attempt, SubbaRow gained admission to Harvard Medical School but did not receive any financial aid. However, both his father-in-law and the head of the Department of Tropical Medicine, Dr. Richard Strong, contributed money toward SubbaRow's education. He left for Cambridge, Massachusetts, in 1923. To earn the rest of the money, he took a job as an evening janitor at the Peter Bent Brigham Hospital in Boston. He earned a diploma in tropical medicine in 1924.

LIFE'S WORK

SubbaRow made significant discoveries from the onset of his career as an assistant professor of biochemistry at Harvard University. In 1927 he and his mentor, Dr. Cyrus Fiske, developed a new test, called the Fiske-SubbaRow method, to detect phosphorus levels in blood and urine. As a result, they were able to determine that the molecules phosphocreatine and adenosine triphosphate (ATP) provided the energy responsible for a muscle contraction. This discovery was not well received in the scientific community initially, as a Nobel Prize had previously been awarded in 1922 to other scientists who identified a different reason for muscle contractions. SubbaRow and Fiske were eventually proven correct,

SubbaRow's Discovery of Aminopterin and Methotrexate

During and shortly after World War II, no treatment or cure for leukemia existed. When SubbaRow relocated to Lederle Laboratories he was contacted by Dr. Sidney Farber, whose research focused on the treatment of childhood leukemia. Farber was researching folic acid's connection to cancer, and the two men consequently became collaborators. At first, both thought that the treatment for leukemia lay in modifying the vitamin, but they eventually realized that the actual answer was an analogue, or a vitamin with the opposite properties of folic acid. While SubbaRow synthesized new potential drugs, Farber tested these on healthy and affected rats in the laboratory. They eventually discovered that aminopterin destroyed leukemia cells as well as some healthy cells. The duo tested a derivative of aminopterin, termed methotrexate, in children with acute lymphoblastic leukemia (ALL). The initial 1946 treatment was so successful that it began the modern era of chemotherapy with drugs that targeted specific cancers.

and their discovery earned SubbaRow a PhD in biochemistry from Harvard in 1930.

The Fiske-SubbaRow method continues to be used by scientists today. Unfortunately, SubbaRow was unable to capitalize on his groundbreaking work at Harvard, and was denied tenure because he was considered to be only Fiske's laboratory technician. Hence, SubbaRow left the institution.

In 1940 SubbaRow accepted a position at the pharmaceutical company Lederle Laboratories in Pearl River, New York. Here, SubbaRow was finally acknowledged as a leader in his field. He was appointed director of research and development. SubbaRow and his team continued to make new discoveries, including the isolation and synthesis of the vitamins folic acid and B12. Folic acid was later shown to cure sprue, the disease that killed so many of SubbaRow's family members. SubbaRow and his team also created the antibiotics gramicidin, aureomycin, hetrazan, and aminopterin. Aureomycin became the first oral tetracycline antibiotic that covered a broad spectrum of infections. Hetrazan cured filariasis, an infectious parasitic tropical disease that causes elephantitis. It was used to treat soldiers with malaria and filariasis fighting in the Pacific during World War II.

SubbaRow's work extended to early cancer treatment as well. When he and his colleagues created aminopterin, they noted that the medication stopped cancer cell growth. SubbaRow also helped develop other chemotherapeutic agents to treat leukemia.

Awards and honors for SubbaRow include the Bharat Ratna, India's highest civilian honor. The one-hundredth anniversary of his birth was widely celebrated in India in 1995, and a series of memorial lectures exists in his name.

SubbaRow married his wife, Seshagiri, in 1919. After four years of marriage, SubbaRow left India for the United States. SubbaRow vowed to return to his wife in India three years later. However, he did not return and did not see her again after choosing to devote his life to his career. SubbaRow died at the age of fifty-three in his sleep from a heart attack. Although he lived in the United States for twenty-five years, SubbaRow was never granted American citizenship because of laws banning most Asians from becoming citizens. When the ban was lifted after World War II, SubbaRow did not file the paperwork and remained an Indian citizen.

SIGNIFICANCE

Early in his career, SubbaRow was denied almost all of his educational and career aspirations. However, he persevered, and eventually made countless contributions to the medical field that have helped later generations. SubbaRow initially proposed using folic acid to treat anemia, but this vitamin is now known to prevent significant birth defects in pregnancy. Consequently, since 1988 the United States government has mandated that food be fortified with it. Methotrexate, a derivative of aminopterin, is now used for treating ailments such as childhood leukemia, other cancers, and ectopic pregnancies. The antibiotics he discovered continue to be some of the most-prescribed medications in the world.

Janet Ober Berman

FURTHER READING

Bhargava, Pushpa Mitra. "Dr. Yellapragada SubbaRow (1895–1948): He Transformed Science; Changed Lives." *Indian Academy of Clinical Medicine Journal* 2.1–2 (January–June, 2001): 96–100. Print. Summary of SubbaRow's most notable accomplishments and his being denied of US citizenship.

Nathan, David G. *The Cancer Treatment Revolution: How Smart Drugs and Other New Therapies Are Renewing Our Hope and Changing the Face of Medicine.* Hoboken, NJ: Wiley, 2007. Print. Details the work of SubbaRow and Farber that proved aminopterin and methotrexate were successful chemotherapeutic agents for treating leukemia.

Simoni, Robert, Robert Hill, and Martha Vaughan. "The Determination of Phosphorus and the Discovery of Phosphocreatine and ATP: The Work of Fiske and SubbaRow." *Journal of Biological Chemistry* 277.32 (August, 2002): e1–e2. Print. Summary of the monumental papers published by SubbaRow and Fiske as well as their competition and controversies with rival colleagues.

Henry Sugimoto

Japanese-born artist

Sugimoto established his reputation as an artist in California during the Great Depression and became best known for his paintings created during his time in the Japanese American internment camps of World War II. Later in life, he worked to call attention to the experiences of internees.

Born: March 12, 1900; Wakayama, Japan
Died: May 8, 1990; New York, New York
Full name: Henry Yuzuru Sugimoto (YEW-zew-rew SEW-gee-MOH-toh)
Also known as: Yuzuru Sugimoto
Area of achievement: Art

Early Life

Henry Yuzuru Sugimoto was born in Wakayama, Japan, and raised by his maternal grandparents. In 1919, he joined his parents in California, where he began his formal education in art. He graduated from the California School of Arts and Crafts in 1928 and then studied at the Académie Colarossi in Paris, France. He returned to California in 1932; in 1934, he married Susie Tagawa, with whom he had two children.

Life's Work

In the 1930s, Sugimoto enjoyed a successful artistic career in California and also made a significant trip to Mexico, during which he studied the work of the Mexican muralists. Following the Japanese attack on Pearl Harbor in 1941, Japanese Americans on the West Coast were relocated to internment camps. Sugimoto and his family were interned in the Fresno Assembly Center in May of 1942 and relocated to the Jerome Relocation Center in Arkansas in October. Sugimoto continued to draw and paint throughout his detention, and his work was featured in an exhibition at Hendrix College in Conway, Arkansas.

The Sugimotos were transferred to the nearby Rohwer War Relocation Center in June of 1944. They left the camp the following year and moved to New York.

Sugimoto worked at a textile company until 1962, returning to full-time artistic production only after retirement. He traveled to France and Japan and began to exhibit work in the United States and abroad. Sugimoto also worked to raise awareness of the detention-camp experience, returning to the motif in his art and donating significant works from his internment to museums.

Significance

Sugimoto is best known for the large body of work that he produced during his years in the Jerome and Rohwer detention camps. This mature work presents powerful renderings of human actions and activities that capture the experiences endured during internment, raising awareness of the issue and commenting on the actions of the US government.

Julia A. Sienkewicz

Further Reading

Gesensway, Deborah, and Mindy Roseman. *Beyond Words: Images from America's Concentration Camps.* Ithaca: Cornell UP, 1987. Print. Considers Sugimoto alongside other Japanese American artists working within the internment camps.

Inada, Lawson Fusao. *Only What We Could Carry: The Japanese American Internment Experience.* Berkeley: Heyday, 2000. Print. Gathers images and texts related to the experience of Japanese Americans in internment camps during World War II.

Kim, Kristine. *Henry Sugimoto: Painting an American Experience.* Berkeley: Heyday, 2000. Print. Offers a biography of Sugimoto, placing the work produced during his internment within the context of his full career.

ANNA SUI

Designer

Known for her clothing, accessories, and fragrance, Anna Sui has been a successful designer in the world of New York fashion. Her clothes are inspired by the 1960s and rock and roll, among other cultural and historical trends.

Born: August 4, 1955; Dearborn, Michigan
Full name: Anna Sui (SWEE)
Area of achievement: Fashion

EARLY LIFE

Anna Sui was born in Dearborn, Michigan, outside Detroit, to Paul and Grace Sui, who were both born in China. They met in Paris, where her father was studying structural engineering and her mother was studying painting. After getting married, Sui's parents traveled throughout Europe for three years and then settled down in Dearborn, where her father began his engineering career and her mother was a homemaker. While the community of Dearborn included several ethnic minorities, there were not many Asians, and Sui's was the only Chinese family in the neighborhood. Sui never felt any

Anna Sui. (WireImage)

any racial hostility, as such, but rather she felt that she was a kind of novelty.

Sui was the middle child between two brothers. She was a good student and decided early that she wanted to be a fashion designer. As she grew older, Sui learned how to sew and began making her own clothes. She even took the fabric that she used for a dress and stretched it out to glue on her shoes, so that her outfit would match. It was during this period that Sui started what would be called her "genius files," made of pictures clipped from magazines and catalogues of things that inspired her. One of the early inspirations that would resurface in her mature designs was rock and roll from the 1960s and 1970s, in particular the Rolling Stones, specifically Keith Richards and his girlfriend, actress Anita Pallenberg.

During high school, Sui decided her goal was to attend the Parsons School of Design in New York to study fashion. By the end of her senior year, Sui was accepted to Parsons and received a scholarship as well. In her first year, Sui moved out of the dorms and began experiencing the life of the city, dressing up, going to clubs, and drawing inspiration from the street life of New York. During this time she became good friends with photographer Stephen Meisel, also a student at Parsons, and he would later help her in her career. After two years, feeling that school had become boring and that she required work experience to progress in her career, Sui left Parsons and went to work in 1975.

In the period that followed, Sui worked for a number of junior sportswear companies, including Charlie's Girls and Glenora. She was doing her own sketching and designing as well, and in 1981 she was toying with the idea of starting her own business. She designed five clothing items to be displayed at the fashion trade show the Boutique Show, during which Sui received orders from department stores such as Macy's and Bloomingdale's. Macy's later featured one of her designs in an advertisement in the *New York Times*. But when her supervisor at the Simultanee sportswear firm saw the advertisement, she gave Sui an ultimatum—she could either design for herself or for the company. Sui decided to start her own business and left the company, using her last paycheck to buy fabric for her own clothing business.

LIFE'S WORK

Although Sui struggled financially during the early years of her business, she reinvested her earnings back

Anna Sui's Trademark Fashion Shows

Sui's biannual New York fall and spring fashion shows showcase the designer's creative inspirations and influences. Clothing is usually defined by a theme or an idea, and much historical research goes into a collection. Sui attends museums where she might be influenced by an exhibition, as well as flea markets where vintage finds might spur an idea. She has also found inspiration from attending concerts of the latest rock bands. Sui uses fabric as the starting point for her designs before creating hundreds of sketches. She narrows these sketches down to seventy or eighty that she then accessorizes with shoes, hats, and jewelry. The last step is developing music and staging for the fashion show that reflect the theme of the collection. Highlights of past collections include the 1997 Autumn/Winter Collection, in which Goth, a street style from the 1980s club scene in London, predominated in black lacy and velvet designs accessorized with blood-red lipstick; the 2004 Autumn/Winter Collection, which was influenced by the 1930s fashion designer Elsa Schiaparelli, with highly embellished jackets and surrealist touches; and the 2008 Spring/Summer Collection, influenced by Busby Berkeley musicals of the 1930s and 1940s.

into it. After borrowing thirty thousand dollars from the bank, Sui was able to pay off the loan in six months. She did odd jobs to earn extra money, working as a stylist on fashion shoots for Meisel. Sui worked out of her apartment in the early days, but in 1987 she moved to the Annette B showroom. During this time, Sui also moved her workspace to a loft in the Garment District. An important moment came in 1990, when Sui attended a Jean-Paul Gaultier show in Paris with Meisel. It was at this show that the popular singer Madonna decided to wear one of Sui's signature baby doll dresses of black chiffon and was photographed in it. This was just the encouragement that Sui needed to boost her confidence, and she decided to do her first runway show in 1991.

For Sui's first runway show, top models Naomi Campbell and Linda Evangelista (whom she had met through Meisel) agreed to be paid in dresses. The collection was heavily influenced by the swinging London style of the 1960s, with miniskirts, matching shoes, jackets, and hats. The show was a great success; orders poured in, and Sui made plans to expand her business. She moved out of the Annette B showroom, opening a space of her own in 1992. With this expansion, Sui also opened her own boutique on Greene Street in the Soho area of Manhattan. This store reflected her personal

taste and style, boasting purple walls, Victorian furniture, and vintage rock and roll posters.

In 1992, Sui won the Council of Fashion Designers in America Perry Ellis Award for New Fashion Talent. Throughout the 1990s, Sui's fashion collections were influenced by the 1960s, rock and roll themes such as grunge, French designer Yves Saint Laurent, and American designer Halston. Sui's company continued to grow, her production line expanding to include shoes in 1997 and with boutiques opening in Tokyo and Osaka, Japan; the Japanese department store Isetan distributed her clothing. In 1999, a signature fragrance called Anna Sui was launched along with a line of makeup, and in the same year another boutique opened in Los Angeles (though it has since closed).

From 2000 to 2011, Sui's company continued to flourish and expand. In 2000, she developed a skin-care line and a unique packaging design in purple, her favorite color. In 2003, her fourth fragrance, Dolly Girl, was released in a bottle shaped like a mannequin's head. The year 2005 saw Sui expand her Greene Street flagship store from 947 to 1,875 square feet, a growth that incorporated space for a new line of menswear. As of 2011, over thirty-two independent boutiques and stores and three hundred sales outlets were selling Anna Sui clothing and accessories across more than thirty countries.

SIGNIFICANCE

Anna Sui has combined many different influences to create a unique and compelling fashion vision. The unisex and rock and roll look of the 1960s was combined with the influence of British designer Mary Quant to reflect a hip, swinging London of the 1960s. A girlish sensibility also permeates Sui's designs, as seen in the youthful looks of her miniskirts and baby doll dresses. On the other hand, the dramatic influence of another British designer, Zandra Rhodes, and early twentieth-century French designer Paul Poiret can be seen in some of her collections' colorful clothes, bold fabrics, and overall design. Rich velvets reflect a vintage, Victorian gothic influence in collections rendered in dark hues accessorized with jet-black jewelry. In spite of her diverse and creative influences, Sui has tried to keep a realistic approach in mind when designing for her customers, making her clothes unique, original, and also wearable.

Sandra Rothenberg

FURTHER READING

Bolton, Andrew. *Anna Sui*. San Francisco: Chronicle, 2010. Print. Chronicles the influences and themes of the designer's biannual fashion shows, from her debut in 1991 through 2009.

Darraj, Susan Muaddi. *Anna Sui*. New York: Chelsea, 2009. Print. A book in a series on notable Asian Americans that gives an excellent chronological overview of the designer's success in the fashion world.

Sui, Anna. "Sui Generis." Interview with Josh Patner. *Wall Street Journal*. Dow Jones, 6 Nov. 2010. Web. 29 Mar. 2012. Sui briefly discusses her favorite music, books, hotels, and so on.

EILEEN TABIOS

Philippine-born poet and writer

Eileen Tabios is a poet and writer best known for inventing the hay(na)ku, a poetic form patterned after Japanese haiku. Tabios is the founder of Meritage Press, a multidisciplinary literary and arts press based in San Francisco and St. Helena, California; Babaylan, an imprint of the press, specializes in Filipino literature.

Born: September 11, 1960; Galimuyod, Ilocos Sur, Philippines
Full name: Eileen Rose Tabios (TAHB-yos)
Areas of achievement: Activism, literature

EARLY LIFE

Eileen Tabios was born in the town of Galimuyod, Ilocos Sur, Philippines, on September 11, 1960, to Filamore and Beatriz Tabios. Tabios grew up with her three brothers in a mountaintop home in Baguio City, the country's summer capital. Her primary education until fifth grade was at Saint Louis University, Baguio City. Her father was a teacher and businessman. Her mother taught English literature at Saint Louis University. She also taught at the Brent School, the American school for children of US expatriates. In the late 1960s, Filamore Tabios joined the exodus of professionals disillusioned by the pervasive political corruption in the country and hoping for a better future abroad. Tabios Sr. left for the United States, and a year later the entire family joined him. Tabios was ten years old when, in 1970, she arrived in Fresno, California. Two years later, on September 21, 1972, martial law was declared by Philippine president Ferdinand Marcos to put an end to labor strikes and student rallies.

Meanwhile, the family settled in Gardena, California, where Tabios continued her education at Gardena High School, graduating in 1978. Tabios's teen years were a difficult time, as she navigated her relationship with her parents. She decided that, if given the choice, she would attend college as far from home as possible. She applied and was accepted to Barnard College in New York City and graduated in 1982, majoring in journalism and political science. She pursued an MBA in economics and international business from New York University's Graduate School of Business.

Her first job was with the *New York Times*, where Tabios was assigned to the business section. In 1984, however, she accepted an offer to join a private investment firm. She was living in Manhattan when she met and married her husband, attorney Thomas Pollock. In the mid-1990s, Tabios traded her ten-year career in international project finance to devote herself to writing full time.

LIFE'S WORK

In 1996, Tabios published her first poetry chapbook, *After the Egyptians Determined the Shape of the World Is a Circle*. Two years later, her poetry collection *Beyond Life Sentences* won the Manila Critics Circle National Book Award. Tabios's poetry has been translated into Tagalog, Spanish, Italian, Japanese, Portuguese, Polish, and Greek. Her work has also found its way into modern dance, paintings, sculpture, performance art, visual art, mixed media, Kali martial arts, and music.

Drawn to experimental poetry, Tabios considers the poets Mei-Mei Berssenbrugge, John Yau, and Arthur Sze as major influences on her work. Her prolific output, as well as her prodigious use of multimedia, pushes her beyond mere writing and publishing. As Tabios mentions in her hybrid book *I Take Thee, English, for My Beloved* (2001), her devotion to poetry and language is pervasive, and it explains the creative commitment to and passion for poetics that she carries over to every facet of her life: the colonial history of her birth country, the dynamics of her social and political activism, her work in the visual arts, literature, and writing. According to "Looking for M"—a chapter in *The Thorn Rosary: Selected Prose Poems & New (1998–2010)*—poetics was even involved in her process of becoming an adoptive parent.

In 2000, Pollock's law firm opened an office in San Francisco for its international practice, and after living in New York for twenty years, Tabios returned to the West Coast. They lived in San Francisco before moving to St. Helena, California. Following the death of Tabios's father in 2006, her mother came to live with her. In 2009, Pollock and Tabios formally adopted a twelve-year-old son, Michael, from Columbia, and in 2011 they adopted their daughter Francy.

By 2011, Tabios had published eighteen books and founded Meritage Press, a multidisciplinary literary and arts press based in San Francisco and St. Helena. Tabios also curated *Galatea Resurrects (A Poetry Engagement)*, an online poetry review journal. In memory of her late father, Tabios and her mother established the Filamore Tabios Sr. Memorial Prize for Poetry.

Eileen Tabios is the recipient of numerous honors, including the PEN/Oakland–Josephine Miles National Literary Award and the Potrero Nuevo Fund Prize, as well as grants from the National Endowment for the Arts, the Witter Bynner Foundation, the New York State Council for the Humanities, and the California Council for the Humanities. In 2011, the Library of Congress established a repository for her papers as part of the Asian American Pacific Islander Collection.

SIGNIFICANCE

Tabios is best known for inventing the hay(na)ku, a poetic form patterned after the Japanese haiku with a Filipino flavor. The name comes from the Tagalog phrase "*Ay, naku!*," which can convey an affirmative or negative response, expressing regret, exasperation, or delight. Hay(na)ku favors brevity and a syllabic count similar to that of its haiku predecessor, but verses can be strung together to form a longer poem. Tabios's formal experimentation and inventiveness with poetic conventions are directly related to her interest in transcolonialism. Like many contemporary poets of immigrant or ethnic minority descent, Tabios attempts to articulate the silences in history and cultural memory. Yet Tabios's poetry avoids direct narrative, instead maintaining the natural music and rhythm of poetry. She imbues poetry with power through her work in a variety of media, articulating the identities of women throughout the ages. As a poet who traded a career in finance for a literary art form, Tabios leaves a legacy that will enrich generations and reverberate with readers worldwide.

Remé A. Grefalda

FURTHER READING

Eileen Tabios. *I Take Thee, English, for My Beloved.* East Rockaway: Marsh Hawk, 2005. Print. Excellent resource on the various formats Tabios has used to present her poetry.

---. Interview by Purvi Shah. *Readme.* Readme, Winter 2000. Web. 30 Mar. 2012. Interview in an online journal in which Tabios discusses her poem "Beginning Lucidity" and how it relates to her other work.

---. *The Light Sang as It Left Your Eyes: Our Autobiography.* East Rockaway: Marsh Hawk, 2007. Print. Excellent resource on Tabios's early life, her relationship with her father, and her struggle in coping with his illness.

ANTONIO TAGUBA

Philippine-born military leader

Major General Antonio Taguba issued the Taguba Report in March 2004, detailing the abuse of Iraqi prisoners in Baghdad's Abu Ghraib prison by US military police. The report damaged the reputation of the United States Army and raised the possibility that the US government would be accused of war crimes.

Born: October 31, 1950; Sampaloc, Manila, Philippines
Full name: Antonio Mario Taguba (tah-GOO-bah)
Also known as: Tony Taguba
Area of achievement: Military

Antonio Taguba. (AFP/Getty Images)

EARLY LIFE

Antonio Mario Taguba was born on October 31, 1950, in Manila, the capital of the Philippines. In 1961, he moved to Hawaii with his father, Tomas, who had enlisted in the US Army; his mother, Maria; and his five siblings. He became a US citizen later the same year, and in 1968 he graduated from Leilehua High School in Oahu. Taguba studied history at Idaho State University in Pocatello, graduating in 1972, and through the Reserve Officer Training Corps he was commissioned a second lieutenant in the US Army. His subsequent education included master's degrees in public administration from Webster University, international relations from Salve Regina College, and national security and strategic studies from the US Naval War College. He married his wife Debbie in 1981, with whom he had two children.

LIFE'S WORK

Taguba rose swiftly through the officer ranks, commanding combat units from company to brigade levels, and served in South Korea, Germany, Kuwait, and the United States. His initial specialty was in armored warfare, and he gained experience as a staff officer in support and logistics roles. As he advanced, Taguba earned

a reputation as a rigorously moral, hardworking, and plainspoken officer.

Taguba was promoted to brigadier general in 1997, becoming the second Filipino American to reach the rank of general. He advanced to major general in 2002, and was stationed in Kuwait during Operation Iraqi Freedom. In April 2003, the army appointed him deputy commanding general for support with the Coalition Forces Land Component Command of the Third Army. Among his duties, he oversaw logistical and support services to coalition forces, coordination of support from the governments of Kuwait and Saudi Arabia, military training for Jordanian and Egyptian forces, force deployment support for Qatar, and a budget of about $20 billion.

In early 2004, information and images were leaked to the press depicting the abuse of Iraqi detainees at Baghdad's Abu Ghraib prison (also called the Baghdad Correctional Facility), which was under the control of the 800th Military Police Brigade. The US Army swiftly launched an investigation, and on January 24, 2004, Taguba received the assignment to lead the investigation staff of twenty-three interrogators and researchers. His orders were specific: to follow up on all facts pertaining to the accusations of abuse at Abu Ghraib, to inquire into detainee escapes and misplacement, and to investigate the training, standards, and command policies and procedures of the brigade.

What Taguba found shocked him, and he vowed to his staff to report the investigation's results with objectivity and integrity in spite of the potentially serious political repercussions. The Taguba Report, as it came to be known, was published in March 2004, although Taguba had submitted copies to his superiors earlier. The report recounted numerous incidents of "sadistic, blatant, and wanton criminal abuses" by soldiers of the 372nd Military Police Company from October through December 2003. These abuses included forcing male prisoners to disrobe while female guards pointed at their genitals, forcing female prisoners to expose themselves to male guards, forcing detainees to commit indecent acts with one another, beating and dragging detainees by chains, and, in one case, a male guard sodomizing a female detainee.

In May, Taguba testified before the Senate Armed Services Committee on Abu Ghraib. Emphasizing that only a small number of army personnel were involved, he stood firm on the nature of the abuses and faulted their superiors for inadequate training. He also accused military and civilian intelligence agents of encouraging

The Taguba Report

In 2004, the commander of coalition forces in Iraq ordered US Army major general Antonio Taguba to conduct a covert internal investigation into alleged abuses at Abu Ghraib. An excerpt from Taguba's March 9 report follows.

Regarding part one of the investigation, I make the following specific findings of fact:

That between October and December, 2003, at the Abu Ghraib Confinement Facility (BCCF), numerous incidents of sadistic, blatant, and wanton criminal abuses were inflicted on several detainees. This systemic and illegal abuse of detainees was intentionally perpetrated by several members of the military police guard force. . . .

The allegations of abuse were substantiated by detailed witness statements and the discovery of extremely graphic photographic evidence. . . . I find that the intentional abuse of detainees by military police personnel included the following acts:

- Punching, slapping, and kicking detainees; jumping on their naked feet
- Videotaping and photographing naked male and female detainees
- Forcibly arranging detainees in various sexually explicit positions for photographing
- Forcing detainees to remove their clothing and keeping them naked for several days at a time

the enlisted personnel who engaged in abuse at Abu Ghraib, as well as reprimands and reductions in rank for some of their superiors, one of whom was the brigadier general in command of the 800th Military Police Brigade. Taguba himself was a casualty of his own report, he claimed later, as he was forced into retirement on January 1, 2007, after thirty-four years of service. His report was a source of embarrassment for the administration of President George W. Bush, and awakened the nation to the inadequate training of troops, slipshod leadership, and overzealousness of intelligence agents who contravened international treaties such as the Geneva Convention in torturing prisoners as a means of obtaining information. Accusations of war crimes raised as a result of Taguba's report damaged the reputation of American military forces worldwide; on the other hand, many have praised Taguba as a hero who unflinchingly told the truth under difficult circumstances, holding his own organization, the US military, accountable for its missteps.

Roger Smith

FURTHER READING

Hersh, Seymour. *Chain of Command*. New York: HarperCollins, 2004. Print. A detailed and readable account on the scandal of prisoner treatment at Abu Ghraib, including Taguba's report and its unfriendly reception at the Pentagon; places the Abu Ghraib scandal in the larger context of the US war on terror.

———. "The General's Report." *New Yorker* 25 June 2007: 58–63. Print. Combines a biographical sketch of Taguba with an extended discussion of his report on Abu Ghraib and the Pentagon's reaction.

Jehl, Douglas. "The Struggle for Iraq: The Report, Head of Inquiry on Iraq Abuses Now in Spotlight." *New York Times*. New York Times, 11 May 2004. Web. 1 Mar. 2012. An examination of Taguba's reputation as a man of integrity with regard to the reliability of his report about Abu Ghraib.

Taguba, Antonio. *Article 15–6 Investigation of the 800th Military Police Brigade*. Lanham: Bernan, 2004. Print. The text of Taguba's report on prisoner abuse at Abu Ghraib.

the abuse as a part of preparation for interrogation. According to army doctrine, the guarding and the interrogation of prisoners are duties to be kept separate.

After the report was published, Taguba was, by his own account, treated coldly by his superiors, including Secretary of Defense Donald H. Rumsfeld. On the day of his testimony to the Senate, it was announced that Taguba was being transferred to the Office of the Assistant Secretary of Defense for Reserve Affairs, an effective demotion.

SIGNIFICANCE

The immediate effects of Taguba's unflinching report were courts-martial and convictions for eleven of

TOSHIKO TAKAEZU

Artist and educator

An artist best known for her functional and closed ceramic sculptures, Toshiko Takaezu had a prolific career, exhibiting her work internationally and teaching at institutions such as the Cleveland Institute of Art and Princeton University. Over the course of Takaezu's sixty-five-year career, her work was grounded in nature and consistently expanded the boundaries of modern ceramics.

Born: June 17, 1922; Pepeekeo, Hawaii
Died: March 9, 2011; Honolulu, Hawaii
Full name: Toshiko Takaezu (toh-SHEE-koh taka-AY-zew)
Areas of achievement: Art, education

EARLY LIFE

Toshiko Takaezu was born in Pepeekeo, in the US Territory of Hawaii, on June 17, 1922; she was the sixth of eleven children. Her parents were immigrants to Hawaii from Okinawa, Japan. During her early years, Takaezu experienced a traditional Japanese upbringing. Her father worked as a laborer in the sugarcane fields, and her mother raised her and her ten siblings. In 1931, Takaezu and her family moved to Maui, Hawaii, where she completed high school. In 1940, she went to live with her sisters in Honolulu, where she worked at the Hawaii Potter's Guild. She met and studied art with the New York sculptor Carl Massa in 1944.

In 1947, Takaezu met Claude Horan, a ceramics professor at the University of Hawaii, and from 1948 to 1951, Takaezu studied ceramics, design, and weaving at the university. She taught ceramics classes at the Honolulu YWCA beginning in 1949. Takaezu decided to attend the Cranbrook Academy of Art in Bloomfield Hills, Michigan, to study ceramics with Finnish ceramist Maija Grotell, whom Takaezu credits for teaching her students to become individuals in their pursuit of art. Takaezu remained a strong supporter of her former teacher. The relationship was one of mutual respect, as Takaezu became Grotell's assistant in her third year of graduate school and taught summer courses at Cranbrook in 1954.

LIFE'S WORK

In the 1954–55 academic year, Takaezu served as a replacement for Harvey Littleton at the University of Wisconsin–Madison. From 1955 to 1956, she spent eight months in Japan, where she met master Japanese potters Shoji Hamada, Rosanjin Kitaoji, and Toyo Kaneshige and spent time at a Zen Buddhist monastery, which proved a formative experience in the years to come. Upon her return from Japan, Takaezu began work as a faculty member and head of the ceramics department at the Cleveland Institute of Art in Ohio, where she remained for ten years.

Around this time, Takaezu began to move from functional ceramic forms, such as multiple spouted vases, to a more closed, rounded, and sculptural form. Takaezu is credited as the first American ceramic artist to produce this type of closed ceramic sculpture. In the late 1950s, Takaezu began to establish herself as a formidable professional artist, as well as a teacher. Her work gained wide acceptance and critical acclaim in museums, collections, and shows across the United States.

In 1964, Takaezu established a studio in Clinton, New Jersey, where she would move the following year, leaving her position at the Cleveland Institute of Art. She won a Tiffany Foundation grant that year as well. Having traveled in South America, Takaezu returned to New Jersey in 1967 and accepted a teaching position in the ceramics department at Princeton University; she remained in that position until 1992. During her tenure at Princeton, Takaezu taught ceramics to countless students; she taught Queen Noor of Jordan and actor Brooke Shields. Maintaining a reputation as a dynamic and disciplined educator, Takaezu also continued a prolific career as a ceramic artist, showing nationally in many individual and group exhibitions.

Her work in the 1970s and 1980s took on a more sculptural form. While she continued to make functional ceramics, her closed vessel forms were exhibited more frequently. These forms—globular closed ceramic pieces—often incorporated sound, and small pieces of ceramics were sometimes enclosed inside the pieces. Takaezu often pointed to the importance of the interior of the piece, which remained invisible to the viewer. She stated that she would often write a word with a powerful message on the interior of a piece—a word known only to her. Of equal importance to her, however, was the outside of the piece, which she often glazed (in a painterly fashion) with vibrant, bright glazes.

After her retirement from teaching in 1992, Takaezu focused full time on her ceramic sculpture. Unlike many ceramic artists, she increased the scale of her work after retirement. Her pieces grew to heights ranging from five to nine feet. The sculptures took on a deeper connection to nature as well, the theme of sculptural arrangement connecting to trees, stars, the ocean, and other natural elements. In the 1980s Takaezu also began to cast bells and closed sculptures in bronze.

In the late 1980s, and through the beginning of the 2000s, Takaezu received many honors, including honorary doctorates from Lewis and Clark College, Moore College, and Princeton University. Her work is among the permanent collections of many museums and galleries, and she has had a number of retrospectives both nationally and internationally. In 2001, Takaezu donated a bronze bell to the sculpture garden at Princeton, honoring the students of the university who lost their lives on September 11, 2001.

SIGNIFICANCE

Toshiko Takaezu is remembered as a respected sculptor and teacher, challenging her students to treat ceramics as a true art form and accepting students as apprentice artists. Her artwork presented a vision of ceramics that blurred the line between the natural world and made

objects, and as her career advanced, her pieces grew in scale and depth. Having spent time at a Zen Buddhist monastery during her time in Japan, she was strongly influenced by the Zen tradition throughout her career.

Idris Kabir Syed

FURTHER READING

Sewell, Darrel. *The Poetry of Clay: The Art of Toshiko Takaezu*. Philadelphia: Philadelphia Museum of Art, 2005. Print. Catalog from an exhibit of the same title; contains biographical information and provides images of the artist's work from the 1980s through 2003.

Takaezu, Toshiko. *Toshiko Takaezu: A Retrospective*. Kyōto: Kokuritsu Kindai Bijutsukan, 1995. Print. Catalog from an exhibit of the same title; contains biographical information, short essays by Takaezu and art critics, and a retrospective from the early 1950s through 1994.

Yake, J. Stanley. *Toshiko Takaezu: The Earth in Bloom: A Tribute*. New York: MEAM, 2005. Print. Tribute to Takaezu includes a short preface, a poem, and 142 pages of images of the artist's process and work.

RONALD TAKAKI

Educator, scholar, and writer

Ronald Takaki was an ethnic studies scholar and professor at the University of California, Berkeley. He taught the very first African American history course at the University of California Los Angeles, and established Berkeley's doctoral program in ethnic studies. Takaki is an ethnic studies legend who advocated for multiethnic education and civic equality regardless of race or ethnicity.

Born: April 12, 1939; Honolulu, Hawaii
Died: May 26, 2009; Berkeley, California
Full name: Ronald Toshiyuki Takaki (toh-shee-YOO-kee tah-KAH-kee)
Areas of achievement: Scholarship, education, and sociology

EARLY LIFE

Ronald Toshiyuki Takaki was born on April 12, 1939, in Honolulu, in the US Territory of Hawaii. His grandfather immigrated to Hawaii from Japan during the nineteenth

century and worked on a sugarcane plantation. Takaki's father died when he was seven years old, and his mother and Chinese stepfather raised him and his two siblings. His stepfather owned a Chinese restaurant in Honolulu. At the suggestion of a teacher, Takaki attended the College of Wooster in Ohio, earning a bachelor's degree in history in 1961. Takaki continued studying history in graduate school at the University of California (UC), Berkeley, earning a master's degree in 1962 and a doctorate in 1967. His doctoral dissertation was about slavery in the United States and was published in 1971 as his first book, *A Pro-Slavery Crusade: The Agitation to Reopen the African Slave Trade*.

LIFE'S WORK

Takaki taught history at the College of San Mateo in California from 1965 to 1967, after which he taught at UCLA (1967–72), introducing the university's first African American history course. In 1972, he helped to found the doctoral program in ethnic studies at UC

Ronald Takaki. (© Christopher Felver/Corbis)

Berkeley, where he taught until his retirement in 2004. He also developed the American cultures requirement, the university's multicultural requirement for graduation.

Takaki wrote over twenty books about ethnic studies. While in his early career he concentrated on African Americans and slavery, his later career focused on Asian Americans. Takaki's first book, *A Pro-Slavery Crusade*, examines the white South and the reasoning behind slavery in the United States. In *A Different Mirror: A History of Multicultural America* (1993), Takaki writes about the history of Africans, Native Americans, as well as immigrants of Irish, Chinese, and Japanese descent.

Takaki's works include books such as *Violence in the Black Imagination: Essays and Documents* (1972), *Raising Cane: The World of Plantation Hawaii* (1994), *Issei and Nisei: The Settling of Japanese America* (1994), *Double Victory: A Multicultural History of America in World War II* (2000), and *Strangers from a Different Shore: A History of Asian Americans* (1989), which was nominated for the Pulitzer Prize.

Takaki was the recipient of several awards, including a fellowship from the National Endowment for the Humanities (1970–71), a distinguished teaching award from UC Berkeley, and honorary degrees from Northeastern University, Wheelock College, Macalester College, and the College of Wooster. He gave lectures all over the world, including in Austria, the Netherlands, Japan, Russia, South Africa, Armenia, and New Zealand. He also debated other scholars such as Arthur Schlesinger Jr. and Nathan Glazer on issues such as affirmative action and multicultural education.

Takaki died on May 26, 2009, in Berkeley, California, having lived with multiple sclerosis for several decades. The cause of death was suicide. He was seventy years old. Takaki was married to Carol Rankin. They had two sons, Troy and Todd, and one daughter, Dana.

SIGNIFICANCE

Ronald Takaki was a pioneer in ethnic studies. Not only did he teach ethnic studies, he also helped to define it as an academic field. He dedicated his career to writing a multiethnic history of the United States, because ethnic groups had traditionally been excluded from standard history textbooks. He sought to educate university students and scholars about the cultural diversity that permeates the United States. Takaki was passionate about equality for Asian Americans and other ethnic groups. He passed on his scholarly pursuits to his students by creating the ethnic studies program at UC Berkeley.

Tina Chan

FURTHER READING

Chan, Sucheng. *Asian Americans: An Interpretive History*. Boston: Twayne, 1991. Print. Chronicles the history of Asian immigration, discussing such factors as discrimination, work lives, and social organization.

Lim, Shirley, and Amy Ling. *Reading the Literatures of Asian America*. Philadelphia: Temple UP, 1992. Print. Themes in this collection include Asian American identity, gender, and race; various Asian American writers discuss topics such as culture, beliefs, and history.

Okihiro, Gary. *Common Ground: Reimagining American History*. Princeton: Princeton UP, 2001. Print. Discusses factors that have shaped American history, such as race, gender, and sexuality.

Takaki, Ronald. *Strangers from a Different Shore: A History of Asian Americans*. Boston: Little, 1998. Print. A history of Asian Americans that includes

Japanese, Chinese, Vietnamese, Korean, Vietnamese, Filipino, and Indian perspectives; documents immigration from the early 1800s and other issues.

Wu, Frank. *Yellow: Race in America Beyond Black and White*. New York: Basic, 2002. Print. Investigates Asian American racial identity and stereotypes, including legal cases and scholarly studies.

Zia, Helen. *Asian American Dreams: The Emergence of an American People*. New York: Farrar, 2000. Print. Analyzes the political and cultural history of Asian Americans, including the author's personal stories.

GEORGE TAKEI

Actor, writer, and political activist

George Takei is best known for his role in the television series Star Trek *as helmsman Hikaru Sulu. Takei has appeared in more than 140 roles in film and television and performed as a voice actor and narrator. Takei is an outspoken supporter of gay rights and has received awards for his activism, as well as for his contributions to American-Japanese relations.*

Born: April 20, 1937; Los Angeles, California
Full name: George Hosato Takei (haw-sah-TOH tah-KAY)
Areas of achievement: Entertainment, activism

EARLY LIFE

George Hosato Takei was born in Los Angeles, California, on April 20, 1937, to Japanese American parents Takekuma Takei and Fumiko Emily Takei. He has one brother and one sister. After the Japanese attack on Pearl Harbor in 1941, Takei and his family were placed in internment camps for the duration of World War II. In 1942, they were sent to Rohwer War Relocation Center in southeastern Arkansas and later transferred to the Tule Lake Segregation Center in California.

In 1946, the family returned to Los Angeles. Takei attended Mount Vernon Junior High and Los Angeles High School, where he enjoyed acting in school plays. After graduating in 1956 Takei enrolled at the University of California, Berkeley as an architecture major. Takei later transferred to the University of California, Los Angeles to study theater, receiving his bachelor of arts in 1960 and his master of arts in 1964.

In 1957, Takei replied to a newspaper ad for a voice acting role for the Japanese movie *Rodan*, in which he performed voices for eight characters. In 1959, he made his television debut in the series *Playhouse 90* and his movie debut in Warner Brothers' film *Ice Palace*.

Takei traveled to England and Japan, where he attended the Shakespeare Institute in Stratford-upon-Avon and the Sophia University in Tokyo. Upon his return to the United States, Takei trained at the Desilu Workshop in Los Angeles.

LIFE'S WORK

In the early 1960s, Takei worked briefly in theater when he appeared in the play *Fly Blackbird* at the Billy Rose Theatre in New York City, but soon returned to Los Angeles and began working in television. In 1963, Takei was cast in a supporting role in the film *PT 109*. In 1964, Takei appeared in an episode of *The Twilight Zone*, in which he played a Japanese American gardener looking

George Takei. (WireImage)

George Takei's Role as Mr. Sulu in *Star Trek*

Takei's role as Mr. Sulu in the television series *Star Trek* (1966) was his first major break in television and remains his best-known role. *Star Trek*'s creator Gene Roddenberry was keen on having a diverse crew for his starship, which made the show the first to have a multicultural cast. Takei was cast as Mr. Sulu, the *Enterprise*'s helmsman, a nonstereotypical role for an Asian American and one that would make him famous.

Takei's role was to be expanded in the second season, but he was also working on the film *The Green Berets* (1968), which limited his availability. *Star Trek* was canceled in its third season and Takei moved on to other projects. In 1973, he returned to the role of Mr. Sulu, providing the voice of the character for an animated version of *Star Trek*. Takei continued his role in the first six *Star Trek* feature films: *Star Trek: The Motion Picture* (1979), *Star Trek: The Wrath of Khan* (1982), *The Search for Spock* (1984), *The Voyage Home* (1986), *The Final Frontier* (1989), and *The Undiscovered Country* (1991).

Takei continues to contribute to the *Star Trek* universe through his appearances at science fiction conventions and by providing narration for *Star Trek* computer games. He has also appeared in several of the *Star Trek* franchise shows and an internet series entitled *Star Trek New Voyages* (2004).

for work at an American World War II veteran's house. The episode received many complaints about its racial overtones and was so controversial that it was never run in syndication in the United States.

In 1965, Takei was cast in the role of Mr. Sulu for a second pilot episode of the science fiction program *Star Trek*. The episode aired as the third in the series on September 22, 1966. Takei stayed with *Star Trek* for the duration of its run, which lasted until June 3, 1969.

In the 1970s Takei became increasingly involved with public affairs, and in 1973 he ran for a city council seat in Los Angeles. He narrowly lost the race and decided to put acting first, but Takei did not lose his passion for public involvement. In 1973, Los Angeles mayor Tom Bradley appointed Takei to a position on the board of directors for the Southern California Transit District. In 1978, Takei's vote was the tiebreaker in favor of creating the Los Angeles subway system. Takei served on the transit board until 1984.

Takei appeared in numerous television shows during his career, including *Perry Mason*; *The Courtship of Eddie's Father*; *Voyage to the Bottom of the Sea*; *The Six Million Dollar Man*; *Mission: Impossible*; *Hawaii Five-O*; *Death Valley Days*; *MacGyver*; *Murder,*

She Wrote; *Will & Grace*; and *Malcolm in the Middle*.

From 1973 to 1974 Takei did the narration for the animated version of *Star Trek*. In 1979 he teamed up with Robert Asprin to co-author the science fiction novel *Mirror Friend, Mirror Foe*. That same year, Takei appeared in the first *Star Trek* movie. In 1986, Takei received a star on the Hollywood Boulevard Walk of Fame, and in 1991 he put his signature and handprint in the sidewalk in front of Grauman's Chinese Theatre.

Takei continued to perform as a voice actor. His vocal credits include *The National Parks: America's Best Idea*, a documentary series directed by Ken Burns. He provided voices for the animated Disney *Mulan* movies, as well as *Star Wars: The Clone Wars*, *The Simpsons*, and *Futurama*. Some of his other voice credits include the computer game *Command & Conquer: Red Alert 3*, *Star Trek* audio novel recordings, and guest narration for symphony orchestra performances.

Takei wrote his autobiography, *To the Stars*, in 1994, and was invited onto radio host Howard Stern's radio program to promote his book. Takei and Stern hit it off and Takei was asked to record sound bites for the show. In 2006, Takei became the official announcer for Stern's show on Sirius XM Radio. He has continued to make appearances on television, film, and stage, while also becoming a presence on the internet to communicate with fans and promote his activism.

In 2005, Takei went public in *Frontiers* magazine and officially announced that he was gay. On September 14, 2008, Takei married Brad Altman, his partner of eighteen years, in a ceremony held outside the Los Angeles Japanese American National Museum. Takei serves as a spokesperson for the Human Rights Campaign and has participated in public service announcements denouncing antigay politicians and homophobia. In 2006 he went on a national speaking tour called "Equality Trek."

SIGNIFICANCE

When George Takei began his acting career in the late 1950s, World War II had been over for just slightly more than a decade and events of the war years continued to stain ethnic relations in the United States. There were few opportunities for minorities in the entertainment industry and Takei faced considerable difficulties, but worked very hard to overcome bigotry and prejudice.

Takei was also deeply affected by his time spent in the Japanese internment camps as a youth. As an adult he turned his energies to political activism. In 1972, Takei was a delegate to the Democratic National Convention and in 1973 ran for mayor of Los Angeles. In 1981 he testified before Congress about his childhood experiences in the internment camps.

Takei has won numerous awards for his acting and his public service work. These include the Order of the Rising Sun, Gold Rays with Rosette, which was awarded to him by the Japanese Emperor Akihito in 1994 for his work in improving relations between the United States and Japan. In 2007, Takei received a Lifetime Achievement Award at the 8th Annual San Diego Asian Film Festival, and in 2009, the Ivy Bethune Tri-Union Diversity Award.

Karen S. Garvin

FURTHER READING

Knapp, Alex. "How George Takei Conquered Facebook." *Forbes* 23 March 2012. Web. 10 Apr. 2012. Presents an interview with George Takei in which he discusses his followers on online social networks and the role of the internet in his activism.

Steele, Bruce C. "Short Answers: George Takei." *Advocate* 6 Dec. 2005: 26. Print. An interview with Takei that includes his revelation that he is gay and explains why he decided to become active in promoting gay rights.

Takei, George. *To the Stars: The Autobiography of George Takei,* Star Trek*'s Mr. Sulu*. New York: Pocket, 1994. Print. Describes Takei's childhood in internment camps, his early interest in theater, and the motivation for his political activism. Takei talks about his success and reveals behind-the-scenes stories about his days in *Star Trek*.

AMY TAN

Writer, novelist

Amy Tan's literary works have incorporated the universal themes of love and family relationships, making her a popular writer. Although works of fiction, Tan's stories are loosely based on events from her life and offer realistic portrayals of the Chinese American as well as the universal human experience.

Born: February 19, 1952; Oakland, California
Full name: Amy Ruth Tan
Birth name: An-Mei Ruth Tan
Area of achievement: Literature

EARLY LIFE

Amy Ruth Tan was born February 19, 1952, in Oakland, California. Her father, John Yuehhan Tan, had been an electrical engineer in Beijing, but left China in 1947 to escape the Chinese Civil War. After arriving in the United States, he became a Baptist minister. Tan's mother, Du "Daisy" Ching, had divorced an abusive husband to whom she was married for twelve years in China, and had lost custody of their three daughters. After Ching left China in 1949, she married John Tan in the United States. The family settled in Oakland, where they had three children: Peter, born in 1950, Amy, born in 1952, and John, born in 1954.

When Tan was fifteen years old, both her older brother and her father, diagnosed with brain tumors, began undergoing chemotherapy. They died within eight months of each other in 1967 and 1968. Following their deaths, Tan's mother took her and her brother John to Europe. The family traveled through the Netherlands and Germany before finally settling in Montreaux, Switzerland. In Switzerland, Tan attended the Institut Monte Rosa Internationale, an American school with children from different cultures. During this time, Tan's mother told her and her brother about her abusive first marriage and that they had three half sisters in China.

When Tan graduated from high school in 1969, the family moved back to San Francisco. For one year, Tan attended Linfield College, a small Baptist school in Oregon, before transferring to San Jose City College in California to be with her new boyfriend, Louis DeMattei, an Italian American law student she met on a blind date. Tan switched from pre-medicine to a double major in English and linguistics, eventually transferring to San Jose State University. Although she still thought of being a writer or artist, she never took a course in creative writing.

Tan graduated with honors from San Jose State in 1973 and won a scholarship to attend the Summer

Amy Tan. (Getty Images)

Linguistics Institute at the University of California at Santa Cruz. In 1974, Tan earned a master's degree in linguistics at San Jose State, and received a graduate minority fellowship for doctoral work at the University of California. On April 6, 1974, she married DeMattei, who had begun working as a tax lawyer.

Tan dropped out of the doctoral program during her second year and, from 1976 to 1980, worked as a language-development consultant in Alameda County, directing training projects for developmentally disabled children. After five years, emotional and work-related stress caused her to resign. From 1981 to 1983, Tan worked as an editor and reporter for the medical journal *Emergency Room Reports*. She briefly wrote speeches, pamphlets, and brochures for corporate clients before becoming an independent freelance writer.

LIFE'S WORK

Tan had always thought of writing as a hobby because she believed that she could not make money as writer, but her work in the medical journal field and as a freelance writer convinced her otherwise. Tan began reading fiction and writing short stories. Her short story "Endgame" earned her an invitation to join the Squaw Valley

Community of Writers at the University of California at Irvine. This selective workshop for beginning writers helped Tan learn the processes of editing and rewriting. It also helped her to realize that she had many stories to tell. "Endgame" was published by a local literary magazine, *FM Five*, and later was reprinted in the November 1986 issue of *Seventeen* as "Rules of the Game."

Literary agent Sandra Dijkstra saw the story and contacted Tan, offering to be her agent and encouraging her to continue writing. Tan sent Dijkstra some stories and they began planning for a book. However, in 1986, Tan's work was delayed following her mother's hospitalization for chest pains. When her mother recovered, she and Tan traveled to China for three weeks in October 1987. While in China, Tan met her half sisters, an experience that helped her better understand both her American and her Chinese heritage.

When Tan's book proposal was completed, it sold to the publisher G. P. Putnam's Sons for an advance of $50,000. Tan immediately stopped freelancing and began working on the book, drawing inspiration from her experiences in China and from stories she had heard from her mother and aunt when she was growing up. The result was a novel about Chinese American mothers and daughters called *The Joy Luck Club*, publishing rights for which were sold to the Book of the Month Club in September 1987. Serial rights were sold to the *Atlantic Monthly*, *Ladies' Home Journal*, and *San Francisco Focus*. In addition, audio rights were sold to Dove Entertainment and to foreign markets in Italy, France, Holland, Japan, Sweden, and Israel. The book's commercial and critical success made Tan famous.

Tan started numerous drafts for a second book, but she was uninspired and threw them away. Eventually, Tan decided to fictionalize the story of her mother's life in China during World War II, her abusive marriage, and her experience of leaving three daughters in China and coming to the United States. Although she made some changes to the story, Tan kept the book close to her mother's experience. *The Kitchen God's Wife* was published in 1991. Like *The Joy Luck Club*, the book also received positive reviews and became a best-seller.

Tan's next work was a children's storybook called *The Moon Lady*, published in 1992. Her planned third adult book, *The Year of No Flood*, was never finished because Tan grew tired of writing it after talking about it too much in advance. In 1994, Tan published a children's book entitled *The Chinese Siamese Cat*. Based on her memories of her cat, the book was adapted into a PBS television series that debuted in 2001 as *Sagwa the*

The Joy Luck Club

Amy Tan's first novel, *The Joy Luck Club*, was published in 1989 and remained on the *New York Times* bestseller list for thirty-four months in hardcover and nine months in paperback. The book sold over two million copies and was translated into thirty-five languages. Critics praised the book for its intimate storytelling about mother/daughter relationships and themes of love and redemption. The novel was nominated in 1989 for the National Book Critics Circle's Best Novel Award and the *Los Angeles Times* Best Book of the Year. The book won the National Book Award and the Commonwealth Gold Award in 1989, as well as the Bay Area Book Reviewers Award in 1990.

Tan's novel is a collection of sixteen interlocking stories about four Chinese immigrant mothers and their Chinese American daughters. The stories are based on Tan's own relationship with her mother and her experience of being torn between two cultures as a young person, as well as stories that she had heard from her mother and aunt.

In 1993, *The Joy Luck Club* was made into a film that grossed more than $32 million. Tan was the co-screenwriter and co-producer. Also in 1993, the novel was adapted for the stage by American playwright Susan Kim and produced through a collaboration between the Yale-China Association, the Shanghai People's Art Theatre, and Connecticut's Long Wharf Theatre. The play featured a predominantly Chinese cast and was performed in several Chinese cities, including Shanghai and Beijing.

Chinese Siamese Cat. Tan served as the creative consultant for the show. In 1995 Tan published *The Hundred Secret Senses*, a novel that follows the relationship between two half-sisters. It received mixed reviews but was still a *New York Times* best-seller.

In the late 1990s, Tan began working on a book about her mother's diagnosis of Alzheimer's disease. During this time, she was also helping a close friend who was battling cancer. Her mother died on November 22, 1999, at age eighty-three, and her friend died two weeks later. Although Tan had already given her publisher the manuscript of her newest book, Tan took the manuscript back and rewrote it. *The Bonesetter's Daughter* debuted in 2001. It too became a best-seller. The book was made into an opera performed by the San Francisco Opera in 2008.

Tan became very ill in 1999. After suffering for eighteen months from serious flu-like symptoms, she was diagnosed with late-stage Lyme disease, which doctors said she had contracted from a tick bite. Following treatment, it took almost two years before Tan fully recovered. The disease left her with lesions in her brain, resulting in epilepsy and neuropathy—a numbness in the feet that causes balance problems—and a sleep disorder.

In 1999, Tan selected and edited the annual edition of *The Best American Short Stories*, published by Houghton Mifflin Harcourt. In 2003 she published *The Opposite of Fate: A Book of Musings*, a collection of nonfiction essays. Her 2005 novel, *Saving Fish from Drowning*, was an Editor's Choice Selection in *Booklist*. Also in 2005, Tan received the Commonwealth Award for Literature. In 2006, Tan wrote the foreword for the collection *Tails of Devotion: A Look at the Bond Between People and Their Pets*, proceeds from which benefited San Francisco animal charities.

Throughout her career, Tan has supported numerous charitable organizations, including organizations working for orphans, Lyme disease research, animal rescue, lung cancer research, and freedom of speech, among others. Tan's essays and short stories appear in numerous anthologies and textbooks. She also lectures at universities worldwide.

SIGNIFICANCE

Tan's work connects with readers on many levels. In addition to shedding light on the Asian American experience, Tan's works focus on relationships and family—especially mothers and daughters—as well as the universal themes of love, loss, redemption, and forgiveness. It is difficult to classify Tan's novels and short stories as pure fiction, because they contain elements of biography, history, mythology, personal memories, and folk tales. In addition to receiving critical praise, Tan has become one of the most commercially successful writers of her generation.

Virginia L. Salmon

FURTHER READING

"Amy (Ruth) Tan." *Feminist Writers*. Ed. Pamela Kester-Shelton. Detroit: St. James, 1996. Offers a brief chapter on Tan that discusses her life, works, and themes.

Huntley, E. D. *Amy Tan: A Critical Companion*. Westport, CT: Greenwood, 1998. Print. Discusses Tan's life, first three novels, and place in Asian American literature. Includes bibliography and index.

Rosinsky, Natalie M. *Amy Tan: Author and Story-teller*. Minneapolis: Compass Point, 2007. Print. Presents information written for younger readers. Includes information about Tan's background.

Shields, Charles J. *Amy Tan*. Philadelphia: Chelsea House, 2002. Print. Discusses Tan's early life, career, and literary works.

TAN DUN

Chinese-born composer and musician

Most popularly known for writing the score to the 2000 film Crouching Tiger, Hidden Dragon, *which won both a Grammy and an Academy Award, Tan Dun has also distinguished himself as a prolific composer of dance, symphonic, choral, solo, and operatic works that employ an array of instruments and techniques. His compositions can be described as eclectic fusions of Western, Asian, and organic elements that explore a wide range of sound.*

Born: August 18, 1957; Si Mao, Changsha, Hunan, China
Full name: Tan Dun
Also known as: Tán Dùn
Area of achievement: Music

Tan Dun. (AFP/Getty Images)

EARLY LIFE

Born in the Hunan province of China during the rule of Mao Zedong, Tan Dun was deemed a child of "intellectuals"—his father, Tan Xiang Qiu, was a food research facility worker, and his mother, Fang Qun Ying, was a medical doctor. The family was separated for "reeducation" during the Cultural Revolution, and Tan Dun was assigned to plant rice in a countryside commune. It was there that he learned from the villagers how to play such instruments as the *erhu*, the *yangqin*, and the violin.

Tan Dun's musical exposure came primarily through regional folk and ritual songs and a variety of forbidden operas. To circumvent government restrictions, he would often set Maoist texts to banned peasant tunes, and by age seventeen he was the leading musician in his community, often performing for community festivities. He became skilled at improvising on every available instrument and commonly turned everyday items into new instruments. This musical ingenuity, along with a rich mélange of Taoist, Buddhist, and folk beliefs, would form the core of his personal philosophy.

In the time after Mao's death, as the Cultural Revolution ended and traditional operas reemerged, several members of a traveling Beijing opera troupe were drowned in a riverboat accident, and the Communist Party appointed Tan Dun as a replacement violinist and arranger for the group. It was during this time that he first heard, on the radio, Western classical music—works by Ludwig van Beethoven and Johann Sebastian Bach. When the Central Conservatory of Music in Beijing reopened in 1978, Tan Dun became one of thirty composition students admitted from thousands of applicants. There, he studied with Zhao Xindao and Li Yinghai. Lectures by visiting composers, including Chou Wen-Chung, George Crumb, Alexander Goehr, Hans Werner Henze, Toru Takemitsu, and Isang Yun, broadened his perspective on the wide array of twentieth-century music that had previously been suppressed in China.

Tan Dun became a leader of the so-called new wave of Chinese composition. In 1980, he produced a symphony based on a Hunan lament from the fourth century BCE, for which he won a prize at the first National Symphonic Competition. He came to international attention in 1983, when his *String Quartet: Feng-Ya-Song* (Ballad-Hymn-Ode) took second prize in the Dresden International Weber Chamber Music Composition Competition. The atonal elements in the work also spawned some debate in China, and the Communist Party temporarily banned performances of the piece, which they labeled as "spiritual pollution."

In 1986, Columbia University offered Tan Dun a fellowship to study composition with Chou Wen-Chung, Mario Davidovsky, and George Edwards. In New York City, he learned to temper his predominately atonal studies through private sessions with musicians such as John Cage, Philip Glass, and Meredith Monk. Tan Dun's works were frequently featured by a variety of performance groups and assorted dancers during this time, usually to mixed reviews. He graduated from Columbia in 1993 with a doctorate in musical arts.

LIFE'S WORK

Nontraditional orchestration and unusual techniques became a hallmark of Tan Dun's work. His *Organic Music Trilogy*, created to commemorate the 150th anniversary of Gustav Mahler's birth, comprised *Water Concerto for Water Instruments and Orchestra* (1998), *Paper Concerto for Paper Instruments and Orchestra* (2003), and *Earth Concerto for Stone and Ceramic Instruments and Orchestra* (2009). In *The Map* (2002), Tan Dun melded technology and tradition by creating a concerto that featured solos from live and prerecorded performers. He explored the limits of the Internet age with Internet Symphony No. 1, "Eroica" (2008), commissioned by Google for the YouTube Symphony Orchestra, an online collaborative ensemble.

Marco Polo (1996), a commission for the Edinburgh Festival, marked the first of four operas Tan Dun would write over the ensuing decade. Commissions for his work have also come from Suntory Hall in Tokyo, Japan; the New York Philharmonic; the Metropolitan Opera; the International Bach Academy in Stuttgart, Germany; the Association for the Celebration of Reunification of Hong Kong with China; and the International Olympic Committee.

Tan Dun's work in film includes music for the supernatural thriller *Fallen* (1998), Zhang Yimou's martial arts film *Hero* (2004; released as *Yīngxióng* in 2002), and Ang Lee's internationally lauded action-adventure film *Crouching Tiger, Hidden Dragon* (2000). In addition to winning a Grammy and an Academy Award for his work on the latter, Tan Dun has been honored with a Eugene McDermott Award in the Arts from the Council for the Arts of the Massachusetts Institute of Technology, the triennial Glenn Gould International Protégé Award, the Grawemeyer Award from the University of Louisville, and *Musical America* magazine's Composer of the Year Award. In addition, he was appointed cultural ambassador to the world for the 2010 Shanghai World Exposition.

SIGNIFICANCE

By successfully crossing between the worlds of classical music, popular music, and multimedia performance, Tan Dun has composed an array of accessible works that consistently blend multicultural elements and musical techniques. In 2011, he adapted his music from several popular martial-arts films into *Martial Arts Trilogy*, a concerto for cello, piano, and violin, which premiered with the National Symphony Orchestra. His international achievements transcend cultural labels of East versus West, and his work promotes an increasingly globalized musical culture.

Gary Galván

FURTHER READING

Buruma, Ian. "Of Musical Import." *New York Times Magazine* (4 May 2008): 46–51. Print. Offers glimpses into Tan Dun's hectic schedule during a festival celebrating his work, as well as retrospectives and reminiscences of his influences and inspirations.

Klein, Christina. "*Crouching Tiger, Hidden Dragon*: A Diasporic Reading." *Cinema Journal* 43.4 (2004): 18–42. Print. Examines the cultural phenomenon of Ang Lee's film and its reflection of globalized culture.

Witzleben, J. Lawrence. "Music in the Hong Kong Handover Ceremonies: A Community Re-Imagines Itself." *Ethnomusicology* 46.1 (2002): 120–33. Print. Reviews and examines the day of musical celebration in the 1997 transfer of sovereignty over Hong Kong to China.

TERENCE TAO

Mathematician and educator

Mathematician Terence "Terry" Tao's collaborative nature and ingenuity have led to several innovations in the fields of prime numbers and wave motion.

Born: July 17, 1975; Adelaide, Australia
Full name: Terence Chi-Shen Tao
Also known as: Terry Tao
Area of achievement: Mathematics

EARLY LIFE

Terence Tao was born in Adelaide, South Australia, on July 17, 1975, to Billy and Grace Tao. His father was a pediatrician of Chinese descent; his mother had been born in Hong Kong and was employed as a secondary-school math and science teacher. Tao has two younger brothers, Trevor and Nigel.

Tao was exceptionally bright from a young age. At the age of two, he taught himself arithmetic using magnetic numbers on his home refrigerator and learned how to read and write by watching the children's television program *Sesame Street*. By 1983, at eight years of age, Tao was attending classes at Blackwood High School, where he scored in the ninety-ninth percentile of seventeen-year-olds in an international aptitude test for mathematics. At ten years old, he became the youngest competitor ever in the International Mathematical Olympiad (IMO), a high-school student competition in Australia. Two years later, he won the IMO gold medal.

Tao completed his high-school education in 1988 and enrolled at Flinders University of South Australia in 1989. In December 1991, at age sixteen, Tao received an honors bachelor of science degree in mathematics from Flinders University. In August of the following year, he received his master of science degree in mathematics, also from Flinders.

After earning his master's degree, Tao traveled to the United States to continue his education at Princeton University. He received his PhD in mathematics in 1996, under the supervision of Professor Elias Stein, and was hired by the University of California, Los Angeles (UCLA) as an E. R. Hedrick Assistant Professor. In 2000, Tao was made the youngest full professor in UCLA history.

Tao became the James and Carol Collins chair in mathematics at UCLA in 2007. He has also been a visiting professor and an honorary professor at the University of New South Wales and Australian National University, respectively. In 2002, he married his wife, Laura, an engineer at NASA's Jet Propulsion Laboratory; the couple has one son, William. In 2009, Tao became a dual citizen of the United States and Australia.

LIFE'S WORK

As a mathematician, Tao's areas of research include harmonic analysis; partial differential equations; geometric, arithmetic, and algebraic combinatorics; analytic number theory; and compressed sensing. He specializes in analysis, including calculus and differential equations. In addition to Tao's inequality theorem, which explores the field of information theory, he is perhaps best known for his theorem on the topic of prime numbers, which he developed with Cambridge University mathematician Ben Green. The Green-Tao theorem proves that prime numbers contain arithmetic progressions, which was previously held to be impossible. Green and Tao's work bridged a gap between analysis and number theory and established Tao as a mathematician with a proclivity for crossing disciplinary boundaries.

Terence Tao. (AFP/Getty Images)

Terence Tao's Strategy and His *What's New* Blog

While Tao has been described as the "Mozart of Math" because of his creativity and the ease with which complex mathematical equations seem to flow out of him, Tao attributes his success to strategies that enable him to break up difficult problems into easier ones. Often, he focuses on one question at a time and tries a variety of techniques.

In addition to his papers and books, Tao is a well-respected and prolific blogger. On his *What's New* blog, Tao frequently posts remarks about his ongoing projects, links to and commentary on current articles, and other mathematical topics. There are numerous active mathematical blogs at all levels of sophistication, but many consider *What's New* to be the "grandfather" of mathematical blogging and an important and influential source of information. As of 2010, the American Mathematics Society had published two books of excerpts from Tao's blog.

Between 1986 and 2010, Tao was recognized over thirty times with awards and honors for his contributions to the field of mathematics. In 2000, he won the Salem Prize; from 2001 to 2003, he was a Clay Mathematics Institute fellow; in 2002, he won the American Mathematical Society Bochner Prize; and in 2005, he was awarded the American Mathematical Society Conant Prize jointly with mathematician Allen Knutson.

In 2006, at the age of thirty-one, Tao received the prestigious Fields Medal from the International Mathematical Union, making him the first Australian to be awarded this high honor. That same year, he received the Ramanujan Prize from India's SASTRA (Shanmugha Arts, Science, Technology, and Research Academy) University. In 2007, he was named a fellow of the MacArthur Foundation and was a finalist for the

Australian of the Year Award, bestowed by the National Australia Day Council.

SIGNIFICANCE

Tao has made many important contributions to the field of mathematics, with special breakthroughs in wave motion and prime numbers that have practical applications in fiber optics and information security. His interdisciplinary, open-minded approach allows him to bridge perceived divisions within mathematics and yields innovative results. In addition to his many other accomplishments, Tao has published over two hundred papers on the topic of mathematics, collaborated with numerous mathematicians on papers and research, and authored over a dozen books on higher-level math.

Jae Jerkins

FURTHER READING

Clements, M. A. "Terence Tao." *Educational Studies in Mathematics* 15.3 (1984): 213–38. Print. Provides an accounting of the interviews and math testing completed with a young Tao, beginning when he was eight years old.

Tao, Terence. *Nonlinear Dispersive Equations: Local and Global Analysis*. Providence, RI: Amer. Mathematical Soc., 2006. Print. Introduces the reader to solutions to nonlinear wave, Schrödinger, and KdV equations.

---. *Solving Mathematical Problems: A Personal Perspective*. New York: Oxford UP, 2006. Print. Describes Tao's tactics and provides samples of a variety of problems in number theory, algebra, analysis, and geometry.

Mary Tape

Chinese-born activist and photographer

Tape is best known for her role in the 1885 California Supreme Court case Tape v. Hurley, *in which her eight-year-old daughter Mamie sued a San Francisco school that denied her admission due to her Chinese heritage. She also received local acclaim for her talent as an amateur photographer.*

Born: 1857; China
Died: October 9, 1934; Berkeley, California

Full name: Mary Tape (TAYP)
Also known as: Mary McGladery
Areas of achievement: Activism, art

EARLY LIFE

Mary Tape was born in China in 1857 and immigrated to the United States by 1868, settling in San Francisco. She lived in Chinatown for a time before becoming a resident of the children's home run by the Ladies' Protection and Relief Society. While at the home, Tape met the institution's matron, Mary McGladery, who taught her to speak and read English. Tape was so strongly influenced by McGladery that she adopted her teacher's name as her own; her original name is not known.

In the spring of 1875, Mary met Joseph Tape (originally Jeu Dip), a deliveryman who had emigrated from China in 1869. They married on November 16, 1875, and later had four children. Joseph established a successful business that allowed the family to purchase a home as well as vacation and rental properties.

LIFE'S WORK

The Tapes valued education, and as established residents of San Francisco, they wanted their children to be educated in the local public school system that they supported through taxes. Although California state law provided for segregated public education for nonwhite students, children of Chinese ancestry were denied even this between 1871 and 1885, reflecting the significant anti-Chinese sentiment of the period. Many Chinese American children received no education, while others had tutors, were homeschooled, or attended religious schools. In 1878, the Chinese community in California petitioned the state legislature for public education opportunities, but the petition was rejected.

When their eldest daughter, Mamie, was refused admittance to the local public school because of her Chinese heritage, the Tapes first enlisted the Chinese consulate to argue on their behalf. In response, the superintendent of San Francisco schools cited the California Constitution, which referred to the Chinese as "dangerous to the well-being of the state," as justification for barring Mamie and other Chinese American children from enrolling. The Tapes then sued the principal of the Spring Valley School, Jennie Hurley, and the San Francisco Board of Education. In March of 1885, the Supreme Court of California ruled in *Tape v. Hurley* that Chinese American children born in the United States and residing within a public school district were guaranteed the right to a public school education by both the US Constitution and California law.

Following this decision, the California legislature passed a law that allowed the establishment of segregated schools for Chinese children and prohibited students from attending any other public school when a Chinese school was available. Tape wrote a strongly worded letter to the board of education protesting this injustice and pledging that her own children would never attend a segregated school. Despite her pledge, Tape eventually sent her eldest children to the newly established Chinese school. Early in the 1890s, Tape moved with her family to Berkeley, California, where her children were able to attend nonsegregated schools.

While living in Berkeley, Tape, a skilled amateur photographer, became known for developing her own photographs and creating slides for use with a magic lantern, an early image-projecting device. She received a great deal of attention for her artistic talent and knowledge of chemicals and darkroom principles, though many of the reports on her work focused on the fact that she was a Chinese woman participating in an activity dominated by Caucasian men. Tape also created paintings and decorative dishes, some of which appeared in exhibits decades after her death.

SIGNIFICANCE

Tape played a significant role in the movement against school segregation, establishing in *Tape v. Hurley* a precedent that continued to be referenced in cases of discrimination. Though Chinese American children remained segregated in some California communities into the 1930s, the process of school segregation ultimately came to an end nationwide following the 1954 Supreme Court case *Brown v. Board of Education*.

Judy A. Johnson

FURTHER READING

Kuo, Joyce. "Excluded, Segregated, and Forgotten: A Historical View of the Discrimination against Chinese Americans in Public Schools." *Chinese America: History and Perspectives* (2000): 32–48. Print. Provides an overview of anti-Chinese discrimination in public schools and includes several references to the Tape case.

Ngai, Mae. *The Lucky Ones: One Family and the Extraordinary Invention of Chinese America*. Boston: Houghton, 2010. Print. Details the history of the Tape family, including the lives of Mary and Joseph's children.

Thompson, Daniella. *The Tapes of Russell Street: An Accomplished Family of School Desegregating Pioneers*. Berkeley Architectural Heritage Association, 30 Apr. 2004. Web. 7 Mar. 2012. Discusses Tape's early life, experience with segregation, and artistic talents and includes several of her photographs.

CHRIS TASHIMA

Actor, director, and writer

Chris Tashima is an actor and director best known for his independent films such as Americanese, Day of Independence, *and* Visas and Virtues.

Born: March 24, 1960; Cambridge, Massachusetts
Full name: Christopher Inadomi Tashima
Areas of achievement: Film, theater, and activism

EARLY LIFE

Chris Tashima was born Christopher Inadomi Tashima in Cambridge, Massachusetts, on March 24, 1960. The year after he was born, his father, Atsushi Wallace Tashima, graduated from Harvard Law School. Along with his wife, Nora Kiyo Inadomi, Atsuchi Tashima relocated to Pasadena, California, where he became deputy state attorney general. In 1968, Tashima's father joined Amstar Corporation, a major sugar producer. As a young man, Tashima attended the College Preparatory School, a private academy in the Claremont district of Oakland. In 1978, Tashima finished high school in Los Angeles. Tashima's father was later appointed to a seat on the United States District Court by President Jimmy Carter. In 1996, the elder Tashima was appointed to the United States Court of Appeals by President Bill Clinton.

Tashima's courses in film theory and film direction at Porter College, the performing arts school of the University of California Santa Cruz, inspired him to transfer to the film program at the University of California Los Angeles (UCLA). Tashima's academic plans were delayed due to high enrollment. He left school to work as an extra, and developed an interest in performance. After several auditions with East West Players, Tashima's childhood violin training helped to land him his first professional acting role. He was hired to play violin for the group's 1985 production of composer Kurt Weill's *Threepenny Opera*. Shortly thereafter, Tashima understudied for the lead role in *Song of a Nisei Fisherman*. He took the main role when the principal actor dropped out unexpectedly. Over the next three years, Tashima's work with East West Players, and a mentorship with the theater group's founder, Mako, broadened his performance skills and deepened his cultural awareness. Tashima became increasingly aware of the absence of Asian American characters in American film, theater, and television.

LIFE'S WORK

While designing sets for East West Players in the mid-1990s, Tashima met Tim Toyama in a playwriting workshop, and their association led to his earning a role in Toyama's one-act play *Visas and Virtues*. Tashima appeared in the lead role of Chiune "Sempo" Sugihara in the small but successful North Hollywood production. Deeply impressed by the story of the Japanese consul general to Lithuania who risked his career to provide exit visas for more than six thousand Jews during World War II, Tashima followed a suggestion by the play's director to adapt the script to film. Together with Toyama, he formed Cedar Grove Productions, taking the name from the literal translation of the name Sugihara. At the outset, the project faced numerous challenges. The loss of two financial backers delayed production by nine months. After a year and a half, with the help of a volunteer cast and crew, which included the prominent cinematographer Hiro Narita, the film was shot in seven days. The film adaptation of *Visas and Virtues* earned an Academy Award for Best Short Film, Live Action, in 1998.

Tashima again collaborated with Toyama to create a film version of the playwright's one-act script *Day of*

Chris Tashima. (WireImage)

Independence. The work is based on the life of Toyama's father, who was interned as a Japanese American during World War II. With a cast and crew of approximately two hundred volunteers that included actors and technical assistants, the film was shot in six days in Stockton, California, using replica internment barracks that were built for the production. The completed film appeared at numerous film festivals, earning more than twenty awards. It also received an Emmy Award following its 2005 airing on PBS.

Tashima appeared in director Eric Byler's *Americanese* in 2006. The film was awarded Outstanding Ensemble Cast Award at the South by Southwest Film Festival. Adapted from the novel *American Knees*, by Shawn Wong, who also edited the seminal 1974 Asian American collection *Aiiieeeee!*, the film explores the tensions of Asian and American identity within a larger white culture.

SIGNIFICANCE

In a career that has lasted over twenty-five years, Tashima has established himself as a prominent stage actor, director, and set designer. His awards include a shared Drama-Logue Scenic Design Award for East West Players' 1992 production of *Into the Woods* and a 1995 Best

Set Design Ovation Award for *Sweeney Todd*, also at East West Players. Tashima has also been long committed to advocacy for Asian American performing artists. He has worked with the Asian American Committee of the Directors Guild of America and the Asian Pacific American Media Task Force of the American Federation of Radio and Television Artists, and served on five nominating committees of the Academy of Motion Picture Arts and Sciences.

Tashima has become one of the best-known actors and directors in the film and theater industry. His film company, Cedar Grove Productions, and its partner theater company, Cedar Grove OnStage, continue to produce and promote the work of Asian American Artists.

Ron West

FURTHER READING

Feng, Peter X. *Identities in Motion: Asian American Film and Video*. Durham: Duke UP, 2002. Print. Presents a historical overview and cultural analysis of Asian American film.

Xu, Wenying. *Historical Dictionary of Asian American Literature and Theater*. Lanham: Scarecrow, 2012. Print. Presents a chronological history of Asian American theater.

HAO JIANG TIAN

Chinese-born singer

Hao Jiang Tian is known as one of the world's best bassi cantanti (a type of operatic bass voice), having made regular appearances at the Metropolitan Opera since his debut in 1991. He has performed on many of the world's best opera stages, often alongside such renowned opera singers as Plácido Domingo and Luciano Pavarotti, and has been widely celebrated as one of the finest contemporary Chinese American opera singers.

Born: 1954; Beijing, China
Full name: Hao Jiang Tian (how chee-ANG tee-AN)
Also known as: Haojiang Tian; Tián Hàojiāng
Areas of achievement: Music, theater, entertainment

EARLY LIFE

Hao Jiang Tian was born in Beijing in 1954. His father, Tian Yun, was the director of the influential People's Liberation Army Song and Dance Ensemble; his mother, Lu Yuan, was a composer for the ensemble. During

the Cultural Revolution (1966–76), Tian's parents were banished from their posts. Observing the hardships that befell his family and others enabled Tian to defy adversity and channel his emotions and passions, all of which would later prove to be remarkable strengths, into his career as an opera singer.

After middle school, Tian was assigned to work in the Beijing Boiler Factory to cut steel sheets, but his gifted voice was soon discovered, and he was selected from more than five hundred candidates in Beijing to enroll in a class that trained singers for the "model drama" (Beijing operas and ballets featuring proletarian protagonists during the Cultural Revolution). Following the end of the Cultural Revolution, Tian continued his vocal training with the Central Conservatory of China. He graduated in 1980 and started working at the Central Philharmonic Society Chorus.

Tian's first exposure to opera was in 1980, in a master class taught by the Italian opera star Gino Bechi.

Subsequently, Tian's defiance of social norms and his exploration of Western music, including his Elvis-like hip movements during a performance in northern China, motivated him to go abroad. With a full scholarship from the Lamont School of Music at the University of Denver, Tian came to the United States to study vocal arts in 1983. He earned his master's degree at the University of Denver in 1987.

LIFE'S WORK

The turning point in Tian's career came in 1991, when his voice won him a contract with the Metropolitan Opera. Between then and 2010, he performed at the Metropolitan Opera every year, appearing in twenty-six operas and more than 300 performances. Worldwide, Tian has sung in over forty major roles in over 1,300 performances, collaborating with more than thirty world-class theaters and opera houses in Italy, Germany, the Netherlands, Japan, and other countries and frequently sharing the stage with legendary singers such as Luciano Pavarotti. He has earned special acclaim for his performances in the roles of Philip II in *Don Carlos* and Mephistopheles in Charles Gounod's *Faust*, among others.

One of the operas in which Tian has performed most often is *Turandot*, a classic by the Italian composer Giacomo Puccini. Tian sang the character of King Timur and performed in the opera more than two hundred times worldwide, including one 2009 performance in Beijing's Bird's Nest Stadium, as it is popularly known, before an audience of fifty thousand. However, while *Turandot* incorporates many Chinese cultural elements, such as the melody of the Chinese folk song "Jasmine Flower," Tan Dun's opera *The First Emperor* provided Tian with his first opportunity to sing the role of an actual Chinese character in an authentic Chinese story written and designed by Chinese artists. Tian sang the role of General Wang alongside Plácido Domingo, who sang the title role. The opera was premiered at the Metropolitan Opera in 2006 to mixed reviews, although it was commended for its visual scale and design.

In the late 2000s, Tian's other endeavors involving new works, many of which combined Asian and Western cultures, included Guo Wenjing's *Poet Li Bai* (2007, premiering at Denver's Central City Opera), Amy Tan's *The Bonesetter's Daughter* (2008, the San Francisco Opera), and *The Memory Palace of Matteo Ricci* (2010, Hong Kong), the latter a play based on the 1984 book of the same name by eminent historian Jonathan Spence. In 2008, Tian received the Alumni Professional Achievement Award from the University of Denver and was nominated for a Grammy Award. He is a member of the Committee of 100, an influential organization of Chinese American leaders in various fields.

SIGNIFICANCE

About ten years after his arrival in the United States, Tian won recognition as an internationally preeminent basso cantante, attesting to his ability to overcome language hurdles and cultural gaps in order to compete and excel in opera on an international level. Tian is the first opera singer of Chinese origin to achieve such prominent status, and he has been praised as "the most shining Chinese American opera singer on stage." As a renowned Asian American artist, Tian has also lectured widely in China, Singapore, and other Asian countries. Together with his wife, Martha Liao, he has nurtured young, talented Asian artists and worked to bridge Western and Eastern cultures.

Lisong Liu

FURTHER READING

Bristow, Michael. "Singer Uses Opera to Build China-US Bridges." *BBC News*. BBC, 19 Aug. 2011. Web. 30 Mar. 2012. Discusses Tian's history with music and his I Sing Beijing project.

Hao Jiang Tian, Opera Bass. Hao Jiang Tian, n.d. Web. 30 Mar. 2012. Tian's personal website, including valuable information, images, video links, and news reports.

Tian, Hao Jiang, and Lois B. Morris. *Along the Roaring River: My Wild Ride from Mao to the Met*. Hoboken, NJ: Wiley, 2008. Print. Tian's memoir, detailing his family history, musical career, and personal life.

CHANG-LIN TIEN

Chinese-born scientist and educator

A noted researcher in the field of thermal science, Tien taught at the University of California, Berkeley for

much of his career. From 1990 to 1997, he served as the campus's seventh chancellor, becoming the first

Asian American to hold the position at a major US research university.

Born: July 24, 1935; Wuhan, China
Died: October 29, 2002; Redwood City, California
Full name: Chang-Lin Tien
Areas of achievement: Science, education

EARLY LIFE

Chang-Lin Tien was born in Wuhan, China, in 1935 and relocated to Taiwan with his family at the age of fourteen following the outbreak of the Chinese Civil War. Tien received a bachelor's degree from National Taiwan University in Taipei in 1955. The following year, Tien was awarded a fellowship at the University of Louisville, in Kentucky, from which he earned a master's degree in 1957. He went on to earn another master's degree and his doctorate in mechanical engineering from Princeton University in 1959.

LIFE'S WORK

In 1959, Tien joined the faculty of the Department of Mechanical Engineering at the University of California (UC) campus in Berkeley. He was awarded Berkeley's Distinguished Teaching Award in 1962, becoming the youngest recipient of the honor in the school's history. Tien was elected to the National Academy of Engineering in 1976 and served as the chair of Berkeley's Department of Mechanical Engineering throughout the late 1970s, carrying out groundbreaking research in areas such as nuclear reactor safety and cryogenics. He also served as a consultant to NASA engineers during the development of the space shuttle program. Over the course of his research career, Tien published several hundred journal articles and made editorial contributions to several of the field's important texts, including *Molecular and Microscale Heat Transfer* (1994) and *Microscale Energy Transport* (1998).

After two years as executive vice chancellor of UC Irvine, Tien returned to Berkeley in 1990 as chancellor, becoming the first Asian American to hold that post at a major research university. His seven-year tenure as chancellor was hampered by economic difficulties in California, which resulted in the reduction of the school's operating budget by more than seventy million dollars. Tien also received a great deal of attention for his well-publicized battles with university regents over their 1995 elimination of the school's affirmative action policy, of which Tien was a leading supporter. Despite this economic and administrative upheaval,

Chang-lin Tien. (Getty Images)

Tien succeeded in raising more than one billion dollars for UC Berkeley through his "Campaign for the New Century" fundraising efforts.

SIGNIFICANCE

Through his research and publications, Tien paved the way for further studies in the field of thermal science. While his tenure as chancellor of UC Berkeley was marked by economic uncertainty, his lifelong dedication to the institution has since been memorialized with the construction of the school's Center for East Asian Studies and establishment of a graduate fellowship in the environmental sciences, both named in his honor.

John Pritchard

FURTHER READING

"Chang-Lin Tien: Chancellor, 1990–1997." *Days of Cal.* Bancroft Library, n.d. Web. 13 Mar 2012. A biography of Tien from UC Berkeley's Bancroft Library dealing primarily with his accomplishments as chancellor.

"Chang-Lin Tien, UC Berkeley Chancellor from 1990–97 and an Internationally Known Engineering

Scholar, Dies at Age 67." *Campus News*. University of California, Berkeley, 30 Oct. 2002. Web. 13 Mar. 2012. An obituary detailing Tien's life and career, with particular focus on his tenure as chancellor of UC Berkeley.

Cummins, John, et al. "In Memoriam." *University of California*. University of California, 2002. Web. 13 Mar 2012. A memorial written by colleagues of Tien focusing particularly on his research and contributions to the field of thermal science.

JENNIFER TILLY

Actor

Jennifer Tilly is an award-winning actor who has also been nominated for an Academy Award. Over the course of her career, she has performed on stage, in film, and on television. With hundreds of acting credits to her name, Tilly has a successful career in the entertainment industry.

Born: September 16, 1958; Harbor City, California
Full name: Jennifer Tilly
Birth name: Jennifer Elizabeth Chan
Areas of achievement: Film, entertainment

EARLY LIFE

Jennifer Tilly was born Jennifer Chan in Harbor City, California, to parents Harry Chan, a car salesman, and Patricia Tilly, a teacher and former stage actress. She was the second of four children, one of whom is the Academy Award nominee Meg Tilly. Tilly is of Chinese, Irish, and Native American descent. Her parents divorced when she was five years old, and her family moved to Texada Island in British Columbia, Canada. Growing up in this rural area without television, Tilly entertained her family by performing. As a child, she was introduced to ballet, theater, and the movies and grew to love the arts.

After high school, Tilly returned to the United States to attend Stephens College in Missouri, where she majored in acting. She helped put herself through college with money she won in writing competitions. While still in college, she began developing her trademark voluptuous and ditzy character style, accentuated by a distinctive, breathy voice. After college, Tilly moved to Los Angeles to pursue an acting career. She was soon followed by her sister, Meg. Tilly was aggressive in seeking out roles, working odd jobs to support herself while performing on stage. She approached each acting role with a perfectionist's frame of mind, and sought to give the best performance she could, even if it was a low-budget production. In 1983, she landed

a recurring role on a television series called *Boone*. A year later, she made her way into film, playing Mona in the movie *No Small Affair* (1984). She married director Sam Simon in 1984.

LIFE'S WORK

Throughout the 1980s, Tilly appeared regularly on numerous television shows, including *Hill Street Blues*, *Cheers*, *Remington Steele*, and *Moonlighting*. She appeared in numerous films as well, including *Remote Control* (1987) and *Johnny Be Good* (1988). In 1989, she broke out of the stereotypical sexpot role for which she had become known, for a role in the movie *The*

Jennifer Tilly. (FilmMagic)

Fabulous Baker Boys, which was nominated for several Academy Awards. In 1991, Tilly appeared in an uncredited role in the Oliver Stone film *The Doors*. That same year, her marriage with Simon ended in divorce.

In 1992, Tilly appeared in a stage production of *One Shoe Off*. Her performance as Clio earned her a Theater World Award for "Most Promising Newcomer." Tilly played Olive Neal in the Woody Allen movie *Bullets over Broadway* in 1994, which garnered her an Academy Award nomination for Best Actress in a Supporting Role. In 1995, she made *Sleuth* magazine's list of the Top 25 Sexiest Women. In 1996, Tilly starred in the movie *Bound*, opposite Gina Gershon. The crime drama features an affair between Tilly's character, Violet, and Gershon's character, Corky. The movie became a cult classic, and increased Tilly's popularity among gay and lesbian audiences. In 2006, Tilly was awarded the Golden Gate Award for media professionals who promote understanding of the LGBT (lesbian, gay, bisexual, and transgendered) community.

Tilly appeared in the film *Liar, Liar* with Jim Carrey in 1997. In 1998, she lent her voice to the character Tiffany in the horror film *Bride of Chucky*, a role that earned her a Best Actress award at the Fanta Festival and a nomination for Best Actress from the Academy of Science Fiction, Fantasy & Horror Films. Tilly reprised the role in the 2004 feature *Seed of Chucky*.

Tilly has earned numerous roles as a voice actor. She is the voice of Bonnie on the animated television series *Family Guy*, and she has also done voice-over work for animated feature films such as *Monsters, Inc.* (2001) and *Home on the Range* (2004).

In addition to being an actor, Tilly is also a skilled poker player. In 2005, she won the much-coveted World Series of Poker bracelet, after rising to the top of a six-hundred-player pool. She has written numerous articles for the poker magazine *Bluff*. Tilly splits her time between acting and professional poker, having won over $500,000 as a professional card player.

SIGNIFICANCE

In a career that has lasted over two decades, Tilly has established herself as a successful film, television, and theater actor. In 2011, she appeared in the television sitcom *Modern Family* and the television drama series *Drop Dead Diva*. In addition to accruing a large audience of fans from her work in entertainment, Tilly has become a popular figure in the world of professional poker.

James J. Heiney

FURTHER READING

"Jennifer Tilly." *New York Times*. New York Times, 2012. Web. 30 Mar. 2012. Includes information on Tilly's career as an actor.

Lee, Joann Faung Jean. *Asian American Actors: Oral Histories from Stage, Screen, and Television*. Jefferson: McFarland, 2000. Print. Discusses Asian American actors, and covers prejudices that were and still are found in the industry.

Ono, Kent A., and Vincent N. Pham. *Asian Americans and the Media*. Cambridge: Polity, 2009. Print. Discusses the representation of Asians in many media markets in the context of the times and responses by Asian America.

MEG TILLY

Actor and writer

Actor Meg Tilly won a Golden Globe and was nominated for an Academy Award for Best Supporting Actress in 1985 for her work in the film Agnes of God. *The younger sister of actor Jennifer Tilly, Meg left films in 1994 to raise her family and begin a second career as a writer of books for children and young adults.*

Born: February 14, 1960; Long Beach, California
Full name: Margaret Tilly
Birth name: Margaret Elizabeth Chan
Areas of achievement: Acting, film, literature

EARLY LIFE

Meg Tilly was born on February 14, 1960, in Long Beach, California, the third of four children. Her father, Harry, was a Chinese American car salesman, and her mother, Patricia, was a schoolteacher. Tilly's parents divorced when she was three. Patricia moved her children to Texada Island, British Columbia, to live with their grandmother; the family later moved to Victoria. Tilly's family was poor and sometimes lived on wild game, including squirrels and snakes.

After her mother remarried, Tilly was abused by her stepfather, and later by her mother's boyfriends.

Tilly, her older sister Jennifer, and her younger sister Becky were known in school as the Three Musketeers. When Tilly went public with her memories of abuse as an adult, Jennifer refused to discuss the matter, but Becky corroborated her accounts.

Tilly began taking dancing lessons at the age of twelve. She won a scholarship to a New York ballet school and became associated with the Connecticut Ballet Company and, later, the Throne Dance Theater. A back injury ended Tilly's career as a dancer, but not before she earned a small part as an auditioning dancer in the film *Fame* (1980).

Over the next five years, Tilly, who had previously acted in community theater productions in Canada, appeared in six more films, one television movie, and an episode of the television series *Hill Street Blues*. One of those appearances was as the character Chloe in director Lawrence Kasdan's film *The Big Chill* (1983). In an ensemble cast that included Glenn Close, Kevin Kline, and William Hurt, Tilly held her own as the young, free-spirited girlfriend of Alex, the man whose suicide brings his friends together for the first time since college.

Meg Tilly. (FilmMagic)

LIFE'S WORK

Tilly's performance in the film *Agnes of God* (1985) won her an Oscar nomination for Best Supporting Actress, as well as a Golden Globe. Still only twenty-five, she found herself working alongside stars such as Jane Fonda and Anne Bancroft. Over the next ten years, Tilly appeared in numerous films and television movies, including *Off Beat* (1986), *Masquerade* (1988), *Leaving Normal* (1992), and *Body Snatchers* (1993). Although she was originally cast as Mozart's wife in *Amadeus* (1984), she tore a ligament in her leg while playing soccer with her children and could not play the part.

Tilly has a daughter and a son by her first husband, producer Tim Zinnemann, son of famed film director Fred Zinnemann. When her first marriage ended in divorce in 1989, Tilly began a five-year relationship with actor Colin Firth, whom she had met while filming director Milos Forman's *Valmont* (1989) and with whom she had another son. In 1990, Tilly starred in the CBS television movie *In the Best Interests of the Child*, which concerned child abuse; during this time, she began writing a book based on her own childhood.

In 1994, Tilly appeared in the romantic comedy *Sleep with Me* and wrote an episode of the NBC television series *Winnetka Road*. Her first book, *Singing Songs*, was also published in that year. The semiautobiographical book tells the story of Anna, one of four siblings whose mother marries a man with three children of his own. The stepfather abuses all seven of the children. In the *New York Times Book Review*, Donna Rifkind described the family as "a supremely dysfunctional version of the Brady Bunch" and called Tilly's work "a book of considerable quality." Tilly once said that other than her children, *Singing Songs* was the best work she had ever done.

In 1995, Tilly married film producer John Calley. The couple divorced in 2002, and Tilly married writer Don Calame the same year. While raising her three children, she stepped away from her work as an actor to focus solely on her writing, producing several books for children and young adults. Tilly's second book, *Gemma* (2006), tells the story of a twelve-year-old girl, her alcoholic mother, and the mother's abusive boyfriend; her third, *Porcupine* (2007), concerns a twelve-year-old girl whose father is killed in the war in Afghanistan. Tilly's fourth book, *First Time*, published in 2008, is about a high-school girl who fends off advances from her mother's lecherous boyfriend.

In 2010, Tilly returned to acting with a role in the Syfy television series *Caprica*. She then went on to play a lead role in the Canadian series *Bomb Girls*, which debuted in January 2012.

SIGNIFICANCE

As a young woman, Tilly worked hard to leverage her talents as a dancer and an actor to escape an abusive home. She met with great success during her career as an actor, starring in several films. Still dealing with unresolved issues from her past and wanting to spend more time raising her children, Tilly left a lucrative profession while she was still in high demand to pursue work as a writer. In this capacity, she wrote books aimed at helping children who live in situations similar to those in which she was raised, offering them strategies and hope

Randy L. Abbott

FURTHER READING

Chiu, Alexis. "Scars of Her Youth." *People* 66.11 (2006): 101–2. Print. Discusses Tilly's home life as a child growing up amid poverty and abuse.

Rifkind, Donna. "The Brady Bunch from Hell." *New York Times Book Review* 5 June 1994: 37. Print. A review of Tilly's first book, *Singing Songs*.

Tilly, Meg. *Singing Songs*. New York: Dutton, 1994. Print. Tilly's first book, a story of abuse told from the perspective of a five-year-old.

SAMUEL C. C. TING

Scientist

Physicist Samuel C. C. Ting shared the Nobel Prize with fellow researcher Burton Richter for the discovery of a new and unpredicted particle, the J/psi particle. The discovery not only opened a new field of particles for discovery and analysis but also necessitated the refinement of nuclear quark theories.

Born: January 27, 1936; Ann Arbor, Michigan
Full name: Samuel Chao Chung Ting
Also known as: Dīng Zhàozhōng; Tin Chao-chung
Areas of achievement: Science and technology

EARLY LIFE

Samuel Chao Chung Ting became a United States citizen by accident. His parents, graduate students at the University of Michigan, were going back to China when Ting was born prematurely. The family returned to China two months after Ting's birth. His father, Kuan Hai Ting, was an engineer, and his mother, Tsun-Ying Wang, was a psychologist. He has a younger brother, John, and a younger sister, Susan.

When Japan invaded China the family lived like refugees, moving often. Ting does not remember this as a time of lacking food or shelter, but his education was nontraditional. In 1948, the family moved to Taiwan, and Ting began a traditional education at the prestigious Provincial Chien Kuo High School (now Municipal Taipei Chien-Kuo Senior High School). His parents were professors of engineering and psychology at the National Taiwan University in Taipei, Taiwan. As his mother worked, Ting was cared for by his maternal grandmother, who had lost her husband many years earlier and raised Tsun-Ying as a single mother. Ting gives much of the credit for his success to his grandmother's strength of character. He attended National Cheng Kung University in Tainan City for one year, and in 1956 he transferred to the University of Michigan, where he earned bachelor degrees in mathematics and physics. He earned a PhD in physics three years later.

Ting married Kay Kuhne in 1960 and had two daughters, Jeanne Ting Chowning, the director of education at the Northwest Association for Biomedical Research, and Amy Ting, an artist. Ting and Kuhne later divorced, and in 1985 Ting married Dr. Susan Carol Marks. Their son, Christopher, attended law school at the University of Michigan.

LIFE'S WORK

Ting was awarded a Ford Foundation Fellowship to work at the European Organization for Nuclear Research (CERN), near Geneva, Switzerland. In the spring of 1965, Ting moved to New York's Columbia University to teach. In 1966, he read about an experiment at the Cambridge Electron Accelerator that appeared to violate quantum electrodynamics. He took leave from Columbia to go to Hamburg, Germany, to work with Deutsches Elektronen-Synchrotron (DESY), repeating the Cambridge electron-positron pair production experiment. Although the original experiment appeared to be inconsistent with nuclear theory, Ting's experiment confirmed

Samuel C. C. Ting. (© Gene Blevins/LA DailyNews/Corbis)

the theory's prediction. Since that time, he has searched for new particles that decay to electron or muon pairs.

He became a professor of physics at the Massachusetts Institute of Technology (MIT) in Cambridge, Massachusetts, in 1969. In 1971, he returned with his research group to the Brookhaven National Laboratory in Upton, New York, in order to look for new particles of higher mass than the electron. In 1974, an experiment showed evidence of a new particle of heavy mass; Ting named this the J particle, and the discovery opened up a whole field of new particles. Ting discussed his findings with Burton Richter at Stanford University and discovered that Richter's group had found the same particle, calling it the Ψ (psi) particle. The two published papers simultaneously and proposed that the particle be referred to as a J/Ψ (J/psi) meson. In 1976, Ting and Richter shared the Nobel Prize for their pioneer work discovering new types of heavy elementary particles. Their experiments provided evidence for a fourth type of quark called a charm.

Ting was appointed the first Thomas Dudley Cabot Institute Professor of Physics at MIT in 1977. He lives

with his family in Switzerland so that he can work with CERN, but he travels frequently to MIT. As of 2011, Ting was searching for a particle called the Higgs boson, the discovery of which could answer the question of how elementary particles have mass. He is the principal investigator for the Alpha Magnetic Spectrometer, a cosmic ray detector that was successfully installed on the International Space Station in May 2011. It is hoped that the spectrometer will be able to detect dark matter. This project was slated for a shuttle flight, then canceled in the aftermath of the space shuttle *Columbia* disaster in 2003. Ting had to fight to get the project rescheduled for 2011. The project carries a budget of $1.5 billion and involves five hundred scientists in fifty-six institutions and sixteen countries.

Significance

Samuel C. C. Ting achieved wide prominence for discovering the J/psi particle, a very massive meson thought to be composed of a charmed quark and its antiquark. Ting has also had many other scientific accomplishments, including advancing the understanding of dark matter, validating quantum electrodynamics, establishing that electrons, muons, and tau mesons are point masses (that is, masses with no volume), and validating the Standard Electroweak Model. With the launch of the Space Shuttle *Endeavor* in 2011, the Alpha Magnetic Spectrometer project began an unprecedented study of charged cosmic rays.

C. Alton Hassell

Further Reading

Aguilar, M., et al. *The Alpha Magnetic Spectrometer (AMS) on the International Space Station*. Amsterdam: Elsevier, 2002. Print. Provides a discussion of the test results of the AMS on the shuttle test flight.

Kim, Hyung-chan. *Distinguished Asian Americans: A Biographical Dictionary*. Westport: Greenwood, 1999. Print. Offers a nice but short review of Ting's lifework.

Lundqvist, Stig, ed. *Physics, 1971–1980*. Singapore: World Scientific, 1992. Print. Offers biographies and lectures of the Nobel Prize winners of the 1970s in physics.

The Discovery of the J/psi Subatomic Particle

In order to determine how many heavy photons existed and what their properties were, Samuel Ting began an experiment on the thirty giga-electron-volt (GeV) proton accelerator at Brookhaven National Laboratory in Upton, New York. In the summer of 1974, Ting's team saw an unexpected narrow peak in electron-positron pair production at a mass of 3.1 GeV. The group concluded that they had observed a massive new particle with a relatively long lifetime. They named it the J particle.

Meanwhile, at the Stanford Linear Accelerator Center (SLAC), in Menlo Park, California, Burton Richter's team was looking into the unexplained production of hadrons at energies where they should be very rare. They discovered that at slightly more than 3.1 GeV, the hadron production increased by a factor of seventy. With a different experimental technique and no knowledge of Ting's results, Richter's team reached the same conclusion. They named the new particle psi.

The Richter group announced their findings at SLAC's Program Advisory Committee (PAC) on November 11, 1974. Ting, a member of PAC, attended the meeting. It was there that he and Richter learned of each other's discoveries. The hadron class of subatomic particles was previously thought to be composed of three kinds of quarks: the up, down, and strange quarks. The J/psi particle's relatively long life called for the addition of a fourth kind of quark, the charm quark. This discovery changed the way physicists understand the structure of matter.

Morey, Janet, and Wendy Dunn. *Famous Asian Americans*. New York: Cobblehill, 1992. Print. Features a nice biography of Ting; written for young audiences.

Veltman, Martinus. *Facts and Mysteries in Elementary Particle Physics*. River Edge: World Scientific. 2003. Print. Includes discussions of Higgs, dark matter, and the particles that Ting has studied.

ALEX TIZON

Philippine-born journalist

A notable journalist in the United States, Tomas Alex Tizon saw his national reputation boosted in 1997 when, with two colleagues, he won the Pulitzer Prize for investigative work at the Seattle Times. *The winning series uncovered fraud in the federal housing program for American Indians, as well as the deplorable state of housing on reservations. Tizon is one of only three Filipino Americans to have won a Pulitzer Prize, and the first to win the prize for investigative reporting.*

Born: October 30, 1959; Manila, Philippines
Full name: Tomas Alex Tizon (TAE-sohn)
Area of achievement: Journalism

EARLY LIFE

Born in 1959 in Manila, the Philippines, Tomas Alex Tizon immigrated to the United States with his family at the age of four. His father, Francisco Tizon Jr., was a commercial attaché for the Philippine consulate. Leticia Asuncion Tizon, his mother, was a doctor at the Swedish Medical Center in Seattle, Washington. Tizon earned his undergraduate degree in political science at the University of Oregon, where in 2000 he won the Outstanding Young Alumnus Award. Tizon also holds a master's degree in communications from Stanford University. Tizon lived for more than twenty years in Seattle, where he met his wife Melissa, a writer and editor, and raised two children, Dylan and Maya.

LIFE'S WORK

Working at the *Seattle Times* for over fifteen years, Tizon wrote about crime, law enforcement, immigration issues, and ethnic groups. In the prizewinning series on American Indian reservation housing (published in the *Seattle Times* in 1996), Eric Nalder, Deborah Nelson, and Tizon provided a glimpse into why American Indians had grown weary of the federally sponsored program. Many were living in shacks and counting themselves lucky not to spend their nights in cars or under highway overpasses. Tizon and his colleagues described the home of Muckleshoot Thelma Moses, a mother of nine and a grandmother of twenty-five. It was ten feet by twelve feet, with no running water, electricity, or toilet. She had lived on the Muckleshoot Reservation for almost fifty-six years, ten of those years spent on a waiting list with one hundred other Muckleshoots for a government-subsidized house. During the mid-1990s, 40 percent of American Indians nationwide were living in overcrowded conditions or in houses with serious deficiencies. The piece won Tizon and his colleagues a Pulitzer Prize for journalism in 1997.

Tizon has written about the terrorist attacks of September 11, 2001, Hurricane Katrina, the war in Iraq, and two presidential campaigns. He specializes in personal profiles, which have ranged from murderers to heads of state, and he has reported from all regions of the United States, China, Singapore, the Arctic, Canada, and his homeland, the Philippines.

After September 11, Tizon began his "Crossing America" series. The project began with a suggestion from *Times* reporter Ralph Thomas that someone drive from Seattle to New York City, gathering stories on what ordinary Americans were thinking. Fourteen stories with photos were published over twenty-one days. Two months after they completed their cross-country journey to New York City, Tizon and photographer Alan Berner set out once again for "postcards" from Hawaii, New England, and the Pacific Northwest.

Leaving the *Seattle Times* in 2003, Tizon become a national correspondent for the *Los Angeles Times*. He has contributed to *Newsweek* magazine and CBS News's *60 Minutes*. Tizon has taught as a visiting professor at the University of Oregon and lectured at schools such as Harvard University, University of California at Berkeley, and Stanford University. He has written for *Sierra* and other magazines, his work in the former magazine describing the damage to fishing that was wrought by mountaintop coal mining in Kentucky and other Appalachian states.

In 1998 Tizon was awarded a Jefferson Fellowship from the East-West Center in Hawaii for his work in Japan, the Philippines, China, and Indonesia. In 2002, having received an Asia Pacific Journalism Fellowship, he worked in Singapore and Taiwan. Tizon also received a Knight International Press Fellowship, which he used for work in Manila. *Filipinas Magazine* named him among the one hundred most noteworthy Filipino Americans of the twentieth century. Additionally, Tizon has won more than a dozen national awards in journalism.

As an author, Tizon has expanded his focus to include book-length projects. As of 2011, he was due to publish a book about race and manhood with Houghton

Alex Tizon. (University of Oregon)

Mifflin Harcourt entitled *Big Little Man: The Asian Male at the Dawn of the Asian Century*. His lectures at Harvard's Nieman Conference on Narrative Journalism have been published in the collection *Telling True Stories* (2008). He has also lectured several times at the Poynter Institute, a journalism school in St. Petersburg, Florida, where he was a visiting faculty member from 1997 to 2007.

SIGNIFICANCE

In winning the Pulitzer Prize for journalism, Alex Tizon followed in the footsteps of Carlos P. Romulo, a Filipino American who won the Pulitzer Prize for journalism in 1941. He has brought readers into a variety of regions and subcultures, ranging from urban gangs in Seattle to American Indian communities. His work led to his creating a system with which the media can monitor the governmental alleviation of poverty in poor areas.

Bruce E. Johansen

FURTHER READING

Kramer, Mark, and Wendy Call, eds. *Telling True Stories: A Nonfiction Writers' Guide from the Nieman Foundation at Harvard University*. New York:

Plume, 2008. Print. Tizon joins other Nieman fellows with advice on the art and craft of writing.

Scanlan, Chip. "The Power of Serendipity: Alex Tizon's Journey." *Poynter*. Poynter Institute, 2 Mar. 2011. Web. 7 Mar. 2012. Tizon's travels across the country gathering stories after the September 11, 2001, terrorist attacks.

Tizon, Alex. *Big Little Man: The Asian Male at the Dawn of the Asian Century*. Boston: Houghton, 2012. Print. Examines changes in the male role across Asia as the region achieves economic prominence.

---. "Dept. of Shameless Self-Promotion."*Alex Tizon*. Alex Tizon, n.d. Web. 20 Mar. 2011. Tizon's own brief biography.

Iva Toguri D'Aquino

Radio broadcaster

Iva Toguri D'Aquino was an ordinary woman devoted to the United States when circumstances during World War II trapped her in Japan. She was coerced into becoming a radio broadcaster for the Japanese, which led to a terrible postwar debacle in which she was convicted of treason and served a six-year prison term in the United States.

Born: July 4, 1916; Los Angeles, California
Died: September 26, 2006; Chicago, Illinois
Full name: Iva Ikuko Toguri D'Aquino (EE-kew-koh toh-GEW-ree dah-KEE-noh)
Birth name: Iva Ikuko Toguri
Also known as: Orphan Annie; Tokyo Rose
Areas of achievement: Radio and television

Early Life

Iva Ikuko Toguri was born in the United States to Japanese immigrants Jun Toguri and Fumi Imuro, who sought to fully assimilate themselves into American society even though American laws prevented them from becoming citizens. They avoided Japanese communities as they moved around California, though Toguri's father's business sold imported Japanese goods. Toguri and her younger sisters were American citizens by birth. They learned English rather than Japanese, grew up in an American lifestyle, and ate typical American food. Toguri attended the University of California Los Angeles, earning generally good grades and a degree in zoology; she hoped to study medicine in the future.

In the summer of 1941, Toguri's maternal aunt in Japan became ill. Although Toguri had no passport and did not speak Japanese, the family sent her to visit her relative. She brought many gifts, as well as trunks of American foodstuffs to reduce her need for unfamiliar Japanese food. (Later, her visit and the large amount of luggage would be used against her during her court case.) When Japan attacked the United States in December of 1941, Toguri found herself increasingly under pressure as an enemy alien. She often had no ration card and was frequently malnourished, suffering bouts of scurvy and beriberi. Toguri faced extreme pressure to become a Japanese citizen but always refused. She had no contact with her family, who were interned with other Japanese Americans until late 1943, her mother dying while interned in 1942. As her presence created difficulties for her relatives, Toguri left them and got clerical

Iva "Tokyo Rose" Toguri D'Aquino. (Getty Images)

The Trial of "Tokyo Rose"

On July 5, 1949, Iva Toguri D'Aquino, known as "Tokyo Rose," went on trial for treason against the United States. She was accused of broadcasting demoralizing propaganda to US troops during World War II. The trial's two lead prosecutors had earlier advised Attorney General Tom Clark of the lack of a case against Toguri, but he still had them move forward with the trial. FBI agents interviewed hundreds of witnesses, occasionally manufacturing evidence that did not exist. The FBI also harassed and intimidated witnesses on the side of the defense. Particularly important to the prosecution were Kenkichi Oki and George Mitsushio, who had worked with Toguri on Radio Tokyo (NHK) and provided the key proof needed. Both later admitted that their testimony was false.

The grand jury indicted Toguri on eight counts of treason. Prosecutors supplied testimony from men who claimed to have heard Tokyo Rose broadcasts. They provided selected transcripts and tapes of Toguri's work without informing anyone that they had full sets of both. The prosecutors called additional colleagues of Toguri's as witnesses, most of whom were Japanese Americans vulnerable to legal charges themselves. Japanese officer Shigetsugu Tsuneishi testified that fourteen women had announced for NHK, and that thirteen other Japanese radio stations had at some point used female broadcasters. Toguri's Allied supervisors testified to her trustworthiness and loyalty. Nevertheless, Judge Michael Roche persuaded the jury to convict Toguri on a single count. She was issued a sentence of ten years.

work in 1942, first translating American broadcasts at the Domei News Agency and then at NHK (commonly called Radio Tokyo) in 1943.

Japan attempted to demoralize Allied forces using short-wave radio broadcasts. Some of their broadcasters were women, and early on Allied forces came to refer to these broadcasters broadly as Tokyo Rose. In late 1942, Japanese forces began coercing captured Allied radio professionals to help with their broadcasts. One such group, led by Australian Major Charles Cousens and American Captain Wallace Ince, started a radio show called *Zero Hour*, which secretly sought to sabotage the Japanese goal. In November 1943, Cousens hired Toguri as an announcer. She used her improved situation to supply much-needed fresh vegetables to prisoners of war at the NHK camp.

At the Domei News Agency, Toguri met Felipe D'Aquino, a Portuguese national of Japanese and Portuguese descent; they married in 1945.

Life's Work

Toguri D'Aquino introduced her broadcasts as Orphan Annie, her on-air persona, a friendly enemy of American sailors and soldiers. Over time, Toguri D'Aquino recorded several hundred broadcasts and became popular among listeners. The propaganda content of her broadcasts would become the subject of some debate, as the effect on Army troops appeared to be positive rather than negative. General Robert Eichelberger of the US Army, for instance, arranged for an airdrop of additional records, and near the end of the war the Navy issued a mock citation honoring Tokyo Rose for helping to improve the morale of listeners. Toguri D'Aquino played popular music of the day and spoke in American slang. For several months Cousens wrote her scripts, but illness forced him to stop writing, leaving Toguri D'Aquino and others to write new material (she reported herself ill with increasing frequency as well).

In 1945, and with the end of the war, the mysterious Tokyo Rose was a popular target for interviews, and NHK workers pointed reporters to Toguri D'Aquino. Two reporters offered her two thousand dollars for an exclusive interview in which she falsely identified herself as the only Tokyo Rose. Toguri D'Aquino never received the money, and in other interviews she correctly identified herself as one of many women broadcasters. She was arrested by the US Army and held for over a year while her case was considered. Deciding that there was no case against her, the Federal Bureau of Investigation and army intelligence released Toguri D'Aquino but refused to let her return to the United States. Her efforts to return, however, came to the attention of the American Legion and radio broadcaster Walter Winchell, who denounced her and demanded that she be tried for treason.

In the election year of 1948, Attorney General Tom Clark placed political expediency over justice and ordered her trial. She was sent to San Francisco, where anti-Japanese prejudice was strong, rather than the relatively multiracial region of Hawaii, since laws required that she be tried in the region she reached first. After another year spent in jail Toguri D'Aquino was tried, and on October 6, 1949, she was convicted of treason on a single count. She was sentenced to ten years in prison and required to pay a fine of $10,000.

After the trial, Toguri D'Aquino was sent to a federal women's prison in Alderson, West Virginia, where she worked in the infirmary and became a model prisoner. Released in 1956, she moved to Chicago to work in her family's business. For a time, she was threatened with deportation, but eventually the government allowed her to stay, although not as a citizen. In 1976, after *Chicago Tribune* reporter Ron Yates investigated the case and exposed the massive perjury that had secured her conviction, an effort began to pardon Toguri D'Aquino. The effort paid off in 1977, when President Gerald Ford, at the end of his term, finally granted her a pardon and thereby restored her citizenship. She continued with the family business, taking over its management after her father died. She and her husband Felipe D'Aquino, who had been deported from the United States in 1948, were never able to meet again; they divorced in 1980.

SIGNIFICANCE

Iva Toguri D'Aquino, an American citizen, was forced to participate in Japanese propaganda broadcasts during World War II, and was charged with treason in a case that unfairly dubbed her as the Japanese broadcaster "Tokyo Rose," a popular moniker among Allied forces. Over the years, and with the help of President Gerald Ford's pardon, Toguri D'Aquino's struggle has become representative of the injustices perpetrated against Asian Americans in the United States during World War II. On January 15, 2006—less than a year before her death—the World War II Veterans Committee honored Toguri D'Aquino's patriotism and courage with the Edward J. Herlihy Citizenship Award.

Timothy Lane

FURTHER READING

Duus, Masayo. *Tokyo Rose: Orphan of the Pacific.* Tokyo: Kodansha, 1979. Print. A careful study of Toguri D'Aquino's life, including the story of the *Zero Hour* Radio Tokyo broadcasts and her postwar ordeal; based primarily on interviews.

Howe, Russell Warren. *The Hunt for "Tokyo Rose."* Lanham: Madison, 1990. A detailed, factual, but sometimes excessively polemical study of Toguri's life, the *Zero Hour* broadcasts, and her postwar ordeal, taking advantage of government documents viewed through the Freedom of Information Act.

WENDY TOKUDA

Journalist, author, and community service leader

Journalist Wendy Tokuda has worked as a television news anchor in the Los Angeles area and the San Francisco Bay Area for over thirty years. In addition to working as a journalist, she cofounded the nonprofit organization Students Rising Above to assist underprivileged students in attending college. She has also written several children's books.

Born: 1950; Seattle, Washington
Full name: Wendy Tokuda
Areas of achievement: Journalism, literature, philanthropy

EARLY LIFE

Wendy Tokuda was born in 1950 in Seattle, Washington, to Japanese American parents. Growing up in Seattle, she earned high grades in school and graduated at the top of her high-school class. She briefly attended Whitman College before transferring to the University of Washington. After graduating with a bachelor's degree in political science, Tokuda traveled to Japan, where she taught English, an experience that gave her a broader perspective on her own cultural heritage and identity as a Japanese American.

After returning to the United States, Tokuda began working as a staff member at a television station in Seattle, and very soon started anchoring the news at the local station. She worked in Seattle as a news anchor until 1978, when she moved to San Francisco to coanchor the local news at KPIX in the Bay Area. Tokuda's early work as a news anchor took place during a time when women were just beginning to break into television journalism. Her success continued to grow in the Bay Area news market, due in part to her decision to avoid the lighter stories often assigned to female anchors. As a news reporter, she focused on covering important issues and significant news events.

Tokuda reported the local evening news in San Francisco until 1992, when she relocated to Los Angeles to continue her career in the larger Southern

Wendy Tokuda.

California market. From 1992 to 1996, she coanchored the evening news on KNBC Los Angeles. Tokuda's work as a journalist made important inroads for Asian American women in television news. After a successful and well-received career in Los Angeles, she returned to the Bay Area in 1997, where she coanchored the local news at KRON in San Francisco. Tokuda also began reporting on local underprivileged youth in the news series "Students Rising Above," an award-winning segment about the challenges and obstacles facing students from disadvantaged homes in the Bay Area who desired to attend and graduate from college. In 1998, Tokuda cofounded the Students Rising Above program, a nonprofit organization in the San Francisco area dedicated to providing support to underprivileged students.

LIFE'S WORK

Tokuda is an award-winning television news anchor and has established herself as one of California's best-known journalists. Throughout her career, she has maintained a commitment to community service. Students Rising Above continues to provide support services to disadvantaged students in California, helping them enroll in colleges. Although the program started small, it now offers a range of services and support systems

to at-risk students entering college for the first time. In particular, the program offers financial support, medical and dental care, and counseling and mentoring, all with the goal of improving students' academic performance and success rates in graduating from college. The Students Rising Above program has been very successful, with a 90 percent graduation rate for its student candidates; many students who otherwise would never have had the chance to attend college have become the first in their families to earn a college degree.

In addition to working as a journalist, Tokuda has written and cowritten several children's books, including *Shiro in Love* (1989), *Humphrey the Lost Whale* (1986), and *Samson the Hot Tub Bear* (1998). The latter two books are drawn from local news stories in the Bay Area; *Humphrey the Lost Whale* is based on the true story of a whale that wandered into San Francisco Bay and was guided back out to sea by animal rescue officials, while *Samson the Hot Tub Bear* was inspired by a news report about a bear who appeared in several suburban backyards, availing himself of swimming pools, hot tubs, and leftover food. Tokuda is also an avid gardener, a proponent of recycling, and a volunteer in local conservation projects in the Bay Area—all pursuits that reflect her commitment to preserving the environment.

SIGNIFICANCE

Tokuda has won numerous awards for her journalism as well as for her community service, including a Peabody Award for her work as a television news anchor and a National Emmy Award for Public Service for her reporting on and support for disadvantaged students. Tokuda has said that her Japanese American family roots have provided her with sensitivity to and awareness of the challenges that young people from diverse backgrounds face growing up in the United States. Tokuda's own family experienced extreme hardship, as her grandparents and parents were sent to live in a Japanese American internment camp during World War II, and Tokuda credits her ability to see social issues from an informed and insightful perspective to her family's loving support and her cultural heritage. She carries on these values in both her personal life and her professional career, demonstrating compassion for the many young people facing obstacles and challenges today.

William Teipe

FURTHER READING

Kilduff, Paul. "At Home with Wendy Tokuda." *SF Gate.* Hearst, 11 Nov. 2006. Web. 30 Mar. 2012. Reviews the environmentally conscious changes Tokuda has made to her Oakland home.

Peterson, Gary. "Rising on the Wings of Education." *Inside Bay Area*. MediaNews Group, 17 Feb. 2012. Web. 30 Mar. 2012. Discusses the work of the Students Rising Above organization and their successes.

"Wendy Tokuda." *CBS San Francisco*. CBS, n.d. Web. 30 Mar. 2012. A brief biography of Tokuda and summary of her career.

LAUREN TOM

Actor

With an award-winning career that spans over three decades and one hundred and fifty film, stage, and television productions, Lauren Tom is a highly successful Chinese American actor. From the stage she moved to bit parts on television, and then to more substantial film roles, including in the prominent 1993 film The Joy Luck Club. *For more than a decade, she voiced two Laotian characters on the animated television comedy series* King of the Hill.

Born: August 4, 1959; Chicago, Illinois
Full name: Lauren Judith Tom
Areas of achievement: Film, television, theater

EARLY LIFE

Lauren Tom was born on August 4, 1959, in Highland Park, Illinois, to Nancy and Chan Tom. Her grandparents immigrated to the United States from Hoping, China, and settled in Chicago's Chinatown. Her father owned five businesses that supplied Chinese restaurants with noodles, bean sprouts, take-out containers, tripe, and egg rolls. She and her older brother, Chip, grew up in a predominantly Jewish neighborhood. Although she did not learn to speak Chinese, Tom maintained ties to her ethnic heritage by visiting her grandparents and participating in cultural events such as Chinese New Year. A self-described shy teenager, Tom pursued her love of dance at the Hubbard Street Dance Company in Chicago.

Tom graduated early from Highland Park High School and attended Northwestern University for one semester. At seventeen, she was cast as Connie Wong in the touring production of *A Chorus Line* and moved to New York City to join the Broadway production. Tragedy struck when Tom's father suffered a fatal heart attack on his way to New York City to watch Tom on her opening night on Broadway. She immediately returned home to be with her family and later rejoined the production in New York City.

Encouraged by friends and cast members from *A Chorus Line* to further pursue an acting career, Tom gradually transitioned from dance to acting and began booking roles in plays and Broadway productions such as *Doonesbury* (1983) and *Hurlyburly* (1984). She also graduated from New York University with a B.A. in liberal arts.

Tom's early television work included guest roles on *The Facts of Life*, *The Equalizer*, and *The Cosby Show*. In 1990, Tom was cast as a dim sum waitress in the comedy film *Cadillac Man*, which led to a guest spot on *The Tonight Show* with Johnny Carson. Her positive experience and newfound recognition from the show convinced Tom to move to Los Angeles, where she landed

Lauren Tom. (Getty Images)

the role of Lena St. Clair in the film *The Joy Luck Club* (1993). Based on the best-selling novel by Amy Tan, the groundbreaking film raised the profiles of many Asian American actors in Hollywood, including Tom's. Subsequently, Tom was cast as Ross's girlfriend on the hit television show *Friends*. Her role as Julie was written especially for Tom by a writer/producer who was impressed with her work.

LIFE'S WORK

Tom's multifaceted career spans more than three decades. She has starred in over one hundred and fifty film, television, and theater productions. After *A Chorus Line*, Tom pursued acting in off-Broadway productions in New York City. She has worked with theatrical directors and playwrights such as David Henry Hwang, Joanne Akalaitis, and Peter Sellars. In 1988, she won an Obie Award for her off-Broadway performance in *American Notes*. In the early 1990s, she returned to Chicago to star in *'Tis Pity She's a Whore* and also won two Drama-Logue Awards for *25 Psychics*, her one-woman show, which premiered at HBO's US Comedy Arts Festival in Aspen, Colorado.

Her feature film work in the 1980s included *Wall Street* (1987) and *See No Evil, Hear No Evil* (1982). In 1992, she starred as Jack Nicholson's wife in *Man Trouble*. The following year, she was cast in *The Joy Luck Club* and in *Mr. Jones*. She played a nanny in the 1994 film *When a Man Loves a Woman*.

Besides *Friends*, Tom's television work in the 1990s included shows such as *Chicago Hope*, *The Nanny*, *Quantum Leap*, *thirtysomething*, *Homicide: Life on the Street*, and *Grace Under Fire*.

In 2000, Tom was cast as Ginger Chin in the television series *DAG* opposite Delta Burke. Subsequently, she played Nora Chin in *The Division* for six episodes. In 2006, she starred as mail-order bride Mai Washington in the one-hour television drama *Men in Trees*, starring Anne Heche. She also appeared in hit series such as *Grey's Anatomy*, *The Closer*, *Hawthorne*, and *Without a Trace*.

Tom is also a prolific voiceover artist for animated series and videogames. In 1997, she joined the cast of the long-running series *King of the Hill*, playing the Laotian mother and daughter characters of Minh and Connie Souphanousinphone for thirteen seasons. She is also the voice of Amy Wong on *Futurama*, an animated series that aired on Fox Television and was revived by Comedy Central after successful DVD sales. Voiceover acting allowed Tom to pursue non-Asian roles, and from 2004 to 2006, she played Susan Vandom, a mother on the animated series *W.I.T.C.H.* She voiced the male villain, Gizmo, on *Teen Titans*, as well as Jinx, an East Indian character.

As a writer, Tom has published essays in *Brain, Child: The Magazine for Thinking Mothers*, *The Fresh Yarn*, and *East Meets Woman*.

In 1999, Tom married actor Curt Kaplan. They have two sons and live in Los Angeles, California.

SIGNIFICANCE

Her work in television and film has made Tom's face recognizable to many. Her accomplishments in voiceover work have ensured that the characters she voices are just as familiar. Tom's work on stage, whether as part of a Broadway production or performing in a one-woman show, is impressive, and she is known for her commitment and hard work, regardless of the project or entertainment genre she is involved with. With her success in film, television, theater, and voiceover work, the multitalented Lauren Tom is regarded as one of the most prolific and versatile Asian American actors of her generation.

Jenny Cho

FURTHER READING

Amatangelo, Amy. "TV Insider: Lauren Tom." *Boston Herald*. 9 Mar. 2008: 41. Print. Discusses the television program *Mail-Order Bride*.

Breslauer, Jan. "A Bit of Joy and Luck." *Los Angeles Times* 24 Nov. 1996: 4. Print. Profiles Tom's stage career through 1996.

Pryor, Tim. "China Girl." *Detour Magazine* October 1993: 21–23. Print. Discusses Tom's early childhood in Chicago and her early work on Broadway and in films.

Trachtenberg, Robert. "House of the Spirits." *InStyle* May 2001: 381–86. Print. Presents a personal profile of Tom and highlights the interior design of her home.

TAMLYN TOMITA

Actor

Tamlyn Tomita is best known for her breakout role as Kumiko in the film The Karate Kid, Part II. *She also appeared in the 1993 film* The Joy Luck Club. *Throughout her career, Tomita has been active in supporting organizations that advocate for Asian American political empowerment.*

Born: January 27, 1966; Okinawa, Japan
Full name: Tamlyn Naomi Tomita
Areas of achievement: Film, television, activism

EARLY LIFE

Tamlyn Naomi Tomita was born as an American citizen on a US Army base in Okinawa, Japan on January 27, 1966. She is the daughter of Shiro and Asako Tomita. Her father, a second-generation Japanese American soldier, was raised in Los Angeles. He met Tomita's mother, an Okinawan Filipina, while stationed in Okinawa, where she worked as a USO singer. When Tomita was six months old her family moved to Los Angeles. She and her two younger brothers grew up in Pacoima, in California's San Fernando Valley, among a farming

Tamlyn Tomita. (Getty Images)

community of Japanese American families. Tomita's father joined the Los Angeles Police Department, rising to the rank of sergeant. Tomita graduated from Granada Hills High School with aspirations to become a nurse, and enrolled at the University of California Los Angeles (UCLA). However, Tomita instead became a British history major, and thought of becoming a teacher. As a student at UCLA, she took an Asian American film class taught by filmmaker Robert Nakamura. As a student in the class, Tomika attended a performance by the renowned Asian American theater company the East West Players.

In 1984, Tomita represented her San Fernando Valley community in the annual Los Angeles Nisei Week Queen Pageant. After winning the pageant, she was noticed by Helen Funai, a local community singer and entertainer. In 1985, Tomita won the Miss Nikkei International pageant in Brazil.

LIFE'S WORK

During her junior year at UCLA, Tomita was asked by Funai to audition for the film *The Karate Kid, Part II* (1986). The audition changed Tomita's life. Despite the fact that her only previous acting experience consisted of performing for her church's Easter plays, Tomita won the role of Kumiko. She spent the summer of 1985 filming *The Karate Kid, Part II* in Hawaii and on studio sound stages in Burbank, California. Under pressure from Tomita's father, Helen Funai became her manager for the film. She later found Tomita another agent. Tomita credits her director and fellow cast members for helping her during her debut film performance.

On the set of *The Karate Kid, Part II*, Tomika met Nobu McCarthy. Like Tomika, McCarthy had experience in beauty pageants, and the two became close friends. Actor Ralph Macchio, the star of the film, taught Tomita how to swing dance, and the "Okinawan folk dance" that Tomita's character uses to teach karate to Macchio's character was made up by Tomita and her mother to fit the demands of the script. After filming was complete, Tomika returned briefly to UCLA, but following the success of *The Karate Kid* and offers for other film roles, she left school.

Throughout the 1980s, Tomita found many roles in television, but turned down roles that she felt utilized Asian Americans negative stereotypes. In 1987, she made her first appearance as Lily Murakami in the TV series *Santa Barbara*. She reappeared on the show in the role of Ming Li in 1988. Throughout her career, Tomita has appeared on such television shows as *Law and Order: Los Angeles*, *Babylon 5*, *Chicago Hope*, *Nash Bridges*, *The Sentinel*, *Quantum Leap*, and *The Shield*. She appeared in *Come See the Paradise* in 1990. In 1993, Tomita appeared as Waverly Jong in the popular film *The Joy Luck Club*. In 2004, she played the role of Janet Tokada in *The Day After Tomorrow*.

In 1991, Tomita was chosen by *People* magazine as one of the 50 Most Beautiful People in the world. After a long relationship with actor Stan Egi, Tomita was briefly married and then divorced in 1998.

SIGNIFICANCE

Outside of her work in the entertainment industry, Tomita has worked with numerous charities and nonprofit organizations. She has emceed and hosted numerous community benefits for charity groups, including the Little Tokyo Service Center, Visual Communications,

and the East West Players. She has also encouraged community empowerment by appearing in public service announcements for voter registration. Tomita has also appeared in productions of *The Vagina Monologues* to benefit Asians for Miracle Marrow Matches (A3M) (Tomita's father died of leukemia in 1990). Tomita has said she feels blessed to be a mixed-race actor (Okinawan, Japanese, and Filipina).

Florante Peter Ibanez

FURTHER READING

Lipton, Lauren. "Role in 'Paradise' Helps Tomita Trace Her Cultural Roots."*Los Angeles Times*. Los Angeles Times, 15 Dec. 1990. Web. 15 Mar. 2012. Discusses Tomita's role in the film *Come See the Paradise*.

Maslin, Janet. "The Joy Luck Club (1993)." *New York Times*. New York Times, 8 Sep. 1993. Web. 15 Mar. 2012. Reviews the film *The Joy Luck Club*.

TRITIA TOYOTA

Journalist, educator, scholar

For nearly three decades Tritia Toyota was a pioneering Asian American broadcast journalist in Los Angeles, California. She was a cofounder of the Asian American Journalists Association. After leaving her career in journalism, Toyota earned a PhD in anthropology and turned her advocacy toward the university classroom and academic publishing. In 2010 Toyota wrote the book Envisioning America: New Chinese Americans and the Politics of Belonging *about the growth and sophistication of Asian American political power in Southern California.*

Born: March 29, 1947; Portland, Oregon
Full name: Tritia Toyota
Birth name: Letritia R. Miyake
Areas of achievement: Journalism, sociology, education

EARLY LIFE

Tritia Toyota was born Letritia R. Miyake on March 29, 1947, in Portland, Oregon, to Japanese American internment camp survivors. Toyota moved to Southern California, where she earned a bachelor's degree and then a master's degree in 1970 from the University of

California, Los Angeles (UCLA). Toyota met Michael R. Yamaki at UCLA and the couple married in the 1970s. Yamaki worked as a lawyer and the couple lived in Brentwood, California, a suburb of Los Angeles.

In 1970, the Los Angeles–area news media were virtually all white and male. Toyota broke in as a self-identified "three-fer"—young, female, and of Asian descent—as a reporter at the KNX radio station. Toyota worked there until 1972, when she moved to the KNBC television network, where she worked as a reporter until she began anchoring in 1975. Toyota was a pioneer as one of the first Asian Americans to anchor the news in Los Angeles, if not California, an area with substantial numbers of Chinese and Japanese American citizens who had been rooted there since the mid-1800s.

LIFE'S WORK

Toyota was a popular on-camera personality. In 1979, she was the inspiration for the punk rock song "I'm Stuck in a Pagoda with Tricia Toyota" by the Dickies. Despite the mirth, the journalist was concerned about stereotypical portrayals of Asian Americans and outright discrimination and exclusion. In her 2010 book *Envisioning America: New Chinese Americans and the Politics of*

The Asian American Journalists Association

In 1981, Toyota, KNBC-TV colleague Frank Kwan, *Los Angeles Times* journalists Bill Sing, Nancy Yosihana, David Kishiyama, and others founded the Asian American Journalists Association (AAJA). It was the third national association of journalists of color since 1975.

AAJA members, who largely worked in mainstream daily media, advocated for fair and in-depth coverage of Asian Americans and Pacific Islanders. Bill Wong, in a 1987 dispatch for *East-West News*, identified the "Connie Chung" syndrome, the pattern of news managers to pair an attractive Asian female anchor with a white male anchor to the exclusion of Asian males. Asian American journalists were aware of the backhanded "model minority" compliment bestowed on studious and high-achieving citizens and immigrants, but they were also aware of research that said white decision makers rejected many they perceived as aggressive, sneaky, and different.

Leaders from the National Association of Black Journalists, the National Association of Hispanic Journalists, AAJA, and the newest group, the Native American Journalists Association, met in 1988 in Baltimore, Maryland. In 1990, the groups formed the Unity: Journalists of Color alliance; their first convention was held in 1994 in Atlanta, Georgia. There, Toyota reminded her colleagues that many Asian Americans were recent immigrants and the news media needed to recognize and reflect their experiences.

AAJA has continued to grow its membership, hold annual conventions, and participate in Unity conventions. In August 2010, eight hundred members gathered for the AAJA convention in Los Angeles.

Belonging, Toyota noted that occasional coverage of the Chinese New Year or the Nisei Week parade did not amount to adequate coverage of the Asian American population.

In 1981 Toyota cofounded the Asian American Journalists Association with several other journalists of Asian descent. The organization advocates for increased participation of Asian Americans in the industry and improved coverage in the media.

In 1985, Toyota moved to the KCBS television station in Los Angeles to work as an anchor. She followed the familiar custom for broadcast news anchors of contractually staying off the air for several months—in her case three—when switching to a competing station in the same market.

Once settled in, Toyota took advantage of her prominent positions as a reporter and anchor to insinuate herself into social processes where people identified as Asian American. She acknowledged that she was not always welcome, yet her frequent infiltration allowed her to develop a deeper understanding of communities and report authoritatively on evolving Asian American political and social power in California.

In one example she reported on Lily Chen, a naturalized immigrant from Taiwan who made history as the first Chinese American woman mayor of a United States city when she was elected in Monterey Park, California. Toyota tracked other evidence of the rise of Chinese political power and civic engagement in California. In 1994, during the O. J. Simpson murder trial, Toyota conducted a five-part interview with Judge Lance Ito, the Japanese American who attracted harsh media scrutiny for what some perceived as unorthodox judicial decisions.

Toyota's twenty-nine years in broadcast journalism ended quietly in 1999. On November 17 of that year, the *Los Angeles Times* reported that the high-profile anchor was removed from the early morning and noon newscasts but was offered an opportunity to continue working at the station. Toyota declined the offer, according to the *Times*, and left without rancor.

She returned to UCLA and earned a PhD in anthropology. During her time in the doctoral program she was a student of Don T. Nakanishi, director of the Asian American Studies Center. Toyota was also a friend and academic colleague of Lucie Cheng, a sociology professor and founding dean of a graduate program in Taiwan. Toyota wrote an appreciation of Cheng in a 2010 issue of *Amerasia Journal*. Toyota became an adjunct assistant professor in the departments of anthropology and Asian American studies at her alma mater. Toyota's scholarly work focuses on the fusion of multiple generations of native-born Chinese Americans and naturalized immigrant Chinese who came to America after the 1965 liberalization of immigration regulations.

SIGNIFICANCE

Toyota was the most recognizable Asian American journalist in the 1980s on the West Coast and paved the way for newscasters such as Connie Chung and Ann Curry in the 1980s, 1990s, and 2000s. After leaving the news industry, Toyota continued to advocate for Asian Americans by using academia as a vehicle for raising awareness about Asian American issues. Along with *Envisioning America*, Toyota has authored a number of scholarly journal articles. Her awards include a Golden Mike and an Emmy for writing and producing the documentary program *Asian America*.

Wayne Dawkins

FURTHER READING

Toyota, Tritia. *Envisioning America: New Chinese Americans and the Politics of Belonging*. Palo Alto: Stanford UP, 2009. Print. Toyota's study of the many aspects of Chinese American civic involvement in Southern California.

---. "Paying Attention to the Margins." *Amerasia Journal* 35.3 (2009): 47–50. Print. Toyota's contribution to a special issue paying tribute to her mentor at UCLA, Don T. Nakanishi, longtime director of the Asian American Studies Center.

MING TSAI

Chef, business executive, and entrepreneur

Recognized for introducing a fusion of Eastern and Western cuisines to the masses, celebrity chef Ming Tsai is a first-generation Chinese American and third-generation Yale graduate. He has hosted an Emmy Award–winning cooking show, written several Asian-inspired cookbooks, and earned national distinction from his peers for his work as an innovator in the culinary world.

Born: March 29, 1964; Newport Beach, California
Full name: Ming Tsai
Areas of achievement: Entertainment, business

EARLY LIFE

Ming Tsai was born in Newport Beach, California on March 29, 1964. His parents, both Chinese Americans, raised him in Dayton, Ohio, where they operated an Asian restaurant. Tsai first developed his passion for the culinary arts as a small child, spending many hours in the family kitchen. When he was ten years old, he cooked a dish of friend rice for himself and his friends. Tsai's love for the restaurant business grew as he learned to cook alongside his parents in the family restaurant, Mandarin Kitchen, where he also helped seat customers at the front of the house.

Tsai attended high school at Phillips Academy, a boarding school in Andover, Massachusetts. After graduating, he enrolled at the Yale School of Engineering, following in the footsteps of his father and grandfather. As a college student, Tsia traveled to Paris and fell in love with French cuisine. During the summer of his junior year, he attended Le Cordon Bleu cooking school. While studying at the French culinary institute, Tsia was inspired to blend Eastern and Western cuisines,

incorporating signature flavors such as ginger and Chinese five-spice powder into French cuisine. After graduating from Yale with a degree in mechanical engineering, Tsai trained under famed pastry chef Pierre Hermé, while continuing to travel. He spent time in Osaka, Japan, working under sushi master Kobayashi.

Ming Tsai. (WireImage)

Tsai returned to the United States and continued his education at Cornell University, earning a master's degree in hotel administration. Realizing the importance of developing a well-rounded background in his chosen field, Tsai worked as a sous chef at restaurants in Atlanta, Chicago, and San Francisco. In San Francisco, he met and married his wife Polly while working as an executive chef. The couple has two sons. Following a failed business partnership with restaurant owner Bruce Cost, Tsai and his wife moved to New Mexico. Tsai declined an offer by casino developer Steve Wynn to come and work in Las Vegas. Although he applied for a slot at the New York restaurant Union Pacific, the position was filled by chef Rocco DiSpirito. Unable to find a position at an existing restaurant, Tsai decided to branch out on his own.

LIFE'S WORK

In 1998, Tsai's Western and Asian-style restaurant, Blue Ginger, opened in Wellesley, Massachusetts. The establishment quickly became a hit with customers, as well as Tsai's culinary peers. That same year, Blue Ginger earned a Best New Restaurant nod from *Boston* magazine and a nomination for a Best New Restaurant 1998 by the James Beard Foundation. The restaurant has been regularly rated one of the most popular Boston restaurants in the *Zagat* restaurant guide. Tsai was named Chef of the Year by *Esquire* magazine in 1998. From 1998 to 2003, Tsai starred in the Food Network's *East Meets West*, which focused on combining the culinary traditions of Asia and Europe. Tsai was awarded a Daytime Emmy in 1999 for Outstanding Service Show Host. In 2002, the Beard foundation named Tsai Best Chef Northeast.

In 2007, Blue Ginger was recognized by *Restaurants & Institutions*, a publication that showcases the best in the foodservice industry. Tsai's restaurant was again honored in 2009 by the International Foodservice Manufacturers Association, receiving its Silver Palate Award in the independent restaurant category.

Tsai's son David, born in 2000, suffers from a number of food allergies. In an effort to increase awareness and stress the importance of dining safety, Tsai contributed to the PBS children's television program *Arthur*, assisting producers with creating content for preschoolers and their parents concerning the dangers of peanut allergies. Tsai has served as national spokesperson for the Food Allergy and Anaphylaxis Network. In 2009, he served as honorary chair of the organization's Walk for Food Allergy: Moving Toward a Cure in Boston.

Tsai has served as host and executive producer of the award-winning television show *Simply Ming*, which first debuted on the Food Network before transitioning to public television. In 2006, the show joined the Culinary Podcast Network, which provides access to episodes of the *Simply Ming* television series. The podcasts feature information on food allergies, as well as cooking tutorials and culinary tips and tricks. Each recipe utilizes Tsai's signature East-West style and flavors. Tsai has also appeared regularly on *Ming's Quest*, a travel-based show that features him cooking in various countries around the world using regional ingredients.

In 2005, Tsai defeated Bobby Flay on the Food Network show *Iron Chef America*. He appeared in the third season of *The Next Iron Chef*, but was eliminated in the series' seventh week. Tsai also appeared as a judge on the Bravo cable television series *Top Chef* in 2008.

Tsai has put his Yale engineering degree to good use, assisting in the development of a unique line of cutlery bearing his name. His line of Kyocera cooking tools is a product of his longtime collaboration with and endorsement of Kyocera Advanced Ceramics, a premier manufacturer of kitchen items. In 2000, the retail chain Target began carrying his Blue Ginger products on its shelves across the country.

Over the course of his career, Tsai has penned four cookbooks: *Blue Ginger: East Meets West Cooking with Ming Tsai* (1999), *Simply Ming* (2003), *Ming's Master Recipes* (2005), and *Simply Ming One-Pot Meals* (2010).

SIGNIFICANCE

Tsai's unique method of fusing Eastern and Western cuisines makes him a pioneer in the culinary arts. He has succeeded in broadening the palate of his audience, inspiring them with his love of food and cooking. Dedicated to eradicating the misconception that Chinese food is overly sauced and sweetened, Tsai has managed to combine the best of both hemispheres in the kitchen, while raising awareness of the diversity and complexity of the world's different culinary cultures. In addition, Tsai has been a tireless advocate for those afflicted with food allergies, working with restaurants and the media to help ensure that people can dine worry free.

Mavis Carr

FURTHER READING

Schillinger, Liesl. "Ming's Thing." *New Yorker* 15 Nov. 1999: 60+. Print. Profiles Tsai, including his background, education, opening of Blue Ginger, and television popularity.

Tsai, Ming. *Blue Ginger: East Meets West Cooking with Ming Tsai*. New York: Clarkson Potter, 1999. Print. Includes many of the dishes Tsai introduced at his first restaurant, Blue Ginger, in Wellesley, Massachusetts.

---. "Squash, a Growing Sport, and Nutritious, Too." *New York Times*. New York Times, 28 Jan. 2012. Web. 27 Mar. 2012. Tsai discusses his love of the sport of squash. Includes details about his career in the culinary arts.

ROGER Y. TSIEN

Scientist

A pioneer in biological imaging, Roger Tsien characterized and exploited green fluorescent protein from jellyfish as an agent for visualizing biological processes within living cells. Tsien's ingenious use of the protein and its variants revolutionized the ability of scientists to visualize a broad range of biological processes that were thought to be beyond imaging technologies.

Born: February 1, 1952; New York City, New York
Full name: Roger Yonchien Tsien
Also known as: Qian Yongjian
Area of achievement: Science

EARLY LIFE

Roger Yonchien Tsien was born in New York City to Hsue Chu Tsien, a prominent engineer who had worked as a liaison officer for the Chinese government and several American companies, and Yi Ying Tsien, who had trained as a nurse. He grew up in Livingston, New Jersey, the youngest of three boys. Tsien's earliest memories are of his fascination with building sand paths and bridges. Because he suffered from asthma, Tsien had to spend a great deal of time indoors, so his parents bought him a chemistry set, which he used to make colored crystals of metal silicates and solutions of potassium permanganate that changed colors when filtered through paper. These experiments cultivated a lifelong preoccupation with colors.

Tsien attended Livingston High School, where he was frequently bored. In 1967, he spent the summer at Ohio State University in the laboratory of Robert Kline, examining the binding of metals to thiocyanate. The next summer, when he was sixteen years old, he won first prize in the nationwide Westinghouse Talent Search for this work.

With the help of a National Merit Scholarship, Tsien matriculated at Harvard University in the fall of 1968. The dullness of his chemistry classes caused him to search for a new focus, and he became entranced by neuroscience. In 1972, at age twenty, Tsien graduated from Harvard with a bachelor's degree in chemistry and physics. In order to continue his study of neuroscience, he won a Marshall Scholarship to Cambridge University, where he worked with Jeremy Sanders on the design of small molecules that could detect calcium ion changes in nerve cells. He received a PhD in physiology from Churchill College, Cambridge in 1977 and remained as a research fellow at Gonville and Caius College, Cambridge from 1977 to 1981. During this time, he met his wife, Wendy.

Roger Y. Tsien. (Getty Images)

Life's Work

In 1982, Tsien received an appointment to the Department of Physiology-Anatomy at the University of California, Berkeley. Despite a cut in funds, he was able to make some significant achievements, developing synthetic dyes for calcium ions and sodium. In 1989, he left Berkeley for the University of California, San Diego, where he was given funding from the Howard Hughes Medical Institute, more space, and a dual appointment in the chemistry and biology departments to facilitate his research interests, which lay in a combination of these two fields.

Tsien's ultimate goal was to express genes in cells that had fluorescent molecules attached to them. This would allow scientists to observe the appearance and movement of proteins in single living cells. The problem was finding a molecule that could be engineered directly into the gene that encodes the protein of interest. In 1992, green fluorescent protein (GFP) was discovered in the marine jellyfish *Aequorea victoria* by Douglas Prasher and his colleagues at Woods Hole Oceanographic Institute. The instant he read about this protein, Tsien knew that he had found the fluorescent molecule that would do what he wanted.

In Tsien's laboratory, researcher Roger Heim and his coworkers identified the color-emitting (chromophore) portion of GFP and worked out the enzyme-free, oxygen-dependent mechanism by which the chromophore is constructed inside cells. Heim also isolated several mutants of GFP that glow more intensely and emit different colors. In 1995, Mats Ormö and Jim Remington at the University of Oregon solved the crystal structure of mutant GFP, suggesting new ways to engineer GFP to generate a protein that was more stable than the blue version of GFP. These discoveries contributed to Tsien's own research in the field.

One of Tsien's greatest aspirations was to use GFP and its sundry variants to image biological processes within living cells. Atushi Miyawaki, a postdoctoral research fellow in Tsien's lab, used fluorescence resonance energy transfer (FRET), in which an excited GFP molecule transfers its energy to a nearby dye molecule that then fluoresces at a distinct wavelength, to image protein and calcium ion binding in cells. Miyawaki called these calcium-ion-sensing proteins "chameleons," and the research group used them to image cell signaling and cell division in many different cell types under various conditions.

In 2009, Xiaokun Shu from Tsien's lab engineered plant molecules called phytochromes to fluoresce in the infrared spectrum. This achievement, in combination with

---

Roger Tsien's Nobel Prize in Chemistry

Tsien initially worked on molecules that measure calcium ion changes, and thus he was familiar with a protein made by luminescent marine jellyfish, called aequorin, which fluoresces blue when bound by calcium ions. Tsien also noted that upon isolation, aequorin was typically contaminated with green fluorescent protein (GFP), and that GFP, unlike aequorin, glowed without the need of any exogenously added cofactor. This motivated him to turn to GFP as a potential biological imaging agent.

Original experiments with GFP in yeast showed such weak fluorescence that it was not usable. However, in the 1990s, Tsien's team member Roger Heim identified three amino acids—serine[65], tyrosine[66], and glycine[67]—as the components of the GFP chromophore. Heim further showed that synthesis of the chromophore resulted from an intramolecular reaction between serine[65] and glycine[67], followed by oxidation (electron loss) by molecular oxygen (O_2) of a bond to the nearby tyrosine[66]. These reactions create the p-hydroxybenzylidene-imidazolidone chromophore, which occurs without any exogenous factors. Elucidation of this mechanism suggested ways to increase the fluorescence of GFP and change the color it emitted. These variants in color provided tools that laboratories could use to label biological molecules and visualize them in cells. In 2008, Tsien was awarded the Nobel Prize in Chemistry for his discovery of the utility of GFP and the elucidation of its mechanism, as well as his engineering of GFP to create variants that revolutionized biological imaging studies.

---

the earlier isolation of a red fluorescent protein from corals in a Moscow aquarium by researchers from the Russian Academy of Sciences, greatly enhanced the ability of fluorescent proteins to function in living cells and emit light at a wide spectrum of colors and frequencies.

Significance

Roger Y. Tsien won the 2008 Nobel Prize in Chemistry for his work on GFP. His introduction of GFP to biological research caused seismic shifts in biological imaging; in addition to allowing such imaging to be done easily and cheaply, it also vastly increased the applications of fluorescent imaging in general. For example, by fusing GFP to the control regions of various genes, geneticists can easily quantify gene expression. Protein chemists have used GFP fusions to study protein folding and other parameters of protein function. Cell biologists have also used GFP to visualize a range of phenomena, including waves of increased calcium ion concentrations during cell division, activation of receptors in cancer cells, and the entrance of viruses into cells during viral infection. Drug developers have used GFP-protein fusions to screen for drugs that inhibit the formation of amyloid bodies, those protein agglomerations in the brain that are responsible for most of the pathology associated with Alzheimer's disease. These are just a few of the myriad uses of GFP imaging.

The ease of GFP visualization also made it a prime choice for educational demonstrations. Several science education equipment suppliers now sell GFP-based gene expression kits that illustrate gene expression, protein function, bacterial transformation, and other biological processes through the ingenious use of GFP. Thus Tsien's discoveries revolutionized not only biological research but also science education.

Michael A. Buratovich

FURTHER READING

Tsien, Roger Y. "Autobiography." *Nobelprize.org*. Nobel Media, 2008. Web. 30 Mar. 2012. An extensive overview of Tsien's life, including his childhood and the development of his research.

---. "The Green Fluorescent Protein." *Annual Review of Biochemistry* 67.1 (1998): 509–44. Print. A technical summary of the work on GFP that won Tsien the Nobel Prize.

---. "Molecular Designer: An Interview with Roger Y. Tsien." By Steven Adler. *A Passion for Ideas: How Innovators Create the New and Shape Our World*. Ed. Heinrich von Pierer and Bolko von Oetinger. West Lafayette: Purdue UP, 2002. 133–50. Print. Discusses specific aspects of Tsien's work, education, and approach to research.

Zimmer, Marc. *Glowing Genes: A Revolution in Biotechnology*. Amherst, NY: Prometheus, 2005. Print. An introduction to new advances in biotechnology, highlighting many usages of GFP in the field.

DANIEL CHEE TSUI

Chinese-born physicist

Best known for his work associated with the fractional quantum Hall effect, Tsui, along with colleagues, was awarded the 1998 Nobel Prize in physics for the discovery of a new form of quantum fluid with fractionally charged excitations. Tsui's research focuses on the electrical properties of thin films, microstructures of semiconductors, and solid-state physics.

Born: February 28, 1939; Henan, China
Full name: Daniel Chee Tsui (SHOO)
Birth name: Chee Tsui
Areas of achievement: Science and technology

EARLY LIFE

Daniel Chee Tsui was born in a village in Henan, China, on February 28, 1939. He spent the first eleven years of his life helping his father farm. Although his parents had never learned how to read or write, they recognized the importance of a good education for their son. There were few educational opportunities in their village, so they sent Tsui to the British colony of Hong Kong for schooling.

In 1951, Tsui began attending school in Hong Kong, unfamiliar with the territory and the Cantonese dialect spoken there. His classmates helped him adapt to the daily regimen. A year later, Tsui entered Pui Ching Middle School, a high school with a renowned natural sciences curriculum. Most of Tsui's teachers were graduates of China's top universities. They inspired him to pursue knowledge instead of financial gain. Upon graduation in 1957, Tsui was admitted to the medical school of the National Taiwan University. However, after receiving a full scholarship from his church pastor's alma mater, Tsui chose to go to the United States for his postsecondary education.

In 1958, Tsui entered Augustana College in Rock Island, Illinois. He graduated in 1961 with Phi Beta Kappa honors and a degree in mathematics. Inspired by his compatriots Tsung-Dao Lee and Chen Ning, winners of the 1957 Nobel Prize in Physics, Tsui next enrolled at the University of Chicago. As a physics research assistant, he helped a new and young faculty develop a new laboratory and research facility. At the University of Chicago, he acquired a wide range of skills, including engineering, soldering, machining, design, and construction of laboratory apparatus. While attending graduate school in Chicago, he met an undergraduate

Daniel Chee Tsui. (AP Photo)

named Linda Varland. They were married after Linda's graduation.

After earning a PhD in 1967, Tsui stayed on at the University of Chicago for another year to conduct post-doctoral work. In 1968, he was hired as a researcher by Bell Laboratories in New Jersey. In 1982, he accepted a faculty position at Princeton University.

Life's Work

After joining the Solid State Electronics Research Group at Bell Laboratories, Tsui began work in semiconductor research. In 1982, he and colleague Horst Störmer discovered that electrons exhibiting wave characteristics were best described by using quantum mechanics. In 1998, Tsui and his colleagues Robert B. Laughlin and Horst Störmer were awarded a Nobel Prize in physics for their discovery of the fractional quantum Hall effect. The effect uncovered new behavior by electrons exposed to extremely strong magnetic fields at very low temperatures, and has applications in the creation of extremely small and precise transistors used in cell phones and other sophisticated electronic devices. Tsui was later named Arthur Legrand Doty

Professor Emeritus of Electrical Engineering and Senior Scholar at Princeton.

For his pioneering work in physics, Tsui received the Oliver E. Buckley Prize from the American Physical Society (1984) and the Benjamin Franklin Medal in Physics from the Franklin Institute (1988). Augustana College has honored Tsui's accomplishments with a Distinguished Alumni Award (1989) and an honorary degree (2004). The Daniel Tsui Fellowship at the University of Hong Kong provides opportunities for outstanding young physicists from China, Taiwan, or Singapore to carry out research at the school.

Tsui attributes his scientific achievements to intellectual curiosity. When delivering his 1998 Nobel lecture, Tsui admitted that his journey to discovering the fractional quantum Hall effect would not have been possible without the contributions of his graduate students and postdoctoral fellows, along with the contributions of his collaborators at the Bell Laboratories and Princeton University.

For Tsui, scientific discoveries are always possible if a person is willing to venture into uncharted territory, do and redo experiments, talk and work with others, think over ideas, and take advantage of technical advances. In retirement, Tsui continues to share his experiences and insights with students in the United States and abroad.

Significance

Tsui's life story and scientific accomplishments have inspired countless students to pursue scientific careers. By any measure, he has lived up to the expectations of his parents and childhood teachers. In addition to his curiosity, Tsui's confidence and ability to work with others have helped him achieve much in his field. Fulfilling his goal of leading a life of learning, he has conducted research in new fields and made important discoveries in experimental physics.

Joyce Tang

Further Reading

Jonson, Mats. "The Nobel Prize in Physics 1998: Presentation Speech." *Nobelprize.org*. Nobel Foundation, 1998. Web. 30 Mar. 2012. A concise explanation of Laughlin, Störmer, and Tsui's discovery of the fractional quantum Hall effect.

Wong, Cheuk-Yin. *The Joy of the Search for Knowledge: A Tribute to Professor Dan Tsui*. Hackensack: World Scientific, 1999. Print. Essays by Tsui's colleagues, discussing his personality, life, and work.

KITTY TSUI

Hong Kong–born writer, activist, and bodybuilder

Novelist Kitty Tsui is recognized as one of the first Asian American writers to explore homosexuality and feminism in her work. Drawing from personal experiences, her work has helped challenge conventional wisdom about sexuality and gender roles. Tsui's writing has been published throughout the world, translated into German, Italian, and Japanese.

Born: 1952; Hong Kong
Full name: Kitty Tsui (KIHT-tee CHOY)
Birth name: Kit Fan Tsui
Areas of achievement: Literature, activism

EARLY LIFE

Kitty Tsui was born in 1952 in Hong Kong. She demonstrated a talent for writing at a young age and was first published in the *South China Morning Post*, an English-language daily, when she was twelve years old. After living for a time in Hong Kong and England, her family settled in San Francisco, California, in 1968.

Tsui's grandmother, Kwan Yong Lin, who lived in San Francisco's Chinatown, had a significant impact on her during her childhood. Lin was an actress and a Cantonese opera singer, and she had endured many hardships as an immigrant. The adult Tsui would identify with her grandmother as a creative but marginalized woman. Tsui wrote several poems about Lin and dedicated her book *The Words of a Woman Who Breathes Fire* (1983) to her.

Tsui left home at age seventeen. She received her BA in creative writing from San Francisco State University in 1975. Only a few years prior to her enrollment as a freshman, the campus had been an epicenter of a series of demonstrations that led to the recognition of Asian studies as an academic discipline. During the 1970s, Tsui became increasingly interested in activism, and along with such writers as Merle Woo and Willyce Kim, she became part of a group of lesbian Asian American women who began to publish their work nationwide.

In 1981, at the age of twenty-nine, Tsui found herself struggling with alcoholism. In an effort to change her life, she began working out and started an intensive bodybuilding program. She won a bronze medal in bodybuilding at the second Gay Games in 1986 and a gold medal at the next Games in 1990. Tsui has said that her interest in bodybuilding was motivated in part by her desire to challenge conventional perception, especially with respect to race, gender, and sexuality.

LIFE'S WORK

Tsui published her first major work, *The Words of a Woman Who Breathes Fire*, in 1983. The book is a collection of prose and poetry that addresses such topics as class, gender, sexuality, and identity. In addition to being Tsui's debut for a larger audience, it was also the first book published by an out Chinese American lesbian.

During the 1980s, Tsui became an inspirational figure for Asian American lesbians. She gained national exposure presenting a program called *Asian/Pacific Lesbians: Our Identities, Our Movements*, a collection of her performance art paired with a friend's slide show, in San Francisco, New York City, Chicago, and Washington, DC. Her reputation as a vocal proponent of GLBT (gay, lesbian, bisexual, and transgender) arts continued to grow throughout the 1990s. She was the first Asian American model to feature in the lesbian erotica magazine *On Our Backs*, appearing on the front cover of the summer 1988 issue. In 1990, the Lambda Book Report named Tsui one of the fifty most influential people in GLBT literature. She won the Center for Lesbian and Gay Studies' Ken Dawson Award in 1995 for her work in gay and lesbian history.

Tsui's second book, *Breathless: Erotica* (1995), is a collection of daringly erotic short stories featuring lesbian sex and celebrating the female body. The book was awarded the Firecracker Alternative Book Award the following year. In 1997, Tsui published *Sparks Fly*, written from the point of view of Tsui's nom de plume, Eric Norton, a San Francisco gay man.

SIGNIFICANCE

Tsui's influence on modern lesbian and Asian American literature cannot be overstated. In the 1980s, she was one of the first well-known Asian American lesbian writers, part of a larger movement that helped lead to such advancements as the establishment of ethnic studies departments at many universities. Her works became a part of modern Asian American studies curricula nationwide.

As a writer, Tsui has broken ground in many ways. She is the first Chinese American lesbian to publish an "out" book. Her work exploring female identity and sexuality in a non-patriarchal, non-Western frame of reference has proved influential for both her audience and her fellow writers. Tsui has worked to develop a Chinese lesbian literary tradition, establishing a new canon that is separate from the Western lineage of Sappho, Radclyffe Hall, Gertrude Stein, and Virginia Woolf, and has continually challenged mainstream perceptions, particularly the idea that an individual's identity is a discrete, singular construct. Her long-term examination of what it means to be both Asian American and a lesbian is a reminder of the richness and complexity of cultural identity.

Leigh E. Barkley

FURTHER READING

Tsui, Kitty. "Breaking Silence, Making Waves, and Loving Ourselves: The Politics of Coming Out and Coming Home." *Lesbian Philosophies and Cultures.* Ed. Jeffner Allen. New York: State U of New York P, 1990. Print. Includes autobiographical material.

---. "Give Joan Chen My Phone Number Anytime." *Lesbian Erotics.* Ed. Karla Jay. New York: New York UP, 1995. Print. Provides insight into Tsui's past and tackles issues of coming out and writing lesbian sexuality, among others.

---. *The Words of a Woman Who Breathes Fire.* San Francisco: Spinsters, 1983. Print. Tsui's first book, a collection of poetry and prose that reveals her interest in the interplay of cultural identities.

Wei, William. *The Asian American Movement.* Philadelphia: Temple UP, 1993. Print. Helps to contextualize Tsui's activism.

GEORGE TSUTAKAWA

Artist

In over sixty years as a painter and sculptor, George Tsutakawa produced art that creatively combined his observations of nature with forms and styles adapted from Japanese, European, and American traditions. His monumental public fountains are considered his best-known and most influential work.

Born: February 22, 1910; Seattle, Washington
Died: December 18, 1997; Seattle, Washington
Full name: George Tsutakawa (SOO-tah-kah-wah)
Area of achievement: Art

EARLY LIFE

George Tsutakawa was born in Seattle, Washington, the fourth child of Shozo and Hisa Tsutakawa. His parents came to the United States from Japan in 1905, and Shozo Tsutakawa ran an export-import business based on trade between Japan and the United States. The business prospered and the family lived comfortably in an affluent Seattle neighborhood.

Tsutakawa grew up speaking English and attended elementary school in Seattle until 1917, when he and his older brother were sent to Fukuyama, Japan, to live with their maternal grandmother, Mutsu Naito. When Hisa Tsutakawa died in the influenza epidemic of 1918, Shozo sent the rest of his children to live with their grandmother as well. She introduced the nine Tsutakawa siblings to classical Japanese arts. Tsutakawa also grew close to his paternal grandfather, Kiichi Tsutakawa, an expert in Japanese flower arranging and other traditional arts.

Strongly inspired by young Japanese artists who had studied in Paris, Tsutakawa dropped out of high school to become an artist. This unsettled his father, who had returned to Japan, and he sent Tsutakawa back to Seattle in 1927. Working hard to relearn English, Tsutakawa returned to school while working part time with his uncles in the grocery branch of the family business. Art remained his passion, however, and he studied printmaking and watercolor in high school until he graduated in 1932. Tsutakawa went on to attend the University of Washington, where he graduated with a bachelor of fine arts in 1937.

LIFE'S WORK

In the 1930s, Tsutakawa joined a diverse network of Seattle-based artists, including Mark Tobey and Morris Graves (later internationally recognized as leaders in the Northwest school of painting), as well as Kenjiro Nomura and Kamekichi Tokita, Tsutakawa's close friends and painters of urban scenes. While Tsutakawa won some art competitions and earned the esteem of Seattle artists, his livelihood depended on his job with the family business, and his family's circumstances changed after the Japanese attack on Pearl Harbor in December 1941. Blocked legally from becoming American citizens, Tsutakawa's father and uncles were considered enemies of the United States, and their business was confiscated.

Much of Tsutakawa's extended family in the United States was relocated to internment camps in 1942, but Tsutakawa himself was inducted into the US Army instead. Although he trained for combat, health problems and his bilingual skills led to a position teaching Japanese to army officers in Minnesota. Throughout World War II, Tsutakawa perfected his artistic skills and studied art whenever possible, occasionally painting murals and portraits. He traveled to Chicago and New York to tour museums and art exhibits.

When the war ended and Tsutakawa returned to Seattle, he decided to commit himself fully to art. In 1947, he married Ayame Iwasa, whom he had met while visiting family in the internment camp where she was being held, and joined the faculty of the University of Washington's School of Art. He earned his master's degree in fine arts in 1950 and remained at the School of Art until 1976.

In the 1950s, although he had won praise for his work in many genres, Tsutakawa emerged mainly as an important sculptor. He worked first with wood, drawing upon Himalayan *obos*, or stacked stones, for inspiration. When he was commissioned to design a fountain for a downtown Seattle plaza in 1958, he turned to metal, creating patterns in the flowing water by having it move across a variety of surfaces and shapes. Additional commissions quickly followed; in all, Tsutakawa created over seventy public fountains in the United States, Canada, and Japan.

During the 1960s and 1970s, Tsutakawa alternated between designing distinctive public sculptures and creating intimate ink-stroke paintings in Japanese sumi style. His work often reflected his close examination of shapes in natural settings, and he turned more frequently for inspiration to the shores and mountains near his Seattle home.

SIGNIFICANCE

Upon his death in 1997, George Tsutakawa left behind a powerful legacy of artistic accomplishment and influence. From the late 1960s to the 1990s, he received numerous major awards, including lifetime achievement recognitions from the emperor of Japan, the Japanese American Citizens League, and the University of Washington. His work as an educator and spokesperson for the arts helped shape artistic careers for many young people, including his own four children, and his ability to create beautiful works in almost every artistic medium remains noteworthy. Tsutakawa's work reflected a unique fusion of classical Japanese art traditions with modern European and American styles, the product of his diverse life experiences and constant desire to experiment with new combinations of materials and genres.

Beth Kraig

FURTHER READING

Chang, Gordon, Mark Dean Johnson, and Paul J. Karlstrom, eds. *Asian American Art: A History, 1850–1970*. Stanford: Stanford UP, 2008. Print. An overview of Asian American art history that situates Tsutakawa in a critical discussion of whether Asian American art can be distinguished from work by non–Asian Americans.

Kingsbury, Martha. *George Tsutakawa*. Seattle: U of Washington P, 1990. Print. Includes dozens of illustrations of Tsutakawa's artwork, analysis of his artistic development, and extensive biographical material.

Poon, Irene. *Leading the Way: Asian American Artists of the Older Generation*. Wenham: Gordon College, 2001. Print. Useful for comparing Tsutakawa's art with that of other Asian American artists active in his lifetime.

Wechsler, Jeffrey, ed. *Asian Traditions, Modern Expressions: Asian American Artists and Abstraction, 1945–1970*. New York: Abrams, 1997. Print. Includes numerous references to Tsutakawa, as well as an essay on Asian American artists in Seattle.

U

YOSHIKO UCHIDA

Writer

Writer Yoshiko Uchida portrays in her works the hard-ships, endurance, and courage of Japanese Americans living in US internment camps during World War II. Over the course of her career, she created a large body of Japanese American literature for children and young adults.

Born: November 24, 1921; Alameda, California
Died: June 21, 1992; Berkeley, California
Full name: Yoshiko Uchida (yo-SHE-koh oo-CHEE-dah)
Area of achievement: Literature

EARLY LIFE

Yoshiko Uchida was born in 1921 in Alameda, California, to Japanese immigrants Dwight Takashi Uchida and Iku Umegaki Uchida. Both parents were educated at Doshisha University in Kyoto, Japan. Working as an assistant manager at a large Japanese import-export firm, Uchida's father provided the family with a comfortable life. Uchida and her older sister grew up in a happy home in a Japanese American community. Her mother wrote classical Japanese poetry, known as *tanka*, and her father was an avid writer of letters. Influenced by her parents, young Uchida found pleasure in books and writing at an early age.

Uchida's family observed Japanese customs and socialized with other Japanese Americans, but she considered herself American and longed to be accepted as such. However, she experienced racial discrimination and was mistreated by her peers. Motivated to escape her unpleasant life, Uchida completed high school in two and a half years. She enrolled at the University of California, Berkeley, at age sixteen. As a college student, she was excluded from white social groups. Out of shyness and fear, she never spoke to white classmates unless spoken to first. Fortunately for Uchida, Japanese student clubs on campus held dances, picnics, and other activities.

Uchida was in her senior year of college when Japan attacked the US naval base at Pearl Harbor on December 7, 1941. The surprise military aggression by Japan led US government officials to mistrust Japanese Americans, fearing they might feel more loyal to Japan than the United States. Therefore, the government rounded up all Japanese people on the West Coast, including American citizens, and moved them to internment camps. Uchida's father was sent to an internment camp in Missoula, Montana. The rest of the Uchida family was taken to the Tanforan Racetrack outside San Francisco on May 1, 1942, and assigned to live in a small, dark horse stall. Despite terrible living conditions, camp residents organized schools and recreational activities, and found other ways to cope with their situation. Yoshiko helped teach small children at camp schools.

Later, her father was released from Missoula so he could join his family at Tanforan. In September 1942, the family was transported to the Topaz War Relocation Center in Utah's Sevier Desert. This new camp was no better: Their room was frequently covered with a layer of dust that had sieved through the cracks of the roof and walls. When sand storms struck, the sand whirled in the air, and people could hardly see or walk. They lived in the barracks behind barbed wire, and were watched constantly by guards in a tower that overlooked the facility. Uchida also taught school in Topaz. Finally, through the efforts of the National Japanese American Student Relocation Council, Uchida and her sister were released in May 1943. Uchida went to pursue graduate work in education at Smith College in Massachusetts.

LIFE'S WORK

After earning a master's degree in education from Smith, Uchida taught at the Frankford Friends School near Philadelphia, Pennsylvania, for one year. She then moved to New York City, where she worked as a secretary for several years. Between 1952 and 1957, Uchida was a full-time writer. She took an administrative position at the University of California, Berkeley in 1957, where she remained until 1962. While working professionally as a secretary, Uchida devoted most of her personal life to writing. She collected Japanese folktales, wrote picture books, children's books, novels, and autobiographies, and published over thirty children's and young adult titles.

Uchida's work can be categorized into four genres: Japanese folktales, picture and children's books, historical fiction, and autobiography. She published a total of forty Japanese tales between 1949 and 1965 in the books *The Dancing Kettle and Other Japanese Folk Tales* (1949), *The Magic Listening Cup: More Folk Tales from Japan* (1955), and *The Sea of Gold and Other*

Yoshiko Uchida's *Desert Exile*

The autobiography *Desert Exile* (1982) is a true account of Yoshiko Uchida's family, her childhood, and her experiences at the internment camps in Tanforan, California, and Topaz, Utah, during World War II. Growing up in a closely knit Japanese family, Uchida had a happy childhood. As she got older, she became more conscious of being different from her white classmates and uncomfortable about being rejected and discriminated against. The Pearl Harbor attack interrupted her college education and shattered her happy family. All Japanese people living on the West Coast were sent to the internment camps. The Uchida family was taken to Tanforan Racetrack first and then to the Topaz camp. Living in barracks behind barbed wire, Uchida suffered deeply yet tried to cope. One way she dealt with internment was by teaching small children at camp schools. Her incarceration finally came to an end in May, 1943, and she was released to attend Smith College.

Tales from Japan (1965). Uchida was the first author to publish such a large collection of Japanese folktales. Her picture and children's books are set in both Japan and America. The picture books *The Forever Christmas Tree* (1963), *The Birthday Visitor* (1975), and *The Bracelet* (1976) tell stories of friendships between Japanese American girls and their neighbors, among others. *Takao and Grandfather's Sword* (1958), *Sumi and the Goat and the Tokyo Express* (1969), and *The Smallest Boy* (1970) are each set in Japan. Uchida's writings drew upon her personal experiences. The Rinko trilogy—*A Jar of Dreams* (1981), *The Best Bad Thing* (1983), and *The Happiest Ending* (1985)—includes stories about an eleven-year-old named Rinko living in a prejudiced society during the Great Depression.

In her autobiographies, *Desert Exile* (1982) and *The Invisible Thread* (1991), Uchida recounts stories of her family, childhood, student days, and experiences at the internment camps. Her works *Journey to Topaz* (1971) and *Journey Home* (1978) are also based on her internment camp experience. The historical novel *Paper Bride* (1987) describes the main character Hana's journey to America, where she weds a man in an arranged marriage.

Uchida received numerous awards, honors, and citations for her work. In 1952, she was awarded the Ford Foundation Foreign Study and Research Fellowship. One of her collections, *The Magic Listening Cup*, was chosen by the *New York Herald Tribune* as the Children's Spring Books Festival honor book in 1955. *Samurai of Gold Hill* (1985) and *A Jar of Dreams* (1993) won the silver medal for the best juvenile book by a California author. The California Association of Teachers of English honored her with the Award of Merit for her entire body of work. Other organizations, such as the International Reading Association, Children's Council for Social Studies, and Children's Book Council, selected many of Uchida's works as notable books. In addition, Uchida received an award from the Japanese American Citizen League for promoting understanding of Japanese culture and Japanese American experiences in the United States. Uchida died on June 21, 1992, in Berkeley, California.

SIGNIFICANCE

Uchida introduced many Japanese folktales to American children, and enhanced the cultural diversity of children's literature in the United States. Her portrayal of the hardships endured by Japanese Americans is authentic and truthful. Many characters in her books are painfully aware of their differences in a white-majority society; they feel caught between two cultures. Through her works, Uchida has spoken not only to Japanese American children but also to children in other ethnic groups about identity and personal worth. She has created characters with whom ethnic minority children identify.

From Uchida's books, Japanese American children can find continuity with their own personal history. They learn about their parents and grandparents. Uchida's work helps them to appreciate their culture and heritage and learn to treat those who are different with respect. In her autobiographies, Uchida gives a true account of the Japanese American internment camp during World War II. In addition, her works of fiction help make younger readers aware of an unfortunate chapter in American history, when the US government treated some of its own citizens like enemies.

Shu-Hsien L. Chen

FURTHER READING

McDiffett, Danton. "Prejudice and Pride: Japanese Americans in the Young Adult Novels of Yoshiko Uchida." *English Journal* 90 (January, 2001): 60–65. McDiffett discusses discrimination against Japanese Americans and other hardships during the Great Depression and World War II, as portrayed in Uchida's work.

Uchida, Yoshiko. *Desert Exile: The Uprooting of a Japanese-American Family.* Seattle: U of Washington P, 1982. Print. Uchida's autobiography relates her childhood and her time in the internment camps during World War II.

---. *The Invisible Thread.* Englewood Cliffs, NJ: Messner, 1991. Another autobiographical work, this one aimed at middle grades.

MIYOSHI UMEKI

Actor, singer

The first person of East Asian descent to win an Academy Award for acting, Miyoshi Umeki was a trailblazer for Asian performers in the United States. Famous for her acting skills and her singing, Umeki was a star of film, theater, and television, in addition to being an international recording star.

Born: May 8, 1929; Otaru, Hokkaido, Japan
Died: August 28, 2007; Licking, Missouri
Full name: Miyoshi Umeki (mee-YOH-shee oo-MEHK-ee)
Birth name: Umeki Miyoshi
Also known as: Nancy Umeki
Areas of achievement: Film, theater

EARLY LIFE

Miyoshi Umeki was born on the island of Hokkaido, Japan, on May 8, 1929, into a large family. Her father owned a successful ironworks factory, and Umeki was surrounded by her family and a large number of servants and apprentices during her early life. As a young girl, Umeki started listening to American pop and standards recordings. She especially loved Billy Eckstine and tried to copy the singing styles of Doris Day and other female American pop stars. Because her family disapproved of American music, Umeki would practice singing under her covers and in secret places, but one of her older brothers encouraged her love of music and

helped her learn to play instruments such as the mandolin and piano.

As a young girl, under the more westernized name Nancy Umeki, she began singing with American military bands and in a jazz group, becoming very popular on Japanese radio. Her popularity led to a record contract with the RCA Victor Japan record label, for which she produced standards albums sung in both Japanese and English. She starred in a 1953 Japanese musical film, *Seishun jazu musume* (Youthful jazz daughter). While singing at a nightclub, Umeki was approached by an American talent scout who urged her to move to the United States and expand her career opportunities. Umeki immigrated to the United States in 1955 and became a naturalized citizen.

LIFE'S WORK

After moving to the United States, Umeki landed a regular job on the television show *Arthur Godfrey and Friends*, appearing throughout the 1955 season, and was featured in the film short *Around the World Revue* (1956), billed as Nancy Umeki. While performing on Godfrey's show, Umeki was noticed by famed Broadway director Joshua Logan, who cast her in his upcoming film *Sayonara* (1957), opposite actor Red Buttons. This was a breakout opportunity for Umeki, who played the doomed war bride of an American soldier. Kept apart by prejudice and army red tape, she and her

Miyoshi Umeki. (AP Photo)

husband commit suicide. The film was a great success, earning Umeki the 1957 Academy Award for Best Supporting Actress. She was the first East Asian actor ever to win an Academy Award and, as of 2010, the only female East Asian actor to have received this accolade.

This was followed by Umeki's being cast as a mail order Chinese bride in the Rodgers and Hammerstein Broadway musical *Flower Drum Song* (1958). Although some disapproved of a Japanese actress playing a Chinese character, Umeki received rave reviews for her quiet and delicate performance, which earned her a Tony Award nomination for best supporting actress. She followed this by reprising the role in the film version, released in 1961. Umeki also continued to record music and put out albums and singles on the Mercury label.

Between 1961 and 1963, Umeki appeared in three other movies, each concerned in some way with East-meets-West plot contrivances. None of these movies was a great success. Also, between 1962 and 1964 Umeki acted in a handful of television shows, such as *The Virginian*, *The Donna Reed Show*, *Dr. Kildare*, *Rawhide*, and *Mister Ed*. During this time she also appeared on game shows and variety shows including

The Ed Sullivan Show, *The Tonight Show*, and *The Dinah Shore Chevy Hour*. However, it was not until 1969 that Umeki landed another major role, this time on the television series *The Courtship of Eddie's Father*, on which she played Mrs. Livingstone, a Japanese housekeeper. Umeki was featured in the show for its entire three years and was nominated for a Golden Globe for best supporting actress in a television comedy. When the show was canceled in 1972, Umeki retired from show business.

From 1958 to 1967, Umeki was married to television producer Frederick W. Opie; she married Randall Hood in 1968 and had one son. After her retirement, Umeki and Hood ran a business renting editing equipment to the film industry, and Umeki devoted herself to being a wife and mother. Hood died in 1976. Umeki later moved to Licking, Missouri, where she died of complications from cancer on August 28, 2007, at the age of seventy-eight.

SIGNIFICANCE

Miyoshi Umeki was the first Asian actress to receive top billing in Hollywood and on Broadway. Her quiet charm and great talent opened doors for a generation of Asian American actors after her. Although diminutive in height, she had a commanding presence on the stage and a beautiful singing voice that made her an audience favorite.

Leslie Neilan

FURTHER READING

"Broadway: The Girls on Grant Avenue." *Time* 22 Dec. 1958: 42–47. Print. An interview with Umeki and Pat Suzuki, stars of *Flower Drum Song*, discussing their roles and the rise of Asian American performers in the United States.

Lewis, David H. *Flower Drum Songs: The Story of Two Musicals*. Jefferson: McFarland. 2006. Print. Describes the controversies and success surrounding the original 1958 production of *Flower Drum Song* and the 2002 Broadway revival, as well as the positive and negative views of the Asian American issues raised by the play and its productions.

Lim, Shirley Jennifer. *A Feeling of Belonging: Asian American Women's Public Culture, 1930–1960*. New York: New York UP, 2006. Print. Examines the lives of Asian American women as they discovered an identity for themselves as native-born Americans; includes discussion of Miyoshi Umeki.

LOUNG UNG

Cambodian-born activist and writer

As a child in Cambodia, Loung Ung witnessed extreme violence at the hands of the Khmer Rouge, the Communist dictatorship that gripped the country in the 1970s. Her powerful memoir, First They Killed My Father *(2000), helped to raise global awareness of the genocide that occurred in Cambodia. Although she was able to flee to the United States, Ung has since returned to Cambodia, where she has worked as a peace activist and advocate for the removal of landmines that remain from the country's brutal past.*

Born: 1970; Phnom Penh, Cambodia
Full name: Loung Ung (LOY-uhng UHNG)
Areas of achievement: Social issues and activism

EARLY LIFE

Loung Ung was born in 1970 into a privileged Chinese Cambodian family. She is the daughter of Seng Im Ung and Ay Choung Ung. Her father was a high-ranking military official in the Cambodian government. Ung led a quiet, sheltered life until April 17, 1975, when the Khmer Rouge took over the government of Cambodia. The Khmer Rouge waged a campaign to purge the country of all associations with the old government and return Cambodia to an agrarian society. Many upper-class and educated Cambodians were identified as threats by the regime and quickly executed or forced into labor camps where starvation was rampant.

In their attempts to rid society of industrial capitalism, the Khmer Rouge forced the evacuation of all of Cambodia's cities. Everyone in Phnom Penh was required to leave for the countryside. Although the Ungs were able to hide their identities as allies of the old government, they were required to work in labor camps, receiving small rations as compensation. Ung's older sister was sent to a teenage labor camp where she died of apparent food poisoning.

The family stayed in a village known as Ro Leap until December 1976, when Ung's father was taken away by soldiers and never seen again. Presumably he was killed. Ung's mother decided that it was safer for her children to pretend to be orphans. Taken to a child labor camp, Ung was separated from her older sister Chou and put in a training camp for child soldiers. In 1977, she escaped and went to find her mother and youngest sister. She found that they had been taken by soldiers.

When the Vietnamese invaded Cambodia in 1979, toppling the Khmer Rouge regime, the remaining members of the Ung family were reunited. Meng, Loung's oldest brother, intended to immigrate to the United States and could only take one other person. Loung and Meng ended up in a refugee camp in Thailand, and eventually settled in the northern New England state of Vermont.

LIFE'S WORK

Still a child, Ung had some difficulty adjusting to life in the United States, unable to forget the bloodshed she had witnessed and the hardships she experienced in Cambodia. Encouraged to write about her experiences as a high school student, she amassed hundreds of pages in a journal. Continuing on to St. Michael's College in Vermont, Ung met her husband and continued to write. After graduating in 1993, she worked at a women's shelter in Maine, eventually joining the US Veterans Administration's Campaign for a Landmine-Free World. The group works to discourage the use of landmines

Loung Ung. (AP Photo)

The Cambodian Genocide

The 1975 takeover of Cambodia by the Khmer Rouge led to one of the bloodiest genocides in modern history. Almost immediately upon completing the conquest of Cambodia, the Khmer Rouge, led by Pol Pot, began to implement their practice of uprooting the populace of cities and towns. Pol Pot had been influenced by the writings of Marxist Andre Gunder Frank, who held that only rural labor created wealth and that urban society exploited peasants. The Khmer Rouge intended to move entire populations of cities to the countryside and create a new social order that would be based on agriculture, free of outside, imperialist influences. In implementing the evacuation policy, the Khmer Rouge moved large numbers of people from the capital. Almost all were taken to the countryside. The exodus included the infirm, the sick, and the elderly. Many thousands died as a result of their forced relocation.

In addition to forcing people to leave the cities, the Khmer Rouge began a systematic campaign of eliminating Western influences. During almost four years of rule, the Khmer Rouge executed its suspected enemies: intellectuals, ethnic minorities, and anyone who had traveled abroad, spoke another language, or even wore eyeglasses. Hundreds of thousands left the country as refugees. Estimates of the number of people who died as a direct result of Khmer Rouge policies range to well over two million people.

in war, and works to help clear areas of the world that were mined during past conflicts.

In 1995, Ung returned to Cambodia. She visited with her remaining relatives, including her grandmother, and learned of the fate of other members of the family. Following her visit to Cambodia, Ung continued to devote herself to raising awareness of the dangerous conditions remaining in the country because of unexploded landmines.

In 2000, Ung's first memoir was released. *First They Killed My Father: A Daughter of Cambodia Remembers* was a *New York Times* best-seller, and helped expose the Cambodian war experience of the 1970s to a new generation. The book traces Ung's early life in Cambodia and documents her family's struggle to survive the Khmer Rouge regime, as they tried to hide her father's role in the previous government. The book is written from a first-person perspective, and ends with Ung and her brother Meng and his wife traveling to a refugee camp in Thailand, where they await a plane to the United States.

Ung's second book, *Lucky Child* (2006), details her adjustment to life in the United States, contrasting it with her sister Chou's life in Cambodia. Close in age, the two were inseparable until the war, when Ung went to a child labor camp to be trained as a child soldier. Later, her older brother Meng chose her to go to the United States, and they were forced to leave the rest of their family members behind. *Lucky Child* tells the story of her sister's survival in postwar Cambodia. Ung's work has brought widespread attention to the atrocities committed during the reign of the Khmer Rouge. Both of her memoirs were best-sellers, and she has been asked to speak at many events about the Cambodian genocide. Today, Ung lives in Ohio, but regularly visits Cambodia.

SIGNIFICANCE

Ung has devoted her life to raising awareness of the atrocities perpetrated by the Khmer Rouge and the dangers of active landmines that are still buried throughout Cambodia. Her two best-selling memoirs have helped to bring the horrific history of the Khmer Rouge to the attention of the increasing numbers of Americans too young to have any memory of those events, and to remind those who do remember them.

Susan Hoang

FURTHER READING

Memmott, Carol. "Haunted by Cambodia." *USA Today.* 3 Feb. 2000: 1A. Print. Interview with Ung done after publication of *First They Killed My Father.*

Ung, Loung. *First They Killed My Father: A Daughter of Cambodia Remembers*. New York: Harper Perennial, 2006. Print. Ung's first memoir recounts her life as a child facing the trauma of war.

EDISON UNO

Activist, social reformer, and educator

After spending several years in internment camps as a teen, Uno worked to obtain legal redress for the many Japanese Americans who were interned during World War II. He encouraged people to speak about their wartime experiences and the hardships endured as a consequence of racism.

Born: October 19, 1929; Los Angeles, California
Died: December 24, 1976; California
Full name: Edison Tomimaro Uno (TOH-mee-MAH-roh EW-noh)
Areas of achievement: Activism, social issues, education

EARLY LIFE

Edison Tomimaro Uno was born in California in 1929, one of ten children. Following the Japanese attack on Pearl Harbor in 1941, Uno's father, George, was taken into FBI custody and relocated to several different internment camps. The rest of the family was sent to the temporary assembly center in Santa Anita, California, and then on to Colorado's Amache War Relocation Center. Uno and his family finally reunited with George in an internment camp in Crystal City, Texas. Uno's mother and siblings were later released, but he remained in the camp with his father, becoming one of the last internees to leave.

In 1946, Uno returned to Los Angeles, where he became president of his senior class at John Marshall High School. He also became the youngest president of the East Los Angeles chapter of the Japanese American Citizens League (JACL), elected at the age of eighteen. Uno went on to earn a degree in political science from Los Angeles State College, later known as California State University at Los Angeles. He married Rosalind Kido, with whom he later had two daughters.

LIFE'S WORK

Uno managed an import-export company for a time before accepting the first of several positions at the University of California, San Francisco. He worked as an operations manager and a financial aid officer and, in 1969, assumed the role of assistant dean of students, a position he held until 1974. In addition, he lectured on Asian American studies and Japanese American history at several colleges and universities.

Uno served in the JACL for much of his life and devoted himself to lobbying for the repeal of the Emergency Detention Act, Title II of the Internal Security Act of 1950, which allowed "subversive" people to be held without trial during a national security emergency. The legislation was repealed in 1971. During the late 1960s, Uno supported students who went on strike for freedom of speech and the rights of minority students at San Francisco State College. In 1969, he joined other activists in a pilgrimage to Manzanar, one of the internment camps, to restore what remained and bear witness to the injustice. He later served on the Manzanar Committee, which convinced the California government to name the Manzanar camp a historical landmark in 1972. Uno and others also succeeded in altering the landmark plaque's wording to include the term *concentration camp*, rather than a more innocuous phrase such as *relocation center*.

During the 1970s, Uno was part of a group that called for redress for the thousands of former internees who had been unjustly deprived of property and civil rights during World War II. He also aided in obtaining a presidential pardon for Iva Toguri D'Aquino, better known as Tokyo Rose, a woman wrongly convicted of spreading pro-Japanese propaganda during the war. Uno coauthored a children's book, *Japanese Americans: The Untold Story*, published in 1970. He served as an advisor for several television productions, including a documentary produced by NBC, *Guilty by Reason of Race* (1972).

SIGNIFICANCE

Uno received a number of awards in recognition of his work, including the San Francisco Bar Association's Liberty Bell Award. Both an institute at San Francisco State University and a civil-rights award issued by the JACL were named in his honor. Largely due to the efforts of activists such as Uno, in 1988 President Ronald Reagan approved the Civil Liberties Act, which granted monetary reparations to former internees and issued an official apology for the internment of Japanese Americans.

Judy A. Johnson

FURTHER READING

Hongo, Florence M., ed. *Japanese American Journey: The Story of a People*. San Mateo: Japanese Amer. Curriculum Project, 1985. Print. Provides a biographical sketch, including photographs, that highlights Uno's humor and passion for justice.

Hosokawa, Bill. *JACL in Quest of Justice*. New York: Morrow, 1982. Print. Discusses the JACL's efforts to obtain compensation for those relocated to internment camps.

Murray, Alice Yang. "Edison Uno: The Experience and Legacy of the Japanese American Internment." *The Human Tradition in California*. Ed. Clark Davis and David Igler. Wilmington: Scholarly Resources, 2002. 161–76. Print. Explores the political reasons for the internment of Japanese Americans and places Uno's efforts in context.

---. *Historical Memories of the Japanese American Internment and the Struggle for Redress*. Palo Alto, CA: Stanford UP, 2007. Print. Covers Uno's involvement in the movement for redress as well as his experience of detention.

EDDIE VAN HALEN

Dutch-born musician

Eddie Van Halen is the cofounder and lead guitarist for the American hard rock band Van Halen. He is widely considered one of the greatest guitarists of all time, known for his unique style that has been copied by countless guitarists after him.

Born: January 26, 1955; Amsterdam, Netherlands
Full name: Edward Lodewijk van Halen
Area of achievement: Music

EARLY LIFE

Eddie Van Halen was born Edward Lodewijk van Halen on January 26, 1955, in Amsterdam, the Netherlands. His father, Jan, was a Dutch clarinetist, saxophonist, and pianist, and his mother, Eugenia, was originally from the former Dutch colony of Indonesia and was half Dutch and half Indonesian. The family moved to Nijmegen, the Netherlands, shortly after Eddie was born. He and his older brother Alex began taking piano lessons at the ages of six and nine, continuing for nearly a decade.

In 1962 the van Halens moved to Pasadena, California, to be near some of Eugenia's family. Upon arriving in the United States, Jan decided to Americanize the family name, changing it to Van Halen. In Pasadena, Jan worked as a janitor at the Masonic Temple, washed dishes at Arcadia Methodist Hospital, and played in wedding bands, while Eugenia cleaned houses. Eddie knew no English when they arrived in the United States.

Eddie and Alex formed their first band, the Broken Combs, in elementary school, with Alex playing saxophone and Eddie playing piano. Despite their parents' emphasis on classical music, Eddie and Alex were drawn to the rock and roll of their new American home by the time they were in junior high school. Reluctantly, their parents bought Alex a guitar while Eddie used the money from his paper route to buy a drum set. Alex found the guitar frustrating and took advantage of Eddie's delivery schedule to play his drums. Eddie, as

Eddie Van Halen. (Getty Images)

769

Eddie Van Halen's Technique and Style

A dominant figure in rock music, Eddie Van Halen expanded the techniques of the electric guitar by constantly pushing its boundaries. He showed an affinity for power chords, distorted amplifiers, and feedback associated with rock music. He also elevated the practice of two-handed tapping and promoted the extended solo.

Van Halen's incredible talent is evident in his extended guitar solo in the song "Eruption." Released in 1978 on *Van Halen*, "Eruption" is one of the most influential guitar solos in the history of rock music. The instrumental opens with a single power chord, establishing a tonal center. Then Van Halen explores the pentatonic scale, employing a series of passages using hammer-ons, pull-offs, and artificial harmonics. The opening section closes with the use of the whammy bar. The next section also begins with the striking of power chords, which changes to string bends reminiscent of legendary rock guitarist Chuck Berry. A tremolo section—a series of rapid repetitions of a single note—follows, and Van Halen punctuates with another whammy bar dive. He returns to the use of fast passages involving repeated notes, reintroducing passages with hammer-ons and pull-offs. The climax of the celebrated guitar solo commences with two-handed tapping, outlining chords with arpeggios with the use of the right hand to tap, working in conjunction with the left hand. After a lengthy tapping section, the guitar instrumental concludes with harmonics and feedback, amplified by the use of the whammy bar.

an act of revenge, began learning blues guitar solos on Alex's guitar. By the time he was twelve, Eddie was studying guitar legend Eric Clapton's solos from Clapton's recordings with the Yardbirds and Cream.

LIFE'S WORK

In 1972, the Van Halen brothers formed a trio called Mammoth with Alex on drums, Eddie on guitar and vocals, and friend Mark Stone on bass. They rented their sound equipment from a young singer named David Lee Roth. As Eddie became increasingly frustrated singing the lead, he decided he could save the band money by inviting Roth to join as the lead vocalist in 1974. That same year, bassist Michael Anthony replaced Mark Stone. They soon discovered there was another band named Mammoth based in Los Angeles. At Roth's suggestion, they changed the band's name to Van Halen.

By 1977, Van Halen was a popular local band, playing night clubs all over California. It was in one of those clubs that Van Halen caught the attention of KISS bassist and cofounder Gene Simmons, who financed their first demo tape. The band signed with Warner Brothers Records in 1977 and released their eponymous debut album in 1978. Van Halen released a total of six albums between 1978 and 1984, despite internal conflicts between members.

Eddie married television actress Valerie Bertinelli, popular for her role on *One Day at a Time,* on April 11, 1981. Their son, Wolfgang William Van Halen (named for the composer Wolfgang Amadeus Mozart), was born March 16, 1991. The couple separated in 2001, and Bertinelli filed for divorce in 2005; it was finalized in 2008. Eddie married his publicist, Janie Liszewski, in 2009.

In 1982, Eddie was asked by producer Quincy Jones to perform the guitar solo on the song "Beat It" from Michael Jackson's *Thriller* album. The band's 1984 album, *1984*, produced their first set of number-one hits, "Jump," "Panama," and "Hot for Teacher." It would be their final album with Roth, who left to pursue a solo career.

Sammy Hagar, who had been the lead singer of the rock band Montrose, was hired to replace Roth in 1985. Van Halen's music took on a less aggressive, more commercial sound that featured Eddie's keyboard playing over his virtuosic guitar playing. They released five albums before Hagar left in 1996. After a brief reunion with Roth, former Extreme vocalist Gary Cherone joined the band for the poorly received *Van Halen III* album (1998). Following Cherone's departure, the band announced they were going on hiatus.

Over the course of his career, Eddie suffered numerous injuries from onstage falls and crashes while performing the acrobatics for which the band became known. As a result, he had hip replacement surgery in 1999. In May 2000, he began treatment for oral cancer and was declared cancer-free the next year.

In 2004, Hagar rejoined the band for a brief reunion tour. In 2007, the band announced a similar reunion tour with Roth; however, this tour was delayed after Eddie entered a rehabilitation center for undisclosed reasons. The tour launched in the fall of 2007 with Eddie's son replacing Anthony as the bassist. The band was inducted into the Rock and Roll Hall of Fame that same year. Rumors persisted through 2009 and 2010 of an album of new material and a supporting tour, but none materialized.

SIGNIFICANCE

Eddie Van Halen is one of the foundational performers of virtuosic hard rock and heavy metal guitar styles of the 1980s. His combination of classically grounded technique and innovative performance techniques such as two-handed fretboard tapping made Van Halen one of the most decorated and imitated guitarists of the era. He is regularly regarded alongside Jimmy Page, Jimi Hendrix, and Steve Vai as one of the most influential guitarists in rock.

Eric S. Strother

FURTHER READING

Christe, Ian. *Everybody Wants Some: The Van Halen Saga*. Hoboken, NJ: Wiley. 2008. Print. Band history and biography.

Tolinsky, Brad, ed. *Guitar World Presents Van Halen*. New York: Leonard, 1997. Collection of interviews from the magazine on the band.

Zlozower, Neil, and David Lee Roth. *Van Halen: A Visual History 1978–1984*. San Francisco: Chronicle, 2008. Print. Images and quotes from the bad during the years they recorded and toured with David Lee Roth.

ALI VELSHI

Kenyan-born journalist and writer

Recognized by television viewers worldwide as the chief business correspondent on the Cable News Network (CNN), Velshi is an anchor on the popular shows CNN Newsroom *and* Your Money, *as well as* World Business Today *on CNN International. He has published numerous articles and books about finance.*

Born: October 29, 1969; Nairobi, Kenya

Full name: Ali Velshi

Areas of achievement: Television, business, and journalism

EARLY LIFE

Ali Velshi was born in Kenya in 1969 to Muslim parents of Indian descent. They moved to Toronto, Canada, where Ali was raised. Ali's father, Murad, became the first Indian Canadian member of Ontario's Legislative Assembly.

Velshi attended Queen's University in Kingston, Ontario, and completed his degree in religious studies in 1994. At college he was involved in politics and worked at the student newspaper and radio station. After graduation, he became a reporter for the Canadian television station CFTO-TV. In 1996, his interest in politics led to an American Political Science Association fellowship working with US Representative Lee Hamilton, Democrat of Indiana.

Returning to Canada in 1997, Velshi became a business anchorman for Cable Pulse 24 and CITY TV, and in 1999 moved to ROB-TV (Report on Business Television), which later became the Business News Network. Ali was hired by CNN's now-defunct financial channel, CNNfn, in 2001, and began working in New York that

September, during the week of the terrorist attacks on the United States. His shows on CNNfn included *The Money Gang, Business Unusual, Your Money,* and *Insights.* When CNNfn went off the air, Velshi was retained as a reporter and business commentator for the main CNN programs. He began to attract a more general

Ali Velshi. (Getty Images)

audience who appreciated his warmth and good humor. Although his primary work was on financial and business news, Ali also reported on significant events and breaking news such as Hurricane Katrina, which he covered from the vantage point of an oil rig in the Gulf of Mexico.

LIFE'S WORK

In 2005, Velshi served as host for CNN's *The Turnaround*, a show that traveled across the United States featuring struggling small business owners. Velshi introduced them to highly successful individuals who could advise them on ways to improve their enterprises. Velshi was included when CNN created a new program, *The Situation Room*, in 2005. He appeared on the show until 2006, when he became a business reporter for the very popular *American Morning* program. Recalling the success of Velshi's 2005 program *The Turnaround*, CNN sent him on the road again in 2008 for the *Election Express* to cover the Texas primaries.

He continued to cover special events, and in 2008, when a financial meltdown signaled the beginning of a new recession, Velshi was in great demand for appearances and programs. By this time, his ability to explain financial trends in layman's terms had earned the trust of CNN viewers. He continued the *Your Money* program, begun during the CNNfn years, and in 2011 cohosted the weekly program with financial anchor Christine Romans. Velshi has been featured on podcasts and radio programs, and as an author of articles in publications such as *Money* magazine. He also writes his own blog.

Velshi, who was married for a brief time in the 1990s, met Lori Wachs, an investment manager, when she appeared on his program. They married in 2009. In 2010, he moved from New York to be near the global CNN headquarters in Atlanta, Georgia.

He returned to *American Morning* as a coanchor in 2011. Also in 2011, he presented several programs for *CNN Newsroom*. Although serious and insightful, Velshi balanced this with a self-deprecating sense of humor, sometimes making fun of his own baldness during his exchanges with other journalists. Audiences welcomed his touch of empathy as their anxieties rose over concerns about the global economy and its impact on their own well-being.

SIGNIFICANCE

Ali Velshi is a familiar media figure who began sharing his ideas on finances with CNN's vast audiences in 2001. He has participated in the interpretation of crucial and often traumatic events such as the assassination of Benazir Bhutto in 2008, the financial crash of 2008, the bailouts of automakers and financial institutions that followed, the Gulf oil spill of 2010, and the debt ceiling crisis of 2011. In 2010 he received the National Headliner Award for Business and Consumer Reporting for CNN's *How the Wheels Came Off*, a program about the American auto industry's near collapse. His coverage of the attempted terrorist attack on a Delta Airlines flight into Detroit in December 2009 earned a 2010 Emmy Award nomination for CNN. Along with his CNN colleagues Sanjay Gupta and Kiran Chetry, Velshi became a role model for young Americans of South Asian descent.

Alice Myers

FURTHER READING

Laise, Eleanor. "How to Survive the 2009 Boom in Money Books." *Wall Street Journal* Eastern Edition, 20 Jan. 2009: B9. Print. Comparative review of several financial books, including Velshi's *Gimme My Money Back*.

Potter, Deborah. "Business Blather: The Financial Meltdown Was a Missed Opportunity for Cable News." *Journalism Review* 30.6 (Dec. 2008): 50. Print. Critical description of the major cable news networks' handling of the financial crisis of 2008, including statements by Velshi and others on CNN as well as MSNBC.

Velshi, Ali. *Gimme My Money Back: Your Guide to Beating the Financial Crisis*. New York: Sterling, 2009. Print. Velshi provides practical advice for beginning investors or those recovering from major losses resulting from the global economic crisis.

BRANDON VERA

Mixed martial artist

Brandon Vera established himself as a rising star in mixed martial arts by winning the 2005 heavyweight tournament in World Extreme Cagefighting (WEC). Since then, he has had a successful career with the Ultimate Fighting Championship (UFC).

Born: October 10, 1977; Norfolk, Virginia
Full name: Brandon Michael Vera
Also known as: The Truth
Area of achievement: Sports

EARLY LIFE

Brandon Michael Vera was born in Norfolk, Virginia, on October 10, 1977. Vera was raised by his Filipino father, Ernesto Mendoza Vera Sr., and his adoptive Filipina mother, Amelia Guerra Vera. His biological mother was Italian. Vera grew up in a close-knit family that includes a sister, Michelle (who is also a mixed martial artist), as well as his grandmother and aunts and uncles.

Vera began as a wrestler at Norfolk's Lake Taylor High School. Going undefeated for his first two years of

Brandon Vera. (Zuffa LLC via Getty Images)

competition, Vera wrestled well enough to earn a four-year athletic scholarship to Old Dominion University, also in Norfolk. However, Vera realized after only a year and a half that college was not for him. He subsequently left school and enlisted in the United States Air Force. He was sent to Colorado Springs, Colorado, where he continued his wrestling training at the US Olympic Training Center.

Vera intended to compete in the Olympic trials for the 2000 games, but his wrestling career came to an abrupt halt in 1999 after he tore ligaments in his right elbow. He underwent arthroscopic surgery to repair the ligaments, but he suffered nerve damage and was released from the Air Force on a medical discharge. Vera spent a year and a half rehabilitating his arm and working as a telecommunications installer, but the job was only temporary. As soon as he was medically able, Vera began training in martial arts and continued his wrestling training. In 2002, Vera won the Grapplers Quest tournament in the 225-pound class. His natural ability caught the eye of Lloyd Irvin, who introduced Vera to the sport of mixed martial arts.

LIFE'S WORK

For the first few years of his mixed martial arts training, Vera served as an assistant trainer at Irvin's gym. After two fights in three years, Vera began his career officially in 2005. Winning both of his fights by technical knockout (TKO), Vera defeated both of his opponents in the one-night World Extreme Cagefighting (WEC) tournament in January 2005, earning a call from the Ultimate Fighting Championship (UFC). After his successful debut in October 2005, defeating Fabiano Scherner with knee strikes, Vera followed up the next year with three victories over the top UFC heavyweight fighters. Vera, who specializes in Muay Thai kickboxing, defeated former UFC heavyweight title challenger Justin Eilers at UFC 57 with a head kick. In May 2006 at UFC 60, Vera demonstrated his ability in submission holds, forcing Assuerio Silva to submit with a guillotine choke in the first round. Vera was then put in the cage against former UFC heavyweight champion Frank Mir to determine if he was worthy of challenging then-champion Tim Sylvia for the title. Vera earned his title shot with a first-round knockout over Mir.

Before his title fight, Vera got into a contract dispute with the UFC and found himself out of competition from

November 2006 until October 2007. Vera's return fight at UFC 77 was against his original opponent, Tim Sylvia, who had lost his title to UFC Hall-of-Famer Randy Couture during the time Vera was renegotiating his contract. Vera suffered his first loss against Sylvia, losing a unanimous decision. Vera also suffered a broken left hand in the fight, resulting in another long break from competition.

Vera returned at UFC 85, losing a controversial fight to Fabricio Werdum wherein Vera alleged the referee stopped the fight prematurely. Frustrated with his heavyweight quest, Vera dropped down to the light heavyweight division and defeated Reese Andy by unanimous decision at UFC Fight Night 14. He then lost a hard-fought split decision against Keith Jardine at UFC 89 in October 2008, but rebounded with two strong wins in 2009 against Michael Patt and Krzysztof Soszynski. He then lost a controversial split decision to Couture, despite Vera offering one of his strongest performances to date. He even dropped Couture with a knee strike.

After the loss to Couture, Vera suffered two more losses to current UFC Light Heavyweight Champion Jon Jones and Thiago Silva. The second loss was changed to a no-contest by the Nevada State Athletic Commission after Silva failed the athletic commission's drug test. Originally let go from his UFC contract following the loss, Vera has since been reinstated.

SIGNIFICANCE

Brandon Vera is currently the premier Filipino mixed martial artist. After the calamitous 2009 Pacific typhoon season, Vera aided the Their Fight Is Our Fight charity by hosting mixed martial arts seminars to raise money for relief funds. Vera is proud of his Filipino heritage, and he encourages all aspiring Filipino mixed martial artists to work hard and raise awareness in their country about the sport of mixed martial arts. On July 9, 2011, Vera hosted a mixed martial arts seminar for autism awareness, and later that month, he was inducted into the Grapplers Quest Hall of Fame for his accomplished submission wrestling career.

Kyle Barrowman

FURTHER READING

Sievert, Steve. "With Brandon Vera, UFC Expansion Poised for Warm Response in Philippines." *MMAjunkie.com*. 26 Aug. 2008. Web. 2 Apr. 2012. Sievert reveals the UFC's plans to expand the sport internationally, with the help of Brandon Vera.

"The Truth about Brandon Vera." *Philippine Star*. Philstar, 20 June 2010. Web. 2 Apr. 2012. Explains Brandon Vera's product endorsements in the Philippines and his connection to his father's homeland.

PHILIP VERA CRUZ

Philippine-born labor activist

Vera Cruz was part of the first generation of Filipinos—or manongs, as they were respectfully called in the Filipino dialect of Ilocano—who immigrated to the United States in the 1920s and early 1930s. He helped found the United Farm Workers, serving as the union's vice president from its founding in 1966 to his departure in 1977. Vera Cruz embodied the ideals of internationalism as he dedicated his life to the causes of immigrant and human rights, especially for workers located in the United States and the Philippines.

Born: December 25, 1904; Saoag, Ilocos Sur, Philippines
Died: June 12, 1994; Bakersfield, California
Full name: Philip Villamin Vera Cruz
Also known as: Manong Philip
Areas of achievement: Activism, social issues

EARLY LIFE

Philip Vera Cruz was born in Saoag, Ilocos Sur, the Philippines. Due to his father's ill health, the impoverishment of his country, and a desire to support his siblings' educational endeavors, Vera Cruz immigrated to the United States in 1926. Like that of many Filipinos of his generation—affectionately called *manongs*—Vera Cruz's arrival in the United States was precipitated by the passing of the Immigration Act of 1924. This legislation placed a restriction on Japanese, Chinese, and other East Asian immigrants into the country, but not on Filipino immigrants. As a result, single Filipino males became the new source of inexpensive labor for the nation's industry. Vera Cruz would travel throughout the United States, finding himself in such cities as Seattle, Chicago, and Spokane, working various menial jobs throughout his young life. He picked seasonal crops and worked in canneries, doing whatever he could find for work.

Philip Vera Cruz and the United Farm Workers Union

Although Philip Vera Cruz served as the second vice president of the Californian United Farm Workers Union (UFW) from 1966 to 1977, he did not always agree with UFW policies. Vera Cruz believed in an immigrant labor struggle that transcended the boundaries of the United States to encompass justice for workers of every race, nationality, religion, and gender. This internationalist position clashed with what he believed to be the UFW's insularity. Vera Cruz has said that he was the only UFW board member to express objection to the union's policy against undocumented immigrant workers. He spent many years suppressing his differences with Cesar Chavez's leadership, especially in regard to Chavez's views toward undocumented immigrants and what Vera Cruz deemed as undemocratic union practices. Still, Vera Cruz stayed with the union because he believed in the ideals of labor solidarity as well as the UFW's ability to mobilize immigrant workers for better wages and improved working conditions. In 1977, however, he left the union. Chavez had accepted an invitation from the US-supported dictatorship of Ferdinand Marcos to visit the Philippines, and Vera Cruz was no longer able to compromise with the contradictory decisions of UFW leadership.

Vera Cruz attended school when he could, after sending large portions of his wages to his family in the Philippines. Eventually, he was able to save enough money to complete a few courses at Gonzaga University in Spokane, Washington. However, without the necessary funds for his matriculation he was unable to complete more than a year of higher education. In 1942, at the age of thirty-eight, Vera Cruz was drafted into the US military and stationed in San Luis Obispo, California. Because of his older age, Vera Cruz did not serve in World War II; instead he was discharged from military service to work in the fields. In 1943 he followed a cousin to the town of Delano in California's Central Valley, where he would become one of the most important Filipino labor leaders in US history.

LIFE'S WORK

Vera Cruz's early years diverged greatly from those of other Filipino labor leaders, such as Chris Mensalvas, Ernesto Mangaong, and Carlos Bulosan, who helped organize the labor movement in the United States from the 1930s through the early 1950s. Through a culmination of various life experiences, Vera Cruz would realize that the rhetoric of the American Dream was a far cry from the reality of racial exclusion and labor exploitation that his compatriots experienced every day. His politicization would continue to mature

through his participation and leadership role in the Agricultural Workers Organizing Committee (AWOC) in the 1960s, which consisted primarily of Filipino farm workers. On September 8, 1965, Vera Cruz played an instrumental role in AWOC's decision to refuse the grape growers' proposal to work below an hourly wage of $1.40. The decision to strike, initiated by Filipino farm workers, served as the catalyst for a nation-wide movement to defy the exploitative wages and oppressive working conditions of America's agricultural workers. In August 1966, as a result of the Delano Grape Strike (1965–70), Vera Cruz's AWOC would merge with the National Farm Workers Association (NFWA), led by Cesar Chavez, to form the United Farm Workers of America (UFW). Vera Cruz served as second vice president, the highest-ranking Filipino officer of the UFW. During his tenure, he was instrumental in the formation of a Farm Workers Credit Union as well as Agbayani Village, a retirement community for elder Filipino farm workers.

Vera Cruz resigned from the UFW in 1977 to protest UFW leadership and, in particular, Chavez's decision to accept an invitation to the Philippines from the then-dictator Ferdinand Marcos. After his departure from the union, Vera Cruz remained politically active by speaking at various college campuses and community events as well as to audiences of youth, activists, and students who would travel to Agbayani Village. In sharing his life experiences, he urged the younger generation of Filipino Americans to engage in global democratic struggles and link the social problems facing immigrants at home with US policies of aggression and support for military dictatorships abroad.

In 1987, Vera Cruz received the Ninoy M. Aquino Award for his lifelong service to the Filipino community in the United States. This award allowed him to return to the Philippines more than sixty years after he first departed, where he was reunited with his siblings and family members. In 1992, Vera Cruz was also honored at the founding convention of the American Federation of Labor and Congress of Industrial Organizations' (AFL-CIO) Asian Pacific American Labor Committee. On June 12, 1994, Vera Cruz died of emphysema at Mercy Hospital in Bakersfield, California.

SIGNIFICANCE

Vera Cruz dedicated his life to the causes of immigrant, worker, and human rights. As a labor organizer he championed the ideals of international solidarity. As a Filipino immigrant in the United States, he created links with other marginalized groups as he realized that any immigrant community acting by itself for social change would not be able to attain sustainable victories in a labor or social movement. His life is a testament to the possibilities of collective democratic struggle and his legacy continues to inspire those struggling to create a more just and peaceful world.

Michael Joseph Viola

FURTHER READING

Fujita Rony, Dorothy. "Coalitions, Race, and Labor: Rereading Philip Vera Cruz." *Journal of Asian American Studies* 3.2 (June 2000): 139–62. Print. Revisits the important contributions of Vera Cruz and explores the challenges and possibilities for coalition building across the terrains of race and social difference.

San Juan, Epifanio, Jr. "Parallel Lives: Carlos Bulosan and Philip Vera Cruz." *Balikbayang Sinta: An E. San Juan Reader*. Manila: Ateneo de Manila UP, 2008. Print. Provides a comparative analysis of these two important Filipino labor leaders, situating both of their lives in their appropriate historical context and exploring why Vera Cruz's life is still widely unknown while Bulosan has been canonized in such fields as American ethnic and cultural studies.

Scharlin, Craig, and Lilia V. Villanueva. *Philip Vera Cruz: A Personal History of Filipino Immigrants and the Farmworkers Movement*. Seattle: U of Washington P, 2000. Print. A powerful biography that offers an important window into his life and the oppressive conditions of the manong generation that fueled their militancy and resistance.

Valledor, Sid Amores. *The Original Writings of Philip Vera Cruz*. Indianapolis: Dog Ear, 2006. Print. Contains Vera Cruz's recollections of his involvement with the farm workers' movement as well as reflections from Valledor, who knew Vera Cruz personally.

ABRAHAM VERGHESE

Ethiopian-born physician, writer, educator

Abraham Verghese is a physician, novelist, and teacher. In addition to his achievements as a clinician, Verghese is known for his work in combating the global AIDS epidemic. He has published several best-selling books and numerous articles in professional medical journals.

Born: 1955; Ethiopia
Full name: Abraham Verghese (vuhr-GEEZ)
Areas of achievement: Medicine, publishing, education

EARLY LIFE

Abraham Verghese was born in 1955 in Ethiopia to Indian parents who were both teachers. He was raised in a Christian household. Although he started medical school in Ethiopia, Verghese left for the United States in 1973 when Ethiopia's political climate became unstable following the deposition of Emperor Haile Selassie. Verghese completed his medical education at Madras Medical College in Chennai, India. He returned to the United States in 1980 to complete his internship and residency at East Tennessee State University in Johnson City, Tennessee.

After completing his residency in 1983, Verghese took a fellowship at the Boston University School of Medicine. He worked at the Boston City Hospital while training as a specialist in infectious diseases. There, Verghese witnessed the beginning of the HIV epidemic as cases increased throughout the United States. Verghese returned to Johnson City as an assistant professor of medicine and studied Tennessee's rural epidemic of AIDS and HIV from 1985 to 1989. He compassionately cared for AIDS patients during a time when little could be done except to provide support and palliation.

LIFE'S WORK

Verghese moved to Iowa in 1990 and took a position at an AIDS outpatient clinic at the University of Iowa. His role as an orderly providing patient care, along with his efforts with AIDS patients, provided Verghese with many insights. He became interested in writing about his experiences, and enrolled in a masters in fine arts program at the University of Iowa. After earning his MFA in 1991, Verghese relocated to El Paso, Texas to become a professor of medicine and chief of the

Abraham Verghese. (AFP/Getty Images)

infectious disease division at the Texas Tech Health Sciences Center. Verghese's first book, *My Own Country: A Doctor's Story* (1995), recounts his experience working with AIDS patients in Johnson City. The book was selected by *Time* magazine as a Best Book of the Year. While in Texas, Verghese wrote and published his second book, *The Tennis Partner*, in 1998. Also a bestseller, the book tells the story of Verghese's colleague who struggled with drug addiction.

Verghese founded the Center for Medical Humanities and Ethics located at the University of Texas Health Science Center in San Antonio. He defined the core mission of the center as "imagining the patient's experience." Verghese stressed to the center's medical students the importance of compassion and sensitivity toward patients. He led patient rounds with small groups, demonstrating physical examinations and mentoring students in their behavior toward patients' families as part of ultimate patient care. Verghese's unique approach to bedside medicine gained him recognition in the greater medical community. Verghese later took a position at Stanford University School of Medicine as Professor of Theory and Practice of Medicine and senior Associate Chair of the Department of Internal Medicine.

Verghese continues to reach out with his mission of patient care through both his writing and his medical practice. In 2008, he shared his commitment to bedside medicine and physical assessment along with technological advances in an article entitled "Culture Shock: Patient as Icon, Icon as Patient" in the December issue of the *New England Journal of Medicine*. His third book, *Cutting for Stone*, was published in 2009. This book, Verghese's first novel, became his third bestseller, and it was recognized as a "Notable Book" by the *New York Times*.

SIGNIFICANCE

As a young doctor, Verghese faced prejudices against foreign medical graduates. Through perseverance and hard work, he became a successful author and an innovator of clinical care practices. His writing has appeared in the *New York Times*, the *New Yorker*, *Sports Magazine*, and the *Wall Street Journal*. Verghese personifies

Abraham Verghese's Autobiography *My Own Country*

Verghese's autobiography, *My Own Country: A Doctor's Story of a Town and Its People in the Age of AIDS* (1995), is more than a series of case histories or a chronicle of the doctor-patient relationship. It is also an intensely personal story of one man's search for a sense of belonging and a country to think of as home. He finds it, at least for a short while, among his AIDS patients and their families in a small, out-of-the-way corner of the world in rural Tennessee.

Due to the unexpected presence of a considerable number of AIDS cases, Verghese became, by virtue of his specialization in infectious diseases, the area's AIDS expert. He began receiving AIDS patients a year after he moved to Tennessee. When a former coworker asked him to examine her brother, Verghese was drawn inexorably into the emotionally charged world of AIDS.

AIDS patients began seeking out Verghese with increasing frequency. Many managed to summon up courage, dignity, and humanity from the most desperate circumstances. As these patients struggled to come to terms with their disease, their doctor underwent his own odyssey. Aware of the parallels between his own status as a "foreigner" and that of his homosexual patients, he gained insight into the plight of gays in "straight" society. The autobiography, despite its subject of death and disease, is rich in stories of compassion, courage, humanity, and humor.

the ancient Greek ideal of the Hippocratic physician, as much of his work has focused on the preservation and improvement of the patient-physician relationship. His leadership and mentoring at Stanford University School of Medicine, along with his prolific writing, have made a significant impact on patient care worldwide.

Marylane Wade Koch

FURTHER READING

Srikanth, Rajini, and Esther Yae Iwanaga, eds. *Bold Words: A Century of Asian American Writing*. Piscataway, NJ: Rutgers UP, 2001. Print. Anthology of Asian American writings including a contribution from Verghese about his experience with AIDS patients.

Verghese, Abraham. "Culture Shock–Patient as Icon, Icon as Patient." *New England Journal of Medicine* 359.26 (25 Dec. 2008): 2748–50. Print. Offers Verghese's perspective on the modern physician's education, and the need to return to bedside medicine and physical assessment, while appreciating the role of technology in optimal patient care.

---. *The Tennis Partner*. New York: Harper Collins, 1998. Print. Presents the true story of the author's physician friend and tennis partner and his struggle with drug addiction.

SHANE VICTORINO

Professional baseball player

Victorino is one of a small number of Hawaiian-born players in baseball's major leagues. A fleet switch-hitting outfielder, he was an important member of the Philadelphia Phillies World Championship 2008 team.

Born: November 30, 1980; Wailuku, Hawaii
Full name: Shane Patrick Victorino
Also known as: The Flyin' Hawaiian, the Pineapple Express
Areas of achievement: Sports, philanthropy

EARLY LIFE

Shane Patrick Victorino was born on November 30, 1980 in Wailuku, Maui, Hawaii, to Jocelyn and Michael Victorino. As a child, Victorino struggled with attention deficit hyperactivity disorder (ADHD). He excelled at soccer, football, track, and baseball, assisted by his father, who coached youth sports. In 1999, at St. Anthony's High School on Maui, Victorino won the 100-, 200-, and 400-meter races at the state level, setting the state record of 10.80 seconds for the 100-meter event. The Los Angeles Dodgers selected Victorino in the sixth round of the 1999 Major League Baseball (MLB) draft, 194th overall. He began his minor league career with the Dodgers, where he stayed until December 2002, when the San Diego Padres selected him in the Rule 5 Draft.

Victorino made his major league debut with the Padres on April 2, 2003. However, he hit only .151 in thirty-six games and was returned to the Dodgers minor league system. Victorino's fortunes changed when the Philadelphia Phillies picked him as a Rule 5 draftee from the Dodgers on December 13, 2004. At the Phillies' minor league Scranton/Wilkes Barre Red Barons game in 2005, Victorino won the league's Most Valuable Player award after batting .310. He was selected as an All-Star and made a brief appearance in the major

Shane Victorino. (Getty Images)

leagues with the Phillies at the end of their regular season. He became a full-time major leaguer in 2006.

LIFE'S WORK

Victorino has become a mainstay in the Phillies outfield and a popular player among fans of the Phillies. In 2007, the Phillies and their fans even celebrated "Shane Victorino Day." Victorino's father was in attendance. Victorino was an integral part of the 2008 Phillies World Championship season. In Game 2 of the National League Division Series against the Milwaukee Brewers, Victorino hit a grand slam into the left field bleachers to break the game open and helped propel the Phillies on to the next round. They faced the Dodgers in the National League Championship Series (NLCS).

Victorino had a solid series against the Dodgers. In Game 2, he drove in four runs and made a tremendous catch at the left-center field wall. In Game 3, Dodgers pitcher Hiroki Kuroda and Victorino engaged in an argument after Kuroda threw a pitch over Victorino's head. Both benches emptied and fines were later imposed by league officials. In Game 4, Victorino slugged a two-run homer in the eighth inning. The Phillies won 7-5 and earned the opportunity to play in the World Series against the Tampa Bay Rays. Victorino invited many friends and relatives to attend the World Series, and many Hawaiians wore Phillies hats and jerseys in a show of solidarity with Victorino. The Phillies defeated the Rays in five games, earning Victorino his first World Series ring. In the post-season, he was honored with the first Gold Glove award of his career, as well as the Lou Gehrig Memorial Award.

In 2009, Victorino was selected for the National League All-Star Team in a special All-Star final vote and started in center field, the first Hawaiian non-pitcher to play in an MLB All-Star Game. He had one hit and scored a run in a 4-3 National League loss. Victorino was involved in a bizarre incident at Chicago's Wrigley Field while playing the Cubs on August 12, 2009. As Victorino was playing a fly ball, a Chicago Cubs fan threw a cup of beer on him. The fan was charged with illegal conduct at a sports facility and battery. During the 2009 post-season, Victorino hit .353 as his team defeated the Colorado Rockies in the National League Division Series. Once again, the Phillies faced the Dodgers in the NLCS. Victorino hit .368 with two home runs and six runs batted in as the Phillies again defeated the Dodgers to earn their second consecutive trip to the World Series.

In the 2009 World Series, Victorino hit only .182 against the New York Yankees. The Yankees defeated the Phillies in six games. In November 2009, Victorino married Melissa Smith. The couple has three children.

On January 21, 2010, the Phillies signed Victorino to a three-year contract for $22 million. He had a somewhat unsuccessful year in 2010, when his batting average dropped to .259. The playoffs were frustrating for the Phillies in 2010. Although they were heavily favored to win the pennant over the San Francisco Giants, the Phillies lost the series in six games, with Victorino hitting only .208. In 2010, Shane and his wife established the Shane Victorino Foundation to help underprivileged youth. Following the 2010 season, he was awarded his third consecutive Gold Glove. Victorino was designated the Phillies Charities Community Service Award winner in 2010, and was the Phillies Roberto Clemente Award winner. Victorino has also been selected Humanitarian of the Year by the Philadelphia Sportswriters Association.

SIGNIFICANCE

As one of a small number of Hawaiian-born major league players, Victorino has emerged as a positive role model and inspiration for young Hawaiian athletes by virtue of being a star player, World Series Champion, and winner of prestigious awards related not only to his success as an athlete but also to his work with charitable organizations.

Mark C. Herman

FURTHER READING

Maimon, Alan. *Shane Victorino: The High Flyin' Hawaiian*. Chicago: Triumph, 2011. Print. Offers a biography of Victorino, focusing on his overcoming personal struggles related to ADHD to become a star.

Stark, Jayson. *Worth the Wait: Tales of the 2008 Phillies*. Chicago: Triumph, 2009. Print. Victorino's accomplishments in the 2008 season are placed within the context of the Phillies World Championship season.

JOSÉ GARCÍA VILLA

Poet, writer

José García Villa was an experimental modernist poet who made significant innovations in poetic form. His work was a major force in the development of creative writing in English in the Philippines.

Born: August 5, 1908; Singalong, Manila, Philippines
Died: February 7, 1997; New York, New York
Full name: José García Villa
Also known as: The Comma Poet, Doveglion, the Pope of Greenwich Village
Area of achievement: Literature

EARLY LIFE

Villa was born in Singalong, Manila in the Philippine Islands on August 5, 1908. He was the son of Simeon Villa and Guía García. Villa graduated from the University of the Philippines High School in 1925. Planning to pursue a medical career, he enrolled in pre-med courses at the University of the Philippines. He later changed his concentration to pre-law, but realized that neither medicine nor law suited his interests. Villa realized his true passion was art. He was first attracted to painting, but upon reading Sherman Anderson's *Winesburg, Ohio*, he began writing short stories and poems.

In 1929, he published his first collection of poetry, entitled *Man Songs*. The experimental, erotic poems caused considerable controversy in the Philippines and resulted in Villa's suspension from the university. He was also fined for obscenity by the Manila Court of First Instance. Villa's short story "Mir-i-Nisa" was also published in 1929 and earned him increased recognition as a writer. The Philippine Free Press selected it for its 1929 Best Story of the Year Award. Villa used the prize money from the award to travel to the United States in 1930. He enrolled at the University of New Mexico and graduated with a bachelor of arts degree in 1933. While at the university, he pursued literary studies and was one of the founders of the magazine *Clay*, where he worked as an editor. During this period, Villa wrote several short stories, several of which were published in American magazines. Edward O'Brien included Villa's work in his anthology of *The Best Short Stories of 1932*.

LIFE'S WORK

In 1933, Villa published a collection of his short stories entitled *Footnotes to Youth*. The collection earned

Villa praise both for his literary talent and for his ability to write in a second language. As a Filipino, he was not a native speaker of English. During the late 1930s and early 1940s, Villa published several collections of poetry, including *Many Voices* (1939), *Poems* (1941), *Have Come, Am Here* (1942), *Selected Poems* (1942) and *New* (1942). In *Have Come, Am Here*, Villa utilized a new type of poetic rhyming, known as reversed consonance, where the last consonant sound of a word becomes the first consonant of the word in the rhyming pair (for example, following the word "said," with the word "days").

In 1942, Villa began doing postgraduate work at Columbia University. His poetry had gained the admiration of many American poets including Conrad Aiken, Richard Eberhart, and Mark Van Doren. Villa received a Guggenheim Fellowship in Creative Writing in 1943. Readers and critics of his day considered him a member of the group of influential writers in New York known as the modernists. This group consisted of E. E. Cummings, Mark Van Doren, Tennessee Williams, W. H. Auden, and Gore Vidal. Villa also used the pen name Doveglion (composed of dove, lion, and eagle) to represent himself and an imaginary country that he claimed as his native land. In 1949, Villa introduced the "comma poem," in which he placed a comma after each word to control the rhythm and speed. For Villa, the form of the poem was as essential as the content.

From 1949 to 1951, Villa served as associate editor at New Directions Publishing. He directed poetry workshops at City College of New York from 1952 to 1960. He published four books in the 1960s and then stopped writing to devote himself to teaching aspiring poets full-time. From 1963 to 1973, Villa taught at The New School for Social Research. Villa also held private workshops at his apartment for students. Late in his career, Villa served as a cultural attaché to the United Nations and as a cultural advisor to the president of the Philippines.

Villa received two honorary doctorates and many awards, including the Philippines National Artist Award for literature. He died in New York City on February 7, 1997. In 1999, a collection of his work entitled *The Anchored Angel* helped reintroduce his work to a new audience. In August 2008, there was a Centennial Celebration of Villa in New York City.

José García Villa's *Have Come, Am Here*

As Villa began collecting and preparing poems for *Have Come, Am Here* (1942), he increasingly pushed the boundaries of his poetic technique. In six of the collection's poems, Villa introduced a new method of rhyming which he called "reversed consonance." As he explained it, "a rhyme for *near* would be *run, green, reign*," with the initial *n–r* combination reversed in each instance. The device is one more variation among Villa's many attempts to break down conventional poetic forms.

Much more successful than Villa's reversed consonance technique was the forward force of both his love lyrics and his "divine poems." These poems are occasionally indistinguishable from one another because the protagonist addresses both his beloved and his god with the same possessive rhetoric: "Between God's eyelashes I look at you, / Contend with the Lord to love you. . . ." Such interplays of ambiguity are made inevitable by the poems' brevity and density, constant ellipses, and startling juxtapositions.

Some of Villa's poems have elements of the French symbolists, E. E. Cummings's curtailments of standard grammar, or the equivalent of cubist/surrealist transformations of reality. Mostly, however, Villa was an original. Feeling emotionally homeless, he fortified his exile by offering in his poetry a universal protagonist. For Villa, that meant a rejection of common codes and orders and a rising above all local circumstances. *Have Come, Am Here* reflects this profound need for self-justification.

SIGNIFICANCE

Although Villa's work is not particularly widely known in the United States, he made significant contributions to poetry and to the short story form. He was the foremost Filipino writer among "artsakists," a group of people who valued art for its own sake and did not believe it needed a political or social purpose. Villa also played an important role in establishing English-language literature as a Filipino genre and was one of the major modernist poets in the United States. Villa's innovative and experimental poetry introduced the reversed consonance rhyme scheme into poetry and made punctuation a significant element of poetry.

Shawncey J. Webb

FURTHER READING

Espiritu, Augusto Fauni. *Five Faces of Exile: The Nation and Filipino American Intellectuals*. Stanford, CA: Stanford UP, 2005. Print. Analyzes works by five Filipino American writers from the viewpoint of diaspora.

Ponce, Martin Joseph. *Beyond the Nation: Diasporic Filipino Literature and Queer Reading*. New York: New York UP, 2011. Print. Discusses eroticism in Villa's poetry, suggesting that he combines poetics and politics in the theme of eroticism.

Villa, José García. *Poems 55: The Best Poems of José García Villa*. Manila, Phil. Florentino, 1962. Print. Includes poems chosen by Villa as his best, also featuring critical commentary by David Daiches, Richard Eberhart, and Horace Gregory.

JOHN DAVID WAIHEE III

Politician

John Waihee was the first Native Hawaiian to be elected governor of Hawaii. The state's fourth governor and a Democrat, he served two terms, from 1986 to 1994. Waihee placed an increased emphasis on restoring the prominence of Native Hawaiian culture and political sovereignty in state government. Prior to his role as an elected official, Waihee was a pivotal force behind the establishment of the Office of Hawaiian Affairs, a land trust for Native Hawaiians. Waihee's tenure as governor took place during a period of economic prosperity for the state, spurred by increased tourism and foreign real estate investment.

Born: May 19, 1946; Honokaa, Hawaii
Full name: John David Waihee III (WAH-ee-ee)
Areas of achievement: Government and politics, social issues

EARLY LIFE

John David Waihee III was the oldest child and only son born to rancher parents in the small town of Honokaa, a plantation village in the Hamakua District on the northern coast of the island of Hawaii. Waihee attended Andrews University in Berrien Springs, Michigan, where he received an undergraduate degree in business. He was a member of the 1976 inaugural graduating class of the William S. Richardson School of Law at the University of Hawaii at Honolulu, where he earned his law degree.

Waihee practiced law in Honolulu for two years prior to his 1978 election to the state constitutional convention, where he served as the unofficial Democratic majority leader. The panel was crucial in the design and implementation of the future makeup of Hawaiian state government through its creation of a state budgetary platform and establishment of term limits for elected state officials.

Waihee's most notable achievements at the constitutional convention came during the negotiations surrounding the creation of the Office of Hawaiian Affairs. Influenced by the political events that had recently restored rights to native Alaskans, the late 1970s saw an upsurge in Native Hawaiian interest in utilizing state-controlled resources and programs as a means of cultural preservation and future financial benefit. Waihee played a key role in convincing convention delegates to consider referenda brought forth by the convention's Hawaiian Affairs Committee designed to address sensitive issues that lingered from the overthrow of the Hawaiian monarchy by the United States in 1893. This agenda included the preservation of agricultural territory, distribution of profits from real estate sales to foreign investors, mandatory Hawaiian cultural education in the state's public school system, and the establishment of Hawaiian as the state's official language. The comprehensive legislation was accepted by the convention with the formal establishment of the Office of Hawaiian Affairs, an effort that reestablished Hawaiian cultural identity and sovereignty.

LIFE'S WORK

Waihee capitalized on the political cachet he established at the state constitutional convention with a successful run for Hawaii state representative in 1980. In 1982 he successfully ran for the office of lieutenant governor, a position he would hold during the third and final two-year term of popular Democratic governor George Ariyoshi. Waihee's notoriety and popularity increased during his years as lieutenant governor, in large part due to his work in a well-publicized contract negotiation with regional airline carriers and his role in the implementation of the state's first liquor tax.

Waihee was one of seven candidates who vied for the seat left vacancy by Ariyoshi's retirement in the 1986 Hawaiian gubernatorial election. He was an upset victor in a heated nomination battle with fellow Democrat Cecil Heftel, a race in which his campaign was outspent by a four-to-one margin. Waihee and running mate Ben Cayetano ran on a platform promising an invigorated "new generation" of Democratic leadership that propelled them to a narrow victory against Republican candidate D. G. Anderson.

Waihee's first term as governor was notable for an intensive development of the state's private and public infrastructure. He was also credited with stimulating the Hawaiian economy with his overhaul of the state's tax code, easing the tax burden on state businesses. The governor drew national acclaim for his widespread development of affordable housing units throughout the state. Green initiatives were also a major priority of Waihee's administration, which increased funding to state nature reserves and oversaw the enactment of a variety of legislation to protect island wildlife.

Waihee won reelection in 1990 with 61 percent of the popular vote against Republican contender Fred Hemmings. The margin of victory was the largest of any Hawaiian candidate for governor since the implementation of Hawaiian statehood in 1959.

Waihee's second term was diminished by natural disaster and economic downturn. Hurricane Iniki all but destroyed the Hawaiian island of Kauai in 1992, resulting in a major blow to the state's tourism. It would take several years for the industry to recover.

Waihee took a staunch anti-gambling stance against proposed casinos, claiming that it would asphyxiate inter-island tourist movement and discourage visitors from spending much needed tourist dollars throughout the state.

In 1993 Waihee received criticism and national media attention for his refusal to fly the US flag at Iolani Palace, Hawaii's capitol building, during the festivities recognizing the one hundredth anniversary of the overthrow of Queen Liliuokalani. His refusal demonstrated that Waihee's allegiance to Native Hawaiian culture was still strong some twenty years after his role in the establishment of the Office of Hawaiian Affairs.

SIGNIFICANCE

John Waihee remained a staunch advocate of Native Hawaiian culture his entire political career, placing himself in stark opposition to previous governors, who were either federally appointed or easily swayed by outside investors and mainland politicians. His political savvy was crucial in the development of legislation that would insure Native Hawaiians could forever reap the benefits of large-scale property transactions and infrastructure development while solidifying their role as key players in the islands' political landscape for decades to come.

John Pritchard

FURTHER READING

Gordon, Mike. "John Waihee." *Honolulu Advertiser*. Honolulu Advertiser, 2 July 2006. Web. 12 Feb. 2012. Profile of John Waihee.

---. "Onipa'a." *Honolulu Advertiser*. Honolulu Advertiser, 2 July 2006. Web. 12 Feb. 2012. Discussion of Waihee's refusal to fly the American flag over selected state buildings during the one-hundredth anniversary of the overthrow of Queen Liliuokalani.

"Present at the Creation: Former Gov. Waihee Ponders OHA's 25 Years." *Office of Hawaiian Affairs*. Office of Hawaiian Affairs, n.d. Web. 9 Feb 2012. An interview with Waihee discussing the formation of the Office of Hawaiian Affairs and where the state agency has succeeded and failed since then.

AN WANG

Chinese-born entrepreneur, inventor, scientist

Best known for founding Wang Laboratories, An Wang originally achieved success through patents for early computer components. His inventions made the magnetic core memories in early computers possible. His company was one of the most successful during the formation of the computer, or "information," industry.

Born: February 7, 1920; Shanghai, China
Died: March 24, 1990; Boston, Massachusetts
Full name: An Wang (Ahn Wahng)
Areas of achievement: Science and technology, business

EARLY LIFE

Wang was born in Shanghai, China, in 1920, the oldest of five children. His father practiced traditional Chinese medicine, passing on a sense of long family history and culture to his son. He was also an English teacher and began teaching Wang at home. Wang grew up in a country of feuding warlords, political corruption, and brutality. He was often separated from his family, and he lost both parents and a sister to the chaos and warfare.

In 1940, Wang graduated with a bachelor's degree in science from Jiao Tong University in Shanghai. He spent the rest of World War II designing radio receivers and transmitters for the Chinese army.

In 1945, Wang immigrated to the United States and continued his education at Harvard University. He married Lorraine Chiu in 1949, and they eventually had three children. While Lorraine was also from Shanghai, she and Wang met in Boston in 1948. Both became naturalized US citizens in 1955. Wang believed that the

An Wang. (Time & Life Pictures/Getty Images)

attitudes and values he acquired in China greatly influenced the way he lived and did business in the United States.

LIFE'S WORK

After receiving a PhD in applied physics in 1948 from Harvard University, Wang worked at Harvard's Computation Laboratory, where one of the first computers had been developed. He was assigned the task of developing faster and more reliable computer memory. He invented a method by which one could retrieve information stored in small rings of highly magnetized material by passing a current around the ring. He published his work in a 1950 article co-authored by Way Dong Woo, another Shanghai native who also worked at Harvard. He also patented his work, which made magnetic core memories for computers practical. Such memories became the standard for computers until the introduction of silicon chips.

In 1951, Wang left Harvard to found Wang Laboratories and focus on practical, commercial applications. He sold his memory patents to IBM for $500,000 in 1956, and he reinvested the money in his company. Wang developed a digital logarithmic converter, which made high-speed electronic arithmetic possible at a relatively low cost. He used this as the basis for some of the earliest desktop calculators.

Despite Wang Laboratories' large market share in the desktop calculator business in the late 1960s, Wang made a radical decision to refocus the company away from calculators. He developed and began manufacturing word processors that appealed to those unfamiliar with computers. His company eventually became the largest distributor of office word processors in the world. By 1989, they had over thirty thousand employees and $3 billion a year in sales.

In the 1980s, Wang tried to relinquish some of the personal control he had over the company and give responsibility to his son, Fred, who became president in 1986. Wang's sense of history and family may have led him to put the family's role in the company ahead of the health of the business. Many in the company felt that John F. Cunningham, the only non-Asian ever to have attained a powerful position in the company, would have been the better choice.

Wang focused on philanthropy. Part of his philosophy was social responsibility. He felt that organizations and businesses needed to give back to their communities. He established the Wang Institute of Graduate Studies, which offered degrees in software engineering. He also contributed to the restoration of a Boston landmark, the Metropolitan Theater, which became the Wang Center for the Performing Arts.

As Wang Laboratories began to falter in the late 1980s, Wang refocused his attention back to the company. He died of esophageal cancer on March 24, 1990. The company he had spent a lifetime building ended up filing for bankruptcy in 1992.

SIGNIFICANCE

Wang developed some of the original basic components for early computers and word processors. He took a great risk when he left the relative security of research at Harvard University to found a new company at a time when many in the United States still did not trust people of Asian descent after World War II. He continued his technical inventiveness (eventually earning more than thirty-five patents) while he built a multi-billion-dollar company. During the early development of computers, Wang was unique in his ability to achieve both technical, engineering success and practical, commercial business success.

Linda Eikmeier Endersby

FURTHER READING

Hargrove, Jim. *Dr. An Wang, Computer Pioneer.* Chicago: Children's, 1993. Print. Offers a readable account of Wang's life and work for a young audience.

Kenney, Charles C. *Riding the Runaway Horse: The Rise and Decline of Wang Laboratories.* Boston: Little, Brown, 1992. Print. Focuses mainly on Wang's business but includes personal details as well, based on interviews with Wang's staff and associates.

Wang, An, and Eugene Linden. *Lessons: An Autobiography.* Reading, MA: Addison-Wesley, 1986. Print. Provides an autobiographical account of Wang's life, also discussing his company's successes and failures.

Yost, Jeffrey R. *The Computer Industry.* Westport, CT: Greenwood, 2005. Print. Provides some information on Wang's company rather than his personal life; provides background information on the industry and context in which Wang developed his company.

CHARLES B. WANG

Chinese-born business executive, entrepreneur, writer

Charles Wang is a founder and former chairman and chief executive officer of Computer Associates International (now CA Technologies). Over the course of nearly four decades, this humble startup company grew to become a billion-dollar enterprise and a leader in the computer software industry. Having retired from Computer Associates in 2002, Wang is perhaps best known now as the owner of the New York Islanders hockey team.

Born: August 19, 1944; Shanghai, China
Full name: Charles B. Wang
Birth name: Wang Jialian
Areas of achievement: Business, science and technology

EARLY LIFE

Charles B. Wang is the second of three sons, born in Shanghai, China, to Kenneth, a lawyer and judge in China and later a professor, and Mary Wang. In 1952, the family left China and immigrated to Queens, New York. Wang graduated from Brooklyn Technical High School. In 1967, he earned a bachelor's degree in mathematics from the City University of New York's Queens College. Wang began his career as a programming trainee at Columbia University's Riverside Research Institute. He later worked for Standard Data Corporation of New York, where he became vice president of sales. Standard Data rejected an opportunity to begin a franchise business for a Swiss software company, Computer Associates International Ltd. Instead, Wang seized the opportunity and started his own business.

LIFE'S WORK

In 1976, Wang, his friend Russell Artzt, and two other associates began to distribute one of Computer Associates' management software programs, called CA-SORT, through a subsidiary they started and named Trans-American Computer Associations. Within a year, Trans-American Computer Associations added its own merchandise to its sales and opened a data center in Danbury, Connecticut. The small subsidiary quickly grew, and Wang's brother Tony, who initially provided the company with outside legal counsel, joined the company as president and chief operating officer. By 1980, Wang's business had bought out its parent company and become Computer Associates (CA) International. The following year, CA went public. As the company expanded, it bought out many of its competitors, including in 1987 Uccel Corporation, which had established a business market in Europe. Uccel's software development director, Sanjay Kumar, joined CA. In 1989, CA International had sales of over one billion dollars, had added computers to its distribution line, and had become the largest software company in the world.

Over the next ten years, CA continued to grow by aggressively acquiring other businesses. These acquisitions were sometimes seen as ruthless undertakings made at the expense of former companies' employees, who were sometimes fired or forced to sign new contracts. CA acquired Legent Corporation in 1995 and Cheyenne Software in 1996, and then AI Ware, an artificial intelligence company. Next, CA bought out Platinum Technology in 1999 and Sterling Software in 2000.

Meanwhile, Wang published two books for executives: *Techno Vision: The Executive's Survival Guide to Understanding and Managing Information Technology* (1994) and *Techno Vision II: Every Executive's Guide to Understanding and Mastering Technology and the Internet* (1997). In 1996, Wang donated $25 million for the creation of the Charles B. Wang Center at the State University of New York's Stony Brook campus. In 1999, Wang and his brothers honored their father by donating funds to create the Kenneth Wang School of Law at Soochaw University in China.

As the turn of the century approached, CA began to encounter controversy. The company's top executives received exorbitant financial incentives, which angered many shareholders. By 2000, Kumar and Wang, previously good friends, had begun to disagree on company operations, and CA's stock plummeted. Wang stepped down and declared Kumar chief executive officer.

Class-action lawsuits claiming that company revenues were misrepresented from 1997 to 2000 led the US attorney in Brooklyn, New York, and the US Securities and Exchange Commission to investigate the company. Extremely high executive compensations, as well as accounting and bookkeeping problems, were revealed, and in November 2002, Wang resigned from the board of directors. In 2006, Kumar and a number of other CA executives pled guilty to charges of securities fraud and obstruction of justice, and Kumar was sent to prison. The company survived these challenges, however, and continues to thrive.

Charles B. Wang. (Getty Images)

Wang is also known for being the majority owner of the New York Islanders hockey team, in which he invested with Kumar starting in 2000, eventually buying out Kumar's share. Wang set about rebuilding the team, which has not won a Stanley Cup since the early 1980s, or even made it to the finals since 1993. Wang has invested significantly in the Islanders, and they are regarded as more competitive than they were, but ultimate success continues to elude the team. A looming question is where the Islanders will play after 2015, when the team's lease with Long Island's aging Nassau Coliseum expires. The arena needs to be replaced, but local voters in 2011 defeated Wang's ambitious redevelopment plans; the team's options include moving to Brooklyn—geographically part of Long Island—or leaving New York state entirely.

SIGNIFICANCE

Throughout his career, Wang has developed a reputation for philanthropy. He is the cofounder and chairman of Smile Train, a nonprofit organization that provides free surgery to children in developing countries with cleft palates. In 1999, the Chinatown Health Clinic, which provides free health services to Asian Americans in New

York City, was renamed the Charles B. Wang Community Health Center, after Wang made a significant donation. He has also been involved with the Make-a-Wish Foundation, which fulfills the wishes of terminally ill children.

Despite the controversy that followed Wang throughout his career, his commitment to building businesses and delivering innovative technology products has made him very successful. He has acknowledged this success through his many philanthropic endeavors.

Cynthia J. W. Svoboda

FURTHER READING

Berenson, Alex. "Chairman of Computer Associates Resigns." *New York Times*. New York Times, 19 Nov. 2002. Web. 3 Apr. 2012. On the occasion of his retirement, recapitulates Wang's twenty-six years building Computer Associates.

Diamos, Jason. "Owner of the Islanders Dares to Be Different." *New York Times*. New York Times, 20 July 2006. Web. 3 Apr. 2012. Discusses Wang's unorthodox management decisions as owner of the New York Islanders.

GARRETT WANG

Actor

Chinese American actor Garrett Wang became recognizable in the late 1990s as Ensign Harry Kim on the television series Star Trek: Voyager. *He played only the second Asian main character in the television franchise's history.*

Born: December 15, 1968; Riverside, California
Full name: Garrett Richard Wang
Also known as: Wang Yi-Chung
Area of achievement: Television

EARLY LIFE

Garrett Wang was born to Chinese immigrant parents in Riverside, California. Shortly after he was born, Wang's parents moved with Garrett and his sister Laura to Indiana, and then to Bermuda. The Wang family moved back to the United States and settled in Memphis, Tennessee, where Wang attended high school at Harding Academy. After graduating, Wang attended the University of California, Los Angeles (UCLA), where he majored in Asian studies. While at UCLA, his professors encouraged Wang to pursue theater and drama. One professor, Jennifer Roundtree, was particularly influential and helped Wang develop as an actor and encouraged him to pursue acting after college. After graduating from UCLA, Wang began a career in the theater. His first performance was as John Lee in *Porcelain* at the Burbage Theatre in West Los Angeles. He also performed in *Model Minority* at the Los Angeles Theatre Center, *Woman Warrior* at the Mark Taper Forum, and *A Language of Their Own* at the Intiman Theatre.

In 1994 Wang appeared in an episode of the short-lived television series *All-American Girl* (1994–95),

about a Korean American family, with plotlines loosely based on the life experiences of comedian Margaret Cho. The next year, Wang was cast in his best-known role, Ensign Harry Kim on the science fiction television series *Star Trek: Voyager* (1995–2001).

LIFE'S WORK

Wang's character on *Star Trek: Voyager* was a loyal and dedicated officer whose intelligence and dedication often helped the entire crew on the wayward spacecraft. As Kim, Wang was the first Asian main character on a *Star Trek* television franchise since George Takei as Mr. Sulu in the original *Star Trek* series (1966–69). Prior to *Star Trek: Voyager*, two previous incarnations, *Star Trek: The Next Generation* (1987–94) and *Star Trek: Deep Space Nine* (1993–99) sought to follow Star Trek creator Gene Roddenberry's vision of a command crew that was inclusive of women and minorities. However, neither *Star Trek: The Next Generation* nor *Star Trek: Deep Space Nine* included Asians in their main cast.

Wang has voiced complaints about his character in *Star Trek: Voyager*, having asked producers and writers to give Kim more personality and depth. In addition, his was the only main character that received no promotions over the course of the series, implying in the minds of some a glass ceiling for Asians. Nonetheless, Wang has been involved in other aspects of the Star Trek franchise, lending his voice to the 2001 video game *Star Trek: Voyager—Elite Force* and playing the new role of Commander Garan in the 2008 unofficial three-part fan miniseries *Star Trek: Of Gods and Men*.

Wang has also had roles in smaller films such as *Ivory Tower* (1998) and *Demon Island* (2002).

Garrett Wang. (Getty Images)

SIGNIFICANCE

Wang is one of only four Asian American actors regularly associated with the *Star Trek* franchise. As a result, he is significant for examining how Asians and Asian Americans are portrayed in a science fiction narrative. In addition to achieving success with acting, Wang was chosen by *People* magazine as the eighteenth most beautiful person in their 1997 Most Beautiful People issue. In 2001, E! Entertainment Television named Wang one of the coolest bachelors. Wang has aimed to change the perception of Asian Americans by becoming a recognizable face in Hollywood.

Norma Jones

FURTHER READING

Bernardi, Daniel. *Star Trek and History: Race-ing Toward a White Future.* Piscataway, NJ: Rutgers UP, 1998. Print. A discussion of race through the Star Trek franchises.

Mok, Theresa. "Getting the Message: Media Images and Stereotypes and Their Effect on Asian Americans." *Cultural Diversity and Mental Health* 4.3 (1998): 185–202. Print. How media is a source of influence in perceptions of Asian Americans as well as consequences of monolithic portrayals.

Ono, Kent A., and Vincent N. Pham. *Asian Americans and the Media.* Malden, MA: Polity, 2009. Print. Further reading on Asians and Asian Americans in media.

VERA WANG

Fashion designer and entrepreneur

Since she launched her successful haute couture wedding gown business in 1990, American designer and entrepreneur Vera Wang has become best known for modernizing bridal fashion. Her work has inspired countless designers to enter a once-overlooked and creatively stagnant area of the fashion industry.

Born: June 27, 1949; New York, New York
Full name: Vera Wang
Birth name: Vera Ellen Wang
Areas of achievement: Fashion, business

EARLY LIFE

Vera Ellen Wang was born on June 27, 1949, in New York City. Her father, Cheng Ching Wang, and her mother, Florence Wu, both came from wealthy and influential families in China. They immigrated to the United States

in 1947 to escape the Communist Revolution. Starting a new life in America, Wang's father established the US Summit Company, a subsidiary of the Summit Group, which produced pharmaceuticals for Asian markets. Wang's mother became a translator for the United Nations. As a result of their parents' success, Wang and her brother, Kenneth, were raised in an affluent home.

Throughout her youth, Wang took part in extended family trips around the world on ocean liners, and often spent summers living in Paris. While in Paris, she regularly accompanied her fashion-loving mother to fashion shows, where they would purchase couture garments. Together, Wang and her mother frequented the boutiques of many exclusive designers, including Christian Dior, Hubert de Givenchy, and Yves Saint Laurent. In addition to developing an eye for fashion, Wang learned to speak several languages, including French and Mandarin Chinese.

Vera Wang. (Getty Images)

From kindergarten through high school, Wang attended the elite, all-girls Chapin School in Manhattan. She was a strong student, and was able to balance her studies with involvement in the arts and athletics. At age eight, Wang dreamed of becoming a competitive figure skater. She devoted many hours before and after school both on the ice and at the School of American Ballet at the famed Lincoln Center in Manhattan. In 1968 and 1969, Wang and pairs partner James Stuart placed sixth and fifth, respectively, at the US Figure Skating Championships. However, after failing to place at Nationals, Stuart decided to pursue a solo career, and Wang made the difficult decision to drop figure skating as a viable career option.

Wang enrolled at Sarah Lawrence College. On the advice of her father, she began taking classes to prepare for medical school, but the void figure skating left in her proved difficult to fill. Wang left Sarah Lawrence during her sophomore year and moved to Paris to pursue a relationship with French figure skater Patrick Pera. While in Paris, she took courses in art history and foreign language at the Sorbonne and found that the architecture and fashion of the city rekindled her early love of clothing and fashion design. She returned to Sarah Lawrence to earn her degree in art history.

LIFE'S WORK

Wang began her career in fashion as an editorial assistant at *Vogue* magazine in 1971. Frances Patiky Stein, an editor at *Vogue*, saw talent and potential in Wang and offered her the job after she graduated from college. Before that, she had worked summers as a sales girl at an Yves Saint Laurent boutique in New York. Although Wang intended the job at *Vogue* to be a temporary stepping stone to design school, she remained at the magazine for sixteen years. After only a year at the magazine, Wang was promoted to senior fashion editor. She credits *Vogue* for giving her an invaluable insider education on working in the fashion industry. Each day at *Vogue* challenged Wang to re-envision recurring fashions in new ways as she directed the composition of the magazine's trendsetting, high-fashion editorial photographs. The magazine helped Wang hone her creative talent, confidence, and instincts, and gave her the opportunity to build close working relationships with many top designers.

In 1987, Wang made the decision to leave *Vogue* and accepted an offer to become a fashion director for designer Ralph Lauren. As fashion director, she oversaw the production of thirteen different lines of accessories, and was given the opportunity to design sportswear and lingerie. In 1989, Wang married businessman Arthur Becker, and made yet another career-altering decision. Wang worried that the stress of her job at Ralph Lauren was adversely affecting her efforts to start a family with Becker, and so she decided to leave her job. However, it became clear with time that despite fertility treatments and reduced stress levels, Wang was unable to conceive.

Wang was disappointed with the news. She was also becoming restless without a job. Her spirits were once again lifted by a long-withheld blessing from her father to continue pursuing her dream of becoming a fashion designer. He suggested that she focus on bridal wear, an idea she resisted at first before reflecting on her own experience as a bride. Unable to find something that appealed to her, she had designed on her own dress for her wedding. She saw that a niche existed for applying her elegant yet simple fashion aesthetic to a lucrative industry largely overlooked by high fashion.

Having borrowed four million dollars from her father, she and business partner Chet Hazzard opened Vera Wang Bridal House, Ltd., in September 1990. Wang began by selling the dresses of other more well-known

Vera Wang's Wedding Gown Collections

Wang's wedding gown collections are renowned for their exquisite quality of construction and attention to detail. For her couture gowns, which start at $3,500 and cost up to tens of thousands of dollars, Wang uses only the finest of fabrics, such as tulle, silk, and duchess satin. Her hand-sewn, hand-beaded gowns each take months to create. They come in two separate lines—as one-of-a-kind, made-to-order gowns personally designed for each client, or as ready-to-wear gowns in standard sizes sold at high-end department stores. Since

she began her business in 1990, Wang has become the designer of choice for many affluent and famous brides, including Sharon Stone, Vanessa Williams, and Victoria Adams ("Posh Spice"). Being a former dancer and competitive figure skater, Wang has prided herself in understanding a woman's shape and how her body moves. She strives to design gowns that women with a diversity of sizes and shapes can feel confident in, using fabric to accentuate their best assets and camouflage the parts of their bodies they might be less comfortable showing.

designers at her two-story boutique inside the Carlyle Hotel on the Upper East Side of Manhattan. With hard work and the support of friends, Wang built up her business and reputation, and began making a profit in 1994. It was at this time that Wang felt it opportune to begin designing her own gowns. As Wang grew her business, she and Becker also grew their family. In 1991, they adopted daughter Cecilia and in 1994, Josephine.

SIGNIFICANCE

Before Wang entered bridal fashion, wedding gown selection was rather limited, and consisted primarily of traditional designs: white, floor-length, voluminous dresses. The standard had been set in the Victorian era, when brides began imitating the voluminous corseted white gown Queen Victoria wore down the aisle to marry Prince Albert in 1840. Wang's couture wedding gowns revolutionized bridal fashion, opening the door for a multitude of bridal industry designers to follow. Many brides now take for granted the availability of a wide selection of gowns suiting a diverse range of tastes and budgets. Wang's continued success has shown that she is not only a ground-breaking designer, but also a savvy businesswoman. She has managed to use her success in bridal fashion as a springboard for expanding her brand into lines of couture evening wear, bridesmaid

fashion, ready-to-wear clothing lines, fragrance, a wedding advice book, interior décor, crystal and china, and stationery. Wang has striven to expand her clientele from affluent women to average working women of all body types and sizes desiring comfort, quality, and simple elegance.

Yung Hua Nancy Ng Tam

FURTHER READING

Todd, Anne M. "Vera Wang." *Asian Americans of Achievement.* 16 vols. New York: Infobase, 2007. Print. Detailed biographical account of Wang's life.

Wang, Vera. "Envision." *33 Things Every Girl Should Know: Stories, Songs, Poems, and Smart Talk by 33 Extraordinary Women.* Ed. Tonya Bolden. New York: Crown Publishers, 1998. Print. Autobiographical essay about Wang's start in the fashion business.

---. "The Power of Reinvention." *Come to Win: Business Leaders, Artists, Doctors, and Other Visionaries on How Sports Can Help You Top Your Profession.* Ed. Venus Williams. New York: HarperCollins, 2010. Print. Wang discusses how competitive figure skating in her youth instilled in her skills and lessons she applies to the competitive fashion industry.

WAYNE WANG

Hong Kong–born film director

Wayne Wang was the first Chinese American director to have a successful career, making films about both Chinese characters and those from other ethnic groups.

Born: January 12, 1949; Hong Kong
Full name: Wayne Wang
Area of achievement: Film

EARLY LIFE

Wayne Wang was born in Hong Kong a few days after his parents and older brother fled from Shanghai, China, during the Communist Revolution. His father—Wang Shen Lin, an engineer—was fluent in English and imparted to his son a passion for American films, naming him for actor John Wayne. Wang was encouraged in his artistic interests by his mother, an amateur painter.

After graduating from an English-language Jesuit high school in 1967, Wang moved to the United States to attend Foothill College in Los Altos Hills, California, intending to become either a dentist or a doctor. Instead, he transferred to the California College of Arts and Crafts in Oakland, where he received a degree in painting. He later earned a master's degree in film and television. Wang returned to Hong Kong to direct a television comedy series and act as assistant director on *Golden Needles* (1974) before moving to San Francisco.

LIFE'S WORK

Wang developed material for his first film while working as a job counselor at a Chinatown community center. He adapted the struggles of his clients into the film *Chan Is Missing* (1982), shot for only $22,000 and

Wayne Wang. (FilmMagic)

financed through grants from the American Film Institute and the National Endowment for the Arts. One of the most notable successes among the burgeoning independent American film movement, *Chan Is Missing* is also considered one of the first films to realistically depict Chinese Americans. The simple plot—two taxi drivers search for a man who disappeared with their $4,000—gave Wang the opportunity to humorously and sympathetically present the daily lives of working-class Chinese Americans.

Wang, who became an American citizen in 1984, explored similar themes in his second film, *Dim Sum: A Little Bit of Heart* (1985). In this warm-hearted comedy, a widow is told by a fortune teller that she has a year to live. She resolves to see her daughter married and to return to China to pay her respects to her ancestors. The communication barriers between Chinese immigrants and their American-born children is a frequent subject for Wang's early films.

Wang next made *Slam Dance* (1987), a poorly received murder mystery set in Los Angeles. He returned to form with *Eat a Bowl of Tea* (1989), the story a first-generation Chinese American and his Chinese wife after their arranged marriage. The film stars Cora Miao, a former Miss Hong Kong and Wang's wife. Wang returned to Hong Kong for *Life Is Cheap . . . but Toilet Paper Is Expensive* (1989), an unusual satire about the effects of the global economy.

Though he did not want to be stereotyped as simply an interpreter of Chinese American life, Wang was inspired to adapt Amy Tan's acclaimed 1989 novel about the relationships between several Chinese American women and their Chinese mothers. *The Joy Luck Club* (1993) became Wang's most popular film, blending humor and sensitivity into a universal portrait of the immigrant experience, though it was criticized by some for perpetuating stereotypes of Chinese American men. After years of making low-budget films with small casts, Wang proved he could make a bigger-budget film, featuring multiple locations and more than sixty speaking roles.

Wang followed *The Joy Luck Club* with *Smoke* (1995), his best-received film addressing subjects other than Chinese Americans. With a screenplay by novelist Paul Auster, *Smoke* focuses on the interlocking lives of the customers of a Brooklyn cigar store and features outstanding performances from a large cast, including William Hurt, Harvey Keitel, and Forrest Whitaker. Wang and Auster had such a good time making *Smoke* that they made a companion film, *Blue in the Face* (1995). Largely improvised, *Blue in the Face* was shot in five days.

Wang next directed the film *Chinese Box* (1997), focusing on the handover of Hong Kong to the People's Republic of China. Actors Jeremy Irons, Gong Li, and Maggie Cheung star as people striving to find meaning in their lives amid this enormous political change. Wang's subsequent films did not achieve the same critical and commercial success as his earlier work. After the disappointing performances of *Anywhere But Here* (1999), *The Center of the World* (2001), *Maid in Manhattan* (2002), *Because of Winn-Dixie* (2005), and *Last Holiday* (2006), Wang returned to his roots with *The Princess of Nebraska* (2007), a film about a pregnant Chinese girl's life in the United States, and *A Thousand Years of Good Prayers* (2007), in which a man travels from China to America to visit his estranged daughter and becomes friendly with an Iranian woman.

SIGNIFICANCE

Wang's films are notable for their low-key, relaxed style and their even-handed approach to subjects that might turn maudlin in other hands. *Chan Is Missing*, selected in 1995 for preservation in the National Film Registry by the Library of Congress, *Dim Sum*, *Eat a Bowl of Tea*, *The Joy Luck Club*, and *Smoke* constitute a body of highly regarded work rivaled among Chinese American directors only by the films of Ang Lee.

Michael Adams

FURTHER READING

Feng, Peter. "Being Chinese American, Becoming Asian American: *Chan Is Missing*." *Cinema Journal* 35.4 (1996): 88–118. Print. Examines Wang's film as an argument for the fluidity of Chinese American identity.

Lu, Alvin. "Invisible Cities: Wayne Wang." *Film Comment* 34.4 (1998): 31–37. Print. Analyzes the themes in Wang's films through *Chinese Box*.

Tibbetts, John C. "A Delicate Balance." *Literature Film Quarterly* 22.1 (1994): 2–6. Print. Wang is interviewed about the making of *The Joy Luck Club*.

HINES WARD

South Korean–born athlete

In 2011, Pittsburgh Steelers wide receiver Hines Ward became the first Korean American to win the Super Bowl Most Valuable Player (MVP) award. Since retiring from football in 2012, Hines has continued to work with a foundation he established to benefit Korean youth.

Born: March 8, 1976; Seoul, South Korea
Full name: Hines E. Ward Jr
Also known as: Woe-dee; Wardy; Silent Assassin
Areas of achievement: Sports, philanthropy

EARLY LIFE

Hines E. Ward Jr. was born on March 8, 1976, in Seoul, South Korea to Kim Young He, a Korean, and Hines E. Ward Sr., an African American. When he was a year old, his family relocated to East Point, Georgia. Soon after, Ward's parents divorced. Ward went to live with his paternal grandmother, Martha Ward, after his father convinced a family court that his mother did not speak English well enough to raise him independently. Nonetheless, Ward was raised by his mother and grandmother.

As a child, Ward was mocked at school because of his ethnicity. Being of both African American and

Hines Ward. (Getty Images for GQ)

Hines Ward and the Super Bowl

Ward's professional career with the Pittsburgh Steelers began slowly. During his rookie season in 1998, he was confined mostly to special-teams play. He started no games and caught only fifteen passes. The next year, however, he moved to a starting offense position and caught sixty-one passes. Although he lacked the speed to be a threat, he was known as a tough and reliable possession receiver. Ward established himself as a valuable player by working hard, running reliable routes, fighting for every pass thrown in his direction, and undertaking the unglamorous work of blocking for his teammates.

In the 2006 Super Bowl in Detroit, the Steelers were matched against the Seattle Seahawks. The Steelers had long been known for trick plays, and having two wide receivers with quarterback experience—Ward and Antwaan Randle El—offered them unique opportunities for unusual plays. In the fourth quarter, after the Seahawks had come within only four points of taking the lead, the Steelers ran a trick play. Randle El took a handoff on a reverse and threw to Ward for a forty-three-yard touchdown that sealed the victory for Pittsburgh. In 2008, Ward enjoyed one of his finest seasons and played an important role in the Steelers' return to the Super Bowl. When the Steelers faced the Arizona Cardinals for the NFL title, Ward was hobbled by a sprain. Nevertheless, he caught two passes that helped his team win.

Korean heritage, he was teased for being outside of the norm. Ward did not let the teasing bother him, deciding instead to focus on his schoolwork and football.

At Forest Park High School, football coach Mike Parris selected Ward as the team's quarterback. During Ward's high school football career, he was a two-time Clayton County Offensive Player of the Year. He also earned All-American honors from *Blue Chip Illustrated*, *Super Prep*, and *USA Today*.

Between 1994 and 1997, Ward's football career progressed, and he became a versatile star player at the college level. He played quarterback, running back, and, most often, wide receiver for the University of Georgia (UGA) Bulldogs. At UGA, Ward's 149 career receptions for 1,965 yards placed him second in team history. As running back, he totaled 3,870 all-purpose yards, which placed him second only to legendary running

back Herschel Walker in Bulldogs history. Ward received All-SEC honors and held Georgia records for Pass Attempts, Pass Completions, and Passing Yards. In the 1995 Peach Bowl, Ward completed 31 of 69 passes for 413 yards. In 1997, Ward earned a bachelor's degree in consumer economics from UGA.

LIFE'S WORK

In 1998, Ward was drafted by the Pittsburgh Steelers in the third round of the National Football League (NFL) Draft. He was selected for the NFL Pro Bowl each season between 2001 and 2004. In 2002, Ward set a Steelers franchise record with 112 receptions and 12 touchdowns. Ward signed a contract extension with the Steelers worth over $25 million. On November 13, 2005, Ward became the Steelers' all-time leading receiver. He has been named team MVP three times over the course of his professional career.

On February 5, 2006, the Pittsburgh Steelers defeated the Seattle Seahawks in Super Bowl XL. In addition to earning his first Super Bowl Championship ring, Ward was named the game's MVP. He caught five passes for 123 yards and scored one touchdown, a 43-yard TD reception that helped the Steelers seal their victory in the fourth quarter. This was a 21–10 win over the Seattle Seahawks. Upon being named Super Bowl MVP, Ward gave full credit to his teammates.

Ward is considered one of the best blocking wide receivers of all time. He signed another contract extension with the Steelers in April 2009 worth $22 million. On September 12, 2010, in a game against the Atlanta Falcons, Ward became the first player in Steelers history to surpass 11,000 receiving yards. During that same game, he became the twelfth player in NFL history to earn 900 career receptions.

In February 2009, Ward won his second Super Bowl Championship as a member of the Pittsburgh Steelers. He appeared on the television dancing competition *Dancing with the Stars* in 2011.

SIGNIFICANCE

During his playing career, Ward established himself as one of the best wide receivers in the NFL. In 2006, he established the Hines Ward Helping Hands Foundation, which works with mixed-race children in South Korea, partnering with host families to provide opportunities for Korean youth to experience life in the United States. Through the foundation's work, many children have traveled to Pittsburgh and attended Steelers home games as Ward's guests.

In September of 2010, Hines was appointed by President Barack Obama to the President's Advisory Commission on Asian Americans and Pacific Islanders. He announced his retirement from professional football in March 2012. Upon news of his retirement, Steelers fans and sports media entities worldwide celebrated his illustrious career.

Willette F. Stinson

FURTHER READING

Beith, Malcolm. "Living a Dream: Hines Ward's Return to Korea." *Newsweek* 27 Mar. 2006. Print. Discusses Ward's return to South Korea with his mother.

Chastain, Bill. *Steel Dynasty: The Team That Changed the NFL*. Chicago: Triumph, 2005. Print. Discusses how Chuck Noll turned the Pittsburgh Steelers into one of the most fearsome and successful teams in NFL history.

Keveney, Bill. "You'll Recognize the Names on *Dancing*." *USA Today* 1 Mar. 2011. Print. Discusses Ward's appearance on *Dancing with the Stars*.

Schmalzbauer, Adam. *The History of the Pittsburgh Steelers*. Mankato, MN: Creative Education, 2005. Print. Highlights Pittsburgh Steelers history, including Ward's accomplishments in football and as an MVP award-winner.

GEDDE WATANABE

Actor

Most famous for playing Long Duk Dong in Sixteen Candles, *Watanabe has been in numerous films and plays and is a popular voice actor in animated movies, television shows, and video games.*

Born: June 26, 1955; Ogden, Utah
Full name: Gedde Watanabe (GEH-dee wah-tah-NAH-bee)
Birth name: Gary Watanabe
Areas of achievement: Entertainment, theater, film

EARLY LIFE

Gedde Watanabe was born in Ogden, Utah, on June 26, 1955. Asian Americans were a very small minority in Utah when Watanabe was growing up and he often felt alone and separate from his peers. His parents' volatile relationship made his home life unhappy, as well. He took refuge in singing to avoid thinking about their fights. Breaking out of his shell, he performed in school plays during high school. He came to love the connections with people that performing gave him. After graduation he decided to move to San Francisco, California, to try to make his living as a performer.

Watanabe found happiness for the first time working as a street musician in an area of Chinatown. At first he was not successful and was often pelted with vegetables by restaurant workers, but he persevered. Simultaneously, he attended the American Conservatory Theater in San Francisco. After spending a few years in San Francisco, Watanabe moved to New York City. He spent the next thirteen to fourteen years making his living as a successful street musician.

In 1976 Watanabe got his first break when he was hired to appear in Stephen Sondheim's musical *Pacific*

Gedde Watanabe. (Getty Images)

Overtures, about American attempts to westernize Japan beginning in the mid-1800s. Watanabe sang one of the three parts in "Someone in a Tree." Despite this opportunity, there were few roles for Asian actors in the United States and Watanabe had difficulty finding work.

Several years later, Watanabe made his film debut in the independent film *The Long Island Four* (1980). This little-known work, starring some of New York's underground performers and celebrities, was based on the true story of the capture of four Nazis in Long Island during World War II. Although the film was not a success, Watanabe began contemplating a return to California to try to be an actor full time.

LIFE'S WORK

Watanabe's breakout role came in director John Hughes's 1984 comedy *Sixteen Candles.* Watanabe played a foreign exchange student from China living with the main character's grandparents. The role, Long Duk Dong, was broadly comic, overtly sexual, and based on extreme stereotypes. The film proved so popular that the character "The Donger" became an icon in the 1980s. His success in *Sixteen Candles* was followed by the second lead in *Gung Ho* (1986), a film about a Japanese automobile plant in America.

Despite the exposure that these roles gave him, Watanabe found it difficult to land major roles due to the continued lack of parts for Asian American actors. He found some success on television, appearing on the short-lived television version of *Gung Ho* in 1986 and playing Hiroshi on *Sesame Street* in 1988. In 1989 he was featured in comedian and spoof songwriter Weird Al Yankovic's cult film *UHF.* Guest roles on series such as *Seinfeld* and *Murphy Brown* followed. From 1997 to 2003 he had a recurring role as Nurse Yosh Takata on the award-winning television drama *ER.* Watanabe also worked as a voice actor for animated programs such as *The Simpsons,* *Rugrats,* *American Dad,* and *What's New Scooby-Doo?* In 1998 and 2004 he provided the voice of Ling in Disney's *Mulan* movies, although he did not sing for his part because the producers thought his singing voice was too good for the character.

In 1999 Watanabe appeared in two films playing roles that were not Asian-specific parts: *Guinevere* and *EdTV.* Throughout the 1990s and 2000s Watanabe continued to appear on stage, most notably in the all-Asian productions of the East West Players in Los Angeles, starring in *A Funny Thing Happened on the Way to the Forum* and *Pippin,* among others.

SIGNIFICANCE

Watanabe remains both famous and infamous for his portrayal of Long Duk Dong in *Sixteen Candles.* Many moviegoers loved the character for his racy humor and slapstick antics. However, many, including a large and vocal Asian contingent, were horrified at the blatant racial stereotyping. Watanabe played Dong with a thick accent and spoke in broken English, creating the quintessential caricature of an Asian geek. Watanabe had doubts about playing such a character, but ultimately felt that making people laugh was a good thing and embraced the role. Although he understands that some took offense at the character, Watanabe believes that Asians should be able to poke fun at themselves and play a broad spectrum of characters.

Leslie Neilan

FURTHER READING

Benshoff, Harry M., and Sean Griffin. *America on Film: Representing Race, Class, Gender, and Sexuality at the Movies.* 2nd ed. Malden: Wiley, 2009. Print. Examines different ethnic and social groups and their representation in film. The section on Asian actors, including Watanabe, addresses stereotypes and the problems Asians have in finding serious roles.

Christie, Thomas A. *John Hughes and Eighties Cinema.* Maidstone: Crescent Moon, 2009. Print. Discusses John Hughes, the creator of Long Duk Dong, and his influence on film and culture.

Gora, Suzanna. *You Couldn't Ignore Me If You Tried: The Brat Pack, John Hughes, and Their Impact on a Generation.* New York: Three Rivers, 2011. Print. Discusses all of Hughes's work with material on *Sixteen Candles,* Long Duk Dong, and Gedde Watanabe.

G. J. WATUMULL

Business executive, investor, philanthropist

Businessman G. J. Watumull contributed to Hawaii's retail industry and the growth in popularity around the United States of what became known as "Hawaiian shirts." He also invested in Hawaii real estate and established the Watumull Foundation for the promotion of the economic and educational development of India, as well as to support educational and cultural activities in Hawaii.

Born: June 26, 1891; Hyderabad, Sindh, British India (now Pakistan)
Died: August 13, 1959; Honolulu, Hawaii
Full name: Gobindram Jhamandas Watumull (WAH-tuh-muhl)
Areas of achievement: Business, philanthropy

EARLY LIFE

G. J. Watumull was born in 1891 in Hyderabad, Sindh, British India (today Pakistan), one of nine children born to Jhamandas Naraindas, his father, and Hekandbai, his mother. His family was part of a merchant clan in the Sindhi ethnic group. His father worked as a contractor and suffered a debilitating accident when Watumull was eight years old. Because his father was unable to work, Watumull's older brother Jhamandas left British India to find work in retail management, first in the Philippines, then in Hawaii.

In the meantime, Watumull's other two elder brothers supported their parents and siblings by working for four cents a day. Even though times were difficult, Watumull remained in school. He attended a village school from which he graduated in 1909. In 1911 Watumull attended the University of Bombay and completed a two-year engineering program with the financial help of Jhamandas. Soon after he completed his studies, Watumull was hired for a government job and worked on an irrigation project in the Sindh region. He continued his work with the government and became a chief clerk, earning ten dollars a month. In 1917, Jhamandas persuaded Watumull to leave India and move to Hawaii to manage the retail business.

LIFE'S WORK

Watumull arrived in the US Territory of Hawaii on October 30, 1917, and assumed the management of his brother's Far East India Store, which later became known as Watumull's East India Store. The original store was located in Manila, the Philippines; the store in Hawaii opened in 1913. Watumull began as the store's manager and major buyer. Many of the store's goods were imported from places such as Bombay, Shanghai, and Tokyo. Located in the downtown area of Honolulu, the business thrived under Watumull's direction. By 1922, the store was one of two major retailers in Hawaii that specialized in aloha attire—typified by the so-called Hawaiian shirt—clothing printed with the bright colors and large floral designs that became a symbol of Hawaii.

In 1937, Watumull and the company moved the store to a new three-story building more centrally located within the downtown Honolulu area. Despite the Great Depression of the 1930s, the business survived and even expanded. In 1936, Watumull began a Hawaiian sportswear clothing line and commissioned his sister-in-law, artist Elsie Das, as the designer. She used nature as her source for creating unique aloha-wear designs specifically for the store.

When World War II began, Watumull found it difficult to import goods from Asia. He adapted the store's inventory, moving from a store featuring import goods to a men's and women's clothing store that specialized in Hawaiian sportswear. Eight years after the war ended, the company began importing Asian goods once more. The retail business continued to expand. By the time of Watumull's death in 1959, eleven stores bearing the Watumull name were in existence, including one in Waikiki. By 1964, there were seventeen stores in Hawaii.

In addition to the retail business, Watumull also invested in real estate. In 1952, Watumull Enterprises secured a fifty-five-year lease for property on the main road through the town of Kailua, Oahu, and began building Kailua Shopping Center, which would house several stores and a supermarket. The half-million-dollar center opened in June 1954. A year later, Watumull began building an apartment hotel in Waikiki. It was his first tourist and apartment hotel business in Waikiki. Later, the company would expand and build the Waikiki Beach Shops as well as an office building in the business district of downtown Honolulu. Other business interests included the management of Kauai Beachboy Hotel on the island of Kauai. For Watumull, however, the real estate aspect of his business was more of a hobby than his main focus.

Throughout most of his career, he was helped by his wife, Ellen Jensen, who was born in Portland,

The Watumull Foundation

Formed in 1942 by G. J. and Ellen Jensen Watumull, the Watumull Foundation had three main purposes. The first of these was to assist India in increasing its national efficiency through education and social activities. The second purpose was to promote cultural exchange between India and the United States. The final purpose was to support philanthropic, cultural, and educational work. In order to achieve these objectives, the Foundation helped to sponsor the International Planned Parenthood Conference in 1952 in Bombay. The Foundation also awarded scholarships to students in India for higher education and contributed funds and materials for research. To meet its second goal, the Foundation sponsored Indian professors to study in the United States, gave prizes for books published about India, and arranged for a gift of a baby female elephant to the Honolulu Zoo, among its other activities. Its Hawaii-based projects included awarding scholarships to students at the University of Hawaii at Manoa; supporting construction projects for local private schools, hospitals, and other organizations; assisting the Pacific Asian Affairs Council; and conducting an oral history project that interviewed more than one hundred prominent Hawaiians.

Oregon, and arrived in Hawaii in 1920 to teach music. The couple met through mutual friends. They were married in Redwood City, California, on July 5, 1922. Their marriage would be one of the first Indian-American unions. They had three children, Lila, David, and Radha. Lila joined her father in the business as a buyer while David assisted in the management of the company. Watumull officially retired in 1957.

When Watumull and Jensen married, Watumull was not a US citizen, and the laws at the time required Jensen to forfeit her US citizenship upon marrying a foreign national. Watumull had begun applying for citizenship immediately after his arrival in Hawaii and obtained his first papers in 1918. However, five years later, when he would have been eligible for citizenship, US immigration law was revised to exclude Asians from eligibility to become citizens. Watumull campaigned for years against these immigration restrictions, and when they were finally lifted following World War II, Watumull became a citizen in 1946.

Watumull's involvement in civic affairs did not end there. In 1942, he and his wife formed the Watumull Foundation to promote India and its culture. In 1943, Watumull assisted with the formation in Washington, DC, of the National Committee for India's Freedom, a group that supported the movement for Indian independence from Great Britain. As another means by which to promote a better understanding of India and its culture, Watumull was a member of the East-West Philosophers' Conference, a gathering of intellectuals to discuss the coming together of Eastern and Western thought. For Watumull, promoting cultural understanding and working toward peace were essential to creating a better world.

Only two years following his retirement, Watumull died of a heart condition at the age of sixty-eight, just eight days before Hawaii became a state. He was survived by his wife, three children, five grandsons, two brothers, and a nephew, who had been assisting him with the family business.

SIGNIFICANCE

Watumull's achievements are plentiful and helped to shape Hawaii's merchandising history. As one of the major retailers that promoted Hawaiian sportswear and its themes, Watumull helped to shape the direction of Hawaiian clothing. In addition, he built one of the first shopping centers in Kailua, Oahu, which was still operating in 2011. Through the Watumull Foundation, he sponsored the exchange of students between India and the United States and supported Hawaiian cultural activities, including the Honolulu Symphony and the Honolulu Academy of Arts. Upon his death, a tribute to Watumull in Hawaiian newspapers noted that good will was the legacy he left behind.

Regina Pfeiffer

FURTHER READING

Arthur, Linda. *Aloha Attire: Hawaii Dress in the Twentieth Century*. Atglen, PA: Schiffer, 2000. Print. Highlights the development of the manufacturing and retail merchandising of Hawaiian sportswear.

Hope, Dale, with Gregory Tozian. *The Aloha Shirt: Spirit of the Islands*. Hillsboro, OH: Beyond Words, 2000. Print. Quotes Lila Sahney, the eldest of G. J. Watumull's children, about the growth in popularity of the aloha shirt. The book also includes information about the designers of aloha shirts, including Elsie Das and Ellen Jensen.

Markovits, Claude. *Global World of Indian Merchants, 1750–1947: Traders of Sind from Bukhara to Panama*. New York: Cambridge UP, 2000. Print. Gives the reader more background information about the diaspora of Indian merchants to other parts of the world.

MICHI WEGLYN

Activist, fashion designer, writer

In Years of Infamy: The Untold Story of America's Concentration Camps *(1976), Michi Weglyn provided an accurate history of the Japanese American internment and contributed to the movement for government reparations. Weglyn also had a successful career as a costume designer.*

Born: November 29, 1926; Stockton, California
Died: April 25, 1999; New York City, New York
Full name: Michi Nishiura Weglyn (MEE-chee NEE-
    shee-yoo-rah WEHG-lihn)
Birth name: Michi Nishiura
Areas of achievement: Activism, fashion

EARLY LIFE

Michi Nishiura Weglyn was born in Stockton, California, on November 29, 1926. Her parents, Tomojiro Nishiura and Misao Yuwasa Nishiura, were Japanese immigrants. She had one younger sister, Tomi. The family lived in Brentwood, California, and earned their living as tenant farmers raising fruits and vegetables. On

Michi Weglyn. (AP Photo)

December 7, 1941, the Japanese bombed Pearl Harbor, Hawaii, and life in the United States became very difficult for Japanese immigrants, including the Nishiuras. In 1942, Weglyn and her family were relocated from their home to an internment camp. They were taken to Arizona, first to the Turlock Assembly Center and then to the Gila River Relocation Center, where they lived for the next three years. At the camp, her parents did menial work; Weglyn and her sister went to school at Butte High School. Weglyn did well both academically and in her extracurricular activities.

As a result of the establishment of the National Japanese American Student Relocation Council (NJASRC) in May 1942, Weglyn was able to leave the internment camp and attend college. In 1944, she received a scholarship to Mount Holyoke College in Massachusetts, where she majored in biology. The following year she was forced to leave school when she was diagnosed with tuberculosis. After a period of treatment, she continued her education but did not return to Mount Holyoke. While a student at the college, she had designed a stage set and discovered that her real interest was in design, not biology. In 1947, she took classes at Barnard College in New York City, and then in 1948, she studied at the Fashion Academy of New York. In 1949, she was again treated for tuberculosis.

During her time as a student in New York City, she lived at the International House, a graduate student residential community for students from other countries. There she met Walter Matthys Weglyn (Weglein). Walter Weglyn had escaped from Nazi Germany to Holland as a child through the Kindertransport program, which saved many Jewish children by moving them through Holland out of Nazi-occupied Europe. After the war, he had moved to the United States, where he worked for a branch of a Dutch perfume company. On March 5, 1950, they were married.

LIFE'S WORK

In 1952, Weglyn was hired to design costumes for an ice show presented on stage at New York's Roxy Theatre. This job led to more opportunities in costume designing, including for additional ice shows at the theater and shows at nightclubs such as the famed Copacabana. In 1954, she broke into designing for television shows with a job as designer for the *Kraft Television Theatre.* From 1954 to 1956, she worked as a costume designer for various television programs, including actress and singer Dinah Shore's variety show. In 1957, she accepted a costume designer position with *The Perry Como Show,* one of the biggest variety shows of its time. She held this position until the show moved to Los Angeles in 1966. In 1964, she had already entered another area of costume design with her own company, Michi Associates, Ltd., which manufactured and rented costumes.

By the early 1960s, Weglyn had become interested in researching and bringing to public attention the plight of Japanese Americans interned during World War II. Her husband, who as a German Jew had suffered from extreme ethnic discrimination during World War II, was instrumental in helping her with her research and in encouraging her to pursue her project. After seven years of intense research in the holdings of the New York Public Library, the Franklin Roosevelt Library, and the National Archives, Weglyn wrote *Years of Infamy: The Untold Story of America's Concentration Camps*, published in 1976.

The book was praised by members of Congress and the military, educators, journalists, and others for its well-documented account of the government program that deprived Japanese Americans of their rights as citizens. While researching her book, Weglyn met Edison Uno, president of the Japanese American Citizens League, and became a staunch activist for the redress movement—a push for a formal government apology and financial reparations for the internment episode. Up until her death in 1999, she continued to work for redress, which was granted starting in 1988. In 2009, she was honored with a celebration at California State Polytechnic University, Pomona, where the Michi and Walter Weglyn Endowed Chair of Multicultural Studies was established in 1999.

SIGNIFICANCE

Michi Nishiura Weglyn played a significant role in American life both as a costume designer and as an author and activist. Her costume designs artistically enhanced performances on both stage and screen. *Years of Infamy: The Untold Story of America's Concentration Camps* was and continues to be praised for its well-documented account of the Japanese internment program and as a significant contribution to US historiography. Her dedication to researching and presenting an accurate factual account of the internment of Japanese Americans during World War II played a key role in achieving redress for Japanese Americans. Michi Weglyn's book and her work for redress have made a significant contribution to the Japanese American community both in reparations awarded to those interned and as an affirmation of Japanese Americans as citizens who suffered racial discrimination and internment at the hands of their own government.

Shawncey Webb

FURTHER READING

Murray, Alice Yang. *Historical Memories of the Japanese American Internment and the Struggle for Redress.* Stanford: Stanford UP, 2008. Print. Coverage of the reasoning behind internment, the redress movement, and Weglyn's role in it.

---. *What Did the Internment of Japanese Americans Mean?* Boston: Bedford/St. Martin's, 2000. Print. Discusses the government's role in the internment program, the resistance of Japanese Americans, and their incarceration.

Weglyn, Michi. *Years of Infamy: The Untold Story of America's Concentration Camps.* 1976. Seattle: U of Washington P, 2003. Print. Thoroughly researched and documented history of Japanese American internment.

MING-NA WEN

Macau-born actor

In a career spanning more than a quarter century, actor Ming-Na Wen has had prominent roles in film and television. She is perhaps best known for her role in the television show ER. *Other notable roles include an appearance in the soap opera* As the World Turns *and a leading role in the film adaptation of* The Joy Luck Club.

Born: November 20, 1963; Coloane Island, Macau
Full name: Ming-Na Wen
Also known as: Ming-Na, Ming Na, Ming Wen, Ming Na Wen
Areas of achievement: Acting, film, television

Ming-Na Wen. (FilmMagic)

EARLY LIFE

Ming-Na Wen and her brother, Jonathan, were born to mother Lin Chan on Coloane Island, Macau, then a territory of Portugal. Lin Chan, a Cantonese nurse, divorced Wen's father and moved both children to Hong Kong when Wen was still a toddler; she then married Chinese American Soo Lim Yee when Wen was four years old. The family moved to Queens, New York, and then eventually to Yee's hometown of Pittsburgh, Pennsylvania. Wen's first foray into acting was in her third-grade Easter play, where she played the role of a bunny; she fell in love with acting when she earned the audience's laughter and applause.

Growing up Asian in Pittsburgh was not easy on Wen, and she tried going by the names Maggie and Doris in order to fit in with her classmates and downplay her heritage. She graduated from Mount Lebanon High School in Pittsburgh in 1981. As a nurse, Lin Chan hoped that her daughter would pursue a career in medicine; despite her mother's wishes, however, Wen elected to study theater and drama, earning her bachelor of fine arts in drama from the prestigious Carnegie Mellon University. Her early on-screen roles included work on the children's television program *Mister Rogers' Neighborhood* in 1985.

LIFE'S WORK

Since her appearance in *Mister Rogers' Neighborhood*, Wen's multimedia acting career has spanned television, film, stage, and video games. In 1988, she was cast as Lien Hughes on the long-running daytime soap opera *As the World Turns*. Her character was significant because she was one of the few Asian characters in daytime soaps at the time who were not domestic employees. The character later became a lawyer working in Washington, DC.

After leaving the show, Wen was cast as Jing-Mei "June" Woo, a lead character in the film adaptation of Amy Tan's *The Joy Luck Club* (1993), which won praise from critics and fans alike for refusing to portray Asians and Asian Americans as monolithic stereotypes or confined within simplified racial identities. A year later, Wen expanded her repertoire as the female lead in the film *Street Fighter* (1994), based on the video game of the same name. The movie also featured action star Jean-Claude Van Damme and Golden Globe winner Raul Julia. Wen's character, Chun-Li Zang, defies the stereotype of Asian women as passive and compliant; instead of waiting for stronger men to save her, Zang infiltrates an enemy organization to avenge her father's murder.

Wen married Eric Michael Zee in 1995 and later dropped her last name, noting that her family went by either the surname Yee or Zee and that she no longer wanted to be Wen professionally or privately. After 1998, she is credited on screen as simply Ming-Na.

Wen continued her film career by lending her voice to the title character in *Mulan* (1998), Disney's first animated full-length movie set in an Asian culture. She then became a regular cast member of the television drama *ER* from 1999 to 2004, reprising a recurring role she had played during its first season in 1994. Her character, originally named Deb Chen, went by the name Jing-Mei upon her reappearance in the sixth season, harking back to her character in *The Joy Luck Club*. In 2009, Wen won the role of Camile Wray in the science-fiction series *Stargate Universe*, where, as the first openly gay character in the *Stargate* franchise, she once again broke new ground as an Asian American actress.

SIGNIFICANCE

As one of the few Asian American female actors in prime-time television and major motion pictures, Ming-Na Wen has shaped audience perceptions of the minority. The characters she has played have defied the passive, submissive, and sexualized stereotypes of Asian and Asian American women, and the proliferation of her work across numerous platforms has elevated the visibility of Asian American women beyond mere caricature. In recognition of her work, Ming-Na won the Annie Award in 1998 for her voice acting in *Mulan.*

Norma Jones

FURTHER READING

Breaux, Richard, M. "After 75 Years of Magic: Disney Answers Its Critics, Rewrites African American History, and Cashes In on Its Racist Past." *Journal of African American Studies* 14.4 (2010): 398–416. Print. A commentary on images of race in Disney movies.

Lowe, Lisa. "Heterogeneity, Hybridity, Multiplicity: Marking Asian American Differences." *A Companion to Asian American Studies*. Ed. Kent A. Ono. Malden: Blackwell, 2005. Print. Discusses Wen's character and her portrayal in *The Joy Luck Club.*

Lu, Sheldon H. *Transnational Chinese Cinemas: Identity, Nationhood, Gender*. Honolulu: U of Hawaii P, 1997. Print. Includes biographical information regarding Wen.

Ono, Kent A., and Vincent N. Pham. *Asian Americans and the Media*. Malden: Polity, 2009. Print. Discusses Wen's portrayal of Dr. Chen on *ER*.

Tewari, Nita, and Alvin Alvarez, eds. *Asian American Psychology: Current Perspectives*. New York: Psychology, 2008. Print. Addresses how Wen's portrayals have affected perceptions of Asian Americans and related psychology.

MICHELLE WIE

Professional golfer

Michele Wie became a golf and media sensation before she was a teenager. Known for 300-yard drives, she competed against men and women professionals before turning fifteen. She has earned millions of dollars from endorsements, and ranked as high as second in the world rankings. Wie was one of the top female athletes in total earnings before she won her first tournament in 2009, helping to popularize the LPGA Tour.

Born: October 11, 1989; Honolulu, Hawaii
Full name: Michelle Wie
Birth name: Michelle Sung Wie
Also known as: Wie Seong-mi
Area of achievement: Sports

EARLY LIFE

Michelle Sung Wie was born in Honolulu, Hawaii, to parents who had immigrated to the islands from South Korea. Her mother's background as a former Korean national amateur golf champion in the mid-1980s inspired Wie to take up the game as a four-year-old. From her earliest days on the course, she had a passion for hitting the ball hard, sometimes as far as one hundred yards. Her first eighteen-hole round at age seven resulted in a score of eighty-six; she broke par as a nine-year-old. By that age Wie was outscoring her parents, and she soon established herself as a top junior champion, winning tournaments against both girls and boys.

In 2000, Wie became the first ten-year-old to qualify for the US Women's Amateur Public Links championship, and began a remarkable amateur career. Possessing a golf swing that was described as nearly perfect, she captured the attention of the local golf community with her trademark power off the tee, driving 300-yard

Michelle Wie. (Getty Images)

tee shots at the age of twelve. In 2002, Wie won the Hawaii Open Women's Golf championship by thirteen strokes, and qualified for her first Ladies Professional Golf Association (LPGA) event, the Takefuji Classic in Hawaii. For five years, Wie held the record as the youngest golfer to qualify for an LPGA event.

Wie's family sought to expand her opportunities in competitive golf after she won the Hawaii Junior Golf Association's Tournament of Champions in 2001 and 2002. At the time, Wie was excelling in her studies at Punahou Academy in Honolulu, the same high school once attended by President Barack Obama. She suspended her schooling in order to train full-time in golf, traveling to the Leadbetter Golf Academy in Florida in 2002. Before Wie turned professional in 2005, she became the youngest winner of a United States Golf Association (USGA) adult event (the 2003 US Women's Amateur Public Links), the youngest to make the cut in an LPGA major tournament (the 2003 Kraft Nabisco Championship), the youngest to play in the Curtiss Cup for amateur women golfers (2004, at age fourteen), and the youngest to play in a men's Professional Golf Association (PGA) event (2004 Sony Open at age fourteen), where she scored the lowest round by a female in a PGA event (a sixty-eight).

LIFE'S WORK

Inspired by the success of golfer Tiger Woods, and seemingly ready for the highest level of competition, Wie turned professional a week before her sixteenth birthday and immediately secured multi-million-dollar endorsements from shoe brand Nike and electronics giant Sony. However, Wie was barred from regular participation in LPGA events due to her age. She was able to compete in tournaments, including some LPGA events, by gaining a sponsor exemption—when the sponsor of a tournament allows non-qualifying golfers to play—or by completing qualifying rounds of play.

Her first two professional events in 2005 resulted in no earnings, despite admirable play and a fourth-place finish in the Sony World Championship. (The fourth place finish was later vacated due to her signing an incorrect scorecard.) In early 2006, she was ranked third in the world, and attained the second-place spot by mid-year. Due to her infrequent playing, Wie eventually dropped to seventh. Through 2006, she alternated play between PGA and LPGA events. Wie's first full professional year yielded six top-five finishes in women's tournaments, including the LPGA Championship and the US Open, but no championships. She made the cut

---

Michelle Wie at the 2003 Kraft Nabisco Championship

Already a seasoned golfer and the youngest to qualify for a Ladies Professional Golf Association (LPGA) event in 2002, thirteen-year-old Michelle Wie broke new ground in the 2003 Kraft Nabisco Championship. Wie posted the overall lowest score by an amateur and became the youngest golfer to make the cut in an LPGA major, eventually finishing in the top ten. Wie's opening round of par seventy-two was punctuated by drives that exceeded three hundred yards; her distance averaged in the 280s for the tournament, outpacing eventual champion Annike Soremstan by about twenty yards. Her third round sixty-six tied the lowest amateur score in an LPGA major and enabled her to compete in the final grouping of players because she was in third place. Despite a final round of seventy-six, Wie finished in ninth place, serving notice that her future was bright. She used the momentum from this event to become the youngest champion of an adult United States Golf Association (USGA) event, the 2003 Women's Amateur Public Links tournament, and the youngest to make the cut in the 2003 United States Women's Open later that year—all before her fourteenth birthday.

---

once for a men's PGA event. *Time* magazine named the seventeen-year-old Wie as one of the "Time 100," a list of popular and influential people.

In early 2007, Wie suffered a wrist injury that limited her participation in tournaments. Some critics questioned the severity and nature of the injury. She did compete in nine LPGA events, and made the cut three times. Wie finished the year enrolled as a freshman communications major at Stanford University, with total golf and endorsement earnings of approximately $19 million. In many cases, her ability to compete in professional tournaments was due to sponsor exemption and qualifying play, a point that made her somewhat controversial, and further shaped her image as a phenomenon. However, as she was a popular figure in golf, her performance on the course did not hamper her marketability.

It was not until 2009 that Wie was able to earn a membership in the LPGA after successfully completing the LPGA Qualifying School. This enabled her to compete full-time without having to seek sponsor exemptions or play qualifying tournaments. In late 2009, Wie contributed to the United States team's victory at the Solheim Cup, a tournament in which professional women golfers compete on two teams representing Europe and the United States. Three months later, in her sixty-seventh LPGA event, she won the Lorena Ochoa Invitational in Guadalajara, Mexico, against a limited field of competitors, with a 15-under-par 275. This victory, her first since she began playing LPGA events in 2002, heralded for many the arrival of a matured athlete who had proven her ability to persevere by shaking off past disappointments and challenging expectations. Wie's second tour victory came at the 2010 CN Canadian Open, a three-stroke, twelve-under-par win against a full field of women professional golfers.

SIGNIFICANCE

Wie has become one of professional golf's most recognizable figures. Though her endorsement contracts have dwarfed her golf earnings, Wie has ignored her detractors. Wie challenged golf's gender barriers when she openly sought competition against top male players before she turned professional at fifteen. An outstanding student, Wie has multiple interests outside of golf. Regardless of her future accomplishments, Wie has established herself as a pioneer in women's golf, who has helped add vitality to the game.

P. Graham Hatcher

FURTHER READING

Adelson, Eric. *The Sure Thing: The Making and Unmaking of Golf Phenom Michelle Wie*. Ballentine: 2009. Print. Reviews ten years of coverage about Wie's career.

Hawkins, John. "Wie-markable." *Golf World*. 23 Jan 2004: 14. Print. Discusses Wie's 2004 Sony Open performance, where she was the youngest female to compete in a full-field PGA event.

Mario, Jennifer. *Michelle Wie: The Making of a Champion*. New York: St. Martin's Griffin, 2006. Print. Chronicles the rise of Wie's career to her turning professional in 2005.

SUNITA WILLIAMS

Astronaut

United States Navy Captain Sunita Williams is a highly versatile pilot and astronaut who has set several milestones while in space as both a woman and an Asian American. She is best known for her work on the International Space Station and her space walks.

Born: September 19, 1965; Euclid, Ohio
Full name: Sunita Lyn Pandya Williams
Birth name: Sunita Lyn Pandya
Also known as: Suni Williams
Areas of achievement: Science and technology, military

EARLY LIFE

Sunita Williams was born to Deepak N. Pandya, a neuroanatomist from the Indian state of Gujarat, and Ursuline "Bonnie" Zalokar Pandya, an x-ray technician of Slovenian ancestry from Cleveland, Ohio. When her father accepted a new appointment in Boston, Massachusetts, in 1966, the family moved to nearby Needham, where Williams was raised and graduated from high school in 1983. She was active in athletics, especially competitive swimming, and contemplated a career in veterinary medicine because she loved animals. When both Columbia University and the United States Naval Academy offered her admission, she selected the latter, in part because she could avoid assuming student loans, and in part because her brother Jay was already enrolled there. After graduating in the middle of her Naval Academy class in 1987, Williams attended flight school in Pensacola, Florida. In 1989, she joined a helicopter support squadron in Norfolk, Virginia, and was deployed to the Middle East as part of Operation Desert Shield in 1990 and Operation Provide Comfort in 1991 during the first Gulf War.

In 1969, a nearly four-year-old Williams had watched Neil Armstrong and Buzz Aldrin walk on the moon, but never imagined that she might become an astronaut herself. However, after meeting several astronauts at the Johnson Space Center in Houston, Texas, Williams realized she had many of the skills necessary for piloting spacecraft. She graduated from the United States Naval Test Pilot School in Patuxent, Maryland, in 1993 and in 1995 earned a master's degree in engineering management from the Florida Institute of Technology. In 1998, NASA selected her for astronaut training.

Sunita Williams. (Getty Images)

LIFE'S WORK

As a new NASA astronaut, Williams received extensive training in additional skills, including water and wilderness survival techniques, piloting the supersonic T-38 training jet, and operating robotic arms. She lived underwater for eight days in NASA's Aquarius laboratory in 2002. As a result of working with the Russian Space Agency in Moscow, Williams learned to speak Russian, a talent that proved useful when she served with Russian flight engineers on board the International Space Station.

Williams first traveled into space in December 2006 on board the space shuttle *Discovery*. She brought with her a copy of the Hindu scripture *Bhagavad Gita* and a statue of Ganesha, the Hindu god of beginnings, from her Hindu father, as well as a Christian cross from her Slovenian Catholic grandmother. After docking with the International Space Station, Williams joined Expedition 14 and then remained with Expedition 15 until June 2007. In all, Williams spent 195 days on the station, establishing a record for space endurance by women that had not been broken by 2011. During these two expeditions, Williams also logged 29 hours, 17 minutes, of walking in space, setting a new record for

women until it was broken by astronaut Peggy Whitson in 2008.

Several noteworthy events occurred during Williams's six months in space. Shortly after arriving, her long black hair was cut by fellow astronaut Joan Higginbotham and brought back to Earth, where it was donated to children who had lost their hair due to medical problems. In April 2007, while the Boston Marathon was taking place in her home state of Massachusetts, Williams became the first astronaut to run a marathon in space. Williams ran the 26.2 miles in 4 hours, 23 minutes, and 46 seconds, while strapped to a stationary treadmill inside the Space Station. In May 2007, she spoke with Queen Elizabeth II of Great Britain via video communication.

By 2011, Williams had logged more than three thousand flight hours as a Navy pilot in more than thirty different aircraft, rising in rank to captain. She is scheduled to take part in Expeditions 32 and 33 on board the International Space Station in 2012 where she will serve as commander.

SIGNIFICANCE

By 2011, Williams was only the second female of Indian heritage to fly in space; she holds the record for the longest spaceflight for a woman. Her numerous honors include two Navy Commendation Medals, the Navy and Marine Corps Achievement Medal, and the Humanitarian Service Medal. She has also received international awards such as Russia's Medal of Merit in Space and India's Sardar Vallabhai Patel Vishwa Pratibha Award.

James I. Deutsch

FURTHER READING

Kanin, Zachary. "One Small Step." *New Yorker* 83.15 (2007): 47. Print. A humorous parody, written after Williams ran her own Boston Marathon on the International Space Station, in which author Kanin imagines some other feats Williams might accomplish in space.

Mahanti, Subodh. *Pioneer of Space Travel, Sunita Williams*. New Delhi: Indian Ministry of Information and Broadcasting, 2007. Print. Places Williams's achievements in the context of recent spaceflight history.

Seshadri, S., and Aradhika Sharma. *Astronaut Sunita Williams: Achiever Extraordinaire* New Delhi: Rupa, 2007. Print. Contains many details of Williams's personal life and Indian American identity, thanks to the cooperation of her parents.

Andrea Wong

Business executive

Andrea Wong is among the most important executives working in the television and media industry. She has managed and developed highly successful programming for television networks such as ABC and Lifetime. Wong is known for her ability to oversee and consistently generate creative solutions to meet the challenges networks face in competing for and retaining audiences.

Born: 1966; Sunnyvale, California
Full name: Andrea Wong
Areas of achievement: Business, entertainment

Early Life

Andrea Wong was born in the town of Sunnyvale, in northern California, to Chinese American parents; her father is a teacher, her mother a nurse. Growing up, Wong wanted to work for computer giant Apple Inc., and studied to become an engineer. Wong studied electrical engineering for four years at the Massachusetts Institute of Technology (MIT), graduating with a bachelor's of science degree. After finishing her undergraduate studies, however, she decided that rather than continue in engineering she would attend the Stanford Graduate School of Business, where she went on to graduate with an MBA in 1993.

During her time at Stanford, Wong worked as an intern for the American Broadcasting Company (ABC). Wong has said that it was this opportunity that helped her to discover her passion for television. Upon graduating from Stanford, she began her career working in banking and finance, but she soon transitioned into television, working as a researcher for the news program *Primetime Live*. Over the next few years, Wong demonstrated her talent in the field of news media and began her rise through the ranks at ABC. Wong was the senior vice president of network programming at ABC by 2000.

Life's Work

During Wong's tenure at ABC, she oversaw the development and acquisition of a number of successful television shows, including *The Bachelor*, *Extreme Makeover: Home Edition*, *Dancing with the Stars*, and the *Country Music Awards*. While each show was distinct, each one, in Wong's words, tapped into broad and resonant themes in people's lives, an element that she points out as essential to quality television programming. Wong has described the themes of these shows as "aspirational" and resonating with strong values for the viewing public. Her insights into and understanding of television audiences are evident in the success of these shows. Wong's tenure at ABC lasted until 2007, during which time she brought the network higher ratings, increased audience viewership, and enhanced ABC's brand as a channel focused on family programming.

In 2007, Wong left ABC to run Lifetime and the Lifetime Movie Network, television channels geared toward programming for women, where she became president and chief executive officer (CEO). Wong brought a new approach to Lifetime that included not only a fresh lineup of shows aimed at expanding the network's traditional audience, but also a larger budget apportioned to the production of movies for Lifetime. As CEO, Wong oversaw the debut of several new shows, including *Army Wives*, as well as the acquisition of Bravo's successful reality series, *Project Runway*.

Andrea Wong. (FilmMagic)

In addition to developing programming, Wong further enhanced the Lifetime Movie Network by recruiting well-known actors to appear in big-budget movie productions. Wong increased budgets for Lifetime movies, strove for higher production value, and broadened the themes and content of the already well-known Lifetime movie brand. By expanding the appeal of movies to a wider audience, particularly younger female viewers, Wong succeeded in both maintaining traditional viewership and attracting newer demographics.

In her career as a network executive, Wong has met the challenge of creating appealing, high-quality programming by using her knowledge of what audiences like to watch. She has brought to her projects both business acumen and a sense of the creative and financial demands of television. Additionally, Wong has worked actively to inspire young women and support issues important to the female public, developing television that offers role models to young female viewers. In 2008, Lifetime ran its fifth Every Woman Counts campaign, aiming to encourage participation and leadership in the political process by women of all ages.

While a CEO at Lifetime, Wong promoted the network's ongoing drive to collect signatures in support of the Breast Cancer Patient Protection Act, for which she received a public award. The Breast Cancer Patient Protection Act proposes improved support and care for women undergoing surgery and treatment for breast cancer. Among other things, the act stipulates that women should be allowed at least a twenty-four-hour hospital stay after surgery in order to recover, as well as the choice to remain in the hospital for up to forty-eight hours, if necessary. As of 2011, the bill was still in House subcommittees.

After Lifetime and the A&E Television group were consolidated in 2010, Wong oversaw the transitional phase of the merger before leaving the company. She served as a media advisor on the board of directors for Liberty Media Corporation. In September 2011, Wong joined Sony Pictures Television as the president of international production, representing Sony Pictures Entertainment abroad.

SIGNIFICANCE

As a television executive, Andrea Wong has developed highly successful programming in drama and reality television. Wong's tenure at major television networks such as ABC and Lifetime demonstrates her talent for appealing to viewers across the general viewing public. Wong notes that she was fortunate to work with excellent mentors during her early years. To young people just beginning their careers, she suggests taking the time to find one's passion in life, then learning as much as possible about the business that surrounds it and pursuing it wholeheartedly. As of 2011, Wong continues to be one of the most prominent business executives in the television industry.

William Teipe

FURTHER READING

Halpern, Jake. "Project Lifetime." *Stanford Magazine*. Sanford Alumni Association, July/August 2009. Web. 16 Mar. 2012. Article provides extensive business-related information on Wong's career, focusing specifically on her work with Lifetime.

James, Meg. "Lifetime CEO Andrea Wong to Step Down." *Los Angeles Times*. Los Angeles Times, 6 Feb. 2010. Web. 16 Mar. 2012. Article describes the events leading up to and immediately following Lifetime's consolidation with A&E, and includes quotations from Wong's statement upon resigning.

Wong, Andrea. "Q&A: Lifetime's Andrea Wong." Interview with Jon Lafayette. *TV Week*. Crain Communications, n.d. Web. 16 Mar. 2012. Transcript of an interview with Wong, in which she describes the process of getting started with Lifetime and beginning to revitalize the network.

ANNA MAY WONG

Actor

A popular actor during the early twentieth century, Anna May Wong overcame typecasting and the prejudices of her time to become a highly respected artist. She managed to challenge negative stereotypes with her own projects and inspired a generation of Asian American actors to follow her into the world of film and theater.

Born: January 3, 1905; Los Angeles, California
Died: February 3, 1961; Santa Monica, California

Full name: Anna May Wong
Birth name: Wong Liu Tsong
Also known as: Huáng Liǔshuāng
Areas of achievement: Film, theater, television

EARLY LIFE

Anna May Wong was the second child of Wong Sam Sing and Lee Gon Toy, both second-generation Chinese Americans. The family lived near Chinatown in Los Angeles. Wong Sam Sing was a laundryman, a typical occupation for his family, and as their children grew up, they joined their parents in the family business. Liu Tsong (as Wong was called as a child) and her older sister were the only Chinese children at their school; they were constantly teased and sometimes even physically abused by their classmates. To protect his daughters from bullying in school, Wong Sam Sing sent them to a Presbyterian Chinese school; they also attended Chinese language school on Saturdays.

During the early days of the film industry, major studios were in the process of relocating from New York to Los Angeles. In spite of her family's disapproval, Wong became a great fan of the short silent films being shown in nickelodeons. She started to position herself

Anna May Wong. (Getty Images)

around the studios and use her English name, Anna May. Soon she landed her first role as an extra in the 1919 silent film *The Red Lantern*. After more experience, she dropped out of high school and at the age of sixteen secured her first role, as the wife of Lon Chaney's Asian character in the film *Bits of Life* (1921).

LIFE'S WORK

The following year, Wong was cast in a leading role in *The Toll of the Sea* (1922), the first Technicolor film to be made in Hollywood. The plot was a variation on Italian composer Giacomo Puccini's tragic opera *Madame Butterfly*, in which the Asian heroine commits suicide because of her non-Asian lover's infidelity. The popularity of the plotline reflected general fears of racial mixing. This fear also interfered with Wong's career, as studios were afraid of casting an Asian American actor as a love interest alongside European and American costars. Nevertheless, Wong won critical acclaim for her acting.

Her next major project was *The Thief of Bagdad*, produced in 1924 and starring Douglas Fairbanks, in which she played a beautiful Mongol slave girl. Loosely based on a story from the *Arabian Nights*, the film was a huge success. Her next major film, released as *The Dragon Horse* in 1927, was set in Ming China, and had an Asian cast. Although not well known, the film provided a welcome relief from typecasting. In her next film, *Old San Francisco*, Wong played another kind of stereotypical character—an evil, manipulative role later termed the "dragon lady." Soon afterward she decided to pursue her career in Europe.

In Germany and throughout Europe, Wong was treated with respect, but she also experienced the isolation of being away from the Chinese American community. She and her sister Lulu first went to Berlin, where Wong studied German and acted in the film *Schmutziges Geld* (1928; titled *Show Life* in English). She met many German intellectuals, including the philosopher Walter Benjamin. She used her newly acquired German language skills in Vienna, where she played the title character in the operetta *Tschun Tschi*. Wong also appeared on stage in London in *The Circle of Chalk* with Laurence Olivier. She starred in five English films.

English broadcaster Eric Maschwitz fell in love with Wong, and upon their separation he composed the wistful lyrics of the song "These Foolish Things (Remind Me of You)," which would become a jazz standard. With her international stardom assured, Wong confidently returned to the United States in 1930,

Anna May Wong's Screen Image as the "Dragon Lady"

The term "dragon lady" first appeared in popular culture thanks to a villain with the name in the 1930s comic strip *Terry and the Pirates*. The character was based on Anna May Wong's film *Daughter of the Dragon* (1931), in which she played a treacherous Asian femme fatale. Together with the "Madame Butterfly" stereotype, in which the character is essentially punished with death for the mistake of falling in love with a Caucasian, the character typified many of the roles that Wong played throughout her career. The subject of a large body of critical theory exploring the roles of racism and misogyny in literature and film, the term "dragon lady" is now connected with the "Yellow Peril" political hysteria of early twentieth-century America. The term eventually became associated with any strong, politically clever Asian or Asian American woman.

starring in the successful Broadway play *On the Spot*, which was later adapted as the film *Dangerous to Know* (1938).

Signing a contract with Paramount, Wong could not escape the typecasting and pervasive racism that infected Hollywood and popular culture at large. In *Daughter of the Dragon* (1931), she played the daughter of Fu Manchu, another predictably evil character. In 1932, she appeared with her friend Marlene Dietrich in Josef von Sternberg's *Shanghai Express*. Wong was insulted when she was passed over in favor of Caucasian actors for MGM's adaptation of Pearl S. Buck's *The Good Earth* (1931), which follows a Chinese family.

During this period, Wong became a spokesperson for Chinese resistance to the invasion of China by Japan, which culminated in the outbreak of the Second Sino-Japanese War in 1937. In spite of Wong's loyalty to the cause, Chinese audiences resented her for her portrayals of Chinese characters. During her 1936 tour of China, Wong experienced this hostility firsthand. In the late 1930s, however, Wong was able to make a few films in which she portrayed more positive characters, including *Daughter of Shanghai* (1937). Wong continued

acting in film and on television until her death in 1961. She was given a star on the Hollywood Walk of Fame in 1960.

SIGNIFICANCE

Like many actors of ethnic minority descent in twentieth-century Hollywood, Anna May Wong was forced to conform to racial stereotypes and exaggerate her ethnicity. Wong persevered, challenging professional and cultural conventions, and was able to transcend these limitations. Film historians have increasingly recognized Wong's role in cultural history and her considerable talents as an actress. Asian Americans in particular have been inspired by her courage. *Anna May Wong: In Her Own Words*, a documentary film by Korean American filmmaker Yunah Hong, was shown in 2010 at the Pusan International Film Festival. Several recent biographies have also examined her personal story and life's work.

Alice Myers

FURTHER READING

Chan, Anthony B. *Perpetually Cool: The Many Lives of Anna May Wong (1905–1961)*. Lanham: Scarecrow, 2003. Print. Detailed biography provides a great deal of historical context; illustrated, with filmography and index.

Hodges, Graham Russell. *Anna May Wong: From Laundryman's Daughter to Hollywood Legend*. New York: Palgrave, 2004. Print. Comprehensive biography covers childhood and entire career; illustrated, with bibliography, filmography, and index.

Leibfried, Philip, and Chei Mi Lane. *Anna May Wong: A Complete Guide to Her Film, Stage, Radio, and Television Work*. Jefferson: McFarland, 2004. Print. A well-researched guide providing details on all of Wong's works; illustrated, with bibliography and index.

Leong, Karen J. *The China Mystique: Pearl S. Buck, Anna May Wong, Mayling Soong, and the Transformation of American Orientalism*. Berkeley: U of California P, 2005. Print. Study of American orientalism in 1930s and 1940s; shows how Wong created an identity embracing both Chinese and American cultures; illustrated, with bibliography and index.

B. D. Wong

Actor

B. D. Wong is a leading Asian American figure in entertainment who has found fame on Broadway, on television, and in movies.

Born: October 24, 1960; San Francisco, California
Full name: Bradley Darryl Wong
Also known as: Bradd Wong
Areas of achievement: Acting, television, theater

EARLY LIFE

Chinese American actor B. D. Wong was born Bradley Darryl Wong in San Francisco, California, to Roberta Christine and William D. Wong. He became interested in the arts and acting as a young boy. While attending Lincoln High School, he participated in community theater around the Bay Area. Shortly after graduating from San Francisco State University, Wong moved to New York to pursue acting. He made his debut in 1982 in *Androcles and the Lion*, a dramatic adaptation of a folktale, presented at the New York Town Hall.

LIFE'S WORK

As an actor, Wong has had many important, ground-breaking roles on both stage and screen. His first such role was that of opera singer Song Liling in the Broadway play *M. Butterfly*, opposite actor John Lithgow. The play, written by David Henry Hwang, ran from 1988 to 1990. For the role, Wong changed his stage name from Bradd Wong to B. D. Wong to keep his character's gender ambiguous. Wong won a Tony Award, a Drama Desk Award, an Outer Critics Circle Award, a Clarence Derwent Award, and a Theatre World Award for his performance, making him the only actor to win all five awards for the same role.

Since *M. Butterfly*, Wong has played a variety of roles both in movies and on television. He starred in the short-lived series *All-American Girl*, which was based on stand-up routines of Asian American comedian Margaret Cho. He also provided the voice of Captain Li Shang in the Disney films *Mulan* (1998) and *Mulan II* (2004) and appeared in various other films, including *Father of the Bride* (1991), *Jurassic Park* (1993), and *Seven Years in Tibet* (1997). From 1997 to 2003, he played Father Ray Mukada in the HBO television series *Oz*. One of Wong's best-known roles is that of Dr. George Huang, the psychiatrist on NBC's *Law & Order: Special Victims Unit*, for which he won an Asian

Excellence Award for Outstanding Television Actor in 2008. He left *Law & Order* in 2011 to take on the role of another psychiatrist in the NBC series *Awake*.

Wong is also known for his few musical theater roles. In 1999, he starred in the Broadway revival of *You're a Good Man, Charlie Brown* alongside actors Anthony Rapp and Kristin Chenoweth. Wong played the role of Linus, a role that was not specifically Asian American, and showed his versatility as an actor. He also starred in the 1998 production of *As Thousands Cheer*.

In 2003, Wong published a book, *Following Foo: The Electronic Adventures of the Chestnut Man*, which documents the path to parenthood for him and his then-partner, producer Richie Jackson. It takes the reader through the trials and tribulations of watching his and Jackson's prematurely born son, Jackson Foo, fight for his life following the death of his twin brother, Boaz Dov. The book is a collection of e-mails Wong wrote to his friends and family about the birth and death and their responses.

B. D. Wong. (Getty Images)

SIGNIFICANCE

B. D. Wong is an openly gay Asian American actor, writer, and father. Through his work, he has brought awareness to both Asian American and gay, lesbian, bisexual, and transgender (GLBT) issues, starting with his explosive role as Song Liling in *M. Butterfly*. The play makes incisive statements about the gendered notions of the East versus the West, and Wong's portrayal of a character who transitions from a man to a woman and back again reflects his versatility as an actor. The role gives visibility and voice to the historical oppression of people of Asian descent as well as members of the GLBT community. Wong also stood in solidarity with fellow Asian American entertainers against the Broadway production of *Miss Saigon* when Jonathan Pryce, a white actor, was cast as the Engineer, a Eurasian character. He is outspoken about the underrepresentation of Asian Americans in the media and is involved with several organizations centered on such issues, such as the Coalition of Asian Pacifics in Entertainment (CAPE). He is also outspoken about GLBT causes and has made appearances at the GLAAD Media Awards and AIDS-related charity functions.

Cynthia Wang

FURTHER READINGS

Stone, Christopher. "B. D. Wong: Out Author, Actor and Parent." *AfterElton*. AfterElton.com, 16 Nov. 2005. Web. 13 Mar. 2012. Article and biography about Wong, focusing on his role as a gay parent.

Summers, Claude J. "B. D. Wong." *Glbtq*. Glbtq, 13 Mar. 2012. Web. Summary of Wong's life and work, centered on his involvement with the GLBT community.

Wong, B. D. *Following Foo: The Electronic Adventures of the Chestnut Man*. New York: Harper, 2003. Print. Wong's account of the fight for his son's life.

DELBERT WONG

Judge

Delbert Wong was the first Chinese American to be appointed as a judge in the continental United States. He joined the Los Angeles Municipal Court in 1959 and the Superior Court in 1961.

Born: May 17, 1920; Hanford, California
Died: March 10, 2006; Glendale, California
Full name: Delbert Earl Wong
Area of achievement: Law

EARLY LIFE

Delbert Earl Wong was born to Alice and Earl Quong Wong in Hanford, California, in 1920. Wong's father was an immigrant from Guangdong, China, and his mother was from Weaverville, California. In 1921, the family settled in Bakersfield, California, in a community with approximately five hundred Chinese citizens. Wong's younger brother, Ervin, was born in 1924; two other siblings passed away as infants. His father was co-owner of Lincoln Market, a grocery store that sustained his family throughout the Great Depression.

Wong graduated from Kern County Union High School and received an associate of arts degree from Bakersfield College. He was a business major at the University of California, Berkeley when Pearl Harbor was attacked on December 7, 1941. In 1942, Wong graduated from Berkeley and joined the Army Air Corps with his brother, Ervin. He was assigned as a navigator with the 401st Bomb Group, a unit that flew B-17 Flying Fortresses, due to his mathematical skills. Wong completed thirty mandatory combat missions.

Tragedy struck Wong's family in 1944 when Ervin died in a flight accident and the family grocery store burned down in a fire. Wong went home on leave, then returned to the military to train as a statistical officer. By the end of World War II, he had received four Air Medals, the Distinguished Flying Cross, and two Presidential Distinguished Unit Citations.

While Wong was stationed in San Bernardino, California, the base legal officer encouraged him to become a lawyer. Wong's parents objected because they feared he would experience discrimination as a Chinese lawyer. The GI Bill changed their minds, and Wong enrolled in Stanford Law School in 1945.

In 1948, Wong married Dolores Wing, whom he had met at Berkeley. That same year, he became the first Chinese American to graduate from Stanford Law School. The couple had four children: Kent, Shelley, Duane, and Marshall.

LIFE'S WORK

Wong was hired as junior counsel by the Office of Legislative Counsel in Sacramento. In 1952, he joined the Los Angeles office of then–attorney general Edmund G. "Pat" Brown. He was the first Asian American deputy attorney general and endorsed Brown for California governor. On January 31, 1959, Wong was sworn in as the first Chinese American judge in the United States (excluding Hawaii, then a territory). In 1953, the Wongs played a role in diversifying the Silver Lake neighborhood of Los Angeles after a realtor rebuffed their attempt to purchase a lot because they were Chinese; Wong informed the property owner, who ordered the realtor to negotiate or be fired.

Wong's career reflects a number of achievements for Asian Americans. As the first Asian American deputy attorney general in California, Wong represented the state in numerous cases. After Brown appointed him as a judge, Wong was assigned to arraignment court, traffic court, and trial court. He was inducted to the Los Angeles Superior Court in 1961 and reelected until his retirement.

In 1968, Wong joined the Appellate Department of the superior court. In the midst of the Vietnam War, Wong and two other judges reversed the ruling of *People v. Cohen* (1969), in which Paul Robert Cohen was convicted for wearing a profanity-laced jacket inside Los Angeles Municipal Court. The case reached the Supreme Court, which agreed with Wong's appellate panel and released Cohen. The renamed *Cohen v. California* became a textbook case in constitutional law classes.

Wong presided over thousands of cases throughout his career. A decorated war hero, he dedicated his life to service to the judiciary and his country. After retiring in 1982, he became an arbitrator for legal disputes.

In 1986, Wong's investigation of the Los Angeles Airport Police Bureau revealed racial discrimination in the promotion of Caucasian officers over minorities. His report resulted in advancement reforms within the bureau. Wong also played a role in writing the first ethics code for the City of Los Angeles when he was appointed to the Ethics Commission by then-mayor Tom Bradley in 1989. During the O. J. Simpson murder trial, Wong entered the media spotlight when he was designated as a special master by the court and asked to retrieve evidence from Simpson's home in 1994. He was required to remain silent about the evidence for over two years.

Wong and his wife supported several organizations, including the Asian Pacific American Legal Center, Friends of the Chinatown Library, Chinese Historical Society of Southern California, and Asian Pacific American Friends of the Center Theater Group. Wong passed away at Glendale Memorial Hospital in 2006.

SIGNIFICANCE

Following in the footsteps of You Chung Hong, the first Chinese American lawyer to practice in California, Delbert E. Wong helped to further pave the way for Chinese Americans in the field of law. His appointment as a judge was a first for Chinese Americans in the continental United States. He was also the first Asian American deputy attorney general in California and the first Chinese American to graduate from Stanford Law School.

Jenny Cho

FURTHER READING

Thurber, Jon. "Delbert E. Wong, 85; First Chinese American Judge in the Continental US." *Los Angeles Times* 12 Mar. 2006: B14. Print. Wong's obituary, chronicling his life and work as a judge.

Wong, Delbert Earl. "Reflections of a World War II Veteran." *Gum Saan Journal* 23.2 (2000): 17–27. Print. Wong's first-person account of his World War II experiences.

Wong, Marshall. *Delbert Wong: First Chinese American Judge*. Spec. issue of *Gum Saan Journal* (2004). Print. Written by Wong's son, covering Wong's life and career and featuring essays by Stewart Kwoh, Linda Wong Smith, and Phillip H. Lam.

---. "Delbert E. Wong, Pioneer Chinese American Judge." *Bridging the Centuries: History of Chinese Americans in Southern California*. Ed. Susie Ling. Los Angeles: Chinese Historical Society of Southern California, 2001. 108–11. Print. A chapter on Wong's career, written by his son.

JADE SNOW WONG

Artist and writer

Jade Snow Wong was an author and a significant Chinese American artist of ceramics and enamel who helped to advance ceramics as an art form. Through her memoirs, sculptures, and personal lifestyle, Wong made significant cultural contributions to the independence of Chinese American women, as well as helping to integrate the Chinese American community into the American community at large.

Born: January 21, 1922; San Francisco, California
Died: March 16, 2006; San Francisco, California
Full name: Jade Snow Wong
Also known as: Wong Jade Snow; Constance Wong; Constance Ong; Constance Wong Ong
Areas of achievement: Art, literature

EARLY LIFE

Jade Snow Wong was born in 1922 in San Francisco, California, the fifth daughter of Chinese immigrants. Her parents had nine children in total, six girls and three boys. Wong's family lived in San Francisco's Chinatown; her parents, who operated a small overalls factory, spoke only Chinese. The building that housed the factory also served as the family's residence.

Wong grew up in a traditional Chinese home in which unquestioning obedience to parents and older family members was required. During the day, Wong attended public schools, where classes were taught in English; in the evenings, she took classes at Chinese school, where she learned Chinese language and penmanship. In addition to studying, Wong had many duties at home, among them helping to prepare meals, doing household chores, and taking responsibility for younger siblings.

After nine years of study, Wong graduated from Chinese school. While she was completing her American high-school education, she worked as a domestic helper for several different American families in order to earn money to attend college. She found herself in a world that contrasted sharply with her life in Chinatown. Upon graduating from high school and lacking adequate funds to attend the state university, she enrolled at San Francisco Junior College (now City College of San Francisco). In sociology classes, she was introduced to different attitudes about family and the role of parents and children. This brought about a period of conflict between Wong and her parents, as she tried to meld the two opposing cultures that informed her world.

While completing her two years of classes at the junior college, Wong continued to work as a domestic helper in Caucasian households. During the summer that followed her graduation from San Francisco Junior College, she was given the opportunity to attend Mills College. Her experiences at Mills further convinced her that while she did not wish to sever her ties with her family, neither did she wish to accept all of the traditions and mores of her Chinese heritage. She graduated Phi Beta Kappa from Mills College in 1942 with a major in sociology and economics.

LIFE'S WORK

During her senior year at Mills College, Wong took a course entitled Tools and Materials, in which she was introduced to the making of pottery and enamel and copper pieces. She found herself fascinated and continued her study in a summer class. Afterward, Wong took a secretarial job at the local shipyard, where

Jade Snow Wong. (AP Photo)

Jade Snow Wong the Ceramist

When Wong set up her potter's wheel in the window of the China Bazaar on Grant Avenue in San Francisco's Chinatown, she began a lifelong career which would permit her to express her individuality and to harmoniously combine her Chinese heritage and the American culture that she had discovered as a college student. In her pottery, she employed the techniques that she had learned in her classes at Mills College in Oakland, California, but she also drew upon Chinese techniques of decoration. Working in clay, enamel, and copper, Wong earned the respect of her family and ful-filled her father's desire to give his daughters an independence they would not have enjoyed in China. Wong was able to both earn a living as a ceramist and affect American cultural attitudes, as her work played a significant role in elevating pottery-making from a craft to an art. The pieces that she created for an exhibit at the Chicago Art Institute in 1952 remained an integral part of her life; she crated them after the exhibit and moved them with her, exhibiting them once again fifty years later at the San Francisco Chinese Historical Society of America Museum and Learning Center.

she discovered that there would be little opportunity for advancement in the business world for a Chinese American woman. She then decided to pursue a career in writing.

While working at the shipyard, Wong published some of her research on problems arising in the war industry, then began work on an autobiography. She also decided to continue working in pottery. Unable to find a studio, she convinced the owner of the China Bazaar near Clay Street in Chinatown to let her set up her potter's wheel in his window. Although many Chinatown residents disapproved of her project, Wong's pottery appealed to nonresidents, and her business thrived. In 1947, a red enamel plate that she had made was included in the national show *100 Objects of Fine Design*. One of her bowls became part of the permanent collection at the Metropolitan Museum of Art.

In 1950, Wong published her first book, *Fifth Chinese Daughter*, in which she recounts her experiences as the daughter of Chinese immigrants. Also in that year, she married Woodrow Ong, another artist living in Chinatown. The two artists worked together and expanded their pottery and enamel business, Ong spinning the copper forms for Wong's enamel work. Wong and her husband had four children, two sons and two daughters.

Wong was asked to present a show of her work at the Art Institute of Chicago in 1952. The successful exhibition was subsequently shown at several other art institutes and museums. As a result of the success of *Fifth Chinese Daughter*, which was a Book-of-the-Month Club selection and was translated into several Asian languages, Wong and her husband were sent by the US government on a four-month speaking tour of Asia in 1953. In addition to working as artists, Wong and her husband established a travel agency and conducted many trips to Asia for cultural exchange.

In 1975, Wong published her second book, *No Chinese Stranger*. The following year she received an honorary doctorate from Mills College. When she and her husband moved their studio from Chinatown to Polk Street on Russian Hill, Wong stopped creating pottery but continued working in enamel and copper. In 2002, she was honored with a showing of her work at the Chinese Historical Society of America Museum and Learning Center. Wong died on March 16, 2006, in San Francisco, California. Her work is exhibited at museums and art institutes throughout the United States, including the Smithsonian Institute.

SIGNIFICANCE

With the memoirs *Fifth Chinese Daughter* and *No Chinese Stranger*, Jade Snow Wong provided an intimate look at the traditions, customs, and lifestyles that define the heritage of Chinese American immigrants and also enabled non-Chinese Americans to better understand the Chinese experience in the United States. *Fifth Chinese Daughter* in particular has proved to be a popular book in grade-school curriculums. Wong's work in ceramics and enamel contributed significantly to the increase in recognition of Chinese American artists in the art world, as well as helping to further the acceptance of ceramics as a true art form. Moreover, Wong's courage and determination in pursuing a career in the arts provided an important demonstration of independence for Chinese American women.

Shawncey J. Webb

FURTHER READING

Wong, Jade Snow. *Fifth Chinese Daughter*. Seattle: U of Washington P, 1989. Print. Details Wong's childhood in a traditional Chinese home and her search for both independence and her family's approval.

---. *No Chinese Stranger*. New York: Harper, 1975. Print. Wong's second memoir, covering her achievements as a potter and an enamelist, her work with her artist husband, and their family life.

Wong, Jade Snow, et al. *Jade Snow Wong: A Retrospective; July 23–December 22, 2002*. San Francisco: Chinese Hist. Museum of Amer., 2002. Print. Catalog of the exhibit, including pieces from the 1952 exhibit at the Art Institute of Chicago, some pieces from Wong's storefront studio, and commentary by Wong and other artists.

Yung, Judy. *Unbound Feet: A Social History of Chinese Women in San Francisco*. Los Angeles: U of California P, 1995. Print. Drawing from oral histories and interviews, places Wong in a broader context of Chinese American women seeking independence and the conflict with Chinese tradition.

RUSSELL WONG

Actor

Known for his good looks and his talent for dancing and martial arts, Russell Wong is the first Asian American actor to have played the main character in two American television series.

Born: March 1, 1963; Troy, New York
Full name: Russell Girard Wong
Areas of achievement: Acting, film, television

EARLY LIFE

Russell Girard Wong was born in Troy, New York, to William Wong, who immigrated to the United States from the northern Chinese province of Shandung, and Dutch American artist Connie Van Yserloo. The sixth of seven children, Wong was raised in Albany, where his father ran a Chinese restaurant called the House of Wong. After his parents divorced, Wong went with his mother to live in California. He was seven years old at the time.

After high school, Wong attended Santa Monica City College, where he studied fashion illustration. He also took acting lessons and trained as a dancer. After performing in a junior ballet company's production of *The Nutcracker*, Wong appeared as a dancer in various music videos, including ones for David Bowie and Janet Jackson, and toured with singer Donna Summer.

In 1983, Hong Kong movie producer Nansun Shi, wife of director Tsui Hark, came to the United States looking for new talent and found Wong and his younger brother Michael. The brothers were invited to Hong Kong and signed for a few movies, although the American-born Wong had some trouble because of his limited ability to speak Chinese. His appearance in the 1985 film *Ge Wu Sheng Ping*, or *Musical Dancer*, attracted the attention of Italian film producer Raffaella De Laurentiis, who signed him for the part of Gordon Chen in *Tai-Pan* (1986), based on author James Clavell's bestselling novel.

LIFE'S WORK

Wong returned to the United States, where he found various roles on television and in films. In 1989, he caught the American public's attention in an episode of *21 Jump Street* and played a leading role in the romantic comedy *Eat a Bowl of Tea*, directed by Wayne Wang. Following his supporting roles in the films *China Cry: A True Story* (1990) and *New Jack City* (1991), Wong was cast as the abusive husband in *The Joy Luck Club* (1993), based on author Amy Tan's novel and also directed by Wang.

In 1994, Wong starred in the television series *Vanishing Son*, playing a Chinese political activist exiled to America. As heroic martial artist and violin virtuoso Jian-Wa Chang, Wong was an uncommon phenomenon: an authentic Asian hero in an American series of the type in which Asian protagonists were traditionally played by non-Asian actors. Although the show attracted a number of devoted fans, it was canceled after thirteen episodes.

It looked as if Wong had landed a major role in 1997 when he was cast as the lead in Miramax's new production about Charlie Chan, directed by Steven Soderbergh; Wong was to have portrayed Chan's grandson, a detective and martial artist. The film was shelved, however, and Wong continued to play secondary but important roles in film, such as the part of Danyael in

Russell Wong. (WireImage)

The Prophecy II (1998) opposite Christopher Walken. In *Takedown* (2000), also called *Track Down*, he played Tsutomu Shimomura, the computer-security expert who wrote the book on which the film was based. Also in 2000, his role in *Romeo Must Die*, starring Jet Li, developed his reputation as a screen stealer; as bodyguard Kai, he shows off his martial-arts abilities in one scene by defeating seven opponents in hand-to-hand combat. The following year, Wong costarred in *The Lost Empire*, also known as *The Monkey King*, a four-hour television series written by *M. Butterfly* playwright David Henry Hwang and based on the sixteenth-century Chinese novel *Journey to the West*. As the Monkey King, Wong was given ample opportunity to demonstrate his dance and martial-arts talents.

In 2003, due to his growing fan base, Wong was cast in the television series *Black Sash* as main character Tom Chang, an undercover narcotics cop who was framed and sent to prison. In the series, Chang seeks to recover his reputation and his family with the aid of his mentor, Master Li, played by actor Mako. Despite the efforts of Wong's fans, the series ran for only six episodes, and Wong returned to film; since then, he has played roles in a number of movies, including *Inside Out* (2005); *Dim Sum Funeral* (2008); and *The Mummy: Tomb of the Dragon Emperor* (2008).

Wong has also worked as a photographer and continued his interest in design by taking classes at the Parsons School of Design in New York City. In 2000, he launched a clothing line, RGW, named for his initials. He also runs a costume company for the film industry with his wife, designer Flora Cheong-Leen, whom he married in 2003.

SIGNIFICANCE

Russell Wong is the first Asian American actor to have starred in two American television series. In 1994, he won both the Image Award, sponsored by the Organization of Chinese Americans, and the Media Achievement Award, sponsored by the Media Action Network for Asian Americans. He was named one of *People* magazine's fifty most beautiful people the following year and was honored by the Asian American Arts Foundation in 1997.

Marcia B. Dinneen

FURTHER READING

Beltran, Mary C. "The New Hollywood Racelessness: Only the Fast, Furious, (and Multiracial) Will Survive." *Cinema Journal* 44.2 (2005): 50–67. Print. Discusses Wong's effectiveness in playing the role of Kai in *Romeo Must Die*.

Darling, Cary. "Groundbreaker: Russell Wong Changes Image of Asian Americans in *Vanishing Son*." *Chicago Tribune*. Tribune, 8 Feb. 1995. Web. 2 Apr. 2012. Addresses Wong's television series as an opportunity for Asian action heroes.

Wong, Russell. "My Favorite Weekend." Interview by Lisa Boone. *Los Angeles Times* 29 May 2003: E67. Print. Provides information on Wong's career and hobbies.

SHAWN WONG

Writer

Wong is one of the most prominent figures in Asian American literature. The 1974 anthology he coedited, Aiiieeeee!, *is considered a seminal work of Asian American criticism, identifying and naming the canonical works of Asian American literature. Wong has published two novels,* Homebase *and* American Knees. *He is one of the most prolific Asian American critics, writers, and editors.*

Born: August 11, 1949; Oakland, California
Full name: Shawn Hsu Wong
Birth name: Chung-Hsing Ellsworth Hsu
Area of achievement: Literature

EARLY LIFE

Shawn Hsu Wong was born Chung-Hsing Ellsworth Hsu in Oakland, California, to Peter Shih-Yi Hsu, a civil engineering graduate student at the University of California, Berkeley, and Maria H. C. Hsu, a student at UC Berkeley and the California College of Arts and Crafts in Oakland. Maria was an artist and draftsperson. Wong's parents were from Tianjin, China, making Wong a second-generation Chinese American. Although raised in Berkeley, Wong lived in Guam, Taiwan, and Los Angeles as a child before returning to Berkeley. In 1957, Wong's father died at the age of forty. His mother remarried in 1960 to Henry W. Wong. Henry adopted Shawn, and Shawn took his stepfather's surname. His mother died in 1965, at the age of thirty-nine.

Wong attended San Francisco State College (now University) from 1967 to 1969 and then transferred to Berkeley in 1969. Wong received his BA in English in 1971. Later that year, he began the creative writing master's program at San Francisco State University. He received an MA in creative writing in 1974. While in school, Wong noticed a distinct lack of Asian and Asian American literature in the curriculum. He decided to create his own anthology with the help of writers Jeffrey Paul Chan, Frank Chin, and Lawson Inada.

LIFE'S WORK

In 1972, the four writers published "Aiiieeeee! An Introduction to Chinese American and Japanese American Literature," in the *Bulletin of Concerned Asian Scholars* (renamed *Critical Asian Studies* in 2001). This essay was expanded upon and republished as the landmark anthology *Aiiieeeee! An Anthology of Asian American Writers* (1974), edited by Wong, Chan, Chin, and Inada.

The anthology *Aiiieeeee!* has been hailed as the preeminent source defining Asian American literature. The title refers to the cry "aiiieeeee!" that Asian characters stereotypically whine in film and on television. *Aiiieeeee!* argues against a perceived homogeneous Asian American identity, introduces the existence of Asian American literature from as early as the nineteenth century, and reclaims and excerpts earlier, lesser-known works. Its preface was listed as one of the key documents of Asian American history in noted historian Franklin Odo's *The Columbia Documentary History of the Asian American Experience* (2002).

After graduating, Wong taught at various colleges and universities. In 1976, he moved to Seattle, Washington. In 1977, he married his first wife, Barbara Lui. They divorced in 1985.

Wong published his first novel, *Homebase*, in 1979. In this book, Rainsford Chan, a fourth-generation Chinese American orphan, searches for a "homebase."

Shawn Wong. (Erin Malone)

Aiiieeeee! An Anthology of Asian American Writers

Some of the earliest critical voices who attempted to define a new Asian American aesthetic were Frank Chin, Jeffrey Paul Chan, Lawson Fusao Inada, and Shawn Wong. They assembled one of the first literary anthologies featuring the work of Asian American writers, *Aiiieeeee! An Anthology of Asian American Writers* (1974, 1991). In this trailblazing anthology, the editors outline in an introductory manifesto the long history of racism against Asians in the United States. They discuss the erasure of "real" forms of Asian American history, literature, and culture by the publishing industry, the Hollywood film industry, and the educational and capitalist economic systems in the United States.

The editors discuss how difficult it was to convince the white, male-dominated publishing industry to consider seriously the literature of Asian American writers. Their literary anthology was likely perceived as too hostile, alien, and marginal to the interests of an American reading public. That is, it did not present the "Oriental" in ways that were comfortable for mainstream white readers. The editors remind writers and readers of the serious political implications in making choices about the style, language, and content by which one articulates oppositional forms of subjectivity. They stress the need to challenge why publishing institutions, cultural products, consumers, and critics choose one text or writer over another. *Aiiieeeee!* was repeatedly turned down by mainstream presses in the early 1970s, although it was eventually published in 1974 by the African American Howard University Press.

Through real and imaginary travels, Chan claims his history as a Chinese American. The novel won the Pacific Northwest Booksellers Award as well as the Fifteenth Annual Governor's Writers Day Award of Washington.

In 1984, Wong began teaching in the Department of American Ethnic Studies at the University of Washington in Seattle. In 1987, Wong married Vicki Tsuchida.

In 1991, Wong, Chan, Chin, and Inada published *The Big Aiiieeeee!*, a sequel to their first anthology. Four years later, Wong published his second novel, *American Knees*, an accessible, sexy, and humorous story about Asian American romantic relationships that explores intra–Asian American stereotypes. It shattered stereotypes of Chinese American men by being one of the first Asian American novels featuring a man comfortable with his sexuality, complete with explicit sexual dialogue. He wrote the novel for his second wife, who died two years later at the age of forty-eight.

He remarried once more in 2000, to Erin Malone. The couple had a son, Peter, in 2002.

In the meantime, *American Knees* was adapted as an independent feature film, *Americanese,* released in 2006. Produced by Lisa Onodera and directed by Eric Byler, it was acquired by IFC Entertainment and planned for a rerelease in 2009. As of 2011, the project was still shelved.

Wong has edited or coedited six literary anthologies, as well as a number of scholarly journals. Wong has also written short stories, poems, and plays. As of 2011, Wong remained a professor in the Department of English at the University of Washington. He was director of the creative writing program in the department from 1995 to 1997, and department chair from 1997 to 2002. Beginning in 1997, he taught at the University of Washington's Rome Center in Italy.

Wong has been honored on several occasions for his work in Asian American studies. He was awarded a Creative Writing Fellowship in Fiction from the National Endowment for the Arts in 1981 and the Rockefeller Foundation Bellagio Residency in Italy in 1994. Wong was also featured in two PBS documentaries: *Shattering the Silences* (1997) and Bill Moyers's *Becoming American: The Chinese Experience* (2004).

In 2011, he began writing his third novel, *The Ancient and Occupied Heart of Greg Li.*

SIGNIFICANCE

Wong is a leading figure in Asian American literature. He coedited *Aiiieeeee!*, the landmark Asian American literature anthology. A pioneer in rediscovering earlier Asian American literature, Wong has been instrumental in defining and shaping the course of Asian American literature. As a writer, he is best known for his novels, *Homebase* and *American Knees*, both about searching for genuine ethnic identity. Wong's prolific writing, both original and critical, reinforces his standing as a major presence within Asian American literature.

Christina Fa

FURTHER READING

Chan, Jeffery Paul, Frank Chin, Lawson Fusao Inada, and Shawn Wong, eds. *The Big Aiiieeeee! An Anthology of Chinese American and Japanese American Literature.* New York: Penguin, 1991. Print. The second of the editors' two anthologies on Asian American literature and writers.

de Marcken, Anne. "Part of One's Life: An Interview with Shawn Wong," *Writer's Chronicle* 40.3 (December 2007): 66–71. Print. Interview illuminat-ing Wong's story behind writing *American Knees*, and how he thinks *Americanese* compares to his novel.

Partridge, Jeffrey F. L., and Shawn Wong. "Aiiieeeee! And the Asian American Literature Movement: A Conversation with Shawn Wong," *MELUS* 29.3/4 (2004): 91–102. Print. Thorough interview by a scholar who wrote the *American Knees* introduction (reprint, 2005). Wong discusses the geneses of his published works.

TIMOTHY C. WONG

Hong Kong–born scholar

Timothy C. Wong is best known for his writing and translation of traditional Chinese fiction.

Born: January 24, 1941; Hong Kong
Full name: Timothy C. Wong
Birth name: Huang Tsung-t'ai
Areas of achievement: Literature, education

EARLY LIFE

Timothy C. Wong was born in Hong Kong in 1941. His family relocated to Hawaii, where Wong grew up. Following his 1963 graduation from Saint Mary's College of California in Moraga with a BA, Wong joined the Peace Corps. He was assigned to Thailand for two years, from 1963 to 1965. He used his time as a Peace Corps volunteer to travel extensively throughout Southeast Asia.

After the Peace Corps, Wong decided to return to Hawaii to further his studies. He enrolled in graduate school at the University of Hawaii and selected Asian Studies as his major. His education was funded by a grant from the East-West Center, an organization that promotes understanding between the United States, Asia, and the Pacific Islands. While working on his MA, Wong studied with the Inter-University Program for Chinese in Taipei from 1966 to 1967. He graduated from the University of Hawaii in 1968. He returned from 1972 until 1973 to the Inter-University Program to study Japanese in Tokyo at the time of his PhD studies. Wong completed his PhD in Chinese literature at Stanford University in 1975.

LIFE'S WORK

After earning his PhD, Wong was hired as a professor of Chinese at the Arizona State University campus in Tempe, Arizona. In addition to modern Mandarin, he taught Chinese fiction and literary translation. He taught there from 1974 to 1985. In his last year at Arizona State University, Wong took an assignment as the resident director of the China Cooperative Language and Study program. The program was for American students and was in association with the Council on International Exchange at Peking University.

During the next decade, between 1985 and 1995, Wong taught literature at Ohio State University in Columbus, Ohio. He returned to Arizona State University in 1995 as an assistant professor of Chinese. He also held two other appointments at Arizona State: director of the Center for Asian Studies from the summer of 1995 until 2002, and graduate director of the Department of Language and Literature, where he implemented a new program in Asian languages and civilizations for master's students.

Throughout Wong's tenures at Arizona State University and Ohio State University, he pursued his scholarly interest in the traditional Chinese fiction of the dynastic period and beyond, up to twentieth- and twenty-first-century Chinese fiction. Wong has published a great deal of material on the subject, including numerous articles and three books. The University of Hawaii published his widely read and critiqued compilation, *Stories for Saturday: Twentieth Century Chinese Popular Fiction* (2002). In this volume, Wong presents a collection of Chinese folk literature from the first half of the twentieth century. This work has led to much discussion in scholarly and literary circles about the rightful place of popular reading entertainment in Chinese literature.

Wong's 1978 book, *Wu Ching-tzu*, about the literary work *The Scholars* (c. 1750), has helped fiction from the

Ch'ing Dynasty find its way into broader literary and academic circles. Wu Ching-tzu was a Chinese writer from the mid-Ch'ing period, a dynasty that ruled China from 1644 to about 1912. Wong's work is an exploration of Wu Ching-tzu's satirical novel. *Wu Ching-tzu* is also a seminal work because it introduced the literary world to the first Chinese novel written in satirical form.

In addition to being a respected writer, Wong established himself early in his career as a translator of popular Chinese fiction, such as *Sherlock in Shanghai: Stories of Crime and Detection* (2006), a translation of stories by Cheng Xiaoqing. Wong is also a sought-after sinologist (Chinese studies scholar), public speaker, and presenter.

Wong has served in many leadership roles in the academic and scholarship arenas. He has performed in the capacities of panel member, committee member, lecturer, chairman, director, organizer, coordinator, president, board member, evaluator, and reader. The Chinese Language Teachers Association appointed Wong to the office of associate editor in 1988 and 1989. He also served on their board of directors from 1984 to 1986.

As of 2011, Wong was teaching Ming-Qing Chinese fiction in undergraduate and graduate courses for the School of International Letters and Cultures at Arizona State University.

SIGNIFICANCE

Wong's work introduced the world and new generations of scholars to the relevancy of an obscure, mostly forgotten canon of literary works. Furthermore, Wong's expertise as a sinologist and translator has made other relevant works available to experts and academics around the world.

Jocelyn A. Brown

FURTHER READING

Ching-tzu, Wu. *The Scholars*. Trans. Gladys Yang and Xianyi Yang. Beijing: Foreign Language, 2000. Print. An eighteenth-century satire about the excesses of the upper classes born of the corrupt feudal system.

Ma, Yau-Woon, and Joseph S. M. Lau, eds. *Traditional Chinese Stories: Themes and Variations*. New York: Columbia UP, 2008. Print. A compilation of sixty-one stories that represent the five styles in Chinese fiction, including tables with a chronological listing of each story and its history in Chinese literature.

Wong, Timothy C. *Stories for Saturday: Twentieth-Century Chinese Popular Fiction*. Honolulu: U of Hawaii P, 2003. Print. A compilation of translated popular Chinese stories from the first half of the twentieth century, depicting urban life as it existed at that time, also including an afterword about this type of Chinese literature.

TYRUS WONG

Chinese-born artist and animator

A pioneering artist and animator, Tyrus Wong was one of the first Chinese Americans to work at Walt Disney Studios. In 2001, he was named a Disney Legend for his atmospheric and innovative work on the animated classic Bambi *(1942).*

Born: October 25, 1910; Nan An, Taishan, Guangzhou, China
Full name: Tyrus Yoo Wong
Birth name: Wong Gaing Yoo
Also known as: Ty Wong; Look Tai Yow; Look Ti Yow
Areas of achievement: Art, animation, film

EARLY LIFE

Born in Nan An village in Guangzhou, China, in 1910, Tyrus Yoo Wong immigrated to the United States in 1920. Although Wong and his father arrived together on the SS *China*, Wong was detained alone at Angel Island Immigration Station. His father, who had already immigrated under the paper name Look Get, arranged for Wong to enter the United States as a "paper son" (a term for immigrants whose papers had been purchased) named Look Tai Yow (or Look Ti Yow). Wong's mother, who remained in China, died before he could see her again, though he was able to reunite with his older sister on a later trip to Hong Kong.

Wong and his father headed to Sacramento, California, where Wong started elementary school under the English name Tyrus. They later lived for a time in Los Angeles's Chinatown. In 1926, the two moved to Pasadena, where Wong attended Benjamin Franklin Junior High School. Impressed by his talent, his teacher encouraged him to apply for a scholarship to Otis Art Institute (now the Otis College of Art and Design). To his

Tyrus Wong. (Qi Heng/Xinhua/Landov)

surprise, he received a summer scholarship. Afterward, his father asked for help from the Chinese American community to pay for another term. Wong later received a scholarship from Otis, where he also did janitorial work, and he graduated in 1932 with many top awards.

During the Great Depression, Wong was hired by the Works Progress Administration's Federal Arts Project to create two artworks per month, which were loaned to government buildings around the country. He was also active in Los Angeles's Chinatown, and he and fellow Otis alumnus Benji Okubo, along with Marian Blanchard, were commissioned by Eddy See to paint the walls of his Dragon's Den restaurant. With See's encouragement, Wong recruited his future wife, Ruth Kim, to work as a waitress at Dragon's Den. The couple would later marry and have three daughters: Kay, Tai-Ling, and Kim.

LIFE'S WORK

In 1938, Wong was hired by Walt Disney Studios to work on projects such as Mickey Mouse short films, filling in characters' movements as a kind of "in-between" artist. The monotony of the job frustrated Wong, so he created and submitted background art for the animated classic *Bambi* (1942). His atmospheric forest scenes,

influenced by Sung dynasty paintings, got him hired on the film as an inspirational sketch artist, a job he held from 1938 to 1941.

After a union strike, Wong left Disney and became a preproduction illustrator at Warner Bros. His Warner Bros. credits include *Rebel Without a Cause* (1955), *Calamity Jane* (1953), and *The Wild Bunch* (1969). He was a technical adviser for *Around the World in 80 Days* (1956) and a preproduction illustrator for *Sands of Iwo Jima* (1949). Wong himself appeared in the short instructional film *Oriental Brushwork* (1954), directed by Eliot O'Hara. He also drew storyboards, set sketches, and preproduction illustrations for Republic, Columbia, and RKO Studios.

In 1944, in addition to his film work, Wong began to work part time for the Pasadena-based Winfield Pottery, which sold his hand-painted porcelain designs at Neiman Marcus, Bullocks Wilshire, and Marshall Field department stores. From the 1950s through the 1970s, he illustrated greeting cards for companies such as Hallmark, California Artists, and Duncan McIntosh.

After Wong retired in 1968, he focused his creativity on his beloved hobby of kite making. In 2001, he received the Disney Legends award for his work on *Bambi*. During the same year, his artwork appeared in the group exhibition *Inspiring Lines: Chinese American Pioneers in the Commercial Arts* at the Chinese American Museum's LMAN Studio. Wong was also honored with the Historymakers Award from the Chinese American Museum, which hosted his solo exhibition *Tyrus Wong: A Retrospective* in 2004. In 2007, Wong's art was displayed by the Academy of Motion Picture Arts and Sciences in an exhibition called *The Art of the Motion Picture Illustrator: William B. Major, Harold Michelson and Tyrus Wong*. He is featured in the documentary *Brushstrokes in Hollywood: A Portrait of Tyrus Wong*, directed by Pamela Tom. When Wong reached one hundred years old, he was still flying kites in Santa Monica, California.

SIGNIFICANCE

A celebrated artist in a variety of media, Tyrus Wong helped to pave the way for Chinese Americans in fine arts and animation. He was the second Chinese American to be hired by Walt Disney Studios and was later honored as a Disney Legend for his work on *Bambi*. His signature blend of Chinese and Western artistic styles can be seen in thousands of works, from murals to film storyboards. His art has been exhibited at the Los Angeles Museum of Art, the Art Institute of Chicago, the

Craft and Folk Art Museum, the Chinese American Museum, the Santa Barbara Museum of Art, and more.

Jenny Cho

FURTHER READING

Canemaker, John. *Before the Animation Begins: The Art and Lives of Disney Inspirational Sketch Artists*. New York: Hyperion, 1996. Print. Profiles sketch artists such as Wong who conceptualize the style of a film in preproduction.

Poon, Irene, et al. *Wah Ming Chang and Tyrus Wong: Two Behind the Scenes*. San Francisco: Chinese Hist. Society of Amer., 2003. Print. A profile of artists Wong and Chang.

See, Lisa. *On Gold Mountain*. New York: Vintage, 1996. Print. Memoir about the See family; includes a chapter about Wong.

Wong, Tyrus. "Oral History Interview with Tyrus Wong, 1965 Jan. 30." By Betty Hoag. *Archives of American Art*. Archives of Amer. Art, n.d. Web. 20 Mar. 2012. An interview about Wong's life and art.

Wong, Tyrus, and Bill Stern. *Mid-century Mandarin: The Clay Canvases of Tyrus Wong*. Los Angeles: Museum of California Design, 2004. Print. Catalogue of the exhibition organized by the Museum of California Design and displayed at the Craft and Folk Art Museum.

VICTOR WONG

Actor, entertainer, journalist

From the 1970s to the 1990s, Victor Wong was one of the most visible and versatile Asian American actors in television, theater, and movies, known particularly for his roles in John Carpenter's Big Trouble in Little China *(1986) and Bernardo Bertolucci's* The Last Emperor *(1987). Wong was a role model and frequent actor for director Wayne Wang. He was also a noted painter, comedian, and journalist.*

Born: July 31, 1927; San Francisco, California
Died: September 12, 2001; Locke, California
Full name: Victor Keung Wong
Birth name: Yee-Keung Victor Wong
Also known as: Victor K. Wong
Areas of achievement: Acting, entertainment, journalism

EARLY LIFE

Victor Wong was born in San Francisco, California, in July 1927 to parents who had emigrated from China. He had a brother named Zeppelin and several sisters. Wong's father, Sare King Wong, was a respected intellectual in the Chinese American community, and was later considered the unofficial "mayor" of Chinatown. The family moved to the small town of Locke, California, when Victor was a small child, but returned to San Francisco a few years later. As a youth, Wong came down with tuberculosis; the subsequent years spent in a sanitarium made him more introverted. He attended the University of California Berkeley, where he majored in political science and journalism, the University of Chicago, where he studied theology, and the San Francisco Art Institute, where he studied painting under Mark Rothko. While in Chicago, he was also an early member of the Second City comedy troupe.

LIFE'S WORK

Victor Wong was a participant in San Francisco's thriving Beat movement, befriending such figures as writer Jack Kerouac, who later wrote about Wong in the character of Arthur Ma in the novel *Big Sur* (1962). Wong was also a member of author Ken Kesey's so-called Merry Pranksters, a loose confederation that included writer Neal Cassady and the rock group the Grateful Dead, among others. The group lived communally up and down the West Coast and was closely associated with the drug culture of the 1960s. Wong spent some time as an abstract painter, befriending the poet and painter Lawrence Ferlinghetti.

Among the first Chinese Americans to enter into broadcast journalism, Wong worked on the daily program *Newsroom* on his hometown public television station KQED from 1968 to 1974, specializing in photojournalism essays. After an attack of Bell's palsy that caused one of his eyelids to permanently droop, Wong left television and began acting, first in local theater.

Wong later appeared on the New York stage and had a recurring role in the daytime drama *Search for Tomorrow*. By that time he had become a well-known character actor and, already in his late fifties, he made his television movie debut in 1983's *Nightsongs*. He played his first memorable film role in 1985 in Wayne Wang's *Dim Sum: A Little Bit of Heart*; he was to appear in four films for Wang. Many other roles followed in such motion pictures as *Eat a Bowl of Tea* (1989), *The Joy Luck Club* (1993), *The Golden Child* (1986), *The Last Emperor* (1987), *Shanghai Surprise* (1986), and *Seven Years in Tibet* (1997). Wong also appeared prominently in *3 Ninjas* (1992) and its three sequels. He also worked in many well-known made-for-television movies. He was quoted as saying, "If I can't act, I go crazy. I need it every day."

In 1998, Wong retired from acting after suffering two strokes. He struggled with many health issues from that time on. Nonetheless, he continued to be active with his artwork, producing many of his pieces digitally. He died of a heart attack at the age of seventy-four, on the day after the terrorist attacks of September 11, 2001. It was believed that Wong suffered great anxiety for the safety of his two sons, who were living in New York City at the time. Wong was married four times; he had two daughters and three sons, one of whom was killed in a street attack in 1986, the tragedy that triggered his first stroke.

SIGNIFICANCE

In the 1960s, Victor Wong was one of the few Asian Americans working in television to appear on camera. He was honored for his journalistic work by the Chinese

Historical Society of America in 1999. While he was often typecast in movies and television programs with Asian themes, Wong proved to be a well-respected performer, and one of the most sought-after Asian American actors of his time. He projected a reassuring, grandfatherly persona to which moviegoers seemed to respond. Prominent playwright David Henry Hwang described Wong's acting as "electric." Wong was showcased in the award-winning 1997 documentary *My America . . . or Honk If You Love Buddha*, which considered the Asian American experience.

Roy Liebman

FURTHER READING

Chang, Lia. "Remembering Our Merry Prankster." *Asian Week*. Asian Week, 5–11 Oct. 2001. Web. 21 Mar. 2012. Offers an extensive article and obituary on the life and work of Victor Wong.

Kerouac, Jack. *Big Sur*. 1962. New York: Penguin, 1992. Print. Kerouac's novel includes the character of Arthur Ma, a fictionalized version of Wong, who was a friend of the author.

Pulley, Michael. "The Last Days of Victor Wong." *Sacramento News and Review*. Chico Community Publishing, 19 Sept. 2001. Web. 21 Mar. 2012. An informative obituary about Wong, chronicling the different phases of his career.

TIGER WOODS

Athlete

Tiger Woods was once one of the world's most celebrated professional athletes. His success on the golf course as well as his endorsement deals earned him a fortune. He was widely considered to be the greatest golfer in history. However, Woods's reputation was tarnished in late 2009 by revelations of his extramarital affairs.

Born: December 30, 1975; Cypress, California
Full name: Tiger Woods
Birth name: Eldrick Tont Woods
Areas of achievement: Sports, philanthropy

EARLY LIFE

Tiger Woods was born Eldrick Tont Woods on December 30, 1975, in Cypress, California, to Earl and Kultida Woods. Earl nicknamed his son "Tiger" after a South

Vietnamese military officer who had saved his life during his military service in the Vietnam War. Tiger would be closely identified with his parents throughout his celebrity career. Earl Woods had been previously married to Barbara Hart, with whom he had three children before their divorce in 1968. The following year, he married Kultida Punsawad, a native of Thailand whom Earl had met overseas. The couple settled in the small town of Cypress, California. Earl Woods was African American with Caucasian and American Indian ancestry. Kultida Woods was a Buddhist, and had a diverse Asian heritage. Attending Cypress public schools, the young Woods was sometimes taunted for his mixed racial background.

Although Earl Woods was unfaithful to his wife Kultida over the length of their marriage, he was fanatically devoted to his son, who was a golf prodigy.

Tiger Woods. (Getty Images)

The senior Woods taught his son how to swing a golf club when he was a year old. At the age of two, Woods appeared on *The Mike Douglas Show* to demonstrate his putting ability. At age five, he was featured in *Golf Digest* and on the television show *That's Incredible.* Woods's mother was an equally formidable, if unheralded influence on him, imparting to him her self-assured demeanor, competitive drive, and Buddhist faith.

At age seven, Woods began entering golf tournaments. By the time he turned eleven, he could defeat his father in golf. Woods was undefeated in thirty Southern California golf tournaments. Earl entered Woods in the Junior World Golf Championships; he won six times. In 1991, at the age of fifteen, Woods was named Golf Digest Junior Amateur Player of the Year. That same year, he became the youngest golfer ever to win the US Junior Amateur Championship. Woods won the same championship in 1992 and 1993. He became the first golfer to win the US Amateur Championship in three consecutive years, from 1994 to 1996. In 1994, Woods graduated from Western High School in Anaheim, California.

LIFE'S WORK

Woods enrolled at Stanford University in 1994, but left in 1996 to concentrate on his professional golf career. After turning professional, he signed a multi-million-dollar endorsement deal with Nike.

In 1997, he won the prestigious Master's Tournament with a score of 270, far ahead of the other competitors. From 2000 to 2009 Woods was the most dominant player in golf. Although he was hampered by an injured left knee, Woods worked relentlessly on both the technical and the competitive aspects of his game. He worked with coaches Buster Harmon and Hank Haney in seeking to improve what was already a graceful and nearly perfect golf swing. Woods was able to drive the ball over three hundred yards with ease, had an accurate short game, and demonstrated strong putting skills. In 2000, he won the US Open for the first time, a feat that he repeated in 2002 and 2008.

Through 2009, Woods won fourteen major professional championships, second only to golfing legend Jack Nicklaus. He ranked third in Professional Golf Association (PGA) tour victories with seventy-one, and had earned the most PGA prize money: $111 million. Woods won three grand slams, meaning he consecutively won the Masters Tournament, the US Open, the British Open, and the PGA Championship three times. Woods was named PGA Player of the Year a record ten times, and ranked as the world's number-one golfer for the longest period of time in the sport's history.

Woods quickly achieved iconic status as a professional athlete. Nike, his chief sponsor, paid him hundreds of millions of dollars to endorse its products. Woods was credited in part for the increase of Nike's revenue throughout the 2000s. Nike made use of Woods's charisma in a series of memorable television commercials, which featured Woods with children of all races and ethnicities who repeated "I am Tiger Woods." The advertisement emphasized Woods's own racial diversity and broad appeal. In another commercial, Woods inventively bounces a golf ball on his sand wedge forty-nine times to snappy background music before casually hitting the ball in mid air some two hundred yards.

Woods took great pains to maintain his public image. He consistently avoided any kind of political commentary, and refused to become a spokesman for any movement. He also rejected any attempt to categorize him racially, declaring himself to be "Cablinasian," a word he invented symbolizing his ensemble of racial heritages. He likewise refused to inject himself into any kind of racial advocacy or controversy.

On October 5, 2004, Woods married Swedish fashion model Elin Nordegren. The couple moved into a luxurious home in a gated community in Windermere, Florida. The couple's daughter Sam was born on June 18, 2007. Their son Charlie was born on February 8, 2009. Woods's reputation as a doting father and devoted husband enhanced his public image, and his popularity was compared to that of baseball legend Babe Ruth and basketball legend Michael Jordan.

Before Woods, golf had never achieved such a wide following as a spectator sport, but Woods's mastery of the sport, combined with the power of his celebrity, increased golf's popularity worldwide. He earned endorsement contracts from numerous companies, including Electronic Arts, American Express, Gillette, Gatorade, Accenture, General Mills, General Motors, Titleist, Tag Heuer, and Buick. In 2009 *Forbes* magazine reported that Woods was the first athlete in history to have earned a billion dollars. In addition to owning a 155-foot yacht named *Privacy,* it was reported that Woods owned multimillion-dollar homes in California, Wyoming, Sweden, and Dubai.

In addition to his success as a golfer, Tiger Woods has become known for his philanthropy. Established in 1996, the Tiger Woods Foundation focuses on promoting the sport of golf to inner-city children. The foundation also oversees the Tiger Woods Learning Center, which helps low-income children get into college. In addition to his athletic achievements, Woods's clean public image and charitable work made him a role model for children.

On December 5, 2007, Woods was inducted into the California Hall of Fame. Although he eschews politics, Woods spoke at Barack Obama's presidential inauguration at the Lincoln Memorial in 2009.

On November 27, 2010, Woods crashed his car into a tree near his Orlando home at 2:30 in the morning. Rumors began to circulate in the media that he was fleeing a domestic dispute. The police arrived and issued Woods a citation. Over the next several days numerous women, including fashion models and actresses, began making claims of having had extramarital relationships with Woods. In addition, his twenty-one-year-old Orlando neighbor also claimed she and Woods had a relationship. Over the next months, Woods was unmasked in the media as a serial adulterer. Although

Tiger Woods's "Cablinasian" Identity

Woods is from a mixed-race background; his father was African American and his mother hailed from Thailand. When Woods entered the public arena as an eighteen-year-old golfer, he issued a press release stating that he was equally proud of his African American and his Asian heritage. He asked reporters to focus on him as a golfer and person and not as a representative of any race. When Woods appeared on *The Oprah Winfrey Show* on April 24, 1997, he announced that he was "Cablinasian," a word he invented to represent his heritage as one-eighth Caucasian, one-fourth African American, one-eighth American Indian, and one-half Asian (Thai and Chinese). He asked that he not be seen in racial categories. "I'm just who I am," Woods told Winfrey, "whoever you see in front of you." His comments sparked an immediate reaction. For example, Columbia University professor Manning Marable accused Woods of "minimizing" his African American identity. One week later, Winfrey ran a follow-up show devoted to the "Tiger Woods Race Controversy."

Although Woods rarely used the term "Cablinasian" in subsequent years, he never veered from his insistence that he belonged to no single racial group. Woods has been admired for rejecting rigid and divisive racial categorization. By most accounts, he was a successful pioneer in symbolizing a post-racial United States.

he had succeeded over the course of his career in scrupulously preserving his image and privacy, the scandal surrounding his numerous affairs resulted in the details of his personal life being exposed and examined by the media.

On December 11, 2009, Woods admitted to the affairs and announced that he was taking a leave of absence from golf. Many of his commercial sponsors, excluding Nike, canceled his contracts. In January 2010, he entered a clinic to receive therapy and treatment for his personal problems. Woods also spoke of returning to his practice of Buddhism. In February 2010, Woods admitted that he had let the temptations of fame and fortune get the best of him, saying "I was wrong. I was foolish." On August 23, 2010 he and Nordegren divorced. They were awarded joint custody of their children.

When Woods returned to golf on April 8, 2010, at the Masters Tournament, his skills were seemingly diminished. By May 2011, he had fallen out of the top ten in world golf rankings for the first time in fourteen years. His last championship victory was at the 2009 WGC-Bridgestone Invitational.

SIGNIFICANCE

Woods is one of the most important figures in the history of American athletics and one of the few who transcended his sport. It is widely agreed that he is one of the greatest golfers in history, as evidenced by his numerous tournament victories. His only rival in career victories is Jack Nicklaus, who obtained them over a much longer career. Before Woods arrived, golf was perceived by many as an exclusive sport, reserved for elites. When Woods won the Masters Tournament in 1997, he was the first person of African and Asian ancestry to do so. Woods not only broke golf's color barrier, he became one of the most popular and idealized athletes in the world. His ensuing endorsements made him the richest athlete in the world, and the first to reach a billion dollars in career earnings. As a public figure, Woods has treated his own racial identity with sensitivity. He has rejected racial categorization, and he refused to accept the label of African American, in part because he felt that it would diminish the importance of his Asian heritage. For all of his accomplishments, his legacy will no doubt be tarnished by the scandal surrounding his infidelity in 2009. In the years that have followed, Woods has not been the same on the golf course, and his image is no longer featured as prominently in the mainstream media.

Howard Bromberg

FURTHER READING

Callahan, Tom. *His Father's Son: Earl and Tiger Woods.* New York: Gotham, 2010. Print. Quoting extensively from interviews with Earl Woods, Tiger Woods, and others, recounts Earl's influence on Tiger. Lists Woods's career golf victories and PGA total winnings.

Helling, Steve. *Tiger: The Real Story.* Cambridge: Da Capo, 2010. Print. Straightforward account by *People* magazine writer that attempts to sort out the conflicts between Woods's private and public images.

Jones, Lisa. "Are We Tiger Woods Yet?" *Step into a World: A Global Anthology of the New Black Literature.* Ed. Kevin Powell. New York: Wiley, 2000. Print. Argues that America's embrace of Tiger Woods's multicultural identity is more the product of corporate indoctrination and commercialization than progress in racial relations.

Lusetich, Robert. *Unplayable: An Inside Account of Tiger's Most Tumultuous Season.* New York: Atria, 2010. Print. Follows Woods's career from its inception. Reports on his tournament play and travails in 2009.

Perez, Hiram. "How to Rehabilitate a Mulatto: The Iconography of Tiger Woods." *Asian American Studies Now: A Critical Reader.* Ed. Jean Yu-Wen Shen Wu and Thomas Chen. Piscataway: Rutgers UP, 2009. Print. Academic essay that portrays Woods as a celebrity icon of multiracialism and post-modernist racial identity.

Woods, Tiger. *How I Play Golf.* New York: Warner Bros., 2001. Print. Woods's manual on golf, the best-selling golf instructional manual in publishing history.

CHIEN-SHIUNG WU

Chinese-born scientist

Chien-Shiung Wu is best known for conducting the 1956 experiment that proved that "weak" interactions among decaying particles are not always symmetrical. The results disproved the principle of conservation of parity, the basic law of physics that postulated complete symmetry between left and right. Wu was also involved in experiments with uranium and the development of more sensitive radiation detectors for the Manhattan Project.

Born: May 31, 1912; Liuhe, Jiangsu, China
Died: February 16, 1997; New York City, New York

Full name: Chien-Shiung Wu (CHEE-en SHEE-ung WOO)
Also known as: C. S. Wu
Areas of achievement: Science and technology

EARLY LIFE

Chien-Shiung Wu was born near Shanghai, China, to Fuhua Fan and Zhongyi Wu, a former engineer and a principal at an elementary school for girls. Wu's father founded the school in order to educate women, and he advised his daughter to ignore obstacles and keep moving forward. To promote the education and freedom of women, her mother encouraged parents to send their daughters to school, and she also spoke out against the practice of binding the feet of young girls.

Growing up in a family environment that was conducive to learning, Wu was constantly exposed to books about science and mathematics. With the support and encouragement of her father, she developed self-confidence and curiosity. In 1922, after attending her father's school, Wu transferred to a boarding school, the Soochow School for Girls, and enrolled in its normal school program. Because Wu was very interested in mathematics, physics, and chemistry, she studied these subjects by herself from borrowed books. Graduating with high honors in 1930, Wu entered the National Central University in Nanjing. After obtaining a bachelor of science degree in physics in 1934, she taught and did research in X-ray crystallography with Shanghai's National Academy of Sciences. An uncle's financial assistance allowed Wu to travel to the United States in 1936, where, instead of attending the University of Michigan as planned, Wu entered the University of California Berkeley. She received graduate and research training under the guidance of prominent physicists Ernest Lawrence, Emilio Segre, and J. Robert Oppenheimer, and eventually became an expert in nuclear fission.

After obtaining a PhD in physics from UC Berkeley in 1940, Wu married fellow student and physicist Luke Yuan in 1942. They would have one child, Vincent, who is also a physicist. Wu went on to teach at Smith College in Northampton, Massachusetts, and briefly at Princeton University, before joining the Manhattan Project at Columbia University in 1944. Wu worked with a team of Columbia scientists in using diffusion techniques to separate common uranium from its fissionable isotopes.

After World War II, Wu was retained by Columbia as a research scientist. In 1954, she became a US citizen.

LIFE'S WORK

Wu devoted four decades to research and teaching. Her work on beta decay—later discussed in her book *Beta Decay* (1966), a respected publication among physicists—helped to support Enrico Fermi's theory of weak interactions.

In 1956, Wu began an experiment that would come to be known as the "Wu experiment," seeking to prove a theory developed by Tsung-Dao Lee, a colleague at Columbia, and Chen-Ning Yang, a physicist at the State University of New York in Stony Brook. The fundamental laws of physics had shown complete symmetry between left and right. Approached by Lee and Yang to

Chien-Shiung Wu. (Science Source)

test a new theory, Wu and her collaborators designed and executed an experiment to show that the weak interactions among decaying particles were not always symmetrical with respect to left and right. The evidence of their research undermined the principle of conservation of parity, earning Lee and Yang the Nobel Prize in physics in 1957. Although Wu did not share the Nobel Prize with Lee and Yang, she was recognized as a top experimental physicist. As a result, her ideas and work were highly regarded by Nobel laureates and leaders in physics.

Wu was promoted to full professor at Columbia University in 1958, and was appointed Michael I. Pupin Professor of Physics in 1973. After conducting extensive research on beta decay, Wu moved on to study sickle-cell anemia. Throughout her forty-year career at Columbia, she trained numerous graduate students and postdoctoral fellows. She retired from teaching in 1981, as Pupin Professor Emerita of Physics. She then traveled as an advisor and lecturer in China and Taiwan. In 1995, a group that included four Nobel laureates established the Wu Chien-Shiung Foundation in Taiwan. One of the foundation's objectives is to cultivate outstanding talent in the sciences.

The Manhattan Project

In September 1942, the Manhattan Project acquired 59,000 acres of land along the Clinch River in eastern Tennessee with the goal of creating an atomic bomb. The greatest challenge facing the project was the accumulation of sufficient quantities of fissionable material. Physicists had identified a likely candidate in uranium-235 (U-235). Natural uranium is only seven-tenths of 1 percent U-235. The remainder is overwhelmingly uranium-238 (U-238), which could not be made to fission with any process available during the 1940s. U-235 cannot be chemically separated from U-238; it must be physically separated using processes that rely on the 1.2 percent difference in mass between the two isotopes.

The Manhattan Project settled on two methods to separate U-235 from U-238. In electromagnetic separation, the uranium was rendered into a gas (uranium hexafluoride); the gas ionized and was then electrically propelled through a magnetic field. The lighter U-235 followed a more sharply curved path than the U-238, and the isotopes ended their journeys at two different places. In gaseous diffusion, the uranium hexafluoride was pumped through a series of porous barriers with millions of submicroscopic openings per square inch. The gas molecules containing U-235 trickled through the barriers at a slightly higher rate than those with U-238. After the gas passed through several thousand such barriers, the concentration of U-235 was significantly enhanced. In three years, the Y-12 electromagnetic separation team and K-25 gaseous diffusion team together separated enough U-235 for a single atomic bomb.

Wu identified three ingredients vital to her scientific achievements: a supportive husband, a home close to work, and good child care. These arrangements allowed her to work long hours in the laboratory. She observed that the only obstacle that blocks women from making progress in the field of science is "unimpeachable tradition."

SIGNIFICANCE

Chien-Shiung Wu was a pioneer in physics and the only Chinese American woman to play an active role in the Manhattan Project. The results of her famous 1956 experiment held vast ramifications for physicists everywhere, and her subsequent work on beta decay continues to be a standard reference. The significance of her contributions has been recognized by numerous awards and honors, including the National Medal of Science (1975) and the Wolf Prize in Physics (1978), as well as honorary doctoral degrees from colleges and universities such as Princeton, Harvard, and Dickinson. Wu was the first woman to be the president of the American Physical Society (1975). Wu inspired young scientists to pursue scientific careers. Her life experience underscores the significance of growing up in an intellectually stimulating home environment and a willingness to take risks. She managed to make important contributions in a male-dominated, prestigious field.

Joyce Tang

FURTHER READING

Byers, Nina, and Gary Williams, eds. *Out of the Shadows: Contributions of Twentieth-Century Women to Physics*. New York: Cambridge UP, 2006. Print. An introductory examination of Wu's career and significant accomplishments, highlighting many aspects of her biography.

McGrayne, Sharon Bertsch. *Nobel Prize Women in Science: Their Lives, Struggles, and Momentous Discoveries*. 2nd ed. Secaucus: Carol, 1998. Print. Author considers the gender disparities among Nobel laureates, citing Wu as an example of a woman who succeeded in her field.

Reynolds, Moira Davison. *American Women Scientists: 23 Inspiring Biographies, 1900–2000*. Jefferson: McFarland, 1999. Print. Includes an extensive and well-detailed biographical sketch of Wu, describing her education and professional research; also provides background on her family.

JASON WU

Taiwanese-born designer

Jason Wu's designs are sold in select retail stores, including Neiman-Marcus and Bergdorf Goodman. He has an influential fan in Anna Wintour, the editor of Vogue *magazine. His work gained worldwide recognition when First Lady Michelle Obama chose to wear his design to President Barack Obama's inaugural ball in January 2009.*

Born: September 27, 1982; Taipei, Taiwan
Full name: Jason Wu
Area of achievement: Fashion

EARLY LIFE

Jason Wu was born in Taipei, Taiwan, in 1982. His family was in the import-export business, and he credits them for always supporting him in his pursuit of a career in design. Wu's parents recognized his talent early in his life; when he was five years old, his mother would drive him to bridal stores so he could copy the gowns in the window displays.

Believing he would get a better education outside of Taiwan, Wu's parents moved him to Vancouver, British Columbia, when he was nine years old. It was in Canada that Wu became interested in fashion, learning to sew and create patterns while using dolls as mannequins. He carried on his hobby of designing clothes for dolls as a student at the Eaglebrook School, a middle school for boys in Deerfield, Massachusetts, and at Loomis Chaffee, one of the country's leading boarding schools in Windsor, Vermont.

Wu spent several summers studying sculpture in Tokyo, Japan. He also participated in a year-long exchange program at a school in Rennes, France, during which time he traveled to Paris whenever he could. He returned to New York to attend the New School at Parsons School of Design, where he studied for three and a half years.

LIFE'S WORK

While Wu was at Parsons, he won a fashion doll design competition. He went on to develop his own line of dolls, the Fashion Royalty collection, produced by Integrity Toys. The dolls are available exclusively at FAO Schwarz, the famous toy store in New York City, where some sell for several hundred dollars.

Following an internship with Narciso Rodriguez, a Cuban American designer who had also studied at the Parsons School of Design, Wu launched his own label in 2006 with backing from his parents and money he had earned from his doll designs. It did not take long for some members of the fashion world to view Wu as the heir apparent to designers Oscar de la Renta and Carolina Herrera, as his cocktail- and ballroom-gown designs recalled the styles so favored by those fashion houses.

Wu was becoming increasingly well known when his designs appeared in the January 2007 issue of *Vogue* magazine. Its iconic editor, Anna Wintour, became a proponent of his designs and was seen in the front row of Wu's presentation during New York Fashion Week. She nominated him for the Fashion Group International's Rising Star Award in 2008, which he won. Wu's clothes have been described as very feminine, seeming to belong to an earlier time, when women wore conservative jackets, floral prints, and dresses with hourglass shapes.

At the age of twenty-six, Wu drew widespread attention when Michelle Obama wore one of his designs

Jason Wu. (Getty Images)

on national television during an interview with Barbara Walters. Wu spent a lot of time visiting stores across the country to develop ideas for specific clients and climates; one such store was Ikram in Chicago, Illinois, and he credits the owner, Ikram Goldman, with bringing his designs to the attention of Mrs. Obama.

SIGNIFICANCE

Wu came to national prominence when First Lady Michelle Obama chose his design for her inaugural gown when President Barack Obama was sworn into office in 2009. Wu has said that he was shocked when he tuned in to watch the inaugural festivities and saw her in his dress. The dress was subsequently given to the Smithsonian Institution's National Museum of American History, to be stored with other gowns worn by first ladies.

By 2010, Wu's business had gone international. He plans to sell his fashion line to one or two high-end retailers in certain cities because he believes that luxury is based not on price but on availability. He has also developed the Jason Wu for Target clothing line for the Target retail chain.

Jo Ann Collins

FURTHER READING

Alexander, Hilary. "Michelle Obama's Dress Designer: Jason Wu in Profile." *Telegraph*. Telegraph, 22 Jan. 2009. Web. 1 Apr. 2012. Describes Obama's inaugural gown and how it shone a spotlight on the designs of Jason Wu.

Finn, Robin. "Jason Wu: Project Fun Day." *New York Times* 18 June 2009: MB2. Print. Describes how Wu spent a day off in New York City.

Jackson, Jill. "A New Age of Fashion." *Doll Reader* 35.8 (2007): 52–56. Print. A discussion of Jason Wu's life and career, focusing on the designs for his doll collection.

Pasquarelli, Adrianne. "40 under Forty: Jason Wu, 26." *Crain's New York Business*. Crain, 2009. Web. 1 Apr. 2012. Part of a series profiling forty entrepreneurs under the age of forty. Includes biographical information and discusses Wu's plans for the future.

MITSUYE YASUTAKE YAMADA

Japanese-born poet, educator, and writer

Best known for her autobiographical poetry about living in internment during World War II, writer and educator Mitsuye Yamada explores the individual lives, multicultural identities, and unique social pressures of Japanese American women in the uneasy aftermath of wartime. For the past several decades, she has played an active and significant part in the Asian American community in Southern California.

Born: July 5, 1923; Fukuoka, Kyushu, Japan
Full name: Mitsuye Yasutake Yamada (meet-SOO-yeh YAH-su-TA-keh yah-MAH-dah)
Birth name: Mitsuye May Yasutake
Areas of achievement: Literature, education

EARLY LIFE

Mitsuye Yasutake was born to first-generation Japanese American parents during a 1923 family visit to Japan. Her father, Stanford-educated Jack Kaichiro Yasutake, was an interpreter for the United States Immigration Service. Under the pen name Jakki he wrote informal Japanese verse known as *senryu*. Her mother, Hide Shiraki Yasutake, was an observant and sharp-minded housewife. By virtue of her birth abroad, Mitsuye ("May" to her family) was the sole Yasutake child with Japanese citizenship; she was also the only daughter among her four siblings. Returning to America in 1926, Yasutake was raised in Seattle, Washington.

Hours after the bombing of Pearl Harbor on December 7, 1941, the Federal Bureau of Investigation accused Jack Yasutake of spying and incarcerated him as a prisoner of war. In 1942, Yasutake, her brothers, and her mother were sent to Minidoka War Relocation Center on a windswept desert near Twin Falls, Idaho, along with thousands of Japanese Americans from the Pacific Northwest. The internment camp experience, along with the questions it raised about loyalty, identity, intolerance, and Asian family legacy, became pivotal to Yasutake's writing, teaching, and political activities later on in life.

In 1944, after signing the requisite oath renouncing allegiance to the emperor of Japan, Yasutake and her oldest brother were allowed to leave Minidoka to attend the University of Cincinnati. Later, she transferred to New York University, graduating in 1947. In 1953, she earned a master's degree from the University of Chicago, which began her academic career with various American colleges and universities. She married research chemist Yoshikazu Yamada in 1950. The couple had four children. Mitsuye Yamada became a naturalized US citizen in the 1950s.

LIFE'S WORK

After moving to California in the 1960s, Yamada taught literature and creative writing at California State University, Fullerton, and Cypress Community College, specializing in multicultural perspectives. Yamada's literary reputation rests largely on two collections of poetry. Her definitive work, *Camp Notes and Other Poems* (1976), contains excerpts from a journal Yamada kept during World War II and later edited for publication. It chronicles Yamada's life from the 1942 Seattle evacuation of Japanese Americans, through the tedium and indignities of forced internment, to release into an unwelcoming Midwestern city.

Mitsuye Yamada's
Camp Notes and Other Poems

Yamada was one of the first writers to publish a personal account of the US government's internment of citizens of Japanese descent. Originally published by Shameless Hussy, a feminist press, Mitsuye Yamada's *Camp Notes and Other Poems* (1976) is an extremely powerful and personal volume. The actual "Camp Notes" poems are the center of the volume and are bracketed by an opening section on the author's parents and a closing series of poems looking to the present and future.

The section titled "Camp Notes" highlights poems composed while Yamada was imprisoned with her mother and brothers in the Minidoka camp in Idaho. The first poems tally the upheaval of the removal experience with titles such as "Evacuation," "Curfew," and "On the Bus." The title of "Harmony at the Fair Grounds" reflects the irony in many of Yamada's brief, acrid poems: The "grounds" on which the Japanese Americans were imprisoned were anything but "fair."

A subheading, "Relocation," designates poems about life in the Minidoka camp. The author continues to document the grim, degrading aspects of prison life, where monotony and uncertainty intensified the physical stresses of primitive, cramped quarters. Even more demoralizing were the irrationality, stupidity, and lies of the bureaucratic internment system. The remaining poems in the volume reflect the author's life from the end of the war through the 1950s and 1960s and explore themes of illness, raising children, education, discrimination, and activism.

The poetry in *Camp Notes and Other Poems* is concrete and spare, occasionally using irony to point out discrepancies between the starkness of internment camps and the rosy image portrayed by American media. The book records the mess hall meals, outhouse and shower lines, tarpaper-covered barracks, dust storms, curfews, uniformed guards, and barbed wire fences of internment. Two representative poems convey the tenuous political status of Japanese Americans during the war: "The Question of Loyalty" bewails the government's mistrust of citizens loyal to both America and Japan. "Cincinnati" recounts how the poet, greeted with racial epithets upon her emancipation, discards a handkerchief ironed by the mother she had to leave behind in the camp.

In a more complex, lyrical, and sometimes defiant volume, *Desert Run: Poems and Stories* (1988), Yamada makes a pilgrimage to the desert where she spent 547 days in internment. In the title poem, images of death—"lifeless sand," "desolate stillness," a carcass, bones, and a burial—give way to reflections on the slow, persistent growth of desert lichen and blooms, suggesting renewal. Other pieces in the collection explore cultural traditions, family bonds, and social problems from the perspectives of Japanese American grandmothers, mothers, and daughters. "I Learned to Sew" traces an immigrant's quest for education; "Jeni's Complaint" describes a grandmother proffering heirlooms; and the short story "Mrs. Higashi Is Dead" shows how language differences affect a mother-daughter relationship. Throughout *Desert Run* Asian ancestral ties run deep.

Yamada helped to establish the Asian American Studies Program at the University of California Irvine, and was guest instructor at several other colleges and universities. She founded the Multicultural Women Writers of Orange County, coediting the group's collection of narratives, poems, and essays published as *Sowing Ti Leaves: Writing by Multicultural Women* (1991). Additionally, Yamada has served on the board of Amnesty International USA and campaigned to compensate Japanese Americans for their treatment by the US government during World War II.

The 1981 documentary film *Mitsuye and Nellie: Two Asian-American Poets* brought national attention to Yamada's writing. The film blends historical photos and newsreels with the poetry of Yamada and Chinese American poet Nellie Wong. In 1982, Yamada received a Vesta Award for her contributions to the arts in Southern California. In 1998, Yamada's two key collections of poetry were combined into a single, comprehensive volume entitled *Camp Notes and Other Writings*.

SIGNIFICANCE

Mitsuye Yamada's first poetry collection, *Camp Notes and Other Writings*, offers a firsthand, historically significant account of how it felt to be a Japanese American excluded from mainstream society in the 1940s. Her subsequent writings have maintained a consistent—if increasingly political—focus on the lives and challenges of Asian women in a diverse and changing world. As a writer and college professor, Yamada has helped to broaden the canon of American literature to include more works by ethnic women.

Wendy Alison Lamb

FURTHER READING

Daniels, Roger. *Prisoners Without Trial: Japanese Americans in World War II*. New York: Hill, 1993. Print. Argues how nineteenth-century racism and 1940s politics led to ethnic internment; includes photos and suggested reading.

Graham, Renee. "A Poet Speaks Painful Truths of Her Past." *Boston Globe* 5 Dec. 1992: 21. Print. Yamada discusses the emotional toll of internment, the silence of Japanese Americans on the subject, and post-camp assimilation.

Inada, Lawson Fusao, ed. *Only What We Could Carry: The Japanese Internment Experience*. Berkeley: Heyday, 2000. Print. An anthology of letters, personal narratives, news accounts, and government declarations concerning the internment of Japanese Americans.

WAKA YAMADA

Japanese-born activist

Waka Yamada was a social critic and the author of several nonfiction collections. She lectured extensively on women's rights in Japan and abroad, and founded one of Japan's first shelters devoted exclusively to supporting homeless women and children. Overcoming her past as a prostitute, Yamada was among the earliest feminist intellectuals to advocate for women's rights in Japan during the early twentieth century.

Born: December 1, 1879; Kurihama, Kanagawa (now Yokosuka), Japan
Died: September 6, 1957; Iga-cho, Japan
Full name: Waka Yamada (WAH-kah YAH-mah-dah)
Birth name: Waka Asaba
Also known as: Yamada Waka
Areas of achievement: Activism, social issues, women's rights

EARLY LIFE

Waka Yamada was born Waka Asaba in Kurihama, a small fishing village near Yokahama, Japan, in December 1879. She was the fifth of seven children, and she received only a fourth-grade education before going to work on the family farm. In 1896, at the age of sixteen and through an arranged marriage, she became the wife of Hichijiro Araki, a local man who was ten years older. Seeking to escape the unhappy union, and due in part to her family's financial difficulties, she was lured to the United States in the late 1890s after being convinced that she could work as a maid and find a better life there. Instead, she became what the Japanese idiomatically call an *Ameyuki-san* or *karayuki-san*, a woman who traveled abroad and was sexually exploited. On her arrival, Yamada Waka was forced to work as a prostitute in a brothel in Seattle, Washington, one that catered exclusively to white men. She was given the name the "Arabian Oyae" or "Oyae of Arabia."

The following year Yamada was befriended by a Japanese American correspondent for a San Francisco–based Japanese newspaper. They were able to escape and evade thugs hired by Waka's pimp, but when funds were depleted she was betrayed and again forced into prostitution, this time in San Francisco's Chinatown. Escaping once more, she fled to the city's Presbyterian Occidental Mission House for Girls (later known as Cameron House), and there she managed to better educate herself and become proficient in English. She married Kakichi Yamada, her teacher and a Japanese immigrant himself, sometime between 1904 and 1905. At the time it was very rare for an educated Japanese man to marry a woman who he knew had been a prostitute. Following the catastrophic San Francisco earthquake of 1906, the couple returned to Japan, where Kakichi taught foreign languages and became a supporter of feminist causes. Their home soon served as a kind of salon for like-minded people. Because of their fourteen year age difference, Waka often referred to her husband as "Daddy."

LIFE'S WORK

Throughout the early twentieth century in Japan, Waka Yamada was an active journalist, writer, and feminist, publishing her work through periodicals such as *Seito* (Bluestocking) and in the newspaper advice column *Tokyo Asahi Shimbrun*. For a time she published her own periodical called *Women and the New Society*. In the 1930s, Yamada became the chair of the Japanese branch of the Motherhood Protection League. She also helped

Waka Yamada's Career as a Japanese Feminist

Yamada was one of several well-known feminists in Japan during the early and mid-twentieth century, along with Akiko Yosano, Raicho Hiratsuka, and Kikue Yamakawa. Yamada was considered to be one of the best public speakers of the group. She was also considered somewhat more traditional than her colleagues, since she held the belief that among women's primary responsibilities was to be "good wives and wise mothers." In her writings, she stated that she did not advocate that women and men be complete equals, but that they should work together in harmony to create a stable home. She also said that there was no shame in having a husband or even receiving money from the government for support. Her opinions alienated some of her colleagues, one of whom wrote a scathing article entitled "A Criticism of the Feminist Theory That Stabs Women in the Back."

One of the publications at which Yamada worked was the feminist literary magazine *Bluestocking* (*Seito* in Japanese), which had been founded in 1911. Her duties there included translating articles by pro-feminist writers into Japanese and writing her own articles. In one article, she branded both abortion and birth control as sinful. The magazine was dubbed "a nursery for Japanese Noras," referring to the independent-minded proto-feminist heroine of Henrik Ibsen's *A Doll's House* (1879). Beginning in 1931, Yamada had a long-running newspaper column in the major newspaper *Tokyo Asahi Shimbun*, in which she offered advice to women.

to get a law passed by the Japanese legislature providing financial aid to poor mothers of young children.

In 1937, through the sponsorship of *Shufunotomo* magazine, Yamada traveled to the United States for two months to lecture on motherhood and other topics. First Lady Eleanor Roosevelt received her at the White House during the trip. Some critics believed this trip served the cause of Japanese propaganda, as Japan was then engaged in a war with China. During the same visit, she returned to Seattle and lectured, only to be heckled by audience members who knew of her previous life as a prostitute. Yamada returned to Japan, and in Tokyo she founded a shelter for homeless mothers and children who were fleeing abusive homes—the first such institution ever established in Japan.

Although Waka Yamada's prominence receded somewhat following World War II, in 1947 she founded a school for young women modeled on the Cameron House. She then devoted the last ten years of her life to the rehabilitation of prostitutes, many of whom had been war widows and lacked employment skills. Acknowledging her early life experiences, Yamada was quoted as saying, "Once I was not worthy of standing before you, but I have been reborn. Because I have been resurrected from hell, I have plenty to tell you."

SIGNIFICANCE

Although opinions about her effectiveness as a women's advocate varied among her peers, Waka Yamada is still considered to be in the front ranks of Japanese feminists. As a member of the Japanese feminist community gathered around *Seito* magazine, Yamada helped to redefine the rights, roles, and responsibilities of women in modern Japan. Many of her essays, such as "Love and Society" and "Women Bow Down to Society," were collected and published in the 1920s, and her newspaper columns were adapted into two books: *Counseling Women* (1932) and *On Love* (1936); another book of hers, *The Social Status of Japanese Women*, was published in Tokyo in 1935.

Roy Liebman

FURTHER READING

Bernstein, Gail Lee, ed. *Recreating Japanese Women, 1600–1945*. Berkeley: U of California P, 1991. Print. An account of the treatment of women and the progress of women's rights in a changing Japanese society; contains information on Yamada.

Sievers, Sharon L. *Flowers in Salt: The Beginnings of Feminist Consciousness in Modern Japan*. Stanford: Stanford UP, 1983. Print. An account of the rise of feminism in Japan, including passages about Yamada.

Yamazaki, Tomoko. *The Story of Yamada Waka: From Prostitute to Feminist Pioneer*. Trans. Wakako Horonaka and Ann Kostant. Tokyo: Kodansha, 1985. Print. An abridged and translated version of the 1978 Japanese-language book about the life of Waka Yamada.

KRISTI YAMAGUCHI

Athlete, entertainer

Kristi Yamaguchi was the first Asian American to win a gold medal in Olympic figure skating and the first Asian American woman to win an Olympic event. An elegant skater, charismatic performer, and civic-minded person, Yamaguchi is one of the most popular figures in the history of the sport.

Born: July 12, 1971; Hayward, California
Full name: Kristine Tsuya Yamaguchi
Areas of achievement: Sports, entertainment

EARLY LIFE

Kristi Yamaguchi was born in Hayward, California, on July 12, 1971, to Jim and Carole Doi Yamaguchi. Her father worked as a dentist, and her mother worked as a medical secretary. Yamaguchi was the second of their three children and grew up in Fremont, California. Yamaguchi is a fourth-generation American of Japanese descent. Her grandparents were sent to the Japanese internment camps after Japan's attack on the US naval base at Pearl Harbor, Hawaii.

Yamaguchi was born with a foot deformity, and was fitted with a cast within weeks of her birth. Until she was three, she wore corrective shoes and leg braces to correct her condition.

At the age of four, she began to take ballet lessons. Yamaguchi's parents felt that ballet would help her overcome her foot problems. At age six, Yamaguchi saw an ice show at a shopping mall and asked her mother for figure skating lessons. She fell in love with the sport, and began spending countless hours on the ice. She also began carrying around a miniature doll of American ice skater Dorothy Hamill, the 1976 Olympic champion. By age eleven, Yamaguchi began competing in figure skating competitions. She began training at five o'clock in the morning, six days a week. Yamaguchi's spent five hours on lessons each day, and even more time practicing. After graduating from Willow Glen High School in San Jose, California, Yamaguchi did not enroll in college, and instead began devoting all of her time to figure skating.

LIFE'S WORK

Yamaguchi excelled in both single and pairs skating, which is an unusual skill in figure skating. Her partner was Rudy Galindo. In 1986, Yamaguchi and Galindo won the junior pairs skating title at the US Figure Skating Championships and a bronze medal at the Olympic

Festival. In 1988, she won the World Junior Championship in Brisbane, Australia, both in the singles competition and in the pairs competition with Galindo. In 1989 and 1990, Yamaguchi and Galindo were the United States pair champions. In addition, the seventeen-year-old Yamaguchi placed second in the 1989 US Championships singles event. Her long program was praised for being beautiful and exuberant in execution. In 1990, Yamaguchi and Galindo placed fifth in the 1990 World Figure Skating Championships in Halifax, Canada.

Following her fifth-place finish with Galindo in 1990, Yamaguchi decided to concentrate exclusively on singles competition. She moved to Edmonton, Canada, to continue training with the highly regarded skating coach Christy Kjarsgaard Ness. Yamaguchi had established herself as one of the world's elite women skaters, along with fellow American figure skaters Tonya Harding, Jill Trenary, and Nancy Kerrigan. Other prominent competitors at the time included Surya Bonaly of France, Chen Lu of China, and Midori Ito of Japan. Yamaguchi was a well-balanced skater, who emphasized

Kristi Yamaguchi. (Getty Images for IMG0)

Kristi Yamaguchi at the 1992 Winter Olympic Games

The highlight of Yamaguchi's skating career was winning the gold medal in ladies figure skating at the 1992 winter Olympic Games in Albertville, France. Although she was at the time the women's world champion in figure skating, she was not necessarily the favorite to win Olympic gold. Her two main rivals, Tonya Harding and Midori Ito, were strong, athletic skaters, capable of performing the demanding triple axel, a jump that was beyond Yamaguchi. However, Yamaguchi performed her routines with both her customary elegance and mistake-free technique, landing several triple jumps. Her routines were expertly choreographed by Sandra Bezic and won plaudits for their grace and speed. Although Yamaguchi slipped at one point in her program, Ito and Harding fell during their routines. Yamaguchi's artistic routine scored enough points to ensure her first-place finish. On December 8, 2005, Yamaguchi was inducted into the US Olympic Hall of Fame for her 1992 performance. Her induction was a fitting tribute to one of America's most dedicated, talented, and popular ice champions.

artistry and elegance in her routines. She began lifting weights to build up her speed and strengthen her jumps. Her hard work paid off the following year when she won the 1991 World Singles Championships with a performance that included six triple jumps.

In 1992, Yamaguchi had one of her most spectacular years as a competitive skater. She won three coveted titles. She first won the US National Senior Ladies Championship. A few months later, Yamaguchi became the first Asian American woman to win an Olympic gold medal at the 1992 Winter Olympics in Albertville, France. Finally, she followed up her Olympic victory by successfully defending her world champion title.

Following her spectacular results in 1992, Yamaguchi left competitive skating to become a professional entertainer. Over the next ten years, she was a star attraction with the *Stars on Ice* dance show. She also performed in numerous television specials and won several professional competitions. A favorite with the public, Yamaguchi appeared in February 1994 in a humorous commercial for the fast-food chain Wendy's with its founder, David Thomas.

In 1996, Yamaguchi established a philanthropic foundation, the Always Dream Foundation, which benefits early literacy programs in underserved neighborhoods. The foundation was named for her personal motto, "Always Dream." On July 8, 2000, Yamaguchi married former professional hockey player Bret Hedican. The couple's first daughter, Keara, was born on October 1, 2003. Their second daughter, Emma, was born on

November 18, 2005. In 2008, Yamaguchi won the Thurman Munson Award for excellence in athletics and philanthropy. That same year, she won the Inspiration award at the Asian Excellence Awards and was the celebrity winner in the television dance competition *Dancing With the Stars*.

In 2011, Yamaguchi published a best-selling children's book, entitled *Dream Big, Little Pig*. The book reflects her "Always Dream" motto, portraying a pig who follows his unlikely dream to become a skating star.

SIGNIFICANCE

Yamaguchi is an outstanding figure skater, who brought her own brand of elegance and graciousness to the sport. She developed near-flawless form and technique through rigorous and persistent practice, becoming one of the most popular skaters of her generation. In her early career, she excelled in both doubles and singles skating. When she skated in both the singles and pairs in the 1989 US Championships, she was the first woman to do so since Margaret Graham in 1954. The highlight of her career was her two world championships in 1991 and 1992 and her winning the Ladies Figure Skating competition in the 1992 Olympics, the first gold medal won by an Asian American woman.

Howard Bromberg

FURTHER READING

Hasday, Judy L. *Kristi Yamaguchi*. New York: Chelsea House, 1997. A volume in the Asian Americans of Achievement series, recounts Yamaguchi's life in light of her Japanese American heritage. Includes a chronology, timeline, and bibliography.

Nicoll, Gregory. *Kristi Yamaguchi: Triumph on Ice*. Kansas City: Andrews McMeel, 2000. Print. Biography of Yamaguchi, focusing on her victories in ice skating competitions. With extensive photographs of Yamaguchi in performance, and a listing of her awards and achievements.

Smith, Pohla. *Superstars of Women's Figure Skating*. New York: Chelsea House, 1997. Print. Includes a chapter that profiles Yamaguchi's stirring Olympic victory.

Swift, E. M. "All that Glitters," *Sports Illustrated* 14 Dec. 1992: 70–75. Print. Describes Yamaguchi's performance at the 1992 Winter Olympics.

HISAYE YAMAMOTO

Writer

One of the few Japanese American writers to receive national literary attention soon after World War II, Yamamoto is best known for sensitive, understated short stories about Japanese Americans. Her work probes the communication gap between first-generation Japanese Americans and their second-generation children and explores relationships between Asian Americans and other ethnic minorities.

Born: August 23, 1921; Redondo Beach, California
Died: January 30, 2011; Los Angeles, California
Full name: Hisaye Yamamoto (hee-SAH-yeh YAH-mah-MOH-toh)
Also known as: Hisaye Yamamoto DeSoto
Area of achievement: Literature

EARLY LIFE

Hisaye Yamamoto was born to first-generation immigrant parents from Kumamoto, Japan, who farmed for a living in Southern California. At fourteen, she began to submit letters and stories to the feature sections of Japanese American newspapers such as *Kashu Mainichi*. Later, at Compton Junior College, Yamamoto studied French, German, Spanish, and Latin.

Twenty-year-old Yamamoto was living with her family in Oceanside, California, when the United States entered World War II in 1941. As mandated by the federal government, the family was forcibly evacuated to an internment camp in 1942. The Yamamotos joined some seventeen thousand other detainees at the Poston Relocation Center, a desert camp established on Native American lands beside the Colorado River in western Arizona.

At Poston, Yamamoto pored over old *New Yorker* magazines in the camp library and served as reporter and columnist for the *Poston Chronicle*, the camp newspaper. In 1943, it published two of her early fictional works—"Death Rides the Rails to Poston," a serialized mystery, and "Surely I Must Be Dreaming." A real woman at Poston inspired "The Legend of Miss Sasagawara" (1950), the only of Yamamoto's stories set in a detention camp. The title character, a seemingly insane dancer housed with a Buddhist father who ignores her, is misunderstood and diminished; the story addresses the effects of the camp experience on the Japanese American community.

LIFE'S WORK

After the war ended in 1945, Yamamoto worked as a journalist for the *Los Angeles Tribune*, an African American weekly seeking new readers among Japanese Americans returning home from internment camps. In 1948, Yamamoto adopted a baby and turned from journalism to creative writing, soon aided by a 1950 John Hay Whitney Foundation Opportunity Fellowship. Published first in regional newspapers and subsequently in literary journals and anthologies, Yamamoto's thought-provoking stories shed light on Japanese American life.

In 1948, the *Partisan Review* published Yamamoto's "The High-Heeled Shoes," a story featuring haunting sensory images and imaginary dialogues that would become hallmarks of her fiction. The following year, the literary magazine published Yamamoto's definitive work, "Seventeen Syllables," a coming-of-age story shadowed by domestic conflict. *Furioso* published "Yoneko's Earthquake" in 1951, and the mother-daughter tragedy was selected to appear in *The Best American Short Stories, 1952*, edited by Martha Foley. In fact, four of Yamamoto's works—including "The Brown House" (1951), a multicultural gambling story, and "Epithalamium" (1960), about an ill-fated marriage—were selected for Foley's annual lists of distinctive short stories, a coveted literary approbation. *Kenyon Review*, *Harper's Bazaar*, and other notable periodicals published Yamamoto's fiction in the 1950s and early 1960s.

Like "Seventeen Syllables," much of Yamamoto's fiction is narrated by adolescent girls. Crafted with irony, layers of meaning, intertwined plots, and light humor, the stories use deceptively simple language to convey upheaval, longing, and stifled attempts for artistry or independence. Yamamoto portrays complex characters caught between traditional Japanese culture and mainstream American society. Her Japanese American protagonists bear disappointments and indignities quietly and often bond with other Asian Americans or people from other minority groups.

After declining a Stanford University writing fellowship, Yamamoto volunteered at a New York farm sponsored by the Catholic Worker Movement, later the setting for "Epithalamium." In 1955, she married Anthony DeSoto, with whom she would have four children, and moved to Los Angeles. Although none of the memoirs, essays, and short stories she penned after

Hisaye Yamamoto's
Seventeen Syllables and Other Stories

In the late 1940s, Yamamoto's short stories about prewar life in Japanese American communities were making their way into national journals, such as the *Kenyon Review, Harper's Bazaar,* and the *Partisan Review.* They gained Yamamoto a national reputation as a fine American short story writer. Yamamoto's debut collection of short stories, entitled *Seventeen Syllables and Other Stories,* appeared in 1988.

Yamamoto has been lauded for her compassionate explorations of characters who have suffered loss or sorrow in the pursuit of love, beauty, art, and spirituality. Her stories are also noted for their fine technical artistry. "Seventeen Syllables" and "Yoneko's Earthquake" are examples of Yamamoto's intricately developed double plots. Through the double plot, the reader sees the story from multiple perspectives—often through the eyes of young, naïve daughter-narrators, who are just beginning to explore new experiences or awakenings, especially in love and sexuality. In contrast, their mothers' submerged stories hint at the darker, more traumatic aspects of adulthood: unfulfilled yearnings, alienation, loneliness, adultery, abortion, domestic violence, and the loss of loved ones or of creativity. Yamamoto's stories portray a full range of generational and gender tensions, especially between mismatched *issei* (first-generation Japanese American) husbands and wives and between issei parents and their *nisei* (second-generation Japanese American) children. In some of her stories, Yamamoto also explores the interracial and cross-cultural relationships of women and men within Japanese American communities, expanding on multicultural themes and interactions in the United States.

The first book devoted entirely to Yamamoto's stories was published in Japan in 1985, and the fifteen-work collection *Seventeen Syllables and Other Stories* was published in the United States three years later. In 1986, Yamamoto was recognized with an American Book Award by the Before Columbus Foundation. PBS's *American Playhouse* presented a television movie combining elements from "Seventeen Syllables" and "Yoneko's Earthquake," *Hot Summer Winds,* in 1991.

SIGNIFICANCE

Yamamoto's compassionate, restrained short stories gave the US public an understanding of Japanese American life before, during, and after World War II. From child's-eye vignettes of immigrant farming families to descriptions of postwar racial tensions on a city bus, Yamamoto's work offers insight into what was, historically, a difficult time for many Japanese Americans. Her literary accomplishments helped writing by Asian Americans attain recognition as respected American literature.

Wendy Alison Lamb

FURTHER READING

Cheung, King-Kok. Introduction. *Seventeen Syllables and Other Stories.* By Hisaye Yamamoto. Rev. ed. New Brunswick: Rutgers UP, 2001. Print. Traces the history of US legislation affecting Japanese Americans and explores the effects of such policies on Yamamoto's writing.

Robinson, Greg. "The Great Unknown and the Unknown Great: The Life and Times of Hisaye Yamamoto." *Discover Nikkei.* Japanese American National Museum, 14 Mar. 2012. Web. 23 Mar. 2012. Provides an overview of Yamamoto's life and career, with particular focus on her work as a journalist.

Yamamoto, Hisaye. "A MELUS Interview: Hisaye Yamamoto." Interview with Charles L. Crow. *MELUS* 14.1 (1987): 73–83. Print. Reveals how internment, parenthood, and community life shaped Yamamoto's storytelling.

1961 achieved the success of her earlier publications, many anthologies of Asian American literature and women's fiction continued to popularize her work.

MINORU YAMASAKI

Architect

One of the first Asian American architects to gain national recognition, Yamasaki designed a number of award-winning buildings that featured a blend of modernism and classical details and emphasized functionality. Though his works are numerous and can be found throughout the United States and elsewhere, he is best known for designing the World Trade Center complex in New York City.

Born: December 1, 1912; Seattle, Washington
Died: February 7, 1986; Detroit, Michigan
Full name: Minoru Yamasaki (mih-NOH-rew yah-mah-SAH-kee)
Areas of achievement: Architecture and design

EARLY LIFE

Minoru Yamasaki was born in Seattle, Washington, the son of Japanese immigrants. Inspired by an uncle who worked as an architect, Yamasaki decided to enroll at the University of Washington to study architecture. He worked for Alaskan fish canneries during the summers to earn money for his tuition. Upon graduating in 1934, Yamasaki moved to New York and enrolled in a master's degree program at New York University. For the next ten years, he worked as a draftsman and designer for several major architectural and design firms. In December 1941, he married Teruko Hirashiki, with whom he had three children. They would later divorce and then remarry.

Minoru Yamasaki. (NY Daily News via Getty Images)

LIFE'S WORK

Yamasaki began a rapid rise to national prominence in 1945, when he was hired by the Detroit firm Smith, Hinchman & Grylls as chief of design. Four years later, he left the firm to become a partner in Hellmuth, Yamasaki & Leinweber, which established offices in Detroit and St. Louis. In St. Louis, Yamasaki built the Pruitt-Igoe housing project and the main terminal at Lambert-St. Louis International Airport, demonstrating his talents as a disciple of modernist architecture. In 1959, he established his own firm, Yamasaki Associates, in Detroit. The following year, he was named a fellow of the American Institute of Architects and was honored by the University of Washington with the Alumnus Summa Laude Dignatus Award.

A serious illness in 1954 required Yamasaki to undergo a long convalescence, which included a sojourn abroad. Seeing the architecture of Europe and Asia prompted Yamasaki to rebel against the sterility and formulaic qualities of much modern architecture by introducing embellishments into his design. Yamasaki became a proponent of new formalism, a style that retains some of the rigid elements of the International Style while adding touches reminiscent of classical design. Yamasaki professed to imbue his work with three qualities: delight, serenity, and surprise.

Over the course of his four-decade career, Yamasaki designed numerous buildings in the United States and abroad, including the US consulate in Kobe, Japan; the Federal Science Pavilion, designed for the 1962 World's Fair in Seattle; and the Michigan Consolidated Gas building in Detroit. He designed buildings on the campuses of Wayne State University, Oberlin College, Princeton University, and Harvard University, as well as the IBM Building in Seattle and various buildings in locales such as Saudi Arabia and Iran.

In 1962, Port Authority officials selected Yamasaki to complete his most prominent commission yet: the World Trade Center in New York City. Modeling his work on Mies van der Rohe's famous twin high-rise apartment complex in Chicago and his own IBM Building in Seattle, Yamasaki created the massive Twin Towers, which were the tallest buildings in the world at the time of their construction. The towers were surrounded by a series of smaller buildings on the sixteen-acre site. Groundbreaking took place in 1966, and Yamasaki worked closely with engineers and construction personnel to ensure that the building met his clients' needs. The complex was completed in 1976.

Minoru Yamasaki and the World Trade Center

In 1962, the New York Port Authority chose Yamasaki as the lead architect for its World Trade Center project. Yamasaki was presented with a set of requirements for office space allocation as well as retail, parking, and other facilities, but he was given complete freedom to design the structures that would house them. He experimented with different approaches before settling on a concept of two 110-story towers with subordinate buildings set amid a large plaza. The plaza would be laid out with landscaping and decorative elements designed to temper the immensity of the towers.

Yamasaki was initially hesitant to plan towers more than eighty stories high, but shorter towers would not accommodate the required ten million square feet of office space. The public reacted favorably to his plans, but architectural experts criticized the scale and design of the towers, arguing that they would be an eyesore. As planning continued, Yamasaki and his builders pioneered several new construction techniques. The exterior walls would bear the towers' weight and withstand the severe wind forces to which they would be exposed. The only interior columns were for the elevator system, allowing virtually unobstructed space on every floor.

As the towers rose, the World Trade Center reinvented the New York skyline. The twin towers quickly became a symbol of Manhattan. Former critics even acknowledged the towers' unique beauty; their aluminum alloy sheathing radiated a range of dramatic hues as light and weather conditions changed.

SIGNIFICANCE

A controversial architect, Yamasaki rebelled against the stark, functionalist designs of modernist architecture, reintroducing classic embellishments to public buildings. He developed a strong personal philosophy regarding the function of architecture, insisting that buildings should be designed to accommodate the people using them. His buildings would continue to inspire later generations of architects for decades after his death.

Laurence W. Mazzeno

FURTHER READING

Mogilevich, Mariana. "Big Bad Buildings: The Vanishing Legacy of Minoru Yamasaki." *Next American City* 3 (2003): 24–27. Print. A retrospective of Yamasaki's contributions to American architecture, stressing his failures.

Van Hoffman, Alexander. "Why They Built Pruitt-Igoe." *From Tenements to the Taylor Homes: In Search of an Urban Housing Policy in Twentieth-Century America*. Ed. John F. Bauman, Roger Biles, and Kristin M. Szylvian. University Park: Pennsylvania State UP, 2000. 180–205. Print. A detailed account of Yamasaki's unsuccessful public-housing project in St. Louis.

Winther-Tamaki, Bert. "Minoru Yamasaki: Contradictions of Scale in the Career of the Nisei Architect of the World's Largest Building." *Amerasia Journal* 26.3 (2000/2001): 162–89. Print. A scholarly assessment of Yamasaki's career designing public buildings and the impact of his Asian American heritage.

Yamasaki, Minoru. *A Life in Architecture*. New York: Weatherhill, 1979. Print. Autobiography providing Yamasaki's perspective on his career and personal life.

Though many in the architectural community did not consider the World Trade Center a triumph of art and design, the Twin Towers became quite popular with the public and were soon recognized as a symbol of the United States' global dominance. Yamasaki took on numerous commissions in the 1970s and early 1980s, but none of his later works matched the scale or the renown of his earlier project.

BRUCE YAMASHITA

Military leader, lawyer

Bruce Yamashita was expelled from Marine Corps Officer Candidate School just days before graduation. The Marine Corps rejected his contention he was barred due to racial discrimination, until Yamashita won a reversal of the decision through a protracted series of appeals. Upon reversing its decision, the Marine Corps apologized to Yamashita and commissioned him.

Born: February 26, 1956; Honolulu, Hawaii
Areas of achievement: Military, law

EARLY LIFE

Bruce Yamashita was born in Honolulu, Hawaii, on February 26, 1956. His father, Paul Yamashita, was a state engineer and his mother, Pearl Yamashita, was a professor at the University of Hawaii. Yamashita attended the university's Laboratory School, which also served as a research facility for the College of Education. He enrolled as an undergraduate student at the University of Hawaii. In 1975, following his freshman year, he took a year off to attend the International Christian University in Tokyo, Japan. Yamashita finished his studies at the University of Hawaii, where he was elected as a student representative to the state's constitutional convention in 1978. Upon graduation in 1979, he took a job at a trading company headquartered in Tokyo, and then became the editor of *Yokomeshi Shimbun*, a newspaper for adults learning Japanese. After four years, he returned to the United States to attend Georgetown University Law Center.

LIFE'S WORK

After graduating from law school, Yamashita considered becoming a military lawyer. The Marine Corps appealed to him because, unlike the other military divisions, the Marines required lawyers to go through the same basic training at Officer Candidate School (OCS) as all other officers. In addition, Yamashita was inspired by the memory of an uncle who had served in the famed all-nisei 442nd US Regimental Combat Team during World War II.

Yamashita reported to OCS on February 6, 1989, for a nine-week training course. At nearly thirty-three years old, he was much older than the average officer candidate, and he was accustomed to the accepting, multicultural environment of Hawaii, as well as the ethnically diverse community he lived in during law school. Immersion in the grinding stress of OCS came as a shock to Yamashita, the more so because the enlisted instructors singled him out with racial slurs.

They purposely mispronounced his name, told him to go back to Japan because he did not belong in the United States, and called him "kamikaze man." The sustained stress of verbal harassment is an established part of Marine training, and all candidates had to endure it, but the use of racial epithets was not in accordance with military doctrine. Nonetheless, the officers in charge of the school not only tolerated the racial taunting, they also ridiculed Yamashita.

Although he was regularly pressured to quit, Yamashita remained in OCS. However, he came to believe that his instructors were looking for excuses to evaluate him unfairly. On April 7, 1989, two days before his class was to graduate, Yamashita was summarily "disenrolled" by a final review board composed of top ranking OCS officers and sent home.

In January 1990, Yamashita appealed the decision. He wrote a letter to the Commandant of the Marine Corps, Gen. Alfred M. Gray, Jr., in which he contended that he had been refused a commission because of racial discrimination. In response to a request on Yamashita's behalf from Senator Daniel Inouye of Hawaii, Gray initiated an inquiry. The inquiry concluded that there was no evidence of discrimination, and Gray accused Yamashita of trying to blame others for his own failure. Yamashita then filed an appeal with review boards under the command of the Navy's Inspector General. The resulting investigations verified some of Yamashita's claims. As a result, the Marine Corps apologized, and offered to let Yamashita reenroll in OCS.

However, Yamashita wanted a commission, not another round of training. He had nearly completed training in 1989. He renewed his appeal. In the meantime, the Hawaii legislature sent a resolution to Congress calling for Yamashita's reinstatement, while Senator Inouye continued to pressure the Marine Corps. With the help of the Japanese American Citizens League, his sister Margaret, and lawyers Ernest Kimoto (a retired Marine Corps major) and Clayton Ikei, Yamashita persevered. In 1994, Secretary of the Navy John H. Dalton directed that Yamashita receive a commission as a captain in the Marine Corps Reserve, the rank he would likely have held had he finished OCS in 1989. He was commissioned on March 18, 1994, before an audience of family, politicians, and representatives of civil rights organizations. Yamashita moved to Washington, DC, to work as a lawyer in criminal and immigration law.

SIGNIFICANCE

Yamashita's lawsuit exposed the prevalence of racial discrimination and harassment in the US Marine Corps. In 2003, Yamashita published an autobiographical account of his struggle, *Fighting Tradition: A Marine's Journey to Justice*. Director Steve Okino made a documentary, *A Most Unlikely Hero*, about Yamashita's experience, which premiered in 2005. As a result, the Marine Corps made public apologies, held a new investigation into race and attrition at OCS, and promised to monitor recruiting and training more carefully in order to stop racial harassment and discrimination.

Roger Smith

Further Reading

Chin, Steven A. "A Matter of Honor: The Bruce Yamashita Story." *San Francisco Examiner* 4 Apr. 1993. Reprint, *ModelMinority.com*, 2012. Web. 4 Apr. 2012. Recounts Yamashita's experience at Marine Corps Officer Candidate School with some background biographical information.

Schmitt, Eric. "Asian American Proves Marine Bias." *New York Times* 2 Jan. 1994: 10. Print. Relates the background of Yamashita's successful legal battle against the Marine Corps for racial discrimination.

Yamashita, Bruce I. *Fighting Tradition: A Marine's Journey to Justice*. Honolulu: U of Hawaii P, 2003. Print. Discusses Yamashita's family background and youth, while relating his experience of racial harassment at Marine Corps Officer Candidate School and the story of his appeals to win redress for it.

Karen Tei Yamashita

Educator, novelist, and playwright

Karen Tei Yamashita is known primarily for her prose narratives on Japanese migration to the United States and to Brazil, although she also has written numerous plays and performance pieces that highlight the dynamic nature and diversity of Asian American culture. Yamashita's fiction shows the influence of the magic realism of Latin American writers such as Jorge Borges. Typically, her stories contain characters of humble or ordinary circumstances dealing with the consequences of corporate capitalism and environmental degradation. Yamashita's literary landscape consists of change as the only constant, of characters with fluid identities that look ahead rather than being mired in the past.

Born: January 8, 1951; Oakland, California
Full name: Karen Tei Yamashita (yah-mah-SHI-ta)
Area of achievement: Literature

Early Life

Karen Tei Yamashita is a *sansei*, or third-generation American of Japanese descent. Her grandparents left Japan for the United States around 1900. She grew up in California's San Francisco Bay Area and graduated from Carleton College with Phi Beta Kappa honors in 1973, with degrees in both English and Japanese literature. A Thomas J. Watson Fellowship funded three years of travel and study, first to Japan, then Brazil, where she lived from 1975 to 1984. In 1977 Yamashita married Ronaldo Lopes de Oliveira, an architect; they have two children, Jon and Jane. After returning to the United States with her family in the mid-1980s, Yamashita continued her research and writing on communities of Japanese ancestry in the Americas. She worked for public television in Los Angeles until 1997 when she joined the faculty of literature and creative writing at the University of California Santa Cruz.

Life's Work

By 2010, Karen Tei Yamashita had published five books: *Through the Arc of the Rainforest* (1990), *Brazil-Maru* (1992), *Tropic of Orange* (1997), *Circle K Cycles* (2001), and *I Hotel* (2010), which was a finalist for the National Book Award in the fiction category. Her first novel received both an American Book Award and the Janet Heidinger Kafka Award. Notable short stories by Yamashita include "The Orange," "The Bath," "Tucano," and "Asaka-no-Miya." She has also written performance pieces and plays such as *Omen: An American Kabuki* (1978), *Hiroshima Tropical* (1984), *Hannah Kusoh: An American Butoh* (1989), *Noh Bozos* (1993), and *Anime Wong: A CyberAsian Odyssey* (2008).

Change is an enduring topic in Yamashita's writing. *Through the Arc of the Rainforest*, her first novel, is a fast-paced, humorous satire set in Brazil in the late twentieth century. The characters—crafted in the best tradition of magical realism—must change their habitual attitudes if they are to overcome the encroachment of global capitalism.

Brazil-Maru, Yamashita's second novel, depicts the beginning of the saga of Japanese immigration to Brazil, a topic of abiding interest. This historical novel consists of the accounts of four main characters belonging to a group that sought to establish a community based on socialist values and Christianity. The book portrays this experiment taking hold as well as the cost exacted by the South American frontier.

Yamashita's third novel, *Tropic of Orange*, is set in Mexico and Los Angeles. This fictive world is seen through the perspective of several characters: recent immigrants, an African American, descendants of immigrants, and a character who is several hundred years old. In this novel, as well as Yamashita's memoir, *Circle K Cycles*, ethnic identity is shown to be porous, hybrid, and often strategic, involving constant remixing; it is not primordial or essentialist. *Circle K Cycles*—written in Japanese, English, and Portuguese—explores the experiences of contemporary Japanese Brazilian guestworkers in Japan. *I Hotel* is based on the Asian American civil rights movement of the 1960s. The novel is a multigenre work that uses nonlinear collages and textual representations of dance, music, and filmmaking to characterize a pivotal, complex, and multifaceted period in Asian American and American history.

Yamashita has continued to teach as a professor of literature and work as the codirector of the Creative Writing Program at the University of California Santa Cruz. The university presented her with the Chancellor's Award for Diversity in 2009. Yamashita's awards and honors also include the 2011 California Book Award. Yamashita was made a Fellow of the United States Artists in 2011 as well.

SIGNIFICANCE

Yamashita's body of work broadens the definition of Asian American literature to include not only the United States, but North and South America as well. Her stories were among the first in Asian American literature to use magical realism and concepts from quantum physics. Recurrent themes in Yamashita's writing—including global capitalism, the environment, mass media, and new formulations of community—broaden the scope of Asian American literature, and indeed American literature as a whole.

Ruth Y. Hsu

FURTHER READING

Chang, Yalan. "Nature, Body and Society: The Fluidity/Cyborgization in Karen Tei Yamashita, Margaret Atwood and Bruce Sterling." *Ecology and Literature: Global Perspective*. Ed. Neerja Arun and Bakesh Saraswat. New Delhi: Creative, 2009. Print. Examines the ecological concerns explored in Yamashita's work.

Rody, Caroline. *The Interethnic Imagination: Roots and Passages in Contemporary Asian American Fiction*. Oxford: Oxford UP, 2009. Print. Contains a chapter on Yamashita's novels in terms of the formation of Asian American ethnic identity.

---. "The Transnational Imagination: Karen Tei Yamashita's *Tropic of Orange*." *Asian North American Identities: Beyond the Hyphen*. Ed. Eleanor Rose Ty and Donald C. Goellnicht. Bloomington: Indiana UP, 2004. Print. Reconfigures Asian American literary studies in light of the transnational links fictionalized in *Tropic of Orange*.

WAKAKO YAMAUCHI

Writer, playwright

Wakako Yamauchi endured the indignities of wartime internment to become one of the most respected Japanese American playwrights and chroniclers of immigrant life in California. Stressing precise detail, unadorned narration, and poignant realism, her writing captures a full range of complex, often devastating human encounters.

Born: October 25, 1924; Westmorland, California
Full name: Wakako Yamauchi
Birth name: Wakako Nakamura
Areas of achievement: Literature and theater

EARLY LIFE

Wakako Yamauchi was born in Westmorland, California on October 25, 1924, the third of five children. Her father, Yasaku, and mother, Hamako, were both natives of Shizuoka, Japan. Like other *issei* (first-generation Japanese Americans), they maintained cultural and linguistic ties to their homeland. These bonds were sustained through shared recollections of the past, food, social customs, and the arts, especially through song. Pressured to assimilate into American society, Yamauchi's family found companionship in neighboring families throughout Southern California. Yamauchi's later work would explore this sense of connection to Japan.

Like many Japanese immigrants who lived on the West Coast, the Nakamuras eked out a living as tenant farmers. They settled in Imperial Valley, suffering through drought, economic depression, racism, a major earthquake in 1940, and wartime suspicion. The Alien Land Law of 1913 prohibited people of Asian descent from owning land, so the Nakamuras had to lease their property. This lifestyle required frequent moves and climate-dependent subsistence living. The work was arduous and socially isolating, especially for those without families. The Nakamuras briefly ran a hotel for migrant laborers, many of whom were desperate for companionship and kindness.

Yamauchi's senior year of high school was marked not by graduation ceremonies but by World War II and detainment in Poston, Arizona. Internment of Japanese Americans had begun in 1942, after the Japanese attack on the naval base at Pearl Harbor, Hawaii. In the camp, Yamauchi befriended Hisaye Yamamoto, a journalist with the *Poston Chronicle*, who later became an author. Yamauchi became a layout artist for the newspaper. After earning an early release from the internment camp in 1944, she moved to Chicago to work in a candy factory. She returned to California a short while later to attend her father's funeral. He had succumbed to drink, illness, and the emotional trauma of war. Yamauchi then accompanied her remaining family to San Diego after the camps were disbanded in 1945. Working as a photo developer, she expanded her creative talents, eventually reuniting with Yamamoto in Los Angeles, rooming with her friend, and attending night classes at the Otis Art Center.

Introduced to Chester Yamauchi through her brother, Wakako married in 1948. The couple had a daughter in 1955. While her husband studied, Yamauchi became the breadwinner, working temporary jobs. Her writing was not a priority. Henry Mori, editor of the Los Angeles-based Japanese newspaper *Rafu Shimpo*, solicited Yamauchi's graphic arts expertise for this local newspaper. After some negotiation, he agreed to publish Yamauchi's stories in exchange for artwork. This agreement provided Yamauchi with steady publication opportunities from 1960 to 1974. After editors Frank Chin, Lawson Fusao Inada, Shawn Wong, and Jeffrey Paul Chan included one of her works in *Aiiieeeee! An Anthology of Asian American Writers* (1974), Yamauchi's identity as a *nissei* writer rose to sudden prominence.

LIFE'S WORK

Yamauchi and her husband divorced in 1975. She continued to write, infusing her work with emotional sensitivity and philosophical irony. Yamauchi's work explores emotional turbulence and the residual stress of internment camp life. She adapted her popular short story "And the Soul Shall Dance" into a full-length play with a Rockefeller playwright-in-residence grant. The

story details the miserable pairing of a brusque farmer and his artistic, temperamental wife. Transplanted to America to replace her dead sister, the character Emiko finds her new rural homestead devoid of inspiration. Without financial means and any possibility of return to Japan, her only solace is drink and traditional music, which accompanies her recollections.

In 1977, the Asian American theater group The East West Players of Los Angeles staged a performance of Yamauchi's *And the Soul Shall Dance* to great acclaim. It won the Los Angeles Drama Critics Circle Award that same year. Shortly thereafter, the Public Broadcasting Service (PBS) produced a version for television, which aired nationally between 1977 and 1978. Yamauchi composed six other full-length plays that were performed at major venues in New York, San Francisco, and Seattle. *The Music Lessons*, based on her short story "In Heaven and Earth," focuses on family struggles in a farming community. Kaoru, a musician and migrant, joins a widow and her children in the fields. Pushed into an awkward love triangle with the mother and her underage daughter, he catalyzes the release of repressed sexuality, anger, and accumulated disappointments. Drama departments at Yale and the University of California Los Angeles produced the work, cementing Yamauchi's status as major American playwright.

Yamauchi's oeuvre includes numerous short stories and nine plays. Her major works illuminate the disparity between a rich inner life and scarcity of resources in the external world. The ambitions of Japanese Americans during her upbringing were not far-reaching: boys usually worked in farming or manual labor and girls married or became domestics. The tragic heroes of Yamauchi's work are rootless bachelors, gambling away their loneliness and social emasculation, or artistic, sensitive women who find their secret delights crushed by the weight of daily survival.

SIGNIFICANCE

Yamauchi writes as a historical witness invested in recuperating compromised human dignity. Her texts explore the difficulties of the early Japanese immigrants to the West Coast, conveying their stories as a heavy braid of longing, loss, and self-restraint. Scholarship on her work has appeared in feminist, genre-based, and ethnic literature monographs and periodicals. The symbolic scarcity evoked in such stories as "That Was All," "The Sensei," and "Otoko" is not just material; often, the deficiency Yamauchi illuminates is in fundamental sympathy for fellow human beings. Bitter but not cynical, her camp survivors explain their shame and silence. Other speakers, usually mature women, expose the foundations of failed love as insufficient flexibility and faulty communication. Many of Yamauchi's characters desire to express themselves through art, but are prevented from doing so by their limited circumstances.

Nancy Kang

FURTHER READING
McDonald, Dorothy Ritsuko. "Relocation and Dislocation: The Writings of Hisaye Yamamoto and Wakako Yamauchi" *MELUS* 7.3 (1980): 21–38.

Print. Comparative analysis of these literary contemporaries in the context of internment and other thematic continuities.
Osborn, William P., and Sylvia A. Watanabe. "A MELUS Interview: Wakako Yamauchi." *MELUS* 23.2 (1998): 101–110. Print. Discusses Yamauchi's primary inspirations and understanding of historical and personal witnessing.
Yamauchi, Wakako. *Songs My Mother Taught Me: Stories, Plays, and Memoir*. Ed. Garrett Hongo. New York: Feminist Press of CUNY, 1994. Print. Features Yamauchi's stories and two major plays, extracted from over three decades of writing.

MARTIN YAN

Entertainer, writer, entrepreneur

Martin Yan is a master chef who has written over thirty cookbooks and hosted numerous cooking shows, notably Yan Can Cook *for PBS. Credited with making Chinese home cooking popular with Americans, Yan's simple recipes feature dishes from all over China, representing its many regions, especially Guangzhou. Yan's television shows mix entertainment, education, and humor to demystify the art of preparing Chinese cuisine.*

Born: December 22, 1948; Guangzhou, Guangdong, China
Full name: Martin Yan
Areas of achievement: Entertainment, business

EARLY LIFE

Martin Yan was born in Guangzhou, Guangdong, China on December 22, 1948. The son of Tat Ming, a restaurateur, and Xi Mei, a grocery store owner and operator, Yan began to cook at age twelve. When he was thirteen, he moved to Hong Kong to work in his uncle's restaurant. Yan attended Munsang College and received a diploma from the Overseas Institute of Cookery, Hong Kong in 1967. After completing his undergraduate education, Yan moved to Canada, where he began teaching Chinese cooking and got his first job on television, appearing on a Calgary talk show. In 1975, Yan earned a master's degree in food science from the University of California, Davis.

In 1982, Yan began hosting the PBS cooking show *Yan Can Cook*, the first and most popular of his cooking

shows. *Yan Can Cook*, with its catchphrase "If Yan can cook, so can you," featured Chef Yan as an educator, entertainer and wok master.

Yan has over 3,000 television cooking shows to his credit, and his cooking lessons have been broadcast in

Martin Yan. (AP Photo)

over fifty countries. In addition to *Yan Can Cook*, he has also hosted *Martin Yan Quick & Easy*, *Martin Yan's Chinatown Cooking*, *Martin Yan's Hong Kong*, and *Martin Yan's Hidden China*. In researching his work on Chinatown cooking, Yan visited eleven Chinatowns in seven countries, including the five Chinatowns of Toronto. He has also appeared as a guest judge on several episodes of *Iron Chef America*.

Yan considers legendary chef Julia Child, who once lived in China, to be one of his mentors. Child wrote the introduction to Yan's book *Martin Yan's Chinatown Cooking*. Yan has influenced American cooking with his Chinese dishes, but he has also been influenced by American and European chefs, including Paul Prudhomme, Jacques Pepin, and Wolfgang Puck.

LIFE'S WORK

Yan is the founder of the Yan Can Restaurant Group, which operates a chain of Yan Can restaurants in California. In 1985, he founded the Yan Can International Cooking School near San Francisco. Yan also established the Martin Yan Culinary Arts Center in the port city of Shenzhen, China in 2007.

In the United States as of 2012, there are over 66,000 Asian restaurants, of which over 52,000 are Chinese restaurants. The Chinese restaurant industry earns over $17.5 billion in annual sales. There are more Chinese restaurants in the United States than McDonald's, Burger King, and Wendy's branches combined. Chinese dishes once featured exotic recipes with hard-to-find lists of ingredients. Today, entire grocery store aisles or even entire grocery stores will stock nothing but those once-elusive ingredients. Asian foods are generally healthier, usually featuring one portion of meat protein for every three portions of vegetables. A wok, because of its shape, cooks food faster, using less fuel and requiring less oil for frying. Yan has been at the vanguard of significant changes in American cooking, both in restaurants and in homes across the country. As American tastes have developed, other Asian cultures and foods such as Thai and Vietnamese cuisines have grown in popularity.

A recognized expert in the practice of fusion cooking, Yan stresses the combination of flavors from varying ethnic cultures. Yan, who speaks four different dialects of Chinese, points out that China itself is a multiethnic country with over fifty ethnic groups, each with its own culture, history, and foods. As a teacher and traveler, Yan has visited all regions of China and gathered recipes from their differing styles of cooking, such

---

Yan Can Cook

The Chinese cuisine cooking show *Yan Can Cook* (1982) did for Chinese cuisine what Julia Child's show *The French Chef* (1962) did for French cuisine: *Yan Can Cook* introduced Chinese cuisine to an American market. Yan made the cuisine accessible to the American cook who was watching at home, thoroughly illustrating the ingredients, their preparation, and the whole cooking process in a non-threatening, bold manner flavored with Yan's self-deprecating wit.

Like any good teacher, Yan mixes patience, humor, and an encyclopedic knowledge of his subject to bring the art of Chinese cuisine down to the skill level of the average home viewer. Reinforcing his programs with several popular cookbooks and a website, Yan is mindful of his audience, never talking over the heads of his viewers or assuming a high level of expertise. For these reasons, *Yan Can Cook* has endured and has become a classic of its genre. In 2009, the show was named one of the greatest cooking shows of all time by the popular culinary website www.SlashFood.com.

---

as Cantonese, Sichuan, Hunan, Shanghai, Hong Kong, and Taiwan. Yan has described Taiwan as a microcosm of all Chinese cuisine and culture. Food in much of China is produced locally. Eating locally has been the rule in Chinese cooking for centuries.

Yan married Susan Yoshimura in December 1980. The couple has two sons. Yan, who jokes that he started at the bottom, "sampling food from the floor of my father's restaurant," was inducted into MenuMasters Hall of Fame in 2004. In 2005, Yan starred as one of the lead actors in the Hong Kong film *Rice Rhapsody*.

SIGNIFICANCE

A renowned food consultant and culinary instructor and author of over thirty cookbooks, including *Chinese Cooking for Dummies* (2000), *Martin Yan's Feast: The Best of Yan Can Cook* (1998), and *Martin Yan's Cooking at Home* (1999), Yan's influence on American cooking, from his home base in the San Francisco area, has been widespread. One of the prime movers in the fusion movement, Yan has garnered many honors, including the James Beard Award for best cooking show in 1994, an honorary doctorate in culinary arts from the prestigious Johnson and Wales University of Rhode Island in 1995, and the World's Cookbook Fair Award in 1999 for authoring *Martin Yan's Feast: The Best of Yan Can Cook* (1998).

Randy L. Abbott

FURTHER READING

Mallett, Evan F. "It's All in a Day's Wok for This Celebrated Chef." *Christian Science Monitor* 26 Feb. 1998: 15. Print. Highlights Martin Yan's *Yan Can Cook* show, featuring the chef's style and art of putting flavors together.

McEvoy, Hugh J. "The Cutting Edge of Culinary." *Prepared Foods* 171.9 (Sept. 2002): 32–34. Print. Coverage of the American Culinary Federation conference in Las Vegas, Nevada in 2002, including information on a seminar presented by Martin Yan.

Reiley, Laura. "Forefather of the Asian Invasion: Chef Martin Yan Encouraged Everyday Americans to Welcome the Wok into Their Homes." *St. Petersburg Times* 15 July 2009: 2E. Print. Presents a brief interview profiling Yan's experience as a chef, author, and teacher of the art of cooking Chinese food.

Yan, Martin "The Food Culture on Asia—A Personal View." *Harvard Asia Pacific Review* 8.2 (Winter 2005): 32–34. Print. Details Yan's personal history and experience with Asian food culture.

CHEN NING YANG

Scientist

Chen Ning Yang and his colleague Tsung-Dao Lee were jointly awarded the 1957 Nobel Prize in physics. Their work helped overturn a fundamental law of physics known as the Conservation of Parity Law, which held that elementary particle reactions always had right and left symmetry. Yang also partnered with Robert Mills to develop the Yang-Mills theory, which became an important fundamental of quantum physics. His research with Rodney J. Baxter resulted in the Yang-Baxter equation for statistical mechanics. In addition to his work as a scientist, Yang was a strong advocate for improving relations between China and the United States.

Born: October 1, 1922; Hefei, Province of Anhui (Anwhei), China
Full name: Chen Ning Yang
Birth name: Yáng Zhènníng
Also known as: Franklin Yang, Frank Yang, Yáng Zhènníng
Areas of achievement: Science and technology

EARLY LIFE

Chen Ning Yang was born on October 1, 1922 in Hefei, in the province of Anhui, China. Growing up, Yang lived in Peking (now Beijing), where he attended Chung Te Middle School before transferring to the Provincial Middle School in Hefei. The family later moved to Kunming, where Yang attended Kun Hua Middle School. He earned his BS from National Southwest Associated University in 1942 and received his MS from Tsinghua University in 1944. After graduating, Yang conducted research at National Southwest Associated University and taught classes at its affiliated middle school. During his early life, Yang read a biography of Benjamin Franklin that inspired him to later select Franklin as a nickname. Eventually Franklin was shortened to Frank.

In 1945, Tsinghua University awarded Yang a fellowship at the University of Chicago, where he studied particle physics and statistical mechanics. In Chicago, he met his colleague Tsung-Dao Lee. Yang completed his doctoral thesis, "On the Angular Distribution in Nuclear Reactions and Coincidence Measurements," in 1948, and earned his PhD. During the next year, he taught courses at the University of Chicago. He also spent time in Princeton, New Jersey, where he became affiliated with the Institute for Advanced Study in 1949. On August 26, 1950, Yang married Chih Li Tu. Their son, Franklin, was born in 1951. In 1953, Yang accepted an opportunity to work at the Brookhaven National Laboratory in Upton, New York. It was here that he and R. L. Mills devised the Yang-Mills theory. Yang became a full professor at the Princeton Institute for Advanced Study in 1955.

LIFE'S WORK

In 1956, Yan and Lee published an article "The Question of Parity Conservation in Weak Interactions" in the journal *Physical Review*. Their work with the subatomic particles known as k-mesons, also called the tau-theta puzzle, had surprising results. Yang and Lee projected that the conservation of parity law was invalid, because the particles did not react according to the law, which assumed that their behavior would be symmetrical.

Chen Ning Yang. (Getty Images)

After publishing their findings and suggesting tests that might be conducted to prove their hypothesis, Yang and Lee had their results verified by other scientists and were subsequently awarded the Nobel Prize in Physics in 1957. In 1958, Yang's second son, Gilbert, was born. That same year, Yang earned an honorary doctorate from Princeton. His daughter Eulee was born three years later, and after several more years, Yang became a US citizen. Yang taught at the Institute for Advanced Study until 1965. He spent the next summer at Brookhaven National Laboratory and became an Albert Einstein Professor of Physics and Director of the Institute of Theoretical Physics at the State University of New York (SUNY), Stony Brook.

In the 1970s, Yang visited China to promote work in the sciences. He helped establish a program that supported visiting scientists' research at SUNY. He also participated in the launching of the Foundation for the Center for Advanced Research at Zhongshan University. Yang became the first president of the National Association of Chinese Americans and a member of the Asian Pacific Physical Society. He began serving as Distinguished Professor-at-Large at the Chinese University of Hong Kong in 1986.

After his retirement in 1999, Yang returned to Tsing-hua University. Yang's first wife died in October 2003, and at the age of eighty-two, Yang married his second wife, Weng Fan, a twenty-eight-year-old graduate student.

SIGNIFICANCE

As attested by his many awards, honors, and prizes, and his multiple research articles, Yang's contributions to physics are many and varied. Yang's expertise has been applied in the fields of particle physics, nuclear physics, and theoretical physics. In addition to the Nobel Prize he shared with Lee, his public recognitions have included the Liberty Award (1986), the National Medal of Science (1986), the Oskar Klein Memorial Lecture and Medal (1988), the Benjamin Franklin Medal (1993), and the King Faisal International Prize (2001).

Yang's articles have been published in many science journals, including the *Bulletin of the American Mathematical Society*, *Physical Review*, the *Review of Modern Physics*, and the *Chinese Journal of Physics*. Yang has also served as a member of the Board of Trustees at the Woods Hole Oceanographic Institute, the Salk Institute for Biological Studies, the Stony Brook Foundation, and Rockefeller University. He has also served on the Board of Directors for the Neuroscience Institute and for Scientific American, Inc.

Cynthia J. W. Svoboda

FURTHER READING

Wu, Fa Yueh. "Professor C. N. Yang and Statistical Mechanics." *Exactly Solved Models: A Journey in Statistics Mechanics (Selected Papers with Commentaries (1963–2008)*. Print. London: World Scientific, 2009. Discusses Yang's contributions to physics, statistical mechanics, and mathematical physics.

Yang, Chen Ning. *Elementary Particles: A Short History of Some Discoveries in Atomic Physics*. Princeton, NJ: Princeton UP, 1962. Print. Presents a revised and illustrated edition of Yang's lecture on elementary particles delivered to students at Princeton University in 1959.

---. *Selected Papers 1945–80*. London: World Scientific, 2005. Print. Contains commentaries, letters, photos, articles, and lists of papers from Yang's personal collection of writings.

GENE LUEN YANG

Artist, writer, and educator

Chinese American comic artist Gene Luen Yang is best known for his graphic novel American Born Chinese *(2006), winner of the American Library Association's Michael L. Printz Award and finalist for the National Book Award. He has published several other comic books as well, and his work has appeared in various anthologies.*

Born: August 9, 1973; Alameda, California
Full name: Gene Luen Yang
Also known as: Gene Yang
Areas of achievement: Art, literature, education

EARLY LIFE

Gene Luen Yang began drawing comics when he was in the fifth grade and took a class on comics in high school. He attended the University of California, Berkeley, where he majored in computer science and minored in creative writing, then went on to earn his master's degree in education from California State University,

Gene Luen Yang. (Courtesy of Gene Luen Yang)

Hayward (now East Bay). While in graduate school, he explored the educational potential of the comic-book medium in his final project and used comics in an algebra class that he taught as a substitute teacher.

Yang started publishing comic books under the name Humble Comics in 1996. Parts of *American Born Chinese* originally appeared on the Internet and as mini-comics before First Second Books published the book as a graphic novel in 2006. Prior to this, Yang had published several other graphic novels featuring Asian American protagonists.

LIFE'S WORK

Yang has published a number of comic books. *The Rosary Comic Book* (2003), written and illustrated by Yang and colored by Lark Pien, tells the story of Jesus and his mother, Mary. The reader can read it or pray with it. Funded by the Xeric Grant, a prestigious comics industry grant, Yang wrote and illustrated *Gordon Yamatomo and the King of the Geeks* (2004). The story weaves together the title character's life as a school bully with his unexpected encounter with alien technology, showing how this encounter changes everything. *Loyola Chin and the San Peligran Order* (2004) centers on a high-school sophomore's adventures in dreams and her exploration of faith and love. In January 2010, SLG Publishing released *Gordon Yamatomo and the King of the Geeks* and *Loyola Chin and the San Peligran Order* in one volume under the title *Animal Crackers*.

Yang is probably best known for *American Born Chinese*, a graphic novel incorporating autobiographical elements from the artist's personal experience. This book features three main characters: Jin Wang, who was born in the United States, is of Chinese heritage, and constantly makes efforts to fit in at school; Danny, who is troubled by his cousin Chin-Kee's annual visit, as Chin-Kee's character represents multiple racial stereotypes of Asian Americans; and the Monkey King, who has to cope with the fact that, despite his superb martial arts skills and deity-like qualities, the other characters still view him as a monkey. All three characters are unhappy about who they are and have to struggle with identity. The book weaves these stories together with coherence and complexity. An excerpt from *American Born Chinese* was collected in *The Best American Comics 2008*, edited and introduced by comic artist Lynda Barry.

Gene Luen Yang's *American Born Chinese*

The tremendous success of Yang's 2006 graphic novel, *American Born Chinese*, established Yang as one of the most important new voices in American comics during the 2000s. Yang's visual style is remarkable; it is a modified clear-line style involving thick black lines, flat colors, and no shading. The book details the life of a young second-generation Chinese American alongside the legendary folktale of the Monkey King.

Like Yang, the novel's Jin Wang does not fit in either the world of his first-generation immigrant parents or the world of the white suburban mainstream. Instead, Jin must make his own way. Yang's art similarly makes its own way through the comic genre, fusing a Disney-esque style with Asian overtones. Yang also reconciles Eastern and Western religion as the Monkey King recovers his identity. A devout Catholic, Yang depicts the Monkey King giving offerings to baby Jesus after completing his journey to the West.

Jin is a typical teenage boy, and Yang treats his young-adult readers as such, indulging in many low-brow gags and relatable cultural references. Yang's slapstick delivers comic relief as he delves into the darker themes of alienation, shame, and prejudice while exploring cultural identity. *American Born Chinese* juxtaposes American teenage angst against a backdrop of anti-Asian prejudice, both among society at large and among Asian Americans trying to escape their roots.

Yang's short piece "The Motherless One" is collected in *Up All Night: A Short Story Collection* (2008), targeted at young adult readers. Drawing inspiration from the Monkey King's tale, Yang tells the story of a monkey trying to figure out why he was born out of a rock. In 2008 and 2009, he published *Prime Baby*, an eighteen-week comic series, in the *New York Times Magazine*. First Second, an imprint of Roaring Brook Press, released *Prime Baby* in book format in 2010.

Collaborating with Derek Kirk Kim, Yang published *The Eternal Smile* in 2009. The three stories in this collection—"Duncan's Kingdom," "Gran'pa Greenbax and the Eternal Smile," and "Urgent Request"—explore the connection between reality and fantasy. Yang also contributed a short story, "The Blue Scorpion and Chung," to the collection *Secret Identities: The Asian American Superhero Anthology* (2009). His graphic novel *Level Up*, illustrated by Thien Pham and published by First Second in 2011, was named a *New York Times* Notable Children's Book for young adults.

SIGNIFICANCE

American Born Chinese was the first graphic novel to be nominated for a National Book Award. It won the American Library Association's Michael L. Printz Award and an Eisner Award for Best Graphic Album—New and has been published in more than ten languages. *The Eternal Smile* won an Eisner Award as well. Many of Yang's works feature teenage characters and explore the issue of identity and school life, thus appealing to young adult readers of differing cultural heritages. Besides his artistic and literary contribution to comics, Yang is also an advocate for the educational value of comics, and he has spoken at various events and venues about the potential of comics as a medium.

Lan Dong

FURTHER READING

Fu, Binbin. "*American Born Chinese*." *MELUS* 32.3 (2007): 274–76. Print. A review that praises Yang's contribution to challenging racial stereotypes of Asian Americans in comics.

Krajewski, Sarah, and Melissa Wadsworth-Miller. "Graphic Novels + Teacher Research = Student Success." *English Record* 50.1 (2009): 9–16. Print. Investigates the usage of graphic novels in English classrooms by using *American Born Chinese* as an example.

Yang, Gene Luen. "The *Booklist* Interview: Gene Luen Yang." By Gillian Engberg. *Booklist* 103.13 (2007): 75. Print. Addresses Yang's experience in creating comics, how he reconfigured the Monkey King's story in *American Born Chinese*, and the possibilities of incorporating comics into education.

JEFF YANG

Entrepreneur, journalist, writer

Jeff Yang is a prolific columnist, writer, and entrepreneur in the Asian American media and entertainment industry. His articles have appeared in the Village Voice, Vibe, Spin, *and the* San Francisco Chronicle, *where he contributed to the Asian Pop column for eight years. He founded* A. Magazine *and* Stir, *the first nationally distributed Asian American television show, and most recently he edited* Secret Identities, *the first Asian American superhero anthology.*

Born: March 14, 1968; Brooklyn, New York
Full name: Jeffrey Chih-Ho Yang
Also known as: Yang Zhìhé
Areas of achievement: Journalism, business, entertainment

EARLY LIFE

Jeffrey Chih-Ho Yang was born on March 14, 1968, in Brooklyn, New York. His parents, Dr. David C. Yang and Bailing Yang, were immigrants from Taiwan. Yang attended St. Ann's School in Brooklyn, where he graduated in 1985. He entered Harvard University and graduated in 1989 with a BA in psychology and social relations.

Eventually, Yang was recruited to relaunch Harvard's Asian American student newsletter *East Wind*, running it as an independent publication. Initially, the publication was supported by student grants, later by advertising and sponsorship of businesses and corporations.

LIFE'S WORK

Upon graduation, Yang and a small group of like-minded friends decided to create the pilot issue of *A. Magazine*, a periodical devoted to Asian American culture and lifestyle. Yang recruited a volunteer staff and began publishing the magazine on a quarterly basis, adding the subtitle "Inside Asian America." The magazine soon began to publish on a bimonthly basis and hired its first full time staff, which ultimately included Yang as editor in chief. In 1997, the staff wrote the magazine's first book, *Eastern Standard Time: A Guide to Asian Influence on American Culture from Astro Boy to Zen Buddhism.*

During this period, Yang wrote for the alternative weekly the *Village Voice*, serving first as a regular television and film critic and later as an official columnist. For the Ballantine Publishing Group, Yang cowrote the *New York Times* best-selling autobiography *I Am Jackie Chan: My Life in Action* (1997).

In 1999, Yang launched the Asians United to Raise Awareness Fund (AURA) in commemoration of *A. Magazine*'s tenth anniversary. On the first anniversary of the September 11, 2001, terrorist attacks, the AURA Fund organized the concert and commemorative event My America. Yang collaborated with musical artist Kevin So on an anthem celebrating the legacy of Asian immigrants in America. So later recorded the song "Our America" on his 2010 album *Life Solo Akoustic*.

In the early 2000s, *A. Magazine* raised funds to launch AOnline.com, an online community site for Asian Americans. The company behind *A. Magazine* was renamed A. Media. A. Media expanded quickly, acquiring companies and setting up offices in San Francisco and Los Angeles. Following turbulence in the stock market in 2000, however, the board of directors forced A. Media to merge with Click2Asia, and subsequently Yang left the company.

Yang and several friends and colleagues launched a new consulting company, Factor, Inc, which was then hired by the Starz Encore Group's International Channel and San Francisco–based television station KTSF

Jeff Yang. (© Todd France/Corbis)

to develop and produce *Stir*, a magazine-format television program that targeted Asian American youth. The show was successful, earned a local Emmy, and played an important part on Comcast's AZN TV cable network.

In 2003, Yang took over the column Asian Pop at the *San Francisco Chronicle*. Initially, the column focused solely on Asian popular culture, but over time Yang expanded its content to include wider topics, subjects ranging from technology to politics. During the same year, Yang published *Once Upon a Time in China* (2003), a popular history of Greater Chinese cinema.

When Factor's partners decided to scale back the company, Yang brought the business to the firm Applied Info Partners. Afterwards, Yang joined the consumer trends firm Iconoculture, rising to the position of senior director and consumer strategist, a position he maintained as of 2012.

Yang created the first graphic novel anthology of Asian American superhero stories, *Secret Identities* (2009). His creative partners were actor Parry Shen, education specialist Keith Chow, and indie comics artist/designer Jerry Ma. A second volume of the anthology, *Secret Identities: Shattered*, is planned for 2012.

SIGNIFICANCE

Under Yang's vision and leadership, *A. Magazine* became the most widely circulating Asian American magazine in the United States. Additionally, Yang's books on Asian and Asian American pop culture and cinema remain popular reference works in colleges and universities. Yang was the first regular columnist of Asian American descent to work on the *Village Voice*, and as of 2012 Asian Pop was the only column published by a major newspaper to focus exclusively on Asian and Asian American issues. Yang continues to build his body of work and sphere of influence with his *Wall Street Journal* column and forthcoming volume of *Secret Identities*, to be published in 2012.

Eugenia Beh

FURTHER READING

Yang, Jeff. "Asian Pop." *SF Gate*. Hearst Communications, 9 Sept. 2011. Web. 26 Mar. 2012. An archive of Yang's biweekly online column on Asian and Asian American media and culture.

---. *Once Upon a Time in China: A Guide to Hong Kong, Taiwanese, and Mainland Chinese Cinema*. New York: Atria, 2003. Print. Comprehensive guide to the cinematic history of Hong Kong, Taiwan, and mainland China, including a preface by Yang on his introduction to Chinese cinema, as well as an FAQ and resource guide at the end.

---, ed. *Secret Identities: The Asian American Superhero Anthology*. New York: New Press, 2009. Print. Compilation of twenty-six original stories featuring Asian American superheroes, including a preface by Yang on how he came up with the idea.

JOHN YANG

Broadcast journalist

After beginning his career as a newspaper reporter at the Boston Globe, *John Yang worked as a reporter for* Time *magazine for five years. He later wrote for the* Wall Street Journal *and the* Washington Post. *Yang left the* Washington Post *in late 1999 after being offered a job as a Washington, DC–based correspondent with ABC News. He is best known for his career in broadcast journalism, especially with NBC News and ABC News.*

Born: February 10, 1958; Chillicothe, Ohio
Full name: John Yang
Area of achievement: Journalism

EARLY LIFE

John Yang was born on February 10, 1958, in Chillicothe, Ohio. He graduated from Western Reserve Academy, a private boarding school in Hudson, Ohio, in 1975. Yang received his college degree from Wesleyan University in 1980. He had a passion for political journalism and was particularly adept at writing about the US Congress. After college, he took a position at the *Boston Globe* newspaper.

In 1985, Yang joined the *Washington Post*. As both a reporter and an editor, Yang covered economic policy in the paper's business section and also planned political features. He remained with the newspaper for over ten years.

In 2000, Yang moved to ABC News. As a television journalist, he covered Republican Governor George W. Bush's presidential campaign. Following the Republican primaries, Yang covered Democratic Party candidate Al Gore's presidential campaign through the general election and the state of Florida's recount. Following the terrorist attacks of September 11, 2001, Yang reported from the Pentagon, sharing in a George Foster Peabody and an Alfred I. DuPont–Columbia University Award for ABC's coverage. For the next two years, Yang was based in Jerusalem, working as ABC's Middle East correspondent. In 2005, Yang was part of ABC's news team covering the death of Pope John Paul II. In 2006, Yang reported on the sex scandal involving former Congressman Mark Foley.

LIFE'S WORK

In 2007, Yang joined NBC News and became the network's White House correspondent. The 2008 election cycle found Yang once again covering political campaigns leading up to the presidential race. After the election, Yang was transferred from NBC's Washington bureau to its Chicago bureau in 2009. Contributing to *NBC Nightly News with Brian Williams*, *Today,* and MSNBC, Yang has reported from a wide variety of venues across the Midwest.

Yang is one of the few openly gay journalists reporting for a major network. Yang once said that being both Asian and gay in a professional arena that is not known for employing openly gay or Asian people has given him insight into being an advocate for minority issues and how to be respectful of minority viewpoints. Yang is affiliated with the National Lesbian and Gay Journalists Association.

SIGNIFICANCE

Yang is one of the better known journalists in America. As a gay Asian man, he represents two minorities that are underrepresented in the news business. A member of the Asian American Journalists Association, Yang has a knack for covering political stories, which, combined with his considerable knowledge of business, has made him a busy field reporter for both ABC and NBC over the past decade. Whether covering the Israeli-Palestinian conflict as ABC's Middle East correspondent or covering developments at the White House for NBC, Yang has consistently demonstrated an even-handedness and a sense of professionalism in his reporting.

Randy L. Abbott

FURTHER READING

Iwata, Edward. "Stepping Out: Gay Journalists Meet Openly to Debate Their Struggles, and Roles, in the Media." *Editor & Publisher Magazine* (22 Aug 1992): n. page. Print. Reports on the first conference of the National Lesbian & Gay Journalists Association, held in San Francisco in 1992.

Kregloe, Karman. "Gay Newsmen—A Clearer Picture." *Gay Newsmen.* AfterElton.com, 13 May 2007. Web. 4 Apr. 2012. Explores the decisions of gay television newsmen to out themselves, featuring nine journalists' profiles, including one for John Yang.

RODNEY JAMES TAKASHI YANO

Soldier

While serving in the US Army during the Vietnam War, Rodney James Takashi Yano saved members of his helicopter crew from serious injury or death when a white phosphorous grenade exploded prematurely and started to ignite ammunition on board the helicopter. Yano threw exploding ammunition out of the helicopter while suffering severe wounds himself. He died from these wounds, and was posthumously awarded the Medal of Honor.

Born: December 13, 1943; Kealake Kua, Hawaii
Died: January 1, 1969; Near Bien Hoa, Republic of Vietnam
Full name: Rodney James Takashi Yano
Area of achievement: Military

EARLY LIFE

Rodney James Takashi Yano was born on December 13, 1943, in Kealake Kua, Hawaii, to Mr. and Mrs. Richard S. Yano. His military record lists his religion as Roman Catholic. He joined the US Army in Honolulu, Hawaii.

LIFE'S WORK

The US Army stationed Sergeant First Class Yano in Vietnam in January 1968. He served in the Air Cavalry Troop of the Eleventh Armored Cavalry regiment. On January 1, 1969, he was serving as the crew chief on the regiment's command and control helicopter, from which the commander was directing the actions of the unit's troops. While engaging enemy soldiers over heavy jungle terrain, Yano maintained suppressing fire and dropped

Rodney J. T. Yano's Medal of Honor Citation

Sergeant First Class Rodney J. T. Yano distinguished himself while serving with the Air Cavalry Troop in Vietnam in 1969. Yano was the crew chief aboard the troop's command-and-control helicopter during action against enemy forces entrenched in the dense jungle. From an exposed position facing intense small arms and antiaircraft fire, he delivered suppressive fire upon the enemy forces. He marked their positions with smoke and white phosphorous grenades, thus enabling his troop commander to accurately direct artillery fire against the hostile emplacements. A grenade, exploding prematurely, covered him with burning phosphorous and left him severely wounded. Flaming fragments within the helicopter caused supplies and ammunition to detonate. Dense white smoke filled the aircraft, obscuring the pilot's vision and causing him to lose control. Although he only had the use of only one arm and was partially blinded by the initial explosion, Yano completely disregarded his welfare and began hurling blazing ammunition from the helicopter. In so doing, he inflicted additional wounds upon himself, yet he persisted until the danger was past. Yano's courage and concern for his comrades averted loss of life and additional injury to the rest of the crew. For his conspicuous gallantry at the cost of his life, Yano was posthumously awarded the Medal of Honor.

detonate the ammunition on the helicopter, endangering everyone on board. While covered with burning phosphorous, Yano began throwing ammunition out of the helicopter. He was partially blinded by the exploding grenade and could use only one arm, but he continued to throw out the burning ammunition supplies until the danger had passed. He died from the wounds he suffered during the incident. Yano is buried at the National Memorial Cemetery of the Pacific in Honolulu, Hawaii, and his name is on the Vietnam Memorial in Washington, DC.

SIGNIFICANCE

Because of his selfless actions in protecting the lives of his fellow soldiers despite being gravely wounded, Yano was awarded the United States' highest military honor, the Medal of Honor. President Richard M. Nixon bestowed the posthumous award on Yano at a ceremony at the White House on April 7, 1970. His family accepted the medal on his behalf. The Sergeant Rodney J. Yano Main Library at Schofield Barracks, Hawaii, is named in his honor. In January 1997, the Military Sealift Command named a converted merchant containership the USNS *Yano* in his honor. His family attended the dedication service for this vessel, and his mother served as matron of honor for the ceremonies.

Mark S. Joy

FURTHER READING

Murphy, Edward F. *Vietnam Medal of Honor Heroes.* Rev. ed. New York: Ballantine, 2005. Print. Includes the citations from the Medal of Honor award issued by the government.

United States. Congress. Senate. Committee on Veterans Affairs. *Vietnam Era Medal of Honor Recipients, 1964–1972.* Washington, DC: Government Printing Office, 1973. Print. Collection of the award commendations for all U. S. servicemen who earned the Medal of Honor in Vietnam.

smoke grenades. He also dropped white phosphorous grenades to mark the location of the enemy forces so that the troop commander could direct fire efficiently.

White phosphorous grenades burn at an extremely high temperature and are very hard to extinguish. On the helicopter, one of these grenades exploded prematurely, gravely wounding Yano. The resulting fire started to

TARO YASHIMA

Japanese-born artist and writer

Best known for his spare, delicate stories of childhood and prewar Japan, Taro Yashima enjoyed a successful career as an award-winning illustrator and author of children's literature. Drawing from his experiences in Japan, Yashima successfully captured the essence of

childhood for both Japanese and Japanese American children.

Born: September 21, 1908; Kagoshima, Kyushu, Japan
Died: June 30, 1994; Los Angeles, California

Full name: Taro Yashima (TAH-roh ya-SHE-ma)
Birth name: Jun Atsushi Iwamatsu
Also known as: Atsushi Iwamatsu
Areas of achievement: Literature, art, activism

EARLY LIFE

Taro Yashima was born Jun Atsushi Iwamatsu in the small farming village of Nejime in Kagoshima, Japan. The son of a rural physician, Iwamatsu attended school in a neighboring city and later enrolled in the Imperial Art Academy in Tokyo from 1927 to 1930. After three years, Iwamatsu was expelled for not adhering to the military requirements of the university. Around this time, he married artist Tomoe Iwamatsu, and together they became involved in an artist-activist movement that worked to highlight the plight of the common man and educate audiences about Japan's militaristic propaganda. The couple often hosted antiwar art exhibits that included pieces ridiculing the army.

Around 1931, and despite the popularity of Iwamatsu's work, both he and Tomoe were marked as antiestablishment dissidents and imprisoned for several months. Prisoners were starved and beaten into confessions, often for crimes they did not commit. Tomoe, who was pregnant at the time, was also the victim of beatings. She was released during the eighth month of her pregnancy and gave birth to their son Mako Iwamatsu (later a successful actor in the United States) on December 19, 1933. After providing a false confession, Iwamatsu was released from prison toward the end of 1933 as well.

In 1939, with the assistance of Tomoe's father, the two artists fled Japan to avoid Iwamatsu's impending draft into the army. Leaving their young son behind to live with his grandparents, they traveled to New York City with tourist visas to visit art museums. They enrolled in the Art Students' League in New York City, where they remained until 1941. Not long after the beginning of World War II, Iwamatsu joined the US Army, serving in the Office of War Information and the Office of Strategic Services, where he rendered political cartoons aimed at Japanese soldiers fighting against the United States. Due to the nature of his work, he adopted the pseudonym Taro Yashima—his wife adopting the pseudonym Mitsu Yashima—to protect their son and family back in Japan.

In 1943, Yashima published his first book, *The New Sun*, a graphic novel and memoir that described his early years and imprisonment in pre–World War II Japan. Though not a huge success, the work did receive praise from literary critics and successfully humanized the Japanese experience for Americans. Three years later, he published his

only other work for adults, *Horizon Is Calling* (1947), another graphic memoir detailing his life in Japan.

The family was able to send for their son in 1948, and a daughter, Momo, was born soon after. Around that time the Yashimas became naturalized citizens.

LIFE'S WORK

Yashima is best known as a children's book author and illustrator. In the early 1950s, Yashima suffered from stomach ulcers. It was during this time that his daughter was a great comfort to him. As a way to express his gratitude and preserve memories from his childhood in Japan, Yashima began to tell her stories. *The Village Tree* (1953), Yashima's first children's picture book, describes his childhood memory of a tree that grew along the bank of a stream in his village in Japan. Critics praised his sparse, delicate illustrations and his simple prose. His success led him to publish another picture book about childhood in Japan, *Plenty to Watch* (1954), with his wife. Around that time Yashima moved his family to California, where he and his wife established the Yashima Art Institute in Los Angeles, and where Yashima was to spend the rest of his career.

In 1955, he published *Crow Boy*, one of his most well-known children's books. Based on a classmate in Japan, the book received immediate recognition from literary critics and was awarded a 1956 Caldecott Honor for distinguished illustration in an American children's book, as well as the Child Study Association of America's Wel-Met Children's Book Award.

In 1958, Yashima published *The Umbrella*, the first of three books featuring his daughter Momo. Receiving the 1959 Caldecott Honor for illustration (and securing his career as a sought-after Japanese illustrator), *The Umbrella* crossed cultural barriers and portrayed for readers the universality of childhood. Yashima wrote and illustrated several more books representing Japanese culture, including another with his wife, and created artwork for many other picture books. His *Seashore Story* (1967) received a *New York Times* Best Illustrated Children's Books of the Year citation in 1967 and the 1968 Caldecott Honor.

A year later he and filmmaker Glenn L. Johnson traveled back to Yashima's village in Japan, to visit classmates and friends whom he had not seen in over forty years. They created the short film *Taro Yashima's Golden Village* (1971). Throughout his career Yashima received two Southern California Council on Literature of Children and Young People Awards, and was honored with the University of Southern Mississippi's Silver Medallion for contributions to the field of children's literature. Three of his books were adapted into films for educational use.

SIGNIFICANCE

Taro Yashima produced delicate, moving portraits of Japanese life that enabled many American readers to better understand the experiences of Japanese Americans; he accomplished this during a time when Japanese artists were largely stereotyped. A strong activist for peace and social justice, Yashima used his artistic talents to illuminate the universality of the human experience in award-winning picture books for children and his work for the US government. Collectively, his efforts helped to pave the way for future Asian American children's authors and artists.

Jamie Campbell Naidoo

FURTHER READING

Johnson, Glenn L. "Golden Village of Taro Yashima's Books." *Horn Book* Apr. 1967: 183–91. Print. Johnson describes his and Yashima's journey to Nejime to record the film *Taro Yashima's Golden Village*, which details the artist's reunion with classmates he had not seen for over forty years.

Shibusawa, Naoko. "'The Artist Belongs to the People': The Odyssey of Taro Yashima." *Journal of Asian American Studies* 8.3 (October 2005): 257–75. Print. Critically examines elements of Yashima's *The New Sun* and describes his role with the Office of War Information and the Office of Strategic Services during World War II.

"Taro Yashima Papers." *de Grummond Collection*. University of Southern Mississippi, 15 May 2002. Web. 26 Mar. 2012. Archival collection of the Yashimas' letters, original manuscripts, and photographs.

Yashima, Taro. *The New Sun*. Reprint. Honolulu: U of Hawaii P, 2008. Print. This graphic memoir describes the harsh conditions Yashima experienced as an artist-activist in Japan prior to World War II and his immigration to the United States.

MINORU YASUI

Lawyer and social reformer

Minoru Yasui was a Japanese American lawyer and civil rights activist. During the height of World War II, at the age of twenty-six, he gained international notoriety for deliberately violating the wartime curfew established for Japanese Americans in Portland, Oregon. His actions magnified the civil rights debate surrounding the constitutionality of wartime internment and prosecution of Americans from different cultural backgrounds.

Born: October 19, 1916; Hood River, Oregon
Died: November 12, 1986; Denver, Colorado
Full name: Minoru Yasui
Also known as: Min Yasui
Area of achievement: Social issues

EARLY LIFE

Minoru Yasui was the third son born to Shidzuyo and Masuo Yasui in Hood River, Oregon. His father and mother were both born in Japan and came to the United States in 1903 and 1912, respectively. His father was a successful agriculturalist, businessman, and prominent member of the city's community and its Japanese Methodist church. Yasui's parents placed great emphasis on maintaining the cultural traditions of their native Japan, as their son would do throughout his life and work.

Yasui earned a bachelor's degree from the University of Oregon in 1937, supplementing his academics with Army Reserve Officers' Training Corps (ROTC) training and earning a commission as a second lieutenant in the Army Reserve upon graduation. He graduated from the University of Oregon Law School in 1939 and shortly thereafter passed the state bar exam.

In 1940 Yasui officially forfeited his American citizenship in order to accept a job as a clerk at the Japanese Consulate in Chicago, Illinois. In December of 1941, Japanese forces attacked Pearl Harbor. The attacks created a nationwide mistrust of Japanese Americans, which affected Yasui immediately. He returned to Hood River to find that his father had been imprisoned as an enemy alien. When Yasui attempted to report for his army assignment he was ordered off a military base and deemed unfit for service, despite his officer commission.

LIFE'S WORK

Like many Japanese Americans, Yasui was quick to regard the notion that American citizens could so

Minoru Yasui. (Time & Life Pictures/Getty Images)

suddenly be considered second-class citizens, or even as potential enemies, as unconstitutional. Late on the night of March 28, 1942, Yasui entered a Portland police station and demanded to be arrested under violation of Military Proclamation No. 3—a curfew that required all Japanese Americans to be in their homes after 8:00 p.m.

Yasui spent months in jail awaiting trial before a judge determined that the law had in fact applied to Yasui, since he had previously forfeited his US citizenship and was thus an enemy alien. He was sentenced to nine months in solitary confinement. In 1943 the Supreme Court overruled the lower court's designation of Yasui as an enemy alien, because he had forfeited his citizenship as a diplomatic formality for employment. Yasui was

removed from solitary confinement and in 1943 was sent to an internment camp, where he stayed until 1944.

At the end of the war Yasui established a private law practice in Denver, Colorado, where he remained a prominent civil rights litigator. His work in Colorado expanded his civil rights efforts from the plight of Japanese Americans to include work with African Americans, Native Americans, and Hispanics. He also fought diligently against commercial interests eager to develop Denver's oldest residential communities. He died in Denver in 1986 at the age of seventy.

SIGNIFICANCE

In addition to his work in civil rights litigation, Minoru Yasui served prominently in nearly a hundred Denver-area civic organizations during his lifetime. He was a major participant in the Japanese American Citizens League, which sought reparations for the harsh treatment of their citizenry during World War II. The League would play a key role in the conception of the United States Civil Liberties Act, passed by Congress in 1988.

John Pritchard

FURTHER READING

Aitken, Robert, and Marilyn Aitken. "Japanese American Internment." *Litigation* 37.2 (2011): 59–70. Print. Discusses four court cases filed by Japanese Americans against the internment during World War II, including Yasui's court case.

Ng, Wendy. *Japanese American Internment During World War II: A History and Reference Guide*. New York: Greenwood, 2001. 78–82. Print. Includes biographical information on Minoru Yasui.

"Notable Oregonians: Minoru Yasui—Civil Rights Leader." *Oregon Blue Book*. Oregon State Archives, Jan. 2011. Web. 3 Mar. 2012. One-page overview of Yasui's life, with links to other resources.

Yasui, Minoru. "Minidoka." *And Justice for All: An Oral History of the Japanese American Detention Camps*. Ed. John Tateishi. Seattle: U of Washington P, 1984. Print. Presents Yasui's account of his life, work, and imprisonment.

SHING-TUNG YAU

Chinese-born mathematician

During his years of extensive work in geometrical analysis, Yau has made a profound impact in many

areas of mathematics and physics, ranging from new insights and developments in topology, algebraic geometry, and representation theory to a better understanding of partial differential equations, general relativity, and elementary particle physics.

Born: April 4, 1949; Swatow, China
Full name: Shing-Tung Yau (SHIHNG TOONG YOW)
Area of achievement: Mathematics

EARLY LIFE

The fifth of eight children born to Chen Ying Chiou and Yeuk-Lam Leung Chiou, Shing-Tung Yau was encouraged by his parents to get a good education. Shortly after his birth in southern China, his family fled to Hong Kong to escape the new Communist regime. They lived in poverty in a village outside of Hong Kong City, where Yau became the leader of a street gang. Through his father's guidance and influence, however, he gradually left the streets and developed a deep interest in philosophy and mathematics. When his father passed away in 1963, Yau helped supplement his family's income by serving as a math tutor.

After graduating from Pui Ching Middle School in 1965, Yau continued his education at Chung Chi

Shing-Tung Yau. (Getty Images)

College in Hong Kong. In 1969, he received a fellowship from the International Business Machines (IBM) Corporation to pursue his mathematical studies at the University of California, Berkeley. Studying under the tutelage of renowned mathematician Shiing-Shen Chern, Yau earned his doctorate in mathematics in 1971. From 1971 to 1972, he taught at the Institute for Advanced Study at Princeton University. After a short stint at the State University of New York at Stony Brook (1972–74), Yau became an assistant professor of mathematics at Stanford University. Between 1979 and 1984, he again worked at the Institute for Advanced Study at Princeton. After serving as the chairman of the Department of Mathematics at the University of California, San Diego, Yau accepted a position as professor of mathematics at Harvard University in 1988.

LIFE'S WORK

Yau specializes in differential geometry, which deals with the calculations of figures in more than three dimensions. In 1976, he made his mark on the mathematical world when he solved the Calabi conjecture, proposed by celebrated mathematician Eugenio Calabi in 1954. Calabi reasoned that certain specific geometric structures are allowed under specified topological conditions, but he could not mathematically prove it; Yau solved the equation that proved the existence of these geometric structures, now referred to as Calabi-Yau manifolds. The special properties of these manifolds have proved to be indispensable for the compacting of the proposed extra dimensions of superstring theory, which attempts to explain all the particles and fundamental forces of nature by increasing the four observable dimensions typically used in physics to as many as twenty-six. Calabi-Yau manifolds provide the needed conceptual understanding by allowing the extra dimensions to be wrapped or curled upon themselves.

By studying the stability of minimal surfaces—that is, surfaces in which a deformation creates a surface with a large area—and their behavior in space and time, Yau proved Einstein's positive-mass conjecture in 1979 by showing that the sum of all of the mass in the universe is positive. In doing so, he validated a part of Einstein's theory of relativity. Yau then established that black holes can indeed be formed and that they exist in the universe. In addition, he helped resolve the Smith conjecture involving cyclic groups acting on a sphere and played a part in proving the Donaldson-Uhlenbeck-Yau theorem, which established the existence of Hermitian-Einstein metrics.

To help advance the development of mathematics in China, Yau invested his time, money, and energy to help establish the Institute of Mathematical Sciences at the Chinese University of Hong Kong in 1993, the Morningside Center of Mathematics in Beijing in 1996, and the Center of Mathematical Sciences at Zhejiang University in 2002. A strong ambassador for mathematics worldwide, Yau became the director of all three institutes and has helped organize several professional conferences on mathematics throughout the world. He has received numerous awards for his contributions to mathematics and scientific development, including the Oswald Veblen Prize in Geometry (1981), the Fields Medal (1982), the Crafoord Prize of the Royal Swedish Academy of Sciences (1994), the US National Medal of Science (1997), China's International Scientific and Technological Cooperation Award (2003), and the international Wolf Prize in Mathematics (2010).

SIGNIFICANCE

Referred to as the "Emperor of Math" by many of his colleagues, Yau is considered one of the foremost authorities in the field of geometric analysis, including its history, its development, its present status, where it is going, and how it interfaces with theoretical physics. His establishment of Calabi-Yau manifolds provides a conceptual foundation for elementary particle physics and the very nature of the universe. His contributions to solving a variety of nonlinear partial differential equations and better understanding the topology of differentiable manifolds have greatly expanded the field of mathematics. At the institutions of higher learning where he has served, Yau has helped develop some of the most brilliant mathematicians in the world.

Alvin K. Benson

FURTHER READING

Greene, Brian. *The Elegant Universe: Superstrings, Hidden Dimensions, and the Quest for the Ultimate Theory.* New York: Vintage, 2000. Print. Includes a description of Yau's contributions to the conceptual understanding of the geometry associated with multi-dimensions.

Overbye, Dennis. "Shing-Tung Yau: The Emperor of Math." *New York Times.* New York Times, 17 Oct. 2006. Web. 4 Apr. 2012. Discusses Yau's biography, his work, and his status in and relationship with China.

Yau, Shing-Tung, and Steven J. Nadis. *The Shape of Inner Space: String Theory and the Geometry of the Universe's Hidden Dimensions.* New York: Basic, 2010. Print. Contains an explanation of Calabi-Yau manifolds and their applications in differential geometry and theoretical physics.

LAURENCE YEP

Writer and playwright

Best known for his contribution to Chinese American literature for children and young adults, Yep has written numerous books in the fantasy, mystery, science fiction, historical fiction, realistic fiction, and picture book genres. He has also written numerous plays. Much of his work centers on the theme of cultural alienation and racial discrimination against early Chinese immigrants.

Born: June 14, 1948; San Francisco, California
Full name: Laurence Michael Yep
Area of achievement: Literature

EARLY LIFE

Laurence Michael Yep, born in San Francisco, is the second son of Thomas Gim and Franche Lee Yep. His father immigrated to the United States from China at age ten and settled in San Francisco. His mother was born in Ohio, raised in West Virginia, and later moved with her family to California. Yep grew up in a predominately African American neighborhood, living above his father's grocery store.

Yep attended a Catholic grammar school in Chinatown where both Chinese and English were spoken. Because he lived in one neighborhood but went to school in another, Yep often felt isolated. He turned to fantasy and science fiction novels to pass the time. At Ignatius High School, he was very interested in chemistry but was also inclined toward writing. In 1966, he entered Marquette University in Wisconsin to study journalism. He reconsidered his major after failing one of his assignments. His professor commented on the article, noting that Yep seemed to be better at writing fiction than facts. In 1968, his first science fiction story, "The Selchey Kids," was published in a magazine called *If* and included in the anthology *World's Best Science Fiction, 1969*.

Homesick for San Francisco, Yep transferred to the University of California Santa Cruz, and received his BA in 1970. He pursued his graduate degree at the State University of New York (SUNY) at Buffalo and earned his PhD in English in 1975.

LIFE'S WORK

After graduate school, Yep taught at SUNY Buffalo, San Jose City College, and the Mountain View campus of Foothill College in California. Later, he also taught writing and Asian American studies at the University of California, Berkeley and Santa Barbara, but he most enjoyed being a full-time writer. In 1971, Yep's college friend Joanne Ryder, who was then a children's book editor at HarperCollins, asked Yep to write a young adult novel. He agreed and wrote his first science fiction novel, *Sweetwater* (1973). Ryder and Yep later married.

In 1975 Yep received his doctorate and published his second children's novel, *Dragonwings*, which has won a variety of awards. Since Yep's start in writing science fiction and fantasy, he has expanded into other genres, such as historical fiction, realistic fiction, mysteries, folk tales, picture books, and plays, with a total of over sixty titles published by 2010. At times he has produced four or five books in a single year.

Yep is well known for his nine historical novels in the Golden Mountain Chronicles series, which portrays a Chinese American family spanning seven generations from 1849 to 1995. Within the series, *Dragonwings* and *Dragon's Gate* (1993) are highly acclaimed. His fantasy novels, including *Dragon of the Lost Sea* (1982), *Dragon Steel* (1985), *Dragon Cauldron* (1991), and *Dragon War* (1992), tell the tale of Dragon Princess Shimmer as she works to restore her homeland. Using characters from Chinese folklore, Yep fills the books with dragons, the Monkey King of Chinese legend, wizards, and magicians.

He has also tried his hand at writing mystery novels and published four Chinatown mysteries. In addition, Yep has written a number of picture books: *The Man Who Tricked a Ghost* (1993) and *The Boy Who Swallowed Snakes* (1994) are two examples. His realistic fiction, *Ribbons* (1996) and *The Amah* (2002), narrate the stories of the heroines' ballet lessons and

---

Laurence Yep's *Dragonwings*

Dragonwings (1975), Yep's best-known historical fiction novel, won numerous awards, including the Newbery Honor Book in 1976 and the International Children's Book Award. The story is told through the eyes of an eight-year-old boy named Moon Shadow, who left his mother in China to join his father, Windrider, in San Francisco. Windrider works in a clan-owned laundry in Chinatown and dreams about flying. As the clan elder makes fun of him, Windrider leaves to repair small machines for white people. His son respects him and helps him achieve his dream. After much frustration, difficulties, and correspondence with the Wright Brothers, Windrider finally constructs an airplane named Dragonwings and flies it in front of his proud clan. The story was inspired by the account of a Chinese flier named Fung Joe Guey, who built a biplane and flew it in Piedmont, California, in September, 1909. Yep seamlessly builds into the story's plot the 1906 San Francisco fire, which compounds Windrider's hardships in making his dream come true.

---

their families. In 1993, he adapted *Dragonwings* for the stage. His autobiography, *The Lost Garden* (1991), recounts his childhood, family, writing, and identity confusion.

Yep has won many awards for a number of his works. *Dragonwings* won the Newbery Award for children's literature in 1976, the Boston Globe Book Award in 1977, and seven other literary honors. *Dragon's Gate* won the Newbery Award in 1993. Other award-winning books include *Child of the Owl* (1977), *Sea Glass* (1979), *Dragon Steel* (1985), and *The Rainbow People* (1989). In 2005 Yep was awarded the prestigious Laura Ingalls Wilder Medal for his contributions to children's literature.

Much of Yep's work centers on the themes of cultural alienation and racial prejudice. Yep himself had difficulty fitting in at home and within his community. He was the clumsy son in an athletic family and felt inferior to his older brother. He looked Chinese, but spoke no Chinese and lived in a black community. For many years, he was puzzled as to where his niche was in Chinese and American cultures. A sense of inadequacy and feeling of being an outsider are reflected in his characters.

Although he had contacts with his extended family living in San Francisco's Chinatown, he had little knowledge of Chinese culture, heritage, folklore, and the early Chinese immigrant experience during the nineteenth century. To work on his historical novels, Yep conducted extensive research, gathering bits of information here and there. From his research studies, he learned about the hardship, danger, and prejudice encountered by Chinese railroad workers and gold miners, which enabled him to describe vividly their suffering and endurance in his writings.

According to Yep, growing up in his family's store and observing and listening to the people who came in and out served as the best training for him as a writer. His family members and relatives have become the basis for many of his characters. Cassia Young in *The Serpent's Children* (1984), for example, is based on his maternal grandmother. *Dragon's Child* (2008) recounts the journey taken by Yep's father as he came to America. Yep's father, a talented kite builder, is also found in the protagonist Windrider in *Dragonwings*.

Significance

Yep is a talented and prodigious writer of Chinese American literature for children and young adults. His work has not only enriched multicultural literature but also enhanced understanding of the contributions of early Chinese Americans to the United States. In addition, through his books, young readers can learn about Chinese culture and traditions. Until the late 1960s, children of ethnic groups could not find themselves reflected in American literature. Today, young Chinese Americans are able to read about their own culture and history in Yep's books; they see their own images and hear their own voices. As a result, they learn to appreciate their own heritage.

Shu-Hsien L. Chen

Further Reading

Johnson-Feelings, Dianne. *Presenting Laurence Yep*. New York: Twayne, 1995. Print. A biographical study of Yep and his young adult titles drawn from the author's interview with Yep and her research on his works.

Woo, Celestine. "Toward a Poetics of Asian American Fantasy: Laurence Yep's Construction of a Bicultural Mythology." *Lion and the Unicorn* 30.2 (April 2006): 250–64. Print. Discusses Yep's use of European fantasy and Asian traditions of magic to create bicultural Asian American fantasy.

Yep, Laurence. *The Lost Garden*. Englewood Cliffs, NJ: Messner, 1991. Print. Yep's autobiography, recounting his childhood, family, and San Francisco's Chinatown as well as his works and struggles with identity.

---. "Playing with Shadows." *Lion and the Unicorn* 30.2 (April 2006): 157–67. Explains that dreams were a powerful force in giving hope to early Chinese immigrants in their hardships, as reflected in Yep's characters.

Tabitha Yim

Athlete

Tabitha Yim is a Korean American gymnast who won national and international medals while also competing as a figure skater. She went on to compete for the Stanford University women's gymnastics team, winning conference and National Collegiate Athletic Association (NCAA) titles. In 2010 she returned to her alma mater to serve as an assistant coach with the team.

Born: November 2, 1985; Los Angeles, California
Full name: Tabitha Ann Yim
Also known as: Tab
Area of achievement: Sports

Early Life

Tabitha Yim was born on November 2, 1985, to Inja and Howard Yim. Her father worked as a minister at the Crystal Cathedral in Garden Grove, California. She has an older brother named Jonathan. When Yim was three years old she started gymnastics lessons; four years later she started figure skating lessons after watching Kristi Yamaguchi win the gold medal at the 1992 Olympics. By twelve she was training in both sports at least five days a week. Howard Yim drove his daughter to her various lessons, logging over one hundred miles a day, and cheered her on at competitions. When Yim was thirteen, her father died suddenly from a heart aneurism. The following year her figure skating coach, Olympic silver medalist Ronnie Robertson, died after a long illness. Despite these setbacks Yim continued to train in both sports, with her mother taking over most of the driving duties. During that time she continued to earn high grades in school.

LIFE'S WORK

Yim was most successful as a gymnast, winning medals at national and international meets such as the Pan American Championships and the American Cup. Beth and Steve Rybacki were her coaches at the Charter Oak gym. A well-rounded gymnast, Yim was a five-time United States national team member who had the ability to compete in all four events: the vault, the uneven bars, the balance beam, and the floor exercise. In the 2001 season she won the silver in the all-around and the gold on floor exercise at the senior national championships and made the United States women's world team. At the World Championships in Ghent, Belgium, the United States earned the team bronze medal. Yim also finished seventh place in the all-around and sixth on floor exercise. That year's results made her the most successful Asian American gymnast since Olympian Amy Chow.

The following year Yim continued to practice figure skating in the morning and gymnastics in the afternoon while continuing her education. She trained six days a week and played organ in church on Sundays. In skating she competed at the novice level, two levels below the skaters who compete at the Olympics and other major skating competitions. At the 2002 United States National Championship for gymnastics Yim finished second in the all-around behind fellow American gymnast Tasha Schwikert for the second straight year. Yim also won the gold on the balance beam and the silver on floor exercise. Unfortunately she tore her Achilles tendon before the world championships, the first of several major injuries that would keep her from competing for months at a time. In 2003 she broke her leg and also had knee surgery. The next year she suffered from another broken leg. Four months after that last injury Yim finished fourth at the 2004 United States Olympic trials, making her a major contender for the Olympic team. Two days after the trials she tore her Achilles tendon again, ending her Olympic pursuit.

Yim graduated from Northwood High School in Irvine, California, in 2003. In the fall of 2004 she enrolled at Stanford University where she had been offered an athletic scholarship. She went on to become one of the school's most successful female gymnasts. During her collegiate career she earned fourteen All-American honors, thirteen of which were first team selections. Yim won the Pacific-10 Conference and NCAA regional all-around titles twice. She finished in the top ten at the NCAA championships eleven times, more than any other gymnast from Stanford. Four of those top-ten finishes were in the all-around, while two were third-place finishes on the floor exercise. The Stanford Cardinal team made the NCAA final, called the Super Six, during Yim's final two years with the program. They finished fifth in 2007 and third in 2008. Yim was one of the leaders on the team, serving as team captain. In 2008, her senior year, Yim was named the Pacific-10 Conference Gymnast of the Year. After graduating from Stanford, Yim taught ninth-grade science at Animo Ralph Bunche Charter High School in Los Angeles through the Teach for America program. In 2010 she joined the Stanford athletics department as an assistant coach for the women's gymnastics team.

SIGNIFICANCE

Tabitha Yim's achievements should not be measured solely by the number of medals she won. She could compete on all four apparatus in gymnastics while pursuing a secondary sport and achieving high marks in school, ultimately becoming the most decorated gymnast in the history of Stanford University. Yim is an example of a versatile athlete and a student pushing herself to achieve her best and persevering though injuries and personal losses.

Kristin Fance

FURTHER READING

Driscoll, Jenny. "On the Lookout for Tabitha Yim." *Skating* November 2001: 52. Print. Documents Yim's schedule of skating, school, and gymnastics. The different demands the two sports place on the body are also discussed.

FitzGerald, Tom. "Stanford Gymnast Has Overcome Setbacks." *San Francisco Chronicle* 4 April 2008: D7. Print. Yim's international and collegiate gymnastics careers are reviewed. Yim talks about how her religious faith helped her to deal with problems in her life and athletic career.

Norville, Dwight. "Working Overtime." *International Gymnast* February 2000: 14+. Print. Describes how Yim and her family deal with her two-sport career. Yim's gymnastics goals are also discussed.

Poe, Debbie. "Yim, Liukin Take American Classic." *International Gymnast* May 2003: 32+. Print. Recounts the 2003 American Classic/Challenge competition in which Tabitha Yim won the all-around in the senior division.

VERN YIP

Hong Kong-born designer and architect

Vern Yip is an interior designer and architect best known for his television appearances on TLC's Trading Spaces *and HGTV's* Design Star *and* Deserving Design with Vern Yip. *Yip makes frequent appearances on television and runs his own interior design business in Atlanta, Georgia. He has been active in community and charitable organizations.*

Born: June 27, 1968; Hong Kong
Full name: Vern Yip
Areas of achievement: Architecture and design, television

EARLY LIFE

Vern Yip was born in Hong Kong on June 27, 1968. When he was only two months old, his family immigrated to the United States and settled in the northern Virginia suburbs just outside of Washington, DC. He has one sister, Katherine, who is ten years older than he is. Yip's father was a biochemist and businessman, and his mother

Vern Yip. (Getty Images for UNICEF)

ran her own international consulting firm. The young Yip traveled to Europe, Asia, and Latin America, experiences that would influence his designs later in life.

As a young child, Yip was passionate about dinosaurs and collected realistic models. He had a chemistry set and an extensive comic-book collection. Yip developed an early interest in architecture, using his building blocks to build houses and skyscrapers that he would then refuse to take apart. A trip to the National Gallery of Art introduced him to the architecture of I. M. Pei, who would become one of his inspirations.

Yip attended McLean High School, where he played soccer, wrestled, participated in the peer-counseling program, and belonged to an Elizabethan singing group. After graduating in 1986, he pursued his love of chemistry into college and had plans to attend medical school. He obtained two bachelor's degrees, one in economics and one in chemistry, from the University of Virginia. After he was accepted into medical school, however, Yip changed his mind about his future. Instead, he interned at an architectural firm while attending the Georgia Institute of Technology, where he earned both a master's degree in architecture and an MBA.

LIFE'S WORK

For a while, Yip was content to work in architecture, but he also found himself drawn to interior design. He began to work for an Atlanta design firm, where he studied for and passed the exam to become a board-certified interior designer. Yip continued to use his architectural training as part of his interior-design skills, combining the minimalist approach he admired in Pei's work with eclectic styles culled from his childhood travels.

Yip joined TLC's reality design show series *Trading Spaces* in 2000, near the end of its first season, and continued to appear occasionally on the show through its fourth season. During his time on the show, he became known for his use of a monochromatic color palette and a clean, uncluttered look. He then appeared in the pilot episode of NBC's *Home Intervention*, which debuted in the spring of 2005, but the show never made it past the first episode. In 2006, HGTV premiered its show *Design Star*, a program wherein aspiring designers compete for the chance to have their own show; Yip was recruited by HGTV as a judge and appeared in the show's first five seasons.

In 2006, Yip lost his mother to cancer, and he and his sister established the Vera Yip Memorial Scholarship Fund through the Ulman Cancer Fund for Young Adults in her honor. The following year, HGTV gave Yip his own show, *Deserving Design*. The show was nominated in 2009 for a National Association for Multi-Ethnicity in Communications Vision Award for lifestyle programming. Also in 2009, he dedicated one episode of his show to raising awareness for the Ulman Cancer Fund and served as the honorary chair for Ulman's fundraiser, Eleven—The Event.

Yip has other HGTV shows to his credit, including *Summer Showdown*, *Bang for Your Buck*, and *First Time Design*. His design shows began airing internationally through the Asian-based Life Inspired Network in 2010. In November 2010, Yip, a longtime supporter of UNICEF, was appointed an official UNICEF ambassador to the United States; his duties included fundraising and directing educational activities related to reducing preventable deaths among children around the world.

Yip opened his own interior design firm in Atlanta, Georgia, where he designs both commercial and residential spaces. His work has won numerous honors and awards, including the Atlanta Decorative Arts Center's Southeast Designer of the Year Award in 2000 and *Southern Living* magazine's Distinguished Southerner designation in 2003. In January 2010, Gavin Joshua Mannox was born via surrogate to Yip and his partner, Craig Koch. The couple's daughter, Vera Lillian Beatrix, was born in March 2011.

SIGNIFICANCE

Vern Yip's career represents the success that comes from hard work and dedication. His professional expertise in architecture and interior design is matched by the professional courtesy he extends to all of his clients. A popular, well-liked television personality, Yip has been open about his homosexuality. He describes himself as an overachiever, but his busy work schedule does not prevent him from giving his time to worthwhile charitable causes.

Karen S. Garvin

FURTHER READING

Kramer, Brian, ed. *Trading Spaces: Behind the Scenes.* Des Moines: Meredith, 2003. Print. A behind-the-scenes look at TLC's show *Trading Spaces* that includes biographies of the show's designers, including Vern Yip.

Yip, Vern. *Designing Spaces: Transforming Every Room with Easy, Elegant Style.* New York: Regan, 2005. Print. Shows readers how to create an affordable plan for decorating their homes using his strategic design principles.

---. "Vern Yip's Career by Design." Interview by Becky Krystal. *Washington Post.* Washington Post, 11 May 2008. Web. 4 Apr. 2012. Yip's perspective on television and his approach to design.

JOHN YOO

Korean-born lawyer and law professor

As a young lawyer at the US Department of Justice, John Yoo was the strongest defender of the expansion of executive power during the administration of President George W. Bush. From 2001 to 2003, he wrote controversial memos arguing that the president had expansive powers, and that the Geneva Convention did not apply to foreigners suspected of terrorism.

Born: July 10, 1967; Seoul, South Korea
Full name: John Choon Yoo
Areas of achievement: Law, government and politics

EARLY LIFE

John Yoo was born on July 10, 1967, in Seoul, South Korea. He was an infant when his parents immigrated to the United States. Woo's parents were physicians with strong anticommunist convictions. Raised in Philadelphia, Pennsylvania, Yoo attended the Episcopal Academy, where he studied Greek and Latin, and attended church three times per week. Yoo graduated with honors from Harvard University in 1989, earning a bachelor of arts in history. While at Harvard, he met his future wife, Elsa Arnett, while they both worked on the staff of the campus newspaper.

Between college and law school, Yoo worked briefly as a journalist in Washington, DC. While studying for his law degree at the Yale University, he served as editor of the *Yale Law Review*, and was also an active member of the Federalist Society, a moderately conservative organization that emphasizes limited government. After

John Yoo. (Getty Images)

completing his law degree in 1992, Yoo became a member of the Pennsylvania State Bar, and clerked for Judge Lawrence Silberman at the DC Circuit of the Court of Appeals. He then advanced to the position of clerk for Supreme Court Justice Clarence Thomas. As clerk, Yoo was recognized as a brilliant and hard-working attorney with strong conservative instincts. Colleagues also commented on his self-confidence and willingness to challenge conventional wisdom.

LIFE'S WORK

During the years 1995 and 1996, Yoo was general counsel for the Judiciary Committee of the US Senate, working under the supervision of Senator Orrin Hatch, Republican of Utah. A firm defender of Republican philosophy, Yoo often clashed with Democrats over President Bill Clinton's judicial nominations. In 1996, Yoo became a law professor at the University of California Berkeley, where the majority of professors and students were firmly left of center. He has also served as a visiting law professor at other schools and organizations, including the University of Chicago, the Free University of Amsterdam in the Netherlands, and the American Enterprise Institute. In 2000, he represented the

interests of the Republican Party in the legal battle over Florida's electoral votes that followed the presidential election between Texas Governor George W. Bush and Vice President Al Gore.

From 2001 to 2003, Yoo served as Deputy Assistant Attorney General at the Department of Justice's Office of Legal Counsel (OLC). Officials in the administration of President George W. Bush were impressed with Yoo's views of executive powers, and turned to him for help in developing legal defenses for White House policies related to Bush's post–September 11 War on Terror. In various legal memos, Yoo defended the Bush administration's use of warrantless wiretapping of Americans thought to be speaking to terrorist suspects outside the country. One of Yoo's more controversial memos was his 2003 recommendations to the Central Intelligence Agency, entitled "Memorandum on Military Interrogation of Alien Unlawful Combatants Held outside the United States," in which he argued that "unlawful enemy combatants," not being members of national armies, were not entitled to the legal status of prisoners of war under the Geneva Convention. By defining torture narrowly as extreme pain equivalent to death or physical impairment, he concluded that interrogators could use "enhanced interrogation techniques," including waterboarding, which simulates the experience of drowning.

When the 2003 memorandum was released to the public in 2009, liberal critics accused Yoo of authorizing the use of torture. Several lawyers felt he should be prosecuted or disciplined by the American Bar Association. In 2009, President Barak Obama instructed the Department of Justice to investigate the allegations. The department's Office of Professional Responsibility issued a report in January 2010 which concluded that there was no legal basis for disciplinary action against Yoo. The report, nevertheless, was critical of Yoo's views on interrogation and his interpretations of the Geneva Conventions.

An energetic researcher and writer, Yoo has published books and articles on US constitutional law, international law, and US foreign relations. Emphasizing presidential discretion in conducting foreign policy, he has argued that the original understanding of the Constitution was to allow the president to use armed forces abroad without congressional authorization. Yoo has also argued that each of the three branches of the government has the authority to make its own interpretations of the Constitution. Yoo has published three books: *The Powers of War and Peace: The Constitution and Foreign Affairs after 9/11* (2005), *War by Other Means:*

The Bybee Torture Memo

While the full effects of the Bybee Torture Memo on the US government and military may remain unknown, ample evidence indicates that it influenced decision making with regard to the advisability of using coercive forms of interrogation on detainees. For example, in a report dated April 4, 2003, the working group created by the Department of Defense to look at detainee interrogation practices not only adopted the memo's rationale but also quoted select portions. On April 16, 2003, US secretary of defense Donald Rumsfeld relied on the report to issue a list of approved interrogation techniques. He stressed that the techniques could be used only on unlawful combatants held by the United States at Guantanamo Bay, Cuba. He directed that four of the techniques be used only in case of military necessity and only after he was notified.

After the Bybee Torture Memo came to light, both the general public and the legal community were outraged. Harold Koh, then dean of Yale Law School and former attorney-adviser at the Office of Legal Counsel, wrote and testified that the legal opinion therein is perhaps the most clearly erroneous one he has ever read. He noted that under the memo's narrow definition of torture, many of the techniques used by Saddam Hussein's regime that have been cited as atrocities by the Bush administration would no longer qualify as torture.

An Insider's Account of the War on Terror (2006), and *Crisis and Command: A History of Executive Power from George Washington to George W. Bush* (2010). While several liberal scholars have published refutations of his views, they have conceded that Yoo's writing is cogent and based on impressive research.

SIGNIFICANCE

Yoo provided the Bush administration with well-researched arguments defending strong executive prerogatives in fighting the war on terror. His narrow definition of torture provided justification for controversial methods of interrogation of individuals suspected of terrorism. Although some of his work has proved controversial, Yoo is one of the best-known legal minds of his generation.

Thomas Tandy Lewis

FURTHER READING

Cole, David, ed. *Torture Memos: Rationalizing the Unthinkable*. New York: New Press, 2009. Print. Contains the secret memos by John Yoo and other officials that defend "enhanced interrogation techniques," with the editor's critical commentary.

Goldsmith, Jack. *The Terror President: Law and Judgment Inside the Bush Administration*. New York: Norton, 2009. Print. Goldsmith emphasizes the threat and climate of fear during the Bush administration's eight years in office, but in contrast to Yoo, he admits that "constitutional excesses" were committed.

Richardson, John H. "Is John Yoo a Monster?" *Esquire* 13 May 2008. Print. Presents a discussion of Yoo's ideas and legal memos, with his responses to relevant questions.

Sands, Philippe. *Torture Team: Rumsfeld's Memo and the Betrayal of American Values*. New York: Palgrave Macmillan, 2003. Print. Claims that Yoo and other US officials violated international law during the war on terror.

Yoo, John. *War by Other Means: An Insider's Account of the War on Terror*. New York: Atlantic Monthly, 2006. Print. Presents Yoo's defense of his memos on presidential prerogatives, the Geneva treaties, and permissible interrogation methods.

PHIL YU

Activist, writer

Phil Yu is the creator of the blog Angry Asian Man. *Originally a space designed to record his personal views on Asian American issues, Yu's blog is widely read, while Yu himself is part of a new generation of young, tech-savvy Asian Americans who defy traditional stereotypes of Asian Americans as the model minority.*

Born: May 13, 1978; Philadelphia, Pennsylvania
Full name: Philip Minsoo Yu
Areas of achievement: Social issues, journalism, activism

EARLY LIFE

Philip Minsoo Yu was born in Philadelphia, Pennsylvania, to Jason and Boosung Yu, Korean Americans who immigrated to the United States in the 1970s. Yu's family moved to Sunnyvale, California, when he was a baby, and he grew up in Silicon Valley and attended high school in nearby Cupertino. Yu's mother worked as a registered nurse, while his father ran a video store, where Yu became a voracious consumer of popular culture, media, and entertainment at a young age.

Yu became conscious early on of a noticeable absence of Asians in the movies and television shows he watched. He also became more aware of his burgeoning sense of Asian American identity when he began attending Northwestern University in 1996, feeling that there was a lack of discussion about racial representation in his studies of radio, television, and film, especially with regard to Asian Americans. As a result, he sought out screenings at the Chicago Asian American Showcase and interned at the National Asian American Telecommunications Association, which would eventually become the Center for Asian American Media.

During his junior year in college, Yu took a class called Asian Americans and the Media, taught by professor L. S. Kim, who would become Yu's mentor and friend. In Kim's class, Yu saw that the Asian American community had causes worth fighting for, and that they could and did fight for them.

LIFE'S WORK

Yu graduated from Northwestern in 2000 as the dot-com bubble began to collapse. While working at a temporary job where he filed invoices for a technology-testing laboratory, he decided to create a website. On February 14, 2001, he started the blog and the persona *Angry Asian Man* and began blogging about stereotypes and racism related to Asian Americans in the media and popular culture.

Yu's blog began gaining popularity within a year of its inception. In 2002, *Angry Asian Man* received a substantial boost in traffic when clothing retailer Abercrombie & Fitch launched a line of shirts with images and phrases that many Asian Americans found offensive. Yu used his blog to post photographs of the shirts, as well as the contact information for the Abercrombie & Fitch corporate headquarters so readers could send complaints. As a result, *Angry Asian Man* became a central rallying point for many protesters, which helped build the blog's influence.

Traditional media outlets also began to take notice of Yu's website, including the *San Francisco Chronicle* and the *Washington Post*, the latter of which ran a feature-length article on Yu in 2005. Over time, news organizations such as the *Los Angeles Times* and National Public Radio began contacting Yu for commentary on Asian American issues, including the 2007 mass shooting at Virginia Tech by gunman Seung-Hui Cho, a Korean American.

Yu also began speaking on Asian American identity and activism at events such as South by Southwest, the New York Asian American Student Conference, the Korean American Coalition, and the Organization of Chinese Americans National Conference, as well as at individual schools and at film festivals such as the San Francisco Asian American Film Festival, the Asian American International Film Festival, and the Austin Asian American Film Festival.

In 2009, Yu began running a regular series on *Angry Asian Man* called "Angry Reader of the Week," in which he highlights a follower of the blog each week to show his appreciation for his readership over the years. Featured readers have included sociology professor Oliver Wang, actress Lynn Chen, video producer Ted Fu, and Barack Obama's brother-in-law Konrad Ng. *Angry Asian Man* celebrated its tenth anniversary on February 14, 2011.

SIGNIFICANCE

Yu's writings on current events concerning Asian Americans have made *Angry Asian Man* one of the most well-known and widely read blogs in the Asian American community, and Yu has since become a much-sought-after speaker on the college and social-media circuits. His blog has helped raise awareness about Asian American artists, authors, musicians, politicians, and activists who are rarely mentioned in mainstream media outlets, in addition to serving as a central clearinghouse for information on all things Asian American.

Eugenia Beh

FURTHER READING

Vargas, Jose Antonio. "Incensed and Empowered." *Washington Post*. Washington Post, 9 Oct. 2005. Web. 4 Apr. 2012. A feature article about *Angry Asian Man*, revealing Phil Yu as the man behind the blog.

Yu, Phil. *Angry Asian Man*. Angry Asian Man, 2010. Web. 4 Apr. 2012. Yu's blog, which includes archives back to 2007, as well as a partially tongue-in-cheek explanation of how the website began.

---. "Mad Man: Meet Blogger Phil Yu." Interview by Jeff Yang. *KoreAm*. KoreAm Journal, 1 Nov. 2010. Web. 4 Apr. 2012. Discusses some of Yu's early life and college experiences and his process for posting content on his blog.

JUDY YUNG

Scholar and educator

Judy Yung is a prominent scholar whose research has focused on the experience of Chinese American women in the United States. Noted for her extensive use of oral histories and primary source materials, Yung has been highly influential in promoting the voices of her subjects in social history.

Born: 1946; San Francisco, California
Full name: Judy Yung (YOONG)
Areas of achievement: Scholarship, education, and social issues

EARLY LIFE

Judy Yung was born in San Francisco, California, the daughter of Yung Hin Sen and Jew Law Ying, both from the Duomen District in Guangdong Province in China. Yung would later find out that her true family name was Tom. Her father, whose real name was Tom Yip Jing, immigrated to the United States as a "paper son," pretending to be the real son of a Chinese immigrant living in San Francisco. The Chinese Exclusion Act of 1882 forced countless Chinese immigrants to pretend to be related to a person already living in the United States in order to enter the country. Her father was detained for over a month at Angel Island off the San Francisco coast, where he was interrogated by immigration officials about details of his family life. Upon his release, Yung's father worked as a janitor. His wife later became a garment worker to help support their growing family.

Yung grew up in San Francisco's Chinatown. She attended St. Mary's Chinese Language School, where she learned to read and write Chinese fluently. Growing up in a traditional Chinese household, the fifth and last daughter of six children, she experienced pressure to conform to gender roles. She attended San Francisco State University and received a bachelor of arts degree in English language and Chinese culture in 1967. She completed a master of arts degree in Library Science at the University of California Berkeley the following year. After graduation, she took a position as a librarian at the Chinatown branch of the San Francisco library. The job was considered a traditional position for a woman, but Yung's work was influenced by the progressive social changes of the 1960s and 1970s. She leveraged her position to advocate for more services for the Chinatown community. During her ten years at the branch, she helped to organize and promote collections and programs aimed at meeting the various needs of area residents. During that period, she also devoted much of her free time to researching Chinese American history.

LIFE'S WORK

In 1975, park ranger Alexander Weiss found Chinese poetry on the walls of the Angel Island Immigration station in the San Francisco Bay. It had been composed by the many Chinese immigrants who were detained at the center during the time of the Chinese Exclusion Act.

Inspired by this discovery, Yung helped to collect, catalog, and transcribe the poems, collaborating with historian Him Mark Lai and poet Genny Lim. The group published *Island: Poetry and History of Chinese Immigrants on Angel Island* in 1980. It received the American Book Award in 1981.

Yung continued to work for the next five years on research projects aimed at telling the stories of the injustices endured by the Chinese community in the United States. With a grant from the US Department of Education (under the Women's Educational Equity Act), Yung and Lim embarked on a research project devoted to Chinese women. *Chinese Women of America: A Pictorial History*, published in 1986, was the first significant scholarly work on Chinese American women. This research experience motivated Yung to obtain a PhD so that she could more fully devote herself to uncovering and exposing everyday stories of her community.

In 1990, she graduated from the University of California Berkeley with a PhD in ethnic studies. Her dissertation, published in 1995 as *Unbound Feet: A Social History of Chinese Women in San Francisco*, was hailed as a groundbreaking achievement. It was praised for capturing the experiences and voices of Chinese women in San Francisco. Using a combination of oral history, interviews, and primary source materials from immigration records and photographs, the book provides a comprehensive view of the life of Chinese women immigrants.

Throughout her career, Yung has been a prolific scholar, publishing a variety of books and articles on Chinese American history, each of which has served to highlight the accomplishments and challenges of the Chinese American community. After earning her PhD, Yung began a career as a teacher at the University of California Santa Cruz. She was named chair of the American Studies Department in 2001. A proponent of first-person narratives in works of history, Yung helped to popularize the use of oral histories in academia. After retiring formally from full-time academic work in 2004, Yung continued her scholarly activities. In 2010, she and Erika Lee published *Angel Island: Immigrant Gateway to America*. It was the first comprehensive scholarly study of Angel Island, bringing Yung back to the site that was the catalyst for her academic career.

SIGNIFICANCE

Yung is considered a pioneer of Chinese American history and a significant contributor to research on American social history. Her work has shed light on the contributions of Chinese American women to US history.

Yung has influenced and inspired a generation of scholars, promoting ethnic studies as a legitimate academic discipline and a significant part of history.

Susan Hoang

FURTHER READING

Armitage, Sue. "Here's to the Women: Western Women Speak Up." *Journal of American History* 83.2 (Sept. 1996): 551–59. Print. Contextualizes Yung's research in women's history scholarship, praising her for her nuanced use of oral histories in her scholarship.

Yung, Judy. *Unbound Voices: A Documentary History of Chinese Women in San Francisco.* Berkeley: U of California P, 1999. Print. Provides an intimate look into women's lives in San Francisco's Chinatown. Includes the story of Yung's mother, who tells of her experience passing through Angel Island.

VICTOR SEN YUNG

Actor

Victor Sen Yung is an actor best known for small parts in film and television. Educated at the University of California Berkeley, and a veteran of the US Air Force, Yung is most widely remembered for his roles as Jimmy Chan (later Tommy Chan) in the Charlie Chan films and the loyal but irascible cook Hop Sing in the TV series Bonanza.

Born: October 18, 1915; San Francisco, California
Died: November 9, 1980; North Hollywood, California
Full name: Victor Sen Yung (SEHN YUHNG)
Birth name: Sen Yew Cheung
Also known as: Victor Sen Young; Sen Yung, Sen Young
Areas of achievement: Entertainment, acting

EARLY LIFE

Victor Sen Yung was born in San Francisco, California, in 1915. He was placed in a shelter with his sister in 1919, after his mother died in a flu outbreak and his father traveled back to China. Yung's father returned years later with a new bride and reclaimed his children.

Yung worked his way through college at the University of California Berkeley, where he studied animal husbandry and earned a degree in economics. Yung

moved to Hollywood for post-graduate work at the University of California Los Angeles. He was occasionally employed as an extra in films, such as the adaptation of Pearl S. Buck's *The Good Earth* in 1937 and an installment of the Peter Lorre detective series *Mr. Moto Takes a Chance* in 1938.

Early in his time in Hollywood, Yung worked for a chemical company as a salesman; he hoped to sell flame-retardant suits to the technical workers on Hollywood film lots. Hollywood legend maintains that during one of Yung's sales visits it was suggested that he audition for Twentieth Century Fox for the role of Charlie Chan's number-two son Jimmy Chan. In the aftermath of significant changes to the franchise, new leading man Sidney Toler selected Yung to play Jimmy Chan based on his screen test.

LIFE'S WORK

Yung appeared as Jimmy Chan for the first time in 1938's *Charlie Chan in Honolulu*; over the years he would perform in seventeen more Charlie Chan films. His early films included *The Letter* (1940), *Little Tokyo, USA* (1942), *Moontide* (1942), and *Manila Calling* (1942). Like many Chinese American actors at the time, Yung occasionally played Japanese characters (he

---

The Success of *Bonanza*

Bonanza, American television's first family-oriented Western series, ran for fourteen years as the prime-time showpiece of the National Broadcasting Company (NBC). The series premiered on September 12, 1959, but it did not become popular until the fall of 1961. An American classic, *Bonanza* ranks among the most highly rated shows of all time. It transformed the Western genre by centering primarily on familial issues rather than frontier lawlessness and violence. The show centered on widower Ben Cartwright, played by Lorne Greene, and his three sons. Secondary characters proved equally popular with fans. Victor Sen Yung appeared in the appealing role of Hop Sing, the family cook and housekeeper who often intervened as comic relief and choric commentator during serious, emotional scenes.

The series took hold slowly, receiving early criticism for its lush sentimentality, which reviewers compared to that of soap operas. Later public response, indicating a stronger viewer identification with the characters, bolstered sponsor confidence. The series, touted as a revival of family values, featured a blend of comedy and realism along with social themes such as racial prejudice, greed, alienation among families, and political corruption. Critics praised the show for its story lines, many of which featured themes of reconciliation and acceptance.

Bonanza had a tremendous impact on television production. The show stressed the Cartwrights' relationships with a rapidly expanding territory, where law by necessity was augmented by reason. This emphasis helped to shift later broadcast efforts to a more humanistic plane.

---

appeared as the character Joe Totsuiko in the 1942 Humphrey Bogart film *Across the Pacific*). Though he appeared in several films, Yung was often cast in bit parts as a laundryman, houseboy, waiter, or clerk. Yung left the Charlie Chan series in the early 1940s to join the United States Air Force during World War II. (Actor Benson Fong replaced Yung in the role of Jimmy Chan.) Yung was at first assigned to work on training films with the First Motion Picture Unit. He had a role in the Air Force's play and film *Winged Victory*. Yung applied to take an officer's exam and rose to the rank of captain in intelligence.

After the war, Yung resumed his film career in the Charlie Chan films. The series, however, was in transition. Toler having passing away in 1947, the character of Chan was next played by Roland Winters. Yung was assigned the role of not Jimmy Chan but Tommy Chan, the detective's number-three son. Yung's last appearance in a Charlie Chan film was 1948's *The Feathered Serpent*, which also featured Keye Luke reprising the role of number-one son Lee Chan.

Other films in which Yung appeared include *Target Hong Kong* (1953), *Trader Tom of the China Sea* (1954), and *The Flower Drum Song* (1961).

Much of Yung's most popular work was in television. He acted in a variety of comedies and dramas, including *The Lone Ranger* (1956), *Mister Ed* (1965), *Hawaii Five-0* (1969), *Hawaiian Eye* (1959–63), *Get Smart* (1968–70), and *Here's Lucy* (1968–69). Yung also had a recurring role in the last season of the John Forsythe series *Bachelor Father* (1960–61). Yung's best-known television role, however, was as Hop Sing on *Bonanza*, a character that appeared for fourteen seasons. Never a member of the regular cast and always relegated to guest star status, Yung played a character who did not appear in every episode but did appear in the pilot episode and over one hundred others.

While continuing to make television and film appearances, Yung worked other jobs to earn money. A skilled Cantonese chef, Yung sometimes gave cooking demonstrations in department stores. He wrote *The Great Wok Cookbook* in 1974—a book dedicated to his father.

In 1972, Yung was a hostage on a Pacific Southwest Airlines flight that was hijacked out of San Francisco by two Bulgarian nationalists seeking political asylum in Siberia. Yung was one of three passengers wounded by gunfire when the Federal Bureau of Investigation stormed the plane and killed the hijackers.

Yung's last film appearance was in *Sam Marlow, Private Eye* (1980). That same year, the actor died in his sleep of carbon monoxide poisoning; he had been using an oven to cure clayware, which he sold as part of a home business. The actor Pernell Roberts, who played Adam Cartwright on *Bonanza*, delivered the eulogy at Yung's funeral.

SIGNIFICANCE

Victor Sen Yung was a prominent character actor in film and television during a time when Chinese

American actors were mostly relegated to small, stereotypical roles. Even though Yung was never a leading man and often played secondary parts and one-dimensional characters, he is remembered for his roles in the Charlie Chan films and the TV series *Bonanza*. He left a wide array of performances for generations to appreciate.

Randy L. Abbott

FURTHER READING

Berlin, Howard M. *The Charlie Chan Film Encyclopedia*. Jefferson: McFarland, 2000. Print. Reference work contains capsule biographies of cast members and a complete filmography relating the films in the series.

Hanke, Ken. *Charlie Chan at the Movies: History, Filmography, and Criticism*. Jefferson: McFarland, 1989. Print. The films are presented in chronological order with full cast and credits, synopses, and evaluations. Biographical details on the three most famous actors to portray Chan and background information on series directors and supporting players are included.

Shapiro, Melany. *Bonanza: The Definitive Ponderosa Companion*. Nipomo: Cyclone, 1997. Print. Provides summaries of episodes, biographies of main and supporting actors.

YUNG WING

Chinese-born diplomat and social reformer

Recognized as the first Chinese graduate of an American university, Yung Wing served as one of China's first ambassadors to the United States and deputy commissioner of the Chinese Educational Mission, an innovative program that sent Chinese students to study in the United States during a time of modernization in China.

Born: November 17, 1828; Nam Ping (now Zhuhai), Xiangshan, Guangdong, China
Died: April 22, 1912; Hartford, Connecticut
Full name: Yung Wing
Also known as: Rong Hong; Wing Yung
Areas of achievement: Education, government and politics

EARLY LIFE

Yung Wing was born in southern China, the third of four children, to a poor peasant family in a remote village near the Portuguese colony of Macao. Yung was sent to a missionary school to learn English at age seven. In his autobiography, *My Life in China and America* (1909), Yung wrote that his father envisioned opportunities for him as an interpreter for foreign businessmen.

In 1841, Yung enrolled in the school of the Morrison Education Society, which was founded to teach English and Christianity in honor of China's first Protestant missionary, Robert Morrison. The school was directed by Yale University–educated Samuel R. Brown, who would become Yung's benefactor and mentor. It was there that Yung prepared for an American education and was baptized as a Christian. By the late 1840s, the Morrison Society's benefactors had become disenchanted with the school after witnessing young converts using English to broker deals with opium smugglers and sailors. The school closed in 1849, but Brown encouraged promising students to seek higher education. Having secured sponsorships from several Hong Kong families, Brown brought the eighteen-year-old Yung and two other students to Massachusetts, where they entered Monson Academy in 1847.

In 1850, Yung entered Yale College (now Yale University), where he excelled academically and embraced American life, undergoing a brief stint as a football hero during his freshman year. It was during his college years that Yung struggled with his identity. He wrote of failing his family, especially after his older brother died; the ill will caused by his conversion to Christianity; his loss of Chinese language skills; and his worry that he would never marry because of cultural differences between him and traditional Chinese women. Yung became a naturalized American citizen in 1852, and two years later he was the first Chinese American to graduate from an American college. Around that time he befriended Mary Kellogg, the daughter of one of his professors.

LIFE'S WORK

Yung Wing returned to China in 1855. Unable to serve in the government without a Chinese degree, he worked as a translator and started his own trading enterprise. In 1863, reform-minded government official

Autobiography in Chinese American Literature

Toward the end of the nineteenth century, Chinese American immigrants became some of the first Asian American writers to publish in English. These early Chinese American authors predominantly wrote autobiographical works, using the genre to explore and share their personal experiences in China and the United States. Their primary impulse was to combat negative racist stereotypes about the Chinese in the popular American press and literature of the day. In his autobiography, *When I Was a Boy in China* (1887), Yan Phou Lee, who converted to Christianity and immigrated to the United States to study from 1872 to 1875, sought to show that education could enable a young Chinese immigrant to fully participate in American society. A similar goal inspired Yung Wing's autobiography, *My Life in China and America* (1909). Almost a half-century later, celebrated ceramics artist Jade Snow Wong published her first autobiographical work, *Fifth Chinese Daughter* (1950). Maxine Hong Kingston's memoir *The Woman Warrior* (1975) won the National Book Critics Circle Award for general nonfiction for its compelling blend of folklore, autobiography, and sociology.

Zeng Guofan commissioned Yung to travel to Massachusetts to buy machinery for China's first modern arsenal. Yung's success earned him a government position. With support from the Chinese government, he went on to create the Chinese Educational Mission. The mission fulfilled Yung's ambition to send Chinese students to be trained and educated abroad, bringing their skills home to assist with modernization and reform. Encouraged by Yung's experiences abroad and the Burlingame Treaty (1868), which allowed Chinese subjects to attend American public schools, Chinese officials chose to send students to New England. In 1872, conservative government official Chen Lanbin was appointed as the mission's first commissioner, with Yung working as deputy. Over one hundred students between the ages of ten and sixteen traveled to Connecticut from 1872 to 1875.

In 1875, Chen and Yung were also appointed as ambassadors to the United States; they established China's first permanent legation in Washington, DC. During the same year, Yung married Mary Kellogg. They went on to have two sons, Morrison Brown and Bartlett Golden.

Meanwhile, anti-Chinese sentiment exploded in the United States as the consequence of increased numbers of Chinese laborers in western states.

The students sponsored by the Mission excelled academically and socially, but their cultural assimilation concerned Chinese officials. Chen condemned the students' acceptance of American ways. Yung's lifestyle, on the other hand, openly violated Chinese norms. In 1878, Congress passed the Chinese Exclusion Act, which barred Chinese immigrants from entering the country. Despite a presidential veto, the bill became law in 1882. The Chinese Educational Mission ended in 1881 due to tensions on both sides of the Pacific. The Chinese government cited US legislative hostility as a pretext to recall the students. With the closing of the mission, both Chen and Yung were dismissed from their diplomatic posts. Yung was recalled to China but soon returned home when his wife became ill. He cared for her until her death in 1886.

During the late 1890s, Yung's goals were unexpectedly thwarted by both the American and the Chinese governments. While Yung was working to secure American investments in railroads in China, the US government revoked his citizenship. In 1898, Yung supported the ill-fated Hundred Days of Reform movement. Following political turbulence in China, he was forced to flee for his life to Shanghai. He continued to advocate reform, even as he fled to Hong Kong in 1900. Yung returned to the United States in 1902 illegally and without incident. He retired in Connecticut, writing his autobiography and corresponding with Chinese reformers.

SIGNIFICANCE

Yung Wing was a liberal-minded advocate of relations between China and the United States in the late nineteenth century. He is remembered as the first Chinese graduate of an American university, receiving his bachelor's degree from Yale in 1854. His assimilation into American culture made him an effective ambassador, though his lifestyle aroused Chinese criticism. Under his guidance, the Chinese Educational Mission trained many of China's future politicians, doctors, engineers, and diplomats—many of them reformers who worked to create a modern China. He also encouraged the pursuit of Chinese studies at American universities, beginning with Yale, his alma mater. His burial site at Cedar Hill Cemetery in Hartford, Connecticut, attracts many Chinese visitors seeking to honor his legacy.

June Grasso

FURTHER READING

Leibovitz, Leil, and Matthew Miller. *Fortunate Sons: The 120 Chinese Boys Who Came to America, Went to School, and Revolutionized an Ancient Civilization*. New York: Norton, 2011. Print. Impact of Yung Wing's program is examined based on diaries and letters.

Worthy, Edmund H., Jr. "Yung Wing in America." *Pacific Historical Review* 34.3 (1965): 265–87. Print. Analyzes the deep cultural conflicts that Yung encountered, using archival sources.

Yung Wing. *My Life in China and America*. 1909. Memphis: General, 2010. Print. Autobiography looks back on experiences that had an impact on his life.

Z

Fareed Zakaria

Journalist, educator

Fareed Zakaria is an Indian American journalist, broadcast news commentator, and author. He served as an editor of Foreign Affairs *magazine from 1992 to 2000, and editor of* Newsweek International *from 2000 to 2010. In 2010, he became a contributing editor for* Time *magazine. He also serves as a television news analyst for CNN, where he hosts his own show,* Fareed Zakaria GPS. Esquire *magazine has called him the most influential foreign policy advisor of his generation.*

Fareed Zakaria. (Getty Images for Time)

Born: January 20, 1965; Mumbai, India
Full name: Fareed Rafiq Zakaria
Areas of achievement: Journalism, television

EARLY LIFE

Fareed Zakaria was born in Mumbai, India, on January 20, 1965. He was raised in a well-educated, upper-class Muslim family. His father, Rafiq Zakaria, was an Islamic scholar and former deputy leader of the Indian National Congress party. His mother, Fatima Zakaria, was Sunday editor of the *Times of India*. Fareed attended the Cathedral and John Connon School in Mumbai, a private Anglican school that is considered one of the best in the country. Neither his family life nor his education was typical. Zakaria's family was well-connected with all of Mumbai's major players, including government officials, architects, and writers.

A brilliant student who was immersed in politics practically from birth, Zakaria went to the United States and enrolled at Yale University. Majoring in history, he made a name for himself as president of the Yale Political

"Why They Hate Us"

The terrorist attacks of September 11, 2001 immediately shaped a new era in American life. The outpouring of rage was monumental, but so was the need to know why the attack took place. To fulfill this need, Zakaria wrote a seven-thousand-word cover story for *Newsweek* magazine in October 2001 entitled "Why They Hate Us."

In the article, Zakaria states that the Middle East had been generally distrustful of the West but particularly anti-American, jealous of its wealth and hating its concepts of freedom and modernization. Resistant to globalization, the Middle East was highly frustrated by its condition under corrupt authoritarian regimes. As a result, the mosque became the only place to discuss politics and consequently helped breed fundamentalist organizations with political agendas. Zakaria found it disturbing that few moderate Muslims were willing to risk criticizing the fanaticism of fundamentalists.

Arab humiliation during war in 1967 and 1973, as well as the unresolved Palestinian problem, were issues Zakaria pointed to as factors contributing to hostility toward the United States. To reverse these hostilities, Zakaria advocated the creation of a Palestinian state, aiding Arab moderate groups and scholars to beat back anti-modern fundamentalism. He also advocated international cooperation to hunt down terrorists and their supporters. Zakaria's landmark article reverberated across the United States from schoolrooms to the Pentagon. In the midst of the rage over 9/11, "Why They Hate Us" provided a historic understanding of the extreme feelings that led to terrorism.

Union, editor-in-chief of the *Yale Political Monthly*, and a member of the exclusive Scroll and Key Society. Zakaria went on to study at Harvard University, where he earned a PhD in international relations in 1993. While a student at Harvard, Zakaria met Paula Throckmorton, who was completing a business degree. Married in 1997, the couple has a son and two daughters. Zakaria's wife is a well-known jewelry designer, and has written occasionally for the *Wall Street Journal*.

Before receiving his doctorate from Harvard, Zakaria directed a research project on American foreign policy. He became managing editor of *Foreign Affairs* magazine in 1992, at age twenty-eight the youngest editor ever appointed at the publication. Zakaria's position at *Foreign Affairs* brought Zakaria to New York City. Before marrying his wife, he shared an apartment with his older brother Arshad, who later became head of investment banking for Merrill Lynch. Zakaria penned editorials for the *New York Times* and frequently appeared on the *Charlie Rose Show*. He also began writing regular columns on politics and economics for *Newsweek*.

Zakaria was named managing editor for *Newsweek International* in 2000. Following the terrorist attacks of September 11, 2001, he wrote a widely read article in *Newsweek* entitled "Why They Hate Us." The article helped make Zakaria a well-known personality in mainstream journalism.

LIFE'S WORK

Zakaria leveraged his deep understanding of the undercurrents of international affairs to become a news "superstar" in high media demand. He served as a news analyst with ABC's *This Week with George Stephanopoulos* from 2002 to 2007. Zakaria hosted the weekly PBS news show *Foreign Exchange with Fareed Zakaria* from 2005 to 2008. *Fareed Zakaria GPS* premiered on CNN in June 2008. Zakaria has interviewed numerous world leaders on his CNN show, earning an Emmy Award for his interview with Chinese Premier Wen Jiabao.

In addition to his success as a television personality, Zakaria has established himself as an author, publishing several books on politics, economics, and international relations. His first book, *From Wealth to Power* (1998), is a scholarly study of America's rise to global power between the Civil War and World War I. *The Future of Freedom: Illiberal Democracy at Home and Abroad* (2003) examines the different strains of democratic government and political freedoms worldwide. The book was a *New York Times* best-seller, and has been translated into twenty languages. Zakaria's *The Post-American World* was published in 2008. The book describes how globalization, particularly the economic rise of India and China, will influence the role of the United States as a global superpower. In August 2010, Zakaria was named editor-at-large for *Time* magazine. He also writes a regular column for the *Washington Post*.

The broad appeal of Zakaria's work as a television news analyst has help to popularize international affairs in the United States. In addition to writing several popular books on foreign policy and globalization, he has been praised for his political objectivity. Zakaria's career on television and as a writer have made him an icon of the modern-day twenty-four-hour news cycle, while his work as a writer and academic have made him a highly respected figure in the field of international relations. In 2010, Zakaria was awarded the National Magazine Award and appointed a trustee of Yale University.

Irwin Halfond

FURTHER READING
Maneker, Marion. "Man of the World." *New York Magazine*. New York Media, 21 Apr. 2003. Web. 28 Mar.

2012. Discusses Zakaria's career as an international relations expert.

Zakaria, Fareed. *The Future of Freedom: Illiberal Democracy at Home and Abroad.* New York: Norton, 2003. Print. Discusses and analyzes the view that democracy is the best model of government for the present day.

---. *The Post-American World.* New York: Norton, 2011. Print. Discusses the formation of the global economy and the influence of the economic rise of India and China on the United States.

RAJAN ZED

Indian-born religious leader

Born in a small town in India, Hindu chaplain Rajan Zed has emerged as a leading representative of Hinduism in the United States. He has been recognized by the United States Senate as well as the California State Senate.

Born: October 25, 1954; India
Full name: Rajan Zed
Areas of achievement: Religion and theology

EARLY LIFE

Rajan Zed is the son of Indian parents Sohan Lai and Kamla Devi. While in India, he earned a bachelor's degree in journalism from Panjab University, Chandigarh. In England, he obtained diplomas in personnel management and industrial relations from Cambridge Tutorial College. He was also made a fellow of the Institute of Professional Managers and Administrators. Zed traveled to the United States in the 1990s and earned a master of science degree in mass communication from San Jose University in 1996, and a masters in business administration from the University of Nevada in 2001. In 1998 he worked for the United States Postal Service as a supervisor in Reno, Nevada.

LIFE'S WORK

As president of the Universal Society of Hinduism, Rajan Zed works to enhance understanding of Hinduism and to foster interreligious dialogue. The goal of the society is to advance awareness of the history and principles of Hinduism and to promote spiritual renewal, educational outreach, and friendly relations with non-Hindu communities. It aims to further understanding of traditional and historical Hindu architecture, art, music, and sculpture.

In 2007, Senate Majority Leader Harry Reid, a Democrat from Nevada, invited Rajan Zed to read the opening prayer in United States Senate in Washington, DC on July 12, making him the first representative of the Hindu faith to read a prayer before the opening of the Senate. Just before the prayer, three demonstrators disrupted the meeting to protest the idea of a Hindu leading the prayer. They were arrested by Capitol Police. Later, other Christian organizations spoke out against having a non-Christian lead the prayer.

On August 29, 2007, Zed led the opening prayer of the California State Senate without incident. He began the prayer by sprinkling the podium with holy water from the Ganges River, a traditional practice in Hindu worship. While wearing traditional robes, Zed recited the original lines from the Rig-Veda in Sanskrit, and then translated them into English. He ended the prayer with "Om shanti, shanti, shanti," which he translated as "Peace, peace, peace be unto all."

In January 2008, the Nevada Clergy Association nominated Rajan Zed as its director of public affairs and interfaith relations. This association is made up of priests, pastors, and ministers from Roman Catholic, Protestant, Orthodox, Mormon, Muslim, Hindu, Buddhist, Jewish, Baha'i, and Native American faiths. In December 2008 Hans-Gert Pottering, then president of the European Parliament, invited Zed to a meeting to discuss issues of intercultural dialogue. One of Pottering's top priorities as president was to improve relations between the West and the Arab and Islamic worlds.

Rajan Zed has also spoken out in opposition to negative depictions of Hinduism in popular culture and media. He said that the film *The Love Guru* (2008) appeared to make fun of Hinduism and that it used sacred terms in a superficial manner. After a screening, the Hindu American Foundation determined that the film was vulgar and crude, but not necessarily anti-Hindu. In another instance, Zed criticized the way in which President Barack Obama was pictured on the front page of *Newsweek* magazine—the cover depicted Obama as the Hindu deity Lord Shiva with three sets of arms in an attempt to show that the president has to do too many things at once. Zed remarked that Lord Shiva is highly revered and meant to be worshiped, and his image is not to be used for profit or self-serving purposes.

Zed also supports cultural events that honor the Hindu faith. The Frist Center for the Visual Arts in Nashville, Tennessee, received grant money from the National Endowment for the Arts to sponsor an exhibition on a Hindu deity, entitled *Vishnu: Hinduism's Blue-Skinned Savior*. Zed commended the Frist Center for taking the opportunity to educate the general public about Hinduism and encouraged similar projects.

Zed is married to Shipa Zed and has two children, Navgeet and Palkin.

SIGNIFICANCE
Since his emigration from India, Rajan Zed has earned many certificates and degrees. He established the Society of Universal Hinduism, which gives him the ability to voice his concerns and to promote the Hindu religion as well as to protect it from ridicule. Through his work with interfaith relations, Zed has fostered education and tolerance.

Winifred Whelan

FURTHER READING
Bhatia, Sunil. *American Karma: Race, Culture, and Identity in the Indian Diaspora*. New York: New York UP, 2007. Print. The result of interviews conducted with people of Indian descent who live in the United States. Includes personal accounts of experiences with racism.

Boorstein, Michelle. "Hindu Groups Ask '08 Hopefuls to Criticize Protest." *Washington Post* 27 July 2007. Print. Reports on the protests against the reading of a Hindu prayer at the opening of the United States Senate.

Cohen, Sandy. "Hindus Concerned over Myers Parody Movie." *Toronto Star* 30 March 2008: E6. Print. Discusses the controversy over the film *The Love Guru*, which was accused of making fun of Hindus and the Hindu religion.

Zed, Rajan. "My Prayer for the Senate and the Nation." *Washington Post*. Washington Post, 1 Aug. 2007. Web. 5 Apr. 2012. An article by Rajan in which he discusses the protest at his Senate prayer reading.

CAROLINE ZHANG

Athlete

Caroline Zhang is a young figure skater of Chinese extraction living in California. As a junior skater, she showed great promise in the ladies' singles, developing several new moves in her performances. While still in high school, she was selected for the US Winter Olympics team for Vancouver 2010, though she did not actually compete in the singles.

Born: May 20, 1993; Boston, Massachusetts
Full name: Caroline Zhao Zhang
Also known as: Zhang Yuanyuan
Area of achievement: Sports

EARLY LIFE
Caroline Zhang was born on May 20, 1993, in Boston, Massachusetts. Shortly before she was born, her parents had immigrated to the United States from Wuhan, China. The family later relocated to Brea, California. Zhang began ice skating early, after seeing the sport on television and noticing a rink opposite her ballet school. As a young girl, she was very aware of the success of Chinese American figure skater Michelle Kwan, who became her role model.

In addition to skating and ballet, Zhang studied piano and violin. As a high school student, Zhang won many awards for her academic achievements, charity work, and sporting ability. She did most of her figure skating work at the East West Ice Palace in Artesia, in Los Angeles County, California.

Zhang's competitive skating career began in 2002, when she reached the regional amateur championships. She earned a silver medal, which qualified her for the

2003 US Junior Championships. Zhang finish fourth in the female juveniles competition.

In 2004, Zhang began skating at the intermediate level and working with coach Minghzhu Li. She placed third in the national Junior Championships. The following season, she moved up to the novice class, making second regionally and fourth in the national competition.

Zhang competed in her first US Figure Skating Championships in 2006, where she placed eighth in the juniors competition. She also competed in the 2006–07 International Skating Union (ISU) Junior Grand Prix in Mexico. Zhang won three Grand Prix events in total, including the final.

Much of Zhang's success came as a result of her ability to do spins and execute spiral extensions. She was also praised for her musicality. Her general artistic creativity and her musical and ballet training informed her figure skating abilities. She began to be compared to her idol Michele Kwan and also Sacha Cohen, another well-known American figure skater.

LIFE'S WORK

In 2007, Zhang was still involved in junior competition. At the National Championships, she won the silver medal behind a competitor who was to become one of her main rivals, Mirai Nagasu. This placing enabled Zhang to be part of the US team at the World Junior Figure Skating Championships, where she managed to beat Nagasu and take the gold medal. Another rival, Ashley Wagner, won the bronze. The US women's team made a clean sweep of the podium positions.

During the 2007–08 season, Zhang moved up to the senior level of competition, though still eligible to skate at the junior level. At the senior level, she entered the Grand Prix circuit, making her debut at the 2007 Skate America competition. In her first senior competition, she won the bronze medal. Her diminutive frame helped her develop her unique spin move, known as the the "pearl" spin, which became something of a trademark. She won a bronze medal in the 2007 Cup of China, and gained fourth place in the Grand Prix final, scoring her highest-ever score (176.48).

Zhang placed fourth at the 2008 US Figure Skating Championship. She won silver at the World Juniors, behind American colleague Rachael Flatt. Nagasu won the bronze.

In the 2008–09 season, Zhang again entered the Grand Prix circuit, this time skating at the Skate Canada International and the Trophée Eric Bompard. In the

Caroline Zhang. (Getty Images)

latter, she earned the bronze medal. Zhang appeared as a member of the US team for the 2009 Four Continents Championships, placing fourth overall. At the World Juniors she again earned a silver medal. In April 2009, she gained her highest-ever free-skate score (116.80) at the ISU World Team Trophy, winning the bronze medal. The next month she was ranked eighth in the ISU world standings.

Zhang struggled somewhat during the 2009–10 season, her best result being a third-place finish at the ISU Four Continents Championship. She made several coaching changes over the course of the season, working with Charlene Wong, Tammy Gambill, and Peter Oppegard. Zhang was selected as a member of Team USA for the Winter Olympics in 2010 at Vancouver, BC, but was not selected to skate. She finished fourth place overall at the 2012 US Nationals.

SIGNIFICANCE

Zhang has introduced two new spins to women's figure skating: the pearl spin and the hyperextended Biellmann spin. Her achievements as a junior helped solidify the United States as a dominant player in the women's skating field internationally. She has established herself as one of the most talented and accomplished figure skaters in the sport.

David Barratt

FURTHER READING

Borzi, Pat. "Figure Skating's Next Ones Are Closing in on Their Moment." *New York Times*. New York Times, 24 Jan. 2008. Web. 5 Apr. 2012. Discusses the career development of several young American figure skaters, including Zhang.

Fitzpatrick, Frank. "Effortlessly Gliding to Top." *Philadelphia Inquirer*. Philadelphia Media Network, 28 Oct. 2007. Web. 5 Apr. 2012. Discusses Zhang's 2007 debut in senior competition at only fourteen years of age.

Appendixes

CHRONOLOGICAL LIST OF ENTRIES

All people appearing in this list are the subjects of articles in Great Lives from History: Asian and Pacific Islander Americans. *The names of the people are listed chronologically based on their date of birth.*

1701–1850

Kamehameha I (c. 1758)
Kaahumanu (March 17, 1768)
Norman Asing (c. 1800)
John Papa Īī (August 3, 1800)
Chang and Eng Bunker (May 11, 1811)

Samuel Kamakau (October 29, 1815)
Yung Wing (November 17, 1828)
Kalākaua (November 16, 1836)
Joseph Heco (September 20, 1837)
Liliuokalani (September 2, 1838)

1851–1900

Ernest Francisco Fenollosa (February 18, 1853)
Mary Tape (c. 1857)
Lue Gim Gong (c. 1858)
Seito Saibara (c. 1861)
George Shima (c. 1864)
Philip Jaisohn (January 7, 1864)
Edith Maude Eaton (March 15, 1865)
Kyutaro Abiko (June 23, 1865)
Sadakichi Hartmann (November 28, 1867)
Joseph Kekuku (c. 1874)
Winnifred Eaton (August 21, 1875)
Sakharam Ganesh Pandit (November 1, 1875)
Chang-ho Ahn (November 9, 1878)
Waka Yamada (December 1, 1879)
Sudhindra Bose (c. 1883)
Taraknath Das (June 15, 1884)
Har Dayal (October 14, 1884)
Tokunosuke Abe (c. 1885)

Chiura Obata (November 18, 1885)
Sessue Hayakawa (June 10, 1889)
Margaret Chung (October 2, 1889)
Duke Kahanamoku (August 24, 1890)
Pablo Manlapit (January 17, 1891)
G. J. Watumull (June 26, 1891)
Tsuru Aoki (September 9, 1892)
Johnny Noble (September 17, 1892)
Yellapragada SubbaRow (January 12, 1895)
Mary Abigail Kawena Pukui (April 20, 1895)
Toyo Miyatake (October 28, 1895)
Chiang Soong Mei-ling (March 5, 1897)
Y. C. Hong (c. 1898)
James Wong Howe (August 28, 1899)
Dalip Singh Saund (September 20, 1899)
Kiyoshi Hirasaki (March 1, 1900)
Henry Sugimoto (March 12, 1900)

1901–1910

Clarence Takeya Arai (June 25, 1901)
Sol Hoopii (c. 1902)
James Y. Sakamoto (c. 1903)
Younghill Kang (June 5, 1903)
Chinn Ho (February 26, 1904)
Keye Luke (June 18, 1904)
Isamu Noguchi (November 17, 1904)
Philip Vera Cruz (December 25, 1904)
Anna May Wong (January 3, 1905)
Philip Ahn (March 29, 1905)
George Nakashima (May 24, 1905)
Yun Gee (February 22, 1906)

S. I. Hayakawa (July 18, 1906)
Hiram Fong (October 15, 1906)
José García Villa (August 5, 1908)
Taro Yashima (September 21, 1908)
Ben Fee (September 30, 1908)
M. C. Chang (October 10, 1908)
John Aiso (December 14, 1909)
George Tsutakawa (February 22, 1910)
Toshio Mori (March 20, 1910)
Subrahmanyan Chandrasekhar (October 19, 1910)
Tyrus Wong (October 25, 1910)

1911–1920

Bienvenido N. Santos (March 22, 1911)
Dong Kingman (March 31, 1911)
Chien-Shiung Wu (May 31, 1912)
Makio Murayama (August 10, 1912)
Hazel Ying Lee (August 24, 1912)
James Matsumoto Omura (November 27, 1912)
Minoru Yamasaki (December 1, 1912)
Choh Hao Li (April 21, 1913)
Milton Quon (August 22, 1913)
Carlos Bulosan (November 24, 1913)
Henry D. Moon (September 28, 1914)
William K. Hosokawa (January 30, 1915)
Grace Lee Boggs (June 27, 1915)
Dai-Keong Lee (September 2, 1915)
N. V. M. González (September 8, 1915)
Louis H. Chu (October 1, 1915)
Victor Sen Yung (October 18, 1915)
Najeeb Halaby (November 19, 1915)
Ah Quon McElrath (December 15, 1915)
Benny Kalama (June 29, 1916)
Iva Toguri D'Aquino (July 4, 1916)

Barney F. Hajiro (September 16, 1916)
Spark M. Matsunaga (October 8, 1916)
Minoru Yasui (October 19, 1916)
I. M. Pei (April 26, 1917)
Ben Kuroki (May 16, 1917)
Wah Chang (August 2, 1917)
Jack Soo (October 28, 1917)
Gordon Kiyoshi Hirabayashi (April 23, 1918)
Young Oak Kim (c. 1919)
Fred Korematsu (January 30, 1919)
Alfred Apaka (March 19, 1919)
Monica Sone (September 1, 1919)
Mitsuye Endo (c. 1920)
Earl Kim (January 6, 1920)
Wayne Wang (February 7, 1920)
Sun Myung Moon (February 25, 1920)
Delbert Wong (May 17, 1920)
Harold Sakata (July 1, 1920)
Sammy Lee (August 1, 1920)
Eileen Chang (September 30, 1920)
Ted Fujita (October 23, 1920)

1921–1930

Yoichiro Nambu (January 18, 1921)
Gabby Pahinui (April 22, 1921)
Yuri Kochiyama (May 19, 1921)
Hisaye Yamamoto (August 23, 1921)
Larry Ching (August 27, 1921)
Yoshiko Uchida (November 24, 1921)
Nelson Kiyoshi Doi (January 1, 1922)
Har Gobind Khorana (January 9, 1922)
Jade Snow Wong (January 21, 1922)
Ali Akbar Khan (April 14, 1922)
Charles Mingus (April 22, 1922)
Toshiko Takaezu (June 17, 1922)
Sadao Munemori (August 17, 1922)
Yang, Chen Ning (October 1, 1922)
Sue Kunitomi Embrey (January 6, 1923)
Gyo Obata (February 28, 1923)
Anna Chen Chennault (June 23, 1923)
Mitsuye Yasutake Yamada (July 5, 1923)
Chou Wen-chung (July 29, 1923)
John Okada (September 23, 1923)
Wataru Misaka (December 21, 1923)
Daniel Ken Inouye (September 7, 1924)
Daniel Akaka (September 11, 1924)
Wakako Yamauchi (October 25, 1924)

Victoria Manalo Draves (December 31, 1924)
Wing Chong Luke (February 25, 1925)
Richard Kekuni Blaisdell (March 11, 1925)
Alfredo Alcala (August 23, 1925)
Hiroshi Miyamura (October 6, 1925)
Him Mark Lai (November 1, 1925)
Ruth Asawa (January 24, 1926)
George Ariyoshi (March 12, 1926)
Gloria Hahn (March 28, 1926)
Tsung-Dao Lee (November 24, 1926)
Michi Weglyn (November 29, 1926)
Thomas Noguchi (January 4, 1927)
Victor Wong (July 31, 1927)
Patsy Takemoto Mink (December 6, 1927)
James Hong (February 22, 1929)
A. K. Ramanujan (March 16, 1929)
Miyoshi Umeki (May 8, 1929)
Edison Uno (October 19, 1929)
Amar Bose (November 29, 1929)
Toshiko Akiyoshi (December 12, 1929)
Tamio Kono (June 27, 1930)
Don Ho (August 13, 1930)
Ming Cho Lee (October 3, 1930)

1931–1940

Kwang-chih Chang (April 15, 1931)
Norman Mineta (November 12, 1931)
Pat Morita (June 28, 1932)
Nam June Paik (July 20, 1932)
Jose Espiritu Aruego (August 9, 1932)
Ford Konno (January 1, 1933)
Yoko Ono (February 18, 1933)
James Shigeta (June 17, 1933)
Evelyn Kawamoto (September 17, 1933)
Mako (December 10, 1933)
Ved Mehta (March 21, 1934)
Jeanne Wakatsuki Houston (September 26, 1934)
Hae-Jong Kim (January 18, 1935)
Zulfikar Ghose (March 13, 1935)
Chang-Lin Tien (July 24, 1935)
Seiji Ozawa (September 1, 1935)
Edward W. Said (November 1, 1935)
Samuel C. C. Ting (January 27, 1936)
Zubin Mehta (April 29, 1936)
William Marr (September 3, 1936)
Yuan T. Lee (November 19, 1936)
George Takei (April 20, 1937)
Anita Desai (June 24, 1937)

Robert Nakamura (July 6, 1937)
Allen Say (August 28, 1937)
Adeline Yen Mah (November 30, 1937)
Tommy Chong (May 24, 1938)
Lawson Fusao Inada (May 26, 1938)
Bapsi Sidhwa (August 11, 1938)
Bette Bao Lord (November 3, 1938)
Nobu McCarthy (November 13, 1938)
E. San Juan Jr. (December 29, 1938)
Daniel Chee Tsui (February 28, 1939)
Sam Chu Lin (March 3, 1939)
Ronald Takaki (April 12, 1939)
Nancy Kwan (May 19, 1939)
Ben Cayetano (November 14, 1939)
Frank Chin (February 25, 1940)
Haing S. Ngor (March 22, 1940)
Ken Kashiwahara (July 18, 1940)
Bharati Mukherjee (July 27, 1940)
Ernie Chan (July 27, 1940)
Ronald T. Y. Moon (September 4, 1940)
Maxine Hong Kingston (October 27, 1940)
Bruce Lee (November 27, 1940)

1941–1950

Timothy C. Wong (January 24, 1941)
Mike Honda (June 27, 1941)
Rodney Kageyama (November 1, 1941)
Tony DeZuniga (November 8, 1941)
Janice Mirikitani (c. 1942)
Pyong Gap Min (c. 1942)
Gayatri Chakravorty Spivak (February 24, 1942)
Dith Pran (September 23, 1942)
Eric Shinseki (November 28, 1942)
Muzammil H. Siddiqi (c. 1943)
Randall Duk Kim (September 24, 1943)
Rodney James Takashi Yano (December 13, 1943)
Charles B. Wang (August 19, 1944)
Doris Matsui (September 25, 1944)
Shirley Geok-lin Lim (December 27, 1944)
Ben Fong-Torres (January 7, 1945)
Wendy Lee Gramm (January 9, 1945)
Boona Cheema (August 6, 1945)
Masumi Hayashi (September 3, 1945)
Gary Y. Okihiro (October 14, 1945)
Judy Yung (c. 1946)
Ninotchka Rosca (c. 1946)

Alex Hing (January 8, 1946)
Ruthanne Lum McCunn (February 21, 1946)
Norm Chow (May 3, 1946)
John David Waihee III (May 19, 1946)
Ellison Onizuka (June 24, 1946)
Gus Lee (August 8, 1946)
Connie Chung (August 20, 1946)
Dale Minami (October 13, 1946)
Deepak Chopra (October 22, 1946)
Wing Tek Lum (November 11, 1946)
Michio Kaku (January 24, 1947)
Tritia Toyota (March 29, 1947)
Ramani Ayer (May 27, 1947)
Mazie Hirono (November 3, 1947)
Steven Chu (February 28, 1948)
Laurence Yep (June 14, 1948)
Irene Natividad (September 14, 1948)
Martin Yan (December 22, 1948)
Glen Fukushima (c. 1949)
Shing-Tung Yau (April 4, 1949)
Jessica Hagedorn (May 29, 1949)
Vera Wang (June 27, 1949)

Shawn Wong (August 11, 1949)
Terry Teruo Kawamura (December 10, 1949)
Le Ly Hayslip (December 19, 1949)
Peter Bacho (c. 1950)
Wendy Tokuda (c. 1950)

Gary Locke (January 21, 1950)
Lance Ito (August 2, 1950)
Tseng Kwong Chi (September 6, 1950)
Antonio Taguba (October 31, 1950)

1951–1960

Karen Tei Yamashita (January 8, 1951)
Meena Alexander (February 17, 1951)
Theresa Hak Kyung Cha (March 4, 1951)
Garrett Kaoru Hongo (May 30, 1951)
Queen Noor (August 23, 1951)
Kent Nagano (November 22, 1951)
Philip Kan Gotanda (December 17, 1951)
Kitty Tsui (c. 1952)
Patrick Soon-Shiong (c. 1952)
Roger Y. Tsien (February 1, 1952)
Amy Tan (February 19, 1952)
Steven Okazaki (March 12, 1952)
Orhan Pamuk (June 7, 1952)
David Mura (June 17, 1952)
Francis Fukuyama (October 27, 1952)
David D. Ho (November 3, 1952)
Myung-whun Chung (January 22, 1953)
Elaine L. Chao (March 26, 1953)
Yong Soon Min (April 29, 1953)
Judy M. Chu (July 7, 1953)
Parminder Bhachu (October 20, 1953)
Hao Jiang Tian (c. 1954)
David Wong Louie (c. 1954)
Guy Kawasaki (August 30, 1954)
Ang Lee (October 23, 1954)
Rajan Zed (October 25, 1954)
Vincent Chin (c. 1955)
Abraham Verghese (c. 1955)
Michiko Kakutani (January 9, 1955)
Marilyn Chin (January 14, 1955)
Eddie Van Halen (January 26, 1955)
Lisa See (February 18, 1955)
Gedde Watanabe (June 26, 1955)
John Chen (July 1, 1955)
Kimiko Hahn (July 5, 1955)
Anna Sui (August 4, 1955)
Gish Jen (August 12, 1955)
Cathy Song (August 20, 1955)
Yo-Yo Ma (October 7, 1955)
Indra Nooyi (October 28, 1955)
Heather Fong (c. 1956)

James Hattori (c. 1956)
Huping Ling (c. 1956)
Lynda Barry (January 2, 1956)
Ha Jin (February 21, 1956)
Bruce Yamashita (February 26, 1956)
Cynthia Kadohata (July 2, 1956)
Amitav Ghosh (July 11, 1956)
Chitra Divakaruni (July 29, 1956)
Fae Myenne Ng (October 1956)
Ann Curry (November 19, 1956)
Anna Bayle (December 6, 1956)
Johnny Chan (c. 1957)
Anchee Min (January 14, 1957)
Vikram Pandit (January 14, 1957)
Kyoko Mori (March 9, 1957)
Fred Ho (August 10, 1957)
David Henry Hwang (August 15, 1957)
Tan Dun (August 18, 1957)
Li-Young Lee (August 19, 1957)
Rosalind Chao (September 23, 1957)
Mira Nair (October 15, 1957)
Mark Foo (February 5, 1958)
John Yang (February 10, 1958)
Kayo Hatta (March 18, 1958)
Jennifer Tilly (September 16, 1958)
Andrea Jung (1959)
Israel Kamakawiwoole (May 20, 1959)
Lauren Tom (August 4, 1959)
Maya Ying Lin (October 5, 1959)
Alex Tizon (October 30, 1959)
Jim Yong Kim (December 8, 1959)
Cho-Liang Lin (January 29, 1960)
Greg Louganis (January 29, 1960)
Meg Tilly (February 14, 1960)
Chris Tashima (March 24, 1960)
Linda Sue Park (March 25, 1960)
Ron Darling (August 19, 1960)
Eileen Tabios (September 11, 1960)
B. D. Wong (October 24, 1960)
Lang Ping (December 10, 1960)

1961–1970

1971–1980

Tedy Bruschi (June 9, 1973)
Gene Luen Yang (August 9, 1973)
Lisa Ling (August 30, 1973)
Johnny Damon (November 5, 1973)
Aimee Nezhukumatathil (c. 1974)
Chad Hugo (February 24, 1974)
Grace Park (March 14, 1974)
Thakoon Panichgul (September 25, 1974)
Apl.de.ap (November 28, 1974)
David Lat (c. 1975)
Dat Phan (January 25, 1975)
Terence Tao (July 17, 1975)
Dat Nguyen (September 25, 1975)
Tiger Woods (December 30, 1975)
Hines Ward (March 8, 1976)
Jennifer Lee (March 15, 1976)
Jorge Cham (May 1976)
Rena Inoue (October 17, 1976)
Laura Ling (December 1, 1976)
Mike Shinoda (February 11, 1977)
Kal Penn (April 23, 1977)

Brandon Vera (October 10, 1977)
Phil Yu (May 13, 1978)
Amy Chow (May 15, 1978)
Nicole Scherzinger (June 29, 1978)
Mohini Bhardwaj (September 29, 1978)
Shannyn Sossamon (October 3, 1978)
Norah Jones (March 30, 1979)
Jawed Karim (May 1, 1979)
Toby Dawson (May 4, 1979)
Maggie Q (May 22, 1979)
Mindy Kaling (June 24, 1979)
Kelis (August 21, 1979)
Ne-Yo (October 18, 1979)
Bryan Clay (January 3, 1980)
Amerie (January 12, 1980)
Michelle Kwan (July 7, 1980)
Nadia Ali (August 3, 1980)
Raj Bhavsar (September 7, 1980)
Vanessa Lachey (November 9, 1980)
Shane Victorino (November 30, 1980)
Sarah Chang (December 10, 1980)

1981–2000

Troy Polamalu (April 19, 1981)
Apolo Anton Ohno (May 22, 1982)
Jason Wu (September 27, 1982)
Michael Copon (November 13, 1982)
Tim Lincecum (June 15, 1984)
Sameer Bhattacharya (August 31, 1984)
Anthony Kim (June 19, 1985)
Tabitha Yim (November 2, 1985)
Cassie (August 26, 1986)

Hikaru Nakamura (December 9, 1987)
Brenda Song (March 27, 1988)
Vanessa Hudgens (December 14, 1988)
Sanjaya Malakar (September 10, 1989)
Michelle Wie (October 11, 1989)
Malese Jow (February 18, 1991)
Haley Ishimatsu (September 10, 1992)
Ivana Hong (December 11, 1992)
Caroline Zhang (May 20, 1993)

MEDIAGRAPHY

The following list provides the titles of films and television shows useful to the cultural study of Asian and Pacific Islander Americans.

FILMS

Title: *37 Stories about Leaving Home*
Date: 1996
Director: Shelly Silver
Summary: Documentary. Explores the changing roles of Japanese daughters, mothers, and grandmothers in twentieth-century Japanese society.

Title: *62 Years and 6500 Miles Between*
Date: 2005
Director: Anita Wen-Shin Chang
Summary: Documentary. Tells the story of director Chang's grandmother, a Taiwanese political activist. Explores political persecution and the postcolonial condition.

Title: *A Great Wall*
Date: 1985
Director: Peter Wang
Summary: Cultures clash when Leo Fang brings his American-born wife and son to China to visit his traditional family.

Title: *A Thousand Years of Good Prayers*
Date: 2007
Director: Wayne Wang
Summary: Based on story collection by Yiyun Li. A Chinese father comes to America to help his adult daughter cope with her divorce.

Title: *ABCD*
Date: 1999
Director: Krutin Patel
Summary: Follows two second-generation Indian American or "American Born Confused Desi" siblings. Nina rebels against their mother's traditional Hindu values, while Raj struggles with prejudice at work.

Title: *A.K.A. Don Bonus*
Date: 1995
Director: Spencer Nakasako and Sokly Ny
Summary: A teenager refugee (Sokly "Don Bonus" Ny) and his family try to survive in America without their father after escaping Cambodia's Khmer Rouge.

Title: *The Achievers*
Date: 2006
Director: Abraham Lim
Summary: Adapted from the stage play by Michael Golamco. Five Asian American roommates have a month to relocate after receiving an eviction notice.

Title: *Act of War: The Overthrow of the Hawaiian Nation*
Date: 1993
Director: Joan Lander Puhipau
Summary: Documentary. Native Hawaiians' perspectives on the 1893 overthrow of the Hawaiian monarchy.

Title: *Afterbirth*
Date: 1982
Director: Jason Kao Hwang
Summary: Documentary. Explores how Asian American identity is synthesized from appearance, language, and ritual.

Title: *American Desi*
Date: 2001
Director: Piyush Dinker Pandya
Summary: Leaving his parents' traditional Indian home to attend college, a young man questions his identity.

Title: *American Fusion*
Date: 2005
Director: Frank Lin
Summary: A divorced, middle-aged Chinese immigrant thinks she is doomed to care for her extended family. When she falls in love with a Mexican-American, her family must learn to accept him as well as each other.

Title: *American Sons*
Date: 1995
Director: Steven Okazaki
Summary: Documentary. Actors Ron Muriera, Lane Nishikawa, Yuji Okumoto, and Kelvin Han Yee share stories about the impact of racism on Asian American men.

Title: *Americanese*
Date: 2006
Director: Eric Byler
Summary: Based on the book *American Knees* by Shawn Wong. An Asian American woman and Chinese American man find love and heartache with each other as they struggle with their racial identities and incompatible ideas.

Title: *An Untold Triumph: America's Filipino Soldiers*
Date: 2002
Director: Noel Izon
Summary: Documentary. Seven thousand Filipino Americans helped the US Army liberate their homeland from Japanese occupation during World War II.

Title: *Ancestors in the Americas: Coolies, Sailors, and Settlers—Voyage to the New World*
Date: 1996
Director: Loni Ding
Summary: Part 1 of 3 chronicles the history of Asian migration to the Americas including Chinese, Indian, and Filipino immigration to the United States.

Title: *Ancestors in the Americas: Chinese in the Frontier West—An American Story*
Date: 1998
Director: Loni Ding
Summary: Part 2 of 3 explores the social, cultural, legal, and economic challenges faced by the Chinese immigrants between the 1850s and 1880s.

Title: *Animal Appetites*
Date: 1991
Director: Michael Cho
Summary: Documentary about the 1989 Long Beach trial of two Cambodian immigrants charged with animal cruelty for killing and eating a dog, and the subsequent passage of a law prohibiting pet consumption.

Title: *Asian Stories*
Date: 2006
Director: Ron Oda
Summary: Jilted by his fiancée, a Chinese American man living in Los Angeles asks his best friend, a Japanese American hit man, to kill him.

Title: *Banana Split*
Date: 1991
Director: Kip Fulbeck
Summary: Explores Hapa identity and the multiracial experience.

Title: *Beheading the Chinese Prisoner*
Date: 1900
Director: Siegmund Lubin
Summary: A forty-two-second silent reenactment of the trial and execution of a Chinese prisoner during the Boxer Rebellion.

Title: *Better Luck Tomorrow*
Date: 2002
Director: Justin Lin
Summary: Based on the 1992 murder of Stuart Tay by four honor students in Fullerton, California. A group of stereotypical, overachieving Asian American high school seniors become criminals.

Title: *Big Trouble in Little China*
Date: 1986
Director: John Carpenter
Summary: A white truck driver (Kurt Russell) inadvertently becomes involved with an ancient mystical battle in San Francisco's Chinatown.

Title: *Bontoc Eulogy*
Date: 1995
Director: Marlon Fuentes
Summary: Examines the fate of the eleven hundred Filipinos displayed as a living exhibit at the 1904 St. Louis World's Fair.

Title*: Brown Soup Thing*
Date: 2008
Director: Edward Mallillin
Summary: An elementary school student interviews notable Filipinos for a school project that explores what it means to be Filipino.

Title: *Catfish in Black Bean Sauce*
Date: 1999
Director: Chi Muoi Lo
Summary: Vietnamese siblings adopted as children by an African American couple from Los Angeles experience conflicting emotions when their birth mother visits them in the United States as adults.

Title: *Cavite*
Date: 2005
Director: Ian Gamazon and Neill dela Llana

Summary: When a Filipino American attends his father's funeral in the Philippines, he discovers his mother and sister have been kidnapped and will be murdered if he does not meet horrifying demands.

Title: *Chan Is Missing*
Date: 1982
Director: Wayne Wang
Summary: In the first Asian American feature film with an all Asian/Asian American cast, two San Francisco cabbies search for an elusive person who took their money and disappeared in Chinatown.

Title: *Children of the Camps*
Date: 1999
Director: Stephen Holsapple
Summary: Documentary. Six Japanese Americans interned in World War II relocation centers as children discuss the lasting, negative impact of their experiences.

Title: *Close Call*
Date: 2003
Director: Jimmy Lee
Summary: Based on a true story. Korean American teenager Jenny Lim heads for self-destruction before her estranged Korean father intervenes.

Title: *The Color of Fear*
Date: 1994
Director: Lee Mun Wah
Summary: Documentary. Eight men discuss their experiences with racism and what it means to be Asian American, African American, Latino, or Caucasian.

Title: *The Color of Honor: The Japanese American Soldier in WWII*
Date: 1987
Director: Loni Ding
Summary: Documentary. Relates the experiences of Japanese Americans who served in the US armed forces as translators and interpreters in military intelligence during World War II.

Title: *Combination Platter*
Date: 1993
Director: Tony Chan
Summary: An illegal Chinese immigrant works as a waiter in a Chinese restaurant while searching for a

marriage of convenience with an American citizen so he can obtain a green card.

Title: *The Curse of Quon Gwon: When the East Mingles with the West*
Date: 1916
Director: Marion Wong
Summary: Silent film about a Chinese American couple pulled between a traditional mother-in-law (Wong) and American culture. First known feature film made by an Asian American.

Title: *Dim Sum: A Little Bit of Heart*
Date: 1985
Director: Wayne Wang
Summary: Set in San Francisco's Chinatown. Explores the relationship between a widowed Chinese immigrant mother and her unmarried adult daughter.

Title: *Dim Sum Funeral*
Date: 2008
Director: Anna Chi
Summary: Four estranged Chinese-American adult siblings reunite after their mother's death.

Title: *The Displaced View*
Date: 1988
Director: Midi Onodera
Summary: A Japanese American woman researches her Japanese grandmother as a keeper of tradition. Explores how assimilation erodes cultural traditions.

Title: *Dragon: The Bruce Lee Story*
Date: 1993
Director: Rob Cohen
Summary: Based on *Bruce Lee: The Man Only I Knew* by Linda Lee Cadwell, Lee's widow. Chronicles the life and career of the actor and martial arts expert.

Title: *Eat a Bowl of Tea*
Date: 1989
Director: Wayne Wang
Summary: Based on the novel by Louis Chu. A Chinese American couple struggle to start a family in New York's Chinatown during the 1940s.

Title: *Ekleipsis*
Date: 1998
Director: Tran T. Kim-Trang

Summary: Fifth video in Kim-Trang's eight-part Blindness Series. Focuses on the largest known group of people afflicted with hysterical blindness—a group of Cambodian women who fled the Khmer Rouge and now live in Long Beach, California.

Title: *Enter the Dragon*
Date: 1973
Director: Robert Clouse
Summary: An FBI secret agent and master martial artist (Bruce Lee) agrees to spy on a crime lord and compete in a tournament held on a remote island.

Title: *Face*
Date: 2002
Director: Bertha Bay-Sa Pan
Summary: A Chinese American teen must choose between her traditional Chinese grandmother and an African American DJ.

Title: *The Fact of Asian Women*
Date: 2002
Director: Celine Parrenas Shimizu
Summary: Explores the stereotypical sexualization of Asian and Asian American women by reenacting roles played by Anna May Wong (1920s–40s), Nancy Kwan (1960s), and Lucy Liu (1990s).

Title: *Family Gathering*
Date: 1989
Director: Lise Yasui
Summary: Documentary. Masuo Yasui, a Japanese woman living in Oregon, was arrested by the FBI and sent to an internment camp during WWII.

Title: *Fire*
Date: 1996
Director: Deepa Mehta
Summary: Two Indian American women must choose between their expected roles as devoted wives and their desire for love and intimacy.

Title: *Forbidden City, U.S.A.*
Date: 1989
Director: Arthur Dong
Summary: Documentary about San Francisco's famous Forbidden City, the all-Chinese nightclub, during the 1930s and 1940s.

Title: *From Hollywood to Hanoi*
Date: 1992
Director: Tiana Thi Thanh Nga Alexandra
Summary: Documentary follows the director, a Hollywood actress, as she returns to Vietnam. Focuses on her reunion with family and examines lingering effects of the Vietnam War.

Title: *From Spikes to Spindles*
Date: 1976
Director: Christine Choy
Summary: Documentary. Asian American and white residents of New York's Chinatown unite to protest police brutality, real estate developers, and the destruction of their community.

Title: *The Golden Child*
Date: 1986
Director: Michael Ritchie
Summary: An American detective is told he has been chosen to rescue the Tibetan Golden Child, a Buddhist mystic who was kidnapped by an ancient evil sorcerer.

Title: *The Grace Lee Project*
Date: 2005
Director: Grace Lee
Summary: Documentary. Korean American director interviews other women named Grace Lee to demonstrate their individuality and disprove stereotypes of Asian American women.

Title: *Harold and Kumar Go to White Castle*
Date: 2004
Director: Danny Leiner
Summary: Harold Lee (John Cho) and Kumar Patel (Kal Penn) experience a series of misadventures on their way to eat at the fast food restaurant White Castle.

Title: *History and Memory: For Akiko and Takashige*
Date: 1991
Director: Rea Tajiri
Summary: Documentary. Director explores her parents' internment by examining the broader social impact of Japanese internment during World War II.

Title: *Hito Hata: Raise the Banner*
Date: 1980

Director: Duane Kubo and Robert Nakamura
Summary: Discusses challenges and hardships encountered by Japanese Americans from the 1900s through the 1970s.

Title: *Hollywood Chinese: The Chinese in American Feature Films*
Date: 2008
Director: Arthur Dong
Summary: Documentary. Chronicles the historic and modern depiction of Chinese in American films. Includes film clips and interviews with Asian American actors and actresses.

Title: *Hundred Percent*
Date: 1998
Director: Eric Koyanagi
Summary: Created in response to the lack of Asian American males in American films. The lives of six Asian Americans are followed for three days.

Title: *In Between Days*
Date: 2006
Director: So Yong Kim
Summary: A South Korean immigrant teenager is in love with her best friend and struggles to meet the demands of life in America.

Title: *In the Matter of Cha Jung Hee*
Date: 2010
Director: Deann Borshay Liem
Summary: The director uncovers the forty-year-old mystery of her switched identity that began in a Korean orphanage.

Title: *Jazz Is My Native Language: A Portrait of Toshiko Akiyoshi*
Date: 1983
Director: Renee Cho
Summary: Documentary about Toshiko Akiyoshi, a Japanese American jazz pianist, composer, arranger, and big band leader.

Title: *Journey from the Fall*
Date: 2006
Director: Ham Tran
Summary: Stories of those left behind after the fall of Saigon during the Vietnam War.

Title: *The Joy Luck Club*
Date: 1993
Director: Wayne Wang
Summary: Adapted from the novel by Amy Tan. Explores complicated relationships between four modern Chinese-American women and their more traditional mothers.

Title: *The Karate Kid*
Date: 1984
Director: John G. Avildsen
Summary: A handyman and martial arts master (Pat Morita) teaches karate and life lessons to a high school student.

Title: *Kieu*
Date: 2006
Director: Vú T. Thu Há
Summary: Recounts a traditional Vietnamese national epic poem about the eight doors that open in a person's life. Set in modern San Francisco.

Title: *Lilo & Stitch*
Date: 2002
Director: Dean DeBlois and Chris Sanders
Summary: Animation. A Hawaiian girl adopts an unusual pet who is really an extraterrestrial fugitive.

Title: *Living on Tokyo Time*
Date: 1987
Director: Steven Okazaki
Summary: A Japanese immigrant woman in San Francisco marries a westernized Japanese American man when her visa expires to avoid being deported.

Title: *Lt. Watada*
Date: 2010
Director: Freida Lee Mock
Summary: Documentary. Lt. Ehren Watada, a Japanese American military officer, refused his orders to deploy to Iraq and challenged US war policy.

Title: *Maya Lin: A Strong Clear Vision*
Date: 1994
Director: Freida Lee Mock
Summary: Documentary. Recounts the design and creation of the Vietnam War Memorial by Chinese American architect Maya Lin.

Title: *Mississippi Masala*
Date: 1991
Director: Mira Nair
Summary: The peaceful life of an Indian family in Mississippi is disrupted when their daughter (Sarita Choudhury) falls in love with an African American man (Denzel Washington).

Title: *Mississippi Triangle*
Date: 1984
Director: Christine Choy, Worth Long, Allan Siegel
Summary: Explores racial tensions in the Mississippi delta region through interviews with Chinese Americans, African Americans, and white Americans.

Title: *The Mistress of Spices*
Date: 2005
Director: Paul Mayeda Berges
Summary: Based on the book by Chitra Banerjee Divakaruni. An Indian woman in California uses the power of spices to help others.

Title: *Monkey Dance*
Date: 2004
Director: Julie Mallozzi
Summary: Documentary. Follows three teenage members of the Angkor Dance Troupe, founded to preserve Cambodian dance traditions almost lost during the Khmer Rouge genocide.

Title: *The Motel*
Date: 2005
Director: Michael Kang
Summary: A Chinese American teen lives and works at a motel, where he befriends a Korean man who checks in to stay.

Title: *My America . . . or Honk If You Love Buddha*
Date: 1997
Director: Renee Tajima-Peña
Summary: Documentary. The director journeys across America to figure out what it means to be Asian and Asian American.

Title: *My American Vacation*
Date: 1999
Director: V.V. Dachin Hsu
Summary: A Chinese grandmother and her Chinese American family embark on a vacation together in an RV.

Title: *The Namesake*
Date: 2006
Director: Mira Nair
Summary: Based on the book by Jhumpa Lahiri. Follows the lives of an Indian immigrant couple and their Indian American children.

Title: *Never Forever*
Date: 2007
Director: Gina Kim
Summary: Unable to get pregnant with her Korean American husband, an American wife begins an affair with a Korean immigrant worker who resembles her spouse.

Title: *Nisei Soldier: Standard Bearer for an Exiled People*
Date: 1984
Director: Loni Ding
Summary: Documentary about Japanese Americans who fought in the US Army while their families were imprisoned in internment camps during World War II.

Title: *No Hop Sing, No Bruce Lee*
Date: 1998
Director: Janice Tanaka
Summary: Documentary. Asian American men challenge popular media stereotypes.

Title: *Once Upon a Time in China and America*
Date: 1997
Director: Sammo Hung Kam-Bo
Summary: A Chinese man (Jet Li) starts a martial arts school in America. When he is targeted by the Mafia, Master Wong arrives from Hong Kong to help him.

Title: *The People I've Slept With*
Date: 2009
Director: Quentin Lee
Summary: A promiscuous Chinese American woman becomes pregnant and must determine which lover is the father.

Title: *Picture Bride*
Date: 1994
Director: Kayo Hatta
Summary: A Japanese woman goes to Hawaii in 1918 to marry a man she has never met.

Title: *Ping Pong Playa*
Date: 2007

Director: Jessica Yu
Summary: A young ping pong teacher dreams of becoming a professional basketball player and leaving his dull life in the suburbs.

Title: *Pushing Hands*
Date: 1992
Director: Ang Lee
Summary: Grandfather Chu (Sihung Lung) faces generational conflicts as he adapts to his new life in America.

Title: *Rabbit in the Moon*
Date: 1999
Director: Emiko Omori
Summary: Follows the story of a Japanese American family. Examines the complex history of resistance and alliances in an internment camp.

Title *Raspberry Magic*
Date: 2010
Director: Leena Pendharkar
Summary: An immigrant family develops resilience when their life in American becomes difficult.

Title: *Red Doors*
Date: 2005
Director: Georgia Lee
Summary: Dysfunction may destroy the Wongs, a Chinese American family in New York.

Title: *Resettlement to Redress: Rebirth of the Japanese American Community*
Date: 2005
Director: Don Young
Summary: Documentary follows the resettlement of Japanese Americans after World War II through the 1988 formal acknowledgement by President Reagan that internment was based on racism and warranted reparation.

Title: *Romeo Must Die*
Date: 2000
Director: Andrzej Bartkowiak
Summary: When an Asian warlord's son is murdered by a rival African American gang in Oakland, his brother (Jet Li) leaves Hong Kong to avenge his death.

Title: *Rumble in the Bronx*
Date: 1995

Director: Stanley Tong
Summary: A young Chinese man (Jackie Chan) who is visiting his uncle in New York City must use martial arts to defend himself against a local street gang.

Title: *Rush Hour*
Date: 1998
Director: Brett Ratner
Summary: A Hong Kong Detective (Jackie Chan) and an African American FBI agent (Chris Tucker) must overcome cultural differences and work together to rescue the kidnapped daughter of a Chinese diplomat in Los Angeles.

Title: *Sa-I-Gu: From Korean Women's Perspective*
Date: 1993
Director: Dai Sil Kim-Gibson
Summary: Documentary offers the perspective of Korean women shopkeepers on the sociopolitical factors surrounding the 1992 Los Angeles riots.

Title: *Santa Mesa*
Date: 2008
Director: Ron Morales
Summary: An orphaned Filipino American boy is sent to Manila to live with his grandmother whom he has never met.

Title: *Saving Face*
Date: 2004
Director: Alice Wu
Summary: Examines the complex relationships among three generations of a Chinese American family.

Title: *Separate Lives, Broken Dreams: The Saga of Chinese Immigration*
Date: 1994
Director: Jennie F. Lew
Summary: Documentary examines the factors contributing to and lingering effects of the 1882 Chinese Exclusion Act.

Title: *Snow Falling on Cedars*
Date: 1999
Director: Scott Hicks
Summary: Based on the novel by David Guterson. In the Pacific Northwest of the 1950s, a Japanese American fisherman is accused of murder.

Title: *Stolen Ground*
Date: 1993
Director: Lee Mun Wah
Summary: Documentary. Asian American men candidly discuss their experiences with institutionalized and internalized racism.

Title: *Strawberry Fields*
Date: 1997
Director: Rea Tajiri
Summary: A Japanese American teenager confronts her grandfather's past internment and grieves her sister's suicide. Set in the 1970s.

Title: *Surname Viet Given Name Nam*
Date: 1989
Director: T. Minh-Ha Trinh
Summary: Documentary explores the roles of Vietnamese and Vietnamese American women in historical and contemporary society.

Title: *Thousand Pieces of Gold*
Date: 1991
Director: Nancy Kelly
Summary: Based on the biography of Polly Bemis by Ruthanne Lum McCunn. In the 1880s, a Mongolian woman is sold by her family and taken to America to work as a prostitute in a gold mining town.

Title: *Tie a Yellow Ribbon*
Date: 2007
Director: Joy Dietrich
Summary: A photographer, a Korean adoptee estranged from her Midwestern adoptive family, struggles to find herself and resolve her feelings for her white brother Joe.

Title: *Unfinished Business: The Japanese American Internment Cases*
Date: 1984
Director: Steven Okazaki
Summary: Documentary. Three Japanese American men who were convicted during World War II for resisting the Wartime Relocation Act fight to overturn their convictions forty years later.

Title: *Vincent Who?*
Date: 2009
Director: Tony Lam
Summary: Documentary. Examines how the 1982 Vincent Chin murder case unified the Asian American civil rights movement. Explores how far the movement has come and what issues remain to be addressed.

Title: *Wataridori: Birds of Passage*
Date: 1974
Director: Robert Nakamura
Summary: Documentary. Three *issei* who had been interned at Manzanar during World War II discuss their experiences and make a pilgrimage to the camp.

Title: *We Served with Pride: The Chinese American Experience in WWII*
Date: 1999
Director: Montgomery Hom
Summary: Documentary. First-hand accounts by Chinese American WWII veterans. Narrated by actress Ming-Na and television journalist David Louie.

Title: *The Wedding Banquet*
Date: 1993
Director: Ang Lee
Summary: A gay man marries a woman to please his traditional Taiwanese parents.

Title: *Wet Sand: Voices from L.A. Ten Years Later*
Date: 2003
Director: Dai Sil Kim-Gibson
Summary: Documentary. In a follow-up to *Sa-I-Gu*, filmmaker Kim-Gibson revisits the site of the 1992 riots in Los Angeles and discovers through interviews with diverse witnesses that living conditions have deteriorated.

Title: *When You're Smiling: The Deadly Legacy of Internment*
Date: 1999
Director: Janice Tanaka
Summary: Documentary examines how the silence of Japanese Americans released from internment camps negatively impacted their children.

Title: *Who Killed Vincent Chin?*
Date: 1987
Director: Christine Choy and Renee Tajima-Peña
Summary: Documentary about the 1982 murder of Vincent Chin, a young Chinese American man in Detroit. When Chin's killers receive suspended sentences, the Asian American community seeks justice.

Title: *The World of Suzie Wong*
Date: 1960

Director: Richard Quine
Summary: Adapted from the 1957 novel by Richard Mason. The romance of a Hong Kong prostitute (Nancy Kwan) and an aspiring American painter.

Title: *Yellow*
Date: 1998
Director: Chris Chan Lee
Summary: When a Korean American teenager is robbed while working at his dad's grocery store, he en-

lists his friends to recover the money instead of telling his father.

Title: *Yuki Shimoda: Asian American Actor*
Date: 1985
Director: John Esaki
Summary: Chronicles Yuki Shimoda's thirty-year acting career. Includes interviews with Asian American actors Mako, Nobu McCarthy, Soon Teck Oh, and Beulah Quo.

TELEVISION (SERIES, MINISERIES, MADE-FOR-TELEVISION FILMS)

Title: *All-American Girl*
Date: 1994–1995
Summary: Series based on Margaret Cho's comedy. A traditional Korean mother clashes with her Americanized daughter. First sitcom to feature an Asian American cast on a major network.

Title: *Ally McBeal*
Date: 1997–2002
Summary: Series about eccentric lawyers at a Boston law firm. Lucy Liu joined the cast as a regular in 1998 in her role as Ling Woo, a domineering and confrontational lawyer.

Title: *The Amazing Chan and the Chan Clan*
Date: 1972
Summary: Animated series produced by Hanna-Barbera Productions. Based on the Charlie Chan films of the 1930s and 1940s. Keye Luke provides the voice of Mr. Chan.

Title: *American Dragon: Jake Long*
Date: 2005–2007
Summary: Disney cartoon about Asian American teen Jake Long, who is entrusted with mystical powers of the American Dragon, a guardian of magical creatures that secretly exist in the world.

Title: *Anatomy of a Springroll*
Date: 1994
Summary: Documentary delves into cultural assimilation, identity, and memories via traditional Vietnamese foods. Part of the 2008 PBS series *Global Voices*.

Title: *Bollywood Hero*
Date: 2009
Summary: IFC Original miniseries. A Hollywood actor who goes to India to become a Bollywood star must

overcome culture clashes, learn to dance, and discover his leading lady. Starring Chris Kattan, Neha Dhupia, Pooja Kumar, and Ali Fazal.

Title: *Farewell to Manzanar*
Date: 1976
Summary: Television movie adapted from the memoir by Jeanne Wakatsuki Houston and James Houston. Follows the Wakatsuki family before, during, and following imprisonment at the Manzanar concentration camp.

Title: *The Green Hornet*
Date: 1966–1967
Summary: Based on *The Green Hornet* comic book series. A newspaper publisher and his Asian valet and martial arts expert (Bruce Lee) battle crime as Green Hornet and Kato.

Title: *Hawaii Five-O*
Date: 1968–1980
Summary: Series about a fictional Hawaii state police unit, featuring Hawaiian actors Kam Fong Chun, Zulu, and Herman Wedemeyer and Samoan actor Al Harrington.

Title: *Hawaii Five-O*
Date: 2010–2012
Summary: Based on the 1968 series. Cast includes Korean-American actor Daniel Dae Kim and Korean-American actress Grace Park.

Title: *Kung Fu*
Date: 1972–1975
Summary: This series follows Kwai Chang Caine, a Shaolin monk skilled in martial arts, who travels through the American Old West searching for his half-brother.

Title: *Kung Fu: The Legend Continues*
Date: 1993–1997
Summary: Based on *Kung Fu* (1972–75). Follows the adventures of Kwai Chang Caine's grandson.

Title: *Kung Fu: The Movie*
Date: 1986
Summary: Continues the story of Kwai Chang Caine from *Kung Fu* (1972–75). Brandon Lee plays Caine's son, Chung Wang.

Title: *Lilo & Stitch: The Series*
Date: 2003–2007
Summary: Based on the 2002 Disney film. Lilo, a Hawaiian girl, and Stitch, her alien pet, must recover Jumba's missing experimental creatures and change them from evil to good.

Title: *Lois & Clark: The New Adventures of Superman*
Date: 1993–1997
Summary: Clark Kent romances Lois Lane while Superman fights crime. Dean Cain, a Japanese American, plays Clark Kent and Superman.

Title: *Lost*
Date: 2004–2010
Summary: Survivors of a plane crash struggle to escape from a remote island. Asian American actor Daniel Dae Kim plays the role of Jin-Soo Kwon, a man who speaks only Korean.

Title: *Martial Law*
Date: 1998–2000
Summary: A Chinese police officer and martial arts master fights crime in Los Angeles. Cast includes Kelly Hu and Sammo Hung Kam-Bo.

Title: *My Own Country*
Date: 1998
Summary: Television movie. Dr. Abraham Verghese, an East Indian man who moves to Tennessee, treats patients with AIDS.

Title: *Ohara*
Date: 1987–1988
Summary: Pat Morita stars as Lieutenant Ohara, a Japanese American police officer in Los Angeles, who relies on unconventional, spiritual methods to solve crimes.

Title: *Outsourced*
Date: 2010–2011
Summary: At an American company's call center in India, an American manager struggles with Indian culture while explaining American popular culture to his employees.

Title: *A Shot at Love with Tila Tequila*
Date: 2007–2008
Summary: Reality television dating game show featuring Vietnamese American Tila Tequila (Tila Nguyen), who invites thirty-two male and female contestants into her house to compete for her affection.

Title: *Slaying the Dragon*
Date: 1988
Summary: Documentary examines Hollywood's portrayal of Asian American women in film from the 1920s through the 1980s.

Title: *Star Trek*
Date: 1966–1969
Summary: Follows the missions of the Starship *Enterprise* in the twenty-third century. George Takei, a Japanese American actor, played the role of helmsman Hikaru Sulu.

Title: *Survivor: Cook Islands*
Date: 2009; series 2000–2012
Summary: Reality television game show. During the 2009 season, contestants were divided into teams based on their race and ethnicity. Yul Kwon, of the Asian American team, won the season.

Title: *Wendy Wu: Homecoming Warrior*
Date: 2006
Summary: Television movie. A Chinese monk tells Wendy Wu (Brenda Song), a Chinese American teenager, that she is the reincarnation of a powerful warrior who must save the world from an ancient evil spirit.

Pamela Mueller-Anderson

LITERARY WORKS

The works listed below are categorized by genre and offer readers some of the best resources for the study of literature by Asian and Pacific Islander Americans.

AUTOBIOGRAPHIES AND MEMOIRS

Alexander, Meena. *Fault Lines*, 1993 and 2003. The life of a South Asian woman takes her from her native India to England, Sudan, and finally the United States.

Bulosan, Carlos. *America Is in the Heart,* 1946. A powerful memoir chronicling the resentment and discrimination Filipino immigrant laborers faced in pre–World War II America.

Hayslip, Le Ly. *When Heaven and Earth Changed Places*, 1989. An autobiography that juxtaposes a Vietnamese woman's girlhood and wartime immigration to America with her postwar visit to her native country in 1986.

_____. *Child of War, Woman of Peace*, 1993. The second part of Hayslip's autobiography that focuses on the author's struggle to assimilate in America after her first departure from Vietnam in 1970, and her subsequent humanitarian work to heal the wounds of the Vietnam War in both countries.

Houston, Jeanne Wakatsuki, and James Houston. *Farewell to Manzanar*, 1973. A detailed chronicle of Jeanne Houston's experience in a Japanese American internment center that illustrates the racist nature of the camps.

Huynh, Jade Ngoc Quang. *South Wind Changing*, 1994. The author tells of his years in a Communist Vietnamese labor camp and his escape to America where he struggles with culture shock and economic hardship until he wins a college fellowship.

Kingston, Maxine Hong. *The Woman Warrior*, 1975. A literary award–winning memoir mixing autobiographical and fantastic elements from Chinese folk tales in the author's account of her life and that of her Chinese American immigrant mother.

Lee, Mary Paik. *Quiet Odyssey*, 1990. An autobiography that covers almost the entire twentieth century and reflects on personal as well as general issues for Korean Americans during that time.

Lee, Yan Phou. *When I Was a Boy in China*, 1887. The oldest Chinese American literary text; it juxtaposes a Chinese childhood with the author's experiences in America as one of the first exchange students from China.

Lim, Shirley Geok-lin. *Among the White Moon Faces: An Asian American Memoir of Homelands*, 1996. Chronicles the author's multilayered experience with American society as she moved from Malaysia to study, and eventually to remain, in the United States.

Lin Yutang. *My Country and My People*, 1935. A sympathetic description of China and the Chinese for an American audience by a Chinese American academic.

Lowe, Pardee. *Father and Glorious Descendant*, 1943. Describes the relationship of a Chinese immigrant father and his second-generation, American-born son, with some criticism of American treatment of Chinese Americans.

Mehta, Ved. *The Stolen Light*, 1989. A blind Pakistani American author tells of his experience at Pomona College in Claremont, California, in the 1950s, and his quest for an all-American college lifestyle despite his immigrant status and disability.

_____. *All For Love*, 2001. Chronicles the author's relationships with four different women in New York City in the 1960s and 1970s.

Mura, David. *Turning Japanese: Memoirs of a Sansei*, 1991. A record of how one year in Japan changed the self-understanding of a third-generation Japanese American poet.

Nguyen, Bich Minh. *Stealing Buddha's Dinner*, 2007. Reflections on the childhood and teenage years of a Vietnamese American girl during the 1980s in Grand Rapids, Michigan, and her desire to become all-American.

Nguyen, Kien. *The Unwanted: A Memoir of Childhood*, 2001. An account of a boy and his Vietnamese mother that describes their immigration to the United States in 1985 after his American father abandons them in Communist Vietnam.

Nguyen, Qui Duc. *Where the Ashes Are: The Odyssey of a Vietnamese Family*, 1994. Chronicles the plight of the author's family during the war in Vietnam and his early struggles after moving to the United States until he eventually becomes a radio reporter and revisits his homeland.

Pham, Andrew X. *Catfish and Mandala*, 1999. Chronicles the author's bicycle journeys along the American West Coast, Mexico, and in Japan and Vietnam as he reflects on his cultural identity as Vietnamese American.

Pham, Quang. *A Sense of Duty: Our Journey from Vietnam to America*, 2005. Growing up a teenager in California with his mother and siblings while his father languished in a labor camp in Vietnam for twelve years, the author struggles to fit into American society until he becomes a Marine and serves his new country.

Phim, Navy. *Reflections of a Khmer Soul,* 2007. A literary autobiography chronicling the author's journey from her childhood in Cambodia through the horrors of the Killing Fields, to resettlement in America and interaction with the Cambodian American community of Long Beach, California.

Sone, Monica. *Nisei Daughter*, 1953. The author's tranquil childhood in Seattle, Washington, is shattered when the family is sent to an internment camp for Japanese Americans where she experiences humiliation, generational conflict, and an identity crisis.

Sugimoto, Etsu Inagaki. *A Daughter of the Samurai,* 1934. Contrasts upper-class Japanese culture with that of America where the author immigrated to marry a Japanese American merchant.

Uchida, Yoshiko. *Desert Exile: The Uprooting of a Japanese-American Family*, 1982. One of the key memoirs of the internment of Japanese Americans in America during World War II.

Ung, Loung. *Lucky Child*, 2005. The author's second part of her autobiography, juxtaposing her life as a teenager in America in the 1980s with that of her younger sister left behind in Cambodia until the two are finally reunited in Cambodia.

Wong, Jade Snow. *Fifth Chinese Daughter*, 1950. A Chinese American girl goes to college and becomes a ceramic artist in San Francisco's Chinatown.

Yung Wing. *My Life in China and America*, 1909. A comparison of the two countries, including their educational systems, by an American-educated Chinese reformer who settled in the United States.

NOVELS

Alexander, Meena. *Manhattan Music*, 1997. An Indian woman copes with alienation from her Jewish American husband who whisked her from her native land, and she explores romantic alternatives in New York City.

Cao, Lan. *Monkey Bridge*, 1997. A mother and daughter settle in Connecticut as Vietnamese refugees; they cope with culture shock and a dark legacy from the war that brought them to America.

Chin, Marilyn. *The Revenge of the Mooncake Vixen*, 2009. A humorous tale of two Chinese American sisters who are always up to mischief as teenagers and young women in Southern California.

Chin, Yang Lee. *The Flower Drum Song*, 1957. A humoristic look at a Chinese American father and his son in San Francisco's Chinatown.

Choi, Sook Nyul. *Gathering of Pearls*, 1994. Third novel in a young adult trilogy about Sookan, a Korean girl who survived the Korean War to arrive in America in 1955, where she attends college and is plagued by homesickness.

Choi, Susan. *The Foreign Student*, 1998. Set in Tennessee in 1955, a Korean exchange student falls in love with a Southern belle of European American heritage.

_____. *American Woman*, 2003. The relationship of a Japanese American woman, her group of radicals, and the European American daughter of a newspaper

tycoon they have kidnapped, in 1974; fictionalizes the story of Patricia Hearst and her abductors.

_____ . *A Person of Interest*, 2008. An embittered Chinese American professor is suspected of sending a mail bomb to his more popular colleague on a Midwestern campus; modeled on the Wen Ho Lee case of a Chinese American accused of espionage and the Unabomber.

Chun, Pam. *The Money Dragon*, 2002. A historical novel about the legendary Chinese American capitalist Ah Leong building a financial family empire on Hawaii.

Chu, Louis. *Eat a Bowl of Tea*, 1961. A bitter look at the bachelor society among Chinese Americans in New York City, which changed only slowly with the influx of more Chinese women immigrants after the Chinese Exclusion Act was abolished in 1943.

Desai, Kiran. *The Inheritance of Loss*, 2006. A literary award-winning work that contrasts the life of Biju, an illegal Indian immigrant in America, with that of the upper-class Indian woman Sai living in Darjeeling.

Divakaruni, Chitra. *One Amazing Thing*, 2010. Trapped in the basement of an Indian consulate in an American city after an earthquake, nine diverse characters tell the stories of their lives.

_____ . Queen of Dreams, 2004. Mixing contemporary events like the September 11, 2001, terrorist attacks with fantasy, a single Indian American mother and artist tries to discover the secret behind her late mother's claim to be able to interpret dreams.

Eaton, Winnifred. See Watanna, Onoto

Hagedorn, Jessica. *Dogeaters*, 1990. A tragicomic exploration of the influence of America on Filipino culture in 1950s Manila.

____. *The Gangster of Love,* 1996. A Filipina and her two teenage children immigrate to San Francisco in the 1970s where the daughter falls in with an alternative rock music band and embarks on a road trip to New York City.

Hahn, Gloria. *Clay Walls*, 1987. An account of a Korean American family in the Los Angeles of the 1920s; published under the name Ronyoung Kim.

Hosseini, Khaled. *The Kite Runner*, 2003. Describes the protagonist's experience as an Afghan refugee resettling in Fremont, California, amid economic hardships and his return to Afghanistan to face his past..

Jen, Gish (pen name of Lillian Jen). *Typical American*, 1991. The tragicomic tale of three Chinese students stranded in America after the Communist victory in mainland China in 1949, who try their utmost to become typical Americans.

____. *Mona in the Promised Land*, 1996. A humorous novel about a Chinese American woman trying to convert to Judaism.

____. *The Love Wife*, 2004. A humorous novel about a contemporary American family consisting of a Chinese American father, European American mother, two adopted Chinese American daughters, and a mixed-race son, who have to cope with the arrival of a young Chinese woman, who is a relative of the father.

Jin, Ha (pen name of Xuefei Jin). *A Free Life*, 2007. After dropping out of an American graduate school, a young Chinese man, his wife, and their son start immigrant life, leading to a Chinese restaurant and their own home in the suburbs of Atlanta, Georgia.

Kadohata, Cynthia. *The Floating World*, 1989. A young Japanese American girl experiences an ambiguous relationship with her eccentric, strong-willed Japan-born grandmother before moving to California to study.

____. *Kira-Kira*, 2004. A Newbery Medal–winning novel for young adults about two Japanese American sisters isolated in a European American community who must confront personal tragedy as the older sister dies from lymphoma.

Kang, Younghill. *The Grass Roof*, 1931. An autobiographically inspired story of a young Korean man

who chooses immigration to America over a fight for Korean independence from Japan, which he considers futile.

____. *East Goes West,* 1937. Critical of American society at the time, a Korean immigrant faces the bitter truth that the American dream is out of reach for him despite his American college education.

Keller, Nora Okja. *Comfort Woman*, 1997. In Hawaii, a daughter of mixed Korean and European American heritage discovers through spiritual channeling that her Korean American mother was forced into prostitution as a comfort woman for the Japanese Army in World War II.

____. *Fox Girl*, 2002. Three young Korean friends, two of them children of an American soldier and a Korean mother, struggle with harsh life in a bar town outside a United States Army base in South Korea in the 1960s.

Kim, Ronyoung. See Gloria Hahn

Kim, Suki. *The Interpreter*, 2003. A young but disillusioned Korean American court interpreter solves the mystery of the double murder of her parents in New York City in a novel focused on the city's Korean American immigrant community.

Kingston, Maxine Hong. *Tripmaster Monkey: His Fake Book*, 1989. A postmodern, stream-of-conscious novel about a young Chinese American struggling to come to terms with his ethnic and American identity during the 1960s.

Lahiri, Jhumpa. *The Namesake*, 2003. Chronicles a young Bengali couple's immigration to America, the birth of their two children, and their struggles to make it in their new country.

Le, Thi Diem Thuy. *The Gangster We Are All Looking For*, 2003. A Vietnamese American refugee family settles in San Diego and struggles both economically and psychologically as the father has to adapt to his new American life, leaving behind the gangster role he played in Saigon.

Lee, Chang-rae. *Native Speaker*, 1995. A young college-educated Korean American is hired by a shadowy agency to wreck the rising career of a local Korean American politician who ultimately destroys it himself.

____. *A Gesture Life*, 1999. The long shadow of Japanese colonization of Korea catches up with an elderly Korean American seeking a new American life for himself and his young adopted Korean American daughter.

____. *The Surrendered*, 2010. Decades after coming to America, a former Korean war orphan links up with a

European American man who saved her as an American soldier back in Korea, to find her missing son.

Lee, Gus. *China Boy*, 1994. The story of a seven-year-old Chinese American boy growing up in a tough San Francisco neighborhood in the 1950s who learns to fight back against bullies.

Lord, Bette Bao. *In the Year of the Boar and Jackie Robinson*, 1984. A children's book about a Chinese American girl learning English and becoming accepted by her classmates.

Louie, David Wong. *The Barbarians Are Coming*, 2000. A comic novel about a Chinese American man who has to cope with the arrival of his Chinese parents in America.

Mori, Kyoko. *Stone Field, True Arrow,* 2000. In Wisconsin, a Japanese American woman comes to terms with her failing marriage to a European American husband and the past troubles of her Japanese parents.

Mukherjee, Bharati. *The Tiger's Daughter*, 1971. A young Bengali woman visits her native India after being educated in the United States and marrying a European American.

____. *Jasmine*, 1989. Widowed at seventeen after her husband is murdered in her native India, a Hindu woman illegally immigrates to the United States where she survives male violence and personal hardships.

Murayama, Milton. *All I Asking for Is My Body,* 1975. Written in Pidgin English to resemble the characters' actual speech. Two Japanese American sons rebel against their traditional parents in Hawaii during the years leading up to World War II.

Ng, Fae Myenne. *Bone*, 1993. Two generations of Chinese Americans live in San Francisco's Chinatown and face conflicts due to generational differences as they assimilate into mainstream American culture; the husband has to decide if he wants to return to China the bones of his "paper father," or fake relative, who sponsored his immigration.

____. *Steer Toward Rock*, 2008. A picaresque story of an illegal Chinese American man posing as a Chinese American citizen's legal son; describes his years of servitude and his romantic encounters with lonely Chinese American women.

Nguyen, Bich Minh. *Short Girls*, 2009. Two young second-generation Vietnamese American women, one a model wife and one a born rebel, bond again as sisters as both suffer from their disloyal romantic partners.

Okada, John. *No-No Boy*, 1957. A perceptive contrast between the protagonist, Ichiro, who refused to disavow loyalty to the Japanese emperor and register for the draft in the United States Army during World War II, and fellow Japanese American male internees who answered yes to these two questions.

Ong, Han. *Fixer Chao*, 2001. A satirical, countercultural novel in which a gay Filipino hustler and his straight Jewish American friend steal from the rich in New York society, with the hustler pretending to be a feng shui artist.

Pai, Margaret. *The Dreams of Two Yi-Min,* 1989. A daughter tells of her Korean American parents' early immigrant history in Hawaii.

Rosca, Ninotchka. *State of War*, 1988. As three diverse Filipino characters of multiethnic backgrounds travel to a festival on a Philippine island, the author includes reflections on the impact of America's past rule over the Philippines.

Santos, Bienvenido. *The Man Who (Thought He) Looked Like Robert Taylor*, 1983. An elderly Filipino bachelor from a Polish Chicago neighborhood travels to a Filipino gathering in Washington, DC, to overcome his alienation and homesickness in America.

See, Lisa. *Shanghai Girls*, 2009. Two Chinese sisters flee the Japanese invasion of China in 1937 through arranged marriages to Chinese American men; in the 1950s, the younger sister's daughter suddenly runs away to Communist China.

Sidhwa, Bapsi. *An American Brat*, 1993. A sixteen-year-old Pakistani girl is sent to visit her cousin in the United States and decides to stay because she treasures the greater freedom the United States provides for women.

Tan, Amy. *The Joy Luck Club*, 1989. A major Asian American literary text that tells the interrelated stories of four Chinese American mothers and their daughters, with a strong focus on the challenging experiences of first- and second-generation Chinese American immigrants.

____. *The Kitchen God's Wife*, 1991. A Chinese American daughter learns more about her Chinese-born mother, including her suffering at the hands of her first husband.

____. *The Hundred Secret Senses*, 1995. Two estranged sisters, the older Chinese and the younger Chinese American, meet again in America when their father dies.

____. *The Bonesetter's Daughter*, 2001. A young Chinese American daughter learns about her mother's past in China after she comes to terms with her mother's Alzheimer's disease, a difficult subject in her community.

____. *Saving Fish from Drowning*, 2005. A sarcastic novel about the naivety of American travelers in Asia and the cynicism of Myanmar's military junta in exploiting tourism and world opinion.

Tsiang, H. T. *And China Has Hands*, 1937. The life of an oppressed Chinese American laundryman.

Ty-Casper, Linda. *Wings of Stone*, 1986. A Filipino returns home from the United States on the eve of the fall of Ferdinand Marcos and finds himself shocked, yet paralyzed, by the contrast between America and his native country.

Uyemoto, Holly. *Go*, 1995. A twenty-year-old, third-generation Japanese American woman rebels against her parents and treats her mother rather cruelly.

Watanna, Onoto (pen name of Winnifred Eaton). *Mrs. Nume of Japan*, 1899. The first known Asian American novel, a romance with a Japanese American woman protagonist.

Wong, Shawn. *Homebase*, 1979. A young Chinese American man searches for his identity, which is affected by his ethnic heritage and political consciousness.

____. *American Knees*, 1995. The romantic and sexual adventures of a Chinese American man and three Asian American women.

Yamashita, Karen Tei. *Tropic of Orange*, 1997. A magical realism novel about a Japanese American woman television newscaster in Los Angeles that satirizes global capitalist culture.

Xu Xi (pen name of Xu Su Xi). *Habit of a Foreign Sky*, 2007. A Chinese American woman leads a cosmopolitan existence that is shattered by the death of her mother in Hong Kong after which she reconnects with her Asian American half brother.

PLAYS

Chin, Frank. *The Chickencoop Chinaman*, 1972. Characters of diverse racial backgrounds expose mainstream American discrimination and stereotypes designed to emasculate the Asian American male.

____. *The Year of the Dragon*, 1974. Fred, a young Chinese American, finally rebels against his father, who insisted he work for the family business as a tour guide of Chinatown catering to Caucasian tourists.

Gotanda, Philip Kan. *No More Cherry Blossoms: Sisters Matsumoto and Other Plays*, 2005. A collection of four plays about the challenges faced by Japanese American women throughout the twentieth century.

Hartmann, Carl Sadakichi. *A Tragedy in a New York Flat: A Dramatic Episode in Two Scenes*, 1896. An outsider, modeled after the author, wreaks havoc on the marriage of two working-class European Americans with whom he lodges when it is revealed he is the father of the wife's newborn child.

Houston, Velina Hasu. *Tea*, 1988. Dramatization of the experience of Japanese women who marry American servicemen and come to the United States as "war brides" after World War II.

Hwang, David Henry. *FOB*, 1979 and 1980. Illuminates the conflicts of recent Chinese immigrants to America, pejoratively called FOB for "fresh off the boat," with assimilated Chinese Americans.

____. *M. Butterfly*, 1988. A Tony Award–winning play that questions Western notions of Asian sexuality, loosely based on the twenty-year-old relationship of a French diplomat who believed that his lover, a Chinese opera singer, was female, but is really male.

Lim, Genny. *Paper Angels and Bitter Cane/Two Plays*, 1991. The first play is about so-called "paper sons," or fake relatives, during the period of Chinese exclusion from immigration to the United States; the second is about Chinese laborers recruited for Hawaii's cane plantations.

POETRY COLLECTIONS

Ai (pen name of Ai Ogawa, born Florence Anthony). *No Surrender*, 2010. Final poetry collection includes personal pieces telling of the persona's struggle with cancer; other poems look at illegal South Asian immigrants to America and violence in a post-9/11 world.

____. *Vice: New and Selected Poems*, 1999. The poet's characteristic dramatic monologues include references to Asian political figures such as Imelda Marcos and address contemporary American concerns such as domestic violence.

Alexander, Meena. *Raw Silk*, 2004. The poems offer a cosmopolitan, cross-cultural viewpoint, with many personae who have roots in their native India.

Amirthanayagam, Indra. *The Elephants of Reckoning*, 1993. Poems reflecting on how time in the United States has changed the poet's view of his native Sri Lanka.

Berssenbrugge, Mei-Mei. *I Love Artists: New and Selected Poems*, 2006. A selection of the poet's favorite and new works, often reflecting on issues of multiracial identity.

Gotera, Vince. *Fighting Kite*, 2007. A cycle of poems about a Filipino American trickster by an award-winning poet.

Hahn, Kimiko. *The Unbearable Heart*, 1995. All of the poems are influenced by the accidental death of the poet's mother in 1993, and address personal grief as well as anger at violence against non-Western women.

____. *Volatile*, 1999. The poems express outrage over violence against women in both Asia and America.

____. *The Narrow Road to the Interior: Poems*, 2006. Using the medieval Japanese style of zuihitsu, or prose reflections, the poet sheds a unique light on contemporary American themes.

____. *Toxic Flora: Poems*, 2010. Poems link scientific facts and discoveries to reflections on the filial bond between a daughter and her parents, a topic central to the experience of many Asian Americans.

Hongo, Garrett Kaoru. *Yellow Light*, 1982. Tender poems about the joys and tribulations of Asian Americans in their everyday life in 1970s Hawaii.

____. *The River of Heaven*, 1988. The persona's personal reflections include a visit to the grave of his Japanese American immigrant ancestors in a remote Hawaiian location.

Inada, Lawson Fusao. *Legends from Camp*, 1992. An award-winning poetry collection opening with poems about the American internment of Japanese Americans during World War II, continuing with poems about growing up Japanese American in California and Oregon after the war.

Kim, Myung Mi. *Penury*, 2009. Avant-garde poems focus on the humiliation of illegal Asian immigrants by American authorities.

____. *Dura*, 2008. Complex poems look at the issues of Asian immigration to America and the inequities of global society.

Lai, Him Mark, et al., eds. *Island: Poetry and History of Chinese Immigrants on Angel Island, 1910–1940*, 1980. Collects sixty-nine original poems that were written on the walls of this holding center for Chinese American immigrants in the San Francisco Bay.

Lau, Alan Chong. *Blues and Greens: A Produce Worker's Journal*, 2000. Poems created through the author's experience as a worker for a produce wholesaler; includes reflections on Asian American co-workers and customers.

Lee, Li-Young. *Rose*, 1986. Deeply personal poems about a Chinese American son and his father, as well as the son's encounter with European American ignorance about Asian culture as in the often-anthologized poem "Persimmons."

____. *The City in Which I Love You*, 1990. Includes beautiful love poems of the Chinese American persona and his Italian American wife.

____. *Book of My Nights*, 2001. Self-reflective poems about the art of writing poetry and the persona's Chinese American identity.

____. *Behind My Eyes*, 2008. Poems include references to Asian American immigration, the persona's love for his wife in a mixed-race marriage, and the quest for Christian spiritual guidance.

Lew, Walter. *Treadwinds: Poems and Intermedia Works*, 2002. Creative poems with cross-cultural Asian, American, and European references.

Lum, Wing Tek. *Expounding the Doubtful Points*, 1987. Angry poems about stereotypes and racism encountered by Chinese Americans in Hawaii and mainland America, as well as reflections on the persona's family heritage.

Mirikitani, Janice. *Love Works*, 2001. The poems address Japanese American internment during World War II in the United States, fragile family relations, and the plight of people at the margins of society.

Nezhukumatathil, Aimee. *Lucky Fish*, 2011. Reflections on people who observe beauty in places as diverse as New York, the Philippines, and India.

____. *At the Drive-In Volcano*, 2007. The poems evoke the diverse beauty of American and Asian landscapes.

____. *Miracle Fruit*, 2003. The poems feature the experience of different Asian and American cultural and literary heritages.

Ramanujan, Attipat Krishnaswami. *Second Sight*, 1986. The personae of the poems link their lives in the United States to their South Asian, Indian experience.

Song, Cathy. *Picture Bride*, 1983. Poems celebrate the author's grandparents, early immigrants to Hawaii, and reflect on their experiences and those of their descendants.

_____. *Frameless Windows, Squares of Light*, 1988. Intensely personal, yet occasionally abstract poems, many focused on the author's Chinese American mother married to a Korean American airline pilot living in Hawaii.

_____. *The Land of Bliss*, 2001. The poems concern the struggles of an Asian American girl coping with bullying, an Asian American daughter's worry as her mother succumbs to dementia, and the suffering encountered by families dealing with loss.

_____. *Cloud Moving Hands*, 2007. Many poems invoke Buddhist beliefs to cope with loss, and some are highly ironic, as when a noble Japanese lady and her son are reborn in contemporary suburban America.

Tran, Barbara. *In the Mynah Bird's Own Words*, 2002. Poems show a Vietnamese American daughter reflect on the meaning of the Catholic faith of her mother.

Wong, Nellie. *Stolen Moments*, 1997. Poems by an unapologetically radical feminist socialist Chinese American poet expressing her position on Asian American issues.

_____. *Dreams in Harrison Railroad Park: Poems*, 1977. Poems lamenting the existence of racism and social injustice affecting Asian Americans and underprivileged people in America.

Yamada, Mitsuye. *Camp Notes and Other Poems*, 1976. Autobiographical poems about the internment of Japanese Americans in the United States during World War II.

SHORT STORY COLLECTIONS

Chang, Lan Samantha. *Hunger: A Novella and Stories*, 1998. Short fiction primarily about Chinese American experiences.

Chin, Frank. *The Chinaman Pacific and Frisco R.R. Co.*, 1988. Stories juxtaposing the heroic contributions of Chinese American laborers to America's transcontinental railroad in the nineteenth century with the stifling stagnation in 1970s Chinese American communities.

Desai, Anita. *Diamond Dust and Other Stories*, 2000. Key stories tell of Indian characters visiting or returning home after a long stay in the United States, which altered their perspective on Indian life and society.

Easton, Edith Maude. See Sui Sin Far

Kono, Juliet. *Ho'olulu Park and the Pepsodent Smile and Other Stories*, 2004. Stories about the lives of Asian American immigrants in Hawaii and their interactions with both European Americans and Hawaiians.

Lahiri, Jhumpa. *Interpreter of Maladies*, 1999. Stories about the experience of first-generation Indian Americans.

_____. *Unaccustomed Earth*, 2008. A best-seller offering stories that feature identity conflicts of second- and third-generation Indian Americans.

Leong, Russell Charles. *Phoenix Eyes and Other Stories*, 2000. Stories about Asian American immigrants as well as the title story about a transpacific gay call boy ring.

Li, Yiyun. *Gold Boy, Emerald Girl: Stories*, 2010. Includes "Prison," a story about a Chinese American couple returning to China to find a replacement for their own dead teenage daughter.

Mori, Toshio. *Yokohama, California*, 1949. Stories of Japanese Americans and their culture prior, during, and after the internment of Japanese Americans during World War II.

Mukherjee, Bharati. *The Middleman and Other Stories*, 1988. Stories focusing on the immigrant experience of South Asian women in the United States.

Phan, Aimee. *We Should Never Meet: Stories*, 2004. Stories that cover Operation Babylift, the evacuation of Vietnamese orphans from falling Saigon in 1975, and the lives of different Vietnamese American characters including two very different sisters: a gangster and a model daughter.

Santos, Bienvenido. *The Day the Dancers Came*, 1967. Stories focus on Filipinos living in 1950s America who long for their native country, including bachelors desiring romance with Filipinas from home.

Sui Sin Far (pen name of Edith Maude Easton). *Mrs. Spring Fragrance*, 1912. Short stories that portray in a sympathetic and realistic light—very unusual for its time—the challenges faced by early Chinese Americans.

Yamamoto, Hisaye. *Seventeen Syllables and Other Stories*, 1988. A collection of classic stories originally published after 1948 that presents conflicts in Japanese American families, as in the title story, or the experience of internment, as in "The Legend of Miss Sasagawara."

Yamashita, Karen Tei. *I Hotel*, 2010. Ten interrelated novellas irreverently covering the Asian American experience in San Francisco during the 1960s and 1970s.

OTHER

Cha, Theresa Hak Kyung. *Dictée*, 1982. An experimental literary work combining text and unrelated photographs; explores the fate of mythical and real women, including the author and her mother, all trying to speak out about their experiences in a very unique format.

Chin, Frank, et al., eds. *Aiiieeeee!*, 1974. A collection of short stories, plays, and poems by Asian American writers radically challenging the notion of Asian American assimilation into mainstream America.

Say, Allen. *Grandfather's Journey*, 1993. A Caldecott Medal–winning children's book, written and illustrated by the author, tells of a Japanese man of the Meiji era visiting California and returning there with his Japanese wife, only to leave to have his daughter educated in Japan.

See, Lisa. *On Gold Mountain: The One-Hundred-Year Odyssey of My Chinese-American Family*, 1995. A best-selling history beginning with the author's Chinese American grandfather marrying a European American and laying the foundation for a family spanning generations.

Tabios, Eileen. *I Take Thee, English, for My Beloved*, 2005. A multi-genre volume mixing poetry, autobiography, drama, short fiction, and nonfiction to express the Filipina American avant-garde author's love for the English language as her mode to reach out to her reading community.

Yamauchi, Wakako. *Songs My Mother Told Me: Stories, Plays, and Memoir*, 1994. The collected works cover the Japanese American experience in rural California before World War II as well as the Japanese American internment during the war, and its aftermath.

Yep, Laurence. *The Golden Mountain Chronicles* series, nine volumes from *The Serpent's Children* to *Dragons of Silk*, 1984–2011. The adventures of members of the fictional Young family ranging from 1849 in China to 1995 in the United States; written for young adults. Two volumes in the series won the Newbery Medal.

R. C. Lutz

Organizations and Societies

The following are relevant organizations and societies that have national appeal and are headquartered in the United States. The organizations and societies included here were identified through Internet searches conducted in 2011. Organizations are listed first; the list includes organizations with varying purposes ranging from educational and artistic to scientific and charitable. Next is a list of societies, featuring an array of societies geared toward a specific profession, discipline, or ethnicity. Various ethnic groups make up Asian Americans and Pacific Islander Americans, and the organizations and societies listed here recognize this diversity. Although some organizations and societies appear to target one particular ethnicity, such as the Organization of Chinese Americans, they are often inclusive of other Asian American and Pacific Islander ethnic groups as well.

Organizations

Asian American Business Roundtable (AABR)

20224 Thunderhead Way
Germantown, MD 20874
Phone: (301) 601-9038
Fax: (301) 601-9430
info@aabronline.org
http://www.aabronline.org

AABR offers valuable information and business literature for Asian American businesspeople and aims to help members effectively grow businesses.

Asian American Journalists Association (AAJA)

5 Third Street, Suite 1108
San Francisco, CA 94103
Phone: (415) 346-2051
Fax: (415) 346-6343
national@aaja.org
http://www.aaja.org

AAJA enables Asian American and Pacific Islander journalists to stay connected and up to date on issues such as unfair news practices and offers guidance to those interested in becoming journalists.

Asian American Legal Defense and Education Fund (AALDEF)

99 Hudson Street, 12th Floor
New York, NY 10013
Phone: (212) 966-5932
Fax: (212) 966-4303
info@aaldef.org
http://www.aaldef.org

AALDEF aims to ensure that Asian Americans' civil rights are respected. It holds legal clinics, offers legal publications, and is involved in litigation cases, among other activities.

Asian Americans for Equality (AAFE)

108 Norfolk Street
New York, NY 10002
Phone: (212) 979-8381
Fax: (212) 979-8386
askaafe@aafe.org
http://www.aafe.org

A champion of Asian American rights, AAFE makes efforts to ensure that social services, legal services, and assistance related to businesses, homeownership, and immigration are available to Asian Americans.

Asian American Writers Workshop Inc.

110–12 W. 27th Street, Suite 600
New York, NY 10001
Phone: (212) 494-0061
desk@aaww.org
http://www.aaww.org

This organization puts a spotlight on Asian American writers and their works through literary workshops, contests, and events featuring Asian American authors.

Asian Pacific American Labor Alliance (APALA)

815 16th Street NW
Washington, DC 20009
Phone: (202) 508-3733
Fax: (202) 508-3733
apala@apalanet.org
http://www.apalanet.org

APALA enables Asian Pacific American union members to come together to defend civil, labor, immigrant, and political rights. APALA trains union organizers, including female union members, and empowers voters.

Asian and Pacific Islander American Health Forum (APIAHF)

1828 L Street, NW, Suite 802
Washington, DC 20036
Phone: (202) 466-7772
Fax: (202) 466-6444
info@apiahf.org
http://www.apiahf.org

APIAHF's major priority is for Asian and Pacific Islander Americans to have optimum healthcare. APIAHF is involved in healthcare policy decisions and offers health-related webinars and listservs.

Association of Chinese American Physicians (ACAP)

33–70 Prince Street, Suite 703
Flushing, NY 11354
Phone: (718) 321-8893
admin@acaponline.org
http://www.acaponline.org

ACAP brings together Chinese American physicians and medical students. Members are involved in professional development opportunities, conventions, galas, seminars, and healthcare policy decisions.

Center for Asian American Media (CAAM)

145 Ninth Street, Suite 350
San Francisco, CA 94103-2641
Phone: (415) 863-0814
Fax: (415) 863-7428
info@caamedia.org
http://caamedia.org

CAAM puts a spotlight on Asian American television shows, films, and digital media stories through film festivals, public broadcasts, and a film and video distribution program.

Hmong National Development, Inc. (HND)

1628 16th Street NW
Washington, DC 20009
Phone: (202) 588-1661
info@hndinc.org
http://www.hndinc.org

HND focuses on civic involvement and advocacy of policies pertaining to Hmong Americans. Through national conferences and programs, HND reaches out to local Hmong organizations and strives to empower people of Hmong descent.

Japanese American Citizens League (JACL)

1765 Sutter Street
San Francisco, CA 94115
Phone: (415) 921-5225
Fax: (415) 931-4671
jacl@jacl.org
http://www.jacl.org

JACL has been defending the civil rights of Asian and Pacific Islander Americans since 1929. This enormous organization offers enriching programs for youth and scholastic resources on Asian American historical events for teachers.

National Asian American Pacific Islander Mental Health Association (NAAPIMHA)

1215 19th Street, Suite A
Denver, CO 80202
Phone: (303) 298-7910
Fax: (303) 298-8081
djida@naapimha.org
http://www.naapimha.org

NAAPIMHA focuses on fostering the mental health of Asian Americans and Pacific Islander Americans, advocating policies and offering resources such as fact sheets filled with mental health information.

National Asian American Theatre Co., Inc. (NAATCO)

520 8th Avenue, Suite 308
New York, NY 10018
Phone: (212) 244-0447
Fax: (212) 244-0448
info@naatco.org
http://naatco.org

NAATCO aims to highlight Asian American talent through theater productions.

National Asian Pacific American Bar Association (NAPABA)

1612 K Street, NW, Suite 1400
Washington, DC 20006
Phone: (202) 775-9555
Fax: (202) 775-9333
inf@napaba.org
http://www.napaba.org

Through NAPABA, Asian and Pacific Islander American legal professionals and students unite, take part in committees and conventions, and stay abreast of legal issues and job openings.

National Association of Asian American Law Enforcement Commanders (NAAALEC)

PO Box 70561
Oakland, CA 94612
naaalecpresident@gmail.com
http://www.naaalec.org

NAAALEC enables Asian American law enforcement professionals to connect, helps members further their careers, and reaches out to Asian Americans interested in entering this field.

National Association of Asian American Professionals (NAAAP)

PO Box 354
Uwchland, PA 19480
Phone: (215) 715-3046
http://www.naaap.org

NAAAP encourages leadership among Asian American members through career-related workshops, conventions, and its job portal.

National Association of Korean Americans (NAKA)

3883 Plaza Drive
Fairfax, VA 22030
Phone: (703) 267-2388
Fax: (703) 267-2396
nakausa@naka.org
http://www.naka.org

NAKA is devoted to defending Korean Americans' civil rights through activities such as public forums, rallies, marches, voter registration drives, and national conferences.

National Congress of Vietnamese Americans (NCVA)

6433 Northanna Drive
Springfield, VA 22150
Phone: (703) 971-9178
Fax: (703) 719-5764
info@ncvaonline.org
http://www.ncvaonline.org

NCVA advocates on behalf of Asian Pacific Americans including Vietnamese Americans. Among its activities, NCVA holds forums and delivers outreach programs.

National Federation of Filipino American Associations (NaFFAA)

1322 18th Street, NW
Washington, DC 20036-1803
Phone: (202) 361-0296
NaFFAANational@gmail.org
http://www.naffaausa.org

NaFFAA encompasses over five hundred Filipino American organizations and institutions and seeks to address Filipino American issues such as civil rights, health, and education.

National Korean American Service and Education Consortium (NAKASEC)

1628 16th Street, NW, Suite 306
Washington, DC 20009
Phone: (202) 299-9540
Fax: (202) 299-9729
nakasec@nakasec.org
http://nakasec.org

NAKASEC addresses Korean American civil and immigrant rights, education, and health through publications, youth programs, and other activities.

Organization of Chinese Americans, Inc. (OCA)

1322 18th Street, NW
Washington, DC 20036-1803
Phone: (202) 223-5500
Fax: (202) 296-0540
oca@ocanational.org
http://www.ocanational.org

OCA focuses on helping Asian and Pacific Islander Americans meet their goals economically, socially, academically, and politically. Members take part in national conventions as well as scholarship, internship, leadership, and mentorship programs.

Pakistani American Pharmaceutical Association (PAPA)

128 Mansion Avenue
Yonkers, NY 10704
Phone: (914) 613-8645
Fax: (212) 591-6046
info@papausa.com
http://papausa.com

PAPA gives Pakistani pharmacists the chance to join together and focus on issues related to their profession. It holds several events and publishes a gazette of interest to pharmacists.

South Asian Americans Leading Together, Inc. (SAALT)

6930 Carroll Avenue, Suite 506
Takoma Park, MD 20912
Phone: (301) 270-1855

Fax: (301) 270-1882
http://www.saalt.org

Championing justice and equality for South Asian Americans, SAALT reviews and advocates policies, holds forums and conferences, and gives members plenty of chances to be involved in activism opportunities.

Southeast Asia Resource Action Center (SEARAC)

1628 16th Street, NW
Washington, DC 20009
Phone: (202) 667-4690
Fax: (202) 667-6449
searac@searac.org
http://www.searac.org

SEARAC supports the needs of Southeast Asian Americans including Cambodian, Vietnamese, and Laotian Americans, encouraging leadership, advocacy, and community involvement within Southeast Asian American communities.

Taiwanese American Citizens League (TACL)

3001 Walnut Grove
Rosemead, CA 91770
Phone: (626) 551-0227
Fax: (626) 551-0227
tacl@tacl.org
http://www.tacl.org

TACL strives to enhance Taiwanese Americans' lives particularly through youth opportunities such as internships and scholarships.

Vietnamese American Armed Forces Association (VAAFA)

PO Box 8434
Fountain Valley, CA 92728-8434
Phone: (714) 386-9896
vaafa.org@gmail.com
http://www.vaafa.org

VAAFA brings together Vietnamese Americans who have been a part of the United States military. VAAFA offers military news and resources through its website and reaches out to members and their families by offering scholarships and care packages.

Vietnamese American Arts & Letters Association (VAALA)

1600 N. Broadway, Suite 110
Santa Ana, CA 92706
Phone: (714) 893-6145
info@vaala.org
http://www.vaala.org

Through publications, film festivals, art exhibitions, art contests, recitals, book fairs, and its artist resource guide, VAALA showcases the talent of Vietnamese American photographers, filmmakers, poets, and composers.

SOCIETIES

Asian American Music Society (AAMS)

39 Eton Overlook
Rockville, MD 20850-3004
Phone: (301) 424-3379
webmaster@aamsopera.com
http://www.aamsopera.com

AAMS embraces all types of music, helps organize musical events, and provides Asian dance and musical entertainment for special occasions.

Chinese American Medical Society (CAMS)

41 Elizabeth Street
Suite 600
New York, NY 10013
Phone: (212) 334-4760
Fax: (646) 965-1876
jlove@camsociety.org
http://www.camsociety.org

CAMS unites Chinese Americans from the medical field, and members convene on medical-related issues. CAMS offers helpful opportunities such as scholarships, fellowships, and job postings.

Chinese American Society (CAS)

180 Golf Club Road, #139
Pleasant Hill, CA 94523
Phone: (408) 457-0057
help@ca-soc.org
http://ca-soc.org

CAS encourages Chinese Americans to be involved in politics, offers insight about Chinese American history through its publications, and posts important Chinese American news on its website.

Chinese Historical Society of America (CHSA)

956 Clay Street

San Francisco, CA 94108
Phone: (415) 391-1188 x101
Fax: (415) 391-1150
info@chsa.org
http://www.chsa.org

CHSA offers a good glimpse into Chinese Americans' historical past, holds educational programs for youth and adults, and offers traveling exhibits.

Filipino American National Historical Society (FANHS)

810 18th Avenue #100
Seattle, WA 98122-4778
Phone: (206) 322-0203
fanhsnational@earthlink.net
http://www.fanhs-national.org

FANHS has national headquarters and local chapters teeming with information on Filipino American history. FANHS offers video documentaries, oral histories, and exhibits pertaining to Filipino Americans.

Korean American Historical Society (KAHS)

719 S. King St
Seattle, WA 98104-3035
Phone: (253) 235-9393
KAHSinfo@kahs.org
http://www.kahs.org

Since 1985, KAHS has been a rich source of Korean American history and has been involved in festivals, concerts, and oral history projects.

Laotian American Society (LAS)

PO Box 48432
Atlanta, GA 30362
info@lasga.org
http://www.lasga.org

LAS reaches out to people of Laotian descent particularly through youth educational programs. The news section on the LAS website reveals the latest developments concerning people with Laotian heritage.

National Japanese American Historical Society (NJAHS)

1684 Post Street
San Francisco, CA 94115
Phone: (415) 921-5007
Fax: (415) 921-5087
http://www.njahs.org

NJAHS abounds with Japanese American historical information and offers educational resources for teachers, exhibits, and events such as film screenings and workshops.

Brooke Posley

Libraries and Research Centers

This appendix lists selected libraries and research centers—of schools, national organizations, and government agencies—that offer resources focused on Asians and Pacific Islanders in the United States. Such resources are generally useful for librarians, educators, students, researchers, and lay persons. The appendix also lists useful and valuable metasites. Because URLs frequently change, the accuracy of these sites cannot be guaranteed; however, longstanding sites, such as those of educational institutions, national organizations, and government agencies, generally maintain links when sites move or upgrade their offerings.

Libraries and Research Centers

Arizona State University Asian Pacific American Studies
PO Box 874902
Tempe, AZ 85287-4902
Phone: (480) 965-9711
Fax: (480) 727-7911
apas@asu.edu
http://apas.clas.asu.edu/

The Asian Pacific American Studies department serves undergraduate students and the Southwest community at large, promoting Asian studies and fostering greater understanding of Asian history and culture through a variety of activities, such as teacher training, scholarly conferences, public symposia, and other events.

The Asia Collections, Kroch Asia Library, Cornell University
180 Kroch Library
Ithaca, NY 14853
Reference Desk Phone: (607) 255-8199
Circulation Desk Phone: (607) 255-4245
asiaref@cornell.edu
http://asia.library.cornell.edu/ac/

Housed in the Carl A. Kroch Library, the Asia Collections is one of the finest collections of Asian historical and literary resources available, including print materials, electronic documents, and two book stack levels covering regions throughout Asia.

International and Area Studies Library, University of Illinois at Urbana-Champaign
1408 W. Gregory Dr.
Urbana, IL 61801
Phone: (217) 333-1501
Cataloguing Coordinator: ShuYong Jiang (shyjiang@illinois.edu)
http://www.library.illinois.edu/ias/

The International and Area Studies Library includes the Asian studies collection, which acquires and maintains Asian language materials in Chinese, Japanese, Korean, Arabic, Hebrew, Indic, Persian, Indonesian, Vietnamese, and Thai. The Asian collection is interdisciplinary in nature, with a primary focus on services in the humanities, social sciences, and, to a lesser extent, such fields as agriculture and the sciences.

Asian Reading Room, the Library of Congress (LOC)
101 Independence Ave. SE
Thomas Jefferson Building, LJ 150
Washington, DC 20540-4810
Phone: (202) 707-3766 x5426
Fax: (202) 252-3336
Ask a Librarian: http://www.loc.gov/rr/askalib/ask-asian.html
asianrequest@loc.gov
http://www.loc.gov/rr/asian/

The Asian Reading Room serves researchers seeking to explore the Library of Congress's Asian collections. These collections include materials in many Asian languages and cover a wide range of geographic areas. With nearly three million print and electronic resources, these collections are the most comprehensive to be found outside of Asia. Assistance is available from area specialists and reference librarians.

Council on East Asian Libraries (CEAL), the Association for Asian Studies, Inc.
1021 E. Huron St.
Ann Arbor, MI 48104
Phone: (734) 665-2490
Fax: (734) 665-3801
http://www.eastasianlib.org

Membership is open to all members of the Association for Asian Studies. CEAL facilitates the discussion of issues relevant to East Asian libraries. Among its priorities is a commitment to the development of East Asian library resources, services, and organizations, and the promotion of interlibrary and international cooperation.

Statistical data published from 1957 to the present is available through the online CEAL Statistics Database. Also of use is CEAL's online directory of East Asian libraries in North America.

The Council on East Asian Studies at Yale University (CEAS)

Henry R. Luce Hall, Room 320
34 Hillhouse Ave.
PO Box 208206
New Haven, CT 06520-8206
Phone: (203) 432-3426
Fax: (203) 432-3430
eastasian.studies@yale.edu
http://eastasianstudies.research.yale.edu

CEAS is a National Resource Center for the study of East Asian languages and cultures, as designated by the US Department of Education. CEAS hosts a variety of events and discussions to encourage the study of East Asian countries. The East Asia Library of Sterling Memorial Library (also at Yale) provides one of the oldest and largest collections of print resources available in the United States. Through educational activities that emphasize joint endeavors, CEAS takes the lead in East Asia studies on Yale's campus and the region at large. Visiting scholars and lecturers participate in CEAS activities annually.

The Department of East Asian Languages and Literatures (DEALL), the Ohio State University

Hagerty Hall 398
1775 College Rd.
Columbus, OH 43210-1340
Phone: (614) 292-5816
Fax: (614) 292-3225
deall@osu.edu
http://deall.osu.edu/

The DEALL in the College of Humanities at the Ohio State University is among the largest programs in the country. In addition to information about the programs and courses offered by the Department of East Asian Languages and Literatures, the website provides excellent resource links for Chinese, Japanese, and Korean studies.

South Asian Studies, Duke University Libraries

William R. Perkins Library
411 Chapel Dr.
Durham, NC 27708
Phone: (919) 660-5880

Fax: (919) 684-2855
asklib@duke.edu
http://library.duke.edu/research/subject/guides/south_asian_studies/

With over 200,000 titles, which include serials and monographs, Duke University Libraries offers one of the Southeast region's finest collections of South Asian materials in English and selected vernacular languages (Bengali, Hindi, Marathi, Sanskrit, and Urdu). The collection is integrated with the general library and can be searched online. Most items are housed at Perkins Library; however, specialized titles are sent to the appropriate branch library.

The East Asia Library (EAL), Stanford University, J. Henry Meyer Memorial Library

560 Escondido Mall
Stanford, CA 94305
Phone: (650) 725-3435
Fax: (650) 724-2028
eastasialibrary@stanford.edu
http://lib.stanford.edu/eal

The East Asia Library is the primary Asian-language collection of Stanford University, with holdings of more than 520,000 volumes in the social sciences and humanities. The library shares a history with the Hoover Institution, which has been collecting materials on twentieth century history since the 1920s.

The East Asian Collection, Joseph Regenstein Library, the University of Chicago

1100 E. Fifty-Seventh St.
Chicago, IL 60637
Phone: (773) 702-4685
Fax: (773) 702-6623
Ask a Librarian: http://www.lib.uchicago.edu/e/ask/RBICask.html
http://www.lib.uchicago.edu/e/easia/

The Joseph Regenstein Library at the University of Chicago holds over 570,000 volumes in Chinese, Japanese, and Korean. The library's website offers an extensive search guide for East Asian materials; subject guides to Chinese, Japanese, and Korean collections; East Asian serials collection; and links to library and online databases such as WorldCat.

C. V. Starr East Asian Library, Columbia University Libraries

300 Kent Hall
1140 Amsterdam Ave., MC 3901
New York, NY 10027

Phone: (212) 854-4318
Fax: (212) 662-6286
starr@libraries.cul.columbia.edu
http://library.columbia.edu/indiv/eastasian.html

With nearly 870,000 volumes, which include periodical titles and newspapers in a range of Asian and Western languages, the C. V. Starr East Asian Library offers one of the finest collections in the United States, particularly for the humanities and social sciences.

C. V. Starr East Asian Library, University of California-Berkeley

Durant Hall 208
Berkeley, CA 94720-6000
Phone: (510) 642-2557
eal@library.berkeley.edu
http://www.lib.berkeley.edu/EAL/

The East Asian Library at UC Berkeley offers Chinese, Korean, and Japanese materials in a collection that rivals that of the Library of Congress and the Harvard-Yenching Library. The strength of the library lies in the humanities and the social sciences. Resources range from standard library offerings, such as full-text electronic databases, books, and manuscripts, to rare materials, such as early Chinese, Japanese, and Korean woodblock prints. The Center for Chinese Studies Library is a branch of the East Asian Library, holding more than 55,000 volumes and serving as the leading academic research center on contemporary China in the country.

South/Southeast Asia Library, University of California-Berkeley

120 Doe Library
Berkeley, CA 94720-6000
Phone: (510) 642-3095
Fax: (510) 643-8817
ssea@library.berkeley.edu
http://www.lib.berkeley.edu/SSEAL/index.html

In partnership with other libraries on UC Berkeley's campus, the South/Southeast Asia Library provides vernacular research and teaching in Asian studies. The collection serves as the primary reference center for South and Southeast Asian humanities and social sciences. Alongside the C. V. Starr East Asian Library, this library maintains close relations with the Institute of East Asian Studies and the Center of Chinese Studies Library.

East Asian Library and the Gest Collection, Princeton University

33 Frist Campus Center, Room 317
Princeton, NJ 08544
Phone: (609) 258-3182
Fax: (609) 258-4573
gest@princeton.edu
http://eastasianlib.princeton.edu/

The website contains two major sections: an introduction page and a guide page. The introduction page gives brief summaries of the collections of Chinese, Japanese, Korean, and Western-language materials, and a rare book collection. The guide page provides links to East Asian resources, catalogs, subject guides, and several online databases (such as the Electronic Siku Quanshu and China Academic Journals Network).

East Asian Library, University of Kansas

519 Watson Library
1425 Jayhawk Blvd.
Lawrence, KS 66045
Phone: (785) 864-4669
Fax: (785) 864-3850
Ask a Librarian: http://www.lib.ku.edu/aska/
http://www.lib.ku.edu/eastasia/

The resources available from the East Asian Library include Internet articles and databases devoted to individual countries (such as China, Taiwan, Japan, and Korea), multimedia and K–12 resources, bibliographies, a nonprint Chinese newspaper collection, and links to other East Asian libraries and programs.

East Asian Library, University of Pittsburgh

207 Hillman Library
3960 Forbes Ave.
Pittsburgh, PA 15260
Phone: (412) 648-7708
Fax: (412) 648-7683
Ask a Librarian: http://www.library.pitt.edu/reference/
http://www.library.pitt.edu/libraries/eal/index.htm

The EAL is among the most esteemed collections of East Asian items in the country, featuring more than 431,167 volumes of monographs, about 900 periodical titles, thousands of multimedia resources, over 27 newspapers, and 18 online databases. The library ranks as one of the largest East Asian resource centers in the region. The primary mission of the library is to support the Asian Studies Center with regard to Chinese, Japanese and Korean studies.

East Asian Studies, Washington University in St. Louis
East Asian Library
January Hall, 2nd Floor
St. Louis, MO 63130
Phone: (314) 935-4816
Fax: (314) 935-4045
tchang@wustl.edu
http://libguides.wustl.edu/eastasian

East Asian Studies provides links to Chinese studies, Japanese studies, and Korean studies research guides, as well as information about Washington University's East Asian Library collection, electronic databases, and electronic journals and catalogs on East Asian studies. The group's website offers general information about the East Asian Studies programs for current and prospective students.

East Asia Library, University of Washington
322 Gowen Hall
Box 353527
Seattle, WA 98195-3527
Phone: (206) 543-0242
http://www.lib.washington.edu/about/contact.html
http://www.lib.washington.edu/east-asia/

The East Asia Library provides resources on East Asian subjects at the University of Washington and other academic libraries. The collection offers resources in the humanities and social sciences on and from several Asian countries, as well as computing, academic, and library resources, business and commercial news, and links to major East Asian library collections.

East Asian Sites, Five College Center for East Asian Studies (FCCEAS), Smith College
Florence Gilman Pav.
69 Paradise Rd.
Northampton, MA 01063
Phone: (413) 585-3751
Fax: (413) 585-3748
fcceas@fivecolleges.edu
http://www.smith.edu/fcceas/home.html

The FCCEAS is a consortium that is committed to the teaching of East Asian history and culture throughout New England schools. Member institutions University of Massachusetts-Amherst, Hampshire, Mount Holyoke, Amherst, and Smith Colleges work to encourage and improve the teaching of East Asian topics at all levels of education. The FCCEAS website offers useful links on education and travel, arts and culture, and educational conferences and seminars.

Harvard-Yenching Library, Harvard College Library
2 Divinity Ave.
Cambridge, MA 02138
Phone: (617) 496-3347
Fax: (617) 496-6008
hylref@fas.harvard.edu
http://hcl.harvard.edu/libraries/harvard-yenching/

Harvard-Yenching Library's collection joins over one million volumes in Western languages and Chinese, Japanese, Korean, Vietnamese, and more. A number of rarer works distinguish the collection, including Japanese Buddhist scrolls, Korean genealogies, Vietnamese newspapers, and other documents of historical and literary interest. The library website provides links to print and online publications, Western language newspapers, and academic programs.

Archives and Special Collections in Chinese and Japanese, Hoover Institution Library and Archives
Stanford University
434 Galvez Mall
Stanford, CA 94305-6010
Phone: (650) 723-3563
Fax: (650) 725-3445
Archives Reference: Carol Leadenham (carol.leadenham@stanford.edu)
http://www.hoover.org/library-and-archives/collections/east-asia

Since the collection's beginning in 1919, the Hoover Library and Archives has collected historical and political accounts to support Herbert Hoover's vision. With an overall collection of many million archival documents, the Hoover Institution includes East Asia archives and special collections in Chinese and Japanese. The collection also features rare books, newspapers, private letters and diaries, banned and illegal periodicals, internal documents, and business-related documents. Much of the collection was specially acquired and consists of materials that are not available elsewhere.

The National Bureau of Asian Research (NBR)
George F. Russell Jr. Hall
1414 NE Forty-Second St., Suite 300
Seattle, WA 98105
Phone: (206) 632-7370
Fax: (206) 632-7487
nbr@nbr.org
http://www.nbr.org/
1301 Pennsylvania Ave., NW Suite 305
Washington, DC 20004

Phone: (202) 347-9767
Fax: (202) 347-9766
nbrDC@nbr.org

The NBR collaborates with specialists and institutions worldwide in researching issues of energy, globalization, and politics in regard to US relations with Asia. Drawing upon a wide range of educational and corporate alliances, the NBR offers critical insights and resources regarding policies that pertain to Asia.

Richard C. Rudolph East Asian Library, University of California, Los Angeles

21617 Charles E. Young Research Library
Los Angeles, CA 90095-7511
Phone: (310) 825-4836
Reference and Research Help: http://www.library.ucla.edu/questions/1690.cfm
http://www.library.ucla.edu/libraries/eastasian/

UCLA's Richard C. Rudolph East Asian Library offers special collections devoted to Chinese, Japanese, and Korean studies, each of which specializes in specific subject areas and connects to relevant reference databases. A number of electronic periodicals and specialized research guides are available for use online.

Walter H. Shorenstein Asia-Pacific Research Center (Shorenstein APARC), Stanford University

616 Serra St. E301
Stanford, CA 94305-6055
Phone: (650) 723-9741
Fax: (650) 723-6530
http://aparc.stanford.edu/

The Shorenstein APARC collaborates with scholars to produce interdisciplinary research that focuses on Asian and Pacific countries for education and governmental policy. The organization hosts undergraduate and graduate courses and a range of programs for general and specialist audiences; these programs include the Japan Studies Program and the Corporate Affiliates Visiting Fellows Program, among others.

METASITES

Central Intelligence Agency (CIA)

Office of Public Affairs
Washington, DC 20505
Phone: (703) 482-0623
Fax: (703) 482-1739
https://www.cia.gov/library/publications/the-world-factbook/index.html

The CIA's annual World Factbook offers an excellent reference guide on country studies, covering historical, economic, geographic, and transportation-related information for over two hundred world entities. Included are maps of major regions, physical and political maps, flags of the world, and a map divided by time zone.

Countries and Regions, US Department of State

US Department of State
2201 C Street NW
Washington, DC 20520
Phone: (202) 647-4000
http://www.state.gov/countries

The Bureau of Public Affairs, which handles the website, monitors international affairs in regions throughout the world. Pages are devoted to specific world regions and state department bureaus' involvement in their current affairs; these pages also offer resources about the history, government, economy, and foreign relations of the relevant country. The available information is up-to-date and relevant from a global perspective.

Silk Road Foundation

14510 Big Basin Way #269
Saratoga, CA 95070
Phone: (408) 867-1364
info@silk-road.com
http://www.silk-road.com/toc/index.html

A nonprofit organization, the Silk Road Foundation was established in 1996 to promote the study and preservation of Asian and Silk Road–related culture and art. The website offers resources for studies about the Xinjiang and Dunhuang regions, Sven Hedin, and Buddhism, and links to articles, bibliographies, and travel sites.

Willette F. Stinson

BIBLIOGRAPHY

This bibliography offers resources about Asian and Pacific Islander Americans, beginning with general references and then listing more specific references arranged alphabetically by subject area.

CONTENTS

GENERAL REFERENCE

Danico, Mary Yu, and Franklin Ng. *Asian American Issues*. Westport: Greenwood, 2004.

Edwards, Carol A., ed. *Perspectives on Asian Americans and Pacific Islanders*. Reston: Natl. Council of Teachers of Mathematics, 1999.

Garoogian, David, ed. *The Asian Databook: Detailed Statistics and Rankings on the Asian and Pacific Islander Population, Including Twenty-Three Ethnic Backgrounds from Bangladeshi to Vietnamese, for 1,883 U.S. Counties and Cities*. Millerton: Grey, 2005.

Ichioka, Yuji, et al., comps. *A Buried Past: An Annotated Bibliography of the Japanese American Research Project Collection*. Berkeley: U of California P, 1974.

Niiya, Brian, ed. *Encyclopedia of Japanese American History: An A-to-Z Reference from 1868 to the Present*. New York: Facts on File, 2001.

Odo, Franklin, ed. *The Columbia Documentary History of the Asian American Experience*. New York: Columbia UP, 2002.

Kim, Hyung-chan, ed. *Distinguished Asian Americans: A Biographical Dictionary*. Westport: Greenwood, 1999.

ART

Chang, Gordon H., et al., eds. *Asian American Art, 1850–1970*. Stanford: Stanford UP, 2008.

Creef, Elena Tajima. *Imaging Japanese America: The Visual Construction of Citizenship, Nation, and the Body*. New York: New York UP, 2004.

Poon, Irene. *Leading the Way: Asian American Artists of the Older Generation*. Wenham: Gordon Coll., 2001.

See, Sarita Echavez. *The Decolonized Eye: Filipino American Art and Performance*. Minneapolis: U of Minnesota P, 2009.

BIOGRAPHIES AND CASE STUDIES

Bahrampour, Tara. *To See and See Again: A Life in Iran and America*. New York: Farrar, 1999.

Fung, Eddie. *The Adventures of Eddie Fung: Chinatown Kid, Texas Cowboy, Prisoner of War*. Ed. Judy Yung. Seattle: U of Washington P, 2007.

Huang, Guiyou, ed. *Asian American Autobiographers: A Bio-Bibliographical Critical Sourcebook*. Westport: Greenwood, 2001.

Kalita, S. Mitra. *Suburban Sahibs: Three Immigrant Families and Their Passage from India to America*. New Brunswick: Rutgers UP, 2003.

Lee, Joann Faung Jean. *Asian American Experiences in the United States: Oral Histories of First to Fourth Generation Americans from China, the Philippines, Japan, India, the Pacific Islands, Vietnam and Cambodia*. Jefferson: McFarland, 1991.

____, comp. *Asian Americans in the Twenty-First Century: Oral Histories of First to Fourth Generation Americans from China, Japan, India, Korea, the Philippines, Vietnam, and Laos*. New York: New, 2008.

Marshall, Jack. *From Baghdad to Brooklyn: Growing up in a Jewish-Arabic Family in Midcentury America*. Minneapolis: Coffee, 2005.

Rustomji-Kerns, Roshni, Rajini Srikanth, and Leny Mendoza Strobel, eds. *Encounters: People of Asian Descent in the Americas*. Lanham: Rowman, 1999.

Sultan, Masuda. *My War at Home*. New York: Washington Square, 2006.

Ty, Eleanor. *Unfastened: Globality and Asian North American Narratives*. Minneapolis: U of Minnesota P, 2010.

BUSINESS AND FINANCE

Grieco, Elizabeth M. *The Remittance Behavior of Immigrant Households: Micronesians in Hawaii and Guam*. New York: LFB Scholarly, 2003.

Hirahara, Naomi. *Distinguished Asian American Business Leaders*. Westport: Greenwood, 2003.

Hitch, Thomas Kemper. *Islands in Transition: The Past, Present, and Future of Hawaii's Economy*. Ed. Robert M. Kamins. Honolulu: U of Hawai'i P, 1993.

Hu-DeHart, Evelyn, ed. *Across the Pacific: Asian Americans and Globalization*. Philadelphia: Temple UP, 2000.

Lee, Rachel C., and Sau-Ling Cynthia Wong, eds. *Asian America.Net: Ethnicity, Nationalism, and Cyberspace*. New York: Routledge, 2003.

Park, Kyeyoung. *The Korean American Dream: Immigrants and Small Business in New York City*. Ithaca: Cornell UP, 1997.

Park, Lisa Sun-Hee. *Consuming Citizenship: Children of Asian Immigrant Entrepreneurs*. Stanford: Stanford UP, 2005.

Walker-Moffat, Wendy. *The Other Side of the Asian American Success Story*. San Francisco: Jossey-Bass, 1995.

COMMUNITIES

Abraham, Sameer Y., and Nabeel Abraham, eds. *Arabs in the New World: Studies on Arab-American Communities*. Detroit: Wayne State UP, 1983.

Angelo, Michael. *The Sikh Diaspora: Tradition and Change in an Immigrant Community*. New York: Routledge, 1997.

Ansary, Mir Tamim. *West of Kabul, East of New York: An Afghan American Story*. New York: Farrar, 2002.

Bacon, Jean. *Life Lines: Community, Family, and Assimilation Among Asian Indian Immigrants*. New York: Oxford UP, 1996.

Bakalian, Anny P. *Armenian-Americans: From Being to Feeling Armenian*. New Brunswick: Transaction, 1993.

Bonner, Arthur. *Alas! What Brought Thee Hither? The Chinese in New York, 1800–1950*. Madison: Fairleigh Dickinson UP, 1997.

Boosahda, Elizabeth. *Arab-American Faces and Voices: The Origins of an Immigrant Community*. Austin: U of Texas P, 2003.

Curiel, Jonathan. *Al'America: Travels Through America's Arab and Islamic Roots*. New York: New, 2008.

Dasgupta, Sathi Sengupta. *On the Trail of an Uncertain Dream: Indian Immigrant Experience in America*. New York: AMS, 1989.

Gee, Emma, et al., eds. *Counterpoint: Perspectives on Asian America*. Los Angeles: UCLA Asian Amer. Studies Center, 1976.

Lyman, Stanford M. *Chinatown and Little Tokyo: Power, Conflict, and Community Among Chinese and Japanese Immigrants in America*. Millwood: Assoc. Faculty, 1986.

Okamura, Jonathan Y. *Imagining the Filipino American Diaspora: Transnational Relations, Identities, and Communities*. New York: Garland, 1998.

Root, Maria P. P., ed. *Filipino Americans: Transformation and Identity*. Thousand Oaks: Sage, 1997.

Scolnick, Joseph M., and N. Brent Kennedy. *From Anatolia to Appalachia: A Turkish-American Dialogue*. Macon: Mercer UP, 2003.

Takaki, Ronald T. *Strangers from a Different Shore: A History of Asian Americans*. Boston: Little, 1998.

Tsai, Shi-shan Henry. *The Chinese Experience in America*. Bloomington: Indiana UP, 1986.

Williams-León, Teresa, and Cynthia L. Nakashima, eds. *The Sum of Our Parts: Mixed-Heritage Asian Americans*. Philadelphia: Temple UP, 2001.

Zia, Helen. *Asian American Dreams: The Emergence of an American People*. New York: Farrar, 2000.

EDUCATION

Abelmann, Nancy. *The Intimate University: Korean American Students and the Problems of Segregation*. Durham: Duke UP, 2009.

Aman, Mohammed M., ed. *Cataloging and Classification of Non-Western Material: Concerns, Issues, and Practices*. Phoenix: Oryx, 1980.

Chan, Sucheng. *In Defense of Asian American Studies: The Politics of Teaching and Program Building*. Urbana: U of Illinois P, 2005.

Flynn, James R. *Asian Americans: Achievement Beyond IQ*. Hillsdale: Erlbaum, 1991.

Nakanishi, Don T., and Tina Yamana Nishida, eds. *The Asian American Educational Experience: A Source Book for Teachers and Students*. New York: Routledge, 1995.

Food Culture

Coe, Andrew. *Chop Suey: A Cultural History of Chinese Food in the United States*. New York: Oxford UP, 2009.

Dusselier, Jane. *Asian American Food Culture*. Westport: Greenwood, 2009.

Laudan, Rachel. *The Food of Paradise: Exploring Hawaii's Culinary Heritage*. Honolulu: U of Hawai'i P, 1996.

Lee, Jennifer. *The Fortune Cookie Chronicles: Adventures in the World of Chinese Food*. New York: Twelve, 2008.

Mannur, Anita. *Culinary Fictions: Food in South Asian Diasporic Culture*. Philadelphia: Temple UP, 2010.

Ray, Krishnendu. *The Migrant's Table: Meals and Memories in Bengali-American Households*. Philadelphia: Temple UP, 2004.

Xu, Wenying. *Eating Identities: Reading Food in Asian American Literature*. Honolulu: U of Hawai'i P, 2008.

History and Politics

Bautista, Veltisezar B. *The Filipino Americans (1763 to Present): Their History, Culture, and Traditions*. 2nd ed. Naperville: Bookhaus, 2002.

Buck, Elizabeth. *Paradise Remade: The Politics of Culture and History in Hawai'i*. Philadelphia: Temple UP, 1993.

Chang, Iris. *The Chinese in America: A Narrative History*. New York: Penguin, 2004.

Chi, Tsung. *East Asian Americans and Political Participation: A Reference Handbook*. Santa Barbara: ABS-CLIO, 2005.

Chin, Frank, ed. *Born in the USA: A Story of Japanese America, 1889–1947*. Lanham: Rowman, 2002.

Collet, Christian, and Pei-te Lien, eds. *The Transnational Politics of Asian Americans*. Philadelphia: Temple UP, 2009.

Das Gupta, Monisha. *Unruly Immigrants: Rights, Activism, and Transnational South Asian Politics in the United States*. Durham: Duke UP, 2006.

Denoon, Donald, and Stewart Firth, eds. *The Cambridge History of the Pacific Islanders*. New York: Cambridge UP, 1997.

Do, Hien Duc. *The Vietnamese Americans*. Westport: Greenwood, 1999.

Dudley, Michael Kioni, and Keoni Kealoha Agard. *A Call for Hawaiian Sovereignty*. Honolulu: Nā Kāne O Ka Malo, 1993.

Fischer, Steven Roger. *A History of the Pacific Islands*. New York: Palgrave, 2002.

Fujikane, Candace, and Jonathan Y. Okamura, eds. *Asian Settler Colonialism: From Local Governance to the Habits of Everyday Life in Hawai'i*. Honolulu: U of Hawai'i P, 2008.

Gould, Harold Alton. *Sikhs, Swamis, Students, and Spies: The India Lobby in the United States, 1900–1946*. New Delhi: Sage, 2006.

Gulick, Sidney Lewis. *American Democracy and Asiatic Citizenship*. 1918. New York: Arno, 1978.

Gumport, Robert Kugell, and Marcella M. Smith. *The Chinese Experience in Nineteenth Century America*. Champaign: Center for East Asian & Pacific Studies, 2000.

Hess, Julia Meredith. *Immigrant Ambassadors: Citizenship and Belonging in the Tibetan Diaspora*. Stanford: Stanford UP, 2009.

Hezel, Francis X. *Strangers in Their Own Land: A Century of Colonial Rule in the Caroline and Marshall Islands*. Honolulu: U of Hawai'i P, 1995.

Hing, Bill Ong. *Making and Remaking Asian America through Immigration Policy, 1850–1990*. Stanford: Stanford UP, 1993.

Hing, Bill Ong, and Ronald Lee, eds. *The State of Asian Pacific America: Reframing the Immigration Debate*. Los Angeles: LEAP Asian Pacific Amer. Public Policy, 1996.

Hovannisian, Garin K. *Family of Shadows: A Century of Murder, Memory, and the Armenian American Dream*. New York: Harper, 2010.

Iyall-Smith, Keri E. *The State and Indigenous Movements*. New York: Routledge, 2006.

Kayyali, Randa A. *The Arab Americans*. Westport: Greenwood, 2006.

Kinzer, Stephen. *Overthrow: America's Century of Regime Change from Hawaii to Iraq*. New York: Times, 2006.

Kitano, Harry H. L., and Roger Daniels. *Asian Americans: Emerging Minorities*. Englewood Cliffs: Prentice, 1995.

Kung, Shien-woo. *Chinese in American Life: Some Aspects of Their History, Status, Problems, and Contributions*. Westport: Greenwood, 1973.

Kwon, Ho-Youn, and Shin Kim, eds. *The Emerging Generation of Korean-Americans*. Seoul: Kyung Hee UP, 1993.

Kwong, Peter, and Dusanka Miscevic. *Chinese America: The Untold Story of America's Oldest New Community*. New York: New, 2005.

LaViolette, Forrest E. *Americans of Japanese Ancestry*. New York: Arno, 1978.

Lee, Robert G. *Orientals: Asian Americans in Popular Culture*. Philadelphia: Temple UP, 1999.

Leonard, Karen Isaaksen. *The South Asian Americans*. Westport: Greenwood, 1997.

____. *Chinese and Japanese Americans*. New York: Hippocrene, 1984.

Nakanishi, Don T., and Ellen D. Wu. *Distinguished Asian American Political and Governmental Leaders*. Westport: Greenwood, 2002.

Ng, Franklin. *The Taiwanese Americans*. Westport: Greenwood, 1998.

Okihiro, Gary Y. *The Columbia Guide to Asian American History*. New York: Columbia UP, 2001.

____. *Margins and Mainstreams: Asians in American History and Culture*. Seattle: U of Washington P, 1994.

Rangaswamy, Padma. *Indian Americans*. New York: Chelsea, 2007.

Sahlins, Marshall David. *How "Natives" Think: About Captain Cook, for Example*. Chicago: U of Chicago P, 1996.

San Juan, Epifanio Jr. *From Exile to Diaspora: Versions of the Filipino Experience in the United States*. Boulder: Westview, 1998.

Silva, Noenoe K. *Aloha Betrayed: Native Hawaiian Resistance to American Colonialism*. Durham: Duke UP, 2004.

Skeldon, Ronald, ed. *Reluctant Exiles? Migration from Hong Kong and the New Overseas Chinese*. Armonk: Sharpe, 1994.

Smith, Icy, ed. *Voices of Healing: Spirit and Unity After 9/11 in the Asian American and Pacific Islander Community*. Gardena: East West Discovery, 2004.

Trask, Haunani-Kay. *From a Native Daughter: Colonialism and Sovereignty in Hawai'i*. Monroe: Common Courage, 1993.

Wei, William. *The Asian American Movement*. Philadelphia: Temple UP, 1993.

HUMOR

Dumas, Firoozeh. *Funny in Farsi: A Memoir of Growing up Iranian in America*. New York: Random, 2004.

____. *Laughing Without an Accent: Adventures of an Iranian American, at Home and Abroad*. New York: Random, 2008.

JAPANESE AMERICAN INTERNMENT DURING WORLD WAR II

Austin, Allan W. *From Concentration Camp to Campus: Japanese American Students and World War II*. Urbana: U of Illinois P, 2007.

Burgan, Michael. *The Japanese American Internment: Civil Liberties Denied*. Minneapolis: Compass Point, 2007.

Daniels, Roger. *Prisoners Without Trial: Japanese Americans in World War II*. 2nd ed. New York: Hill, 2004.

Gold, Susan Dudley. *Korematsu v. United States: Japanese-American Internment*. Tarrytown: Benchmark, 2006.

Harth, Erica, ed. *Last Witnesses: Reflections on the Wartime Internment of Japanese Americans*. New York: Palgrave, 2001.

Howard, John. *Concentration Camps on the Home Front: Japanese Americans in the House of Jim Crow*. Chicago: U of Chicago P, 2008.

Ishizuka, Karen L. *Lost and Found: Reclaiming the Japanese American Incarceration*. Urbana: U of Illinois P, 2006.

Lange, Dorothea. *Impounded: Dorothea Lange and the Censored Images of Japanese American Internment*. Ed. Linda Gordon and Gary Y. Okihiro. New York: Norton, 2008.

Maki, Mitchell Takeshi, Harry H. L. Kitano, and S. Megan Berthold. *Achieving the Impossible Dream: How Japanese Americans Obtained Redress*. Urbana: U of Illinois P, 1999.

Ng, Wendy. *Japanese American Internment during World War II: A History and Reference Guide*. Westport: Greenwood, 2002.

Shimabukuro, Robert Sadamu. *Born in Seattle: The Campaign for Japanese American Redress*. Seattle: U of Washington P, 2001.

Yancey, Diane. *Life in a Japanese American Internment Camp*. San Diego: Lucent, 1998.

LAW AND CRIME

Chang, Robert S. *Disoriented: Asian Americans, Law, and the Nation-State*. New York: New York UP, 1999.

Chin, Ko-lin. *Chinatown Gangs: Extortion, Enterprise, and Ethnicity*. New York: Oxford UP, 1996.

____. *Chinese Subculture and Criminality: Nontraditional Crime Groups in America*. New York: Greenwood, 1990.

Daniels, Roger, ed. *Anti-Chinese Violence in North America*. New York: Arno, 1978.

Kim, Hyung-chan. *A Legal History of Asian Americans, 1970–1990*. Westport: Greenwood, 1994.

Konvitz, Milton R. *The Alien and the Asiatic in American Law*. New York: Johnson, 1965.

Long, Patrick Du Phuoc, and Laura Ricard. *The Dream Shattered: Vietnamese Gangs in America*. Boston: Northeastern UP, 1996.

McIllwain, Jeffrey Scott. *Organizing Crime in Chinatown: Race and Racketeering in New York City, 1890–1910*. Jefferson: McFarland, 2004.

Yoshino, Kenji. *Covering: The Hidden Assault on Our Civil Rights*. New York: Random, 2006.

LINGUISTICS AND LITERATURE

Bhalla, Jag. *I'm Not Hanging Noodles on Your Ears and Other Intriguing Idioms from around the World*. Washington: Natl. Geographic, 2009.

Bloom, Harold, ed. *Asian-American Writers*. Philadelphia: Chelsea, 1999.

Hussein, Lutfi. *The Internet Discourse of Arab-American Groups: A Study in Web Linguistics*. Lewiston: Mellen, 2009.

Li, David Leiwei. *Imagining the Nation: Asian American Literature and Cultural Consent*. Stanford: Stanford UP, 1998.

Ling, Jinqi. *Narrating Nationalisms: Ideology and Form in Asian American Literature*. New York: Oxford UP, 1998.

Morimoto, Toyotomi. *Japanese Americans and Cultural Continuity: Maintaining Language and Heritage*. New York: Garland, 1997.

Reyes, Angela, and Adrienne Lo, eds. *Beyond Yellow English: Toward a Linguistic Anthropology of Asian Pacific America*. New York: Oxford UP, 2009.

MILITARY

Crost, Lyn. *Honor by Fire: Japanese Americans at War in Europe and the Pacific*. Novato: Presidio, 1994.

McNaughton, James C. *Nisei Linguists: Japanese Americans in the Military Intelligence Service During World War II*. Washington: Dept. of the Army, 2006.

Muller, Eric L. *Free to Die for Their Country: The Story of the Japanese American Draft Resisters in World War II*. Chicago: U of Chicago P, 2001.

Whelchel, Toshio. *From Pearl Harbor to Saigon: Japanese American Soldiers and the Vietnam War*. London: Verso, 1999.

Wong, Kevin Scott. *Americans First: Chinese Americans and the Second World War*. Cambridge: Harvard UP, 2005.

Yenne, Bill. *Rising Sons: The Japanese American GIs Who Fought for the United States in World War II*. New York: Dunne, 2007.

MUSIC

Nguyen, Phong T., Adelaida Reyes Schramm, and Patricia Shehan Campbell. *Searching for a Niche: Vietnamese Music at Home in America*. Kent: Viet Music, 1995.

Reyes, Adelaida. *Songs of the Caged, Songs of the Free: Music and the Vietnamese Refugee Experience*. Philadelphia: Temple UP, 1999.

Tatar, Elizabeth. *Nineteenth Century Hawaiian Chant*. Honolulu: Dept. of Anthropology, Bernice P. Bishop Museum, 1982.

Weintraub, Andrew N., and Bell Yung, eds. *Music and Cultural Rights*. Chicago: U of Illinois P, 2009.

Wong, Deborah Anne. *Speak It Louder: Asian Americans Making Music*. New York: Routledge, 2004.

Yoshihara, Mari. *Musicians from a Different Shore: Asians and Asian Americans in Classical Music*. Philadelphia: Temple UP, 2007.

PROFESSIONS AND LABOR

Dhingra, Pawan. *Managing Multicultural Lives: Asian American Professionals and the Challenge of Multiple Identities*. Stanford: Stanford UP, 2007.

Kwong, Peter. *Forbidden Workers: Illegal Chinese Immigrants and American Labor*. New York: New, 1998.

Mansfield-Richardson, Virginia. *Asian Americans and the Mass Media: A Content Analysis of Twenty United States' Newspapers and a Survey of Asian American Journalists*. New York: Garland, 2000.

Siu, Paul Chan Pang. *The Chinese Laundryman: A Study of Social Isolation*. Ed. John Kuo Wei Tchen. New York: New York UP, 1987.

Sung, Betty Lee. *A Survey of Chinese-American Manpower and Employment*. New York: Praeger, 1976.

Woo, Deborah. *Glass Ceilings and Asian Americans: The New Face of Workplace Barriers*. Walnut Creek: AltaMira, 2000.

RACIAL AND POLITICAL DISCRIMINATION

Ancheta, Angelo N. *Race, Rights, and the Asian American Experience*. New Brunswick: Rutgers UP, 1998.

Chan, Sucheng, ed. *Entry Denied: Exclusion and the Chinese Community in America, 1882–1943*. Philadelphia: Temple UP, 1991.

Gyory, Andrew. *Closing the Gate: Race, Politics, and the Chinese Exclusion Act*. Chapel Hill: U of North Carolina P, 1998.

Joyce, Patrick D. *No Fire Next Time: Black-Korean Conflicts and the Future of American Cities*. Ithaca: Cornell UP, 2003.

Lee, Erika. *At America's Gates: Chinese Immigration during the Exclusion Era, 1882–1943*. Chapel Hill: U of North Carolina P, 2003.

Matsumoto, Toru. *Beyond Prejudice*. New York: Arno, 1978.

McClain, Charles J. *In Search of Equality: The Chinese Struggle Against Discrimination in Nineteenth-Century America*. Berkeley: U of California P, 1994.

Miller, Stuart Creighton. *The Unwelcome Immigrant: The American Image of the Chinese, 1785–1882*. Berkeley: U of California P, 1969.

Pfaelzer, Jean. *Driven Out: The Forgotten War Against Chinese Americans*. New York: Random, 2007.

Rondilla, Joanne L., and Paul Spickard. *Is Lighter Better? Skin-Tone Discrimination among Asian Americans*. Lanham: Rowman, 2007.

Simpson, Caroline Chung. *An Absent Presence: Japanese Americans in Postwar American Culture, 1945–1960*. Durham: Duke UP, 2001.

Takaki, Ronald T. *Issei and Nisei: The Settling of Japanese America*. New York: Chelsea, 1994.

Tehranian, John. *Whitewashed: America's Invisible Middle Eastern Minority*. New York: New York UP, 2009.

Wu, Frank H. *Yellow: Race in America Beyond Black and White*. New York: Basic, 2002.

Yoon, In-Jin. *On My Own: Korean Businesses and Race Relations in America*. Chicago: U of Chicago P, 1997.

RELIGION

Chen, Carolyn. *Getting Saved in America: Taiwanese Immigration and Religious Experience*. Princeton: Princeton UP, 2008.

Chin, Frank. *Bulletproof Buddhists and Other Essays*. Honolulu: U of Hawai'i P, 1998.

Fenton, John Y. *Transplanting Religious Traditions: Asian Indians in America*. New York: Praeger, 1988.

Garlington, William. *The Baha'i Faith in America*. Westport: Praeger, 2005.

Harley, Gail M. *Hindu and Sikh Faiths in America*. New York: Facts on File, 2003.

Lawrence, Bruce B. *New Faiths, Old Fears: Muslims and Other Asian Immigrants in American Religious Life*. New York: Columbia UP, 2002.

Mann, Gurinder Singh, Paul David Numrich, and Raymond B. Williams. *Buddhists, Hindus and Sikhs in America*. New York: Oxford UP, 2001.

Nissimi, Hilda. *The Crypto-Jewish Mashhadis: The Shaping of Religious and Communal Identity in Their Journey from Iran to New York*. Portland: Sussex Academic, 2007.

Phan, Peter C. *Christianity with an Asian Face: Asian American Theology in the Making*. Maryknoll: Orbis, 2003.

Prothero, Stephen, ed. *A Nation of Religions: The Politics of Pluralism in Multireligious America*. Chapel Hill: U of North Carolina P, 2006.

Storhoff, Gary, and John Whalen-Bridge, eds. *American Buddhism as a Way of Life*. Albany: SUNY P, 2010.

Williams, Raymond Brady. *Religions of Immigrants from India and Pakistan: New Threads in the American Tapestry*. New York: Cambridge UP, 1988.

Yee, James, and Aimee Molloy. *For God and Country: Faith and Patriotism Under Fire*. New York: PublicAffairs, 2005.

Yoo, David K., and Ruth H. Chung, eds. *Religion and Spirituality in Korean America*. Urbana: U of Illinois P, 2008.

SCIENCE, HEALTH, AND MEDICINE

Choy, Catherine Ceniza. *Empire of Care: Nursing and Migration in Filipino American History*. Durham: Duke UP, 2003.

Whistler, W. Arthur. *Tongan Herbal Medicine*. Honolulu: U of Hawai'i P, 1992.

Yount, Lisa. *Asian-American Scientists*. New York: Facts on File, 1998.

Zhan, Lin, ed. *Asian Voices: Asian and Asian American Health Educators Speak Out*. Sudbury: Jones, 1999.

SEX AND GENDER ROLES

Baluja, Kaari Flagstad. *Gender Roles at Home and Abroad: The Adaptation of Bangladeshi Immigrants*. New York: LFB Scholarly, 2003.

Gopinath, Gayatri. *Impossible Desires: Queer Diasporas and South Asian Public Cultures*. Durham: Duke UP, 2005.

Masequesmay, Gina, and Sean Metzger, eds. *Embodying Asian/American Sexualities*. Lanham: Lexington, 2009.

Mura, David. *Where the Body Meets Memory: An Odyssey of Race, Sexuality, and Identity*. New York: Anchor, 1996.

Tengan, Ty P. Kāwika. *Native Men Remade: Gender and Nation in Contemporary Hawai'i*. Durham: Duke UP, 2008.

SOCIAL IDENTITY AND CUSTOMS

Bayoumi, Moustafa. *How Does it Feel to be a Problem? Being Young and Arab in America*. New York: Penguin, 2008.

Bhatia, Sunil. *American Karma: Race, Culture, and Identity in the Indian Diaspora*. New York: New York UP, 2007.

Bonus, Rick. *Locating Filipino Americans: Ethnicity and the Cultural Politics of Space*. Philadelphia: Temple UP, 2000.

Chan, Sucheng, ed. *Hmong Means Free: Life in Laos and America*. Philadelphia: Temple UP, 1994.

Espiritu, Yen Le. *Asian American Panethnicity: Bridging Institutions and Identities*. Philadelphia: Temple UP, 1992.

Foster, Jenny Ryun, Frank Stewart, and Heinz Insu Fenzl, eds. *Century of the Tiger: One Hundred Years of Korean Culture in America, 1903–2003*. Honolulu: U of Hawai'i P, 2003.

Gallimore, Ronald, et al. *Culture, Behavior and Education: A Study of Hawaiian-Americans*. Beverly Hills: Sage, 1974.

Halualani, Rona Tamiko. *In the Name of Hawaiians: Native Identities and Cultural Politics*. Minneapolis: U of Minnesota P, 2002.

Haseltine, Patricia, comp. *East and Southeast Asian Material Culture in North America: Collections, Historical Sites, and Festivals*. New York: Greenwood, 1989.

Hein, Jeremy. *Ethnic Origins: The Adaptation of Cambodian and Hmong Refugees in Four American Cities*. New York: Russell Sage Foundation, 2006.

Hong, Maria, ed. *Growing up Asian American*. New York: Perennial, 2003.

Howard, Alan. *Ain't No Big Thing: Coping Strategies in a Hawaiian-American Community*. Honolulu: UP of Hawaii, 1974.

Jensen, Joan M. *Passage from India: Asian Indian Immigrants in North America*. New Haven: Yale UP, 1988.

Kawakami, Barbara. *Japanese Immigrant Clothing in Hawaii, 1885–1941*. Honolulu: U of Hawai'i P, 1993.

Kibria, Nazli. *Becoming Asian American: Second-Generation Chinese and Korean American Identities*. Baltimore: Johns Hopkins UP, 2002.

____. *Family Tightrope: The Changing Lives of Vietnamese Americans*. Princeton: Princeton UP, 1993.

Kirch, Patrick Vinton, and Roger C. Green. *Hawaiki, Ancestral Polynesia: An Essay in Historical Anthropology*. New York: Cambridge UP, 2001.

Knoll, Tricia. *Becoming Americans: Asian Sojourners, Immigrants, and Refugees in the Western United States*. Portland: Coast to Coast, 1982.

Ling, Huping, ed. *Asian America: Forming New Communities, Expanding Boundaries*. New Brunswick: Rutgers UP, 2009.

Lynch, Annette. *Dress, Gender and Cultural Change: Asian American and African American Rites of Passage*. New York: Berg, 1999.

Manalansan, Martin F. IV, ed. *Cultural Compass: Ethnographic Explorations of Asian Americans*. Philadelphia: Temple UP, 2000.

Mangiafico, Luciano. *Contemporary American Immigrants: Patterns of Filipino, Korean, and Chinese Settlement in the United States*. New York: Praeger, 1988.

McCarus, Ernest, ed. *The Development of Arab-American Identity*. Ann Arbor: U of Michigan P, 1994.

Mote, Sue Murphy. *Hmong and American: Stories of Transition to a Strange Land*. Jefferson: McFarland, 2004.

Ng, Franklin, ed. *Asian American Interethnic Relations and Politics*. New York: Garland, 1998.

Proudfoot, Robert. *Even the Birds Don't Sound the Same Here: The Laotian Refugees Search for Heart in American Culture*. New York: Lang, 1990.

Rudrappa, Sharmila. *Ethnic Routes to Becoming American: Indian Immigrants and the Cultures of Citizenship*. New Brunswick: Rutgers UP, 2004.

Seward, George Frederick. *Chinese Immigration: Its Social and Economical Aspects*. New York: Arno, 1970.

Tsui, Bonnie. *American Chinatown: A People's History of Five Neighborhoods*. New York: Free, 2009.

Vang, Chia Youyee. *Hmong America: Reconstructing Community in Diaspora*. Champaign: U of Illinois P, 2010.

SPORTS

Franks, Joel S. *Crossing Sidelines, Crossing Cultures: Sport and Asian Pacific Cultural Citizenship*. 2nd ed. Lanham: UP of Amer., 2010.

King, C. Richard, ed. *Asian Americans in Sport and Society*. New York: Routledge, 2010.

STAGE AND SCREEN ENTERTAINMENT

Eng, Alvin, ed. *Tokens? The New York City Asian American Experience on Stage*. New York: Temple UP, 2000.

Feng, Peter X., ed. *Screening Asian Americans*. New Brunswick: Rutgers UP, 2002.

Hamamoto, Darrell Y., and Sandra Liu, eds. *Counter-visions: Asian American Film Criticism*. Philadelphia: Temple UP, 2000.

Leong, Russell, ed. *Moving the Image: Independent Asian Pacific American Media Arts*. Los Angeles: UCLA Asian Amer. Studies Center, 1991.

WOMEN

Aseel, Maryam Qudrat. *Torn Between Two Cultures: An Afghan-American Woman Speaks Out*. Sterling: Capital, 2003.

Beggs, Marjorie, ed. *InvAsian: Asian Sisters Represent*. San Francisco: Asian Women United of California, 2003.

Bloom, Harold, ed. *Asian American Women Writers*. Philadelphia: Chelsea, 1997.

Bow, Leslie. *Betrayal and Other Acts of Subversion: Feminism, Sexual Politics, Asian American Women's Literature*. Princeton: Princeton UP, 2001.

Chee, Maria W. L. *Taiwanese American Transnational Families: Women and Kin Work*. New York: Routledge, 2005.

Chow, Claire S. *Leaving Deep Water: Asian American Women at the Crossroads of Two Cultures*. New York: Dutton, 1998.

De Jesús, Melinda L., ed. *Pinay Power: Peminist Critical Theory: Theorizing the Filipina American Experience*. New York: Routledge, 2005.

Fountas, Angela Jane, ed. *Waking up American: Coming of Age Biculturally: First-Generation Women Reflect on Identity*. Emeryville: Seal, 2005.

Gupta, Sangeeta R., ed. *Emerging Voices: South Asian American Women Redefine Self, Family, and Community*. Walnut Creek: AltaMira, 1999.

Hune, Shirley, and Gail M. Nomura, eds. *Asian/Pacific Islander American Women: A Historical Anthology*. New York: New York UP, 2003.

Husain, Sarah, ed. *Voices of Resistance: Muslim Women on War, Faith and Sexuality*. Emeryville: Seal, 2006.

Ito, Karen Lee. *Lady Friends: Hawaiian Ways and the Ties that Define*. Ithaca: Cornell UP, 1999.

Kafka, Phillipa. *(Un)doing the Missionary Position: Gender Asymmetry in Contemporary Asian American Women's Writing*. Westport: Greenwood, 1997.

Kang, Hyn Li. *Compositional Subjects: Enfiguring Asian/American Women*. Durham: Duke UP, 2002.

King-O'Riain, Rebecca Chiyoko. *Pure Beauty: Judging Race in Japanese American Beauty Pageants*. Minneapolis: U of Minnesota P, 2006.

Ling, Huping. *Voices of the Heart: Asian American Women on Immigration, Work, and Family*. Kirksville: Truman State UP, 2007.

Read, Jen'nan Ghazal. *Culture, Class, and Work among Arab-American Women*. New York: LFB Scholarly, 2004.

Shakir, Evelyn. *Bint Arab: Arab and Arab American Women in the United States*. Westport: Praeger, 1997.

Vo, Linda Trinh, et al., eds. *Asian American Women: The Frontiers Reader*. Lincoln: U of Nebraska P, 2004.

Yamamoto, Traise. *Making Selves, Making Subjects: Japanese American Women, Identity, and the Body*. Berkeley: U of California P, 1999.

Yuh, Ji-Yeon. *Beyond the Shadow of Camptown: Korean Military Brides in America*. New York: New York UP, 2002.

Susan M. Filler

WEBSITE DIRECTORY

Consult the list below for online resources available to readers for further cultural study of Asian and Pacific Islander Americans.

Asian American Action Fund: Asian American Activism in History
http://www.aaa-fund.org/history/dalip_saund.php
Discusses Asian American involvement in activism and politics and the significant role Dalip Singh Saund, the first Asian American to be elected to Congress, played in paving the way for later Asian American political figures.

Asian American Business Development Center (AABDC)
http://www.aabdc.com
Features information on Asian Americans who have made significant strides in the business world and who have been included in the AABDC's annual list of outstanding Asian Americans in business.

Asian-Nation: Asian American History, Demographics, and Issues
http://www.asian-nation.org
Features articles containing detailed information on the social and political issues faced by Asian Americans and important events throughout Asian American history.

Asian Pacific American Collective History Project: The Rise of Asians and Asian Americans in Vaudeville, 1880s–1930s
http://www.sscnet.ucla.edu/history/faculty/henryyu/APACHP/teacher/research/moon.htm
Discusses Asian American participation in vaudeville and significant Asian American vaudeville performers.

California Cultures: Asian Americans: Early Twentieth Century
http://www.calisphere.universityofcalifornia.edu/calcultures/ethnic_groups/subtopic2b.html
Includes historical photographs and information regarding life for Asian Americans in California during the early twentieth century.

California State University, Sacramento: The Japanese American Archival Collection
http://digital.lib.csus.edu/jaac
Includes an archive of photographs and documents pertaining to Japanese American history and historical figures.

Center for Educational Telecommunications: Asian American History Timeline
http://www.cetel.org/timeline.html
Features a timeline of key events in Asian American history, including events pertaining to civil rights, politics, and education.

Center for Labor Education and Research, University of Hawaii–West Oahu: CLEAR Biographies of Hawaii Labor History Figures
http://clear.uhwo.hawaii.edu/LaborBios.html
Offers biographical information on several Asian and Pacific Islander Americans who played significant roles in Hawaii's labor history, including Koji Ariyoshi, Fred Kinzaburo Makino, and Pablo Manlapit.

County of Los Angeles Public Library: Notable Asian Americans
http://www.colapublib.org/apahm/notable.html
Offers a list of well-known Asian American figures, including Jerry Yang, Michelle Kwan, David Ho, and Steven Chu and discusses their achievements.

Densho: The Japanese American Legacy Project
http://www.densho.org
Sheds light on the experiences of Japanese Americans relocated to internment camps during World War II through lessons, historical photographs, and interviews.

Digital History: Asian American Voices
http://www.digitalhistory.uh.edu/asian_voices/asian_voices.cfm
Provides insight on Asian American history and covers specific social issues such as discriminatory practices in housing.

Education.com: Famous Asian Americans in the Arts
http://www.education.com/magazine/article/famous-asian-americans-arts
Features biographical information about Asian American celebrities, including Maya Lin, Yo-Yo Ma, and Vera Wang.

eFIL: Filipino Digital Archives and History Center of Hawaii

http://www.efilarchives.org

Connects visitors with numerous digital materials pertaining to the Filipino American experience in Hawaii, including oral histories and photographs.

Japanese American Citizens League

http://www.jacl.org

Provides information about Asian American activism and civil rights issues and includes a timeline of important events.

Japanese Americans in the Columbia River Basin: Historical Overview

http://archive.vancouver.wsu.edu/crbeha/ja/ja.htm

Offers historical information on the experiences of Japanese Americans in the nineteenth and twentieth centuries, including discussion of incidents of discrimination.

JARDA: Japanese American Relocation Digital Archives

http://www.calisphere.universityofcalifornia.edu/jarda

Offers oral history transcripts, digitized photographs, and letters pertaining to Japanese American relocation and internment.

Library of Congress: The Chinese in California, 1850–1925

http://memory.loc.gov/ammem/award99/cubhtml/related.html

Includes links to various resources, including collections of historical images pertaining to Chinese American history.

Life Interrupted: The Japanese American Experience in WWII Arkansas

http://ualr.edu/lifeinterrupted

Offers historical photographs as well as links to educational materials and other resources related to Japanese American internment in Arkansas.

Middle Tennessee State University Library: American Women's History: Asian-American Women

http://frank.mtsu.edu/~kmiddlet/history/women/wh-asian.html

Offers a host of resources, including primary sources, pertaining to Asian American women in history.

National Public Radio (NPR): Asian-American Artists Break into Soul Music

http://www.npr.org/templates/story/story.php?storyId=126778643

Features an interview transcript and audio clip in which an Asian American singer discusses the obstacles faced by Asian American performers of soul music.

National Public Radio (NPR): Asian-American Ivy Leaguer Has Tall Hoop Dreams

http://www.npr.org/templates/story/story.php?storyId=123368990

Features an interview transcript and audio clip that reveal the challenges, including racial discrimination, faced by basketball player Jeremy Lin during his college basketball career.

National Public Radio (NPR): South-Asian Americans Discover Political Clout

http://www.npr.org/templates/story/story.php?storyId=130853516

Offers a news story and audio clip about several Indian American politicians and political candidates as well as various South Asian American political organizations.

National Register of Historic Places: Asian-Pacific American Heritage Month

http://www.cr.nps.gov/nr/feature/asia

Includes photographs and descriptions of historic places related to Asian and Pacific Islander Americans, including.

New York University: Asian American Arts Centre Records: Asian/Pacific American Archives Survey

http://dlibdev.nyu.edu/tamimentapa/?q=node/71

Provides access to a variety of collections of primary and secondary sources pertaining to Asian and Pacific Islander American history and individuals.

The Philippine History Site: Filipino Migration to the United States

http://opmanong.ssc.hawaii.edu/filipino/filmig.html

Features historical information pertaining to Filipino immigration to the United States and the experiences of Filipino American migrant workers.

Public Broadcasting Service (PBS): Ancestors in the Americas

http://www.pbs.org/ancestorsintheamericas/aahistorysites.html

Provides a plethora of links to educational resources such as timelines, oral histories, and other primary and secondary sources.

Public Broadcasting Service (PBS): Becoming American: The Chinese Experience

http://www.pbs.org/becomingamerican/chineseexperience.html

Offers links to timelines and resources as well as information about the PBS documentary series *Becoming American: The Chinese Experience* (2003).

SEAAdoc: Documenting the Southeast Asian American Experience

http://seaadoc.lib.uci.edu

Provides information on the social, economic, and political issues faced by Cambodian, Laotian, and Vietnamese Americans since the 1970s.

Seattle Civil Rights and Labor History Project: Seattle's Asian American Movement

http://depts.washington.edu/civilr/aa_intro.htm

Discusses the activities of Asian American activists in Seattle, Washington, particularly during the 1960s and 1970s.

Snapshots of Asian America: Asian American Activism in the 1960s and 1970s

http://www.kqed.org/w/snapshots

Offers an audio webcast that provides insight about early activism activities within the Asian American community, particularly during the 1960s and 1970s.

South Asian American Digital Archive (SAADA)

http://www.saadigitalarchive.org

Offers many digitized materials, including historical photographs and letters, that shed light on the history of South Asian Americans.

University of Minnesota: Voices from the Gaps

http://voices.cla.umn.edu

Offers interview transcripts, essays, and reviews pertaining to female writers of color, including many of Asian descent.

University of Southern California Digital Library: Korean American Digital Archive

http://digitallibrary.usc.edu/search/controller/view/kada-m1.html?view=1

Provides access to several collections of oral histories, private records, historical photographs, and other documents concerning the Korean American experience.

US Department of Defense: Chinese Soldiers Fought in US Civil War

http://www.defense.gov/news/newsarticle.aspx?id=44949

Discusses several soldiers of Chinese descent and their service in the Civil War.

US Department of Defense: 22 Asian Americans Inducted into Hall of Heroes

http://www.defense.gov/news/newsarticle.aspx?id=45241

Discusses Asian American military figures who have been honored for their valuable service to the United States.

US National Archives and Records Administration: ARC Gallery: Japanese American Experiences during World War II

http://www.archives.gov/research/arc/topics/japanese-americans

Presents historical images and information related to Japanese American life during World War II, including images of internment camps and lists of Japanese American soldiers.

Washington State Commission on Asian Pacific American Affairs: Selected Dates and Events of Asian Pacific American History

http://www.capaa.wa.gov/data/timeline.shtml

Features a historical timeline of significant events in the history of Asian and Pacific Islander Americans.

Women Artists of the American West: Asian American Artists

http://www.cla.purdue.edu/waaw/AsianAmerican

Features images of artwork by various Asian American artists living in the western United States and also offers some brief comments on the inspiration behind the artists' works.

Brooke Posley

CONTRIBUTORS

Randy L. Abbott
University of Evansville

Carolyn Anderson
University of Massachusetts

Diana Meyers Bahr
Independent Scholar

David Barratt
Montreat College

Melissa A. Barton
Westminster, CO

Alvin K. Benson
Utah Valley University

Shanita Bigelow
Chicago, IL

Margaret Boe Birns
New York University

Leah Bromberg
Ann Arbor, MI

Jocelyn A. Brown
Independent Scholar

Leon James Bynum
Columbia University

Mavis N. Carr
Hampton University

Tina Chan
State University of New York at Oswego

Alexandra Chang
Asian/Pacific/American Institute at New York University

Shu-Hsien L. Chen
Queens College

Peggy Myo-Young Choy
University of Wisconsin–Madison

Kyle Casey Chu
Independent Scholar

John L. Clark, Jr.
Connecticut College

Michael D. Cummings, Jr.
Madonna University

Miyo Y. Davis
Art Institute of Washington

Rossella De Leon
Portland State University

James I. Deutsch
Smithsonian Institution

Jonathan E. Dinneen
Independent Scholar

Lan Dong
University of Illinois Springfield

Mark R. Ellis
University of Nebraska Kearney

Tim Engles
Eastern Illinois University

Evyn Le Espiritu
Pomona College

Christina Fa
YellowVisions ~ Asian Pacific Americana Collection

Nettie Farris
University of Louisville

Ronald J. Ferrara
Middle Tennessee State University

Keith M. Finley
Southeastern Louisiana University

Macey M. Freudensprung
The University of Texas at San Antonio

Karen S. Garvin
Independent Scholar

Katie S. Greer
Oakland University

Scot M. Guenter
San Jose State University

Fusako Hamao
Independent Scholar

P. Graham Hatcher
Blue Mountain College

Bernadette Zbicki Heiney
Lock Haven, PA

Mark C. Herman
Edison State College

Susan Hoang
Los Angeles, CA

William L. Howard
Chicago State University

Mary Hurd
East Tennessee State University

Karen M. Inouye
Indiana University Bloomington

Bruce E. Johansen
University of Nebraska at Omaha

Mark S. Joy
Jamestown College

Anne Klejment
University of St. Thomas

Marylane Wade Koch
University of Memphis

Beth Kraig
Pacific Lutheran University

Timothy Lane
Louisville, KY

Norma Lewis
Independent Scholar

Jing Li
Duquesne University

Victor Lindsey
Independent Scholar

Lisa Locascio
University of Southern Califorina

M. Philip Lucas
Cornell College

Martin J. Manning
US Department of State

Eugenio Matibag
Iowa State University

Thomas McGeary
Champaign-Urbana, IL

Michael R. Meyers
Pfeiffer University

Pamela Mueller-Anderson
Indiana University, Robert H. McKinney School of Law

Alice Myers
Great Barrington, MA

Jeff Naidoo
University of Kentucky

Leslie Neilan
Virginia Tech

Yung Hua Nancy Ng Tam
Liverpool, NY

Sarah Park
St. Catherine University

Eric Pellerin
Independent Scholar

Barbara Bennett Peterson
University of Hawaii

Allene Phy-Olsen
Austin Peay State University

Janet Pinkley
California State University, Channel Islands

Brooke Posley
Clarion University

R. Kent Rasmussen
Thousand Oaks, CA

Sandra Rothenberg
Framingham State University

Joseph F. Sanders
Western Michigan University

Elizabeth D. Schafer
Independent Scholar

Harvey Schwartz
San Francisco State University

Roger Smith
Independent Scholar

David Steffens
Oklahoma City University

Theresa Stowell
Morenci, MI

Jenny Suh
Claremont Graduate University

Idris Kabir Syed
Kent State University

Elnora Kelly Tayag
California State University, Channel Islands

John Edward Thorburn, Jr.
Independent Scholar

Miriam Tuliao
New York Public Library

Jennifer Samonte Valencia
Design Institute of San Diego

Sarbani Vengadasalam
Independent Scholar

Michael Joseph Viola
Antioch University–Seattle

Cynthia Wang
University of Southern California

Shawncey J. Webb
Taylor University

Winifred Whelan
St. Bonaventure University

K. Kale Yu
Nyack College

Gay Pitman Zieger
Independent Scholar

Indexes

CATEGORY INDEX

GEOGRAPHICAL INDEX

INDEX